Lecture Notes in Computer Science 14589

Founding Editors

Gerhard Goos
Juris Hartmanis

Editorial Board Members

The series Lecture Notes in Computer Science (LNCS), including its subseries Lecture Notes in Artificial Intelligence (LNAI) and Lecture Notes in Bioinformatics (LNBI), has established itself as a medium for the publication of new developments in computer science and information technology research, teaching, and education.

LNCS enjoys close cooperation with the computer science R & D community, the series counts many renowned academics among its volume editors and paper authors, and collaborates with prestigious societies. Its mission is to serve this international community by providing an invaluable service, mainly focused on the publication of conference and workshop proceedings and postproceedings. LNCS commenced publication in 1973.

Arne Meier · Magdalena Ortiz

Editors

Foundations of Information and Knowledge Systems

13th International Symposium, FoIKS 2024
Sheffield, UK, April 8–11, 2024
Proceedings

 Springer

Editors
Arne Meier 🔘
Leibniz University Hannover
Hanover, Germany

Magdalena Ortiz 🔘
TU Wien
Vienna, Austria

ISSN 0302-9743   ISSN 1611-3349 (electronic)
Lecture Notes in Computer Science
ISBN 978-3-031-56939-5   ISBN 978-3-031-56940-1 (eBook)
https://doi.org/10.1007/978-3-031-56940-1

Preface

This volume contains the papers presented at FoIKS24: 13th International Symposium on Foundations of Information and Knowledge Systems, held in Sheffield, UK, April 8–11, 2024.

The FoIKS symposia provide a biennial forum for presenting and discussing theoretical and applied research on information and knowledge systems. The goal is to bring together researchers interested in this topic, share research experiences, foster collaboration, and identify new issues and directions for future research. Past FoIKS meetings have been held in Schloss Salzau (Germany, 2002), Vienna (Austria, 2004), Budapest (Hungary, 2006), Pisa (Italy, 2008), Sofia (Bulgaria, 2010), Kiel (Germany, 2012), Bordeaux (France, 2014), Linz (Austria, 2016), Budapest (Hungary, 2018), Dortmund (Germany, 2020), and Helsinki (Finland, 2022).

The call for papers solicited original contributions that address any fundamental aspect of information and knowledge systems, including submissions that apply ideas, theories, or methods from specific disciplines to information and knowledge systems. Examples of such disciplines are discrete mathematics, logic and algebra, model theory, databases, information theory, complexity theory, algorithmics and computation, statistics, and optimization.

Traditionally, FoIKS symposia have been a forum for intensive discussion, with speakers given ample time to present their ideas and findings in the broader context of their research. In addition, participants are asked to prepare an initial response to another contributed talk to initiate the discussion.

FoIKS 2024 received 42 submissions. Each submission was single blind reviews by three program committee members based on its significance, novelty, technical soundness, and appropriateness for the FoIKS audience. In the end, the committee decided to accept 21 (18 long and 3 short) papers for oral presentation at the symposium and publication in the archival proceedings.

We are very honoured that FoIKS 2024 had a Best Paper Award for the first time. The PC members nominated four papers, and the PC chairs discussed the selection. We congratulate the winner of the Best Paper Award, which is even a single-author paper:

Fausto Barbero. *On the logic of interventionist counterfactuals under indeterministic causal laws.*

The author received a prize of EUR 500, sponsored by Springer.

We were also delighted to have four outstanding keynote speakers. The abstracts of their presentations are included in this volume:

- Georg Gottlob (University of Calabria, Italy and University of Oxford, UK): *Hypertree Decompositions, an Ongoing Project*
- Phokion Kolaitis (University of California Santa Cruz and IBM Research, USA): *Consistency of Relations over Semirings and Monoids*

- Andrei Popescu (University of Sheffield, UK): *Epi-Recursion and Epi-Corecursion*
- Uli Sattler (University of Manchester, UK): *Engineering Ontologies requires more than Automated Reasoning*

We thank all the people who contributed to making FoIKS 2024 a successful meeting. In particular, we thank the invited speakers for their stimulating presentations, the authors for their high-quality submission, revision, and presentation of their work, and all the participants for their contributions to the symposium discussions. We thank the Program Committee and the external reviewers for their prompt and thorough reviews. We thank EasyChair for providing the online submission and proceedings system. Finally, we would like to thank Springer for their help in publishing the proceedings and for their generous sponsorship of the best paper award.

We would like to thank the Local Organizing Committee, chaired by Jonni Virtema, for being proactive and responsive throughout the organizing process, and the members of the FoIKS Steering Committee for their trust and support.

February 2024   Arne Meier
                                                                              Magdalena Ortiz

Organization

Program Committee Chairs

Arne Meier   Leibniz Universität Hannover, Germany
Magdalena Ortiz   Vienna University of Technology, Austria

Program Committee

Shqiponja Ahmetaj	Vienna University of Technology, Austria
Yamine Ait Ameur	IRIT/INPT-ENSEEIHT, France
Christoph Beierle	FernUniversität in Hagen, Germany
Meghyn Bienvenu	CNRS, University of Bordeaux, France
Joachim Biskup	Technische Universität Dortmund, Germany
Elena Botoeva	University of Kent, UK
Fabio Cozman	University of São Paulo, Brazil
Dragan Doder	Utrecht University, The Netherlands
Thomas Eiter	Vienna University of Technology, Austria
Christian Fermüller	Vienna University of Technology, Austria
Flavio Ferrarotti	Software Competence Centre Hagenberg, Austria
Laura Giordano	Università del Piemonte Orientale, Italy
Marc Gyssens	Universiteit Hasselt, Belgium
Miika Hannula	University of Helsinki, Finland
Andreas Herzig	CNRS, IRIT, Univ. Toulouse, France
Tomi Janhunen	Tampere University, Finland
Matti Järvisalo	University of Helsinki, Finland
Gabriele Kern-Isberner	Technische Universität Dortmund, Germany
Elena Kleiman	Braude College, Israel
Sébastien Konieczny	CRIL – CNRS, France
Juha Kontinen	University of Helsinki, Finland
Sebastian Link	University of Auckland, New Zealand
Thomas Lukasiewicz	University of Oxford, UK
Pierre Marquis	CRIL, U. Artois & CNRS, France
Kevin McAreavey	University of Bristol, UK
Thomas Meyer	University of Cape Town and CAIR, South Africa
Nicola Olivetti	Aix-Marseille University, France
Ramon Pino Perez	Université d'Artois, France
Gian Luca Pozzato	Università di Torino, Italy
Elena Ravve	Ort Baude College, Israel
Sebastian Rudolph	TU Dresden, Germany

Attila Sali	Alfréd Rényi Institute of Mathematics, Hungary
Katsuhiko Sano	Hokkaido University, Japan
Klaus-Dieter Schewe	Zhejiang University, China
Kostyantyn Shchekotykhin	Alpen-Adria Universität Klagenfurt, Austria
Guillermo R. Simari	Universidad del Sur in Bahia Blanca, Argentina
Mantas Simkus	Vienna University of Technology, Austria
Michael Sioutis	University of Montpellier, CNRS, France
Umberto Straccia	ISTI-CNR, Italy
Karim Tabia	Artois University, France
Alex Thomo	University of Victoria, Canada
David Toman	University of Waterloo, Canada
Dirk Van Gucht	Indiana University Bloomington, USA
Qing Wang	Australian National University, Australia
Stefan Woltran	Vienna University of Technology, Austria

Additional Reviewers

Hofmann, Jana
Kooi, Barteld
Kuske, Dietrich
Luosto, Kerkko
Mahmood, Yasir
Nakamura, Yoshiki
Sauerwald, Kai
Wotawa, Franz

Local Chair

Jonni Virtema	University of Sheffield, UK

Local Organizers

Timon Barlag	University of Sheffield, UK
Mike Cruchten	University of Sheffield, UK
Nina Pardal	University of Sheffield, UK
Max Sandström	University of Sheffield, UK

Publicity Chair

Lucía Gómez Álvarez	TU Dresden, Germany

Invited Talks

Consistency of Relations over Semirings and Monoids

Phokion Kolaitis

University of California Santa Cruz and IBM Research, USA

Abstract. In several different settings, one comes across situations in which the objects of study are locally consistent but globally inconsistent. Earlier work in probability theory in the 1960s and in relational database theory in the 1980s produced characterizations of when local consistency implies global consistency. We will discuss two different generalizations of these results: the first considers K-relations over an arbitrary positive semiring K, while the second considers K-relations over an arbitrary positive monoid K. In each of these two settings, we explore when a database schema has the property that every pairwise consistent collection of K-relations over that schema is globally consistent; special cases include the earlier results about local vs. global consistency in relational database theory and more recent results about local vs. global consistency of bags.

This is joint work with Albert Atserias at UPC Barcelona.

Epi-Recursion and Epi-Corecursion

Andrei Popescu

University of Sheffield, UK

Abstract. Structural recursion is arguably the most important definitional principle in theoretical computer science. Traditionally, one defines (or programs) functions over an inductive datatype by structural recursion over the datatype's constructors. This amounts to writing clauses indicating how the to-be-defined function is supposed to interact with the constructors. For example, to define the length of a list we can write: length Nil = 0, and length (Cons x xs) = length xs + 1. However, this works out of the box only if the datatype is freely generated by the constructors, in that the constructors are injective and non-overlapping. On the other hand, for non-free datatypes such as finite sets, bags, and terms with bindings under the nominal representation, mathematicians and computer scientists have devised mechanisms for making structural recursion work with the help of verifying certain conditions.

In this talk, I will distill the ideas underlying recursion on non-free datatypes into the notion of epi-recursor. This is a simple piece of categorical logic that separates the constructor layer from a layer that "sits on top" of it, consisting of operators and properties that further support recursion. I will show how this abstract view can shed light on the relative expressiveness of different recursors. Finally, I will look at the dual problem of supporting corecursion via epi-corecursion, and its applications to defining functions that manipulate infinitary structures with bindings such as Boehm trees.

Hypertree Decompositions, an Ongoing Project

Georg Gottlob

University of Calabria, Italy

Abstract. In the contexts of database quertying and constraint satisfaction problems (CSPs), the hypertree decomposition method can be used query optimization and for faster CSP solving and for, whereby problem instances having a low hypertree width (i.e., a low degree of cyclicity) can be recognized and decomposed automatically, and efficiently evaluated. Queries and CSPs having bounded hypertree width are also highly parallelizable. The notion of Hypertree decomposition was introduced in 1999. This talk reviews - in form of questions and answers - the main relevant concepts and algorithms and surveys selected related work including applications and more recent results.

Engineering Ontologies requires more than Automated Reasoning

Uli Sattler

University of Manchester, UK

Abstract. (Co)-authoring, (re)using, and maintaining complex artifacts such as knowledge bases, ontologies, or software are complex tasks that are supported by a range of powerful tools and for which best practice/methodologies have been developed. Some of these relate to modularity and patterns: the former has been investigated for ontology engineering with some interesting results related to re-use and also to automated reasoning and optimisation. (Design) patterns have been hailed as a reusable engineering solution that supports high quality design, reuse, and comprehension in a number of disciplines including software and ontology engineering. For ontologies, a lot of effort has been spent on identifying, collecting, and classifying patterns - with seemingly little effect on ontology engineering practice. SNOMED CT is an interesting case in point as it is increasingly built using modelling templates as well as tools designed to support the usage of these templates, but the resulting OWL ontology has no signs of the usage of these templates. Recently, we developed a generic framework for identifying regularities in formal languages and investigated various variants of the problem of finding minimal rewritings of a given language using macros. We have developed related algorithms and applied these to existing, large OWL ontologies including SNOMET C; we found that we can find minimal rewritings of these in less than a minute. An interesting point of this application relates to the rather unusual syntax of OWL that poses some non-trivial problems due to the presence of a mixture of ranked and unranked symbols such as "SubClassOf" being binary whereas "Disjoint-Classes taking basically any number of symbols. In this talk, I will provide a general overview of the (ontology) engineering challenges mentioned above around modularity and patterns/regularities, and discuss various related solutions and insights gained.

Contents

Nonmonotonicity

Axiomatizations

Logics and Semantics

Argumentation

Answer Set Programming

Repairs

Inconsistency- and Error-Tolerant Reasoning w.r.t. Optimal Repairs of $\mathcal{EL}^{\perp}$ Ontologies

Franz Baader[1,2] , Francesco Kriegel[1,2(✉)] , and Adrian Nuradiansyah[1]

[1] Theoretical Computer Science, Technische Universität Dresden, Dresden, Germany
{franz.baader,francesco.kriegel,adrian.nuradiansyah}@tu-dresden.de
[2] Center for Scalable Data Analytics and Artificial Intelligence (ScaDS.AI),
Leipzig, Germany

Abstract. Errors in knowledge bases (KBs) written in a Description Logic (DL) are usually detected when reasoning derives an inconsistency or a consequence that does not hold in the application domain modelled by the KB. Whereas classical repair approaches produce maximal subsets of the KB not implying the inconsistency or unwanted consequence, optimal repairs maximize the consequence sets. In this paper, we extend previous results on how to compute optimal repairs from the DL $\mathcal{EL}$ to its extension $\mathcal{EL}^{\perp}$, which in contrast to $\mathcal{EL}$ can express inconsistency. The problem of how to deal with inconsistency in the context of optimal repairs was addressed previously, but in a setting where the (fixed) terminological part of the KB must satisfy a restriction on cyclic dependencies. Here, we consider a setting where this restriction is not required. We also show how the notion of optimal repairs obtained this way can be used in inconsistency- and error-tolerant reasoning.

1 Introduction

Description Logics (DLs) [2,3] are a well-investigated family of logic-based knowledge representation formalisms, which have gained particular prominence by the fact that they are the formal basis for the Web ontology language OWL,[1] and are thus employed in many application domains (e.g., biology and medicine [21]). In particular, in the setting of ontology-mediated query answering (OMQA) [16,28], concepts defined in the terminological part (TBox) of a DL knowledge base (KB) can be used as queries or within more complex queries on data, represented in the assertional part (ABox) of the KB.

For example, assume that the TBox $\mathcal{T}$ consists of the concept inclusions (CIs) $Man \sqsubseteq Human$ and $Human \sqcap \exists loves. Human \sqsubseteq Caring$, which say that men are humans and that a human loving some human is caring; and that the ABox $\mathcal{A}$ consists of the assertions $Man(n)$, $loves(n, n)$, and $Egoistic(n)$, which say that Narcissus (represented by the individual name n) is an egoistic man who loves

---

[1] https://www.w3.org/TR/owl2-overview/.

© The Author(s), under exclusive license to Springer Nature Switzerland AG 2024
A. Meier and M. Ortiz (Eds.): FoIKS 2024, LNCS 14589, pp. 3–22, 2024.
https://doi.org/10.1007/978-3-031-56940-1_1

himself. Given this KB, the instance query (IQ) $(Caring \sqcap Man)(n)$, which checks whether the individual n is an instance of the concept $Caring \sqcap Man$, returns true as an answer, and the conjunctive query (CQ) $Human(x) \wedge loves(x,x)$, which looks for self-loving humans, returns n. Note that, for both queries, we would not obtain this answer if we considered only the data (i.e., the ABox without the TBox). Also note that, in most DLs, this CQ cannot be expressed by instance queries due to the fact that it looks for a cycle in the data.

The DL community has spent considerable effort on designing sound, complete, and terminating inference algorithms for DLs of various degrees of expressiveness, not just for query answering, but also for other inference problems, such as the consistency and the subsumption problem [2,3]. However, even a sound inference procedure can produce consequences that are plainly wrong in the application domain that is modeled by a KB in case this KB contains errors. Inconsistency of a KB is a sure sign that there is something wrong with it, but errors can also be detected if consequences are produced that are not supposed to hold in the application domain. In our example, one may wonder whether it really makes sense to have a KB implying that Narcissus is both egoistic and caring. To correct this, one may thus try to construct a repair of it, i.e., a new KB from which the unwanted consequence $(Caring \sqcap Egoistic)(n)$ no longer follows. As pointed out in [4], it is not reasonable to use as a repair an arbitrary KB that does not have the unwanted consequences. Additionally, the repaired KB should (a) not introduce new knowledge and (b) be as close as possible to the original KB. More formally, (a) can be reformulated as saying that every repair must be entailed by the original KB, and the optimality condition (b) chooses repairs that are not strictly entailed by another repair. This still leaves different possibilities for how to formalize the notion of an (optimal) repair, depending on which entailment relation is employed.

Classical repair approaches [15,25,27] read (a) as talking about the explicitly represented knowledge, and thus use the superset relation as the "entailment" relation. Thus, a *classical repair* is a subset of the original KB that does not have the unwanted consequences, and it is *optimal* if it is a maximal such subset. In our example, if we assume that the TBox is correct (and thus should not be changed) there are three optimal classical repairs, obtained by removing one of the three assertions from the ABox. As pointed out in [13], this classical approach has the disadvantage that it is syntax-dependent. If, in our example, we had used the single assertion $(Man \sqcap Egoistic)(n)$, which is equivalent to the two assertions $Man(n)$ and $Egoistic(n)$, then a classical repair would need to remove the information that Narcissus is an egoistic man as a whole, thus leading to an optimal classical repair that is weaker than the one obtained when only the assertion $Egoistic(n)$ is removed. Even for the original version of our example, the optimal classical repair obtained by removing the assertion $loves(n,n)$ loses more consequences than necessary. In fact, this repair retains no information at all about love-relationships, though one could actually have kept the information that Narcissus loves something not known to be human (this could, e.g., be a pet), and even more (see below).

To be able to retain such entailed knowledge, we use in [5, 14] as entailment relation the usual logical entailment induced by the semantics of TBoxes and ABoxes, and extend ABoxes to quantified ABoxes (qABoxes), which may contain anonymous individuals. For example, the qABox $\exists \{x, y\}.\mathcal{B}$ with $\mathcal{B}$ equal to

$$\{Man(n), Egoistic(n), loves(n, x), loves(x, y), loves(y, y), Man(y), Egoistic(y)\}$$

is a (still not optimal) repair, which says that Narcissus is an egoistic man who loves something that in turn loves an egoistic man loving himself, where the existentially quantified variables x, y represent anonymous individuals whose names are not known. Using logical entailment is appropriate if we are interested in the answers to CQs that a KB yields. For this reason, this entailment relation is also called CQ-entailment in [5]. CQ-entailment is too strong if we are only interested in instance queries. In this case, it is sufficient to employ IQ-entailment, which looks at what concept assertions a given KB entails, i.e., the KB $\mathcal{K}_1$ IQ-entail the KB $\mathcal{K}_2$ if every concept assertion entailed by the latter is also entailed by the former.

In [5], we investigate the repair problem for the DL $\mathcal{EL}$, which has the top concept ($\top$), conjunction ($C \sqcap D$), and existential restrictions ($\exists r. C$) as concept constructors. More precisely, we consider KBs consisting of an $\mathcal{EL}$ TBox and a qABox, where the TBox is static (i.e., cannot be changed), and repair requests consisting of $\mathcal{EL}$ concept assertions. In the IQ-case, the set of optimal IQ-repairs can always be computed in exponential time, and this set covers all repairs in the sense that every IQ-repair is IQ-entailed by an optimal repair. In the CQ-case, this covering property need no longer hold; in particular, there are repair problems that have a CQ-repair, but no optimal one. To regain this important property, which implies that one does not lose repair options when concentrating on optimal repairs, one must restrict the TBox to being cycle-restricted.[2] With respect to cycle-restricted TBoxes, the set of optimal CQ-repairs can be computed in exponential time, but this computation requires the use of an NP-oracle.[3] These results show that it makes sense to tailor the employed entailment relation to the repair problem at hand. It must be strong enough to take the queries one is interested in and the ones used to specify the repair request into account, but also should not be stronger than that to avoid unnecessary complications such as non-coverage or higher computational complexity.

In this paper, we consider repairs in $\mathcal{EL}^\perp$, which extends $\mathcal{EL}$ with the bottom concept $\perp$, and in which inconsistency can be expressed. In our example, we could then use the CI $Caring \sqcap Egoistic \sqsubseteq \perp$ to say that no one can both be caring and egoistic. With this additional CI, the KB of our example becomes inconsistent. To repair the inconsistency, it is no longer enough to request that Narcissus should not be both caring and egoistic, one must also forbid this for all other individuals, also anonymous ones. For example, the qABox $\exists \{x, y\}.\mathcal{B}$

---

[2] For example, the CI $Human \sqsubseteq \exists loves. Human$ destroys cycle-restrictedness, whereas the CI $\exists loves. Human \sqsubseteq Human$ does not.

[3] In the CQ-case, using conjunctive instead of instance queries as repair requests may appear to be more appropriate, but this may destroy the covering property [9].

introduced above would still be inconsistent w.r.t. the extended TBox. Since anything follows from an inconsistent KB, condition (a) can no longer enforce that the repair is related in a reasonable way to the original KB. This problem is solved in [9] for a more expressive DL, according to which any $\mathcal{EL}^{\perp}$ TBox can be transformed into a normal form that is the union of a positive part $\mathcal{T}_{+}$ not containing $\perp$ and a bottom part $\mathcal{T}_{\perp}$ consisting of CIs of the form $C \sqsubseteq \perp$ for $\mathcal{EL}$ concepts C. As entailment relation, one then uses entailment w.r.t. $\mathcal{T}_{+}$, and the repair request must be extended by global requests $\exists\{x\}.\{C(x)\}$ for all CIs $C \sqsubseteq \perp$ in $\mathcal{T}_{\perp}$, expressing that C must not be populated by any individual, be it named or anonymous. In our extended example, $\mathcal{T}_{\perp}$ consists of the CI $Caring \sqcap Egoistic \sqsubseteq \perp$, and $\mathcal{T}_{+}$ of all other CIs. If we want to repair the inconsistency, then this boils down to repairing the original ABox $\mathcal{A}$ for the global repair request $\exists\{x\}.\{(Caring \sqcap Egoistic)(x)\}$ w.r.t. the TBox $\mathcal{T}_{+}$. In [9], such repair problems were investigated using CQ-entailment, which takes care of global repair requests since they can be represented as CQs. In the present paper, we investigate the IQ-case, which has the advantage that TBoxes need not be cycle-restricted. However, in addition to instance queries, the entailment relation now also needs to take global requests of the form $\exists\{x\}.\{C(x)\}$ into account. Following [11], we additionally allow role assertions to be contained in the repair request, which means that we have to consider gloIRQ-entailment, which takes these three types of queries (instance and roles assertions as well as global requests) into account. Dealing with such extended repair requests and the stronger entailment relation requires non-trivial changes to our repair approach in [5], but in the end we can again show that the set of optimal gloIRQ-repairs can be computed in exponential time, and this set covers all gloIRQ-repairs.

Both in $\mathcal{EL}$ and in $\mathcal{EL}^{\perp}$, a given repair problem may have exponentially many repairs, in the classical as well as in the optimal sense, and it is often hard to decide which one to use. Error-tolerant reasoning does not commit to a single repair, but rather reasons w.r.t. all of them: cautious reasoning returns the answers that follow from all repairs whereas brave reasoning returns the answers that follow from some repair. For classical repairs of $\mathcal{EL}$ TBoxes, it was investigated in [23,26], but for more expressive DLs that can create inconsistencies, error-tolerant reasoning w.r.t. classical repairs had been considered before, for the case where the error is an inconsistency, under the name of inconsistency-tolerant reasoning [17,18,22]. In [10], we investigate error-tolerant reasoning in $\mathcal{EL}$ w.r.t. the optimal repairs introduced in [5], and in [11], this work is extended to take also role assertions in the repair request into account. Here, we make the further extension from $\mathcal{EL}$ to $\mathcal{EL}^{\perp}$, which then also allows us to do inconsistency-tolerant reasoning. Again, the stronger entailment relation requires non-trivial changes of the approaches developed in [5,11].

For space restrictions, some proofs of technical results can only be found in the extended version [12] and proof sketches are given instead.

2   Preliminaries

First, we briefly recall syntax and semantics of the DL $\mathcal{EL}$ and of quantified ABoxes, but refer the reader to standard texts on DLs [3] and to [5,14] for more detailed expositions. Then, we introduce the relevant entailment relations and recall some useful results regarding them from [5,7,11]. Finally, we define the notion of optimal repairs, and recall our previously obtained results for them [5, 7,9,14].

2.1   The Description Logic $\mathcal{EL}$ and Quantified ABoxes

The *syntax* of $\mathcal{EL}$ concepts is defined inductively as follows. Starting with disjoint sets Σ_C of *concept names* and Σ_R of *role names*, $\mathcal{EL}$ concepts are built using the constructors top concept ($\top$), conjunction ($C \sqcap D$), and existential restriction ($\exists r.C$). An $\mathcal{EL}$ *atom* is either a concept name or an existential restriction. We use $\mathsf{Conj}(C)$ to denote the set of all $\mathcal{EL}$ atoms that occur as a top-level conjunct of C. Such concepts can be used to define both terminological and assertional knowledge. An $\mathcal{EL}$ *concept inclusion (CI)* is of the form $C \sqsubseteq D$ for $\mathcal{EL}$ concepts C, D. An $\mathcal{EL}$ *TBox* $\mathcal{T}$ is a finite set of such CIs. Given an additional set Σ_I of *individual names*, disjoint with Σ_C and Σ_R, an $\mathcal{EL}$ *concept assertion* is of the form $C(a)$, where C is an $\mathcal{EL}$ concept and $a \in \Sigma_I$, and a *role assertion* is of the form $r(a,b)$, where $r \in \Sigma_R$ and $a, b \in \Sigma_I$. An $\mathcal{EL}$ *ABox* $\mathcal{A}$ is a finite set of $\mathcal{EL}$ concept assertions and role assertions.

The *semantics* of $\mathcal{EL}$ concepts, TBoxes, and ABoxes is defined in a model-theoretic way. An *interpretation* $\mathcal{I}$ is a pair $(\Delta^{\mathcal{I}}, \cdot^{\mathcal{I}})$, where the *domain* $\Delta^{\mathcal{I}}$ is a non-empty set, and the *interpretation function* $\cdot^{\mathcal{I}}$ maps each $a \in \Sigma_I$ to an element $a^{\mathcal{I}}$ of $\Delta^{\mathcal{I}}$, each concept name $A \in \Sigma_C$ to $A^{\mathcal{I}} \subseteq \Delta^{\mathcal{I}}$, and each role name $r \in \Sigma_R$ to a binary relation $r^{\mathcal{I}} \subseteq \Delta^{\mathcal{I}} \times \Delta^{\mathcal{I}}$. The interpretation $C^{\mathcal{I}}$ of an $\mathcal{EL}$ concept C is defined inductively as follows: $\top^{\mathcal{I}} := \Delta^{\mathcal{I}}$, $(C \sqcap D)^{\mathcal{I}} := C^{\mathcal{I}} \cap D^{\mathcal{I}}$, and $(\exists r.C)^{\mathcal{I}} := \{d \in \Delta^{\mathcal{I}} \mid \exists e \in \Delta^{\mathcal{I}}\text{such that } (d, e) \in r^{\mathcal{I}} \text{ and } C^{\mathcal{I}}\}$. The interpretation $\mathcal{I}$ *satisfies* the CI $C \sqsubseteq D$ (denoted by $\mathcal{I} \models C \sqsubseteq D$) if $C^{\mathcal{I}} \subseteq D^{\mathcal{I}}$, the concept assertion $C(a)$ ($\mathcal{I} \models C(a)$) if $a^{\mathcal{I}} \in C^{\mathcal{I}}$, and the role assertion $r(a, b)$ ($\mathcal{I} \models r(a, b)$) if $(a^{\mathcal{I}}, b^{\mathcal{I}}) \in r^{\mathcal{I}}$. We further say that $\mathcal{I}$ is a *model* of the $\mathcal{EL}$ TBox $\mathcal{T}$ (ABox $\mathcal{A}$) if each CI in $\mathcal{T}$ (assertion in $\mathcal{A}$) is satisfied by $\mathcal{I}$.

A *quantified ABox (qABox)* $\exists X.\mathcal{A}$ consists of a finite set X of *variables*, which is disjoint with $\Sigma = \Sigma_I \cup \Sigma_C \cup \Sigma_R$, and a *matrix* $\mathcal{A}$, which is a finite set of concept assertions $A(u)$ and role assertions $r(u, v)$, where $A \in \Sigma_C$, $r \in \Sigma_R$ and $u, v \in \Sigma_I \cup X$. Thus, the matrix is an ABox built over the extended signature $\Sigma \cup X$, but cannot contain complex concept descriptions. An *object* of $\exists X.\mathcal{A}$ is either an individual name in Σ_I or a variable in X. We denote the set of objects of $\exists X.\mathcal{A}$ with $\mathsf{Obj}(\exists X.\mathcal{A})$. The interpretation $\mathcal{I}$ is a *model of a qABox* $\exists X.\mathcal{A}$ ($\mathcal{I} \models \exists X.\mathcal{A}$) if there is a variable assignment $\mathcal{Z} : X \rightarrow \Delta^{\mathcal{I}}$ such that the augmented interpretation $\mathcal{I}[\mathcal{Z}]$ that additionally maps each variable x to $\mathcal{Z}(x)$ is a model of the matrix $\mathcal{A}$, i.e., $u^{\mathcal{I}[\mathcal{Z}]} \in A^{\mathcal{I}}$ for each $A(u) \in \mathcal{A}$ and $(u^{\mathcal{I}[\mathcal{Z}]}, v^{\mathcal{I}[\mathcal{Z}]}) \in r^{\mathcal{I}}$ for each $r(u, v) \in \mathcal{A}$. As pointed out in [14], qABoxes are syntactic variants of Boolean conjunctive queries [19], i.e., CQs with an empty tuple of answer variables. In addition, $\mathcal{EL}$ ABoxes can be expressed by qABoxes.

2.2 Queries and Entailment Relations

Let α, β be any of the syntactical objects (CI, assertion, ABox, qABox) introduced above, and $\mathcal{T}$ be an $\mathcal{EL}$ TBox. Then, α *entails* β *w.r.t.* $\mathcal{T}$ ($\alpha \models^{\mathcal{T}} \beta$) if each model of α and $\mathcal{T}$ is also a model of β. If $\exists X.\mathcal{A} \models^{\mathcal{T}} C(a)$, then a is called an *instance* of C in $\exists X.\mathcal{A}$ w.r.t. $\mathcal{T}$. In case $\mathcal{T} = \emptyset$, we will sometimes write $\models$ instead of $\models^{\emptyset}$. If $\emptyset \models^{\mathcal{T}} C \sqsubseteq D$, then we also write $C \sqsubseteq^{\mathcal{T}} D$ and say that C *is subsumed by* D *w.r.t.* $\mathcal{T}$; in case $\mathcal{T} = \emptyset$ we simply say that C is subsumed by D. The subsumption and the instance problems in $\mathcal{EL}$ are decidable in polynomial time [1]. With respect to the empty TBox, the instance problem can be characterized as follows:

Lemma 1. [14] *The following statements hold for each qABox* $\exists X.\mathcal{A}$:

1. $\exists X.\mathcal{A} \models C(a)$ *iff* $\mathcal{A} \models C(a)$ *for each concept assertion* $C(a)$.
2. *For each* $\mathcal{EL}$ *concept* C *and each object* u *of* $\exists X.\mathcal{A}$, *we have* $\mathcal{A} \models C(u)$ *iff* $A(u) \in \mathcal{A}$ *for each* $A \in \mathsf{Conj}(C)$, *and for each existential restriction* $\exists r.D \in \mathsf{Conj}(C)$, *there is some role assertion* $r(u, v) \in \mathcal{A}$ *such that* $\mathcal{A} \models D(v)$.

Tractability also holds (w.r.t. an $\mathcal{EL}$ TBox) for entailment between $\mathcal{EL}$ ABoxes and entailment of a concept assertion by a qABox. A role assertion between individuals is entailed by a qABox iff it is contained in its matrix. The entailment problem between qABoxes (with or without $\mathcal{EL}$ TBox) is NP-complete [5, 14].

For our purposes, a query language QL is a set of Boolean conjunctive queries. The qABox $\exists X.\mathcal{A}$ QL-entails the qABox $\exists Y.\mathcal{B}$ w.r.t. the TBox $\mathcal{T}$ ($\exists X.\mathcal{A} \models^{\mathcal{T}}_{\mathsf{QL}} \exists Y.\mathcal{B}$) if, for each query $\alpha \in \mathsf{QL}$, $\exists Y.\mathcal{B} \models^{\mathcal{T}} \alpha$ implies $\exists X.\mathcal{A} \models^{\mathcal{T}} \alpha$. In our previous work, we have considered three query languages: IQ consists of all $\mathcal{EL}$ concept assertions [5, 10, 14], IRQ extends IQ by all role assertions between individuals [7, 11], and CQ consists of all Boolean conjunctive queries (equivalently: qABoxes) [5, 9, 14]. As shown in [5], CQ-entailment and model-based entailment coincide, and thus deciding $\models^{\mathcal{T}}_{\mathsf{CQ}}$ is also NP-complete.

In contrast, IQ-entailment between qABoxes can be decided in polynomial time. This is a consequence of the following result from [5]. Given a qABox $\exists X.\mathcal{A}$ and a TBox $\mathcal{T}$, one can compute the IQ-saturation $\mathsf{sat}^{\mathcal{T}}_{\mathsf{IQ}}(\exists X.\mathcal{A})$ of $\exists X.\mathcal{A}$ w.r.t. $\mathcal{T}$ in polynomial time, and this saturation satisfies $\exists X.\mathcal{A} \models^{\mathcal{T}}_{\mathsf{IQ}} \exists Y.\mathcal{B}$ iff $\mathsf{sat}^{\mathcal{T}}_{\mathsf{IQ}}(\exists X.\mathcal{A}) \models_{\mathsf{IQ}} \exists Y.\mathcal{B}$. Basically, the IQ-saturation process works as follows: while there is an object u and a CI $C \sqsubseteq D$ in $\mathcal{T}$ such that the matrix of the current qABox entails $C(u)$, but not $D(u)$, the qABox is extended by adding $D(u)$ and then representing this assertion as a qABox. To ensure termination, new variables introduced to express existential restrictions are re-used, i.e., for every concept E occurring in an existential restriction, a single variable x_E is introduced (see [5] for details).

Example 2. Starting with the qABox $\exists \emptyset. \{A(a)\}$ and the TBox $\{A \sqsubseteq \exists r. A \sqcap \exists s. (B \sqcap \exists s. A)\}$, we obtain the IQ-saturation $\exists \{x_A, x_{B \sqcap \exists s. A}\}. \{A(a), r(a, x_A), A(x_A), s(a, x_{B \sqcap \exists s. A}), B(x_{B \sqcap \exists s. A}), s(x_{B \sqcap \exists s. A}, x_A), r(x_A, x_A), s(x_A, x_{B \sqcap \exists s. A})\}$.

The equivalence $\exists X. \mathcal{A} \models_{\mathsf{IQ}}^{\mathcal{T}} \exists Y. \mathcal{B}$ iff $\mathsf{sat}_{\mathsf{IQ}}^{\mathcal{T}}(\exists X. \mathcal{A}) \models_{\mathsf{IQ}} \exists Y. \mathcal{B}$ provides us with a polynomial-time reduction of IQ-entailment w.r.t. a TBox to IQ-entailment w.r.t. the empty TBox. The latter in turn corresponds to the existence of a simulation in the other direction [14]. A *simulation* from $\exists Y. \mathcal{B}$ to $\exists X. \mathcal{A}$ is a relation $\mathfrak{S} \subseteq \mathsf{Obj}(\exists Y. \mathcal{B}) \times \mathsf{Obj}(\exists X. \mathcal{A})$ such that:

(S1) If a is an individual name, then $(a, a) \in \mathfrak{S}$.
(S2) If $(u, u') \in \mathfrak{S}$ and $A(u) \in \mathcal{B}$, then $A(u') \in \mathcal{A}$.
(S3) If $(u, u') \in \mathfrak{S}$ and $r(u, v) \in \mathcal{B}$, then $(v, v') \in \mathfrak{S}$ and $r(u', v') \in \mathcal{A}$ for some v'.

Since existence of a simulation can be decided in polynomial time [20], IQ-entailment between qABoxes (with or without TBox) is also in P.

This implies that IRQ-entailment is also tractable. In fact, as shown in [11], $\exists X. \mathcal{A} \models_{\mathsf{IRQ}}^{\mathcal{T}} \exists Y. \mathcal{B}$ iff $\exists X. \mathcal{A} \models_{\mathsf{IQ}}^{\mathcal{T}} \exists Y. \mathcal{B}$ and $r(a, b) \in \mathcal{B}$ implies $r(a, b) \in \mathcal{A}$ for all $r \in \Sigma_{\mathsf{R}}$ and $a, b \in \Sigma_{\mathsf{I}}$. The second condition can clearly be checked in P.

2.3   Optimal Repairs of Quantified ABoxes w.r.t. Static $\mathcal{EL}$ TBoxes

Assume that we have a qABox (and possibly an $\mathcal{EL}$ TBox) and use the query language QL to extract information from this KB. Usually, one notices that there is something wrong with the given KB if queries are entailed that do not hold in the application domain. Thus, we specify what is to be repaired by a finite set of queries $\mathcal{P}$, which we call a *repair request*, i.e., a repair request is a finite set $\mathcal{P} \subseteq \mathsf{QL}$. As pointed out in the introduction, when defining the notion of an (optimal) repair, it is sufficient to use as entailment relation the one induced by the employed query language.

Definition 3. *Let* QL *be a query language,* $\exists X. \mathcal{A}$ *be a qABox,* $\mathcal{T}$ *be an $\mathcal{EL}$ TBox, and* $\mathcal{P}$ *a repair request for* QL. *Then, a* QL-repair *of* $\exists X. \mathcal{A}$ *for* $\mathcal{P}$ *w.r.t.* $\mathcal{T}$ *is a qABox* $\exists Y. \mathcal{B}$ *such that*

(Rep1) $\exists X. \mathcal{A} \models_{\mathsf{QL}}^{\mathcal{T}} \exists Y. \mathcal{B}$
(Rep2) $\exists Y. \mathcal{B} \not\models^{\mathcal{T}} \alpha$ *for each* $\alpha \in \mathcal{P}$.

This repair is optimal *if it is not strictly* QL-*entailed by another repair. The set* $\mathfrak{R}$ *of* QL-*repairs of* $\exists X. \mathcal{A}$ *for* $\mathcal{P}$ *w.r.t.* $\mathcal{T}$ QL-*covers all* QL-*repairs of* $\exists X. \mathcal{A}$ *for* $\mathcal{P}$ *w.r.t.* $\mathcal{T}$ *if, for each* QL-*repair* $\exists Y. \mathcal{B}$ *of* $\exists X. \mathcal{A}$ *for* $\mathcal{P}$ *w.r.t.* $\mathcal{T}$, *there is* $\exists Z. \mathcal{C} \in \mathfrak{R}$ *such that* $\exists Z. \mathcal{C} \models_{\mathsf{QL}}^{\mathcal{T}} \exists Y. \mathcal{B}$.

In our previous work on optimal repairs we have determined situations in which the set of optimal QL-repairs can effectively be computed, and covers all repairs: (1) QL = IQ and arbitrary $\mathcal{EL}$ TBox [5]; (2) QL = IRQ and arbitrary $\mathcal{EL}$ TBox [7,11]; (3) QL = CQ, but $\mathcal{P} \subseteq$ IQ and $\mathcal{T}$ is cycle-restricted [5]; (4) QL = CQ, but $\mathcal{P} \subseteq$ gloIRQ and $\mathcal{T}$ is a terminating Horn-$\mathcal{ALCROI}$ TBox [9]. The computation of all optimal QL-repairs can be performed in exponential time for situations (1) and (2), and may additionally require an NP-oracle for (3). For situation (4), the exact complexity of the computation problem has not been determined yet.

3   Global Instance Queries

As mentioned in the introduction, in the presence of CIs of the form $C \sqsubseteq \bot$, we need to express, in the repair request, that concept C must not have any element. This is possible using *global instance queries*, which are of the form $\exists\{x\}.\{C(x)\}$ where C is an $\mathcal{EL}$ concept. Such a query is satisfied in an interpretation $\mathcal{I}$ if $C^{\mathcal{I}} \neq \emptyset$. The query language gloIRQ is obtained from IRQ by adding all global IQs. Since $\mathcal{EL}$ concepts can be expressed by (tree-shaped) conjunctive queries, the inclusions IRQ $\subseteq$ gloIRQ $\subseteq$ CQ hold, which imply the inverse inclusions between the induced entailment relations: $\models_{\mathsf{CQ}}^{\mathcal{T}} \subseteq \models_{\mathsf{gloIRQ}}^{\mathcal{T}} \subseteq \models_{\mathsf{IRQ}}^{\mathcal{T}}$. It is easy to see that these inclusions are strict.

In this section, we give a characterization of gloIRQ-entailment that is based on the existence of certain simulations, and which implies that $\models_{\mathsf{gloIRQ}}^{\mathcal{T}}$ is decidable in polynomial time. We call a simulation $\mathfrak{S}$ from $\exists Y.\mathcal{B}$ to $\exists X.\mathcal{A}$ *total* if, for each object $u \in \mathsf{Obj}(\exists Y.\mathcal{B})$, there is an object $v \in \mathsf{Obj}(\exists X.\mathcal{A})$ with $(u,v) \in \mathfrak{S}$.

Lemma 4. $\exists X.\mathcal{A} \models_{\mathsf{gloIRQ}} \exists Y.\mathcal{B}$ *iff there is a total simulation from* $\exists Y.\mathcal{B}$ *to* $\exists X.\mathcal{A}$ *and* $r(a,b) \in \mathcal{B}$ *implies* $r(a,b) \in \mathcal{A}$ *for all* $r \in \Sigma_\mathsf{R}$ *and* $a,b \in \Sigma_\mathsf{I}$.

Proof. Recall from [5,7,14] that $\exists X.\mathcal{A} \models_{\mathsf{IRQ}} \exists Y.\mathcal{B}$ iff there is a simulation from $\exists Y.\mathcal{B}$ to $\exists X.\mathcal{A}$ and $r(a,b) \in \mathcal{B}$ implies $r(a,b) \in \mathcal{A}$. Thus, it remains to relate the entailed global IQs with totality of the simulation.

For the only-if direction, we assume that $\exists X.\mathcal{A} \models_{\mathsf{gloIRQ}} \exists Y.\mathcal{B}$. The proof of Proposition 23 in [14] shows (under the weaker assumption $\exists X.\mathcal{A} \models_{\mathsf{IQ}} \exists Y.\mathcal{B}$) that $\mathfrak{S} := \{ (u,v) \mid \mathcal{B} \models C(u)$ implies $\mathcal{A} \models C(v)$ for each $\mathcal{EL}$ concept $C \}$ is a simulation. *Assume that* $\mathfrak{S}$ *is not total.* Then there exists an object $u \in \mathsf{Obj}(\exists Y.\mathcal{B})$ for which there is no object $v \in \mathsf{Obj}(\exists X.\mathcal{A})$ with $(u,v) \in \mathfrak{S}$. Thus, for each $v \in \mathsf{Obj}(\exists X.\mathcal{A})$, there must be an $\mathcal{EL}$ concept C_v with $\mathcal{B} \models C_v(u)$, but $\mathcal{A} \not\models C_v(v)$. Let C be the conjunction of these finitely many concepts. Then $\exists Y.\mathcal{B} \models \exists\{x\}.\{C(x)\}$, and thus $\exists X.\mathcal{A} \models_{\mathsf{gloIRQ}} \exists Y.\mathcal{B}$ yields $\exists X.\mathcal{A} \models \exists\{x\}.\{C(x)\}$. By Proposition 2 in [14], this implies that there is a homomorphism[4] h from $\exists\{x\}.\{C(x)\}$ (expressed as a qABox) to $\exists X.\mathcal{A}$ such that $\mathcal{A} \models C(h(x))$. However, since $C_{h(x)}$ is a conjunct of C, this contradicts the fact that the concepts C_v satisfy $\mathcal{A} \not\models C_v(v)$. Thus, the simulation $\mathfrak{S}$ must be total.

To show the if direction, consider a total simulation $\mathfrak{S}$ from $\exists Y.\mathcal{B}$ to $\exists X.\mathcal{A}$, and assume that $\exists Y.\mathcal{B} \models \exists\{x\}.\{C(x)\}$. According to Proposition 2 in [14], there is a homomorphism h from $\exists\{x\}.\{C(x)\}$ (expressed as a qABox) to $\exists Y.\mathcal{B}$. It is easy to construct, by induction on the structure of C, a homomorphism g from $\exists\{x\}.\{C(x)\}$ to $\exists X.\mathcal{A}$: we choose each value $g(u)$ from the non-empty (!) set

---

[4] A homomorphism is a total and functional simulation.

$\{\, v \mid (h(u), v) \in \mathfrak{S} \,\}$. Another application of Proposition 2 in [14] yields $\exists X. \mathcal{A} \models \exists \{x\}. \{C(x)\}$. □

The proof of the following lemma is similar to the proof of Proposition IV in [6] (see [12] for details).

Lemma 5. $\exists X. \mathcal{A} \models^{\mathcal{T}} \exists \{x\}. \{C(x)\}$ *iff* $\mathsf{sat}^{\mathcal{T}}_{\mathsf{IQ}}(\exists X. \mathcal{A}) \models \exists \{x\}. \{C(x)\}$

Before we can show the main result of this section, we need one more technical lemma.

Lemma 6. $\exists X. \mathcal{A} \models^{\mathcal{T}} \exists \{x\}. \{C(x)\}$ *iff there exists a global IQ* $\exists \{y\}. \{D(y)\}$ *with* $\exists X. \mathcal{A} \models \exists \{y\}. \{D(y)\}$ *and* $\exists \{y\}. \{D(y)\} \models^{\mathcal{T}} \exists \{x\}. \{C(x)\}$.

Proof. Since the if direction is trivial, we turn our attention to the only-if direction. First note that each global IQ $\exists \{x\}. \{C(x)\}$ is equivalent to the IQ $(\exists u. C)(a)$, where u denotes the universal role with semantics $u^{\mathcal{I}} := \Delta^{\mathcal{I}} \times \Delta^{\mathcal{I}}$ in every interpretation $\mathcal{I}$ [24], and a is an arbitrary individual name. Thus, the assumption $\exists X. \mathcal{A} \models^{\mathcal{T}} \exists \{x\}. \{C(x)\}$ yields that $\exists X. \mathcal{A} \models^{\mathcal{T}} (\exists u. C)(a)$. According to Statement 2 of Lemma 22 in [24], there is an $\mathcal{EL}$ concept D such that one of the following two statements holds:

- $\exists X. \mathcal{A} \models^{\mathcal{T}} D(a)$ and $D \sqsubseteq^{\mathcal{T}} \exists u. C$
- $\exists X. \mathcal{A} \models^{\mathcal{T}} (\exists u. D)(a)$ and $\exists u. D \sqsubseteq^{\mathcal{T}} \exists u. C$.

Clearly, the first statement implies the second, and the second statement directly yields the claim. □

Proposition 7. *Let* $\exists X. \mathcal{A}$ *and* $\exists Y. \mathcal{B}$ *be qABoxes and* $\mathcal{T}$ *be an* $\mathcal{EL}$ *TBox. Then,* $\exists X. \mathcal{A} \models^{\mathcal{T}}_{\mathsf{gloIRQ}} \exists Y. \mathcal{B}$ *iff* $\mathsf{sat}^{\mathcal{T}}_{\mathsf{IQ}}(\exists X. \mathcal{A}) \models_{\mathsf{gloIRQ}} \exists Y. \mathcal{B}$. *In addition,* $\models^{\mathcal{T}}_{\mathsf{gloIRQ}}$ *can be decided in polynomial time.*

Proof. To see that the equivalence holds, note that IQs were already treated in the proof of the corresponding result (Theorem 3) in [5], and role assertions in the proof of Proposition 2 in [7]. Thus, it remains to deal with global IQs.

First, assume $\exists X. \mathcal{A} \models^{\mathcal{T}}_{\mathsf{gloIRQ}} \exists Y. \mathcal{B}$, and let $\exists Y. \mathcal{B} \models \exists \{x\}. \{C(x)\}$. The latter implies $\exists Y. \mathcal{B} \models^{\mathcal{T}} \exists \{x\}. \{C(x)\}$, and therefore $\exists X. \mathcal{A} \models^{\mathcal{T}} \exists \{x\}. \{C(x)\}$. Lemma 5 yields that $\mathsf{sat}^{\mathcal{T}}_{\mathsf{IQ}}(\exists X. \mathcal{A}) \models \exists \{x\}. \{C(x)\}$. Since this holds for all global IQs $\exists \{x\}. \{C(x)\}$ entailed by $\exists Y. \mathcal{B}$, $\mathsf{sat}^{\mathcal{T}}_{\mathsf{IQ}}(\exists X. \mathcal{A}) \models_{\mathsf{gloIRQ}} \exists Y. \mathcal{B}$ follows.

Second, let $\mathsf{sat}^{\mathcal{T}}_{\mathsf{IQ}}(\exists X. \mathcal{A}) \models_{\mathsf{gloIRQ}} \exists Y. \mathcal{B}$, and consider a global IQ $\exists \{x\}. \{C(x)\}$ that is entailed by $\exists Y. \mathcal{B}$ w.r.t. $\mathcal{T}$. By Lemma 6, there is a global IQ $\exists \{y\}. \{D(y)\}$ with $\exists Y. \mathcal{B} \models \exists \{y\}. \{D(y)\} \models^{\mathcal{T}} \exists \{x\}. \{C(x)\}$. Since $\mathsf{sat}^{\mathcal{T}}_{\mathsf{IQ}}(\exists X. \mathcal{A}) \models_{\mathsf{gloIRQ}} \exists Y. \mathcal{B}$, we infer $\mathsf{sat}^{\mathcal{T}}_{\mathsf{IQ}}(\exists X. \mathcal{A}) \models \exists \{y\}. \{D(y)\}$. Lemma 5 yields $\exists X. \mathcal{A} \models^{\mathcal{T}} \exists \{y\}. \{D(y)\}$, and thus $\exists X. \mathcal{A} \models^{\mathcal{T}} \exists \{x\}. \{C(x)\}$. Since this argumentation works for all global IQs $\exists \{x\}. \{C(x)\}$, we obtain $\exists X. \mathcal{A} \models^{\mathcal{T}}_{\mathsf{gloIRQ}} \exists Y. \mathcal{B}$.

To show the complexity result, we use Lemma 4 together with the equivalence we have just shown. First recall that the IQ-saturation $\mathsf{sat}^{\mathcal{T}}_{\mathsf{IQ}}(\exists X. \mathcal{A})$ can be computed in polynomial time [5]. Second, the (unique) maximal simulation from a qABox to another can also be computed in polynomial time [20]. This maximal simulation is total iff there is a total simulation, i.e., it suffices to check whether the maximal simulation from $\exists Y.\mathcal{B}$ to $\mathsf{sat}_{\mathsf{IQ}}^{\mathcal{T}}(\exists X.\mathcal{A})$ is total, which can be done in polynomial time. Finally, checking containment of the role assertions involving only individual names obviously needs only polynomial time.   □

4   Optimal Repairs of qABoxes w.r.t. $\mathcal{EL}^{\perp}$ TBoxes

The description logic $\mathcal{EL}^{\perp}$ extends $\mathcal{EL}$ with the bottom concept $\perp$, which has the semantics $\perp^{\mathcal{I}} := \emptyset$ in every interpretation $\mathcal{I}$. In contrast to $\mathcal{EL}$, a quantified ABox $\exists X.\mathcal{A}$ can be *inconsistent* w.r.t. an $\mathcal{EL}^{\perp}$ TBox $\mathcal{T}$, which means that there is no model of the qABox and the TBox. Since any query is entailed by such an inconsistent qABox, repairing it for unwanted consequences also encompasses resolving the inconsistency. This problem was tackled in [9] for the more expressive DL $\mathcal{ELROI}(\perp)$ and the query language CQ. Here, we restrict the attention to $\mathcal{EL}^{\perp}$, but consider a smaller query language, which has the advantage that TBoxes need not be restricted to being cycle-restricted and repairs can be computed more efficiently.

4.1   Repairing the Inconsistency

For a qABox $\exists X.\mathcal{A}$ that is inconsistent w.r.t. the $\mathcal{EL}^{\perp}$ TBox $\mathcal{T}$, Condition (Rep1) in the definition of repairs is vacuously true, and thus does not enforce the repair to be related in any way to $\exists X.\mathcal{A}$. In [9], this problem is addressed for $\mathcal{ELROI}(\perp)$ TBoxes, according to which any $\mathcal{EL}^{\perp}$ TBox $\mathcal{T}$ can be normalized such that it is the union of a *positive part* $\mathcal{T}_+$ consisting of $\mathcal{EL}$ CIs and an *unsatisfiable part* $\mathcal{T}_{\perp}$ consisting of CIs of the form $C \sqsubseteq \perp$ for $\mathcal{EL}$ concepts C. This separation allows us to characterize inconsistency of qABoxes w.r.t. $\mathcal{EL}^{\perp}$ TBoxes as follows.

Lemma 8. [9, Proposition 17] *Let $\exists X.\mathcal{A}$ be a qABox and $\mathcal{T}$ be an $\mathcal{EL}^{\perp}$ TBox.*

1. *$\exists X.\mathcal{A}$ is inconsistent w.r.t. $\mathcal{T}$ iff there is a CI $C \sqsubseteq \perp \in \mathcal{T}_{\perp}$ with $\exists X.\mathcal{A} \models^{\mathcal{T}_+} \exists\{x\}.\{C(x)\}$.*
2. *If $\exists X.\mathcal{A}$ is consistent w.r.t. $\mathcal{T}$, then $\exists X.\mathcal{A} \models^{\mathcal{T}} \exists Y.\mathcal{B}$ iff $\exists X.\mathcal{A} \models^{\mathcal{T}_+} \exists Y.\mathcal{B}$.*

Specifically, Statement 1 tells us that an inconsistency can be resolved by ensuring that the repair does not entail any global IQ $\exists\{x\}.\{C(x)\}$ for which the unsatisfiable part $\mathcal{T}_{\perp}$ contains $C \sqsubseteq \perp$. Statement 2 in turn states that the unsatisfiable part $\mathcal{T}_{\perp}$ can be ignored when working with a consistent qABox. Thus, to regain a meaningful connection between the original qABox and the repair, $\mathcal{T}_+$ rather than $\mathcal{T}$ is used in Condition (IRep1) below.

Definition 9 [9, Definition 18]. *Let QL be a query language, $\exists X.\mathcal{A}$ be a qABox, $\mathcal{T}$ be an $\mathcal{EL}^{\perp}$ TBox, and $\mathcal{P} \subseteq$ QL a repair request. An* inconsistency QL-repair *of $\exists X.\mathcal{A}$ for $\mathcal{P}$ w.r.t. $\mathcal{T}$ is a qABox $\exists Y.\mathcal{B}$ such that*

(IRep1) $\exists X.\mathcal{A} \models_{\mathsf{QL}}^{\mathcal{T}_+} \exists Y.\mathcal{B}$

(IRep2) $\exists Y.\mathcal{B}$ *is consistent w.r.t.* $\mathcal{T}$,

(IRep3) $\exists Y.\mathcal{B} \not\models^{\mathcal{T}} \alpha$ *for each* $\alpha \in \mathcal{P}$.

We say that $\exists Y.\mathcal{B}$ *is* optimal *if it is not strictly* QL-*entailed by another repair.*

In [9], such repairs were investigated for the query language CQ. Here, we are mainly interested in IRQ-repairs, but since resolving the inconsistency requires us to consider global instance queries as well, we use gloIRQ-entailment and also allow the user to include global instance queries in the repair request. The following proposition shows that inconsistency gloIRQ-repairs for $\mathcal{P}$ w.r.t. $\mathcal{T}$ correspond to gloIRQ-repairs for $\mathcal{P}^{\mathcal{T}_\perp}$ w.r.t. $\mathcal{T}_+$, where $\mathcal{P}^{\mathcal{T}_\perp}$ extends $\mathcal{P}$ with the global IQs $\exists \{x\}.\{C(x)\}$ for all CIs $C \sqsubseteq \perp$ in $\mathcal{T}_\perp$. It can be proved by adapting the proof of Theorem 19 in [9].

Proposition 10. *Let* $\exists X.\mathcal{A}$ *be a qABox,* $\mathcal{T}$ *be an* $\mathcal{EL}^\perp$ *TBox, and* $\mathcal{P}$ *be a repair request. If* $\mathcal{T}$ *is inconsistent, then there are no inconsistency* gloIRQ-*repairs of* $\exists X.\mathcal{A}$ *for* $\mathcal{P}$ *w.r.t.* $\mathcal{T}$. *Otherwise, the set of all (optimal) inconsistency* gloIRQ-*repairs of* $\exists X.\mathcal{A}$ *for* $\mathcal{P}$ *w.r.t.* $\mathcal{T}$ *coincides with the set of all (optimal)* gloIRQ-*repairs of* $\exists X.\mathcal{A}$ *for* $\mathcal{P}^{\mathcal{T}_\perp}$ *w.r.t.* $\mathcal{T}_+$.

For the case where $\mathcal{T}$ is consistent, we compute optimal inconsistency gloIRQ-repairs w.r.t. $\mathcal{T}$ in three stages. To repair the inconsistency of the qABox, we replace $\mathcal{T}$ by the $\mathcal{EL}$ TBox $\mathcal{T}_+$ and $\mathcal{P}$ by the extended repair request $\mathcal{P}^{\mathcal{T}_\perp}$ as described in Proposition 10. Then, we repair for the unwanted role assertions using Proposition 11 below. The main remaining task is then to repair for the unwanted concept assertions and global IQs using gloIRQ-entailment (see Sect. 4.3).

4.2 Repairing for Role Assertions

We assume that $\mathcal{T}$ is an $\mathcal{EL}$ TBox and $\mathcal{P} \subseteq$ gloIRQ is a repair request. We denote the set of the role assertions from $\mathcal{P}$ as $\mathcal{P}_\mathsf{R}$ and the set of remaining elements as $\mathcal{P}_\mathsf{C}$. Given that a role assertion between individuals follows from a qABox iff it is contained in its matrix, one might think that one can deal with role assertions in the repair request by simply removing them. However, this way one may also lose concept assertions involving existential restrictions that could have been retained (see Example 3.3 in [11]). Instead, before removing the role assertions of $\mathcal{P}_\mathsf{R}$, one needs to add a variable x_a as copy of every individual a to the qABox. This copy belongs to the same concept and role assertions as a (see the construction in the proof of Lemma 3.4 in [11] for details). The following proposition can be shown by adapting the proof of Theorem 3.6 in [11] to deal with gloIRQ-repairs rather than IRQ-repairs (see [12] for details).

Proposition 11. *Let* $\exists X.\mathcal{A}$ *be a qABox,* $\mathcal{T}$ *an* $\mathcal{EL}$ *TBox, and* $\mathcal{P}$ *a repair request. Consider the qABox* $\exists Z.\mathcal{C}$ *constructed from* $\exists X.\mathcal{A}$ *by first copying all individual names into fresh variables and then removing all role assertions of* $\mathcal{P}_\mathsf{R}$, *i.e.,*

$$Z := X \cup \{ x_a \mid a \in \Sigma_I \}$$
$$\mathcal{C} := (\mathcal{A} \cup \{ A(x_a) \mid A(a) \in \mathcal{A} \} \cup \{ r(x_a, u) \mid r(a, u) \in \mathcal{A} \}$$
$$\cup \{ r(u, x_a) \mid r(u, a) \in \mathcal{A} \}) \setminus \mathcal{P}_{\mathsf{R}}.$$

The set of all (optimal) gloIRQ-repairs of $\exists X.\mathcal{A}$ for $\mathcal{P}$ w.r.t. $\mathcal{T}$ coincides with the set of all (optimal) gloIRQ-repairs of $\exists Z.\mathcal{C}$ for $\mathcal{P}_C$ w.r.t. $\mathcal{T}$.

When going to the last stage, we can thus assume that we are given a qABox, an $\mathcal{EL}$ TBox, and a repair request that consists of unwanted concept assertions and global IQs. However, we still need to use gloIRQ-entailment rather than gloIQ-entailment to avoid reintroducing role assertions that have been removed.

4.3   Repairing for Concept Assertions and Global IQs

The main tool used in [5] to compute all optimal repairs is the construction of canonical repairs. It is shown that the set of canonical repairs covers all repairs, and thus the optimal ones can be obtained by removing elements strictly entailed by others. We recall the construction of canonical repairs from [5] and explain the modifications that are necessary to treat global IQs. We denote by $\mathsf{Sub}(\mathcal{T}, \mathcal{P})$ and $\mathsf{Atoms}(\mathcal{T}, \mathcal{P})$ the set of subconcepts and atoms occurring in the TBox $\mathcal{T}$ and the repair request $\mathcal{P}$. The objects of the canonical repairs are copies of the objects of the saturation $\exists X'.\mathcal{A}' := \mathsf{sat}_{\mathsf{IQ}}^{\mathcal{T}}(\exists X.\mathcal{A})$ of the input qABox $\exists X.\mathcal{A}$. These copies are of the form $\langle\!\langle u, \mathcal{K} \rangle\!\rangle$, where u is an object of $\exists X'.\mathcal{A}'$ and $\mathcal{K}$ is a repair type (see below). Intuitively, $C \in \mathcal{K}$ says that, in the canonical repair, the object $\langle\!\langle u, \mathcal{K} \rangle\!\rangle$ is not an instance of C. Formally, a *repair type* for an object u of $\exists X'.\mathcal{A}'$ is a set $\mathcal{K} \subseteq \mathsf{Atoms}(\mathcal{T}, \mathcal{P})$ such that

(RT1) The object u is an instance of all atoms in $\mathcal{K}$, i.e., the matrix $\mathcal{A}'$ of the saturation entails $C(u)$ for each atom $C \in \mathcal{K}$.

(RT2) The atoms in $\mathcal{K}$ are pairwise subsumption-incomparable, i.e., $C \not\sqsubseteq^\emptyset D$ for distinct atoms $C, D \in \mathcal{K}$.

(RT3) If C is an atom in $\mathcal{K}$ and E is a subconcept in $\mathsf{Sub}(\mathcal{T}, \mathcal{P})$ with $E \sqsubseteq^\mathcal{T} C$ and $\mathcal{A}' \models E(u)$, then there is an atom D in $\mathcal{K}$ with $E \sqsubseteq^\emptyset D$.

(RT1) is motivated by the fact that instance relationships that do not hold need not be removed. (RT2) avoids redundancies in $\mathcal{K}$ since having D in $\mathcal{K}$ for $C \sqsubseteq^\emptyset D$ also prevents $\langle\!\langle u, \mathcal{K} \rangle\!\rangle$ from being an instance of C. (RT3) ensures that inference with the TBox cannot restore instance relationships for atoms in $\mathcal{K}$.

Given sets $\mathcal{K}$ and $\mathcal{L}$ of $\mathcal{EL}$ concepts (e.g. repair types), we say that $\mathcal{K}$ is *covered by* $\mathcal{L}$ and write $\mathcal{K} \leq \mathcal{L}$ if, for each $C \in \mathcal{K}$, there is $D \in \mathcal{L}$ with $C \sqsubseteq^\emptyset D$. The matrix $\mathcal{B}$ of a canonical repair is defined in a way that ensures that indeed each object $\langle\!\langle u, \mathcal{K} \rangle\!\rangle$ is not an instance of any atom in $\mathcal{K}$ for this repair.

(CR1) $\mathcal{B}$ contains all concept assertions $A(\langle\!\langle u, \mathcal{K} \rangle\!\rangle)$ with $A(u) \in \mathcal{A}'$ and $A \notin \mathcal{K}$.

(CR2) $\mathcal{B}$ contains all role assertions $r(\langle\!\langle u, \mathcal{K} \rangle\!\rangle, \langle\!\langle v, \mathcal{L} \rangle\!\rangle)$ with $r(u, v) \in \mathcal{A}'$ and $\mathsf{Succ}(\mathcal{K}, r, u) \leq \mathcal{L}$, where $\mathsf{Succ}(\mathcal{K}, r, u) := \{ C \mid \exists r.C \in \mathcal{K} \text{ and } \mathcal{A}' \models C(v) \}$.

Finally, for each individual a we select one of its copies $\langle a, \mathcal{K} \rangle$ as representation of a in the repair. However, to obtain a genuine repair, the type $\mathcal{K}$ must satisfy an additional condition. Formally, this selection is made by a *repair seed* $\mathcal{S}$, which maps each individual name a to a repair type $\mathcal{S}_a$ for a such that:

(RS) If $C(a)$ is an IQ in $\mathcal{P}$ with $\mathcal{A}' \models C(a)$, then there is an atom D in $\mathcal{S}_a$ such that $C \sqsubseteq^{\emptyset} D$.

Given a repair seed $\mathcal{S}$, the variable set Y consists of all copies $\langle u, \mathcal{K} \rangle$ except those of the form $\langle a, \mathcal{S}_a \rangle$, which are treated as synonyms of the individual names. We then call $\exists Y. \mathcal{B}$ the *canonical repair* induced by $\mathcal{S}$, and denote it by $\mathsf{rep}_{\mathsf{IQ}}^{\mathcal{T}}(\exists X. \mathcal{A}, \mathcal{S})$.

In [9], global IQs in the repair request were treated in the context of a more expressive DL (also containing inverse roles, role inclusions, and nominals) and for CQ-entailment. Here, we present a simpler treatment, which is also easier to handle algorithmically. The following condition, which is introduced in [9], is a variant of (RS) that deals with global IQs by forbidding their concepts for all objects of the repair, and not just for individual names:

(RT4) If $\exists \{x\}. \{C(x)\}$ is a global IQ in $\mathcal{P}$ and $\mathcal{A}' \models C(u)$, then there is an atom D in $\mathcal{K}$ such that $C \sqsubseteq^{\emptyset} D$.

The following example shows that this condition is not sufficient to repair for global IQs since it does not prevent the TBox from restoring global IQs.

Example 12. Consider the TBox $\{A \sqsubseteq \exists r. B\}$, the ABox $\{A(a)\}$, and the repair request $\{\exists \{x\}. \{B(x)\}\}$. The saturation is $\exists \{y\}. \{A(a), r(a, y), B(y)\}$. With only the above conditions, a repair seed $\mathcal{S}$ could map a to the empty repair type. In the canonical repair induced by this repair seed, the assertion $A(a)$ is not removed, and inference with the TBox will re-introduce an r-successor of a that is an instance of B. Thus, the unwanted global IQ is still entailed.

In [9], this problem is dealt with by introducing a (rather complex) condition on repair seed, called *admissibility*, which also deals with inverse roles, role inclusions, and nominals. Here, we treat it by introducing a new condition on repair types, which is stronger than (RT4) and easier to check than admissibility.

Definition 13. *An $\mathcal{EL}$ concept D is globally forbidden w.r.t. $\mathcal{P}$ if it entails a global IQ in $\mathcal{P}$, i.e. if $\exists \{y\}. \{D(y)\} \models^{\mathcal{T}} \exists \{x\}. \{C(x)\}$ for some $\exists \{x\}. \{C(x)\} \in \mathcal{P}$.*

Repairs must not entail $\exists \{y\}. \{D(y)\}$ for any globally forbidden concept D.

(RT5) If C is a subconcept in $\mathsf{Sub}(\mathcal{T}, \mathcal{P})$ that is globally forbidden w.r.t. $\mathcal{P}$ and $\mathcal{A}' \models C(u)$, then there is an atom D in $\mathcal{K}$ with $C \sqsubseteq^{\emptyset} D$.

Since $\exists\{x\}.\{C(x)\} \in \mathcal{P}$ obviously implies that C is globally forbidden, (RT5) encompasses (RT4). In the remainder of this section, we will verify that repair types additionally satisfying (RT5) correctly treat the global IQs in $\mathcal{P}$. With respect to this extended definition of repair types, we denote the canonical repair induced by the repair seed $\mathcal{S}$ as $\mathsf{rep}^{\mathcal{T}}_{\mathsf{gloIRQ}}(\exists X.\mathcal{A}, \mathcal{S})$.

Lemma 14. *Let $\mathcal{S}$ be a repair seed and consider a subconcept $C \in \mathsf{Sub}(\mathcal{T}, \mathcal{P})$. The matrix of $\mathsf{rep}^{\mathcal{T}}_{\mathsf{gloIRQ}}(\exists X.\mathcal{A}, \mathcal{S})$ entails $C(\langle\!\langle u, \mathcal{K}\rangle\!\rangle)$ iff the matrix of $\mathsf{sat}^{\mathcal{T}}_{\mathsf{IQ}}(\exists X.\mathcal{A})$ entails $C(u)$ and no atom in $\mathcal{K}$ subsumes C.*

Proof (sketch). The proof is almost the same as for Lemma XII in [6], except that we must extend the last case in the if direction, where $C = \exists r.D$ is an existential restriction. According to Lemma 1, $\mathcal{A}' \models \exists r.D$ implies that there is an object v such that $\mathcal{A}'$ contains $r(u, v)$ and entails $D(v)$. In the proof of Lemma XII in [6], a repair type $\mathcal{L}$ is constructed such that $r(\langle\!\langle u, \mathcal{K}\rangle\!\rangle, \langle\!\langle v, \mathcal{L}\rangle\!\rangle)$ belongs to the matrix of $\mathsf{rep}^{\mathcal{T}}_{\mathsf{gloIRQ}}(\exists X.\mathcal{A}, \mathcal{S})$ and induction can be used to show that this matrix entails $D(\langle\!\langle v, \mathcal{L}\rangle\!\rangle)$. This construction must be modified such that $\mathcal{L}$ also satisfies (RT5), which is not hard to achieve (see [12] for details). $\qquad\square$

Proposition 15. *Let $\exists X.\mathcal{A}$ be a qABox, $\mathcal{T}$ an $\mathcal{EL}$ TBox, and $\mathcal{P} \subseteq \mathsf{gloIQ}$ a repair request. For each repair seed $\mathcal{S}$, the induced canonical repair is a gloIRQ-repair of $\exists X.\mathcal{A}$ for $\mathcal{P}$ w.r.t. $\mathcal{T}$. Conversely, every gloIRQ-repair of $\exists X.\mathcal{A}$ for $\mathcal{P}$ w.r.t. $\mathcal{T}$ is gloIRQ-entailed by a canonical repair.*

Proof (sketch). The proof of the first claim is the same as for Proposition 8 in [5,6], but uses Lemma 14 above instead of Lemma XII in [6]. The proof of the second claim is similar to the proof of Proposition 8 in [6], but needs to ensure that the constructed simulation is total and that the employed repair types satisfy (RT4) (see [12] for details). $\qquad\square$

This proposition shows that the set of canonical repairs is a set of gloIRQ-repairs that covers all gloIRQ-repairs. The definition of canonical repairs implies that there are at most exponentially many such repairs of at most exponential size, which can be computed in exponential time. Up to equivalence, the optimal gloIRQ-repairs can be obtained from this set by removing redundant elements, i.e., ones that are strictly gloIRQ-entailed by other elements. Since gloIRQ-entailment is in P (Proposition 7), we obtain the following complexity result for computing the set of all optimal repairs, and clearly this set still covers all repairs.

Proposition 16. *For each qABox $\exists X.\mathcal{A}$, each $\mathcal{EL}$ TBox $\mathcal{T}$, and each repair request $\mathcal{P} \subseteq \mathsf{gloIQ}$, the set of all optimal gloIRQ-repairs can be computed in exponential time, up to gloIRQ-equivalence, and this set covers all gloIRQ-repairs.*

Putting Propositions 10, 11, and 16 together, yields the main result of this section.

Theorem 17. *Given a qABox $\exists X.\mathcal{A}$, an $\mathcal{EL}^{\perp}$ TBox $\mathcal{T}$, and a repair request $\mathcal{P} \subseteq \mathsf{gloIRQ}$, the set of all optimal inconsistency gloIRQ-repairs can be computed in exponential time, up to gloIRQ-equivalence, and this set covers all inconsistency gloIRQ-repairs.*

5   Inconsistency- and Error-Tolerant Reasoning

Error-tolerant reasoning does not commit to a single repair, but rather reasons w.r.t. all of them. In [10,11], we have investigated error-tolerant reasoning in a setting where the query language is IRQ and the TBox is written in $\mathcal{EL}$. Here, we extend the obtained results to $\mathcal{EL}^{\perp}$ TBoxes and the query language gloIRQ. Inconsistency-tolerant reasoning is the special case where the repair request is $\{\perp(a)\}$ for some individual a, which is entailed by a KB iff the KB is inconsistent. We assume in the following that the repair request $\mathcal{P}$ is *solvable*, i.e., has a repair, which is the case if none of the queries in $\mathcal{P}$ is entailed by $\mathcal{T}$ alone.

Definition 18. *Let* $\exists X.\mathcal{A}$ *be a qABox,* $\mathcal{T}$ *an* $\mathcal{EL}^{\perp}$ *TBox,* $\mathcal{P} \subseteq$ gloIRQ *a solvable repair request, and* $\alpha \in$ gloIRQ *a query. Then* α *is* bravely (cautiously) gloIRQ *-entailed by* $\exists X.\mathcal{A}$ *w.r.t.* $\mathcal{P}$ *and* $\mathcal{T}$ *if it is entailed w.r.t.* $\mathcal{T}$ *by some (all) optimal inconsistency* gloIRQ*-repair(s) of* $\exists X.\mathcal{A}$ *for* $\mathcal{P}$ *w.r.t.* $\mathcal{T}$.

As shown in [10] for a restricted setting, brave entailment can be reduced to classical entailment. To this purpose, let $\exists Z.\mathcal{C}$ be the qABox representation of $\exists \emptyset.\{\alpha\}$ if α is a concept or role assertion, and α itself if it is a global IQ. Since every inconsistency gloIRQ-repair is entailed by an optimal one, α is bravely gloIRQ-entailed by $\exists X.\mathcal{A}$ w.r.t. $\mathcal{T}$ and $\mathcal{P}$ iff $\exists Z.\mathcal{C}$ is an inconsistency gloIRQ-repair of $\exists X.\mathcal{A}$ for $\mathcal{P}$ w.r.t. $\mathcal{T}$. This reduces checking brave gloIRQ-entailment to deciding whether a given qABox satisfies Conditions (IRep1)–(IRep3). Since each condition can verified in polynomial time, we obtain the following result.

Theorem 19. *Brave* gloIRQ*-entailment is in* P.

Dealing with cautious entailment is more involved. Since a given repair problem may have exponentially many optimal repairs of exponential size, the naïve approach to solve cautious entailment, which computes all optimal repairs and checks whether each of them entails the query α, would require exponential time. The approach employed in [10] (for a more restricted setting) to reduce the complexity to coNP proceeds as follows: to check whether α is *not* cautiously entailed, it guesses a mapping S from individuals a to sets of atoms S_a and then checks whether

1. S is a repair seed,

2. the repair seed S induces an optimal repair,

3. the optimal repair induced by S does not entail α.

To extend this approach to our setting, we must show that Conditions 1–3 can be checked in polynomial time for the query language gloIRQ and $\mathcal{EL}$ TBoxes. In fact, we have shown in the previous section that the optimal inconsistency gloIRQ-repairs w.r.t. $\mathcal{EL}^{\perp}$ TBoxes we are interested in can actually be obtained as optimal gloIRQ-repairs w.r.t. $\mathcal{EL}$ TBoxes.

Regarding Condition 1, it is easy to see that (RT1)–(RT3), (RT5), and (RS) can be checked in polynomial time. Note that this shows an advantage of (RT5) over the admissibility condition in [9] since for the latter it is less clear how to test it in P. To deal with Condition 2, we use a pre-order on repair seeds that reflects gloIRQ-entailment between the induced canonical gloIRQ-repairs.

Definition 20 [8,11]. *Given repair seeds S and R, we say that S is IRQ-covered by R (write $S \leq_{IRQ} R$) if $S_a \leq R_a$ for each $a \in \Sigma_I$, and $\mathsf{Succ}(R_a, r, b) \leq R_b$ implies $\mathsf{Succ}(S_a, r, b) \leq S_b$ for all $r(a, b) \in A$ with $a, b \in \Sigma_I$.*

Lemma 21. $S \leq_{IRQ} R$ *iff* $\mathsf{rep}^T_{gloIRQ}(\exists X.A, S) \models^T_{gloIRQ} \mathsf{rep}^T_{gloIRQ}(\exists X.A, R)$.

Proof. With respect to the old definition of repair types (without (RT5)), it was shown in [7] that $S \leq_{IRQ} R$ iff $\mathsf{rep}^T_{IQ}(\exists X.A, S) \models^T_{IRQ} \mathsf{rep}^T_{IQ}(\exists X.A, R)$. The same proof, but using Lemma 14 instead of Lemma XII in [6], shows that $S \leq_{IRQ} R$ iff $\mathsf{rep}^T_{gloIRQ}(\exists X.A, S) \models^T_{IRQ} \mathsf{rep}^T_{gloIRQ}(\exists X.A, R)$. Since all can. repairs (for the same input) entail the same global IQs, the latter is actually a gloIRQ-entailment. □

Given any pre-order $\leq$, we write $\alpha < \beta$ if $\alpha \leq \beta$ and $\beta \not\leq \alpha$, and say that α is $\leq$-minimal if there is no β such that $\beta < \alpha$. Lemma 21 implies that, up to gloIRQ-equivalence, the optimal gloIRQ-repairs are exactly the canonical gloIRQ-repairs induced by $\leq_{IRQ}$-minimal repair seeds. Thus, to decide optimality in polynomial time, it remains to show the following result.

Proposition 22. $\leq_{IRQ}$-*minimality of repair seeds is in* P.

Proof. With respect to the old definition of repair types, this result follows from Lemma 5.7 in [11], which states that a repair seed S is not $\leq_{IRQ}$-minimal iff there exists an individual a and an atom $D \in S_a$ such that the lowering $\mathsf{low}(S, D(a))$ is a repair seed. Intuitively, if there is a repair seed S' that is strictly smaller than S, then there must by an individual a and an atom $D \in S_a$ such that $D \notin S'_a$. However, just removing D from S_a is not sufficient since such a removal also has an impact on other parts of the repair seed. The (rather intricate) definition of the lowering function (see Definition 5.3 in [11]) takes care of such effects.

The same proof as in [11] also applies w.r.t. the extended definition of repair types, but in the only-if direction we additionally need to verify that each repair type assigned by the lowering $\mathsf{low}(S, D(a))$ satisfies (RT5).

To see this, assume that S is not $\leq_{IRQ}$-minimal, i.e., there is a repair seed R such that $R <_{IRQ} S$. By Lemma 5.5 in [11], there exists $a \in \Sigma_I$ and $D \in S_a$ such that $R \leq_{IQ} \mathsf{low}(S, D(a))$. As argued in [11], the lowering is a repair seed w.r.t. the old definition of repair types. Since the repair type assigned to an individual b by $\mathsf{low}(S, D(a))$ covers the repair type R_b, and the latter satisfies Conditions (RT5), it follows that also the former covers all globally forbidden concepts, and thus satisfies (RT5). □

It remains to show that Condition 3 can be checked in polynomial time.

Proposition 23. *Given a qABox $\exists X.A$, an $\mathcal{EL}$ TBox T, a repair request $P \subseteq$ gloIRQ, a query $\alpha \in$ gloIRQ, and a repair seed S, we can decide in polynomial time whether α is entailed w.r.t. T by the canonical gloIRQ-repair induced by S.*

Proof. It is sufficient to prove three subclaims depending on the kind of query:

1. $\mathsf{rep}^{\mathcal{T}}_{\mathsf{gloIRQ}}(\exists X.\mathcal{A}, \mathcal{S})$ entails the concept assertion $C(a)$
   iff $\mathsf{sat}^{\mathcal{T}}_{\mathsf{IQ}}(\exists X.\mathcal{A}) \models C(a)$ and no atom in $\mathcal{S}_a$ subsumes C w.r.t. $\mathcal{T}$.
2. $\mathsf{rep}^{\mathcal{T}}_{\mathsf{gloIRQ}}(\exists X.\mathcal{A}, \mathcal{S})$ entails the global IQ $\exists\{x\}.\{C(x)\}$
   iff $\mathsf{sat}^{\mathcal{T}}_{\mathsf{IQ}}(\exists X.\mathcal{A}) \models \exists\{x\}.\{C(x)\}$ and C is not globally forbidden.
3. $\mathsf{rep}^{\mathcal{T}}_{\mathsf{gloIRQ}}(\exists X.\mathcal{A}, \mathcal{S})$ entails a role assertion $r(a,b)$
   iff $r(a,b) \in \mathcal{A}$, $r(a,b) \notin \mathcal{P}$, and $\mathsf{Succ}(\mathcal{S}_a, r, b) \leq \mathcal{S}_b$.

The first and the third claim have been shown in our previous work (see Lemma 3 in [10] and Lemma 4.5 in [11]) for the old definition of repair types, but the proofs can be adapted to take also (RT5) into account. The second claim was not treated in [10,11]. Proofs of all three claims can be found in [12].   □

In sum, we have now shown that the Conditions 1–3 introduced above can be checked in polynomial time. This provides us with an NP-procedure for cautious non-entailment, not only for optimal gloIRQ-repairs w.r.t. $\mathcal{EL}$ TBoxes, but also for optimal inconsistency gloIRQ-repairs w.r.t. $\mathcal{EL}^{\perp}$ TBoxes.

Theorem 24. *Cautious* gloIRQ-*entailment is in* coNP.

It is not clear whether this upper bound is tight. For the case of classical repairs, coNP-completeness of cautious entailment is shown in [11], but the hardness proof cannot easily be adapted to the case of optimal repairs.

6   Conclusion

We have shown that our previous work on optimal repairs [5] and error-tolerant reasoning w.r.t. optimal repairs [10,11] can be extended from TBoxes written in the DL $\mathcal{EL}$ to $\mathcal{EL}^{\perp}$ TBoxes. From a practical point of view, $\perp$ can be used to express disjointness of concepts, which means that certain modelling errors can be detected as inconsistencies, as illustrated in our introductory example. From a theoretical point of view, $\mathcal{EL}^{\perp}$ is a minimal extension of $\mathcal{EL}$ that can express inconsistency. This allows us to investigate the effect that inconsistency has on repairs (such as the need for considering global instance queries in repair requests) without being distracted by clutter caused by other constructors, as e.g. the ones of $\mathcal{ELROI}(\perp)$. In contrast to the treatment of optimal repairs for the DL $\mathcal{ELROI}(\perp)$ in [9], we use here a different entailment relation (gloIRQ-entailment) in the definition of optimal repairs. This relation has the advantage that TBoxes need not be cycle-restricted, and is appropriate if one does not intend to use general conjunctive queries to access the knowledge base. We conjecture that the approach developed in this paper can be extended to $\mathcal{ELRO}(\perp)$ TBoxes, though this would probably cause a higher complexity for computing optimal repairs and for cautious reasoning. As pointed out in [9], in the presence of inverse roles, finite IQ-saturation cannot always work, and thus the motivation for using gloIRQ-entailment rather than CQ-entailment is no longer there. The complexity of error-tolerant reasoning w.r.t. optimal CQ-repairs [5] still needs to be investigated. Since entailment of a CQ by a qABox is already NP-hard, the best complexity for cautious entailment we can hope for is then on the second level of the polynomial hierarchy.

Acknowledgements. This work has been supported by Deutsche Forschungsgemeinschaft (DFG) in projects 430150274 (Repairing Description Logic Ontologies) and 389792660 (TRR 248: Foundations of Perspicuous Software Systems).

References

1. Baader, F., Brandt, S., Lutz, C.: Pushing the $\mathcal{EL}$ envelope. In: Proceedings of the 19th International Joint Conference on Artificial Intelligence (IJCAI), pp. 364–369. Professional Book Center (2005). http://ijcai.org/Proceedings/05/Papers/0372.pdf
2. Baader, F., Calvanese, D., McGuinness, D.L., Nardi, D., Patel-Schneider, P.F. (eds.) The Description Logic Handbook: Theory, Implementation, and Applications. Cambridge University Press (2003). https://doi.org/10.1017/cbo9780511711787
3. Baader, F., Horrocks, I., Lutz, C., Sattler, U.: An Introduction to Description Logic. Cambridge University Press, Cambridge (2017). https://doi.org/10.1017/9781139025355
4. Baader, F., Koopmann, P., Kriegel, F.: Optimal repairs in the description logic $\mathcal{EL}$ revisited. In: Gaggl, S., Martinez, M.V., Ortiz, M. (eds.) JELIA 2023. LNCS, vol. 14281, pp. 11–34. Springer, Cham (2023). https://doi.org/10.1007/978-3-031-43619-2_2
5. Baader, F., Koopmann, P., Kriegel, F., Nuradiansyah, A.: Computing optimal repairs of quantified ABoxes w.r.t. static $\mathcal{EL}$ TBoxes. In: Platzer, A., Sutcliffe, G. (eds.) CADE 2021. LNCS (LNAI), vol. 12699, pp. 309–326. Springer, Cham (2021). https://doi.org/10.1007/978-3-030-79876-5_18
6. Baader, F., Koopmann, P., Kriegel, F., Nuradiansyah, A.: Computing optimal repairs of quantified ABoxes w.r.t. static $\mathcal{EL}$ TBoxes (extended version). LTCS-Report 21-01, Chair of Automata Theory, Institute of Theoretical Computer Science, Technische Universität Dresden, Dresden (2021). https://doi.org/10.25368/2022.64
7. Baader, F., Koopmann, P., Kriegel, F., Nuradiansyah, A.: Optimal ABox repair w.r.t. static $\mathcal{EL}$ TBoxes: From quantified ABoxes back to ABoxes. In: Groth, P., et al. (eds.) ESWC 2022. LNCS, vol. 13261, pp. 130–146. Springer, Cham (2022). https://doi.org/10.1007/978-3-031-06981-9_8
8. Baader, F., Koopmann, P., Kriegel, F., Nuradiansyah, A.: Optimal ABox repair w.r.t. static $\mathcal{EL}$ TBoxes: from quantified ABoxes back to ABoxes (extended version). LTCS-Report 22-01, Chair of Automata Theory, Institute of Theoretical Computer Science, Technische Universität Dresden, Dresden (2022). https://doi.org/10.25368/2022.65
9. Baader, F., Kriegel, F.: Pushing optimal ABox repair from $\mathcal{EL}$ towards more expressive Horn-DLs. In: Proceedings of the 19th International Conference on Principles of Knowledge Representation and Reasoning (KR) (2022). https://doi.org/10.24963/kr.2022/3

10. Baader, F., Kriegel, F., Nuradiansyah, A.: Error-tolerant reasoning in the description logic $\mathcal{EL}$ based on optimal repairs. In: Governatori, G., Turhan, A.Y. (eds.) RuleML+RR 2022. LNCS, vol. 13752, pp. 227–243. Springer, Cham (2022). https://doi.org/10.1007/978-3-031-21541-4_15

11. Baader, F., Kriegel, F., Nuradiansyah, A.: Treating role assertions as first-class citizens in repair and error-tolerant reasoning. In: Proceedings of the 38th ACM/SIGAPP Symposium on Applied Computing (SAC), pp. 974–982. ACM (2023). https://doi.org/10.1145/3555776.3577630

12. Baader, F., Kriegel, F., Nuradiansyah, A.: Inconsistency- and error-tolerant reasoning w.r.t. optimal repairs of $\mathcal{EL}^{\perp}$ ontologies (extended version). LTCS-Report 24-02, Chair of Automata Theory, Institute of Theoretical Computer Science, Technische Universität Dresden, Dresden (2024). https://doi.org/10.25368/2024.6

13. Baader, F., Kriegel, F., Nuradiansyah, A., Peñaloza, R.: Making repairs in description logics more gentle. In: Proceedings of the 16th International Conference on Principles of Knowledge Representation and Reasoning (KR), pp. 319–328. AAAI Press (2018). https://cdn.aaai.org/ocs/18056/18056-78653-1-PB.pdf

14. Baader, F., Kriegel, F., Nuradiansyah, A., Peñaloza, R.: Computing compliant anonymisations of quantified ABoxes w.r.t. $\mathcal{EL}$ policies. In: Pan, J.Z., et al. (eds.) ISWC 2020. LNCS, vol. 12506, pp. 3–20. Springer, Cham (2020). https://doi.org/10.1007/978-3-030-62419-4_1

15. Baader, F., Suntisrivaraporn, B.: Debugging SNOMED CT using axiom pinpointing in the description logic $\mathcal{EL}^{+}$. In: Proceedings of the 3rd International Conference on Knowledge Representation in Medicine (KR-MED). CEUR Workshop Proceedings, vol. 410. CEUR-WS.org (2008). https://ceur-ws.org/Vol-410/Paper01.pdf

16. Bienvenu, M., Ortiz, M.: Ontology-mediated query answering with data-tractable description logics. In: Faber, W., Paschke, A. (eds.) Reasoning Web 2015. LNCS, vol. 9203, pp. 218–307. Springer, Cham (2015). https://doi.org/10.1007/978-3-319-21768-0_9

17. Bienvenu, M., Rosati, R.: Tractable approximations of consistent query answering for robust ontology-based data access. In: Proceedings of the 23rd International Joint Conference on Artificial Intelligence (IJCAI), pp. 775–781. IJCAI/AAAI (2013). https://www.ijcai.org/Proceedings/13/Papers/121.pdf

18. Calì, A., Lembo, D., Rosati, R.: On the decidability and complexity of query answering over inconsistent and incomplete databases. In: Proceedings of the 22nd ACM SIGACT-SIGMOD-SIGART Symposium on Principles of Database Systems (PODS), pp. 260–271. ACM (2003). https://doi.org/10.1145/773153.773179

19. Gottlob, G., Leone, N., Scarcello, F.: The complexity of acyclic conjunctive queries. J. ACM **48**(3), 431–498 (2001). https://doi.org/10.1145/382780.382783

20. Henzinger, M.R., Henzinger, T.A., Kopke, P.W.: Computing simulations on finite and infinite graphs. In: Proceedings of the 36th Annual Symposium on Foundations of Computer Science (FOCS), pp. 453–462. IEEE Computer Society (1995). https://doi.org/10.1109/sfcs.1995.492576

21. Hoehndorf, R., Schofield, P.N., Gkoutos, G.V.: The role of ontologies in biological and biomedical research: a functional perspective. Brief. Bioinform. **16**(6), 1069–1080 (2015). https://doi.org/10.1093/bib/bbv011

22. Lembo, D., Lenzerini, M., Rosati, R., Ruzzi, M., Savo, D.F.: Inconsistency-tolerant query answering in ontology-based data access. J. Web Semant. **33**, 3–29 (2015). https://doi.org/10.1016/j.websem.2015.04.002

23. Ludwig, M., Peñaloza, R.: Error-tolerant reasoning in the description logic $\mathcal{EL}$. In: Fermé, E., Leite, J. (eds.) JELIA 2014. LNCS (LNAI), vol. 8761, pp. 107–121. Springer, Cham (2014). https://doi.org/10.1007/978-3-319-11558-0_8

24. Lutz, C., Wolter, F.: Deciding inseparability and conservative extensions in the description logic $\mathcal{EL}$. J. Symb. Comput. **45**(2), 194–228 (2010). https://doi.org/10.1016/j.jsc.2008.10.007

25. Parsia, B., Sirin, E., Kalyanpur, A.: Debugging OWL ontologies. In: Proceedings of the 14th International Conference on World Wide Web (WWW), pp. 633–640. ACM (2005). https://doi.org/10.1145/1060745.1060837

26. Peñaloza, R.: Error-tolerance and error management in lightweight description logics. Künstl. Intell. **34**(4), 491–500 (2020). https://doi.org/10.1007/s13218-020-00684-5

27. Schlobach, S., Huang, Z., Cornet, R., van Harmelen, F.: Debugging incoherent terminologies. J. Autom. Reason. **39**(3), 317–349 (2007). https://doi.org/10.1007/s10817-007-9076-z

28. Xiao, G., et al.: Ontology-based data access: a survey. In: Proceedings of the 27th International Joint Conference on Artificial Intelligence (IJCAI), pp. 5511–5519. ijcai.org (2018). https://doi.org/10.24963/ijcai.2018/777

Computing Repairs Under Functional and Inclusion Dependencies via Argumentation

Yasir Mahmood[1]($\boxtimes$) (ID), Jonni Virtema[2] (ID), Timon Barlag[3] (ID),
and Axel-Cyrille Ngonga Ngomo[1] (ID)

[1] DICE Group, Department of Computer Science, Paderborn University,
Paderborn, Germany
`yasir.mahmood@uni-paderborn.de`, `axel.ngonga@upb.de`
[2] Department of Computer Science, University of Sheffield, Sheffield, UK
`j.t.virtema@sheffield.ac.uk`
[3] Institut für Theoretische Informatik, Leibniz Universität Hannover,
Hannover, Germany
`barlag@thi.uni-hannover.de`

Abstract. We discover a connection between finding subset-maximal repairs for sets of functional and inclusion dependencies, and computing extensions within argumentation frameworks (AFs). We study the complexity of existence of a repair, and deciding whether a given tuple belongs to some (or every) repair, by simulating the instances of these problems via AFs. We prove that subset-maximal repairs under functional dependencies correspond to the naive extensions, which also coincide with the preferred and stable extensions in the resulting AFs. For inclusion dependencies one needs a pre-processing step on the resulting AFs in order for the extensions to coincide. Allowing both types of dependencies breaks this relationship between extensions and only preferred semantics captures the repairs. Finally, we establish that the complexities of the above decision problems are **NP**-complete and $\mathbf{\Pi_2^P}$-complete, when both functional and inclusion dependencies are allowed.

Keywords: complexity theory · database repairs · integrity constraints · abstract argumentation

1 Introduction

In real-world applications, the provenance of data can be very diverse and include non-trustworthy sources. Thus, databases are often inconsistent in practice when the data does not conform to the imposed integrity constraints. A rich theory has been developed to deal with inconsistent databases. One of the main approaches for handling inconsistency is *database repairing*. The goal is to identify and *repair* inconsistencies in data to obtain a consistent database that satisfies the imposed constraints. In the usual approaches, one would search for a database that satisfies the given constraints and differs minimally from the original database; the

A. Meier and M. Ortiz (Eds.): FoIKS 2024, LNCS 14589, pp. 23–42, 2024.
https://doi.org/10.1007/978-3-031-56940-1_2

obtained database is called a *repair* of the original. Some of the most prominent notions of repairs are set-based repairs [8,14], attribute-based repairs [33], and cardinality-based repairs [28].

Dung's abstract argumentation framework [19] has been specifically designed to model conflicts and support relationships among arguments. An abstract argumentation framework (AF) represents arguments and their conflicts through directed graphs and allows for a convenient exploration of the conflicts at an abstract level. AFs have been explored extensively for representation and reasoning with inconsistent knowledge-bases (KBs) covering datalog, existential rules, and description logics (see e.g., [4–6,11,34,35] and [3] for an overview). The common goal in each of these works is to formally establish a connection between inconsistent KBs and AFs such that the argumentation machinery then outputs extensions equivalent to the set of repairs of the KB. Nevertheless, in the setting of relational databases and integrity constraint, there is still a gap with respect to how or whether a connection between inconsistent databases and AFs can be established. To the best of our knowledge, only functional dependencies (FDs) (or in general, denial constraints) have been investigated in the context of AFs, as discussed in [11]. We expand this area of research by establishing further connections between repairs and abstract argumentation frameworks when further integrity constraints are allowed.

In this paper, we focus on subset repairs of relational databases when the integrity constraints are functional and inclusion dependencies (IDs). We are interested in the computational problems of deciding the existence of a repair, and determining whether a given tuple belongs to some (or every) repair. We show how subset-maximal repairs for a set of functional dependencies and inclusion dependencies can be obtained by computing the naive, preferred, or stable extensions (see Sect. 2 for definitions) in the related AFs. Repairs under functional dependencies correspond to the naive extensions, which also coincide with the preferred and stable extensions in the resulting AFs. For inclusion dependencies one needs a pre-processing step on the resulting AFs for the extensions to coincide. Allowing both types of dependencies breaks this relationship between extensions and only preferred semantics captures the maximal repairs. Finally, we consider the complexity of deciding whether a tuple belongs to at least one or to all repairs, respectively. See Table 1 for the complexity results.

By employing Dung's argumentation framework to model repairs of a relational database, one can effectively abstract away from the detailed content of individual entries in the database and focus solely on their relationships with other entries. This approach provides a clearer understanding of why specific records either appear or do not appear in a repair, as well as the reasons certain values may be absent from query answers. Furthermore, this modeling approach allows for the incorporation of additional information about records, such as priorities among them, directly at an abstract level.

Related Work. The problem of computing subset maximal repairs and its complexity has been explored extensively in the database setting [1,2,15,23,27,31] (see [9,10] for an overview). The notion of conflict graphs and hypergraphs

Table 1. Overview of our main contributions. The complexity results depict completeness, unless specified otherwise. The second column indicates the AF-semantics corresponding to subset-repairs (REP) for dependencies in the first column, and the later three columns present the complexity of each problem. The **P**-results are already known in the literature, whereas the remaining results are new.

Atoms	AF-semantics for REP	Complexity Results		
		REP	∃-REP	∀-REP
FDs	$\sigma \in \{\mathsf{naive}, \mathsf{pref}, \mathsf{stab}\}$ (Theorem 3)	(trivial)	(trivial)	$\in \mathbf{P}$
IDs	pref (Theorem 8)	$\in \mathbf{P}^{[1]}$	$\in \mathbf{P}^{[1]}$	$\in \mathbf{P}^{[1]}$
FDs+IDs	pref (Theorem 14)	**NP** (Theorem 15)	**NP** (Theorem 15)	$\mathbf{\Pi}_2^{\mathbf{P}}$ (Theorem 17)

has been introduced before in the case of functional dependencies [25, 26, 30]. In particular, a correspondence between repairs and subset maximal independent sets of the conflict graph for FDs [2] and denial constraints [15] has been established. Moreover, a recent work defines conflict (hyper)graphs for a richer setting of universal constraints considering symmetric difference repairs [12]. Notice that the same definition also yields a correspondence between repairs and the naive extensions when the conflict graph is seen as an argumentation framework. Nevertheless, up to our knowledge, no work has considered a similar graph representation when inclusion dependencies are taken into account. Hannula and Wijsen [23] addressed the problem of consistent query answering with respect to primary and foreign keys. Their setting allows the insertion of new tuples to fulfill foreign key constraints rather than only deleting. Our work differs from the previous work, since it combines functional dependencies (a subclass of equality-generating dependencies) and inclusion dependencies (a subclass of tuple-generating dependencies). Moreover, one of our main contributions lies in connecting repairs under FDs and IDs to the extensions of argumentation frameworks in Dung's setting [19]. The connection between AFs and preferred repairs has been explored in the context of prioritized description logic [11] and datalog knowledge bases [7, 17, 18, 24]. Employing abstract argumentation, we utilize tuples in a database as arguments, aligning with the approach presented in [11]. In contrast, Croitoru et al.'s work in the datalog setting [17, 18] takes an orthogonal approach, employing structured argumentation to construct arguments from a given knowledge base.

2 Preliminaries

We assume that the reader is familiar with basics of complexity theory. We will encounter, in particular, the complexity classes $\mathbf{P}, \mathbf{NP}$, and $\mathbf{\Pi}_2^{\mathbf{P}}$. In the following, we shortly recall the necessary definitions from databases and argumentation.

We begin by restricting our attention to unirelational databases as these suffice for establishing our desired connections to argumentation frameworks as well as to our hardness results (see Table 1). Towards the end (Sect. 4), we highlight the changes required to expand this approach to the multirelational setting.

The unirelational case is also connected to the literature in team-semantics [32], which is a logical framework where formulae are evaluated over unirelational databases (teams in their terminology). In this setting the complexity of finding maximal satisfying subteams has been studied by Hannula and Hella [22] for inclusion logic formulas and by Mahmood [29] for propositional dependence logic. In the team-semantics literature, FDs are known as *dependence* atoms and IDs as *inclusion* atoms, denoted respectively as $\mathsf{dep}(x; y)$ and $x \subseteq y$.[1]

Databases and Repairs. For our setting, an instance of a database is a single table denoted as T. We call each entry in the table a *tuple* which is associated with an identifier. Formally, a table corresponds to a relational schema denoted as $T(x_1, \ldots, x_n)$, where T is the relation name and $x_1, \ldots, x_n$ are distinct attributes. For an attribute x and a tuple $s \in T$, $s(x)$ denotes the value taken by s for the attribute x. For a sequence $x = (x_1, \ldots, x_k)$, $s(x)$ denotes the sequence of values $(s(x_1), \ldots, s(x_k))$. For a database T, $\mathsf{dom}(T)$ denotes the *active domain* of T, defined as the collection of all the values that occur in the tuples of T.

Let $T(x_1, \ldots, x_n)$ be a schema and T be a database. A *functional dependency* (FD) over T is an expression of the form $\mathsf{dep}(x; y)$ (also denoted as $x \to y$) for sequences x, y of attributes in T. A database T satisfies $\mathsf{dep}(x; y)$, denoted as $T \models \mathsf{dep}(x; y)$ if for all $s, t \in T$: if $s(x) = t(x)$ then $s(y) = t(y)$. That is, every two tuples from T that agree on x also agree on y. Moreover, an *inclusion dependency* (ID) is an expression of the form $x \subseteq y$ for two sequences x and y of attributes with same length. The table T satisfies $x \subseteq y$ ($T \models x \subseteq y$) if for each $s \in T$, there is some $t \in T$ such that $s(x) = t(y)$. We call each such t the *satisfying tuple for s* and the ID $x \subseteq y$. By a dependency atom, we mean either a functional or an inclusion dependency.

Let T be a database and B be a collection of dependency atoms. Then T is *consistent* with respect to B, denoted as $T \models B$, if $T \models b$ for each $b \in B$. Moreover, T is *inconsistent* with respect to B if there is some $b \in B$ such that $T \not\models b$. A *subset-repair* of T with respect to B is a subset $P \subseteq T$ which is consistent with respect to B, and maximal in the sense that no set P' exists such that it is consistent with respect to B and $P \subset P' \subseteq T$. In the following, we simply speak of a repair when we intend to mean a subset-repair. Furthermore, we often consider a database T without explicitly highlighting its schema. Let $\mathcal{B} = \langle T, B \rangle$ where T is a database and B is a set of dependency atoms, then $\mathsf{repairs}(\mathcal{B})$ denotes the set of all repairs for $\mathcal{B}$. Since an empty database satisfies each dependency trivially, we restrict the notion of a repair to non-empty databases. The problem we are interested in (REP) asks to decide whether there exists a repair for an instance $\mathcal{B}$.

Problem: REP

Input: an instance $\mathcal{B} = \langle T, B \rangle$.
Question: is it true that $\mathsf{repairs}(\mathcal{B}) \neq \emptyset$?

---

[1] We borrow this notation and write $\mathsf{dep}(x; y)$ and $x \subseteq y$ for FDs and IDs, respectively.

Two further problems of interest are *brave* and *cautious* reasoning for a tuple $s \in T$. Given an instance $\mathcal{B} = \langle T, B \rangle$ and tuple $s \in T$, then brave (cautious) reasoning for s denoted as $\exists\text{-REP}(s, \mathcal{B})$ ($\forall\text{-REP}(s, \mathcal{B})$) asks whether s belongs to some (every) repair for $\mathcal{B}$.

Abstract Argumentation. We use Dung's argumentation framework [19] and consider only non-empty and finite sets of arguments A. An *(argumentation) framework (AF)* is a directed graph $\mathcal{F} = (A, R)$, where A is a set of arguments and the relation $R \subseteq A \times A$ represents direct attacks between arguments. If $S \subseteq A$, we say that an argument $s \in A$ is *defended by* S *in* $\mathcal{F}$, if for every $(s', s) \in R$ there exists $s'' \in S$ such that $(s'', s') \in R$.

In abstract argumentation one is interested in computing the so-called *extensions*, which are subsets $S \subseteq A$ of the arguments that have certain properties. The set S of arguments is called *conflict-free in* $\mathcal{F}$ if $(S \times S) \cap R = \emptyset$. Let S be conflict-free, then S is

1. *naive in* $\mathcal{F}$ if no $S' \supset S$ is *conflict-free* in $\mathcal{F}$;
2. *admissible in* $\mathcal{F}$ if every $s \in S$ is *defended by* S in $\mathcal{F}$.

Further, let S be admissible. Then, S is

3. *preferred in* $\mathcal{F}$, if there is no $S' \supset S$ that is *admissible in* $\mathcal{F}$;
4. *stable in* $\mathcal{F}$ if every $s \in A \backslash S$ is *attacked* by some $s' \in S$.

We denote each of the mentioned semantics by abbreviations: conf, naive, adm, pref, and stab, respectively. For a semantics $\sigma \in \{\text{conf}, \text{naive}, \text{adm}, \text{pref}, \text{stab}\}$, we write $\sigma(\mathcal{F})$ for the set of *all extensions* of semantics σ in $\mathcal{F}$[2] Now, we are ready to define the corresponding decision problem asking for extension existence with respect to a semantics σ.

Problem: Ext_σ

Input: an argumentation framework $\mathcal{F}$.
Question: is it true that $\sigma(\mathcal{F}) \neq \emptyset$?

Finally, for an AF $\mathcal{F} = (A, R)$ and $a \in A$, the problems Cred_σ and Skep_σ ask whether a is in some σ-extension of $\mathcal{F}$ ("*credulously* accepted") or every σ-extension of $\mathcal{F}$ ("*skeptically* accepted"), respectively. The complexity of reasoning in argumentation is well understood, see [20, Table 1] for an overview. In particular, $\text{Cred}_{\text{naive}}$ and $\text{Skep}_{\text{naive}}$ are in **P**, whereas, $\text{Cred}_{\text{pref}}$ and $\text{Skep}_{\text{pref}}$ are **NP**-complete and $\mathbf{\Pi_2^P}$-complete, respectively. Moreover, the problem to decide whether there is a non-empty extension is in **P** for naive and **NP**-complete for pref-semantics. This makes naive-semantics somewhat easier and pref the hardest among the considered semantics in this work.

---

[2] We disallow the empty set ($\emptyset$) in extensions for the sake of compatibility with repairs. Nevertheless, one can allow $\emptyset$ as an extension in AFs and the empty database as repairs, without affecting our complexity results.

3   Inconsistent Databases via Argumentation Frameworks

In the first two subsections, we consider instances containing only one type of dependency atoms to an AF. Then, we combine both (dependence and inclusion) atoms in the third subsection. Given an instance $\mathcal{B} = \langle T, B \rangle$ comprising a database T and a set B of dependencies, the goal is to capture all the subset-repairs for $\mathcal{B}$ by σ-extensions of the resulting AF $(\mathcal{F}_\mathcal{B})$ for some semantics σ.

In Sect. 3.1, we encode an instance $\mathcal{D} = \langle T, D \rangle$ with database T and a collection D of FDs into an AF $\mathcal{F}_\mathcal{D}$. This is achieved by letting each tuple $s \in T$ be an argument. Then the attack relation for $\mathcal{F}_\mathcal{D}$ simulates the violation between a pair $s, t \in T$ failing some $d \in D$. Although the construction for FDs is similar to the approach adopted by Bienvenu and Bourgaux [11], we do not consider priorities among tuples in the database and therefore establish that a weaker AF-semantics is already enough to capture repairs in our setting.

In Sect. 3.2, we simulate an instance $\mathcal{I} = \langle T, I \rangle$ including a collection I of inclusion dependencies (IDs) via AFs. The first observation is that the semantics of IDs requires the notion of *support* or *defense* rather than *conflict* between tuples. Then, we depict each tuple as an argument as well as use auxiliary arguments to simulate inclusion dependencies (i.e., to model the semantics for IDs). This is achieved by letting s_i be an argument for each $s \in T$ and $i \in I$ such that s_i attacks s. Then, the arguments defending s against s_i correspond precisely to the satisfying tuples $t \in T$ for s and i. Further, we add self-attacks for these auxiliary arguments to prohibit them from appearing in any extension. Consequently, we establish a connection between repairs for $\mathcal{I}$ and the extensions for AFs under preferred semantics. Finally, we establish that after a pre-processing on the resulting AF, the stable and naive extensions also yield repairs for $\mathcal{I}$.

Having established that both FDs and IDs can be modeled in AFs via attacks, Sect. 3.3 generalizes this approach by allowing both types of dependencies.

3.1   Simulating Functional Dependencies via AFs

We transform an instance $\mathcal{D} = \langle T, D \rangle$ with database T and a collection D of FDs to an AF $\mathcal{F}_\mathcal{D}$ defined as follows.

Definition 1. *Let $\mathcal{D} = \langle T, D \rangle$ be an instance of* REP *including a database T and a collection D of FDs. Then, $\mathcal{F}_\mathcal{D}$ denotes the following AF.*

- $A := T$, *that is, each $s \in T$ is seen as an argument.*
- $R := \{(s, t), (t, s) \mid$ *there is some $d \in D$, s.t. $\{s, t\} \not\models d\}$.*

We call $\mathcal{F}_\mathcal{D}$ the argumentation framework generated by the instance $\mathcal{D}$. Moreover, we also call R the conflict graph *for $\mathcal{D}$.*

Note that, for a given instance $\mathcal{D}$, the framework $\mathcal{F}_\mathcal{D}$ can be generated in polynomial time. The attack relation R is constructed for each $d \in D$ by taking each pair $s, t \in T$ in turn and checking whether $\{s, t\} \models d$ or not.

T	Emp_ID	Sup_ID	Dept.	Building
s	TimX3	JonX1	Marketing	B1
t	TimX3	AxeK4	Sales	B2
u	JonX1	JonX1	Production	B1
v	JonX1	AxeK4	Distribution	B4

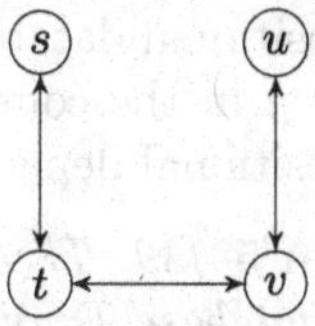

Fig. 1. Argumentation framework for modelling FDs in Example 2.

Example 2. Consider $\mathcal{D} = \langle T, D \rangle$ with database $T = \{s, t, u, v\}$ as depicted inside table in Fig. 1 and FDs $\{\mathsf{dep}(\mathsf{Emp\_ID}; \mathsf{Dept}), \mathsf{dep}(\mathsf{Sup\_ID}; \mathsf{Building})\}$. Informally, each employee is associated with a unique department and employees supervised by the same supervisor work in the same building. Observe that, $\{s, t\} \not\models \mathsf{dep}(\mathsf{Emp\_ID}; \mathsf{Dept})$, $\{u, v\} \not\models \mathsf{dep}(\mathsf{Emp\_ID}; \mathsf{Dept})$, and $\{t, v\} \not\models \mathsf{dep}(\mathsf{Sup\_ID}; \mathsf{Building})$. The resulting AF $\mathcal{F}_\mathcal{D}$ is depicted on the right side of Fig. 1. The preferred (as well as naive and stable) extensions of $\mathcal{F}_\mathcal{D}$ include $\{s, v\}, \{t, u\}$ and $\{s, u\}$. Clearly, these three are the only repairs for $\mathcal{D}$.

It is easy to observe that a subset $P \subseteq T$ satisfying each $d \in D$ contains precisely those tuples $s \in T$, which are not in conflict with each other. Clearly, such subsets correspond to the naive extensions (maximal conflict-free sets) of $\mathcal{F}_\mathcal{D}$. Moreover, since the attack relation in $\mathcal{F}_\mathcal{D}$ is symmetric, i.e., $(s, t) \in R$ iff $(t, s) \in R$, the preferred, stable and naive extensions coincide [16, Prop. 4 & 5].

Theorem 3. *Let $\mathcal{D} = \langle T, D \rangle$ be an instance of* REP *where D is a set of FDs and let $\mathcal{F}_\mathcal{D}$ denote the argumentation framework generated by $\mathcal{D}$. Then for every subset $P \subseteq T$, $P \in \mathsf{repairs}(\mathcal{D})$ iff $P \in \sigma(\mathcal{F}_\mathcal{D})$ for $\sigma \in \{\mathsf{naive}, \mathsf{stab}, \mathsf{pref}\}$.*

Proof. Let $\mathcal{D} = \langle T, D \rangle$ be an instance of REP and $P \subseteq T$ such that $P \models d$ for each $d \in D$. Then, P is clearly conflict-free in $\mathcal{F}_\mathcal{D}$. Moreover, since P is a repair (and hence a maximal subset) of T, there is no $t \in T \backslash P$ such that $P \cup \{t\}$ is also conflict-free. As a result, P is a naive extension in $\mathcal{F}_\mathcal{D}$. Finally, the same holds for preferred and stable extensions since the attack relation in $\mathcal{F}_\mathcal{D}$ is symmetric.

Conversely, let $P \subseteq A$ be naive in $\mathcal{F}_\mathcal{D}$. Then, $\{s, t\} \models d$ for each $s, t \in P$ and $d \in D$ since P is conflict-free. Moreover, P is also subset maximal and therefore a repair for $\mathcal{D}$.   □

An interesting corollary of Theorem 3 reproves that a subset-repair for $\mathcal{D}$ can be computed in polynomial time [20]. Moreover we can also decide if a given tuple $s \in T$ is in some (or all) repairs, in polynomial time. In fact, the basic properties of functional dependencies allow us to make the following observation regarding the acceptability of tuples with respect to $\mathcal{D}$.

Remark 4. Let $\mathcal{D} = \langle T, D \rangle$ be an instance of REP where D is a set of FDs. Then, $\exists\text{-REP}(s, \mathcal{D})$ is true for every $s \in T$, and $\forall\text{-REP}(s, \mathcal{D})$ is true for a tuple $s \in T$ iff $\{s, t\} \models d$ for each $t \in T$ and $d \in D$.

We conclude this section by observing that adding a size restriction for a repair renders the complexity of REP **NP**-hard. Moreover, this already holds for propositional databases, that is, when $\mathsf{dom}(T) = \{0, 1\}$. The following result was proven in the context of team-semantics and maximal satisfying subteams for propositional dependence logic.

Theorem 5 *[29, Theorem 3.32]. There is an instance $\mathcal{D}$ including a propositional database T and FDs D, such that given $k \in \mathbb{N}$, the problem to decide whether there is a repair $P \subseteq T$ for $\mathcal{D}$ such that $|P| \geq k$ is* **NP**-*complete.*

3.2   Simulating Inclusion Dependencies via AFs

Let $\mathcal{I} = \langle T, I \rangle$ be an instance of REP with a database T and collection I of IDs. For $i \in I$ (say $i = \boldsymbol{x} \subseteq \boldsymbol{y}$) and $s \in T$, let $t_1, \ldots, t_m \in T$ be such that $s(\boldsymbol{x}) = t_j(\boldsymbol{y})$ for $j \leq m$. Then we say that, each such t_j *supports* s for the dependency $i \in I$ denoted as $S_i(s) := \{t_1, \ldots, t_m\}$. Clearly, $T \models i$ if and only if $S_i(s) \neq \emptyset$ for each $s \in T$. Moreover, if $S_i(s) = \emptyset$ for some $s \in T$ and $i \in I$, then s cannot belong to a repair for I. In the following, we formalize this notion and simulate the semantics for IDs via AFs.

Definition 6. *Let $\mathcal{I} = \langle T, I \rangle$ be an instance of* REP *including a database T and a collection I of IDs. Then $\mathcal{F}_\mathcal{I}$ is the following AF.*

- $A := T \cup \{s_i \mid s \in T, i \in I\}$.
- $R := \{(s_i, s), (s_i, s_i) \mid s \in T, i \in I\} \cup \{(t, s_i) \mid s \in T, i \in I, t \in S_i(s)\}$.

Intuitively, for each $i \in I$ and tuple $s \in T$, the presence of attacks (t, s_i) for each $t \in S_i(s)$ simulates the support relationship between s and tuples in $S_i(s)$. In other words, each $t \in S_i(s)$ attacks s_i and consequently, defends s against s_i. The whole idea captured in this translation is that a tuple $s \in T$ is in a repair for $\mathcal{I}$ if and only if for each $i := \boldsymbol{x} \subseteq \boldsymbol{y} \in I$, there is some $t \in T$ such that $s(\boldsymbol{x}) = t(\boldsymbol{y})$ if and only if the argument $s \in A$ is defended against each s_i in $\mathcal{F}_\mathcal{I}$.

Example 7. Consider $\mathcal{I} = \langle T, I \rangle$ with database $T = \{s, t, u, v\}$ and IDs $I := \{\text{Sup\_ID} \subseteq \text{Emp\_ID}, \text{Covers\_For} \subseteq \text{Dept}\}$. For brevity, we denote IDs by $I = \{1, 2\}$. The database and the supporting tuples $S_i(w)$ for each $i \in I, w \in T$ are depicted in the table inside Fig. 2. Informally, a supervisor is also an employee and each employee is assigned a department to cover if that department is short on employees. For example, $s(\text{Sup\_ID}) = t(\text{Emp\_ID})$, $s(\text{Covers\_For}) = t(\text{Dept}) = u(\text{Dept})$, and therefore $S_1(s) = \{t\}$, $S_2(s) = \{t, u\}$. Then we have the AF $\mathcal{F}_\mathcal{I}$ as depicted in Fig. 2. The AF $\mathcal{F}_\mathcal{I}$ has a unique preferred extension, given by $\{s, t\}$. Clearly, this is also the only repair for $\mathcal{I}$.

It is worth mentioning that, $\{s, t, u, v\}$ constitutes a naive extension for $\mathcal{F}_\mathcal{I}$ in Example 7, although this is not a repair for $\mathcal{I}$. Clearly, the semantics for IDs in $\mathcal{F}_\mathcal{I}$ requires admissibility (defending against attacking arguments). We now prove that the repairs for $\mathcal{I}$ are precisely the preferred extension in $\mathcal{F}_\mathcal{I}$.

Theorem 8. *Let $\mathcal{I} = \langle T, I \rangle$ be an instance of* REP *where I is a set of IDs and let $\mathcal{F}_\mathcal{I}$ denote the argumentation framework generated by $\mathcal{I}$. Then for every subset $P \subseteq T$, $P \in \mathsf{repairs}(\mathcal{I})$ iff $P \in \mathsf{pref}(\mathcal{F}_\mathcal{I})$.*

T	Emp_ID	Sup_ID	Dept.	Covers_For	S_1	S_2
s	JonX1	AxeK4	Production	Marketing	t	t,u
t	AxeK4	AxeK4	Marketing	Production	t	s
u	TimX3	JonX1	Marketing	Distribution	s,v	v
v	JonX1	AxeK4	Distribution	R&D	t	-

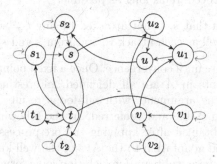

Fig. 2. The AF $\mathcal{F}_\mathcal{I}$ modelling $\mathcal{I}$ in Example 7: the red self-loops together with blue arcs depict the attacks for each tuple $s \in T$ due to IDs $i \in I$ and the black arcs model the attacks due to the support set $S_i(s)$. (Color figure online)

Proof. We first prove the reverse direction. Let $P \subseteq A$ be a preferred extension in $\mathcal{F}_\mathcal{I}$, then P must not contain any auxiliary argument s_i corresponding to some ID $i \in I$ since P is conflict-free. This implies that $P \subseteq T$, which together with that fact P is admissible (every $s \in P$ is defended against each $s_i \in A$) and maximal under set inclusion yields the proof of the claim.

Conversely, let $P \subseteq T$ denote a repair for $\mathcal{I} = \langle T, I \rangle$. Then P is conflict-free in $\mathcal{F}_\mathcal{I}$ since the attacks in R contain at least one argument among the auxiliary arguments (s_i) which are not in P (as $P \subseteq T$). Moreover, for each $s \in P$ and $i := \boldsymbol{x} \subseteq \boldsymbol{y} \in I$, there is some $t \in P$ such that: $s(\boldsymbol{x}) = t(\boldsymbol{y})$. This implies that each $s \in P$ is defended against the attack $s_i \in A$. Consequently, P is admissible. To prove that P is also preferred in $\mathcal{F}_\mathcal{I}$, assume to the contrary that there is an admissible $P' \supset P$ in $\mathcal{F}_\mathcal{I}$. Since P' is also conflict-free, using the same argument as for P we notice that $P' \subseteq T$. Now, P' being preferred (together with the claim in reverse direction) implies that P' is a repair for $\mathcal{I}$ contradicting the fact that P is a subset-maximal repair for $\mathcal{I}$. As a consequence, P is preferred in $\mathcal{F}_\mathcal{I}$.

This proves the correctness of our theorem. □

Notice that a framework $\mathcal{F}_\mathcal{I}$ may not have stable extensions for certain instances $\mathcal{I}$ including databases T and IDs I. This holds because some arguments can neither be accepted in an extension (e.g., when $S_i(s) = \emptyset$ for some $s \in T$ and $i \in I$), nor attacked by arguments in an extension (since arguments in A only attack auxiliary arguments). The argument corresponding to the tuple v in Example 7 depicts such an argument. As a result, the stable and preferred extensions do not coincide in general. Nevertheless, we prove that after a pre-processing, naive, stable and preferred extensions still coincide.

A Pre-processing Algorithm for $\mathcal{F}_{\mathcal{I}}$. Observe that an undefended argument in an AF $\mathcal{F}$ cannot belong to any preferred extension of $\mathcal{F}$. The intuition behind pre-processing is to remove such arguments, which are not defended against some of their attacks in $\mathcal{F}_{\mathcal{I}}$. This corresponds to (recursively) removing those tuples in $s \in T$, for which $S_i(s) = \emptyset$ for some $i \in I$. The pre-processing (denoted $\mathsf{PRE}(\mathcal{F}_{\mathcal{I}})$) applies the following procedure as long as possible.

* For each $s_i \in A$ such that s_i is not attacked by any $t \neq s_i$: remove s and s_j for each $j \in I$, as well as each attack to and from s and s_j.

We repeat this procedure until convergence. Once a fixed point has been reached, the remaining arguments in A are all defended. Interestingly, after the pre-processing, removing the arguments with self-loops results in a unique naive extension which is also stable and preferred. In the following, we also denote by $\mathsf{PRE}(\mathcal{F}_{\mathcal{I}})$ the AF obtained after applying the pre-processing on $\mathcal{F}_{\mathcal{I}}$. Notice that PRE is basically an adaptation to the AFs of the well-known algorithm for finding a maximal satisfying subteam for inclusion logic formulas [22, Lem. 12].

Lemma 9. *Let $\mathcal{I}$ be an instance of REP and $\mathcal{F}_{\mathcal{I}}$ denote the argumentation framework generated by $\mathcal{I}$. Then $\mathsf{PRE}(\mathcal{F}_{\mathcal{I}})$ can be computed from $\mathcal{F}_{\mathcal{I}}$ in polynomial time. Moreover, $\mathsf{PRE}(\mathcal{F}_{\mathcal{I}})$ has a unique naive extension which is also stable and preferred.*

Proof. The procedure $\mathsf{PRE}(\mathcal{F}_{\mathcal{I}})$ removes recursively all the arguments corresponding to assignments s such that $S_i(s) = \emptyset$ for some $i \in I$. Notice that $S_i(s)$ can be computed for each $i \in I$ and $s \in T$ in polynomial time. Then, PRE stores in a data structure (such as a queue) all the arguments s for which $S_i(s) = \emptyset$. Finally, each argument s in this queue can be processed turn by turn, adding possibly new arguments when PRE triggers the removal of certain arguments from A and hence from $S_i(t)$ for some $t \in A$. A fixed-point is reached when every element in the queue has been processed, this gives the size of A as the total number of iterations. Consequently, PRE runs in polynomial time in the size of $\mathcal{F}_{\mathcal{I}}$.

Let $\mathsf{PRE}(\mathcal{F}_{\mathcal{I}}) = (A', R')$ denote the AF generated by the pre-processing. To prove the equivalence between extensions, notice that the set of arguments (S) without self-attacks in A' form an admissible extension since $S_i(s) \neq \emptyset$ for every $s \in S$. Further, since $A' \backslash S$ only includes auxiliary arguments, those are all attacked by S and therefore S is stable. Finally, S is the only naive extension in the reduced AF since S is the maximal and conflict-free in $\mathsf{PRE}(\mathcal{F}_{\mathcal{I}})$ and arguments in $A' \backslash S$ contain self-attacks.

This establishes the correctness of the lemma together with Theorem 8.   □

One consequence of Lemma 9 is that a database in the presence of IDs admits a unique repair (Theorem 8). Moreover, the following observation follows from the proof of Lemma 9. Intuitively, we can also determine $\exists\text{-REP}(s, \mathcal{I})$ and $\forall\text{-REP}(s, \mathcal{I})$ for each $s \in T$, once the pre-processing has terminated resulting in $\mathsf{PRE}(\mathcal{F}_{\mathcal{I}})$.

Remark 10. Let $\mathcal{I}$ be an instance of REP and $\mathcal{F}_\mathcal{I}$ denote the argumentation framework generated by $\mathcal{I}$. Then, $\exists$-REP$(s,\mathcal{I})$ and $\forall$-REP$(s,\mathcal{I})$ is true for every $s \in T$ such that $s \in \mathsf{PRE}(\mathcal{F}_\mathcal{I})$.

Example 11 (Continue). Reconsider the instance $\mathcal{I} = \langle T, I \rangle$ from Example 7. Observe that the argument v is not defended against v_2 and therefore cannot be in a repair. Then the pre-processing removes $\{v, v_1, v_2\}$ and all the edges to/from arguments in this set. This has the consequence that all the arguments which are only defended by v are no longer defended (e.g., u). Consequently, the arguments $\{u, u_1, u_2\}$ have to be removed as well. After repeating the process for u, we notice that no other argument needs to be removed. Hence, the set $\{s, t\}$ is a repair for $\mathcal{I}$ as well as a σ-extension in the reduced AF for $\sigma \in \{\mathsf{naive}, \mathsf{stab}, \mathsf{pref}\}$.

3.3 Simulating Functional and Inclusion Dependencies via AFs

Consider an instance $\mathcal{B} = \langle T, B \rangle$ with a database T such that $B = D \cup I$ includes functional (D) and inclusion (I) dependencies. We apply the pre-processing as a first step, thereby, removing those tuples from T failing some $i \in I$. In other words, we remove (recursively) all the tuples s from T, such that, there is some $i \in I$ with $S_i(s) = \emptyset$. Then, the framework generated by $\mathcal{B}$ is $\mathcal{F}_\mathcal{B} := (A, R_D \cup R_I)$, specified as below.

- $A := T \cup \{s_i \mid s \in T, i \in I\}$.
- $R_D := \{(s,t),(t,s) \mid \text{ there is some } d \in D, \text{ s.t. } \{s,t\} \not\models d\}$.
- $R_I := \{(s_i, s),(s_i, s_i) \mid s \in T, i \in I\} \cup \{(t, s_i) \mid s \in T, i \in I, t \in S_i(s)\}$.

In the presence of both types of dependencies, pre-processing allows to reduce the number of arguments in the resulting AF without affecting the connection between extensions and repairs. The removed tuples are limited to those that cannot belong to any repair. However, to avoid the impression that pre-processing contributes towards the computation of repairs, one may choose not to apply it and consider the original database. Interestingly, even if we apply pre-processing, some tuples may not be accepted in combination with each other, as depicted in the following example.

Example 12. Consider $\mathcal{B} = \langle T, B \rangle$ with database $T = \{s, t, u\}$ and atoms $B = D \cup I$ where $D = \{\mathsf{dep}(\mathsf{Sup\_ID}; \mathsf{Building})\}$ and $I = \{\mathsf{Covers\_For} \subseteq \mathsf{Dept}\}$. Moreover, the database T and the support $S_{\mathsf{Covers\_For} \subseteq \mathsf{Dept}}(w)$ for each $w \in T$ is depicted in the table inside Fig. 3. Then, $\{s, t\} \not\models \mathsf{dep}(\mathsf{Sup\_ID}; \mathsf{Building})$, and $\{t, u\} \not\models \mathsf{dep}(\mathsf{Sup\_ID}; \mathsf{Building})$. The resulting AF $\mathcal{F}_\mathcal{B}$ is shown in Fig. 3, where the edges due to the IDs are depicted in red and blue. Then, the only preferred extensions for $\mathcal{F}_\mathcal{B}$ is $\{t\}$. Also, the only repair for $\mathcal{B}$ is $\{t\}$. Further, although $\{s, u\}$ is preferred for $\mathcal{F}_\mathcal{D}$ where $\mathcal{D} = \langle T, D \rangle$ (ignoring red and blue arcs), and $\{s, t, u\}$ is preferred for $\mathcal{F}_\mathcal{I}$ where $\mathcal{I} = \langle T, I \rangle$ (ignoring black arcs), none of them is preferred for $\mathcal{F}_\mathcal{B}$.

One consequence of allowing both (functional and inclusion) dependencies is that the preferred and naive extensions do not coincide in general. Moreover, both $\exists$-REP and $\forall$-REP are non-trivial and distinct (cf. Remark 4 and 10).

T	Emp_ID	Sup_ID	Dept.	Building	Covers_for	S_i
s	JonX1	AxeK4	Production	B4	Sales	t
t	TimX3	AxeK4	Sales	B2	Sales	t
u	AxeK4	AxeK4	Marketing	B4	Production	s

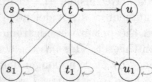

Fig. 3. Argumentation framework for modelling dependencies in Example 12. Black arcs depict conflicts due to functional, and blue ones due to inclusion dependency. (Color figure online)

Example 13 (Cont.). Reconsider the instance $\mathcal{B}$ from Example 12. Then, $\{s, u\}$ is a naive extension for $\mathcal{F}_\mathcal{B}$ but not preferred. Moreover, t is the only tuple for which $\exists$-REP$(t, \mathcal{B})$ and $\forall$-REP$(t, \mathcal{B})$ is true.

As the preceding examples demonstrate, in the presence of both types of dependencies, the repairs correspond to somewhat costly (that is, preferred) semantics for AFs.

Theorem 14. *Let* $\mathcal{B} = \langle T, B \rangle$ *be an instance of* REP *where* B *includes FDs and IDs. Further, let* $\mathcal{F}_\mathcal{B}$ *denote the argumentation framework generated by* $\mathcal{B}$. *Then for every subset* $P \subseteq T$, $P \in$ repairs$(\mathcal{B})$ *iff* $P \in$ pref$(\mathcal{F}_\mathcal{B})$.

Proof. The correctness follows from the proof of Theorem 3 and 8. The conflict-freeness and admissibility of P implies that each FD and ID in B, respectively, is true in P. The converse follows the same line of argument. Finally, the maximality of repairs in $\mathcal{B}$ corresponds to the maximality of extensions in $\mathcal{F}_\mathcal{B}$.   □

The existence of a non-empty extension and the credulous reasoning for preferred semantics are both **NP**-complete, and skeptical reasoning is even harder and $\mathbf{\Pi_2^P}$-complete. Next we establish that when both types of dependencies are allowed, REP, $\exists$-REP and $\forall$-REP actually have the same complexity as, respectively, the existence, credulous and skeptical reasoning for preferred semantics.

Theorem 15. *Let* $\mathcal{B} = \langle T, B \rangle$ *be an instance of* REP *where* B *is a set of FDs and IDs. Further, let* $s \in T$ *be a tuple. Then, the problems* REP *and* $\exists$-REP$(s, \mathcal{B})$ *are both* **NP**-*complete.*

Proof. The membership is easy in both cases. Given $P \subseteq T$ such that $s \in P$ (resp., P is non-empty), one can decide in polynomial time whether $P \models B$. Notice that we do not need to check the maximality, since if there is a repair (non-empty) for $\mathcal{B}$ containing s then there is also a maximal (non-empty) repair containing s.

For hardness, we first reduce from SAT to $\exists$-REP$(s, \mathcal{B})$. Towards the end, we highlight the required changes to reduce SAT to REP. Let $\varphi := \{C_i \mid i \leq m\}$ be a formula over propositions $\{p_1, \ldots, p_n\}$. Then, we construct a database T and a collection B of FDs and IDs over a set $V := \{t_i, u_i \mid 0 \leq i \leq m\}$ of attributes. Our encoding works as follows.

- B contains a single FD $\mathsf{dep}(t_0; u_0)$ to encode that each proposition takes at most one value in $\{0, 1\}$. Moreover, B contains m inclusion dependencies $t_i \subseteq u_i$ for each $1 \leq i \leq m$ to assure that each clause C_i is satisfied.
- The database $T := \{s_\varphi\} \cup \{s_j, \bar{s}_j \mid 1 \leq j \leq n\}$ is constructed in such a way that: (C1) the pair $s_j, \bar{s}_j$ fails the FD $\mathsf{dep}(t_0; u_0)$ for each $1 \leq j \leq n$, thereby ensuring that any repair contains at most one tuple from $\{s_j, \bar{s}_j\}$, and (C2) for each ID $t_i \subseteq u_i$ the value of $s_\varphi(t_i)$ is shared only by the tuple $s \in T \backslash \{s_\varphi\}$ such that their corresponding literal satisfies the clause C_i. Formally, we let $\mathsf{dom}(T) := \{c_i \mid i \leq m\} \cup \{p_1, \ldots, p_n\} \cup \{0, 1\}$. Then, (C1) is achieved by setting $s_j(t_0) = \bar{s}_j(t_0) = p_j$, $s_j(u_0) = 1$, and $\bar{s}_j(u_0) = 0$. Moreover, we also let $s_\varphi(t_0) = s_\varphi(u_0) = 0$. To achieve (C2) we let $s_\varphi(t_i) = c_i$ for each $1 \leq i \leq m$ and $s_\varphi(u_i) = 0$. Then, we let $s_j(t_i) = s_j(u_i) = c_i$ if $p_j \in C_i$, $\bar{s}_j(t_i) = \bar{s}_j(u_i) = c_i$ if $\neg p_j \in C_i$, and we let $s_j(t_i) = s_j(u_i) = 0 = \bar{s}_j(t_i) = \bar{s}_j(u_i)$ in the remaining cases.

Clearly, $T \not\models B$ due to the presence of the pair $s_j, \bar{s}_j$ and the FD $\mathsf{dep}(t_0; u_0)$. Then, a repair $P \subseteq T$ for $\mathsf{dep}(t_0; u_0)$ contains exactly one tuple from each such pair. Finally, $P \models t_i \subseteq u_i$ for $1 \leq i \leq m$ iff P contains at least one tuple $s \in \{s_j, \bar{s}_j\}$ corresponding to $x \in \{p_j, \neg p_j\}$ such that $x \in C_i$ for each $C_i \in \varphi$. This completes the proof since φ is satisfiable if and only if $\exists\text{-REP}(s_\varphi, B)$ is true.

To reduce SAT into REP, we use an additional ID, $t_{m+1} \subseteq u_{m+1}$ and modify T in such a way that every repair P for B necessarily contains s_φ, thereby proving the equivalence as before. This is achieved by adding a new element $c_{m+1} \in \mathsf{dom}(T)$ and setting $s_\varphi(t_{m+1}) = s_\varphi(u_{m+1}) = c_{m+1}$, as well as $s_j(t_{m+1}) = \bar{s}_j(t_{m+1}) = c_{m+1}$ and $s_j(u_{m+1}) = \bar{s}_j(u_{m+1}) = 0$ for each $1 \leq j \leq n$. This has the effect that one cannot construct a subset-repair for B by excluding s_φ and therefore, there is a non-empty repair for B iff φ is satisfiable. This completes the proof for both cases. □

We provide an example for better understanding of the reductions from the proof of Theorem 15.

Example 16. Let $\varphi := \{x \vee y, \neg x \vee \neg y, \neg x \vee y\}$ be a propositional formula. Then, our reduction for $\exists\text{-REP}$ yields a database $T := \{s_\varphi, s_x, s_y, \bar{s}_x, \bar{s}_y\}$ and a collection $B := \{\mathsf{dep}(t_0; u_0)\} \cup \{t_i \subseteq u_i \mid 1 \leq i \leq 3\}$ of dependencies as depicted in the left side of Table 2. Notice that the only satisfying assignment for φ is given by $\{x \mapsto 0, y \mapsto 1\}$, corresponding to the repair $\{s_\varphi, \bar{s}_x, s_y\}$ for B containing s_φ, and consequently $\exists\text{-REP}(s_\varphi, B)$ is true.

Moreover, although each of $\{s_x, s_y\}, \{s_x, \bar{s}_y\}, \{\bar{s}_x, \bar{s}_y\}$ is also a repair for B, none of them contains s_φ. Then, the second part of our reduction (for REP) adds the inclusion dependency $t_4 \subseteq u_4$ to B and expands the database T by two columns in the right side of Table 2. This results in $\{s_\varphi, \bar{s}_x, s_y\}$ being the only REP for B corresponding to the satisfying assignment for φ.

Table 2. The database corresponding to the formula φ from Example 16.

	t_0 u_0	t_1 u_1 t_2 u_2 t_3 u_3	t_4 u_4
s_φ	0 0	c_1 0 c_2 0 c_3 0	c_4 c_4
s_x	x 1	c_1 c_1 0 0 0 0	c_4 0
$\bar{s}_x$	x 0	0 0 c_2 c_2 c_3 c_3	c_4 0
s_y	y 1	c_1 c_1 0 0 c_3 c_3	c_4 0
$\bar{s}_y$	y 0	0 0 c_2 c_2 0 0	c_4 0

Next, we prove that $\forall$-REP$(s, \mathcal{B})$ is even harder and $\mathbf{\Pi_2^P}$-complete.

Theorem 17. *Let $\mathcal{B} = \langle T, B \rangle$ be an instance of REP including a set B of FDs and IDs. Further, let $s \in T$ be a tuple. Then, the problem $\forall$-REP$(s, \mathcal{B})$ is $\mathbf{\Pi_2^P}$-complete.*

Proof. For membership, one can guess a subset $P \subseteq T$ as a counter example for s, that is, $s \notin P$ and P is a subset-repair for $\mathcal{B}$, which can be decided in polynomial time. However, to determine whether P is maximal, one has to use oracle calls for guessing subsets $P' \subseteq T$, with $s \notin P'$ to determine whether $P' \models B$ and $P' \supset P$. This gives an upper bound of $\mathbf{coNP^{NP}}$ (equivalently $\mathbf{\Pi_2^P}$).

For hardness, we use a similar idea as in the proof of Theorem 15 and reduce from an instance Φ of the $\mathbf{\Pi_2^P}$-complete problem 2QBF, where $\Phi = \forall Y \exists Z \varphi(Y, Z)$ and $\varphi := \{C_i \mid i \leq m\}$ is a CNF. We let $X = Y \cup Z$ and construct an instance $\mathcal{B} := \langle T, B \rangle$ over a set $V := \{t_i, u_i \mid 0 \leq i \leq m+1\}$ of attributes. As in the proof of Theorem 15, B contains a FD $\mathsf{dep}(t_0; u_0)$ and a collection of IDs $I := \{t_i \subseteq u_i \mid 1 \leq i \leq m+1\}$ to encode whether each clause $C_i \in \varphi$ is satisfied. Moreover, the additional ID $t_{m+1} \subseteq u_{m+1}$ encodes the existentially quantified variables Z. The database is also constructed as in the proof of Theorem 15, except for the attributes $\{t_{m+1}, u_{m+1}\}$. These attributes encode the effect that s_φ *supports* variables $\{z, \bar{z}\}$ for each $z \in Z$ via the inclusion dependency $t_{m+1} \subseteq u_{m+1}$. This is achieved by letting $s_z(t_{m+1}) = \bar{s}_z(t_{m+1}) = c_{m+1}$ for each such $z \in Z$, as well as $s_z(u_{m+1}) = \bar{s}_z(u_{m+1}) = 0$ and $s_\varphi(t_{m+1}) = s_\varphi(u_{m+1}) = c_{m+1}$.

For correctness, notice that every interpretation I_Y over Y (seen as a subset of Y) corresponds to a subset $P_Y = \{s_y \mid y \in I_Y\} \cup \{\bar{s}_y \mid y \notin I_Y\}$. Then, $P_Y \models B$: $\mathsf{dep}(t_0; u_0)$ is true since P_Y includes only one of $s_y, \bar{s}_y$ and each $t_i \subseteq u_i$ is true since $s(t_i) = s(u_i)$ for each $s \in T \setminus \{s_\varphi\}$ and $i \leq m+1$. Moreover, we have that $s_\varphi \notin P_Y$. Now, in order to extend P_Y by adding s_z or $\bar{s}_z$ for any $z \in Z$, s_φ must be added as well due to the ID $t_{m+1} \subseteq u_{m+1}$. However, in order to add s_φ, we have to find I_Y and I_Z that together satisfy φ due to the IDs $t_i \subseteq u_i$ for $i \leq m$. As a result, for any interpretation I_Y over Y: $I_Y \cup I_Z \models \varphi$ if and only if P_Y is not a repair for $\mathcal{B}$ (since, $P_Y \cup P_Z \cup \{s_\varphi\}$ is a repair in such a case). Equivalently, there is a repair for $\mathcal{B}$ not containing s_φ if and only if the formula Φ is false. As a consequence, Φ is true if and only if every repair for $\mathcal{B}$ contains s_φ if and only if $\forall$-REP$(s_\varphi, \mathcal{B})$ is true. $\qquad\square$

We provide an example for better understanding of the reduction from the proof of Theorem 17.

Table 3. The database corresponding to the instance $\mathcal{B}$ from Example 18.

	t_0	u_0	t_1	u_1	t_2	u_2	t_3	u_3	t_4	u_4
s_φ	0	0	c_1	0	c_2	0	c_3	0	c_4	c_4
s_1	y_1	1	c_1	c_1	0	0	0	0	0	0
$\bar{s}_1$	y_1	0	0	0	0	0	0	0	0	0
s_2	y_2	1	c_1	c_1	c_2	c_2	c_3	c_3	0	0
$\bar{s}_2$	y_2	0	0	0	0	0	0	0	0	0
s_3	z_3	1	c_1	c_1	0	0	c_3	c_3	c_4	0
$\bar{s}_3$	z_3	0	0	0	c_2	c_2	0	0	c_4	0
s_4	z_4	1	0	0	0	0	c_3	c_3	c_4	0
$\bar{s}_4$	z_4	0	0	0	c_2	c_2	0	0	c_4	0

Example 18. Let $\Phi = \forall y_1 y_2 \exists z_3 z_4 ((y_1 \vee y_2 \vee z_3) \wedge (y_2 \vee \neg z_3 \vee \neg z_4) \wedge (y_2 \vee z_3 \vee z_4))$ be a 2QBF. Then, our reduction yields a database $T := \{s_\varphi, s_1, s_2, s_3, s_4, \bar{s}_1, \bar{s}_2, \bar{s}_3, \bar{s}_4\}$ and a collection $B := \{\mathsf{dep}(t_0; u_0)\} \cup \{t_i \subseteq u_i \mid i \leq 4\}$ of dependencies as depicted in Table 3. The reader can verify that the formula Φ is true and that $\forall\text{-REP}(s_\varphi, \mathcal{B})$ is true as well.

We conclude this section by noting that the least requirements for subset-repairs in the presence of both atoms is conflict-freeness and admissibility. Furthermore, although admissible extensions for $\mathcal{F}_\mathcal{B}$ yield subset-repairs for $\mathcal{B}$, those are not guaranteed to be maximal.

4 From Unirelational to Multirelational Databases

A database instance in multirelational setting consists of a collection $\mathcal{T} = (T_1, \ldots T_m)$, where each T_j is a database corresponding to a relational schema $T_j(x_{j,1}, \ldots, x_{j,n_j})$ of arity n_j. As before, T_j denotes the relation name and $x_{j,1}, \ldots, x_{j,n_j}$ are distinct attributes. In the following, we let $T = \bigcup_{j \leq m} T_j$ denote the set of all the tuples in $\mathcal{T}$. A functional dependency over $\mathcal{T}$, and the satisfaction for FDs is defined as before, i.e., an expression of the form $\mathsf{dep}(\boldsymbol{x}; \boldsymbol{y})$ for sequences $\boldsymbol{x}, \boldsymbol{y}$ of attributes in T_j for some $j \leq m$. However, an inclusion dependency may address attributes from two different tables. That is, $i = \boldsymbol{x} \subseteq \boldsymbol{y}$ is an ID between T_j and T_k if $\boldsymbol{x}$ and $\boldsymbol{y}$ are sequences of attributes over T_j and T_k, respectively. We call T_j the *source* and T_k the *target* of i, denoted as $\mathsf{source}(i)$ and $\mathsf{target}(i)$. Then, $\mathcal{T} \models \boldsymbol{x} \subseteq \boldsymbol{y}$ if for each $s \in \mathsf{source}(\boldsymbol{x} \subseteq \boldsymbol{y})$, there is some $t \in \mathsf{target}(\boldsymbol{x} \subseteq \boldsymbol{y})$ such that $s(\boldsymbol{x}) = t(\boldsymbol{y})$. By slightly abusing the notation, if $d := \mathsf{dep}(\boldsymbol{x}; \boldsymbol{y})$ is an FD over attributes in T_j, then we write $\mathsf{source}(d) = T_j$. Finally, we define the notion of (subset-maximal) repairs similar to the case of unirelational databases, i.e., $\mathcal{P} = (P_1, \ldots, P_m)$ where $P_j \subseteq T_j$ for $j \leq m$ such that $\mathcal{P}$ satisfies each dependency in B.

The construction from Sect. 3 for unirelational setting can be expanded to allow databases with more than one relations. The encoding for FDs remains the same as before, whereas for IDs (between T_j and T_k), we create auxiliary arguments only for tuples in $\mathsf{source}(i)$, which can be attacked by arguments corresponding to tuples in the $\mathsf{target}(i)$. As before, we denote by $S_i(s) = \{t \mid t \in \mathsf{target}(i), s(\boldsymbol{x}) = t(\boldsymbol{y})\}$ the tuples supporting s for an ID $i = \boldsymbol{x} \subseteq \boldsymbol{y}$. Given an instance $\mathcal{B} = \langle \mathcal{T}, B \rangle$ of a multirelational database $\mathcal{T}$ and a collection $B = D \cup I$ of FDs D and IDs I, we construct the AF $\mathcal{F}_\mathcal{B} = (A, R_\mathrm{D} \cup R_\mathrm{I})$ as follows.

- $A := \{s \mid s \in T\} \cup \{s_i \mid s \in \mathsf{source}(i) \text{ for } i \in I\}$,
- $R_\mathrm{D} := \{(s, t), (t, s) \mid s, t \in \mathsf{source}(d) \text{ for } d \in D \text{ and } \{s, t\} \not\models d\}$,
- $R_\mathrm{I} := \{(s_i, s), (s_i, s_i) \mid s \in \mathsf{source}(i) \text{ for } i \in I\} \cup \{(t, s_i) \mid t \in S_i(s) \text{ for } i \in I\}$.

Then, a similar argument as in the proof of Theorem 14 allows us to establish that repairs for an instance $\mathcal{B} = \langle \mathcal{T}, B \rangle$ including a multirelational database $\mathcal{T}$ and a collection B of FDs and IDs are precisely the preferred extensions in $\mathcal{F}_\mathcal{B}$.

5   Concluding Remarks

Overview. We simulated the problem of finding repairs of an inconsistent database under functional and inclusion dependencies by Dung's argumentation frameworks. Our main results (See Table 1) indicate that subset maximal repairs correspond to naive extensions when only one type of dependency is allowed, whereas only preferred extensions yield all the repairs when both FDs and IDs are allowed. Further, for the problem to determine whether a tuple is in some (resp., every) repair, we establish the same complexity bounds as the complexity of credulous (skeptical) reasoning for preferred-semantics in AFs.

Discussion and Future Work. We would like to point out that although the conflict relation in the presence of functional dependencies and a connection between preferred extensions and subset maximal repairs is known for FDs [11], the main contributions of our work establishes the relation between extensions of AFs when inclusion dependencies are also allowed. This novel contribution opens up several directions for future work. First and foremost, the authors believe that the connection between repairs in the setting of inconsistent databases and extensions in AFs is stronger than what is established here. Intuitively, one can model the attack relationship via functional, and defense/support via inclusion dependencies. A precise formulation of this transformation will allow us to simulate AFs via inconsistent databases by considering FDs and IDs. However, this intuition needs further exploration and is therefore left for future work.

Further notable future work may consider whether the idea presented here can be generalized to other well-known types of tuple or equality generating dependencies. Then, one can target the richer setting of universal constraints and the symmetric difference repairs [12]. An interesting question is to explore whether the lower bounds for complexity also apply to the sub-classes of FDs and IDs, namely *keys* and *foreign keys* as well as the particular case of acyclic dependencies. Moreover, we would like to explore whether consistent query answering

(CQA) under inconsistency-tolerant semantics can also be tackled via the argumentation approach. The question we pose is the following: Given an inconsistent database $\mathcal{B}$ and a (Boolean) query q, can we construct an AF $\mathcal{F}_\mathcal{B}$ and an argument a_q such that the query q is true in some (resp., every) repair if, and only if, the argument a_q is credulously (skeptically) accepted in $\mathcal{F}_\mathcal{B}$. Finally, one can consider incorporating the information about priorities among tuples into the resulting AFs, that is, extending the translations presented in this work to the setting of prioritized repairing and consistent query answering [21, 25, 26].

Another promising direction to consider next is the exploration of an explainability dimension, similar to that in the setting of ontological KBs [4, 6, 13]. Given an instance $\mathcal{B}$ including a database T and a collection B of dependencies, then the proposed AF $\mathcal{F}_\mathcal{B}$ lets one determine the *causes* why some tuples are not in some repair (or all repairs). We note that, for IDs, the auxiliary arguments modelling each dependency in B can serve this purpose. For FDs, we believe that annotating arguments (or the attack relation between a pair of arguments) by the FDs involved in the conflict can achieve the goal. As a result, one can look at the AF $\mathcal{F}_\mathcal{B}$ and read from it the FDs or IDs which a tuple s failing $\exists\text{-REP}(s, \mathcal{B})$ or $\forall\text{-REP}(s, \mathcal{B})$ participates in. Then, subsets of the atoms and/or possibly tuples in a database can be considered as *explanations*. Such explanations seem interesting in modeling scenarios where the data (database) has higher confidence than the dependencies; for example, if dependencies are mined over some part of the existing data. An explanation then informs that the data (and hence tuples therein) should be kept, whereas dependencies need to be screened and further analyzed.

Acknowledgment. The work has received funding from the European Union's Horizon Europe research and innovation programme within project ENEXA (101070305) and the Deutsche Forschungsgemeinschaft (DFG, German Research Foundation): TRR 318/1 2021 - 438445824 and VI 1045-1/1 - 432788559. The first author expresses gratitude to Arne Meier (Leibniz University Hannover) for the invitation to discuss the topic in Hannover, as well as for motivating and guiding the discussion on this subject.

References

1. Afrati, F.N., Kolaitis, P.G.: Repair checking in inconsistent databases: algorithms and complexity. In: Fagin, R. (ed.) Database Theory - ICDT 2009, 12th International Conference, Proceedings. ACM International Conference Proceeding Series, St. Petersburg, Russia, 23–25 March 2009, vol. 361, pp. 31–41. ACM (2009). https://doi.org/10.1145/1514894.1514899

2. Arenas, M., Bertossi, L.E., Chomicki, J.: Scalar aggregation in FD-inconsistent databases. In: den Bussche, J.V., Vianu, V. (eds.) ICDT 2001. LNCS, vol. 1973, pp. 39–53. Springer, Heidelberg (2001). https://doi.org/10.1007/3-540-44503-X_3

3. Arieli, O., Borg, A., Heyninck, J.: A review of the relations between logical argumentation and reasoning with maximal consistency. Ann. Math. Artif. Intell. **87**(3), 187–226 (2019). https://doi.org/10.1007/S10472-019-09629-7

4. Arioua, A., Croitoru, M.: Dialectical characterization of consistent query explanation with existential rules. In: Markov, Z., Russell, I. (eds.) Proceedings

of the Twenty-Ninth International Florida Artificial Intelligence Research Society Conference, FLAIRS 2016, Key Largo, Florida, USA, 16–18 May 2016, pp. 621–625. AAAI Press (2016). http://www.aaai.org/ocs/index.php/FLAIRS/FLAIRS16/paper/view/12800

5. Arioua, A., Croitoru, M., Vesic, S.: Logic-based argumentation with existential rules. Int. J. Approx. Reason. **90**, 76–106 (2017). https://doi.org/10.1016/J.IJAR.2017.07.004

6. Arioua, A., Tamani, N., Croitoru, M.: Query answering explanation in inconsistent datalog +/- knowledge bases. In: Chen, Q., Hameurlain, A., Toumani, F., Wagner, R.R., Decker, H. (eds.) DEXA 2015. LNCS, vol. 9261, pp. 203–219. Springer, Cham (2015). https://doi.org/10.1007/978-3-319-22849-5_15

7. Arioua, A., Tamani, N., Croitoru, M., Buche, P.: Query failure explanation in inconsistent knowledge bases using argumentation. In: Parsons, S., Oren, N., Reed, C., Cerutti, F. (eds.) Computational Models of Argument - Proceedings of COMMA 2014. Frontiers in Artificial Intelligence and Applications, Atholl Palace Hotel, Scottish Highlands, UK, 9–12 September 2014, vol. 266, pp. 101–108. IOS Press (2014). https://doi.org/10.3233/978-1-61499-436-7-101

8. Barceló, P., Fontaine, G.: On the data complexity of consistent query answering over graph databases. J. Comput. Syst. Sci. **88**, 164–194 (2017)

9. Bertossi, L.E.: Consistent query answering in databases. SIGMOD Rec. **35**(2), 68–76 (2006). https://doi.org/10.1145/1147376.1147391

10. Bertossi, L.E.: Database repairs and consistent query answering: origins and further developments. In: Suciu, D., Skritek, S., Koch, C. (eds.) Proceedings of the 38th ACM SIGMOD-SIGACT-SIGAI Symposium on Principles of Database Systems, PODS 2019, Amsterdam, The Netherlands, 30 June–5 July 2019, pp. 48–58. ACM (2019). https://doi.org/10.1145/3294052.3322190

11. Bienvenu, M., Bourgaux, C.: Querying and repairing inconsistent prioritized knowledge bases: complexity analysis and links with abstract argumentation. In: Calvanese, D., Erdem, E., Thielscher, M. (eds.) Proceedings of the 17th International Conference on Principles of Knowledge Representation and Reasoning, KR 2020, Rhodes, Greece, 12–18 September 2020, pp. 141–151 (2020). https://doi.org/10.24963/KR.2020/15

12. Bienvenu, M., Bourgaux, C.: Inconsistency handling in prioritized databases with universal constraints: complexity analysis and links with active integrity constraints. In: Proceedings of the 20th International Conference on Principles of Knowledge Representation and Reasoning, pp. 97–106 (2023). https://doi.org/10.24963/kr.2023/10

13. Bienvenu, M., Bourgaux, C., Goasdoué, F.: Computing and explaining query answers over inconsistent DL-lite knowledge bases. J. Artif. Intell. Res. **64**, 563–644 (2019)

14. ten Cate, B., Fontaine, G., Kolaitis, P.G.: On the data complexity of consistent query answering. In: Proceedings of the 15th International Conference on Database Theory, ICDT 2012, pp. 22–33 (2012)

15. Chomicki, J., Marcinkowski, J.: Minimal-change integrity maintenance using tuple deletions. Inf. Comput. **197**(1), 90–121 (2005). https://doi.org/10.1016/j.ic.2004.04.007. https://www.sciencedirect.com/science/article/pii/S0890540105000179

16. Coste-Marquis, S., Devred, C., Marquis, P.: Symmetric argumentation frameworks. In: Godo, L. (ed.) ECSQARU 2005. LNCS (LNAI), vol. 3571, pp. 317–328. Springer, Heidelberg (2005). https://doi.org/10.1007/11518655_28

17. Croitoru, M., Thomopoulos, R., Vesic, S.: Introducing preference-based argumentation to inconsistent ontological knowledge bases. In: Chen, Q., Torroni, P., Villata, S., Hsu, J., Omicini, A. (eds.) PRIMA 2015. LNCS (LNAI), vol. 9387, pp. 594–602. Springer, Cham (2015). https://doi.org/10.1007/978-3-319-25524-8_42

18. Croitoru, M., Vesic, S.: What can argumentation do for inconsistent ontology query answering? In: Liu, W., Subrahmanian, V.S., Wijsen, J. (eds.) SUM 2013. LNCS (LNAI), vol. 8078, pp. 15–29. Springer, Heidelberg (2013). https://doi.org/10.1007/978-3-642-40381-1_2

19. Dung, P.M.: On the acceptability of arguments and its fundamental role in non-monotonic reasoning, logic programming and n-person games. AI **77**(2), 321–357 (1995)

20. Dvořák, W., Dunne, P.E.: Computational problems in formal argumentation and their complexity. FLAP **4**(8), 2557–2622 (2017)

21. Fagin, R., Kimelfeld, B., Kolaitis, P.G.: Dichotomies in the complexity of preferred repairs. In: Milo, T., Calvanese, D. (eds.) Proceedings of the 34th ACM Symposium on Principles of Database Systems, PODS 2015, Melbourne, Victoria, Australia, 31 May–4 June 2015, pp. 3–15. ACM (2015). https://doi.org/10.1145/2745754.2745762

22. Hannula, M., Hella, L.: Complexity thresholds in inclusion logic. Inf. Comput. **287**, 104759 (2022). https://doi.org/10.1016/J.IC.2021.104759

23. Hannula, M., Wijsen, J.: A dichotomy in consistent query answering for primary keys and unary foreign keys. In: Libkin, L., Barceló, P. (eds.) PODS 2022: International Conference on Management of Data, Philadelphia, PA, USA, 12–17 June 2022, pp. 437–449. ACM (2022). https://doi.org/10.1145/3517804.3524157

24. Ho, L., Arch-Int, S., Acar, E., Schlobach, S., Arch-Int, N.: An argumentative approach for handling inconsistency in prioritized datalog±ontologies. AI Commun. **35**(3), 243–267 (2022). https://doi.org/10.3233/AIC-220087

25. Kimelfeld, B., Livshits, E., Peterfreund, L.: Detecting ambiguity in prioritized database repairing. In: Benedikt, M., Orsi, G. (eds.) 20th International Conference on Database Theory (ICDT 2017). Leibniz International Proceedings in Informatics (LIPIcs), vol. 68, pp. 17:1–17:20. Schloss Dagstuhl-Leibniz-Zentrum fuer Informatik, Dagstuhl (2017). https://doi.org/10.4230/LIPIcs.ICDT.2017.17. http://drops.dagstuhl.de/opus/volltexte/2017/7048

26. Kimelfeld, B., Livshits, E., Peterfreund, L.: Counting and enumerating preferred database repairs. Theor. Comput. Sci. **837**, 115–157 (2020). https://doi.org/10.1016/J.TCS.2020.05.016

27. Livshits, E., Kimelfeld, B., Roy, S.: Computing optimal repairs for functional dependencies. ACM Trans. Database Syst. **45**(1), 4:1–4:46 (2020). https://doi.org/10.1145/3360904

28. Lopatenko, A., Bertossi, L.: Complexity of consistent query answering in databases under cardinality-based and incremental repair semantics. In: Schwentick, T., Suciu, D. (eds.) ICDT 2007. LNCS, vol. 4353, pp. 179–193. Springer, Heidelberg (2006). https://doi.org/10.1007/11965893_13

29. Mahmood, Y.: Parameterized aspects of team-based formalisms and logical inference (2022). https://doi.org/10.15488/13064. https://www.tib.eu/de/suchen/id/base%3Ae4c211ee856f89407f6d9a67b4c100e3fb7eafdd

30. Staworko, S., Chomicki, J., Marcinkowski, J.: Prioritized repairing and consistent query answering in relational databases. Ann. Math. Artif. Intell. **64**(2–3), 209–246 (2012). https://doi.org/10.1007/S10472-012-9288-8

31. Staworko, S., Chomicki, J.: Consistent query answers in the presence of universal constraints. Inf. Syst. **35**(1), 1–22 (2010). https://doi.org/10.1016/J.IS.2009.03.004

32. Väänänen, J.: Dependence Logic. Cambridge University Press, Cambridge (2007)
33. Wijsen, J.: Condensed representation of database repairs for consistent query answering. In: Calvanese, D., Lenzerini, M., Motwani, R. (eds.) ICDT 2003. LNCS, vol. 2572, pp. 378–393. Springer, Heidelberg (2003). https://doi.org/10.1007/3-540-36285-1_25
34. Young, A.P., Modgil, S., Rodrigues, O.: Prioritised default logic as argumentation with partial order default priorities. CoRR abs/1609.05224 (2016). http://arxiv.org/abs/1609.05224
35. Yun, B., Vesic, S., Croitoru, M.: Sets of attacking arguments for inconsistent datalog knowledge bases. In: Prakken, H., Bistarelli, S., Santini, F., Taticchi, C. (eds.) Computational Models of Argument - Proceedings of COMMA 2020. Frontiers in Artificial Intelligence and Applications, Perugia, Italy, 4–11 September 2020, vol. 326, pp. 419–430. IOS Press (2020). https://doi.org/10.3233/FAIA200526

Dependencies and Constraints

Relational Schemas with Multiplicity Bounds, Diversity Bounds and Functional Dependencies

Joachim Biskup[✉][iD]

Fakultät für Informatik, Technische Universität Dortmund, Dortmund, Germany
joachim.biskup@cs.tu-dortmund.de

Abstract. As yet another semantically enriched data model, we consider relational schemas with finite domain sizes and multiplicity bounds and diversity bounds together with functional dependencies as semantic constraints. As a simple variant of cardinality constraints, for a set of attributes, a multiplicity bound requires that a possible value combination occurs at most as often as the bound extension says. As a new kind of constraint, for a set of attributes, a diversity bound describes how many different value combinations under these attributes may at most occur in a relation instance. A multiplicity bound and a diversity bound together are seen as a weak abstraction of a so-called structure for the set of attributes on the left-hand side of a functional dependency. Such a structure specifies the exact size of the active domain of that set and the respective exact numbers of occurrences, summing up to a given instance size. We study how multiplicity bounds, diversity bounds and functional dependencies under finite sizes of attribute domains interact. We exhibit a powerful sound derivation system for all these items, together with a generation procedure for approximating the entailment closure of such constraints. We further analyze how to construct relation instances that exactly achieve the strongest entailed multiplicity or diversity bound extension, respectively, for some attribute set or even all of them.

Keywords: Armstrong-property · Cardinality constraint · Derivation rule · Diversity bound · Duplicate-freeness · Entailment closure · Finite attribute domain · Functional dependency · Independence atom · Multiplicity bound · Relational schema · Semantic constraint

1 Introduction

Right from the beginning, to capture the "real-world" semantics of an application, the relational model of data has dealt with functional dependencies among sets of attributes for relation instances treated as sets of flat tuples. Since then, a great variety of modifications and extensions have been introduced, leading, e.g., to nested, entity-relationship or object-oriented instances under further semantic constraints, mostly aiming at representing more aspects of an application while preserving the benefits of the relational core.

© The Author(s), under exclusive license to Springer Nature Switzerland AG 2024
A. Meier and M. Ortiz (Eds.): FoIKS 2024, LNCS 14589, pp. 45–63, 2024.
https://doi.org/10.1007/978-3-031-56940-1_3

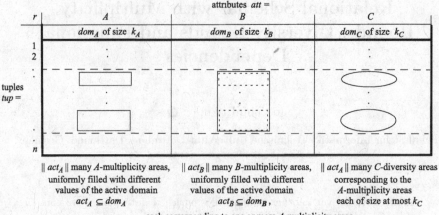

Fig. 1. Multiplicity and diversity areas of an array $r[]$ for a relation instance r with n tuples over attributes A, B and C with given finite domains dom_{att} of size k_{att} and satisfying the functional dependency $fd : A \rightarrow B$ (adapted from [4,8]).

In this work we propose *diversity bounds* as a new kind of a semantic constraint that restricts the size of the active domain of a set of attributes by an upper bound. Such diversity bounds are coming along with functional dependencies, as originally suggested, and multiplicity bounds, as a simple version of earlier introduced cardinality constraints, that only restrict the number of value occurrences under a set of attributes by an upper bound. Once dealing with numbers to declare upper bounds to active domains and multiple occurrences, we also suggest to declare finite domain sizes for the attributes[1]. We will argue that the semantically *enriched data model* provides both useful expressiveness for applications and still manageable means for formal schema analyses.

At first glance, functional dependencies appear to be merely of a qualitative flavor. However, schema design might also be interested in quantitative aspects, like the size of relation instances and their internal structures [3,4,8,10] and the possible or expected amount of redundancy occurring in them [16,17,23,24]. Figure 1 visualizes the potential impact of the qualitative aspects on the quantitative ones. The qualitative aspects are shown as *multiplicity areas*, corresponding to *most elementary selections* that subtuples on some attribute set $\mathcal{X}$ should have a specific value combination ν, and as *diversity areas*, corresponding to subsets of most elementary *full projections* on attribute sets leading to the pertinent active domains. Multiplicity bounds and diversity bounds then introduce quantitative size restrictions on such selections and projections, respectively.

These constraints will be exemplified in the next section and then formally studied regarding entailment, derivation options and instance construction.

---

[1] In the literature, there is no common agreement on the size of domains. Depending on their prevailing interests, whether more logically oriented or more combinatorially, authors deal exclusively with infinite domains, exclusively with finite domains, or both kinds, see, e.g., [1,4,6,16,18,20,21] and many other work.

2   Examples

The following three examples illustrate the expressiveness of our data model regarding applications, the opportunities for formal analyses of its schema declarations, and the issues of the combinatorial flavor of its semantic constraints.

Example 1. Adapting an example given in [1], page 255, we consider a kind of a "real-world" situation of movie theaters. This setting is modeled by a "universal" attribute set $\mathcal{U} = \{$ TITLE, DIRECTOR, TIME, PRICE, THEATER, ADDRESS, PHONE $\}$ and functional dependencies $\mathcal{F} = \{ fd_1 :$ THEATER $\rightarrow$ ADDRESS PHONE, $fd_2 :$ THEATER TIME TITLE $\rightarrow$ PRICE, $fd_3 :$ TITLE $\rightarrow$ DIRECTOR $\}$, enhanced by:

- *multiplicity bounds*, specifying that (i) at any time a title should be shown in at most 10 theaters in parallel, and (ii) only small theaters with at most 3 halls should be delivered:
  $\mathcal{M} = \{ mu_1 :$ TIME TITLE $\leqslant 10$, $mu_2 :$ TIME THEATER $\leqslant 3 \}$;
- *diversity bounds*, specifying that (i) there should be at most 100 movie theaters in operation, and (ii) the overall offering of movie shows should be restricted to 200:
  $\mathcal{D} = \{ di_1 :$ THEATER $\leqslant 100$, $di_2 :$ TIME THEATER $\leqslant 200 \}$;
- *domain declarations* to syntactically denote the respective objects, implying the pertinent *domain sizes*, e.g.:
  $dom_{\text{THEATER}} = \bigcup_{l=2,\dots,20} \{ A, a, B, b, \dots, Z, z \}^l$,
  . . .
  $dom_{\text{PHONE}} = \bigcup_{l=2,\dots,15} \{ 0, \dots, 9 \}^l$.

Example 2. We consider an abstract relational schema with *attributes* A, B_1, B_2, C_1 and C_2, the *domain sizes* k_{att} of which are 25, 4, 5, 3 and 2, respectively. Then, for example, the domain sizes of the attribute sets $B_1 B_2$ and $C_1 C_2$ and $B_1 B_2 C_1 C_2$ can be calculated as $k_{B_1 B_2} = k_{B_1} \cdot k_{B_2} = 4 \cdot 5 = 20$ and $k_{C_1 C_2} = k_{C_1} \cdot k_{C_2} = 3 \cdot 2 = 6$ and $k_{B_1 B_2 C_1 C_2} = k_{B_1 B_2} \cdot k_{C_1 C_2} = 20 \cdot 6 = 120$. These and further declarations as well as some consequences are visualized in Fig. 2.

In a first step, we assume as further *semantic constraints*:

- the attribute set $B_1 B_2$ functionally depends on the single attribute A, formally denoted by the *functional dependency* $fd : A \rightarrow B_1 B_2$,
- the multiplicity of value combinations for the attribute set $B_1 B_2$ is restricted to 3, formally denoted by the *multiplicity bound* $mu : B_1 B_2 \leqslant 3$, and
- the multiplicity of value combinations for the attribute set $C_1 C_2$ is restricted to 2, formally denoted by the *multiplicity bound* $mu : C_1 C_2 \leqslant 2$.

We can then analyze the consequences for the left-hand side A of the functional dependency for any relation instance r of the relational schema:

1. Since r is a *set* containing *no duplicate* tuples, if two or more tuples agree on the attribute A, then they have to be mutually different on the remaining

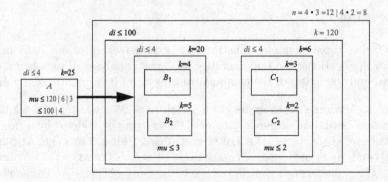

Fig. 2. A declaration of a relational schema with five attributes A, B_1, B_2, C_1 and C_2, a functional dependency, domain sizes k, multiplicity bounds mu and diversity bounds di together with some consequences.

    attributes. Accordingly, a value a of the domain of A can occur in r at most 120 times, i.e., formally, the multiplicity bound $mu : A \leqslant 120$ is *entailed*. Such a reasoning will lead to a derivation rule called *domain-size*.

2. Since r satisfies the functional dependency $fd : A \rightarrow B_1 B_2$, if two or more tuples agree on the attribute A, then they also agree on the attribute set $B_1 B_2$ and thus they have to be mutually different on the now remaining attribute set $C_1 C_2$. Formally, the multiplicity bound $mu : A \leqslant 6$ is *entailed*. Such a reasoning will lead to a derivation rule called *duplicate-freeness*.

3. Extending the argument, the multiplicity of the pertinent value combinations on the right-hand side $B_1 B_2$ of the functional dependency is restricted to at most 3, and thus the multiplicity of the pertinent values on the left-hand side as well. Formally, the multiplicity bound $mu : A \leqslant 3$ is *entailed*. Such a reasoning will lead to a derivation rule called *dependency-satisfaction*.

4. The entailed multiplicity bound $mu : A \leqslant 3$ can actually be achieved, as witnessed by the relation instance shown in Fig. 3. However, the entailment implies that any weaker multiplicity bound $mu : A \leqslant m$ with $3 < m$ could not be met by any relation instance, even if originally declared.

In a second step, we assume additional semantic constraints:

- the diversity of the attribute A is restricted to 4, formally denoted by the *diversity bound* $di : A \leqslant 4$,
- the diversity of value combinations for the attribute set $C_1 C_2$ is restricted to 4, formally denoted by the *diversity bound* $di : C_1 C_2 \leqslant 4$, and
- the diversity of value combinations for the attribute set $B_1 B_2 C_1 C_2$ is restricted to 100, formally denoted by the *diversity bound* $di : B_1 B_2 C_1 C_2 \leqslant 100$.

    We now observe the following adapted consequences:

1. Strengthening the rule *domain-size* to *domain-diversity*, we get the multiplicity bound $mu : A \leqslant 100$.

r	A	B_1	B_2	C_1	C_2
1	1	1	1	1	1
1	1	1	1	2
1	1	1	2	1
2	2	2	2	2
3	3	3	1	1
3	3	3	1	2
3	3	3	2	1
4	4	4	2	2

r_1	A	B_1	B_2
	1	1	1
	2	2	2
	3	3	3
	4	4	4

r_2	A	C_1	C_2
	1	1	1
	1	1	2
	1	2	1
	2	2	2
	3	1	1
	3	1	2
	3	2	1
	4	2	2

Fig. 3. A relation instance r of maximum size $n = 8$ and its redundancy-removing decomposition into normalized relations r_1 and r_2.

2. Adapting the rule *duplicate-freeness* for diversities, we get the multiplicity bound $mu : A \leqslant 4$.
3. Complementing the rule *dependency-satisfaction* dually for diversities, we get the diversity bound $di : B_1B_2 \leqslant 4$.

Analyzing the consequences for the overall size (cardinality) n of any relation instance r of the relational schema, the best bound $n \leqslant 4 \cdot 2 = 8$ is entailed by the diversity bound $di : C_1C_2 \leqslant 4$ together with the multiplicity bound $mu : C_1C_2 \leqslant 2$.

Figure 3 shows a relation instance r that witnesses that the bound can actually be achieved. This instance also achieves the strongest multiplicity bounds and diversity bounds, i.e.: there are four C_1C_2-values, even each of them occurring exactly twice; there are four B_1B_2-values, two of them occurring exactly three times, and there are four A-values, two of them occurring exactly three times as well. Figure 3 also illustrates the impact of the constraints under schema normalization.

Example 3. Specific declarations might be expressive enough to capture classical combinatorial problems [11]. In particular we can describe Latin squares of size $n \times n$ over a set with n elements in their orthogonal array representation by means of a relational schema with three attributes A, B and C, attribute A for denoting *lines* of the square, B for *columns*, and C for entries with *values* from that set. Thus a tuple $\mu = (a, b, c)$ says that the value c occurs in the column b of the line a. Then, for $att = A, B, C$, the *diversity bounds* $di : att \leqslant n$ require that there are at most n lines, at most n columns, and at most n different values for entries, respectively, and the multiplicity bounds $mu : att \leqslant n$ require that each of these items occurs at most n times. Accordingly, if for the attributes A and B the bounds are achieved exactly, there are at least n^2 tuples, at least one for the n^2 many entries, and if the bound for the attribute C is exactly achieved, then each of the n values occurs n times.

Now, if we additionally declare the multiplicity bounds $mu : AB \leqslant 1$, $mu : AC \leqslant 1$ and $mu : BC \leqslant 1$, which are equivalent to the functional dependencies (actually even key dependencies) $fd : AB \to C$, $fd : AC \to B$, and $fd : BC \to$

A, respectively, we have come up with the condition of a Latin square that in each line and in each column each of the values occurs exactly once.

3   Formal Setting of the Enriched Data Model

We now formally define the already intuitively introduced concepts of our data model. Besides standard items like *attributes* and their *domains* and *functional dependencies* we treat *multiplicity bounds* as a special case of cardinality constraints and *diversity bounds* as a new[2] kind of semantic constraints.

Definition 1 (relational schema and relation instances). *A relational schema $R\langle \mathcal{U}, \mathcal{SC}, dom/k \rangle$ comprises*

- $\mathcal{U}$, *a finite set of* attributes;
- $\mathcal{SC} = \mathcal{F} \cup \mathcal{M} \cup \mathcal{D}$, *a set of semantic constraints consisting of* functional dependencies *in* $\mathcal{F}$, multiplicity bounds *in* $\mathcal{M}$ *and* diversity bounds *in* $\mathcal{D}$;
- *dom, a declaration of a* finite domain[3] dom_{att} *satisfying the* domain-size *specification* $k_{att} := \| dom_{att} \| \geqslant 2$ *for each attribute* $att \in \mathcal{U}$[4].

A relation instance r is a set[5],[6] of tuples over the attributes of $\mathcal{U}$ complying with the declared domains and satisfying the multiplicity bounds and diversity bounds and functional dependencies given in $\mathcal{SC}$:

- *duplicate-freeness (as a set): two tuples $\mu_1 \neq \mu_2$ of r differ for at least one attribute;*
- *domain satisfaction, $r \models dom/k$: a tuple $\mu \in r$ assigns a value $\mu(att) \in dom_{att}$ to each attribute $att \in \mathcal{U}$;*
- *functional dependency satisfaction for $fd : \mathcal{X} \to \mathcal{Y} \in \mathcal{SC}$ with the attribute sets $\mathcal{X}$ and $\mathcal{Y}$ being nonempty subsets of $\mathcal{U}$, $r \models fd : \mathcal{X} \to \mathcal{Y}$: if two tuples $\mu_1 \neq \mu_2$ of r agree on all attributes in $\mathcal{X}$, then they agree on all attributes in $\mathcal{Y}$ as well;*
- *multiplicity bound satisfaction for $mu : \mathcal{X} \leqslant m \in \mathcal{SC}$ with the attribute set $\mathcal{X}$ being a nonempty subset of $\mathcal{U}$ and the bound extension m being a non-zero natural number, $r \models mu : \mathcal{X} \leqslant m$: a subtuple (value combination) ν over the attribute set $\mathcal{X}$ occurs at most m times in r, i.e., for all $\nu \in dom_{\mathcal{X}} := \times_{att \in \mathcal{X}} dom_{att}$, for the corresponding selection we have $\| \sigma_{\mathcal{X} = \nu}(r) \| \leqslant m$;*
- *diversity bound satisfaction for $di : \mathcal{X} \leqslant m \in \mathcal{SC}$ with the attribute set $\mathcal{X}$ being a nonempty subset of $\mathcal{U}$ and the bound extension m being a non-zero natural number, $r \models di : \mathcal{X} \leqslant m$: the projection of r on $\mathcal{X}$ contains at most m different value combinations, i.e., $\| \pi_{\mathcal{X}}(r) \| \leqslant m$.*

---

[2] Levene/Loizou [18], Sect. 3.7 briefly mentions it in a note added to Def. 3.100.

[3] W.l.o.g., we only treat attribute domains of the kind $dom_{att} = \{1, \dots, k_{att}\}$.

[4] We use dom/k as an abbreviation to denote these two related functions on $\mathcal{U}$.

[5] An instance r is a finite set, since all declared domains are finite.

[6] W.l.o.g. we always assume that the set is nonempty.

As a special case, a diversity bound $di : \mathcal{X} \leqslant 1$ with the bound extension 1 requires that $\|\pi_{\mathcal{X}}(r)\| \leqslant 1$, i.e., that at most only one value exists for $\mathcal{X}$ in r and, thus (ignoring that r might be empty), r is *constant* under the attribute set $\mathcal{X}$. Such a requirement has already been studied by Hannula/Kontinen/Link [12] as an *independence atom* of the special form $\mathcal{X} \perp \mathcal{X}$ where the right-hand side and the left-hand side are identical.

As another special case, a diversity bound $di : \mathcal{U} \leqslant n$ with the full set of attributes $\mathcal{U}$ requires that relation instances contain at most n many tuples, since $\pi_{\mathcal{U}}(r) = r$ and, thus, $\|\pi_{\mathcal{U}}(r)\| \leqslant n$ means that $\|r\| \leqslant n$.

We can easily observe that the requirements of any such relational schema are *satisfiable*, as witnessed by the singleton set $\{(1, \ldots, 1)\}$. Thus, each such relational schema has a *nonempty* set of relation instances. However, this simple witness does not exactly achieve any bound extensions with a bound extension greater than 1. Moreover, as already observed in Example 2, a declared bound might be strictly weaker than an entailed bound, and then the declared one cannot be achieved exactly. Accordingly, whenever we are interested in *exact achievements* we have to focus on *strongest* entailed bounds.

Definition 2 (entailment). *Let* $R\langle\mathcal{U}, SC, dom/k\rangle$ *be a relational schema.*

1. *A constraint is* entailed *if it is satisfied by each relation instance.*
2. *The (general) closure* SC^* *is the set of constraints (of any kind) that are entailed.*
3. *The fd-entailment closure* $SC_{fd}^{\models}$ *is the set of functional dependencies that are entailed.*
4. *The mu-entailment closure* $SC_{mu}^{\models}$ *is the set of the* strongest *multiplicity bounds among those that are entailed.*
5. *The di-entailment closure* $SC_{di}^{\models}$ *is the set of the* strongest *diversity bounds among those that are entailed.*
6. *The (specific) entailment closure is defined as* $SC^{\models} = SC_{fd}^{\models} \cup SC_{mu}^{\models} \cup SC_{di}^{\models}$.
7. *The entailed relational schema is defined as* $R^{\models}\langle\mathcal{U}, SC^{\models}, dom/k\rangle$.
8. *For an attribute set* $\mathcal{X} \subseteq \mathcal{U}$,
   (a) $\mathcal{X}_{fd}^{\models} := \{ att \mid fd : \mathcal{X} \to att \in SC_{fd}^{\models} \} \subseteq \mathcal{U}$
   is the functional entailment closure *of* $\mathcal{X}$,
   (b) $\mathcal{X}_{mu}^{\models} := \iota m[mu : \mathcal{X} \leqslant m \in SC_{mu}^{\models}]$
   $= Min\{ m \mid mu : \mathcal{X} \leqslant m \in SC^* \} \in \mathbb{N}^+$
   is the bound extension of the strongest *entailed multiplicity bound for* $\mathcal{X}$, *also called the* multiplicity entailment closure *of* $\mathcal{X}$, *and*
   (c) $\mathcal{X}_{di}^{\models} := \iota m[di : \mathcal{X} \leqslant m \in SC_{di}^{\models}]$
   $= Min\{ m \mid di : \mathcal{X} \leqslant m \in SC^* \} \in \mathbb{N}^+$
   is the bound extension of the strongest *entailed diversity bound for* $\mathcal{X}$, *also called the* diversity entailment closure *of* $\mathcal{X}$.

Proposition 1 (decidability and total computability). *The following predicates are decidable:*

1. *The finite set of tuples r is a relation instance of the relational schema*
   $R\langle \mathcal{U}, \mathcal{SC}, dom/k \rangle$.
2. *The semantic constraint Φ, being a functional dependency, a multiplicity bound or a diversity bound, is entailed by the relational schema*
   $R\langle \mathcal{U}, \mathcal{SC}, dom/k \rangle$.

Accordingly, the various entailment closures defined above are totally computable.

Proof. A relational schema has finite domains and, thus, there are only finitely many possible tuples and only finitely many possible sets of such tuples; for each such set the pertinent subpredicates are straightforwardly computable.   □

4   Entailments Between Semantic Constraints

It is well-known [1,2] that there can be entailments among *functional dependencies*. Basically, they can be completely described by a set of *derivation rules*, which we later will call *subset, transitivity* and *augmentation*, respectively. Moreover, the special case of a functional dependency $fd : \mathcal{X} \rightarrow \mathcal{U}$, i.e., actually a *key dependency*, evidently entails the *multiplicity bound* $mu : \mathcal{X} \leqslant 1$, and also vice versa, described by *derivation rules* later called *no-multiplicity/key-equivalence*.

Surprisingly, and apparently never explicitly treated before, the *no-multiplicity* case has a counterpart for diversities (without a direct inverse).

Proposition 2 (no-diversity). *For a relational schema $R\langle \mathcal{U}, \mathcal{SC}, dom/k \rangle$ the premise entails the conclusion:* $\frac{di:\mathcal{Y} \leqslant 1}{fd:\mathcal{X} \rightarrow \mathcal{Y}}$.

Proof. Let a relation instance r satisfy the premise $di : \mathcal{Y} \leqslant 1$ for some $\mathcal{Y} \subseteq \mathcal{U}$, i.e., $\|\pi_{\mathcal{Y}}(r)\| \leqslant 1$ and thus $\pi_{\mathcal{Y}}(r) = \{\nu\}$ for some subtuple ν over $\mathcal{Y}$. Considering any functional dependency $fd : \mathcal{X} \rightarrow \mathcal{Y}$ with some $\mathcal{X} \subseteq \mathcal{U}$, if $\mu_1[\mathcal{X}] = \mu_2[\mathcal{X}]$, then $\mu_1[\mathcal{Y}] = \nu = \mu_2[\mathcal{Y}]$, i.e., the functional dependency is satisfied by r.   □

As shown in Example 2, a functional dependency $fd : \mathcal{X} \rightarrow \mathcal{Y}$ causes entailments between multiplicity bounds and diversity bounds, respectively, for the left-hand side $\mathcal{X}$ and related bounds both for the set of remaining attributes $\mathcal{U} \setminus (\mathcal{X} \cup \mathcal{Y})$ and for the functional entailment closure $\mathcal{X}_{fd}^{\models}$ of $\mathcal{X}$ including the right-hand side $\mathcal{Y}$. The corresponding derivation rules will later be called *duplicate-freeness, dependency-satisfaction* and *dependency-closure*. But the impact of multiplicity and diversity bounds on functional dependencies is limited.

Proposition 3 (non-impact of bound extensions greater than 1). *Let $R\langle \mathcal{U}, \mathcal{SC}, dom/k \rangle$ be a relational schema with $\mathcal{SC} = \mathcal{F} \cup \mathcal{M} \cup \mathcal{D}$ such that all bound extensions m declared in $\mathcal{M} \cup \mathcal{D}$ are greater than 1. Then any entailed functional dependency is entailed by the functional dependencies in $\mathcal{F}$ alone.*

Proof (in contraposition). Assume that the functional dependency $fd : \mathcal{X} \rightarrow \mathcal{Y}$ is *not* entailed by $\mathcal{F}$. Then we can construct the following witness of this non-entailment: it has exactly two different tuples μ_1 and μ_2 that agree on the functional entailment closure of $\mathcal{X}$ and disagree on all remaining attributes. By the assumption, there exists at least one such attribute $att \in \mathcal{Y}$. The agreement-part of this two-tuple relation ensures that all functional dependencies in $\mathcal{F}$ are satisfied indeed, and the disagreement-part immediately shows that the considered functional dependency is not satisfied. Moreover, by the assumption, all multiplicity bounds in $\mathcal{M}$ and all diversity bounds in $\mathcal{D}$ are satisfied as well. $\square$

The described interactions of the functional dependencies with the other more quantitative semantic constraints somehow confirm a useful expressiveness of our data model, whereas the stated limitation suggests that our data model might still be fully computationally manageable. However, the quantitative numerical flavor introduces very subtle combinatorial issues, which might not be completely captured by simple derivation rules, as briefly exemplified for diversities.

A *diversity bound* is inherited to *subsets*, later described by a derivation rule called *subset-monotony*. Given diversity bounds $di : \mathcal{X} \leqslant d_X$ and $di : \mathcal{Y} \leqslant d_Y$, we get the entailments $di : \mathcal{X} \cap \mathcal{Y} \leqslant Min(d_X, d_Y)$ and $di : \mathcal{X} \backslash \mathcal{Y} \leqslant d_X$ and, for the *disjoint case* only, $di : \mathcal{X} \cup \mathcal{Y} \leqslant d_X \cdot d_Y$. For the *overlapping union* we have a disjoint partition $\mathcal{X} \cup \mathcal{Y} = (\mathcal{X} \backslash \mathcal{Y}) \cup (\mathcal{X} \cap \mathcal{Y}) \cup (\mathcal{Y} \backslash \mathcal{X})$. Hence, if we know $di : \mathcal{X} \backslash \mathcal{Y} \leqslant d_{\mathcal{X} \backslash \mathcal{Y}}$ and $di : \mathcal{X} \cap \mathcal{Y} \leqslant d_{\mathcal{X} \cap \mathcal{Y}}$ and $di : \mathcal{Y} \backslash \mathcal{X} \leqslant d_{\mathcal{Y} \backslash \mathcal{X}}$, then we can derive the entailed diversity bound $di : \mathcal{X} \cup \mathcal{Y} \leqslant d_{\mathcal{X} \backslash \mathcal{Y}} \cdot d_{\mathcal{X} \cap \mathcal{Y}} \cdot d_{\mathcal{Y} \backslash \mathcal{X}}$. If we don't know the detailed diversity bounds, then $di : \mathcal{X} \cup \mathcal{Y} \leqslant d_X \cdot d_Y$ might be the strongest satisfied diversity bound, as $di : \mathcal{X} \cup \mathcal{Y} \leqslant d_X$ and $di : \mathcal{X} \cup \mathcal{Y} \leqslant d_Y$ might be as well. More attribute sets might make the situation even more involved.

Example 4. We consider a circular situation with three attributes A, B and C, diversity bounds $di : AB \leqslant 2$ and $di : AC \leqslant 2$ and $di : BC \leqslant 2$, which entail $di : A \leqslant 2$ and $di : B \leqslant 2$ and $di : C \leqslant 2$. We claim that the diversity bound $di : ABC \leqslant 2$ is entailed as well. Though the claim is intuitively very striking, the formal justification is somehow cumbersome and omitted for lack of space. The situation could suggest to define an *extension-instantiated* derivation rule

$$\frac{di : \mathcal{X}\mathcal{Y} \leqslant 2 \quad di : \mathcal{X}\mathcal{Z} \leqslant 2 \quad di : \mathcal{Y}\mathcal{Z} \leqslant 2 \quad \mathcal{X} \cap \mathcal{Y} = \varnothing \quad \mathcal{X} \cap \mathcal{Z} = \varnothing \quad \mathcal{Y} \cap \mathcal{Z} = \varnothing}{di : \mathcal{X}\mathcal{Y}\mathcal{Z} \leqslant 2}.$$

However, the rule would deliver a rather limited contribution to a finite global derivation system that should be both sound and complete, if achievable at all.

Proposition 4 (multiplicity-diversity interaction).   *For a relational schema $R\langle \mathcal{U}, \mathcal{SC}, dom/k \rangle$, the premises entail the conclusion:*

$$\frac{mu : \mathcal{X}_1 \leqslant m_1 \quad di : \mathcal{X}_1 \leqslant d_1 \quad mu : \mathcal{X}_2 \leqslant m_2 \quad di : \mathcal{X}_2 \leqslant d_2 \quad \mathcal{X}_1 \cap \mathcal{X}_2 = \varnothing}{di : \mathcal{X}_1 \mathcal{X}_2 \leqslant Min(Min(m_1, d_2) \cdot d_1), Min(m_2, d_1) \cdot d_2))}.$$

Proof. Assume that the relation instance r satisfies the premises. Let us consider the attribute set $\mathcal{X}_1$ first. By the assumption, the active domain of $\mathcal{X}_1$ in r contains at most d_1 different value combinations. Furthermore, each of the value combinations v can occur at most m_1 times in r and, thus, also in the projection

$\pi_{\mathcal{X}_1 \mathcal{X}_2}(r)$. Moreover, in $\pi_{\mathcal{X}_1 \mathcal{X}_2}(r)$ the multiplicity of v is further constrained by d_2 according to the assumption about the diversity of $\mathcal{X}_2$ in r, since in $\pi_{\mathcal{X}_1 \mathcal{X}_2}(r)$ multiple occurrences of v under $\mathcal{X}_1$ have to be distinguished under $\mathcal{X}_2$ to avoid duplicates. Accordingly, each v can occur at most $Min(m_1, d_2)$ times in $\pi_{\mathcal{X}_1 \mathcal{X}_2}(r)$. In total, there are at most $Min(m_1, d_2) \cdot d_1$ tuples in $\pi_{\mathcal{X}_1 \mathcal{X}_2}(r)$. If we consider the attribute set $\mathcal{X}_2$ in the same way, we get the corresponding bound $Min(m_2, d_1) \cdot d_2$. The minimum of the two bounds restricts the diversity of $\pi_{\mathcal{X}_1 \mathcal{X}_2}(r)$.   □

In the proof above, the multiplicity of v might also be constrained by m_2, since the multiplicity of a value combination w under $\mathcal{X}_2$ is also bounded; this indicates that the proposition does not describe the strongest bound for all cases.

5   Derivation Rules and Axioms for Semantic Constraints

Having investigated entailment between semantic constraints as a *declarative* concept, we now aim at converting our findings into *computational* counterparts.

Definition 3 (derivation system).   *For a relational schema $R\langle \mathcal{U}, \mathcal{SC}, dom/k \rangle$, FDMD consists of the following derivation rules and axioms (for **f**unctional dependencies, **d**iversity bounds, **m**ultiplicity bounds, and **d**omain sizes):*

1. functional dependencies:
   subset: $\dfrac{}{fd:\mathcal{X}\to\mathcal{X}'}$ *for all* $\emptyset \neq \mathcal{X}' \subseteq \mathcal{X}$

   transitivity: $\dfrac{fd:\mathcal{X}\to\mathcal{Y} \quad fd:\mathcal{Y}\to\mathcal{Z}}{fd:\mathcal{X}\to\mathcal{Z}}$

   augmentation: $\dfrac{fd:\mathcal{X}\to\mathcal{Y} \quad \mathcal{X}'\supseteq\mathcal{Y}'}{fd:\mathcal{X}\cup\mathcal{X}'\to\mathcal{Y}\cup\mathcal{Y}'}$

2. diversity bounds:
   pure-diversity: $\dfrac{}{di:\mathcal{X}\leqslant k_{\mathcal{X}}}$

   product-diversity: $\dfrac{di:\mathcal{X}_1\leqslant m_1 \quad di:\mathcal{X}_2\leqslant m_2 \quad \mathcal{X}_1\cap\mathcal{X}_2=\emptyset}{di:\mathcal{X}_1\mathcal{X}_2\leqslant m_1\cdot m_2}$

   diversity-(bound-)monotony: $\dfrac{di:\mathcal{X}\leqslant m}{di:\mathcal{X}\leqslant m'}$ *for all* $m \leqslant m'$

   (attribute-)subset-monotony: $\dfrac{di:\mathcal{X}\leqslant m \quad \mathcal{Y}\subseteq\mathcal{X}}{di:\mathcal{Y}\leqslant m}$

3. multiplicity bounds:
   domain-size: $\dfrac{}{mu:\mathcal{X}\leqslant k_{\mathcal{U}\setminus\mathcal{X}}}$ *(in particular for $\mathcal{X} = \mathcal{U}$:* $\dfrac{}{mu:\mathcal{U}\leqslant 1}$*)*

   multiplicity-(bound-)monotony: $\dfrac{mu:\mathcal{X}\leqslant m}{mu:\mathcal{X}\leqslant m'}$ *for all* $m \leqslant m'$

   (attribute-)superset-monotony: $\dfrac{mu:\mathcal{X}\leqslant m \quad \mathcal{X}\subseteq\mathcal{Y}}{mu:\mathcal{Y}\leqslant m}$

4. interactions of multiplicities and diversities:

domain-diversity: $\dfrac{di:\mathcal{U}\setminus\mathcal{X}\leqslant m}{mu:\mathcal{X}\leqslant m}$ (strengthening the rule domain-size)

multiplicity-diversity: $\dfrac{mu:\mathcal{X}_1\leqslant m_1 \quad di:\mathcal{X}_1\leqslant d_1 \quad mu:\mathcal{X}_2\leqslant m_2 \quad di:\mathcal{X}_2\leqslant d_2 \quad \mathcal{X}_1\cap\mathcal{X}_2=\varnothing}{di:\mathcal{X}_1\mathcal{X}_2\leqslant Min(\,Min(m_1,d_2)\cdot d_1)\,,\,Min(m_2,d_1)\cdot d_2)\,)}$

5. interactions with functional dependencies:

no-diversity: $\dfrac{di:\mathcal{Y}\leqslant 1}{fd:\mathcal{X}\to\mathcal{Y}}$

no-multiplicity/key-equivalence: $\dfrac{fd:\mathcal{X}\to\mathcal{U}}{mu:\mathcal{X}\leqslant 1}$ and $\dfrac{mu:\mathcal{X}\leqslant 1}{fd:\mathcal{X}\to\mathcal{U}}$

duplicate-freeness: $\dfrac{fd:\mathcal{X}\to\mathcal{Y}}{mu:\mathcal{X}\leqslant k_{\mathcal{U}\setminus(\mathcal{X}\cup\mathcal{Y})}}$ (in particular for $\mathcal{X}\cup\mathcal{Y}=\mathcal{U}$: $\dfrac{fd:\mathcal{X}\to\mathcal{U}\setminus\mathcal{X}}{mu:\mathcal{X}\leqslant 1}$)

(redundant by pure-diversity and the next rule)

and $\dfrac{fd:\mathcal{X}\to\mathcal{Y} \quad di:\mathcal{U}\setminus(\mathcal{X}\cup\mathcal{Y})\leqslant m}{mu:\mathcal{X}\leqslant m}$ (strengthening the preceding rule)

dependency-satisfaction: $\dfrac{fd:\mathcal{X}\to\mathcal{Y} \quad \mathcal{X}\cap\mathcal{Y}=\varnothing \quad mu:\mathcal{Y}\leqslant m}{mu:\mathcal{X}\leqslant m}$

and $\dfrac{fd:\mathcal{X}\to\mathcal{Y} \quad \mathcal{X}\cap\mathcal{Y}=\varnothing \quad di:\mathcal{X}\leqslant m}{di:\mathcal{Y}\leqslant m}$

dependency-closure: $\dfrac{fd:\mathcal{X}\to\mathcal{Y} \quad mu:\mathcal{X}\mathcal{Y}\leqslant m}{mu:\mathcal{X}\leqslant m}$

and $\dfrac{fd:\mathcal{X}\to\mathcal{Y} \quad mu:\mathcal{X}\leqslant m}{mu:\mathcal{X}\mathcal{Y}\leqslant m}$ (redundant by superset-monotony)

and $\dfrac{fd:\mathcal{X}\to\mathcal{Y} \quad di:\mathcal{X}\leqslant m}{di:\mathcal{X}\mathcal{Y}\leqslant m}$

and $\dfrac{fd:\mathcal{X}\to\mathcal{Y} \quad di:\mathcal{X}\mathcal{Y}\leqslant m}{di:\mathcal{X}\leqslant m}$ (redundant by subset-monotony)

Then the *derivation closure* $\mathcal{SC}^\vdash = \mathcal{SC}^\vdash_{fd}\cup\mathcal{SC}^\vdash_{mu}\cup\mathcal{SC}^\vdash_{di}$ is the set of functional dependencies, multiplicity bounds and diversity bounds that are *contained* in or can be *derived* from the given semantic constraints $\mathcal{SC}$ by applying the derivation rules and axioms. Obviously, like for entailment, we better remove any redundant element from $\mathcal{SC}^\vdash_{mu}$ and $\mathcal{SC}^\vdash_{di}$ and keep only the strongest ones.

We briefly comment on the relationship of *FDMD* to some other derivation systems. *FDMD* contains the extensively studied rules for functional dependencies [1,2]. Being more explicit and relating active domain sizes only indirectly by bounds, *FDMD* overlaps with a rudimentary treatment of a from relationships derived form of domain size restrictions together with unary structures in [18], Sect. 3.7. *FDMD* shows a weak connection with a note in [22] that $r \models fd : \mathcal{X} \to \mathcal{Y}$ iff $\| \pi_{\mathcal{X}}(r) \| = \| \pi_{\mathcal{X}\mathcal{Y}}(r) \|$. *FDMD* basically generalizes the rule *R8* of [12] dealing with *keys* only to our rule *no-diversity* for *functional dependencies*. *FDMD* is partly overlapping with the approach of [13] that deals with hierarchically structured, cycle-free entity-relationship schemas and considers any set M of multiplicities (and not only upper bounds) but no diversities.

Theorem 1 (soundness). *The system FDMD is sound, i.e., for a given relational schema $R\langle\mathcal{U},\mathcal{SC},dom/k\rangle$, all derivable constraints are actually entailed.*

Proof. Essentially, the claim has already been justified in Example 2 and Sect. 4. The formal details are omitted for the lack of space. To give an example, however, let us inspect the rule *dependency-satisfaction* dealing with *diversity bounds*. Indirectly assume that there exists a relation instance r of the given relational schema such that r satisfies both the functional dependency $fd : \mathcal{X} \to \mathcal{Y}$ with $\mathcal{X} \cap \mathcal{Y} = \emptyset$ and the diversity bound $di : \mathcal{X} \leqslant m$, i.e., $\|\pi_{\mathcal{X}}(r)\| \leqslant m$, and contains different tuples $\mu_1, \ldots, \mu_{m'}$ with $m' > m$ such that $\mu_1[\mathcal{Y}], \ldots, \mu_{m'}[\mathcal{Y}]$ are mutually different. Then, by the satisfied functional dependency, we would also have that $\mu_1[\mathcal{X}], \ldots, \mu_{m'}[\mathcal{X}]$ are mutually different, violating the satisfied diversity bound. $\qquad\square$

Theorem 2 (non-improvability). *Each of the rules and axioms of the derivation system FDMD, with the exception of the rule* multiplicity-diversity, *is non-improvable, i.e., for the given hypotheses the conclusion cannot be strengthened.*

Proof. For each of the rules and axioms, except *multiplicity-diversity*, we can construct a relation r that satisfies the hypotheses and exactly achieves the conclusion (such that a strengthened conclusion would not be satisfied). $\qquad\square$

Unfortunately, the derivation system *FDMD* is expected to be *not complete* due to the issues already mentioned in Sect. 4, and so far we do not know whether completeness could be achieved at all. Nevertheless, exhaustively applying the rules and axioms, we can computationally generate a *sound approximation* of the entailment closure, which might be useful for a database administrator. Exploiting Proposition 3 but still without further optimizations, we outline such a generation procedure:

Procedure derivation

Input	k	domain-size function
	$\mathcal{F}$	functional dependencies
	$\mathcal{M}$	multiplicity bounds (for each $\mathcal{X} \subseteq \mathcal{U}$ at most one)
	$\mathcal{D}$	diversity bounds (for each $\mathcal{X} \subseteq \mathcal{U}$ at most one)
Output	$\mathcal{X}_{fd}^{\vdash}$	functional derivation closure of $\mathcal{X} \subseteq \mathcal{U}$
	$\mathcal{X}_{mu}^{\vdash}$	multiplicity derivation closure of $\mathcal{X} \subseteq \mathcal{U}$
	$\mathcal{X}_{di}^{\vdash}$	diversity derivation closure of $\mathcal{X} \subseteq \mathcal{U}$

ForAll $\mathcal{X} \subseteq \mathcal{U}$ Do   %*initialize*
  $\mathcal{X}_{fd}^{\vdash} := \mathcal{X}$ %*subset*
  $\mathcal{X}_{mu}^{\vdash} := k_{\mathcal{U} \setminus \mathcal{X}}$ %*domain-size*
  $\mathcal{X}_{di}^{\vdash} := k_{\mathcal{X}}$ %*pure-diversity*
  If $mu : \mathcal{X} \leqslant 1 \in \mathcal{M}$ Then $\mathcal{X}_{fd}^{\vdash} := \mathcal{U}$ Fi   %*key-equivalence*
    ForAll $\mathcal{Y} \subseteq \mathcal{U}$ Do
      If $di : \mathcal{Y} \leqslant 1 \in \mathcal{M}$ Then $\mathcal{X}_{fd}^{\vdash} := \mathcal{X}_{fd}^{\vdash} \cup \mathcal{Y}$ Fi   %*no-diversity*
    Od
  If $mu : \mathcal{X} \leqslant m \in \mathcal{M}$ Then $\mathcal{X}_{mu}^{\vdash} := Min(\mathcal{X}_{mu}^{\vdash}, m)$ Fi   %*schema*

IF $di : \mathcal{X} \leqslant m \in \mathcal{D}$ THEN $\mathcal{X}_{di}^{\vdash} := Min(\mathcal{X}_{di}^{\vdash}, m)$ FI   %schema
OD

REPEAT   %exhaustively apply functional dependencies
FORALL $\mathcal{X} \subseteq \mathcal{U}$ DO
  IF $\mathcal{V} \subseteq \mathcal{X}_{fd}^{\vdash}$ and $fd : \mathcal{V} \to \mathcal{W} \in \mathcal{F}$
  THEN $\mathcal{X}_{fd}^{\vdash} := \mathcal{X}_{fd}^{\vdash} \cup \mathcal{W}$ FI   %transitivity, augmentation
OD
UNTIL no changes

FORALL $\mathcal{X} \subseteq \mathcal{U}$ DO   %apply functional derivation closures
 $\mathcal{X}_{mu}^{\vdash} := Min(\mathcal{X}_{mu}^{\vdash}, k_{\mathcal{U} \setminus \mathcal{X}_{fd}^{\vdash}})$ %duplicate-freeness
 $\mathcal{X}_{mu}^{\vdash} := Min(\mathcal{X}_{mu}^{\vdash}, (\mathcal{U} \setminus \mathcal{X}_{fd}^{\vdash})_{di}^{\vdash})$ %strengthened duplicate-freeness
  IF $\mathcal{X}_{fd}^{\vdash} = \mathcal{U}$ THEN $\mathcal{X}_{mu}^{\vdash} := 1$ FI   %special case: key-equivalence
OD

REPEAT   %exhaustively treat multiplicity and diversity bounds
FORALL $\mathcal{X} \subseteq \mathcal{U}$ DO
 $\mathcal{X}_{mu}^{\vdash} := Min(\mathcal{X}_{mu}^{\vdash}, (\mathcal{U} \setminus \mathcal{X})_{di}^{\vdash})$ %domain-diversity, redundant

 IF $\mathcal{Y} \subset \mathcal{X}$ THEN $\mathcal{X}_{mu}^{\vdash} := Min(\mathcal{X}_{mu}^{\vdash}, \mathcal{Y}_{mu}^{\vdash})$ FI   %superset-monotony

 IF $\mathcal{X}_{fd}^{\vdash} \supseteq \mathcal{Y}$ and $\mathcal{X} \cap \mathcal{Y} = \varnothing$ and $\mathcal{Y} \neq \varnothing$
 THEN $\mathcal{X}_{mu}^{\vdash} := Min(\mathcal{X}_{mu}^{\vdash}, \mathcal{Y}_{mu}^{\vdash}, \mathcal{X}\mathcal{Y}_{mu}^{\vdash})$ FI
                    %dependency-satisfaction/closure

 IF $\mathcal{X} = \mathcal{X}_1 \mathcal{X}_2$ and $\mathcal{X}_1 \cap \mathcal{X}_2 = \varnothing$
 THEN $\mathcal{X}_{di}^{\vdash} := Min(\mathcal{X}_{di}^{\vdash}, (\mathcal{X}_1)_{di}^{\vdash} \cdot (\mathcal{X}_2)_{di}^{\vdash})$ FI   %product-diversity

 IF $\mathcal{X} = \mathcal{X}_1 \mathcal{X}_2$ and $\mathcal{X}_1 \cap \mathcal{X}_2 = \varnothing$
   THEN $\mathcal{X}_{di}^{\vdash} := Min(\mathcal{X}_{di}^{\vdash},$
        $Min((\mathcal{X}_1)_{mu}^{\vdash}, (\mathcal{X}_2)_{di}^{\vdash}) \cdot (\mathcal{X}_1)_{di}^{\vdash}), Min((\mathcal{X}_2)_{mu}^{\vdash}, (\mathcal{X}_1)_{di}^{\vdash}) \cdot (\mathcal{X}_2)_{di}^{\vdash}))$ FI
                    %multiplicity-diversity

 IF $\mathcal{Y} \supset \mathcal{X}$ THEN $\mathcal{X}_{di}^{\vdash} := Min(\mathcal{X}_{di}^{\vdash}, \mathcal{Y}_{di}^{\vdash})$ FI   %subset-monotony

 IF $\mathcal{Y}_{fd}^{\vdash} \supseteq \mathcal{X}$ and $\mathcal{Y} \cap \mathcal{X} = \varnothing$
 THEN $\mathcal{X}_{di}^{\vdash} := Min(\mathcal{X}_{di}^{\vdash}, \mathcal{Y}_{di}^{\vdash})$ FI   %dependency-satisfaction

 IF $fd : \mathcal{X}_1 \to \mathcal{X}_2$ and $\mathcal{X} = \mathcal{X}_1 \mathcal{X}_2$ and $\mathcal{X}_1 \cap \mathcal{X}_2 = \varnothing$
 THEN $\mathcal{X}_{di}^{\vdash} := Min(\mathcal{X}_{di}^{\vdash}, (\mathcal{X}_1)_{di}^{\vdash})$ FI   %dependency-closure
OD
UNTIL no changes
ENDPROCEDURE

Theorem 3 (termination, correctness and sound approximation). *Let* $R\langle \mathcal{U}, \mathcal{SC}, dom/k \rangle$ *with* $\mathcal{SC} = \mathcal{F} \cup \mathcal{M} \cup \mathcal{D}$ *be a relational schema. The generation procedure* derivation *always terminates, returns the derivation closure correctly, and approximates the entailment closure soundly.*

Proof. During the repetitions, each assignment to any of the program variables for the functional derivation closures $\mathcal{X}_{fd}^{\vdash}$ or the multiplicity and diversity derivation closures $\mathcal{X}_{mu}^{\vdash}$ and $\mathcal{X}_{di}^{\vdash}$, respectively, either leaves the current value invariant or *increases* or *decreases* it, respectively, by adding one or more additional attributes *bounded* by the finite set $\mathcal{U}$ or by taking the minimum of the current value and one or more other values, *bounded* by the number 1, respectively.

As far as necessary according to Proposition 3, the procedure exhaustively applies the derivation rules of Definition 3, which are sound by Theorem 1.   □

6 Satisfiability and Instance Construction

According to Definition 1, a relation instance r *satisfies* a multiplicity bound or a diversity bound, respectively, with a bound extension m, if the cardinality of all pertinent selections or of the pertinent projection, respectively, is less than or equal to m. In the following we say that r *exactly achieves* the bound m, if for some pertinent selection or for the pertinent projection, respectively, exact equality holds.

Definition 4 (full-satisfiability and partial-satisfiability). *A relational schema $R\langle\mathcal{U}, \mathcal{SC}, dom/k\rangle$ is* multiplicity/diversity fully-satisfiable, *if there exists a relation instance r that exactly achieves all (strongest entailed) multiplicity/diversity bounds in $\mathcal{SC}_{mu}^{\models}/\mathcal{SC}_{di}^{\models}$ simultaneously.*

The schema is multiplicity/diversity partially-satisfiable, *if for all (strongest entailed) multiplicity/diversity bounds in $\mathcal{SC}_{mu}^{\models}/\mathcal{SC}_{di}^{\models}$ there exists a relation instance r that exactly achieves the pertinent bound.*

The schema is fully-satisfiable *if there exists a relation instance r that exactly achieves all (strongest entailed) multiplicity bounds in $\mathcal{SC}_{mu}^{\models}$ and all (strongest entailed) diversity bounds in $\mathcal{SC}_{di}^{\models}$ simultaneously. The schema is* partially-satisfiable *if it is both multiplicity and diversity partial-satisfiable.*

Notably, these definitions refer to the *strongest entailed constraints* that are also the declared ones in the *entailed relational schema*. A relation instance that witnesses a version of full-satisfiability shows a kind of *Armstrong-property*: it satisfies all pertinent entailed bounds but none of the non-entailed and thus stronger ones (with a smaller respective bound extension). As we will see, partial-satisfiability always holds, conceptually by definition for an entailed schema even for the declared constraints, though it remains an open problem to find a concise *construction method* for satisfying instances. However, full-satisfiability does not always hold, and it also remains open to find a concise *decision method*.

Proposition 5 (general partial-satisfiability).   *Each relational schema $R\langle\mathcal{U}, \mathcal{SC}, dom/k\rangle$ is partially-satisfiable.*

Proof. If there existed a strongest entailed bound that all relation instances r do not achieve exactly, then a stronger bound would be entailed.   □

r	$\mathcal{X}$	$\mathcal{X}_{fd}^{\models} \setminus \mathcal{X}$	$\mathcal{Z} := \mathcal{U} \setminus \mathcal{X}_{fd}^{\models}$
μ_1	ν	γ	ξ_1
.	.	.	.
.	.	.	.
.	.	.	.
μ_m	ν	γ	ξ_m

Fig. 4. A relation instance r of minimal size that achieves the bound extension m of $mu : \mathcal{X} \leqslant m$ exactly. For $m = 1$, the $\mathcal{Z}$-part would be void.

To illustrate the open construction problem, let $mu : \mathcal{X} \leqslant m \in \mathcal{SC}_{mu}^{\models}$, and define $\mathcal{Z} := \mathcal{U} \setminus \mathcal{X}_{fd}^{\models}$. Any relation instance $\tilde{r}$ that exactly achieves the bound extension m contains a subrelation r of the structure shown in Fig. 4. For $m > 1$, the following properties are most notable: r satisfies all constraints of the underlying schema; the subtuples ξ_i over $\mathcal{Z}$ are *mutually distinct* and such that in particular all multiplicity bounds $mu : \mathcal{V} \leqslant m' \in \mathcal{SC}_{mu}^{\models}$ with $\mathcal{V} \nsubseteq \mathcal{X}_{fd}^{\models}$ and all functional dependencies $fd : \mathcal{V} \to \mathcal{W} \in \mathcal{SC}_{fd}^{\models}$ with $\mathcal{V} \nsubseteq \mathcal{X}_{fd}^{\models}$ are satisfied. Now, the interesting open challenge would be to construct the suitable complementary subtuples ξ_i explicitly:

- For $mu : \mathcal{V} \leqslant m' \in \mathcal{SC}_{mu}^{\models}$ with $\mathcal{V} \nsubseteq \mathcal{X}_{fd}^{\models}$, we get the following *requirement*:
  if $\quad \xi_i[\mathcal{V} \cap \mathcal{Z}] = \xi_j[\mathcal{V} \cap \mathcal{Z}] \quad$ for some $M \subseteq \{1, \ldots, m\}$, for all $i, j \in M$,
  then $\mu_i[\mathcal{V}] = \mu_j[\mathcal{V}] \qquad$ for all $i, j \in M$, by definition of r, and thus
  $\qquad \|M\| \leqslant m' \qquad\qquad\qquad$ by bound-satisfaction, and
  $\qquad \xi_i[\mathcal{Z} \setminus \mathcal{V}] \neq \xi_j[\mathcal{Z} \setminus \mathcal{V}] \quad$ for all $i, j \in M$
  $\qquad \mathcal{Z} \setminus (\mathcal{V}) \neq \varnothing \qquad\qquad$ by duplicate-freeness.
- For $fd : \mathcal{V} \to \mathcal{W} \in \mathcal{SC}_{fd}^{\models}$ with $\mathcal{V} \nsubseteq \mathcal{X}_{fd}^{\models}$, we get the following *requirement*:
  if $\quad \xi_i[\mathcal{V} \cap \mathcal{Z}] = \xi_j[\mathcal{V} \cap \mathcal{Z}] \qquad$ for $i \neq j$,
  then $\mu_i[\mathcal{V}] = \mu_j[\mathcal{V}] \qquad\qquad\qquad$ by definition of r, and thus
  $\qquad \xi_i[\mathcal{W} \cap \mathcal{Z}] = \xi_j[\mathcal{W} \cap \mathcal{Z}] \qquad$ by dependency-satisfaction and
  $\qquad \xi_i[\mathcal{Z} \setminus (\mathcal{V} \cup \mathcal{W})] \neq \xi_j[\mathcal{Z} \setminus (\mathcal{V} \cup \mathcal{W})]$
  $\qquad \mathcal{Z} \setminus (\mathcal{V} \cup \mathcal{W}) \neq \varnothing \qquad\qquad$ by duplicate-freeness.

So far it remains open how to satisfy the exhibited requirements constructively.

Proposition 6 (no general full-satisfiability). *There exist relational schemas (even without diversity bounds) that are* not *multiplicity fully-satisfiable.*

Proof. Consider a relational schema with three attributes A, B and C, domain sizes $k_A = k_B = k_C = 2$, three multiplicity bounds $mu : A \leqslant 2$, $mu : B \leqslant 2$ and $mu : C \leqslant 2$, and two functional dependencies $fd : A \to B$ and $fd : C \to B$.

As illustrated by Fig. 5, we will construct a counterexample to multiplicity full-satisfiability. Assume that for a relation instance r the bound extension 2 for the attribute A is exactly achieved. Then there are two different tuples $\mu_1 \neq \mu_2$ in r that agree on attribute A, say $\mu_1[A] = \mu_2[A] = 1$. Then, by the functional dependency $fd : A \to B$, we also have agreement on the attribute B, say $\mu_1[B] = \mu_2[B] = 1$. Duplicate-freeness then implies that $\mu_1[C] \neq \mu_2[C]$, say $\mu_1[C] = 1$ and $\mu_2[C] = 2$. Now, additionally assume that the bound extension 2 for the attribute C is exactly achieved as well. Since $k_C = 2$, the value 1 or the value 2 has multiplicity 2 under the attribute C. Say, the value 2 occurs twice, which means that there is a third tuple μ_3, different from both μ_1 and μ_2, with $\mu_3[C] = 2$. Then, however, the functional dependency $fd : C \to B$ requires that $\mu_2[B] = \mu_3[B]$ and, thus, the value 1 has multiplicity at least 3 under the attribute B, violating the multiplicity bound $mu : B \leqslant 2$.   □

r	A	B	C
μ_1	1		
μ_2	1		

r	A	B	C
μ_1	1	1	
μ_2	1	1	

r	A	B	C
μ_1	1	1	1
μ_2	1	1	2

r	A	B	C
μ_1	1	1	1
μ_2	1	1	2
μ_3			2

r	A	B	C
μ_1	1	1	1
μ_2	1	1	2
μ_3	2	1	2

Fig. 5. For functional dependencies $fd : A \to B$ and $fd : C \to B$ and multiplicity bounds $mu : att \leqslant 2$, the construction of a counterexample to multiplicity full-satisfiability under too restricted domain sizes (here: $dom_{att} = \{1, 2\}$).

Just setting the domain sizes to 3, a witness for multiplicity full-satisfiability can easily be found. However, the construction of the counterexample could also be generalized for larger domains. The impact of domain sizes, and similarly of diversity bounds, can also be illustrated by the decision problem of *multiplicity full-satisfiability*. For, unfortunately, the following straightforward attempt for the related construction problem appears to be *not* always successful:

1. For each constraint $sc \equiv mu : \mathcal{X} \leqslant m \in \mathcal{SC}_{mu}^{\models}$ pick a relation instance r_{sc} that achieves the respective bound extension m exactly.
2. Make the respective active domains mutually disjoint by suitable renamings.
3. Take the union of all resulting instances.

Step 1 would *locally* guarantee the satisfaction of all constraints and the exact achievement of the pertinent multiplicity bounds. Step 2 would leave the guaranteed properties invariant and would avoid interactions between the instances. Step 3 would *globally* ensure the satisfaction of all constraints and all the exact bound achievements. But under *finite* domain sizes, Step 2 will not always be possible. Nevertheless, special cases can successfully be handled, as demonstrated by the following example treating diversities (and omitted related ones). The example successfully deals with unary constraints, as suggested by many other investigations, see, e.g., [1,12,18,20,21].

Proposition 7 (diversity unary-full-satisfiability under unary functional dependencies). *Let $R\langle \mathcal{U}, \mathcal{SC}, dom/k \rangle$ be a relational schema with $\mathcal{SC} = \mathcal{F} \cup \mathcal{D}$ such that $\mathcal{F}$ consists of unary functional dependencies and $\mathcal{D}$ contains diversity bounds. Then there exists a relation instance r that exactly achieves all unary diversity bounds in $\mathcal{SC}_{di}^{\models}$ simultaneously.*

Proof (sketch). Consider $\mathcal{SC}_{di}^{\models}$ and let $\mathcal{U} = \{A_1, \ldots, A_n\}$ such that $(A_1)_{di}^{\models} \leqslant \cdots \leqslant (A_i)_{di}^{\models} \leqslant \cdots \leqslant (A_n)_{di}^{\models}$. Define $d_i := (A_i)_{di}^{\models}$ and construct the instance r with d_n many tuples $\mu_1, \ldots, \mu_a, \ldots, \mu_{d_n}$ with $\mu_a(A_i) = Min(a, d_i)$. By the construction, r exactly achieves all unary diversity bounds in $\mathcal{SC}_{di}^{\models}$ simultaneously. A closer inspection shows that all further constraints are satisfied as well. □

7 Conclusions

Complementing functional dependencies as *qualitative* semantic constraints by multiplicity bounds and diversity bounds as *quantitative* semantic constraints, also demanding attribute domains of finite size as additional quantitative requirements, we have enhanced the expressiveness of the traditional relational data model. This enhancement should enable a database administrator to convert numerical insight about a "real-world" application into formal schema declarations for more efficient data manipulations at runtime. From a wider perspective, the enhancement might contribute to the "fundamental problem of database design", as concisely stated by Makowsky/Ravve [19] and already treated in various textbooks, e.g., [1,18,20,21].

In particular, the investigations of multiplicity bounds and diversity bounds exhibit quantitative relationships between data under the left-hand side of a functional dependency, its right-hand side and the remaining attributes. Moreover, regarding a functional dependency $fd : \mathcal{X} \to \mathcal{Y}$, diversity bounds play a complementary role to multiplicity bounds, also dealing with the two special cases of the satisfaction by a relation instance r: (i) there are *no equalities* under the set of attributes $\mathcal{X}$, captured by $r \models mu : \mathcal{X} \leqslant 1$; (ii) there are *no inequalities* under the set of attributes $\mathcal{Y}$, captured by $r \models di : \mathcal{Y} \leqslant 1$ (equivalently by the satisfaction of an independence atom $\mathcal{Y} \perp \mathcal{Y}$ in the sense of [12]).

There are many challenges for further investigations. Besides a better understanding of the relationships mentioned above, a main open problem is whether our setting can be fully axiomatized or not. This includes to find additional sound derivation rules to improve the approximation or even achieve completeness. Closely related are the open questions regarding the partial- or the full-satisfiability of strongest entailed multiplicity bounds and diversity bounds, seen as issues of Armstrong-properties. Moreover, a thorough analysis of the computational complexity of entailment, and sophisticated optimizations of the generation of the derivation closure would be worthwhile.

A *functional dependency* $fd : \mathcal{X} \to \mathcal{Y}$ literally only refers to the attributes $\mathcal{XY}$ under interest, as also reflected by the classical three derivation rules [1,2]. However, a relation instance has to provide *enough diversity* for the multiply occurring values of the left-hand side by the additional remaining attributes $\mathcal{Z} := \mathcal{U} \setminus (\mathcal{X} \cup \mathcal{Y})$, and that diversity also has to come along with *sufficient multiplicity*. Moreover, whenever we complement the left-hand side $\mathcal{X}$ with a multiplicity bound $mu : \mathcal{X} \leqslant m_{\mathcal{X}}$ and a diversity bound $di : \mathcal{X} \leqslant d_{\mathcal{X}}$, the *full-satisfiability* of the combined requirements for $\mathcal{X}$ might depend on the remaining attributes $\mathcal{Z}$. So we should investigate whether and how a kind of a *two-phase* derivation procedure like for multivalued and related dependencies [5,7,15] is theoretically possible and pragmatically reasonable: first focus on the attributes mentioned in the functional dependencies of interest; then add remaining attributes.

Non-key functional dependencies are exploited for *schema normalization* to reduce *potential* redundancy in instances [16,17,23,24]. So it would be worth-while to concisely determine how multiplicity bounds and diversity bounds might affect the *expected amount* of the reduction.

Numerous *other semantic constraints* have been studied [1,18,21], some of them are apparently somehow related to ours, e.g., *afunctional dependencies* [20], general *cardinality constraints* [9,13,14], *independence axioms* [12].

Acknowledgements. I would like to sincerely thank Sven Hartman and Sebastian Link for greatly stimulating discussions on early ideas about the topic of this work, and the anonymous reviewers for helpful and constructive remarks about the submitted version.

References

1. Abiteboul, S., Hull, R., Vianu, V.: Foundations of Databases. Addison-Wesley, Reading (1995)
2. Armstrong, W.W.: Dependency structures of data base relationships. In: IFIP Congress, pp. 580–583 (1974)
3. Berens, M., Biskup, J.: On sampling representatives of relational schemas with a functional dependency. In: Varzinczak, I. (ed.) FoIKS 2022. LNCS, vol. 13388, pp. 1–19. Springer, Cham (2022). https://doi.org/10.1007/978-3-031-11321-5_1
4. Berens, M., Biskup, J., Preuß, M.: Uniform probabilistic generation of relation instances satisfying a functional dependency. Inf. Syst. **103**, 101848 (2022)
5. Biskup, J.: Inferences of multivalued dependencies in fixed and undetermined universes. Theor. Comput. Sci. **10**, 93–105 (1980)
6. Biskup, J., Bonatti, P.A.: Controlled query evaluation with open queries for a decidable relational submodel. Ann. Math. Artif. Intell. **50**(1–2), 39–77 (2007)
7. Biskup, J., Link, S.: Appropriate inferences of data dependencies in relational databases. Ann. Math. Artif. Intell. **63**(3–4), 213–255 (2011)
8. Biskup, J., Preuß, M.: Can we probabilistically generate uniformly distributed relation instances efficiently? In: Darmont, J., Novikov, B., Wrembel, R. (eds.) ADBIS 2020. LNCS, vol. 12245, pp. 75–89. Springer, Cham (2020). https://doi.org/10.1007/978-3-030-54832-2_8
9. Chen, P.P.: The entity-relationship model - toward a unified view of data. ACM Trans. Database Syst. **1**(1), 9–36 (1976)
10. Demetrovics, J., Katona, G.O.H., Miklós, D., Thalheim, B.: On the number of independent functional dependencies. In: Dix, J., Hegner, S.J. (eds.) FoIKS 2006. LNCS, vol. 3861, pp. 83–91. Springer, Heidelberg (2006). https://doi.org/10.1007/11663881_6
11. Flajolet, P., Sedgewick, R.: Analytic Combinatorics. Cambridge University Press, Cambridge (2009)
12. Hannula, M., Kontinen, J., Link, S.: On the finite and general implication problems of independence atoms and keys. J. Comput. Syst. Sci. **82**(5), 856–877 (2016)
13. Hartmann, S.: On the implication problem for cardinality constraints and functional dependencies. Ann. Math. Artif. Intell. **33**(2–4), 253–307 (2001)

14. Hartmann, S., Köhler, H., Leck, U., Link, S., Thalheim, B., Wang, J.: Constructing Armstrong tables for general cardinality constraints and not-null constraints. Ann. Math. Artif. Intell. **73**(1–2), 139–165 (2015)

15. Hartmann, S., Köhler, H., Link, S.: Full hierarchical dependencies in fixed and undetermined universes. Ann. Math. Artif. Intell. **50**(1–2), 195–226 (2007)

16. Katona, G.O.H., Tichler, K.: Encoding databases satisfying a given set of dependencies. In: Lukasiewicz, T., Sali, A. (eds.) FoIKS 2012. LNCS, vol. 7153, pp. 203–223. Springer, Heidelberg (2012). https://doi.org/10.1007/978-3-642-28472-4_12

17. Kolahi, S., Libkin, L.: An information-theoretic analysis of worst-case redundancy in database design. ACM Trans. Database Syst. **35**(1), 5:1–5:32 (2010)

18. Levene, M., Loizou, G.: A Guided Tour of Relational Databases and Beyond. Springer, London (1999). https://doi.org/10.1007/978-0-85729-349-7

19. Makowsky, J.A., Ravve, E.V.: The fundamental problem of database design. In: Plášil, F., Jeffery, K.G. (eds.) SOFSEM 1997. LNCS, vol. 1338, pp. 53–69. Springer, Heidelberg (1997). https://doi.org/10.1007/3-540-63774-5_97

20. Paredaens, J., Bra, P.D., Gyssens, M., Gucht, D.V.: The Structure of the Relational Database Model. EATCS Monographs on Theoretical Computer Science, vol. 17. Springer, Berlin (1989). https://doi.org/10.1007/978-3-642-69956-6

21. Thalheim, B.: Entity-Relationship Modeling – Foundations of Database Technology. Springer, Heidelberg (2000). https://doi.org/10.1007/978-3-662-04058-4

22. Thalheim, B.: Semiotics in databases. In: Schewe, K.-D., Singh, N.K. (eds.) MEDI 2019. LNCS, vol. 11815, pp. 3–19. Springer, Cham (2019). https://doi.org/10.1007/978-3-030-32065-2_1

23. Vincent, M.W., Srinivasan, B.: Redundancy and the justification for fourth normal form in relational databases. Int. J. Found. Comput. Sci. **4**(4), 355–365 (1993)

24. Wei, Z., Link, S.: Discovery and ranking of functional dependencies. In: ICDE 2019, pp. 1526–1537. IEEE (2019)

Minimal Armstrong Databases
for Cardinality Constraints

Bence Király[1] and Attila Sali[1,2](✉) ⓘ

[1] Department of Computer Science and Information Theory,
Budapest University of Technology and Economics, Budapest, Hungary
`kiraly.bence@tuta.io`
[2] HUN-REN Alfréd Rényi Institute of Mathematics, Budapest, Hungary
`sali.attila@renyi.hu`

Abstract. Hartmann et al. proved that calculating Armstrong instance for a collection of cardinality constraints is exactly exponential problem. In fact, they presented a collection of cardinality constraints based on some special graphs, whose minimal Armstrong instance is of exponential size. Motivated by that, graph based cardinality constraints are introduced in the present paper. That is, given a simple graph on the set of attributes, max cardinality constraints on edges end vertices, respectively are set. We take up the task to determine sizes of minimum Armstrong instances of graph based cardinality constraints for several graph classes, including bipartite graphs, complete multipartite graphs. We give exact results for several graph classes or give polynomial time algorithm to construct the minimum Armstrong table for other cases. We show that Armstrong tables of graph based cardinality constraints correspond to another graph defined on the maximal independent vertex sets of the constraint graph. The row graph of an Armstrong table is defined as a pair of rows form an edge if they contain identical entries in some column. It is shown that there exists a minimal Armstrong table for a collection of graph based cardinality constraints such that the line graph of its row graph is a spanning subgraph of the graph defined on the maximal independent sets of the constraint graph. This observation is used to find minimum Armstrong tables for bipartite constraint graphs. Feasible edge colourings of graphs introduced by Folkman and Fulkerson are used to construct minimum Armstrong tables for another class of constraint graphs.

Keywords: cardinality constraint · Armstrong instance · line graphs · complete k-partite graphs · feasible edge colorings

Research of the second author was partially supported by the National Research, Development and Innovation Office (NKFIH) grants K–116769 and SNN-135643. This work was also supported by the BME- Artificial Intelligence FIKP grant of EMMI (BME FIKP-MI/SC) and by the Ministry of Innovation and Technology and the National Research, Development and Innovation Office within the Artificial Intelligence National Laboratory of Hungary.

A. Meier and M. Ortiz (Eds.): FoIKS 2024, LNCS 14589, pp. 64–81, 2024.
https://doi.org/10.1007/978-3-031-56940-1_4

1   Introduction

Armstrong relations are of interest in database theory and practice. A relation r over schema R is said to be *Armstrong* for a collection of integrity constraints Σ of some given type if any constraint σ of that type we have that r satisfies constraint σ if and only if σ is implied by Σ. The practical use of Armstrong relations is nicely explained in [18], they are very useful for the acquisition of meaningful integrity constraints in the design phase of a database system. In order to say something about the usefulness of Armstrong relations experiments were executed. They measured what or how much design teams learn about the application domain in addition to what they already knew prior to using Armstrong relations. Therefore, they first measured the quality without the use of an Armstrong relation, and then measured the quality after the use of Armstrong relations. The conclusion was that use of Armstrong relations improved design quality.

Some other use of Armstrong relations are investigated in [1,13,16,19] that include incomplete databases and fuzzyness as well.

Consequently, the question of minimal Armstrong relations are of particular interest. Their investigation was started by Demetrovics et al. in [3,4,6–8]. These papers dealt with functional dependencies. Branching dependencies, a generalization of functional dependencies were treated in [9]. The research of minimum Armstrong matrices resulted in fruitful interactions between database theory and design theory [10], furthermore coding theory [15,25].

The main topic of the present paper are cardinality constraints that were started by Chen's seminal paper [2] on the entity-relationship model and were systematically studied by Thalheim in [26,27]. Armtrong tables for cardinality constraints were investigated in [12,14,20]. Our starting point is the result of Hartmann et al. [14] that the complexity of constructing an Armstrong matrix is exactly exponential in general. That was proven using a special collection of cardinality constraints, which was actually based on a complete matching of a graph of $2n$ vertices. Motivated by this, we introduce general graph based cardinality constraints. We consider a graph whose vertex set is the set of attributes of the schema given. Max cardinality constraints are defined for the edges and vertices of that graph. We show that Armstrong tables correspond to graphs whose vertex sets are the collection of maximal independent sets of the constraint graphs. In fact, we establish a connection between the line graph of a graph defined on the rows of an Armstrong matrix and the graph of maximal independent sets mentioned above.

It must be emphasized that finite Armstrong tables only exist when every column has some upper bound on it, as it was pointed out by Link et al. [20]. In case some attributes have no explicit upper bounds, Armstrong representations were introduced in [20], which exist even if finite Armstrong tables do not exist. Due to that, the upper bound restriction on vertices in our graph based constraints appear less restrictive.

Then we treat some special graph classes where the size of minimum Armstrong instance can exactly be determined, and give polynomial time algorithm in some other cases to compute the Armstrong table.

The structure of the paper is as follows. Section 2 contains preliminaries and necessary definitions. Section 3 contains our new results. It starts with some easy cases to warm up, then necessary graph theory results are proven and recalled. Then we treat the case when the graph of the maximum independent sets of the constraint graph is bipartite. This involves integer linear programming and integer flows. Finally we generalize to multipartite graphs. Section 4 contains conclusions and further research directions.

2   Preliminaries

In this section the necessary definitions and previous results are recalled. Many of the definitions are well known, they are stated here just for unifying notations. We consider relations that are bags of tuples. Let $R = \{A_1 A_2 \ldots A_n\}$ be relational schema, $dom(A_i)$ be countably infinite $domain$ of $attribute$ A_i. A $relation$ (or $table$) r over schema R is a finite multiset of $tuples$ (functions) $t \colon r \to \cup_{i=1}^{n} dom(A_i)$ such that $t(A_i) \in dom(A_i)$.

Definition 1. A max-cardinality constraint $(max\text{-}CC)$ is an $expression$ $\sigma = card(X) \leq a$ $where$ $X \subseteq R$ and a is a $positive$ $integer.$ A $relation$ r $over$ $schema$ R is $said$ to $satisfy$ $max\text{-}CC$ $card(X) \leq a$ if and $only$ if $there$ $exist$ no $a + 1$ $distinct$ $tuples$ $t_1, t_2, \ldots, t_{a+1} \in R,$ $such$ $that$ for $every$ $attribute$ $C \in X$ we $have$ $t_1[C] = t_2[C] = \cdots = t_{a+1}[C],$ in $notation$ $r \models \sigma.$

Note that a min-cardinality constraint can be defined analogously, however our focus of interest here are max-CC's. Let $\mathcal{C}$ be a class of integrity constraints. A collection Σ of constraints from $\mathcal{C}$ $implies$ $\sigma \in \mathcal{C}$, in notation $\Sigma \models \sigma$, if and only if any relation r that satisfy every constraint in Σ, r also satisfies σ.

Definition 2. Let $\mathcal{C}$ be a $class$ of $integrity$ $constraints$ and Σ be a $collection$ of $constraints$ $from$ $\mathcal{C}.$ A $relation$ r is $\mathcal{C}$-Armstrong for Σ if for any $\sigma \in \mathcal{C},$ r $satisfies$ $integrity$ $constraint$ σ $exactly$ if $that$ $constraint$ is $implied$ by the $collection$ $\Sigma.$

The following collection of cardinality constraints were introduced by Demetrovics and Gyepesi [5] in context of functional dependencies and was later used by Hartmann et al. [14] to prove that the time complexity of computing the minimal Armstrong tables for cardinality constraints is exactly exponential in general. Let $R = \{C_1, C_2, \ldots C_n\}$ and Σ consist of $card(C_i) \leq 2$, if $1 \leq i \leq n$ and $card(C_{2j-1}, C_{2j}) \leq 1$, if $1 \leq j \leq \frac{n}{2}$. Actually, the minimum number of rows of an Armstrong matrix (table) for this collection of max-CC's is exponential in n.

Observe that the cardinality constraints with bound 1 form a maximal matching in the complete graph whose vertices are the attributes of schema R. This motivated the following definition.

Definition 3. *Let $R = \{C_1, C_2, \ldots C_n\}$ be a relational schema, $G = (V, E)$ be a simple graph on n vertices. $CC(G)$ is defined as the following collection of max-CC's. For every attribute C_i set $card(C_i) \leq 2$ and for every edge $\{i, j\} \in E$ of graph G set $card(C_i, C_j) \leq 1$. This collection is called max-CC based on G, furthermore G is called the* constraint graph.

We have that max cardinality constraints satisfy that $card(X) \leq a$ implies $card(X) \leq a + 1$ for any set X of attributes and that if Y is a superset of X then $card(X) \leq a$ also implies $card(Y) \leq a$. From here one may easily deduce the following.

Note 1. If a relation satisfies $CC(G)$ for some constraint graph $G = (V, E)$, then the only max cardinality constraints that could hold but not be implied are $card(A) \leq 1$. This will be used without further mentioning throughout the paper.

The extremal problem studied in the present paper is the following.

Definition 4. *Let $R = \{C_1, C_2, \ldots C_n\}$ be a relational schema, $G = (V, E)$ be a simple graph on n vertices. $ex(CC(G))$ denotes the minimum number of rows of an Armstrong table for $CC(G)$.*

Some simple observations for an Armstrong matrix M for $CC(G)$ are as follows.

Observation 1. *1. A domain value may occur at most twice in a column of M, furthermore in any column there is a pair of identical elements.*
2. If two rows of M agree on a set X of columns (attributes), then X is an independent vertex set in the constraint graph G

Proof. 1. is a direct consequence of Note 1.
2. follows because X cannot contain edges.   □

Two identical domain entries in a column are called *twins*. Different twins are in the *same position*, if they occur in the same pair of rows, a *twin class* is a maximal set of twins in the same position. Note that the columns of an twin class correspond to an independent vertex set in graph G. Also note, that every column contains a pair of twins, according to 1. of Observation 1. We emphasize that twins always refer to a particular column/attribute, while twin class refers to a set of columns/attributes. On the other hand, twins and twin classes both have their associated pair of rows (positions). A twin is said to *cover* the pair of rows where they occur.

Although tables/relations are defined as unordered collections of tuples, as well as tuples are functions from the set of attributes to the union of domains of attributes, we frequently refer to them as matrices, thus imposing order on the rows and attributes. We may do that, because for the studies we undertake this will do no harm.

3 Minimal Armstrong Relations

3.1 Some Easy Cases

In this section some easily solvable cases are presented. Figure 1 shows minimal
Armstrong tables for the two simple, two-vertex graphs.

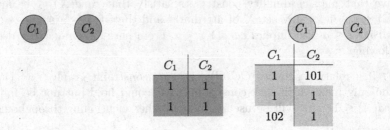

Fig. 1. The two simple graphs on two vertices and their minimal Armstrong tables.

If $G = K_n$, the complete graph on n vertices, then twins of two different
columns cannot occur in the same pair of rows. Thus, the number of pairs of
rows is at least as large as the number of columns, i.e. $\binom{m}{2} \geq n$. If $\binom{m}{2} \geq n$
holds, then to have an Armstrong table for $CC(K_n)$ we assign a unique pair
of rows to every column where entry 1 stands in that column, while all other
entries are pairwise distinct numbers larger than 1 in each column. This shows
that $ex(K_n) = \min\{m : \binom{m}{2} \geq n\}$.

On the other hand, $ex(K_{a,b}) = 3$. Indeed, two tuples can only agree on
attributes in the same partite class, thus if we have m rows, then $\binom{m}{2} \geq 2$, so
$m \geq 3$. On the other hand, a construction is given by two twin classes, one for
each partite class of the vertices, respectively, and the two twin classes have a
row common, as the corresponding (maximal) independent sets of vertices are
disjoint.

When two twin classes have a common row, then they are called *slid together*
(Fig. 2).

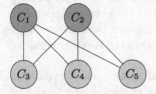

C_1	C_2	C_3	C_4	C_5
1	1	102	103	104
1	1	1	1	1
105	106	1	1	1

Fig. 2. Armstrong table for $CC(K_{2,3})$. $\{C_1, C_2\}$ and $\{C_3, C_4, C_5\}$ are disjoint maximal
independent sets.

Analogously, if the constraint graph is complete k-partite, then the partite
classes are maximal independent sets, so they correspond to twin classes that

can pairwise be slid together. Thus, the argument of $ex(CC(K_n))$ can be applied to show that if G is complete k-partite, then $ex(CC(G)) = \min\{m \colon \binom{m}{2} \geq k\}$.

3.2 Some Necessary Graph Theory

We have seen that maximal independent sets play an important role in constraint graphs.

Definition 5. *Let $\mathcal{I}$ be the system of maximal independent vertex sets of constraint graph $G(V, E)$. Consider the graph $M(\mathcal{I}, D)$, where $\{I_1, I_2\} \in D$ if and only if the maximal independent sets I_1 and I_2 are disjoint. Then $M(\mathcal{I}, D)$ is called the* maximal independent sets graph *of G or shortly* maxindep graph *of G. In notation, $M = \mathcal{M}(G)$*

Example 1. Note that non-isomorphic graphs may have the same maxindep graph. The two graphs shown on Fig. 3 both have $K_{1,2} = \mathcal{M}(G)$.

Fig. 3. Non-isomorphic graphs with the same maxindep graph

Definition 6. *Let R be the set of rows of a relational matrix $\mathbf{A}$. Define graph $S(R, J)$ by $\{r_i, r_j\} \in J$ if there exists twin class in $\mathbf{A}$ covering r_i and r_j. The graph $S(R, J)$ is called the* row graph *of $\mathbf{A}$.*

To formulate the main theorem of this section, the concept of *line-graph* needs to be introduced.

Definition 7. *The line-graph of graph $G = (V, E)$ is the graph $L(G) = (E, F)$, where two edges $e_1, e_2 \in E$ of G form an edge $\{e_1, e_2\} \in F$ if and only if e_1 and e_2 have a common end vertex.*

The following theorem characterizes some minimal Armstrong tables of $CC(G)$ for a constraint graph G.

Theorem 2. *Let $G = (V, E)$ be a constraint graph. Then there exists an Armstrong table $\mathbf{A}$ of $CC(G)$, with $ex(CC(G))$ rows, such that the line-graph $L(S)$ of the row graph $S = S(R, J)$ of $\mathbf{A}$ is a spanning subgraph of the maxindep graph $M = \mathcal{M}(G)$ of G.*

Proof. Let $\mathbf{A}'$ be an Armstrong table of minimum number of rows for $CC(G)$. Note that two distinct non-disjoint twin classes cannot cover the same row, since then there would be three identical entries in a column of $\mathbf{A}'$. Suppose that I is a non-maximal independent vertex set of G, but the columns of $\mathbf{A}'$ corresponding to I are covered by a twin class on rows r_1, r_2. Then there exists a maximal independent vertex set $I \subset I'$, furthermore the max cardinality constraint $card(I') \leq 2$ must be represented by a twin class on rows r_3, r_4. Since $\{r_1, r_2\} \cap \{r_3, r_4\} = \emptyset$, the identical entries of rows r_1, r_2 can be replaced by arbitrary pairwise different new entries to obtain another Armstrong table for $CC(G)$. Keep repeating the transformation above until only maximal independent vertex sets are represented by twin classes in the resulting table $\mathbf{A}$. So the vertex set of $L(S)$, the line-graph of the row graph $\mathbf{A}$ can be identified with the vertices of the maxindep graph $M = \mathcal{M}(G)$ of G. Two vertices (row pairs) in $L(S)$ are connected by an edge iff they are not disjoint, that is the corresponding twin classes are slid together, which can only happen if the corresponding maximal independent vertex sets are disjoint, that is they are connected in $\mathcal{M}(G)$. So the edge set of $L(S)$ is a subset of the edge set of $\mathcal{M}(G)$, while their vertex sets are the same (actually they are identified), so $L(S)$ is a spanning subgraph of $\mathcal{M}(G)$. □

The reverse of Theorem 2 is true in a sense.

Theorem 3. *Let $G = (V, E)$ be a constraint graph, and let $H = (W, F)$ be such a graph that the line graph $L(H)$ is a spanning subgraph of the maxindep graph $\mathcal{M}(G)$. Then there exists a (not necessarily minimal) Armstrong table of $CC(G)$ with $|W|$ rows.*

Proof. Let $\mathcal{I} = \{I_1, I_2, \ldots I_k\}$ be the maximal independent sets of G. Then there is a bijection between F and $\mathcal{I}$, say edge $e_i = \{w_1^i, w_2^i\}$ corresponds to I_i. Construct a table $\mathbf{A}$ of $|W|$ rows and $|V|$ columns by putting entry i in rows w_1^i and w_2^i in columns of I_i, furthermore pairwise distinct entries larger than k into the remaining positions. We claim that $\mathbf{A}$ constructed this way is an Armstrong table for $CC(G)$. Indeed, the construction is valid, that is no conflict exists for entries $1, 2, \ldots, k$ placed in $\mathbf{A}$, since if edges e_i and e_j of H have common vertices, then they are connected in the line graph $L(H)$, so $I_i \cap I_j = \emptyset$, so entries i and j are placed in disjoint column sets.

The maximum number of times an entry appears in a column of $\mathbf{A}$ is at most two by construction. This shows that $card(X) \leq 2$ for any subset X of the columns (attributes). Since rows w_1^i and w_2^i show the max-cardinality constraint for I_i, we have that $card(X) = 2$ for any independent vertex set $X \subseteq V$. On the other hand, if $\{v_a, v_b\} \in E$ is an edge of G, then there exist no two rows of $\mathbf{A}$ that agree in columns corresponding to v_a and v_b. □

Corollary 1. *We have that $ex(CC(G))$ is the minimum number of vertices of a graph $H = (W, F)$ such that the line graph $L(H)$ is a spanning subgraph of $\mathcal{M}(G)$.*

Since we are interested in maxindep graphs it is interesting what graphs are those. Characterization of *clique graphs* is known.

Definition 8. *Let* $G = (V, E)$ *be a graph,* $C \subseteq V$ *is* clique *in* G *if it is a maximal complete subgraph, that is* $\forall v_i, v_j \in C : \{v_i, v_j\} \in E$, *and there does not exist subgraph* D *such that* $C \subset D$ *and* D *is also complete. The* clique graph *of* G *is* $K(G) = (\mathcal{C}, \mathcal{E})$, *where the vertex set* $\mathcal{C} = \{C \subseteq V : C$ *is a clique of* $G\}$ *and two vertices* $C_1, C_2 \in \mathcal{C}$ *are connected by an edge in* $\mathcal{E}$ *if and only if* C_1 *and* C_2 *have non-empty intersection.*

Definition 9. *A set system* $\mathcal{R}$ *satisfies* Helly *property, if every subsystem* $\mathcal{R}' \subseteq \mathcal{R}$ *satisfies the condition that if any two sets in* $\mathcal{R}'$ *have nonempty intersection, then the intersection all sets in* $\mathcal{R}'$ *is nonempty.*

The following characterization was given by Roberts and Spencer [24].

Theorem 4. *Simple graph* $G = (V, E)$ *is a clique graph if and only if there exists a collection* $\mathcal{K} = \{K_1, K_2, \ldots K_n\}$ *of complete subgraphs of* G *that satisfies Helly property and for all edges* $e \in E$ *there exists* $K_i \in \mathcal{K}$ *such that* $e \in E(K_i)$. $\mathcal{K}$ *is called an* edge-cover *of* G.

Now, one has only to observe that $G = (V, E)$ is the maxindep graph of $H = (W, F)$ if and only if it is the complement of the clique graph of $\overline{H}$. So Theorem 4 gives characterization of maxindep graphs, as well.

Theorem 5. *Simple graph* $G = (V, E)$ *is the maxindep graph of another graph if and only if* $\overline{G}$ *has an edge-cover that satisfies Helly property.*

Note that maxindep graphs are special cases of *generalized Kneser-graphs*.

Definition 10. *Let* $\mathcal{F} = \{F_1, F_2, \ldots, F_n\}$ *be a set system. The generalized Kneser-graph of* $\mathcal{F}$ *is* $KG(\mathcal{F}) = (V, E)$, *where* $V = \mathcal{F}$ *and* $\{F_i, F_j\} \in E$ *if and only if* $F_i \cap F_j = \emptyset$

Although it does not belong strictly to the topic of the present paper but it is worth noting that every simple graph is a generalized Kneser-graph. The proof of the following proposition is new.

Proposition 1. *For every finite, simple graph* $G = (V, E)$ *there exists a set system* $\mathcal{F}$ *such that* $G = KG(\mathcal{F})$.

Proof. A construction is given. Let $|V| = n$. Let $\mathcal{F}' = \{F_1, F_2, \ldots, F_n\}$ with $F_i = \{f_{i_1}, f_{i_2}, \ldots, f_{i_n}\}$ pairwise distinct n-element sets. For $1 \leq i < j \leq n$ identify element f_{i_j} with f_{j_i}, that is set $f_{i_j} = f_{j_i}$ if and only if v_i and v_j are not connected by an edge in G. Let $\mathcal{F}$ be the set system obtained after the identifications of vertices. Clearly, for arbitrary $a, b \leq n$ we have $\{v_a, v_b\} \in E$ if and only if $F_a \cap F_b = \emptyset$, so $G = KG(\mathcal{F})$. $\square$

Note, that the set system $\mathcal{F}$ obtained above is an n-uniform Sperner-system, that is members of $\mathcal{F}$ are pairwise distinct n-element sets.

3.3   Bipartite Maxindep Graphs

In this section the case of bipartite maxindep graphs is treated. First we show that every complete bipartite graph is indeed a maxindep graph.

Proposition 2. *Let $G = K_{a,b}$ be a complete bipartite graph with partite classes $|A| = a$ and $|B| = b$. Then G is a maxindep graph of another graph $H = (W, F)$*

Proof. According to Theorem 5 it is enough to present an edge-cover of $\overline{G}$ that satisfies Helly property. Observe that $\overline{G}$ consists of two vertex disjoint cliques, one on A and another one on B. Take the complete subgraphs of $\overline{G}$ spanned by A, respectively by B, they form an edge-cover, and since they are disjoint, trivially satisfy Helly property.   □

Note that a constraint graph $H = (W, F)$ whose maxindep graph $\mathcal{M}(H) = K_{a,b}$ is obtained by taking a complete graph on vertex set $A \cup B$ and two additional vertices v_a and v_b and join v_a by an edge to every vertex in B, and v_b to every vertex in A, respectively. Here maximal independent vertex sets are pairs of the form $\{a, v_a\}$ for $a \in A$ and $\{b, v_b\}$ for $b \in B$ as it is given by [24].

Although the construction in [24] is explicit, we will not always follow through with it. Instead, we speak directly about maxindep graphs, without actually using the construction of [24] to obtain the corresponding constraint graph. Thus, the notation $ex_{MI}(M)$ is introduced that is the smallest number of rows in an Armstrong table of $CC(G)$, where $M = \mathcal{M}(G)$ is the maxindep graph of G. In other words, $ex_{MI}(M)$ is the minimum number of vertices of a graph $H = (W, F)$ whose line graph $L(H)$ is a spanning subgraph of M according to Corollary 1.

Theorem 6. *Let $a < b$ be positive integers. Then $ex_{MI}(K_{a,b}) = 2b$.*

Proof. Let H be the disjoint union of a cycle on $2a$ vertices and $b - a$ pairwise disjoint edges. Then the line graph $L(H)$ consists of a cycle of $2a$ vertices and $b-a$ isolated vertices, that form a spanning subgraph of $K_{a,b}$, showing $ex_{MI}(K_{a,b}) \leq 2b$.

On the other hand, if $L(H)$ is a (spanning) subgraph of $K_{a,b}$, then $L(H)$ is bipartite, so H does not contain odd cycles, furthermore any vertex of H has degree at most 2, since a vertex of degree k in H results in a complete subgraph K_k in $L(H)$. Then the components of H are even cycles and paths, say cycles of sizes $2k_1, 2k_2, \ldots, 2k_e$ and paths of $u_1, u_2, \ldots, u_t$ edges, respectively. As $L(H)$ spans $K_{a,b}$ we have

$$2(k_1 + k_2 + \cdots + k_e) + u_1 + u_2 + \cdots + u_t = a + b. \tag{1}$$

Furthermore, the number of vertices of H is $2(k_1 + k_2 + \cdots + k_e) + (u_1 + 1) + (u_2 + 1) + \cdots + (u_t + 1) = a + b + t$, so it is minimal if t is minimal. The number of vertices covered by a largest matching in $K_{a,b}$ is $2a$. On the other hand, H

has a matching covering at least $2\sum_{i=1}^{e} k_i + \sum_{j=1}^{t}(u_j - 1)$ vertices, namely take every second edge of the even cycles and the paths. Thus,

$$2\sum_{i=1}^{e} k_i + \sum_{j=1}^{t}(u_j - 1) = 2\sum_{i=1}^{e} k_i + \sum_{j=1}^{t} u_j - t = a + b - t \le 2a \qquad (2)$$

This implies $t \ge b - a$, so $ex_{MI}(K_{a,b}) \ge a + b + (b - a) = 2b$. □

For a general bipartite maxindep graph $G = (A, B; E)$ we give an algorithm to determine $ex_{MI}(G)$. First let us observe that if $H = (W, F)$ is such that its line graph $L(H)$ is a spanning subgraph of G, then H is bipartite and its vertices have degree at most 2, by the same argument as above. Also, the components of H are cycles of sizes $2k_1, 2k_2, \ldots, 2k_e$ and paths of $u_1, u_2, \ldots, u_t$ edges, respectively. Assuming $|A| = a$ and $|B| = b$, we obtain again $2(k_1 + k_2 + \cdots + k_e) + u_1 + u_2 + \cdots + u_t = a + b$, since $L(H)$ spans G. This results in $|W| = 2(k_1 + k_2 + \cdots + k_e) + (u_1 + 1) + (u_2 + 1) + \cdots + (u_t + 1) = a + b + t$, so we look for a spanning subgraph of G with a minimum number of path components. (Note, that in this case it is easy to uniquely determine H from $L(H)$.) Let $f : A \cup B \to \{0, 1, 2\}$ where $f(v)$ is the degree of vertex v in the spanning subgraph $L(H)$ of G for all $v \in A \cup B$.

Definition 11. *Let G be a graph and let function $f : V(G) \to \mathbb{Z}$ be given such that for every vertex $x \in V(G)$ we have $0 \le f(x) \le d_G(x)$, where $d_G(x)$ is the degree of x in G. A spanning subgraph F of G is an f-factor of G, if for every vertex $x \in V(G)$, equality $d_F(x) = f(x)$ holds.*

Thus $L(H)$ is a an f-factor of G for some $f : A \cup B \to \{0, 1, 2\}$. Such an f-factor is also called a $\{0, 1, 2\}$-factor. Ore gave a characterization when a bipartite graph has an f-factor [23].

Theorem 7. *A bipartite graph $G = (A, B; E)$ has an f-factor if and only if $\sum_{a \in A} f(a) = \sum_{b \in B} f(b)$ and for all $U \subseteq A$ we have*

$$\sum_{u \in U} f(u) \le \sum_{y \in B} \min\{f(y), |E_G(U, y)|\}, \qquad (3)$$

where $|E_G(U, y)|$ is the number of edges of G, that go between vertex y and elements of vertex set U.

Observation 8. *The number of path components of a $\{0, 1, 2\}$-factor of G is $|A \cup B| - \frac{1}{2}\sum_{v \in A \cup B} f(v)$*

Indeed, every isolated vertex is a path, and every non-degenerate path has exactly two vertices of degree 1.

So in order to minimize the the number of path components in $L(H)$, one has to maximize $\sum_{v \in A \cup B} f(v)$. This can be formulated by the following IP problem by Theorem 7. Let $\underline{c}$ be the identically 1 vector of length $|A \cup B|$, $\underline{x}$ be the vector of variables indexed by the vertices of $A \cup B$. For every vertex $v \in V = A \cup B$, the value of x_v stands for $f(v)$.

$$\max\{\underline{c} \cdot \underline{x}\} = \max\{\sum_{v \in V} x_v\}, \tag{4}$$

with respect to

$$0 \le x_v \le 2 \tag{5}$$

$$\sum_{a \in A} x_a = \sum_{b \in B} x_b \tag{6}$$

$$\forall U \subseteq A : \sum_{u \in U} x_u \le \sum_{y \in B} \min\{x_y, |E_G(U, y)|\} \tag{7}$$

(5) gives that f is a $\{0, 1, 2\}$, (6) holds because of the equality of degree sums on the two partite classes of the bipartite graph, finally (7) is inequality (3). In total there are $2|V(G)| + 2 + 2^{|A|}$ inequalities in the IP problem. However, a polynomial time solution can be found using flows.

Create a network $G'(V', F)$ from bipartite graph $G(A, B; E)$ with capacities $c : F \to \{1, 2\}$ as follows. $V' = A \cup B \cup \{s, t\}$, for every $a \in A$ and $b \in B$ let $(s, a), (b, t) \in F$, furthermore $(a, b) \in F$ if and only if $\{a, b\} \in E$. Let $c((u, v)) = 2$, if $s = u$ or $t = v$, and let $c((u, v)) = 1$ otherwise. Since all capacities are integers, there exists a maximum flow that takes integer values on all of the edges. The edges of G corresponding to directed edges (a, b) of G' with flow value 1 form a $\{0, 1, 2\}$-factor of G with maximum $\sum_{v \in V} x_v$.

Note 2. The graph used by Hartmann et al. [14] to prove that the problem of finding an Armstrong table for cardinality constraints is exactly exponential, consists of $\frac{n}{2}$ independent edges. It is easy to see that the maxindep graph consist of $2^{\frac{n}{2}}$ independent edges. In the row graph the twin classes, corresponding to the vertices of the maxindep graph can be slid together along only those $2^{\frac{n}{2}}$ edges, but each twin class can be slid together with one other twin class, so in total we need 3 rows for each edge of the maxindep graph, so the minimum Armstrong instance has $3 \cdot 2^{\frac{n}{2}}$ rows.

3.4   Complete k-Partite Maxindep Graphs

In this section the statements of the previous section are generalized from bipartite to k-partite graphs. To begin with we show that complete k-partite graphs are maxindep graphs. The following proposition can be proven analogously to Proposition 2.

Proposition 3. *Let $G = K_{q_1, q_2, \ldots, q_k}$ be the complete k-partite graph with partite classes of sizes $q_1, q_2, \ldots, q_k$. Then G is the maxindep graph of some graph $H = (W, F)$.*

Let $q_1 \geq q_2 \geq \cdots \geq q_k$. Since the line graph of the row graph $S(R, J)$ of any Armstrong table $\mathbf{A}$ is a spanning subgraph of $G = K_{q_1, q_2, \ldots, q_k}$, $S(R, J)$ must contain q_1 independent edges corresponding to the large partite class of G, so $\mathbf{A}$ must have at least $2q_1$ rows. On the other hand, by the well-known *fan* construction [22] (see below), the edge set of K_{2q_1} can be partitioned into $2q_1 - 1$ complete matchings (1-factors). If $k \leq 2q_1 - 1$, then pairwise disjoint matchings of sizes $q_1, q_2, \ldots, q_k$ can be chosen from these 1-factors and keeping those edges a graph $S(R, J)$ of $2q_1$ vertices is obtained whose line graph is a spanning subgraph of $G = K_{q_1, q_2, \ldots, q_k}$. So we have just proved the following generalization of Theorem 6.

Theorem 9. *Let $q_1 \geq q_2 \geq \cdots \geq q_k$. If $k \leq 2q_1 - 1$, then $ex_{MI}(K_{q_1, q_2, \ldots, q_k}) = 2q_1$*

Note that $k = 2$ case of Theorem 9 gives another proof of Theorem 6.

If a complete k-partite graph has at least one large partite class, then Theorem 9 gives the answer, it is interesting to consider the case when the partite classes are of some (small) fixed size ℓ, in particular $\ell = 2$.

Since the edges of the row graph that correspond to the vertices of one partite class of $K_{\ell, \ell, \ldots, \ell}$ must be independent, determination of $ex_{MI}(K_{\ell, \ell, \ldots, \ell})$ amounts to finding the minimum n, such that k pairwise disjoint ℓ-element independent edge sets (matchings) exists on a graph of n vertices. Without loss of generality it can be assumed that we look for the k matchings in the complete graph K_n. Consider first the case of $\ell = 2$.

We recall two well-known classical constructions of decomposition of the edge set of a complete graph K_n into $n - 1$ complete matchings if n is even and into $\frac{n-1}{2}$ Hamiltonian cycles if n is odd [21, 22].

The Fan Construction. Let n be even and the vertices of K_n be $\{0, 1, \ldots, n - 1\}$. For $i = 1, 2, \ldots, n - 1$ let the ith matching consist of edges $\{\{0, i\}, \{i - j, i + j\}$ (mod $n - 1$): $j = 1, 2, \ldots, \frac{n}{2} - 1\}$.

Walecki's Construction. Let $n = 2k + 1$ and label the vertices of K_n as $u_0, u_1, \ldots u_{2k}$. Let σ be the permutation of cycle decomposition $(u_0)(u_1 u_2 \ldots u_{2k})$. Let H_1 be the Hamiltonian cycle $u_0 u_1 u_2 u_{2k} u_3 u_{2k-1} \ldots u_k u_{k+2} u_{k+1} u_0$. Then the ith Hamiltonian cycle is $H_i = \sigma^{i-1}(H_1)$ for $i = 1, 2, \ldots, k$.

Theorem 10. *There exists a collection k pairwise disjoint two-edge matchings in K_n if and only if $\binom{n}{2} \geq 2k$.*

Proof. The necessity of the condition is trivial, since k pairwise disjoint two-edge matchings cover $2k$ edges.

We prove the sufficiency by cases according to the mod 4 remainder of n.

$-$ $n \equiv 0$ (mod 4). Then

$$\binom{n}{2} = \frac{4t}{2}(4t - 1) \geq 2k \text{ that implies } k \leq t(4t - 1) \tag{8}$$

The fan construction gives $n - 1 = 4t - 1$ 1-factors of $\frac{n}{2} = 2t$ edges each. From each 1-factor we can chose t pairs of independent edges, in total $t(4t - 1) \geq k$ pairs of independent edges.

– $n \equiv 2 \pmod 4$. Let $n = 4t + 2$, $t \geq 1$. Then

$$\binom{n}{2} = (4t + 1)(2t + 1) \geq 2k \text{ that implies } k \leq 4t^2 + 3t \qquad (9)$$

since $k \in \mathbb{Z}^+$. The fan construction gives $4t + 1$ matchings of $\frac{n}{2} = 2t + 1 \geq 3$ edges each. From each matching t pairs of independent edges can be chosen in total $(4t + 1)t$ pairs. Then each matching has one edge that is not chosen, we can take it to be the edge $\{i - (\frac{n}{2} - 1), i + (\frac{n}{2} - 1)\} \pmod{n - 1}$. These edges form a cycle of length $n - 1 = 4t + 1$. From this cycle additional $2t$ independent edge pairs can be chosen to make the total to $(4t + 1)t + 2t = 4t^2 + 3t$.

– $n \equiv 1 \pmod 4$. Let $n = 4t + 1$, $t \geq 1$. Then

$$\binom{n}{2} = (4t + 1)2t \geq k \text{ that implies } k \leq (4t + 1)t \qquad (10)$$

The Walecki construction decomposes the edge set of K_{4t+1} into $2t$ Hamiltonian cycles of $4t + 1$ edges each. From each cycle $2t$ pairs of independent edges can be chosen, one edge is leftover. Hamiltonian cycle H_i contains the edge $\{u_i, u_{i+1}\}$, choose that as leftover for each $i = 1, 2, \ldots, 2t$. Then additional t independent pairs are obtained by choosing the pairs $\{\{u_i, u_{i+1}\}, \{u_{i+t}, u_{i+t+1}\}\}$. In total we get $(t)(2t) + t = 4t^{+}1$ pairs, as needed.

– $n \equiv 3 \pmod 4$. Let $n = 4t + 3$, $t \geq 1$. Then

$$\binom{n}{2} = (4t + 3)(2t + 1) \geq 2k \text{ that implies } k \leq 4t^2 + 5t + 1, \qquad (11)$$

since $k \in \mathbb{Z}^+$. Walecki's construction gives $2t + 1$ Hamiltonian cycles of $4t + 3$ edges each. From these $(2t + 1)^2$ independent edge pairs can be chosen. The remaining edges can be picked as above so they form a path of $2t + 1$ edges. From this path t pairs of independent edges can be chosen, in total we have $(2t + 1)^2 + t = 4t^2 + 5t + 1$ as needed.

$\square$

The case of general ℓ follows from a theorem of Folkman and Fulkerson [11] if $l|\binom{n}{2}$.

Theorem 11. *[11] The edge set of complete graph K_n can be partitioned into $\frac{\binom{n}{2}}{\ell}$ pairwise disjoint matchings of ℓ edges if $l|\binom{n}{2}$.*

The case, when the divisibility does not hold, requires the concept *feasible edge coloring*.

Definition 12. *Let $P = (p_1, p_2, \ldots, p_n)$ be monotone non-increasing sequence of non-negative integers such that $\sum_{i=1}^{n} p_i = e$ holds. Let G be a simple graph with $|E(G)| = e$. P is* color feasible *on G if there exists a proper coloring of edges of G using n colors, such that the ith color class has size p_i.*

Definition 13. *Let $P = (p_1, p_2, \ldots, p_n)$ and $Q = (q_1, q_2, \ldots, q_n)$ be monotone non-increasing sequences of non-negative integers. P majorizes Q if and only if for all $e \in \{1, \ldots, n-1\}$*

$$\sum_{i=1}^{e} p_i \geq \sum_{i=1}^{e} q_i \tag{12}$$

holds and

$$\sum_{i=1}^{n} p_i = \sum_{i=1}^{n} q_i \tag{13}$$

In notation, $P \succ Q$.

We need the following theorem from [11].

Theorem 12. *If P is color feasible on graph G, and $P \succ Q$, then Q is also color feasible on G.*

The following handles the case of non-divisibility.

Theorem 13. *Let $m, n, k \in \mathbb{N}$. If $m \leq \lfloor \frac{n}{2} \rfloor$ and $mk \leq \binom{n}{2}$, then there exist k pairwise disjoint matchings of size m each in the edge set $E(K_n)$.*

Proof. Since the case $km = \binom{n}{2}$ is treated in Theorem 11, we may assume WLOG that $km < \binom{n}{2} < (k+1)m$. Let $f = \binom{n}{2} - km$ be the number of edges of K_n not appearing in the matchings, $1 \leq f < m$. Consider the matchings as m-element edge-color classes, the remaining edges as single edge color classes. That is we want to have that

$$Q = (\underbrace{m, m, \ldots, m}_{k}, \underbrace{1, \ldots, 1}_{f}, 0, \ldots, 0) \tag{14}$$
$$\underbrace{}_{\binom{n}{2}}$$

is color feasible on K_n. Now, for even n, $E(K_n)$ can be partitioned into $k = n-1$ matchings of size $\frac{n}{2} = \lfloor \frac{n}{2} \rfloor$ each, by the *fan* construction. For odd n we can use Walecki's construction [21] to partition $E(K_n)$ into $k = n$ matchings of size $\lfloor \frac{n}{2} \rfloor = \frac{(n-1)}{2}$ each. These give that the following sequence P is color feasible on K_n:

$$P = (\underbrace{\lfloor \tfrac{n}{2} \rfloor, \lfloor \tfrac{n}{2} \rfloor, \ldots, \lfloor \tfrac{n}{2} \rfloor}_{n-1}, \underbrace{\lfloor \tfrac{n}{2} \rfloor}_{y}, 0, \ldots, 0) \tag{15}$$
$$\underbrace{\phantom{\lfloor \tfrac{n}{2} \rfloor, \lfloor \tfrac{n}{2} \rfloor, \ldots, \lfloor \tfrac{n}{2} \rfloor, 0, \ldots, 0}}_{\binom{n}{2}}$$

where

$$y = \begin{cases} 1, & \text{if } n \equiv 1 \pmod 2 \\ 0, & \text{if } n \equiv 0 \pmod 2 \end{cases} \tag{16}$$

Then $P \succ Q$, since $1 \leq m \leq \lfloor \frac{n}{2} \rfloor$ implies that for every $e \in \{1, \ldots, \binom{n}{2} - 1\}$ inequality $\sum_{i=1}^{e} p_i \geq \sum_{i=1}^{e} q_i$ and equality $\sum_{i=1}^{\binom{n}{2}} p_i = \sum_{i=1}^{\binom{n}{2}} q_i = |E(K_n)| = \binom{n}{2}$ also hold. P is color feasible, then so is Q by Theorem 12. $\qquad \square$

Using this we can solve the case of general k-partite maxindep graph.

Corollary 2. *Let the maxindep graph of constraint graph G be complete k-partite graph $K_{n_1,n_2,...,n_k}$ with $n_1 \leq n_2 \leq \cdots \leq n_k$. Then*

$$ex(CC(G)) = ex_{MI}(K_{n_1,n_2,...,n_k}) = \min\{n : \binom{n}{2} \geq \sum_{i=1}^{l} n_i \text{ and } n \geq 2n_k\}. \quad (17)$$

4   Conclusions, Future Research

In the present paper minimal Armstrong tables of cardinality constraints were investigated. Motivated by a result of Hartmann et al. [14] on the complexity to find minimum Armstrong instances of cardinality constraints, the class of graph-based cardinality constraints $CC(G)$ was introduced for simple graphs $G = (V, E)$. It was shown that the smallest number of rows in an Armstrong table for $CC(G)$ is the smallest number of vertices of a graph $H = (W, F)$ such that the line graph $L(H)$ is a spanning subgraph of the graph of maximal independent sets $\mathcal{M}(G)$ of G. Based on this, the minimum Armstrong instance was determined for several $CC(G)$'s. Also, maxindep graphs were characterized following a known characterisation [24] of clique graphs.

Table 1. Trivial Armstrong table for $k \leq \ell$

a_1	a_2	$\cdots$	a_{n-1}	a_n
1	1	$\cdots$	1	1]
1	1	$\cdots$	1	1
$\vdots$	$\vdots$		$\vdots$	$\vdots$
1	1	$\vdots$	1	1

Graph based cardinality constraints can be generalized as follows. Given a simple graph $G = (R, E)$ where R is the set of attributes of the relational schema, then $CC(G, k, \ell)$ denotes the set of cardinality constraints for all attributes $a \in R$ we have $card(a) \leq k$ and for every edge $\{a_1, a_2\} \in E$, $card(\{a_1, a_2\}) \leq \ell$ holds. Thus, $CC(G) = CC(G, 2, 1)$. $k > \ell$ can be assumed WLOG, since the $k \leq \ell$ case is trivial, as the following Table 1 shows. The concept of twins generalizes to k-tuplets: $(a_{i_1,j}, a_{i_2,j}, \cdots a_{i_k,j})$ form a k-tuplets in the Armstrong matrix if they are in the same column and $a_{i_1,j} = a_{i_2,j} = \cdots = a_{i_k,j}$. k-tuplets represent the $card(a) \leq k$ constraints on attributes, k-tuplets classes are k-tuplets on the same row sets that are independent in the constraint graph. The max cardinality constraints ℓ on edges are represented by sliding k-tuplets classes into position of overlapping in ℓ rows (Fig. 4).

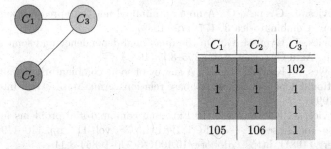

C_1	C_2	C_3
1	1	102
1	1	1
1	1	1
105	106	1

Fig. 4. Constraint graph and its Armstrong matrix for $(k, \ell) = (3, 2)$.

In this case the *row hypergraph* of the Armstrong table $\mathbf{A}$ is defined, where $\{r_{i_1}, r_{i_2}, \cdots r_{i_k}\} \in J$ if there exists a k-tuplets in $\mathbf{A}$ covering rows $r_{i_1}, r_{i_2}, \cdots r_{i_k}$. Then $\mathcal{R} = (R, J)$ is the row hypergraph of $\mathbf{A}$. A necessary condition for $\mathcal{R}$ is that its edges are at most ℓ-intersecting. The investigation of row hypergraphs is the next step in the project of minimum Armstrong instances of cardinality constraints.

Another future research direction is if the upper bounds on vertices and edges are not uniform in the constraint graph, for example some vertices may not have upper bounds. In that case investigation of minimal Armstrong representations may be interesting, as well [20].

In terms of practical work, it may be beneficial to implement some of the constructions in the form of algorithms that can compute the minimal Armstrong tables for any given input in the relevant class. This may be compared to the general construction of an Armstrong table to identify what the reduction in terms of size is.

Finally, Köhler et al. [17] have results on mining cardinality constraints (in particular those with small upper bounds) from given relations/tables. It would be interesting to extend the research of graph based cardinality constraints in that direction.

Acknowledgements. The authors are indebted to the unknown referees for their careful reading of the paper and for the detailed comments that greatly improved the presentation of the paper. They are also grateful for calling their attention to references [17, 20, 26, 27], furthermore for suggesting possible future research directions.

References

1. Balamuralikrishna, N., Jiang, Y., Koehler, H., Leck, U., Link, S., Prade, H.: Possibilistic keys. Fuzzy Sets Syst. **376**, 1–36 (2019)
2. Chen, P.P.S.: The entity-relationship model-toward a unified view of data. ACM Trans. Database Syst. (TODS) **1**(1), 9–36 (1976)
3. Demetrovics, J., Füredi, Z., Katona, G.O.: Minimum matrix representation of closure operations. Discret. Appl. Math. **11**(2), 115–128 (1985)

4. Demetrovics, J., Gyepesi, G.: A note on minimal matrix representation of closure operations. Combinatorica **3**, 177–179 (1983)
5. Demetrovics, J., Gyepesi, G.: On the functional dependency and some generalizations of it. Acta Cybernet. **5**(3), 295–305 (1981)
6. Demetrovics, J., Katona, G.O.H.: A survey of some combinatorial results concerning functional dependencies in database relations. Ann. Math. Artif. Intell. **7**(1–4), 63–82 (1993)
7. Demetrovics, J., Katona, G.O.H.: Extremal combinatorial problems in relational data base. In: Gécseg, F. (ed.) FCT 1981. LNCS, vol. 117, pp. 110–119. Springer, Heidelberg (1981). https://doi.org/10.1007/3-540-10854-8_11
8. Demetrovics, J., Katona, G.O.H.: Extremal combinatorial problems of database models. In: Biskup, J., Demetrovics, J., Paredaens, J., Thalheim, B. (eds.) MFDBS 1987. LNCS, vol. 305, pp. 99–127. Springer, Heidelberg (1988). https://doi.org/10.1007/3-540-19121-6_7
9. Demetrovics, J., Katona, G.O., Sali, A.: The characterization of branching dependencies. Discret. Appl. Math. **40**(2), 139–153 (1992)
10. Demetrovics, J., Katona, G.O., Sali, A.: Design type problems motivated by database theory. J. Stat. Plann. Inference **72**(1–2), 149–164 (1998)
11. Folkman, J., Fulkerson, D.: Edge colorings in bipartite graphs. In: Bose, T., Dowling, J. (eds.) Combinatorial Theory and its Application. University of North Carolina Press (1969)
12. Hall, N., Koehler, H., Link, S., Prade, H., Zhou, X.: Cardinality constraints on qualitatively uncertain data. Data Knowl. Eng. **99**, 126–150 (2015)
13. Hartmann, S., Kirchberg, M., Link, S.: Design by example for SQL table definitions with functional dependencies. VLDB J. **21**, 121–144 (2012)
14. Hartmann, S., Köhler, H., Leck, U., Link, S., Thalheim, B., Wang, J.: Constructing Armstrong tables for general cardinality constraints and not-null constraints. Ann. Math. Artif. Intell. **73**(1), 139–165 (2015)
15. Katona, G.O., Sali, A.: New type of coding problem motivated by database theory. Discret. Appl. Math. **144**(1–2), 140–148 (2004)
16. Köhler, H., Leck, U., Link, S., Zhou, X.: Possible and certain keys for SQL. VLDB J. **25**, 571–596 (2016)
17. Köhler, H., Link, S., Zhou, X.: Discovering meaningful certain keys from incomplete and inconsistent relations. IEEE Data Eng. Bull. **39**(2), 21–37 (2016)
18. Langeveldt, W.D., Link, S.: Empirical evidence for the usefulness of Armstrong relations in the acquisition of meaningful functional dependencies. Inf. Syst. **35**(3), 352–374 (2010). https://doi.org/10.1016/j.is.2009.11.002. https://www.sciencedirect.com/science/article/pii/S0306437909001185
19. Link, S.: Armstrong databases: validation, communication and consolidation of conceptual models with perfect test data. In: Proceedings of the Eighth Asia-Pacific Conference on Conceptual Modelling, vol. 130, pp. 3–22 (2012)
20. Link, S., Koehler, H., Gandhi, A., Hartmann, S., Thalheim, B.: Cardinality constraints and functional dependencies in SQL: taming data redundancy in logical database design. Inf. Syst. **115**, 102208 (2023). https://doi.org/10.1016/j.is.2023.102208. https://www.sciencedirect.com/science/article/pii/S0306437923000443
21. Lucas, É.: Récréations mathématiques, vol. 1. Gauthier-Villars (1882)
22. Lucas, E.: Les jeux de demoiselles (1883)
23. Ore, O.: Studies on directed graphs, I. Annals Math. 383–406 (1956)
24. Roberts, F.S., Spencer, J.H.: A characterization of clique graphs. J. Comb. Theory Series B **10**(2), 102–108 (1971)

25. Sali, A.: Coding theory motivated by relational databases. In: Schewe, K.-D., Thalheim, B. (eds.) SDKB 2010. LNCS, vol. 6834, pp. 96–113. Springer, Heidelberg (2011). https://doi.org/10.1007/978-3-642-23441-5_6
26. Thalheim, B.: Fundamentals of cardinality constraints. In: Pernul, G., Tjoa, A.M. (eds.) ER 1992. LNCS, vol. 645, pp. 7–23. Springer, Heidelberg (1992). https://doi.org/10.1007/3-540-56023-8_3
27. Thalheim, B.: Entity-Relationship Modeling: Foundations of Database Technology. Springer, Cham (2013)

Beliefs

Syntax Splitting and Reasoning from Weakly Consistent Conditional Belief Bases with c-Inference

Jonas Haldimann[1] , Christoph Beierle[1(✉)] , and Gabriele Kern-Isberner[2]

[1] FernUniversität in Hagen, 58084 Hagen, Germany
{jonas.haldimann,christoph.beierle}@fernuni-hagen.de
[2] Technische Universität Dortmund, 44227 Dortmund, Germany
gabriele.kern-isberner@cs.tu-dortmund.de

Abstract. It has been shown that c-inference is an inductive inference operator, mapping belief bases to inference relations, that exhibits many desirable properties put forward for nonmonotonic reasoning. It is based on c-representations which are a special kind of ranking function. However, the definition of c-representation only takes belief bases into account that satisfy a rather strong notion of consistency requiring every world to be at least somewhat plausible. In this paper, we employ the concepts of *strong* and *weak* consistency for conditional belief bases and extend the notions of c-representation and c-inference to also cover weakly consistent belief bases. We adapt a constraint satisfaction problem characterizing c-inference so that it captures extended c-inference and provides a basis for its implementation. Furthermore, we show various properties of extended c-inference and in particular, we prove that the extended notion of c-inference fully satisfies syntax splitting.

1 Introduction

A semantics for conditional belief bases Δ typically provides a means for ordering the underlying possible worlds Ω according to their plausibility. Ranking functions κ [30] do this by assigning a degree of implausibility to the worlds via a mapping $\kappa : \Omega \to \mathbb{N} \cup \{\infty\}$. A ranking function κ models a conditional $(B|A)$, standing for "if A then usually B", if the verification of $(B|A)$ is strictly more plausible than its falsification, i.e., if $\kappa(AB) < \kappa(A\overline{B})$. Defining that Δ is consistent if a κ modelling all conditionals in Δ exists yields a rather strong notion of consistency, enforcing that every world has at least some plausibility. Here, we will take a broader view on consistency and allow also for *weakly* consistent belief bases that allow only some worlds to be considered feasible. Contrary to strongly consistent belief bases that only contain defeasible beliefs, weakly consistent belief bases can also contain *strict* beliefs [10]. Such strict beliefs correspond to the requirement that some worlds are infeasible.

As a semantics for belief bases, we focus on the *c-representations* [20,21] of a belief base Δ, a special kind of ranking functions modelling Δ. c-Representations

A. Meier and M. Ortiz (Eds.): FoIKS 2024, LNCS 14589, pp. 85–103, 2024.
https://doi.org/10.1007/978-3-031-56940-1_5

define inductive inference operators that satisfy most advanced properties of non-monotonic inference, particularly syntax splitting and conditional syntax splitting [19,22]. While initially introduced only for belief bases satisfying the rather strong notion of consistency described above, in this paper we define extended c-representations that also cover belief bases satisfying the weaker notion of consistency where some possible worlds may be assigned a rank of ∞ indicating them to be completely infeasible according to Δ. This allows for realizing a kind of paraconsistent conditional reasoning based on the strong structural concept of c-representations. The notion of c-inference was introduced in [3,4] as nonmonotonic inference taking all c-representations into account, inheriting the restriction that it is only defined for strongly consistent belief bases. Using the extended c-representations we will introduce an extended version of c-inference that also covers weakly consistent belief bases.

The c-representations of a belief base Δ can be characterized by a constraint satisfaction problem (CSP), and in [3,4] it is shown that c-inference can also be realized by a CSP. Here, we develop both a CSP that characterizes all extended c-representations and a simplified version of this CSP the solutions of which still cover all c-representations relevant for c-inference. Furthermore, we show how extended c-inference can be realized by a CSP.

An inductive inference operator satisfies syntax splitting if it satisfies the axioms of independence (Ind) and relevance (Rel) [22]. While these axioms have been developed taking only strongly consistent belief bases into account, here we employ versions of (Ind) and (Rel) adapted to our setting of weakly consistent belief bases and prove that extended c-inference complies with syntax splitting.

This paper revises our workshop contribution [17] and extends it, e.g., by further elaborating and illustrating the concept of strongly and weakly consistent belief bases. In particular, we added a section discussing syntax splitting postulates for inductive inference operators that take also weakly consistent belief bases into account and prove that extended c-inference satisfies them. The paper is organized as follows: After recalling the background on conditional logic in Sec. 2 and inductive inference in Sec. 3 we elaborate and illustrate the different kinds of consistency in Sec. 4. We develop extended c-representations in Sec. 5, extended c-inference in Sec. 6, and present a corresponding characterization of c-representations in Sec. 7. Sec. 8 addresses syntax splitting, and Sec. 9 concludes and points out future work.

2   Conditional Logic

A *(propositional) signature* is a finite set Σ of propositional variables. Assuming an underlying signature Σ, we denote the resulting propositional language by $\mathcal{L}_\Sigma$. Usually, we denote elements of signatures with lowercase letters $a, b, c, \ldots$ and formulas with uppercase letters $A, B, C, \ldots$. We may denote a conjunction $A \wedge B$ by AB and a negation $\neg A$ by $\overline{A}$ for brevity of notation. The set of interpretations over the underlying signature is denoted as Ω_Σ. Interpretations are also called *worlds* and Ω_Σ the *universe*. An interpretation $\omega \in \Omega_\Sigma$ is a *model* of a formula $A \in \mathcal{L}$ if A holds in ω, denoted as $\omega \models A$. The set of models of a formula (over a signature Σ) is denoted as $Mod_\Sigma(A) = \{\omega \in \Omega_\Sigma \mid \omega \models A\}$ or short as Ω_A. The Σ in Ω_Σ, $\mathcal{L}_\Sigma$ and $Mod_\Sigma(A)$ can be omitted if the signature is clear from the context or if the underlying signature is not relevant. A formula A *entails* a formula B, denoted by $A \models B$, if $\Omega_A \subseteq \Omega_B$. By slight abuse of notation we sometimes interpret worlds as the corresponding complete conjunction of all elements in the signature in either positive or negated form.

A *conditional* $(B|A)$ connects two formulas A, B and represents the rule "If A then usually B", where A is called the *antecedent* and B the *consequent* of the conditional. The conditional language is denoted as $(\mathcal{L}|\mathcal{L})_\Sigma = \{(B|A) \mid A, B \in \mathcal{L}_\Sigma\}$. A finite set of conditionals is called a *belief base*. We use a three-valued semantics of conditionals in this paper [12]. For a world ω a conditional $(B|A)$ is either *verified* by ω if $\omega \models AB$, *falsified* by ω if $\omega \models A\overline{B}$, or *not applicable* to ω if $\omega \models \overline{A}$. Popular models for belief bases are ranking functions (also called ordinal conditional functions, OCF) [30,31] and total preorders (TPO) on Ω_Σ [11]. An OCF $\kappa : \Omega_\Sigma \rightarrow \mathbb{N} \cup \{\infty\}$ maps worlds to a *rank* such that at least one world has rank 0, i.e., $\kappa^{-1}(0) \neq \emptyset$. OCFs have been first introduced by Spohn [30] in a more general form. The intuition is that worlds with lower ranks are more plausible than worlds with higher ranks; worlds with rank ∞ are considered infeasible. OCFs are lifted to formulas by mapping a formula A to the smallest rank of a model of A, or to ∞ if A has no models. An OCF κ is a model of a conditional $(B|A)$, denoted as $\kappa \models (B|A)$, if $\kappa(A) = \infty$ or if $\kappa(AB) < \kappa(A\overline{B})$; κ is a model of a belief base Δ, denoted as $\kappa \models \Delta$, if it is a model of every conditional in Δ. For $\Sigma' \subseteq \Sigma$ the *marginalisation* of a ranking function $\kappa : \Omega_\Sigma \rightarrow \mathbb{N} \cup \{\infty\}$ to Σ' is the ranking function $\kappa_{|\Sigma'} : \Omega_{\Sigma'} \rightarrow \mathbb{N} \cup \{\infty\}$ defined by $\kappa_{|\Sigma'}(\omega') = \min\{\kappa(\omega) \mid \omega_{|\Sigma'} = \omega'\}$.

Lemma 1. *Let $\kappa : \Omega_\Sigma \rightarrow \mathbb{N} \cup \{\infty\}$ be a ranking function. Let $\Sigma' \subseteq \Sigma$ and let $\kappa' = \kappa_{|\Sigma'}$. Then, for any formula $A \in \mathcal{L}_{\Sigma'}$ we have that $\kappa(A) = \kappa'(A)$.*

It is also possible to combine ranking functions κ_1, κ_2 over disjoint subsignatures Σ_1, Σ_2. For $\kappa_1 : \Omega_{\Sigma_1} \rightarrow \mathbb{N} \cup \{\infty\}$ and $\kappa_2 : \Omega_{\Sigma_2} \rightarrow \mathbb{N} \cup \{\infty\}$, the combination of κ_1 and κ_2, denoted by $\kappa_\oplus = \kappa_1 \oplus \kappa_2$, is defined by $\kappa_\oplus(\omega) = \kappa_1(\omega_{|\Sigma_1}) + \kappa_2(\omega_{|\Sigma_2})$.

Lemma 2. *Let Σ_1, Σ_2 be disjoint, let $\kappa_1 : \Omega_{\Sigma_1} \rightarrow \mathbb{N} \cup \{\infty\}$ and $\kappa_2 : \Omega_{\Sigma_2} \rightarrow \mathbb{N} \cup \{\infty\}$, and let $\kappa_\oplus = \kappa_1 \oplus \kappa_2$. For formulas $A \in \mathcal{L}_{\Sigma_1}, B \in \mathcal{L}_{\Sigma_2}$ it holds that $\kappa_\oplus(AB) = \kappa_1(A) + \kappa_2(B)$.*

3   Inductive Inference

The conditional beliefs of an agent are formally captured by a binary relation $\vdash\!\!\!\sim$ on propositional formulas with $A \vdash\!\!\!\sim B$ representing that A (defeasibly) entails B; this relation is called *inference* or *entailment relation*. Different sets of properties for inference relations have been suggested, and often the set of postulates called *system P* [1,24] is considered as minimal requirement for inference relations.

Inference relations satisfying system P are called *preferential inference relations*, for details we refer to [1, 24].

Every ranking function κ induces a preferential inference relation $\mathbin{\vrule height 1.2ex depth 0pt width 0pt}\!\sim_\kappa$ by

$$A \mathbin{\vrule}\!\sim_\kappa B \quad \text{iff} \quad \kappa(A) = \infty \text{ or } \kappa(AB) < \kappa(A\overline{B}). \tag{1}$$

Note that the condition $\kappa(A) = \infty$ in (1) ensures that system P's axiom (Reflexivity): $A \mathbin{\vrule}\!\sim_\kappa A$ is satisfied for $A \equiv \bot$. Regarding the inference induced by a marginalized ranking function, the following lemma holds.

Lemma 3. *Let $\kappa : \Omega_\Sigma \to \mathbb{N} \cup \{\infty\}$ be a ranking function. Let $\Sigma' \subseteq \Sigma$ and let $\kappa' = \kappa_{|\Sigma'}$. Then, for formulas $A, B \in \mathcal{L}_{\Sigma'}$ we have that $A \mathbin{\vrule}\!\sim_\kappa B$ iff $A \mathbin{\vrule}\!\sim_{\kappa'} B$.*

Inductive inference is the process of completing a given belief base to an inference relation. To formally capture this we use inductive inference operators.

Definition 4 (inductive inference operator [22]). *An inductive inference operator is a mapping $C : \Delta \mapsto \mathbin{\vrule}\!\sim_\Delta$ that maps each belief base to an inference relation s.t. direct inference (DI) and trivial vacuity (TV) are fulfilled, i.e.,*

(DI) *if $(B|A) \in \Delta$ then $A \mathbin{\vrule}\!\sim_\Delta B$, and*
(TV) *if $\Delta = \emptyset$ and $A \mathbin{\vrule}\!\sim_\Delta B$ then $A \models B$.*

An inductive inference operator C is a *preferential inductive inference operator* if every inference relation $\mathbin{\vrule}\!\sim_\Delta$ in the image of C satisfies system P.

p-Entailment [1, 24] $C^p : \Delta \mapsto \mathbin{\vrule}\!\sim_\Delta^p$ is the most cautious preferential inductive inference operator. It is characterized by system P in the way that it only licenses inferences that can be obtained by iteratively applying the rules of system P to the belief base. Every other preferential inductive inference operator extends p-entailment. While extending p-entailment and adding some more inferences to the induced inference relations is usually desired, p-entailment can act as a basic guidance for inferences of the form $A \mathbin{\vrule}\!\sim \bot$ which can be seen as representations of "strict" beliefs (i.e., A is completely unfeasible).

Postulate (Classic Preservation) (adapted from [9]). *An inductive inference operator $C : \Delta \mapsto \mathbin{\vrule}\!\sim_\Delta$ satisfies (Classic Preservation) if for all belief bases Δ and $A, B \in \mathcal{L}$ it holds that $A \mathbin{\vrule}\!\sim_\Delta \bot$ iff $A \mathbin{\vrule}\!\sim_\Delta^p \bot$.*

4   Consistency of Belief Bases

There are different definitions of consistency of a belief base in the literature. To distinguish two different notions of consistency that commonly occur and are both used in this paper we call one notion of consistency *strong consistency* and the other notion *weak consistency*, as suggested in [18].

Definition 5 ([18]). *A belief base Δ is called* strongly consistent *if there exists at least one ranking function κ with $\kappa \models \Delta$ and $\kappa^{-1}(\infty) = \emptyset$. A belief base Δ is* weakly consistent *if there is a ranking function κ with $\kappa \models \Delta$.*

Thus, Δ is strongly consistent if there is at least one ranking function modelling Δ that considers all worlds feasible. This notion of consistency is used in many approaches, e.g., [15]. The notion of weak consistency is equivalent to the more relaxed notion of consistency that is used in, e.g., [9,13]. Trivially, strong consistency implies weak consistency.

Example 6. Let $\Sigma = \{a, b, c, d\}$. The belief base $\Delta_1 = \{(\bot|\top)\}$ is not weakly consistent. If there were any ranking function κ with $\kappa \models \Delta_1$ then there would be a world ω such that $\kappa(\omega) = 0$ and therefore $\kappa(\top) = 0$. For κ to model $(\bot|\top)$ we need $\kappa(\top \wedge \bot) < \kappa(\top \wedge \top) = 0$ which is clearly impossible. $\Delta_2 = \{(\bot|a), (\overline{b}|\overline{a}), (b|\overline{a})\}$ is also not weakly consistent. The conditional $(\bot|a)$ requires that for every ranking function κ with $\kappa \models \Delta_2$ and any model ω of a we have $\kappa(a) = \infty$. The conditionals $(\overline{b}|\overline{a}), (b|\overline{a})$ in combination require that the rank of any model of $\overline{a}$ must have rank infinity. Because every ranking function must assign rank 0 to at least one world, there is no ranking function modelling Δ_2. Because Δ_1 and Δ_2 are not weakly consistent, they are not strongly consistent.

The belief bases $\Delta_3 = \{(\overline{b}|\overline{a}), (b|\overline{a})\}$ and $\Delta_4 = \{(\bot|a)\}$, both subsets of Δ_2, are weakly consistent but not strongly consistent. Δ_3 requires all ranking functions modelling it to assign rank ∞ to models of $\overline{a}$, and Δ_4 requires all ranking functions modelling it to assign rank ∞ to models of a. The belief base $\Delta_5 = \{(b|a), (d|c)\}$ is strongly consistent and thus also weakly consistent.

Lemma 7. *For every weakly consistent belief base Δ there is an $\omega \in \Omega$ s.t. ω does not falsify any conditional in Δ.*

The original definition of an inductive inference operator in [22] implicitly assumes all belief bases to be strongly consistent. However, the definition can be extended to cover all belief bases. Some inductive inference operators known from literature are defined only for strongly consistent belief bases, while other operators are defined for all belief bases. In particular, inference operators of the second type are able to draw inferences from all weakly consistent belief bases. For example, system Z is an inductive inference operator that is defined based on the Z-partition of a belief base. It was first defined for strongly consistent belief bases [28]. Then an extended version of system Z was introduced [14] that also covers weakly consistent belief bases and that was shown to be equivalent to *rational closure* [26] in [14].

Definition 8 ((extended) Z-partition). *A conditional $(B|A)$ is tolerated by $\Delta = \{(B_i|A_i) \mid i = 1, \ldots, n\}$ if there is a world $\omega \in \Omega$ such that ω verifies $(B|A)$ and ω does not falsify any conditional in Δ, i.e., $\omega \models AB$ and $\omega \models \bigwedge_{i=1}^{n} (\overline{A_i} \vee B_i)$.*

The (extended) Z-partition $EZP(\Delta) = (\Delta^0, \ldots, \Delta^k, \Delta^\infty)$ of a belief base Δ is the ordered partition of Δ constructed by letting Δ^i be the inclusion maximal subset of $\bigcup_{j=i}^{n} \Delta^j$ that is tolerated by $\bigcup_{j=i}^{n} \Delta^j$ until $\Delta^{k+1} = \emptyset$. The set Δ^∞ is the remaining set of conditionals containing no conditional tolerated by Δ^∞.

Because the Δ^i are chosen inclusion-maximal, the Z-partition is unique [28].

Definition 9 ((extended) system Z). *Let Δ be a belief base with $EZP(\Delta) = (\Delta^0, \ldots, \Delta^k, \Delta^\infty)$. If Δ is not weakly consistent, let $A \mathrel{\not\sim^z_\Delta} B$ for any $A, B \in \mathcal{L}$. Otherwise, the (extended) Z-ranking function κ^z_Δ is defined as follows: For $\omega \in \Omega$, if a conditional in Δ^∞ is applicable to ω define $\kappa^z_\Delta(\omega) = \infty$. If not, let Δ^j be the last element in $EZP(\Delta)$ that contains a conditional falsified by ω. Then let $\kappa^z_\Delta(\omega) = j + 1$. If ω does not falsify any conditional in Δ, then let $\kappa^z_\Delta(\omega) = 0$. (Extended) system Z maps Δ to the inference relation $\mathrel{\sim^z_\Delta}$ induced by κ^z_Δ.*

For weakly consistent belief bases Δ the OCF κ^z_Δ is a model of Δ. For strongly consistent belief bases extended system Z coincides with system Z in [15,28].

Lemma 10 ([18]). *For a weakly consistent belief base Δ and a formula A we have $\kappa^z_\Delta(A) = \infty$ iff $A \mathrel{\not\sim^p_\Delta} \bot$.*

Lemma 11 ([18]). *Let Δ be with $EZP(\Delta) = (\Delta^0, \ldots, \Delta^k, \Delta^\infty)$. A world $\omega \in \Omega$ falsifies a conditional in Δ^∞ iff it is applicable for a conditional in Δ^∞.*

It is well-known that the construction of the extended Z-partition $EZP(\Delta)$ is successful with $\Delta^\infty = \emptyset$ iff Δ is strongly consistent [15]. We can also use the extended Z-partition to check for weak consistency. The following proposition summarizes the relations between $EZP(\Delta)$ and the consistency of Δ.

Proposition 12. *Let $\Delta = \{(B_1|A_1), \ldots, (B_n|A_n)\}$ be a belief base with $EZP(\Delta) = (\Delta^0, \ldots, \Delta^k, \Delta^\infty)$.*

(1) *Δ is not weakly consistent iff $\Delta^\infty = \Delta$ and $A_1 \vee \cdots \vee A_n \equiv \top$.*
(2) *Δ is weakly consistent iff $\Delta^\infty \neq \Delta$ or $A_1 \vee \cdots \vee A_n \not\equiv \top$.*
(3) *Δ is strongly consistent iff $\Delta^\infty = \emptyset$.*

Continuing Example 6, for the not weakly consistent Δ_2 we have $EZP(\Delta_2) = (\Delta_2^\infty)$ with $\Delta_2^\infty = \Delta$ and $a \vee \overline{a} \vee \overline{a} \equiv \top$. For the weakly consistent Δ_3 we have $EZP(\Delta_3) = (\Delta_3^\infty)$ with $\Delta_3^\infty = \Delta$ but $a \not\equiv \top$. For the strongly consistent Δ_3 we have $EZP(\Delta_4) = (\Delta_4^0)$ with $\Delta_4^0 = \Delta$ and $\Delta_4^\infty = \emptyset$.

5   Generalizing C-Representations

Before introducing extended c-inference, we have to adapt the notion of c-representations. For strongly consistent belief bases, c-representations have been defined as follows.

Definition 13 (c-representation [20,21]). *A c-representation of a belief base $\Delta = \{(B_1|A_1), \ldots, (B_n|A_n)\}$ over Σ is a ranking function $\kappa_{\vec{\eta}}$ constructed from integers $\vec{\eta} = (\eta_1, \ldots, \eta_n)$, also called impacts, with $\eta_i \in \mathbb{N}_0, i \in \{1, \ldots, n\}$ assigned to each conditional $(B_i|A_i)$ such that $\kappa_{\vec{\eta}}$ accepts Δ and is given by:*

$$\kappa_{\vec{\eta}}(\omega) = \sum_{\substack{1 \leqslant i \leqslant n \\ \omega \models A_i \overline{B}_i}} \eta_i. \tag{2}$$

We will denote the set of all c-representations of Δ by $Mod^c_\Sigma(\Delta)$.

Table 1. Verification (v) and falsification (f) of the conditionals in Δ from Example 15 and their corresponding impacts. The ranking function $\kappa_{\vec{\eta}}$ induced by the impacts $\vec{\eta} = (\eta_1, \eta_2, \eta_3) = (\infty, 1, \infty)$ is an extended c-representation for Δ.

ω	$(b\|p)$	$(f\|b)$	$(\overline{b}\|p)$	impact on ω	$\kappa_{\vec{\eta}}(\omega)$
bpf	v	v	f	η_3	∞
$bp\overline{f}$	v	f	f	$\eta_2 + \eta_3$	∞
$b\overline{p}f$	–	v	–	0	0
$b\overline{p}\overline{f}$	–	f	–	η_2	1
$\overline{b}pf$	f	–	v	η_1	∞
$\overline{b}p\overline{f}$	f	–	v	η_1	∞
$\overline{b}\overline{p}f$	–	–	–	0	0
$\overline{b}\overline{p}\overline{f}$	–	–	–	0	0
impacts	η_1	η_2	η_3		
$\vec{\eta}$	∞	1	∞		

Note that the impact η_i assigned to the conditional $(B_i|A_i)$ decreases the plausibility of a world ω if ω falsifies $(B_i|A_i)$, and that the rank of ω under the c-representation $\kappa_{\vec{\eta}}$ induced by the impact vector $\vec{\eta}$ is the sum of the impacts assigned to the conditionals which are falsified by ω.

A belief base Δ that is not strongly consistent has no c-representation: by Definition 13, a c-representation of Δ is a finite ranking function modelling Δ; if Δ is not strongly consistent, such a ranking function cannot exist. For belief bases that are only weakly consistent, we need a more general definition of c-representations. A ranking function that is a model of a weakly but not strongly consistent belief base must assign rank ∞ to some worlds. To achieve this while keeping a construction of c-representations similar to the one given in (2), we extend the definition of c-representations to allow infinite impacts.

Definition 14 (extended c-representation). *An* extended c-representation *of a belief base* $\Delta = \{(B_1|A_1), \ldots, (B_n|A_n)\}$ *over* Σ *is a ranking function* $\kappa_{\vec{\eta}}$ *constructed from impacts* $\vec{\eta} = (\eta_1, \ldots, \eta_n)$ *with* $\eta_i \in \mathbb{N}_0 \cup \{\infty\}, i \in \{1, \ldots, n\}$ *assigned to each conditional* $(B_i|A_i)$ *such that* $\kappa_{\vec{\eta}}$ *accepts* Δ *and is given by:*

$$\kappa_{\vec{\eta}}(\omega) = \sum_{\substack{1 \leqslant i \leqslant n \\ \omega \models A_i \overline{B}_i}} \eta_i \tag{3}$$

We will denote the set of all extended c-representations of Δ *by* $Mod^{ec}_{\Sigma}(\Delta)$.

Example 15. Let $\Sigma = \{b, p, f\}$ and $\Delta = \{(b|p), (f|b), (\overline{b}|p)\}$. Note that Δ is weakly consistent but not strongly consistent. The OCF $\kappa_{\vec{\eta}}$ displayed in Table 1 is an extended c-representation of Δ induced by the impacts $\vec{\eta} = (\infty, 1, \infty)$.

Every c-representation of a strongly consistent belief base Δ is obviously an extended c-representation of Δ, and every weakly consistent belief base has at least one extended c-representation.

Proposition 16. *Let Δ be a strongly consistent belief base. Every c-representation $\kappa_{\vec{\eta}}$ of Δ is an extended c-representation of Δ.*

Proposition 17. *Let Δ be a weakly consistent belief base. Then $\kappa_{\vec{\eta}}$ with $\vec{\eta} = (\infty, \ldots, \infty)$ is an extended c-representation of Δ.*

Proposition 17 also illustrates that in extended c-representations worlds may have rank infinity without the belief base requiring this. In an extended c-representation of Δ only those worlds need to have rank infinity that have rank infinity in the z-ranking κ_{Δ}^z of Δ.

Proposition 18. *Let Δ be a weakly consistent belief base. If $\kappa_{\Delta}^z(\omega) = \infty$ for a world ω, then $\kappa_{\vec{\eta}}(\omega) = \infty$ for all extended c-representations $\kappa_{\vec{\eta}}$ of Δ.*
Moreover, there is an extended c-representation $\kappa_{\vec{\eta}}$ of Δ with $\kappa_{\vec{\eta}}(\omega) < \infty$ for all worlds ω with $\kappa_{\Delta}^z(\omega) < \infty$.

As a consequence of this proposition, for a weakly consistent Δ, there is an extended c-representation $\kappa_{\vec{\eta}}$ such that $\kappa_{\vec{\eta}}(\omega) < \infty$ iff $\kappa_{\Delta}^z(\omega) < \infty$. Using Lemma 10 we have $\kappa_{\vec{\eta}}(\omega) < \infty$ iff ω does not entail $\bot$ with p-entailment.

Lemma 19. *Let Δ be a weakly consistent belief base. There is an extended c-representation $\kappa_{\vec{\eta}}$ of Δ such that for all $\omega \in \Omega$ we have $\kappa_{\vec{\eta}}(\omega) < \infty$ iff $\omega \not\hspace{1pt}\vdash_{\Delta}^p \bot$, where the world ω is considered as a formula on the right side of the "iff".*

Another consequence of Proposition 18 is the following.

Proposition 20. *Let Δ be a belief base with $EZP(\Delta) = \{\Delta^0, \ldots, \Delta^m, \Delta^{\infty}\}$, and let $\omega \in \Omega$. We have that $\kappa(\omega) = \infty$ for all $\kappa \in Mod_{\Delta}^{ec}$ iff $\omega \models A$ for some $(B|A) \in \Delta^{\infty}$.*

With extended c-representations we can now define extended c-inference.

6   Extending c-Inference

c-Inference [3,4] is an inference operator taking all c-representations of a belief base Δ into account. It was originally defined for strongly consistent belief bases.

Definition 21 (c-inference, $\vdash_{\Delta}^c$ [3]). *Let Δ be a strongly consistent belief base and let A, B be formulas. B is a c-inference from A in the context of Δ, denoted by $A \vdash_{\Delta}^c B$, iff $A \vdash_{\kappa} B$ holds for all c-representations κ of Δ.*

Now we use extended c-representations to extend c-inference for belief bases that may be only weakly consistent.

Definition 22 (extended c-inference, $\vdash_{\Delta}^{ec}$). *Let Δ be a belief base and let $A, B \in \mathcal{L}$. Then B is an extended c-inference from A in the context of Δ, denoted by $A \vdash_{\Delta}^{ec} B$, iff $A \vdash_{\kappa} B$ holds for all extended c-representations κ of Δ.*

First, let us verify that extended c-inference is indeed an inductive inference operator that coincides with c-inference for strongly consistent belief bases.

Proposition 23. *Extended c-inference is an inductive inference operator, i.e., it satisfies (DI) and (TV). For strongly consistent belief bases, extended c-inference coincides with normal c-inference.*

Because extended c-inference is defined as skeptical inference over a set of ranking functions it is also a preferential inference operator.

Proposition 24. *Extended c-inference is preferential, i.e., it satisfies system P.*

Proposition 24 implies that extended c-inference captures p-entailment, i.e., if $A \mathrel{|\!\sim}^{p}_{\Delta} B$ then $A \mathrel{|\!\sim}^{ec}_{\Delta} B$. Furthermore, extended c-inference coincides with p-entailment on entailments of the form $A \mathrel{|\!\sim} \bot$ which can be seen as representations of "strict" beliefs (i.e., A is completely unfeasible).

Proposition 25. *Extended c-inference satisfies (Classic Preservation).*

Extended c-inference does not satisfy *Rational Monotony (RM)* as c-inference already violates (RM).

7   CSPs for Extended c-Representations

In this section, we investigate constraint satisfaction problems (CSPs) dealing with extended c-representations. In Sect. 7.1, we present a constraint system describing all extended c-representations of a belief base. Then we develop a simplification of this constraint system that takes the effects of conditionals in Δ^{∞} into account right from the beginning. In Sect. 7.2 we show how extended c-inference can be realized by a CSP.

7.1   Describing Extended c-Representations by CSPs

The c-representations of a belief base Δ can conveniently be characterized by the solutions of a constraint satisfaction problem. In [4], the following modelling of c-representations as solutions of a CSP is introduced. For a belief base $\Delta = \{(B_1|A_1), \ldots, (B_n|A_n)\}$ over Σ the constraint satisfaction problem for c-representations of Δ, denoted by $CR_{\Sigma}(\Delta)$, on the constraint variables $\{\eta_1, \ldots, \eta_n\}$ ranging over $\mathbb{N}_0$ is given by the constraints cr_i^{Δ}, for all $i \in \{1, \ldots, n\}$:

$$(cr_i^{\Delta}) \qquad \eta_i > \min_{\substack{\omega \in \Omega_{\Sigma} \\ \omega \models A_i B_i}} \sum_{\substack{j \neq i \\ \omega \models A_j \overline{B_j}}} \eta_j - \min_{\substack{\omega \in \Omega_{\Sigma} \\ \omega \models A_i \overline{B_i}}} \sum_{\substack{j \neq i \\ \omega \models A_j \overline{B_j}}} \eta_j.$$

The constraint cr_i^{Δ} is the constraint corresponding to the conditional $(B_i|A_i)$. The sum terms are induced by the worlds verifying and falsifying $(B_i|A_i)$, respectively. A solution of $CR_{\Sigma}(\Delta)$ is an n-tuple $(\eta_1, \ldots, \eta_n) \in \mathbb{N}_0^n$. For a constraint satisfaction problem CSP, the set of solutions is denoted by $Sol(CSP)$. Thus, with $Sol(CR_{\Sigma}(\Delta))$ we denote the set of all solutions of $CR_{\Sigma}(\Delta)$. The solutions of $CR_{\Sigma}(\Delta)$ correspond to the c-representations of Δ.

Proposition 26 (soundness and completeness of $CR_\Sigma(\Delta)$ [4]). *Let $\Delta = \{(B_1|A_1), \ldots, (B_n|A_n)\}$ be a belief base over Σ. Then we have:*

$$Mod_\Sigma^c(\Delta) = \{\kappa_{\vec{\eta}} \mid \vec{\eta} \in Sol(CR_\Sigma(\Delta))\} \tag{4}$$

If we want to construct a similar CSP for extended c-representations, we have to take worlds and formulas with infinite rank into account.

Definition 27 ($CR_\Sigma^{ex}(\Delta)$). *Let $\Delta = \{(B_1|A_1), \ldots, (B_n|A_n)\}$ be a belief base over Σ. The constraint satisfaction problem for extended c-representations of Δ, denoted by $CR_\Sigma^{ex}(\Delta)$, on the constraint variables $\{\eta_1, \ldots, \eta_n\}$ ranging over $\mathbb{N}_0 \cup \{\infty\}$ is given by the constraints $cr_i^{ex}{}^\Delta$, for all $i \in \{1, \ldots, n\}$:*

$$(cr_i^{ex}{}^\Delta)$$

$$\min_{\substack{\omega \in \Omega_\Sigma \\ \omega \models A_i}} \sum_{\substack{1 \leqslant j \leqslant n \\ \omega \models A_j \overline{B_j}}} \eta_j = \infty \quad or \quad \eta_i > \min_{\substack{\omega \in \Omega_\Sigma \\ \omega \models A_i B_i}} \sum_{\substack{j \neq i \\ \omega \models A_j \overline{B_j}}} \eta_j - \min_{\substack{\omega \in \Omega_\Sigma \\ \omega \models A_i \overline{B_i}}} \sum_{\substack{j \neq i \\ \omega \models A_j \overline{B_j}}} \eta_j$$

Again, each constraint $cr_i^{ex}{}^\Delta$ corresponds to the conditional $(B_i|A_i) \in \Delta$.

Proposition 28 (soundness and completeness of $CR_\Sigma^{ex}(\Delta)$). *Let $\Delta = \{(B_1|A_1), \ldots, (B_n|A_n)\}$ be a weakly consistent belief base over Σ. Then we have:*

$$Mod_\Sigma^{ec}(\Delta) = \{\kappa_{\vec{\eta}} \mid \vec{\eta} \in Sol(CR_\Sigma^{ex}(\Delta))\} \tag{5}$$

The requirement for weak consistency in Proposition 28 is necessary because for a belief base Δ that is not weakly consistent it holds that $CMod_\Delta^{ec} = \emptyset$ but $Sol(CR_\Sigma^{ex}(\Delta)) = \{(\infty, \ldots, \infty)\}$.

The resulting CSP $CR_\Sigma^{ex}(\Delta)$ is not a conjunction of inequalities any more, but it now contains disjunctions and is thus more complex. However, for the computation of extended c-inference we can construct a simplified CSP $CRS_\Sigma^{ex}(\Delta)$ that still yields all extended c-representations necessary for c-inference. This is possible, because from Proposition 18 we already know which worlds must have rank infinity and which worlds may have finite rank in the extended c-representations of Δ. The simplified CSP not only uses fewer constraint variables but also fewer constraints than $CR_\Sigma^{ex}(\Delta)$ for weakly but not strongly consistent belief bases. Before stating $CRS_\Sigma^{ex}(\Delta)$, we show some proposition we will use for proving the correctness of $CRS_\Sigma^{ex}(\Delta)$.

We can assume the impacts of conditionals in Δ^∞ to be infinity.

Proposition 29. *Let Δ be a weakly consistent belief base with extended Z-partition $EZP(\Delta) = \{\Delta^0, \ldots, \Delta^m, \Delta^\infty\}$. Let $\vec{\eta}$ be impacts such that $\kappa_{\vec{\eta}}$ is an extended c-representation of Δ. Let $\vec{\eta}'$ be the impact vector defined by $\eta_i' = \infty$ if $(B_i|A_i) \in \Delta^\infty$ and $\eta_i' = \eta_i$ otherwise. Then $\kappa_{\vec{\eta}} = \kappa_{\vec{\eta}'}$.*

For c-inference, it is sufficient to take only a subset of all c-representations of a belief base into account.

Definition 30. *Let Δ be a belief base. Then $CMod_{\Delta}^{ec}$ is the set of c-representations $\kappa_{\vec{\eta}}$ of Δ with $\kappa_{\vec{\eta}}(\omega) < \infty$ for all worlds ω with $\kappa_{\Delta}^{z}(\omega) < \infty$.*

Proposition 31. *Let Δ be a belief base. Then $A \hspace{1mu}\vdash_{\kappa} B$ for all c-representations κ in $CMod_{\Delta}^{ec}$ iff $A \hspace{1mu}\vdash_{\kappa} B$ holds for all c-representations κ in $Mod_{\Sigma}^{ec}(\Delta)$.*

As already indicated above, the c-representations in $CMod_{\Delta}^{ec}$ can then be represented by a simplified CSP.

Definition 32 ($CRS_{\Sigma}^{ex}(\Delta)$). *Let $\Delta = \{(B_1|A_1), \ldots, (B_n|A_n)\}$ be a belief base over Σ with the extended Z-partition $EZP(\Delta) = \{\Delta^0, \ldots, \Delta^m, \Delta^{\infty}\}$. Let*

$$J_{\Delta} = \{j \mid (B_j|A_j) \in \Delta \setminus \Delta^{\infty} \quad s.t. \ A_j\overline{B_j} \wedge \big(\bigwedge_{(D|C)\in\Delta^{\infty}} (\overline{C} \vee D)\big) \not\equiv \bot\}.$$

The simplified constraint satisfaction problem for extended c-inference of Δ, denoted by $CRS_{\Sigma}^{ex}(\Delta)$, on the constraint variables $\{\eta_{j_1}, \ldots, \eta_{j_l}\}$, $j_k \in J_{\Delta}$ ranging over $\mathbb{N}_0$ is given by the constraints $crs_j^{ex}{}^{\Delta}$, for all $j \in J_{\Delta}$:

$$(crs_j^{ex}{}^{\Delta}) \qquad \eta_i > \min_{\substack{\omega\in\Omega_{\Sigma}\\ \omega\models A_iB_i}} \sum_{\substack{j\in J_{\Delta}\\ j\neq i\\ \omega\models A_j\overline{B_j}}} \eta_j - \min_{\substack{\omega\in\Omega_{\Sigma}\\ \omega\models A_i\overline{B_i}}} \sum_{\substack{j\in J_{\Delta}\\ j\neq i\\ \omega\models A_j\overline{B_j}}} \eta_j.$$

The condition $A_j\overline{B_j} \wedge \big(\bigwedge_{(D|C)\in\Delta^{\infty}} (\overline{C} \vee D)\big) \not\equiv \bot$ in the definition of J_{Δ} is equivalent to there being an $\omega \in \Omega_{A_j\overline{B_j}}$ that does not falsify conditionals in Δ^{∞}.

Definition 33. *Let Δ be a belief base, $n = |\Delta|$, and let J_{Δ} be defined as above. For $\vec{\eta}^J \in Sol(CRS_{\Sigma}^{ex}(\Delta))$ let $\vec{\eta}^{J+\infty} \in (\mathbb{N}_0 \cup \{\infty\})^n$ be the impact vector with*

$$\eta_i^{J+\infty} = \begin{cases} \eta_i & for \ i \in J_{\Delta} \\ \infty & otherwise. \end{cases}$$

Then $Sol_{\Delta}^{J+\infty} := \{\vec{\eta}^{J+\infty} \mid \vec{\eta}^J \in Sol(CRS_{\Sigma}^{ex}(\Delta))\}$.

Proposition 34 (soundness and completeness of $CRS_{\Sigma}^{ex}(\Delta)$). *Let Δ be a weakly consistent belief base over Σ. Then*

$$CMod_{\Sigma}^{ec}(\Delta) = \{\kappa_{\vec{\eta}} \mid \vec{\eta} \in Sol_{\Delta}^{J+\infty}\}. \tag{6}$$

Propositions 31 and 34 imply the following result.

Proposition 35 *Let Δ be a weakly consistent belief base. Then $A \hspace{1mu}\vdash_{\Delta}^{ec} B$ iff $A \hspace{1mu}\vdash_{\kappa_{\vec{\eta}}} B$ for every $\vec{\eta} \in Sol_{\Delta}^{J+\infty}$.*

The following example illustrates how $CRS_{\Sigma}^{ex}(\Delta)$ is simpler than $CR_{\Sigma}^{ex}(\Delta)$.

Example 36. Let $\Sigma = \{a, b, c\}$ and $\Delta = \{(\bot|a), (\overline{a}|b), (b|c)\}$. The CSP $CR^{ex}_\Sigma(\Delta)$ over $\eta_1, \eta_1, \eta_3 \in \mathbb{N}_0 \cup \{\infty\}$ contains the constraints

$$(cr^{ex\,\Delta}_1) \quad \min_{\substack{\omega \in \Omega_\Sigma \\ \omega \models a}} \sum_{\substack{1 \leq j \leq n \\ \omega \models A_j \overline{B_j}}} \eta_j = \infty \quad \text{or} \quad \eta_1 > \min_{\substack{\omega \in \Omega_\Sigma \\ \omega \models a \wedge \bot}} \sum_{\substack{j \neq 1 \\ \omega \models A_j \overline{B_j}}} \eta_j - \min_{\substack{\omega \in \Omega_\Sigma \\ \omega \models a \wedge \top}} \sum_{\substack{j \neq 1 \\ \omega \models A_j \overline{B_j}}} \eta_j,$$

$$(cr^{ex\,\Delta}_2) \quad \min_{\substack{\omega \in \Omega_\Sigma \\ \omega \models b}} \sum_{\substack{1 \leq j \leq n \\ \omega \models A_j \overline{B_j}}} \eta_j = \infty \quad \text{or} \quad \eta_i > \min_{\substack{\omega \in \Omega_\Sigma \\ \omega \models b \overline{a}}} \sum_{\substack{j \neq 2 \\ \omega \models A_j \overline{B_j}}} \eta_j - \min_{\substack{\omega \in \Omega_\Sigma \\ \omega \models ba}} \sum_{\substack{j \neq 2 \\ \omega \models A_j \overline{B_j}}} \eta_j,$$

$$(cr^{ex\,\Delta}_3) \quad \min_{\substack{\omega \in \Omega_\Sigma \\ \omega \models c}} \sum_{\substack{1 \leq j \leq n \\ \omega \models A_j \overline{B_j}}} \eta_j = \infty \quad \text{or} \quad \eta_i > \min_{\substack{\omega \in \Omega_\Sigma \\ \omega \models cb}} \sum_{\substack{j \neq 3 \\ \omega \models A_j \overline{B_j}}} \eta_j - \min_{\substack{\omega \in \Omega_\Sigma \\ \omega \models c\overline{b}}} \sum_{\substack{j \neq 3 \\ \omega \models A_j \overline{B_j}}} \eta_j.$$

The extended Z-partition of Δ is $EZP(\Delta) = (\Delta^0, \Delta^\infty)$ with $\Delta^0 = \{(\overline{a}|b), (b|c)\}$ and $\Delta^\infty = \{(\bot|a)\}$. The conditional $(\overline{a}|b)$ cannot be falsified without also falsifying $(\bot|a) \in \Delta^\infty$. Therefore, $J_\Delta = \{3\}$ and the CSP $CRS^{ex}_\Sigma(\Delta)$ over $\eta_3 \in \mathbb{N}_0$ contains only the constraint

$$(crs^{ex\,\Delta}_3) \quad \eta_3 > \min_{\substack{\omega \in \Omega_\Sigma \\ \omega \models bc}} \sum_{\substack{j \in J_\Delta \\ j \neq 3 \\ \omega \models A_j \overline{B_j}}} \eta_j - \min_{\substack{\omega \in \Omega_\Sigma \\ \omega \models b\overline{c}}} \sum_{\substack{j \in J_\Delta \\ j \neq 3 \\ \omega \models A_j \overline{B_j}}} \eta_j$$

which simplifies to $\eta_3 > 0$. For $\vec{\eta} \in Sol^{J+\infty}_\Delta$ it holds that $\eta_1 = \eta_2 = \infty$ and $\eta_3 \in Sol(CRS^{ex}_\Sigma(\Delta))$.

7.2   Characterizing Extended c-Inference by a CSP

In [4] a method is developed that realizes c-inference as a CSP. The idea of this approach is that in order to check whether $A \vdash^c_\Delta B$ holds, a constraint encoding that $A \vdash_{\kappa_{\vec{\eta}}} B$ does not hold is added to $CR_\Sigma(\Delta)$. If the resulting CSP is unsolvable, $A \vdash_{\kappa_{\vec{\eta}}} B$ holds for all solutions $\vec{\eta}$ of $CR_\Sigma(\Delta)$. Based on this idea, we develop a CSP that allows doing something similar for extended c-inference.

First we need a constraint encoding that $A \vdash_{\kappa_{\vec{\eta}}} B$ does not hold for an extended c-representation $\kappa_{\vec{\eta}}$.

Definition 37. *Let $\Delta = \{(B_1|A_1), \ldots, (B_n|A_n)\}$ be a belief base and let J_Δ be as defined in Definition 32. The constraint $\neg CR_\Delta(B|A)$ is given by*

$$\min_{\substack{\omega \models AB \\ i \in J_\Delta \\ \omega \models A_i B_i}} \sum \eta_i \geq \min_{\substack{\omega \models A\overline{B} \\ i \in J_\Delta \\ \omega \models A_i \overline{B_i}}} \sum \eta_i. \tag{7}$$

Using this constraint and the CSP $CRS^{ex}_\Sigma(\Delta)$ developed in Sect. 7.1 we can check if $A \vdash^{ec}_\Delta B$ with the following proposition.

Proposition 38. *Let Δ be weakly consistent. Then $A \vdash^{ec}_\Delta B$ iff either $\kappa^z_\Delta(A\overline{B}) = \infty$ or ($\kappa^z_\Delta(AB) < \infty$ and $CRS^{ex}_\Sigma(\Delta) \cup \neg CR_\Delta(B|A)$ is unsolvable).*

This realization of extended c-inference by a CSP yields a starting point for an implementation of extended c-inference as a SAT or SMT problem [2,7].

8   Syntax Splitting

The concept of *syntax splittings* was originally developed by Parikh [27] describing that a belief set contains independent information over different parts of the signature. The notion of syntax splitting was later extended to other representations of beliefs [22,23]. In [22] not only inductive inference operators were introduced, but also the postulates (Rel), (Ind), (SynSplit) for inductive inference operators that govern inference from strongly consistent belief bases with syntax splitting. Notably, c-inference satisfies these postulates. In this section we show that also extended c-inference respects syntax splittings on belief bases.

Definition 39 (syntax splitting for belief bases [22]). *Let Δ be a belief base over Σ. A partition $\{\Sigma_1, \ldots, \Sigma_n\}$ of Σ is a syntax splitting for Δ if there is a partition $\{\Delta_1, \ldots, \Delta_n\}$ of Δ s.t. $\Delta_i \subseteq (\mathcal{L}|\mathcal{L})_{\Sigma_i}$ for every $i = 1, \ldots, n$.*

In this paper, we only consider syntax splittings with two parts. Such a splitting $\{\Sigma_1, \Sigma_2\}$ of Δ with corresponding partition $\{\Delta_1, \Delta_2\}$ is denoted as [22] $\Delta = \Delta_1 \underset{\Sigma_1,\Sigma_2}{\cup} \Delta_2$. Results for syntax splittings with more than two parts can be obtained by iteratively applying the postulates presented here.

Here, we present slightly adapted versions of the splitting postulates, (Rel$^+$), (Ind$^+$), and (SynSplit$^+$) [18,22], that are intended for inference operators that are defined for all belief bases, including only weakly consistent belief bases.

For belief bases with syntax splitting, the postulate relevance (Rel$^+$) requires that for an inference using only atoms from one part of the syntax splitting only conditionals from the corresponding part of the belief base are relevant.

(Rel$^+$) An inductive inference operator $C : \Delta \mapsto \;\mid\!\sim_\Delta$ satisfies (Rel$^+$) if for a weakly consistent $\Delta = \Delta_1 \underset{\Sigma_1,\Sigma_2}{\cup} \Delta_2$, for $i = 1, 2$, and for $A, B \in \mathcal{L}_{\Sigma_i}$ we have

$$A \mid\!\sim_\Delta B \quad \text{iff} \quad A \mid\!\sim_{\Delta_i} B.$$

The postulate independence (Ind$^+$) requires that an inference using only atoms from one part of the syntax splitting should be drawn independently of additional beliefs about other parts of the splitting.

(Ind$^+$) An inductive inference operator $C : \Delta \mapsto \;\mid\!\sim_\Delta$ satisfies (Ind$^+$) if for any weakly consistent $\Delta = \Delta_1 \underset{\Sigma_1,\Sigma_2}{\cup} \Delta_2$, and for $i, j \in \{1, 2\}, i \neq j$ and for any $A, B \in \mathcal{L}_{\Sigma_i}, D \in \mathcal{L}_{\Sigma_j}$ such that $D \not\mid\!\sim_\Delta \bot$, we have

$$A \mid\!\sim_\Delta B \quad \text{iff} \quad AD \mid\!\sim_\Delta B.$$

The difference of these postulates to (Rel) and (Ind) is that also weakly consistent belief bases are considered. Additionally, in (Ind$^+$) the requirement $D \not\mid\!\sim_\Delta \bot$ was added. Otherwise, the postulate would have some clearly unintended implications. For any formula $A \in \mathcal{L}_{\Sigma_1}$ with (Ind) we would have $AD \mid\!\sim_\Delta \bot$ for any $D \in \mathcal{L}_{\Sigma_2}$ with $D \mid\!\sim_\Delta \bot$. Then, (Ind) would imply that $A \mid\!\sim_\Delta \bot$. The condition $D \not\mid\!\sim_\Delta \bot$ avoids this unintended consequence.

(SynSplit$^+$) An inductive inference operator $C : \Delta \mapsto \mathrel{\vert\!\sim}_\Delta$ satisfies (SynSplit$^+$) if it satisfies both (Rel$^+$) and (Ind$^+$).

For our proof that extended c-inference complies with syntax splitting, we need some lemmas on the behaviour of c-representations in the context of a syntax splitting $\Delta = \Delta_1 \underset{\Sigma_1,\Sigma_2}{\bigcup} \Delta_2$. Differing from the proof that c-inference satisfies (SynSplit) in [22], in the following we argue about the sets of extended c-inferences $Mod^{ec}_\Sigma(\Delta)$ directly instead of the sets of solutions of the corresponding CSPs. This is mainly because the CSPs characterizing all extended c-representations are more involved than the CSPs for c-representations.

First observe that the combination of any extended c-inference of Δ_1 with an extended c-inference of Δ_2 is an extended c-inference of Δ.

Lemma 40. *Let $\Delta = \Delta_1 \underset{\Sigma_1,\Sigma_2}{\bigcup} \Delta_2$ be a weakly consistent belief base with syntax splitting. Let $\kappa_1 \in Mod^{ec}_{\Sigma_1}(\Delta_1)$ and $\kappa_2 \in Mod^{ec}_{\Sigma_2}(\Delta_2)$. Then $\kappa_\oplus = \kappa_1 \oplus \kappa_2$ is an extended c-representation of Δ, i.e., $\kappa_\oplus \in Mod^{ec}_\Sigma(\Delta)$.*

In the other direction, Lemma 41 shows how an extended c-representation of Δ splits for certain formulas.

Lemma 41. *Let $\Delta = \Delta_1 \underset{\Sigma_1,\Sigma_2}{\bigcup} \Delta_2$ be a weakly consistent belief base with syntax splitting. Let $\kappa_{\vec{\eta}} \in Mod^{ec}_\Sigma(\Delta)$ be an extended c-representation induced by impact vector $\vec{\eta}$. Let $\vec{\eta}^1$ be the impact vector containing the impacts from $\vec{\eta}$ for Δ_1 and let $\vec{\eta}^2$ be the impact vector containing the impacts from $\vec{\eta}$ for Δ_2. Then, for $X \in \mathcal{L}_{\Sigma_1}, Y \in \mathcal{L}_{\Sigma_2}$ we have $\kappa(XY) = \kappa_{\vec{\eta}^1}(X) + \kappa_{\vec{\eta}^2}(Y)$.*

Lemma 42 states that marginalizing an extended c-representation of Δ to the subsignature Σ_i, $i \in \{1,2\}$ leads to an extended c-representation of Δ_i.

Lemma 42. *Let $\Delta = \Delta_1 \underset{\Sigma_1,\Sigma_2}{\bigcup} \Delta_2$ be a weakly consistent belief base with syntax splitting. If $\kappa \in Mod^{ec}_\Sigma(\Delta)$ then $\kappa_{|\Sigma_1} \in Mod^{ec}_{\Sigma_1}(\Delta_1)$.*

One of the key observations for proving that c-inference satisfies (SynSplit) in [22] is [22, Proposition 8]. Given a belief base with syntax splitting $\Delta = \Delta_1 \underset{\Sigma_1,\Sigma_2}{\bigcup} \Delta_2$, this proposition states that the c-representations of Δ are exactly the combinations of the c-representations of Δ_1 with the c-representations of Δ_2. In combination, the Lemmas 40, 41, and 42 yield a corresponding observation for extended c-representations as expressed in the following lemma.

Lemma 43. *Let $\Delta = \Delta_1 \underset{\Sigma_1,\Sigma_2}{\bigcup} \Delta_2$ be a weakly consistent belief base with syntax splitting. Then $\kappa \in Mod^{ec}_\Sigma(\Delta)$ iff there are $\kappa_1 \in Mod^{ec}_{\Sigma_1}(\Delta_1)$ and $\kappa_2 \in Mod^{ec}_{\Sigma_2}(\Delta_2)$ such that $\kappa = \kappa_1 \oplus \kappa_2$.*

Extended c-inference does not change if unused atoms are added to or removed from the signature. This is captured by the following Lemma 44.

Lemma 44. *Let Σ be a signature, $\Sigma' \subseteq \Sigma$, and Δ be a belief base over Σ'. For $A, B \in \mathcal{L}_{\Sigma'}$ we have $A \mathrel{\vert\!\sim}^{ec}_\Delta B$ with respect to Σ iff $A \mathrel{\vert\!\sim}^{ec}_\Delta B$ with respect to Σ'.*

Using the lemmas above, we can now show that extended c-inference satisfies (Rel$^+$). Observe that the proof for the next Proposition 45 does not need to deal explicitly with the case that a formula/world is infeasible (i.e., has rank ∞). In this proof, all situations where a world or formula has rank ∞ are already covered by the underlying definitions and results.

Proposition 45. *Extended c-inference satisfies (Rel$^+$).*

Proof. Let $\Delta = \Delta_1 \underset{\Sigma_1, \Sigma_2}{\bigcup} \Delta_2$ be weakly consistent. W.l.o.g. let $i = 1$ and $A, B \in \mathcal{L}_{\Sigma_1}$. We need to show that $A \mathrel{\vert\!\sim}^{ec}_\Delta B$ iff $A \mathrel{\vert\!\sim}^{ec}_{\Delta_1} B$.

Direction $\Rightarrow$:   Assume that $A \mathrel{\vert\!\sim}^{ec}_\Delta B$. Because of Lemma 44 it is sufficient to show that $A \mathrel{\vert\!\sim}^{ec}_{\Delta_1} B$ w.r.t. Σ_1. Let $\kappa_1 \in Mod^{ec}_{\Sigma_1}(\Delta_1)$ be any extended c-representation of Δ_1. We need to show that $A \mathrel{\vert\!\sim}_{\kappa_1} B$.

Let $\kappa_2 \in Mod^{ec}_{\Sigma_2}(\Delta_2)$ and $\kappa_\oplus = \kappa_1 \oplus \kappa_2$. By Lemma 40 we have $\kappa_\oplus \in Mod^{ec}_\Sigma(\Delta)$. Therefore, by assumption we have $A \mathrel{\vert\!\sim}_{\kappa_\oplus} B$. Because $\kappa_1 = \kappa_{\oplus | \Sigma_1}$, with Lemma 3 we have that $A \mathrel{\vert\!\sim}_{\kappa_1} B$.

Direction $\Leftarrow$:   Assume that $A \mathrel{\vert\!\sim}^{ec}_{\Delta_1} B$ (w.r.t. Σ). Let $\kappa \in Mod^{ec}_\Sigma(\Delta)$ be any extended c-representation of Δ. We need to show that $A \mathrel{\vert\!\sim}_\kappa B$.

With Lemma 42 we have that $\kappa_1 = \kappa_{| \Sigma_1}$ is an extended c-representation of Δ_1. With Lemma 44 we have that $A \mathrel{\vert\!\sim}^{ec}_{\Delta_1} B$ w.r.t. Σ_1, and therefore $A \mathrel{\vert\!\sim}_{\kappa_1} B$. Using Lemma 3 we have that $A \mathrel{\vert\!\sim}_\kappa B$.

For proving (Ind$^+$), in contrast to proving (Rel$^+$) in Proposition 45, we have to distinguish explicitly between the case that an entailment holds because its antecedent is infeasible and the case that an entailment holds because its verification has a lower rank than its falsification.

Proposition 46. *Extended c-inference satisfies (Ind$^+$).*

Proof. Let $\Delta = \Delta_1 \underset{\Sigma_1, \Sigma_2}{\bigcup} \Delta_2$ be weakly consistent. W.l.o.g. let $i = 1, j = 2$ and $A, B \in \mathcal{L}_{\Sigma_1}, D \in \mathcal{L}_{\Sigma_2}$ such that $D \mathrel{\not\vert\!\sim}^{ec}_\Delta \bot$. We need to show that $A \mathrel{\vert\!\sim}^{ec}_\Delta B$ iff $AD \mathrel{\vert\!\sim}^{ec}_\Delta B$.

Direction $\Rightarrow$: Assume $A \mathrel{\vert\!\sim}^{ec}_\Delta B$. We show $AD \mathrel{\vert\!\sim}_\kappa B$ for every $\kappa \in Mod^{ec}_\Sigma(\Delta)$.

Let $\kappa \in Mod^{ec}_\Sigma(\Delta)$ be any extended c-representation of Δ. Because $A \mathrel{\vert\!\sim}^{ec}_\Delta B$ we have that $A \mathrel{\vert\!\sim}_\kappa B$. Let $\vec{\eta}$ be the impact vector inducing κ, i.e., $\kappa = \kappa_{\vec{\eta}}$. Because $\Delta = \Delta_1 \cup \Delta_2$, we can sort the impacts in $\vec{\eta}$ into an impact vector $\vec{\eta}^1$ for Δ_1 and an impact vector $\vec{\eta}^2$ for Δ_2. We can distinguish three cases.

Case 1: $\kappa_{\vec{\eta}}(A) = \infty$. Applying Lemma 41, we have $\kappa_{\vec{\eta}}(A) = \kappa_{\vec{\eta}}(A \wedge \top) = \kappa_{\vec{\eta}^1}(A) + \kappa_{\vec{\eta}^2}(\top)$. Because Δ is weakly consistent, there is at least one world ω that does not falsify a conditional in Δ. Therefore, we have $\kappa_{\vec{\eta}^2}(\top) = 0$. Hence, $\kappa_{\vec{\eta}^1}(A) = \infty$. This implies $\kappa_{\vec{\eta}} = \kappa_{\vec{\eta}^1}(A) + \kappa_{\vec{\eta}^2}(D) = \infty + \kappa_{\vec{\eta}^2}(D) = \infty$. Thus, $AD \mathrel{\vert\!\sim}_\kappa B$.

Case 2: $\kappa_{\vec{\eta}}(A) < \infty$ and $\kappa_{\vec{\eta}}(D) = \infty$. With a similar argumentation as in *Case 1*, we have $\kappa_{\vec{\eta}^2}(D) = \infty$. This implies $\kappa_{\vec{\eta}}(AD) = \kappa_{\vec{\eta}^1}(A) + \kappa_{\vec{\eta}^2}(D) = \kappa_{\vec{\eta}^1}(A) + \infty = \infty$. Thus, $AD \mathrel{\vert\!\sim}_{\kappa_{\vec{\eta}}} B$.

Case 3: $\kappa_{\vec{\eta}}(A) < \infty$ and $\kappa_{\vec{\eta}}(D) < \infty$. Because $A \mathrel{\vert\!\not\sim}_{\kappa_{\vec{\eta}}} B$ in this case it is necessary that $\kappa_{\vec{\eta}}(AB) < \kappa_{\vec{\eta}}(A\overline{B})$.

Applying Lemma 41, we have $\kappa_{\vec{\eta}}(AB) = \kappa_{\vec{\eta}}(AB \wedge \top) = \kappa_{\vec{\eta}^1}(AB) + \kappa_{\vec{\eta}^2}(\top)$. Because Δ is weakly consistent, with Lemma 7 there is at least one world ω that does not falsify a conditional in Δ. Therefore, we have $\kappa_{\vec{\eta}^2}(\top) = 0$. Hence, $\kappa_{\vec{\eta}^1}(AB) = \kappa_{\vec{\eta}}(AB)$. Analogously, $\kappa_{\vec{\eta}^1}(A\overline{B}) = \kappa_{\vec{\eta}}(A\overline{B})$ and $\kappa_{\vec{\eta}^2}(D) = \kappa_{\vec{\eta}}(D) < \infty$. Therefore, $\kappa_{\vec{\eta}^1}(AB) < \kappa_{\vec{\eta}^1}(A\overline{B})$. Lemma 41 also yields $\kappa_{\vec{\eta}}(ABD) = \kappa_{\vec{\eta}^1}(AB) + \kappa_{\vec{\eta}^2}(D)$ and $\kappa_{\vec{\eta}}(A\overline{B}D) = \kappa_{\vec{\eta}^1}(A\overline{B}) + \kappa_{\vec{\eta}^2}(D)$. Together, we have that $\kappa_{\vec{\eta}}(ABD) = \kappa_{\vec{\eta}^1}(AB) + \kappa_{\vec{\eta}^2}(D) < \kappa_{\vec{\eta}^1}(A\overline{B}) + \kappa_{\vec{\eta}^2}(D) = \kappa_{\vec{\eta}}(A\overline{B}D)$ and thus $AD \mathrel{\vert\!\sim}_{\kappa_{\vec{\eta}}} B$.

Direction $\Leftarrow$: Assume $AD \mathrel{\vert\!\sim}^{ec}_{\Delta} B$. We show $A \mathrel{\vert\!\sim}_{\kappa} B$ for every $\kappa \in Mod^{ec}_{\Sigma}(\Delta)$.

Let $\kappa \in Mod^{ec}_{\Sigma}(\Delta)$ be any extended c-representation of Δ. Because $AD \mathrel{\vert\!\sim}^{ec}_{\Delta} B$ we have $AD \mathrel{\vert\!\sim}_{\kappa} B$. Because $D \mathrel{\vert\!\not\sim}^{ec}_{\Delta} \bot$, there is a $\kappa' \in Mod^{ec}_{\Sigma}(\Delta)$ such that $D \mathrel{\vert\!\not\sim}_{\kappa'} \bot$ which implies $\kappa'(D) < \infty$. Using Lemma 42 we have $\kappa'_{|\Sigma_2} \in Mod^{ec}_{\Sigma_2}(\Delta_2)$. With Lemma 1 we have $\kappa'_{|\Sigma_2}(D) = \kappa'(D)$. Analogously, we have $\kappa_{|\Sigma_1} \in Mod^{ec}_{\Sigma_1}(\Delta_1)$ and $\kappa_{|\Sigma_1}(A) = \kappa(A)$ and $\kappa_{|\Sigma_1}(AB) = \kappa(AB)$ and $\kappa_{|\Sigma_1}(A\overline{B}) = \kappa(A\overline{B})$. Let $\kappa_{\oplus} = \kappa_{|\Sigma_1} \oplus \kappa'_{|\Sigma_2}$. With Lemma 40 we have $\kappa_{\oplus} \in Mod^{ec}_{\Sigma}(\Delta)$. Because $AD \mathrel{\vert\!\sim}^{ec}_{\Delta} B$ this entails that $AD \mathrel{\vert\!\sim}_{\kappa_{\oplus}} B$. We can distinguish two cases.

Case 1: $\kappa_{\oplus}(AD) = \infty$. Because of Lemma 2 we have $\kappa_{\oplus}(AD) = \kappa_{|\Sigma_1}(A) + \kappa'_{|\Sigma_2}(D)$, and with $\kappa'_{|\Sigma_2}(D) = \kappa'(D) < \infty$ we have $\kappa_{|\Sigma_1}(A) = \infty$. Therefore, $\kappa(A) = \kappa_{|\Sigma_1}(A) = \infty$ and thus $A \mathrel{\vert\!\not\sim}_{\kappa} B$.

Case 2: $\kappa_{\oplus}(AD) < \infty$. Because $AD \mathrel{\vert\!\sim}_{\kappa_{\oplus}} B$ we have $\kappa_{\oplus}(ABD) < \kappa_{\oplus}(A\overline{B}D)$. With Lemma 2 we have $\kappa_{\oplus}(ABD) = \kappa_{|\Sigma_1}(AB) + \kappa'_{|\Sigma_2}(D)$ and $\kappa_{\oplus}(A\overline{B}D) = \kappa_{|\Sigma_1}(A\overline{B}) + \kappa'_{|\Sigma_2}(D)$. This implies that $\kappa_{|\Sigma_1}(AB) + \kappa'_{|\Sigma_2}(D) < \kappa_{|\Sigma_1}(A\overline{B}) + \kappa'_{|\Sigma_2}(D)$ and therefore that $\kappa(AB) < \kappa(A\overline{B})$. Thus, $A \mathrel{\vert\!\sim}_{\kappa} B$.

Note that for *Direction* $\Leftarrow$ of the proof of Proposition 46 for showing that $A \mathrel{\vert\!\sim}_{\kappa} B$ we had to pay special attention to the case where $\kappa(D) = \infty$ even though $D \mathrel{\vert\!\not\sim}^{ec}_{\Delta} \bot$. Therefore, in the proof we employ the extended c-representation $\kappa_{\oplus}$ derived from κ that satisfies $\kappa_{\oplus}(D) < \infty$ and is used to show that $A \mathrel{\vert\!\sim}_{\kappa} B$.

Combining Proposition 45 and Proposition 46 yields that extended c-inference satisfies (SynSplit$^+$):

Proposition 47. *Extended c-inference satisfies (SynSplit$^+$).*

9   Conclusions and Future Work

In this paper, by employing the notions of strong and weak consistency, we extended c-representations and c-inference to cover also weakly consistent belief bases, i.e., belief bases that require some worlds to be completely implausible. We developed a specialized CSP that still describes all extended c-representations relevant for c-inference, and we showed how extended c-inference can be realized by a CSP. Finally, we showed that extended c-inference complies with syntax splitting. For this we proved that extended c-inference satisfies adapted versions of (Rel) and (Ind), that also take inference from weakly consistent belief bases into account.

Future work includes to further investigate the properties of extended c-inference, to broaden the map of relations among inductive inference operators developed in [16] to extended c-inference and to other inductive inference operators taking also weakly consistent belief bases into account. We will also investigate how the reasoning with infeasible worlds relates to approaches to paraconsistent reasoning like Priest's logic LP [29]. Similarly as it has been done for c-inference, we will employ compilation techniques [6] for extended c-inference and we will realize it as a SAT and as an SMT problem [2,7,8] and implement it in the InfOCF reasoning platform [5,25].

Acknowledgments. This work was supported by the Deutsche Forschungsgemeinschaft (DFG, German Research Foundation), grant BE 1700/10-1 awarded to Christoph Beierle as part of the priority program "Intentional Forgetting in Organizations" (SPP 1921). Jonas Haldimann was supported by this grant.

References

1. Adams, E.W.: The Logic of Conditionals: An Application of Probability to Deductive Logic. Synthese Library. Springer, Dordrecht (1975). https://doi.org/10.1007/978-94-015-7622-2
2. Beierle, C., von Berg, M., Sanin, A.: Realization of c-inference as a SAT problem. In: Keshtkar, F., Franklin, M. (eds.) Proceedings of the Thirty-Fifth International Florida Artificial Intelligence Research Society Conference (FLAIRS), Hutchinson Island, Florida, USA, 15–18 May 2022 (2022). https://doi.org/10.32473/flairs.v35i.130663
3. Beierle, C., Eichhorn, C., Kern-Isberner, G.: Skeptical inference based on c-representations and its characterization as a constraint satisfaction problem. In: Gyssens, M., Simari, G. (eds.) FoIKS 2016. LNCS, vol. 9616, pp. 65–82. Springer, Cham (2016). https://doi.org/10.1007/978-3-319-30024-5_4
4. Beierle, C., Eichhorn, C., Kern-Isberner, G., Kutsch, S.: Properties of skeptical c-inference for conditional knowledge bases and its realization as a constraint satisfaction problem. Ann. Math. Artif. Intell. **83**(3–4), 247–275 (2018). https://doi.org/10.1007/s10472-017-9571-9
5. Beierle, C., Eichhorn, C., Kutsch, S.: A practical comparison of qualitative inferences with preferred ranking models. KI - Künstliche Intell. **31**(1), 41–52 (2017). https://doi.org/10.1007/s13218-016-0453-9
6. Beierle, C., Kutsch, S., Sauerwald, K.: Compilation of static and evolving conditional knowledge bases for computing induced nonmonotonic inference relations. Ann. Math. Artif. Intell. **87**(1–2), 5–41 (2019)
7. von Berg, M., Sanin, A., Beierle, C.: Representing nonmonotonic inference based on c-representations as an SMT problem. In: Bouraoui, Z., Jabbour, S., Vesic, S.

(eds.) ECSQARU 2023. LNCS, vol. 14249, pp. 210–223. Springer, Cham (2023). https://doi.org/10.1007/978-3-031-45608-4_17

8. von Berg, M., Sanin, A., Beierle, C.: Scaling up nonmonotonic c-inference via partial MaxSAT problems. In: Meier, A., Ortiz, M. (eds.) FoIKS 2024. LNCS, vol. 14589, PP. xx–yy. Springer, Cham (2024)

9. Casini, G., Meyer, T., Varzinczak, I.: Taking defeasible entailment beyond rational closure. In: Calimeri, F., Leone, N., Manna, M. (eds.) JELIA 2019. LNCS (LNAI), vol. 11468, pp. 182–197. Springer, Cham (2019). https://doi.org/10.1007/978-3-030-19570-0_12

10. Casini, G., Straccia, U.: Defeasible inheritance-based description logics. J. Artif. Intell. Res. **48**, 415–473 (2013). https://doi.org/10.1613/jair.4062

11. Darwiche, A., Pearl, J.: On the logic of iterated belief revision. Artif. Intell. **89**(1–2), 1–29 (1997)

12. de Finetti, B.: La prévision, ses lois logiques et ses sources subjectives. Ann. Inst. H. Poincaré **7**(1), 1–68 (1937). Engl. transl. Theory of Probability. Wiley (1974)

13. Giordano, L., Gliozzi, V., Olivetti, N., Pozzato, G.L.: Semantic characterization of rational closure: from propositional logic to description logics. Artif. Intell. **226**, 1–33 (2015)

14. Goldszmidt, M., Pearl, J.: On the relation between rational closure and System-Z. In: Proceedings of the Third International Workshop on Nonmonotonic Reasoning, 31 May–3 June 1990, pp. 130–140 (1990)

15. Goldszmidt, M., Pearl, J.: Qualitative probabilities for default reasoning, belief revision, and causal modeling. Artif. Intell. **84**, 57–112 (1996)

16. Haldimann, J., Beierle, C.: Approximations of system W between c-inference, system Z, and lexicographic inference. In: Bouraoui, Z., Jabbour, S., Vesic, S. (eds.) ECSQARU 2023. LNCS, vol. 14294, pp. 185–197. Springer, Cham (2023). https://doi.org/10.1007/978-3-031-45608-4_15

17. Haldimann, J., Beierle, C., Kern-Isberner, G.: Extending c-representations and c-inference for reasoning with infeasible worlds. In: Sauerwald, K., Thimm, M. (eds.) 21st International Workshop on Non-monotonic Reasoning, 2–4 September 2023, Rhodes, Greece. CEUR Workshop Proceedings, CEUR-WS.org (2023)

18. Haldimann, J., Beierle, C., Kern-Isberner, G., Meyer, T.: Conditionals, infeasible worlds, and reasoning with system W. In: Chun, S.A., Franklin, M. (eds.) Proceedings of the Thirty-Sixth International Florida Artificial Intelligence Research Society Conference (2023). https://doi.org/10.32473/flairs.36.133268

19. Heyninck, J., Kern-Isberner, G., Meyer, T., Haldimann, J.P., Beierle, C.: Conditional syntax splitting for non-monotonic inference operators. In: Williams, B., Chen, Y., Neville, J. (eds.) Proceedings of the 37th AAAI Conference on Artificial Intelligence, vol. 37, pp. 6416–6424 (2023). https://doi.org/10.1609/aaai.v37i5.25789

20. Kern-Isberner, G.: Conditionals in Nonmonotonic Reasoning and Belief Revision. LNAI, vol. 2087. Springer, Heidelberg (2001). https://doi.org/10.1007/3-540-44600-1

21. Kern-Isberner, G.: A thorough axiomatization of a principle of conditional preservation in belief revision. Ann. Math. Artif. Intell. **40**(1–2), 127–164 (2004)

22. Kern-Isberner, G., Beierle, C., Brewka, G.: Syntax splitting = relevance + independence: new postulates for nonmonotonic reasoning from conditional belief bases. In: Calvanese, D., Erdem, E., Thielscher, M. (eds.) Principles of Knowledge Representation and Reasoning: Proceedings of the 17th International Conference, KR 2020, pp. 560–571. IJCAI Organization (2020). https://doi.org/10.24963/kr.2020/56

23. Kern-Isberner, G., Brewka, G.: Strong syntax splitting for iterated belief revision. In: Sierra, C. (ed.) Proceedings International Joint Conference on Artificial Intelligence, IJCAI 2017, pp. 1131–1137. ijcai.org (2017)

24. Kraus, S., Lehmann, D., Magidor, M.: Nonmonotonic reasoning, preferential models and cumulative logics. Artif. Intell. **44**(1–2), 167–207 (1990)

25. Kutsch, S., Beierle, C.: InfOCF-Web: an online tool for nonmonotonic reasoning with conditionals and ranking functions. In: Zhou, Z. (ed.) Proceedings of the Thirtieth International Joint Conference on Artificial Intelligence, IJCAI 2021, Virtual Event/Montreal, Canada, 19–27 August 2021, pp. 4996–4999. ijcai.org (2021). https://doi.org/10.24963/ijcai.2021/711

26. Lehmann, D.: What does a conditional knowledge base entail? In: Brachman, R.J., Levesque, H.J., Reiter, R. (eds.) Proceedings of the 1st International Conference on Principles of Knowledge Representation and Reasoning (KR 1989), Toronto, Canada, 15–18 May 1989, pp. 212–222. Morgan Kaufmann (1989)

27. Parikh, R.: Beliefs, belief revision, and splitting languages. Log. Lang. Comput. **2**, 266–278 (1999)

28. Pearl, J.: System Z: A natural ordering of defaults with tractable applications to nonmonotonic reasoning. In: Proceedings of the 3rd Conference on Theoretical Aspects of Reasoning About Knowledge (TARK 1990), pp. 121–135. Morgan Kaufmann Publ. Inc., San Francisco (1990)

29. Priest, G.: The logic of paradox. J. Philos. Log. **8**(1), 219–241 (1979). https://doi.org/10.1007/BF00258428

30. Spohn, W.: Ordinal conditional functions: a dynamic theory of epistemic states. In: Harper, W., Skyrms, B. (eds.) Causation in Decision, Belief Change, and Statistics, II, pp. 105–134. Kluwer Academic Publishers (1988)

31. Spohn, W.: The Laws of Belief: Ranking Theory and Its Philosophical Applications. Oxford University Press, Oxford (2012)

Core c-Representations and c-Core Closure for Conditional Belief Bases

Marco Wilhelm[1]([envelope]) [ORCID], Gabriele Kern-Isberner[1] [ORCID], and Christoph Beierle[2] [ORCID]

[1] Department of Computer Science, TU Dortmund University, Dortmund, Germany
marco.wilhelm@tu-dortmund.de, gabriele.kern-isberner@cs.tu-dortmund.de
[2] Department of Mathematics and Computer Science, FernUniversität in Hagen, Hagen, Germany
christoph.beierle@fernuni-hagen.de

Abstract. c-Representations constitute a family of ranking models of symbolic conditional belief bases with outstanding inference properties. In this paper, we identify the subclass of core c-representations which inherit all beneficial properties from c-representations but are stratified, hence, easier to compute. Moreover, this class provides a unique minimal representative, the minimal core c-representation of a conditional belief base. Based on that, we define a novel inference operation, c-core closure, analyze its properties, and compare it to System P, System Z, and skeptical c-inference. Like skeptical c-inference, c-core closure satisfies syntax splitting and does not suffer from the drowning problem. In addition, it satisfies rational monotony and inductive enforcement.

Keywords: conditional reasoning · (minimal) core c-representations · c-core closure · c-representations · System Z

1 Introduction

In logic-based knowledge representation, conditionals $(B|A)$ are used to express defeasible statements of the form "if A holds, then usually B follows". The formal semantics of such conditionals is typically given by *preference relations* over *possible worlds*. A widely used semi-quantitative way of expressing such preferences is constituted by *ranking functions* [27] which assign a degree of implausibility to possible worlds and based on that to formulas. A ranking function κ *accepts* a conditional if its *verification* is more plausible than its *falsification*, $\kappa(A \wedge B) < \kappa(A \wedge \neg B)$, and *models* a finite set of conditionals Δ (a *belief base*) if κ accepts all conditionals in Δ. A family of ranking models with particularly good inference properties are the so-called *c-representations* [16]. c-Representations are characterized by penalizing possible worlds for falsifying conditionals from the belief base and, mathematically, are solutions of a complex constraint satisfaction problem which possibly involves cyclic dependencies among the penalty points. The research question of a "best" c-representation is still unresolved.

© The Author(s), under exclusive license to Springer Nature Switzerland AG 2024
A. Meier and M. Ortiz (Eds.): FoIKS 2024, LNCS 14589, pp. 104–122, 2024.
https://doi.org/10.1007/978-3-031-56940-1_6

In this paper, we identify a subclass of c-representations, the so-called *core c-representations*. Core c-representations are special because they rely on a simplified constraint satisfaction problem and, as a consequence, can be computed much easier. In fact, there is a stratification method for core c-representations which resolves the cyclic dependencies among the penalty points. Furthermore, core c-representations have a *unique* minimal representative which allows us to define an inductive inference operation, the so-called *c-core closure*, that selects for each consistent belief base its *minimal core c-representation* in order to draw inferences from the belief base. Therewith, we bring together the goals of minimizing c-representations (cf. [6]) and stratification for the first time. In our context, stratification was formerly known from the System Z-like *Z-c-representation* only [16] which is another instance of the family of core c-representations.

The rest of the paper is organized as follows. First, we recall some basics on ranking functions in general and on c-representations in particular. Then, we define core c-representations, specify a construction method for them which is based on an extension of *tolerance partitions* of conditional belief bases, and show the existence of a unique minimal core c-representation. Afterwards, we define c-core closure, analyze its properties, and show that it differs from common inference operations such as *System P inference* [1,19], *System Z inference* [24], as well as *skeptical c-inference* [2,3] while satisfying many beneficial inference properties (cf. Table 4). Eventually, we conclude with an outlook.

2 Preliminaries

We consider a *propositional language* $\mathcal{L}(\Sigma)$ defined over a finite *signature* Σ using the common connectives $\wedge$ (conjunction), $\vee$ (disjunction), and $\neg$ (negation). *Formulas* in $\mathcal{L}(\Sigma)$ are interpreted to 1 (true) or 0 (false) as usual, and with $\models$ we denote the *entailment relation* between formulas. For $A, B \in \mathcal{L}(\Sigma)$, we abbreviate $A \wedge B$ with AB, $\neg A$ with $\overline{A}$, arbitrary tautologies $A \vee \overline{A}$ with $\top$, and arbitrary contradictions $A\overline{A}$ with $\bot$. A *conditional* $(B|A)$ with $A, B \in \mathcal{L}(\Sigma)$ is a formal representation of the defeasible statement "if A holds, then usually B follows." A finite set of conditionals Δ is called a *belief base*. Throughout the paper, we allocate $n = |\Delta|$ and enumerate the conditionals in Δ so that we can refer to the conditionals by their indices. Moreover, we identify $\Delta = \{\delta_1, \ldots, \delta_n\}$ with $\delta_i = (B_i|A_i)$ for $i \in [n]$ where $[n]$ abbreviates $\{1, \ldots, n\}$.

The formal semantics of conditionals is given by *ranking functions* over *possible worlds* where a *possible world* is a *propositional interpretation* over Σ represented as a conjunction of those *literals* which are true in the respective interpretation. The set of all possible worlds is denoted with Ω. Further, we denote the sets of possible worlds which *verify/falsify* a conditional $\delta = (B|A)$ with

$$\mathsf{ver}(\delta) = \{\omega \in \Omega \mid \omega \models AB\}, \qquad \mathsf{fal}(\delta) = \{\omega \in \Omega \mid \omega \models A\overline{B}\},$$

and the sets of conditionals from Δ which are *verified/falsified* in $\omega \in \Omega$ with

$$\mathsf{ver}_\Delta(\omega) = \{\delta_i \in \Delta \mid \omega \models A_i B_i\}, \qquad \mathsf{fal}_\Delta(\omega) = \{\delta_i \in \Delta \mid \omega \models A_i \overline{B_i}\}.$$

A *ranking function* $\kappa\colon \Omega \to \mathbb{N}_0^\infty$ [27] assigns to every possible world a *plausibility rank* while satisfying the normalization condition $\kappa^{-1}(0) \neq \emptyset$. The higher the rank $\kappa(\omega)$, the less plausible the possible world ω is, so that $\kappa^{-1}(0)$ is the set of the most plausible possible worlds. Accordingly,

$$\mathsf{Bel}(\kappa) = \bigcap\nolimits_{\omega \in \kappa^{-1}(0)} \{A \in \mathcal{L}(\Sigma) \mid \omega \models A\}$$

is the *belief set* of a reasoner with *belief state* κ, i.e., the consequences of the most plausible beliefs in κ. A ranking function κ *accepts* a conditional $(B|A)$ if $\kappa(AB) < \kappa(A\overline{B})$ where $\kappa(A) = \min\{\kappa(\omega) \mid \omega \models A\}$ for $A \in \mathcal{L}(\Sigma)$,[1] and it is a *ranking model* of a belief base Δ if it accepts all conditionals in Δ. If Δ has a ranking model, then Δ is called *consistent*. Consistent belief bases have infinitely many ranking models of different quality, e.g., in terms of inference properties.

System Z. For consistent belief bases Δ, a well-known ranking model is specified by *System Z* [24] which classifies the conditionals in Δ w.r.t. their normality by making use of a specific *tolerance partition* of Δ. A conditional $(B|A)$ is *tolerated* by Δ if there is a possible world ω such that $\omega \models AB$ and $\omega \models \overline{A_i} \vee B_i$ for $i \in [n]$. Based on that, an ordered partition $(\Delta_1, \ldots, \Delta_m)$ of Δ is a *tolerance partition* of Δ if, for $i \in [m]$, every conditional in Δ_i is tolerated by $\bigcup_{j=i}^m \Delta_j$. The *Z-partition* $Z(\Delta)$ is the unique tolerance partition of Δ where the partitioning sets are chosen maximally, and the *Z-rank* $Z_\Delta(\delta)$ of a conditional $\delta \in \Delta$ is the index i of the subbase $\Delta_i \in Z(\Delta)$ with $\delta \in \Delta_i$. The *System Z ranking model* of Δ is given then by

$$\kappa_\Delta^Z(\omega) = \begin{cases} 0, & \mathsf{fal}_\Delta(\omega) = \emptyset \\ \max_{\delta \in \mathsf{fal}_\Delta(\omega)} Z_\Delta(\delta), & \text{otherwise} \end{cases}, \quad \omega \in \Omega.$$

The ranking model κ_Δ^Z exists iff Δ is consistent. Note that we start the indexing of the subbases in $Z(\Delta)$ from $i = 1$ because it makes the comparison with our approach easier. In literature, you will often find $i = 0$ as the lowest index which means a shift of the Z-ranks $Z_\Delta(\delta)$ by -1. This shift is compensated in the definition of κ_Δ^Z in which alternatively the term $+1$ would occur. System Z coincides with *rational closure* [14].

c-Representations. Another prominent class of ranking models are the so-called *c-representations* [16]. For $\boldsymbol{\eta} = (\eta_1, \ldots, \eta_n) \in \mathbb{N}_0^n$, the ranking function

$$\kappa_\Delta^{\boldsymbol{\eta}}(\omega) = \sum\nolimits_{\delta_i \in \mathsf{fal}_\Delta(\omega)} \eta_i, \quad \omega \in \Omega,$$

is called a *c-representation* of Δ if it is a ranking model of Δ. The entries of $\boldsymbol{\eta}$ can be understood as *penalty points* for falsifying the conditionals in Δ. With

---

[1] Here, the convention $\min \emptyset = \infty$ applies.

Table 1. Verified and falsified conditionals from Δ_{ex} (cf. Example 1).

ω	$\mathsf{ver}_{\Delta_{\mathsf{ex}}}(\omega)$	$\mathsf{fal}_{\Delta_{\mathsf{ex}}}(\omega)$	ω	$\mathsf{ver}_{\Delta_{\mathsf{ex}}}(\omega)$	$\mathsf{fal}_{\Delta_{\mathsf{ex}}}(\omega)$
abc	$\{\delta_1, \delta_4\}$	$\{\delta_3, \delta_5\}$	$\bar{a}bc$	$\{\delta_3\}$	$\{\delta_4\}$
$ab\bar{c}$	$\{\delta_1, \delta_5\}$	$\{\delta_3\}$	$\bar{a}b\bar{c}$	$\{\delta_3\}$	$\emptyset$
$a\bar{b}c$	$\emptyset$	$\{\delta_1, \delta_2, \delta_3\}$	$\bar{a}\bar{b}c$	$\{\delta_2, \delta_3\}$	$\emptyset$
$a\bar{b}\bar{c}$	$\emptyset$	$\{\delta_1, \delta_2\}$	$\bar{a}\bar{b}\bar{c}$	$\{\delta_2\}$	$\emptyset$

Table 2. (Reduced) constraint inducing sets of the conditionals in Δ_{ex} (cf. Example 1 and Example 2).

δ_i	V_i	F_i	V_i^{ψ}	V_i^{ψ}
$\delta_1 = (b\vert a)$	$\{\{\delta_3\}, \{\delta_3, \delta_5\}\}$	$\{\{\delta_2\}, \{\delta_2, \delta_3\}\}$	$\{\{\delta_3\}\}$	$\{\{\delta_2\}\}$
$\delta_2 = (\bar{a}\vert\bar{b})$	$\{\emptyset\}$	$\{\{\delta_1\}, \{\delta_1, \delta_3\}\}$	$\{\emptyset\}$	$\{\{\delta_1\}\}$
$\delta_3 = (\bar{a}\vert b \vee c)$	$\{\emptyset, \{\delta_4\}\}$	$\{\emptyset, \{\delta_5\}, \{\delta_1, \delta_2\}\}$	$\{\emptyset\}$	$\{\emptyset\}$
$\delta_4 = (a\vert bc)$	$\{\{\delta_3, \delta_5\}\}$	$\{\emptyset\}$	$\{\{\delta_3, \delta_5\}\}$	$\{\emptyset\}$
$\delta_5 = (\bar{c}\vert ab)$	$\{\{\delta_3\}\}$	$\{\{\delta_3\}\}$	$\{\emptyset\}$	$\{\emptyset\}$

the *positive* (V_i) resp. *negative (F_i) constraint inducing sets*

$$V_i = \{\{\delta' \in \Delta \setminus \{\delta_i\} \mid \omega \in \mathsf{fal}(\delta')\} \mid \omega \in \mathsf{ver}(\delta_i)\}$$
$$F_i = \{\{\delta' \in \Delta \setminus \{\delta_i\} \mid \omega \in \mathsf{fal}(\delta')\} \mid \omega \in \mathsf{fal}(\delta_i)\}, \quad i \in [n],$$

the acceptance condition $\kappa_\Delta^\eta(A_i B_i) < \kappa_\Delta^\eta(A_i \overline{B_i})$ of the i-th conditional in Δ can be written as (cf. [5])

$$C_i: \quad \eta_i > \min\{\sum_{\delta_j \in S} \eta_j \mid S \in V_i\} - \min\{\sum_{\delta_j \in S} \eta_j \mid S \in F_i\}. \tag{1}$$

The set $\mathsf{CSP}(\Delta) = \{C_1, \ldots, C_n\}$ constitutes a *constraint satisfaction problem* which has to be solved in order to calculate a c-representation of Δ. More precisely, every integer solution of $\mathsf{CSP}(\Delta)$ induces a c-representation of Δ, and every c-representation of Δ can be computed this way.

Example 1. As a running example, we consider the belief base $\Delta_{\mathsf{ex}} = \{\delta_1, \ldots, \delta_5\}$ with

$$\delta_1 = (b\vert a), \quad \delta_2 = (\bar{a}\vert\bar{b}), \quad \delta_3 = (\bar{a}\vert b \vee c), \quad \delta_4 = (a\vert bc), \quad \delta_5 = (\bar{c}\vert ab).$$

The sets $\mathsf{ver}_{\Delta_{\mathsf{ex}}}(\omega)$ and $\mathsf{fal}_{\Delta_{\mathsf{ex}}}(\omega)$ are shown in Table 1 and the resulting constraint inducing sets V_i and F_i in Table 2. The constraint satisfaction problem $\mathsf{CSP}(\Delta_{\mathsf{ex}}) = \{C_1, \ldots, C_5\}$ is given then by

$$
\begin{aligned}
C_1: &\quad \eta_1 > \min\{\eta_3, \eta_3 + \eta_5\} - \min\{\eta_2, \eta_2 + \eta_3\}, \\
C_2: &\quad \eta_2 > \min\{0\} &&- \min\{\eta_1, \eta_1 + \eta_3\}, \\
C_3: &\quad \eta_3 > \min\{0, \eta_4\} &&- \min\{0, \eta_5, \eta_1 + \eta_2\}, \\
C_4: &\quad \eta_4 > \min\{\eta_3 + \eta_5\} &&- \min\{0\}, \\
C_5: &\quad \eta_5 > \min\{\eta_3\} &&- \min\{\eta_3\}.
\end{aligned}
$$

It has three pareto-minimal solutions: $(1,1,1,3,1)$, $(2,0,1,3,1)$, and $(0,2,1,3,1)$, where pareto-minimal means that there is no further integer solution of $\mathsf{CSP}(\Delta_{\mathsf{ex}})$ with any entry less than the respective entries of the solutions above.

For comparing the solutions η of $\mathsf{CSP}(\Delta)$ w.r.t. their induced c-representation κ_Δ^η, the relation $\eta \preccurlyeq_O \eta'$ iff $\kappa_\Delta^\eta(\omega) \leq \kappa_\Delta^{\eta'}(\omega)$ for all $\omega \in \Omega$ leads to a refined notion of minimality: η is minimal w.r.t. $\preccurlyeq_O$, called *ind-minimal*, iff there is no solution η' of $\mathsf{CSP}(\Delta)$ such that $\eta' \preccurlyeq_O \eta$ and $\eta \not\preccurlyeq_O \eta'$ [4]. For Δ_{ex} from Example 1, all three pareto-minimal solutions of $\mathsf{CSP}(\Delta_{\mathsf{ex}})$ induce the same c-representation and are thus ind-minimal. On the other hand, there are belief bases Δ where only some of the pareto-minimal solutions of $\mathsf{CSP}(\Delta)$ are also ind-minimal and the ind-minimal solutions induce different, inferentially non-equivalent ranking models of Δ.

It is useful to simplify $\mathsf{CSP}(\Delta)$ before solving it. For instance, the constraint C_1 in Example 1 can be reduced to $\eta_1 > \eta_3 - \eta_2$. In [5, 8, 28] rewriting rules are suggested which simplify $\mathsf{CSP}(\Delta)$ by manipulating the constraint inducing sets V_i and F_i, $i \in [n]$, without changing the solution set of $\mathsf{CSP}(\Delta)$. These rules are:

R1 If $S, S' \in V_i$ with $S \subsetneq S'$, then $V_i \leftarrow V_i \setminus \{S'\}$.
R2 If $S, S' \in F_i$ with $S \subsetneq S'$, then $F_i \leftarrow F_i \setminus \{S'\}$.
R3 If $V_i \neq \{\emptyset\} \neq F_i$ and $\delta_j \in S$ for all $S \in V_i \cup F_i$, then $V_i \leftarrow \{S \setminus \{\delta_j\} \mid S \in V_i\}$ and $F_i \leftarrow \{S \setminus \{\delta_j\} \mid S \in F_i\}$.
R4 If $V_i = F_i$, then $V_i \leftarrow \{\emptyset\}$ and $F_i \leftarrow \{\emptyset\}$.
R5 If there are $\mathcal{D} \subseteq 2^\Delta$ and $T, T' \subseteq \Delta$ such that $V_i = \{S \dot\cup T \mid S \in \mathcal{D}\}$ and $F_i = \{S \dot\cup T' \mid S \in \mathcal{D}\}$, then $V_i \leftarrow \{T\}$ and $F_i \leftarrow \{T'\}$.
R6 If $F_i = F_j = \{\emptyset\}$ for $i \neq j$ and there is $\mathcal{D} \subseteq 2^\Delta$ such that $V_i = \mathcal{D} \dot\cup \{\{\delta_j\}\}$ and $V_j = \mathcal{D} \dot\cup \{\{\delta_i\}\}$, then $V_i \leftarrow \mathcal{D}$ and $V_j \leftarrow \mathcal{D}$.

The rules R1–R6 rely on simple laws of minimization and arithmetics. Note that some of them take both V_i and F_i into account. For further details, please see [5, 28]. We denote with V_i^ψ and F_i^ψ, $i \in [n]$, the *reduced constraint inducing sets*, i.e., V_i and F_i after applying the rewriting rules R1-R6 exhaustively. In addition, with $\mathsf{CSP}^\psi(\Delta) = \{C_1^\psi, \ldots, C_n^\psi\}$ we denote the *reduced constraint satisfaction problem* where

$$C_i^\psi: \quad \eta_i > \min\{\textstyle\sum_{\delta_j \in S} \eta_j \mid S \in V_i^\psi\} - \min\{\textstyle\sum_{\delta_j \in S} \eta_j \mid S \in F_i^\psi\}. \quad (2)$$

Thus, C_i^ψ is C_i in which V_i and F_i are replaced by V_i^ψ and F_i^ψ.

Example 2. We recall Δ_{ex} from Example 1. The reduced constraint inducing sets V_i^ψ and F_i^ψ are shown in Table 2, and $\mathsf{CSP}^\psi(\Delta_{\mathsf{ex}})$ is given by

$$
\begin{aligned}
C_1^\psi: &\quad \eta_1 > \min\{\eta_3\} && - \min\{\eta_2\} && = \eta_3 - \eta_2, \\
C_2^\psi: &\quad \eta_2 > \min\{0\} && - \min\{\eta_1\} && = -\eta_1, \\
C_3^\psi: &\quad \eta_3 > \min\{0\} && - \min\{0\} && = 0, \\
C_4^\psi: &\quad \eta_4 > \min\{\eta_3 + \eta_5\} && - \min\{0\} && = \eta_3 + \eta_5, \\
C_5^\psi: &\quad \eta_5 > \min\{0\} && - \min\{0\} && = 0.
\end{aligned}
$$

Note that a belief base Δ is consistent iff a c-representation of Δ exists [16], i.e., iff $\mathsf{CSP}^{\psi}(\Delta)$ has an integer solution.

Inductive Inference. Once a ranking model κ of a belief base Δ is determined, this model leads to a *nonmonotonic inference relation* $\mathrel{\vdash}_{\kappa}$ between formulas, telling which formulas B a reasoner with belief state κ should infer from A:

$$A \mathrel{\vdash}_{\kappa} B \quad \text{iff} \quad \kappa(A) = \infty \text{ or } \kappa(AB) < \kappa(A\overline{B}). \tag{3}$$

Compared with this, *inductive inference* is the task of drawing inferences right from the belief base Δ. Thus, it involves the selection of the model(s) of Δ from which the inferences are drawn.

Definition 1 (Inductive Inference Operator [17]). *An inductive inference operator is a mapping $\mathcal{I} \colon \Delta \mapsto \mathrel{\vdash}_{\Delta}^{\mathcal{I}}$ which assigns to every consistent belief base Δ a binary relation $\mathrel{\vdash}_{\Delta}^{\mathcal{I}}$ on $\mathcal{L}(\Sigma)$ such that the properties* direct inference (DI) [21] *and* trivial vacuity (TV) [17] *are satisfied:*

(DI) $(B|A) \in \Delta$ *implies* $A \mathrel{\vdash}_{\Delta}^{\mathcal{I}} B$.
(TV) *If $\Delta = \emptyset$, then $A \mathrel{\vdash}_{\Delta}^{\mathcal{I}} B$ only if $A \models B$.*

This leads to the definition $\Delta \mathrel{\vdash}^{\mathcal{I}} (B|A)$ iff $A \mathrel{\vdash}_{\Delta}^{\mathcal{I}} B$. We give examples of important inductive inference operators (cf. [17]):[2]

- The *System P inference operator* $\mathcal{I}^{P} \colon \Delta \mapsto \mathrel{\vdash}_{\Delta}^{P}$ is defined by $A \mathrel{\vdash}_{\Delta}^{P} B$ if $A \mathrel{\vdash}_{\kappa} B$ for all ranking models κ of Δ [1,19].
- The *System Z inference operator* $\mathcal{I}^{Z} \colon \Delta \mapsto \mathrel{\vdash}_{\Delta}^{Z}$ is defined by $A \mathrel{\vdash}_{\Delta}^{Z} B$ if $A \mathrel{\vdash}_{\kappa_{\Delta}^{Z}} B$ where κ_{Δ}^{Z} is the System Z ranking model of Δ [24].
- The *skeptical c-inference operator* $\mathcal{I}^{c} \colon \Delta \mapsto \mathrel{\vdash}_{\Delta}^{c}$ is defined by $A \mathrel{\vdash}_{\Delta}^{c} B$ if $A \mathrel{\vdash}_{\kappa_{\Delta}^{\eta}} B$ for all c-representations κ_{Δ}^{η} of Δ [2,3].

The System P inference operator is characterized by an axiomatic collection of inference rules [19]. Further, it satisfies *semi-monotony (SM)* [25,26] and *classic preservation (CP)* [11], among others:

(SM) $A \mathrel{\vdash}_{\Delta}^{\mathcal{I}} B$ and $\Delta \subseteq \Delta'$ implies $A \mathrel{\vdash}_{\Delta'}^{\mathcal{I}} B$.
(CP) $A \mathrel{\vdash}_{\Delta}^{\mathcal{I}} \perp$ iff $A \mathrel{\vdash}_{\Delta}^{P} \perp$.

System P is considered to be the "conservative core" of nonmonotonic reasoning systems [19]. System Z extends System P, most notably, by satisfying *rational monotony (RM)* [10,20]:

(RM) $A \mathrel{\vdash}_{\Delta}^{\mathcal{I}} B$ and $A \mathrel{\not\vdash}_{\Delta}^{\mathcal{I}} \overline{C}$ implies $AC \mathrel{\vdash}_{\Delta}^{\mathcal{I}} B$.

---

[2] We write $\mathrel{\vdash}_{\Delta}^{X}$ instead of $\mathrel{\vdash}_{\Delta}^{\mathcal{I}^{X}}$ in order to avoid double superscripts.

Both System P and System Z do not satisfy *syntax splitting* [17,22], though, and suffer from the *drowning problem* [9,24]. *Syntax splitting (SynSplit)* requires that inferences depend on relevant parts of the belief base only, known as the property *relevance (Rel)*, and that strengthening antecedents by irrelevant information has no influence on the inferences, called *independence (Ind)*.

Definition 2 (Syntax Splitting [17]**).** *Let Δ be a consistent belief base, let $\{\Sigma_1, \Sigma_2\}$ be a partition of Σ, and let $\{\Delta_1, \Delta_2\}$ be a partition of Δ such that, for $i = 1, 2$, the subbase Δ_i makes use of atoms from Σ_i only. Then,*

(Rel) $A, B \in \mathcal{L}(\Sigma_1)$ *implies* $A \mathrel{\vert\!\sim}_\Delta^\mathcal{I} B$ *iff* $A \mathrel{\vert\!\sim}_{\Delta_1}^\mathcal{I} B$.
(Ind) $A, B \in \mathcal{L}(\Sigma_1)$ *and* $C \in \mathcal{L}(\Sigma_2)$ *implies* $A \mathrel{\vert\!\sim}_\Delta^\mathcal{I} B$ *iff* $AC \mathrel{\vert\!\sim}_\Delta^\mathcal{I} B$.
(SynSplit) = *(Rel)* + *(Ind)*.

The *drowning problem* describes the circumstance when exceptional subclasses do not inherit properties from their superclass although these properties are unrelated to the reason for the exceptionality. A formalization of the drowning problem is given in [15] based on *conditional syntax splitting*. According to that, an inductive inference operator suffers from the drowning problem if the operator violates a conditional version of the independence property (Ind).

In contrast to System P and System Z, inference operators which are defined over c-representations like skeptical c-inference do not suffer from the drowning problem and satisfy syntax splitting [15,17]. Hence, c-representations constitute a meaningful basis for defining inductive inference operators. However, drawing skeptical c-inferences is a rather challenging task as there is no simple way of validating whether inferences hold w.r.t. *all* c-representations. Further, skeptical c-inference does not satisfy rational monotony (RM) but only the weaker version *weak rational monotony (wRM)* [7]:

(wRM) $\top \mathrel{\vert\!\sim}_\Delta^\mathcal{I} B$ and $\top \mathrel{\not\vert\!\sim}_\Delta^\mathcal{I} \overline{A}$ *implies* $A \mathrel{\vert\!\sim}_\Delta^\mathcal{I} B$.

Inference operators which are defined w.r.t. a single c-representation, similar to the System Z inference operator that is defined w.r.t. the unique System Z ranking model, would additionally satisfy (RM) [7]. Example 1 shows that it is not effective to restrict oneself to minimal c-representations for this purpose as minimal c-representations are not unique either.

With *core c-representations* we establish a subclass of c-representation for which a minimal, thus, outstanding c-representation exists that qualifies for the model selection task. In the remainder of this paper, we define *(minimal) core c-representations*, an inference operator based on the minimal core c-representations, and investigate their properties.

3   Core c-Representations

We define *core c-representations* as a subclass of c-representations. The main features of core c-representations are:

- Core c-representations are easier to compute than general c-representations. While the computation of c-representations requires to solve the constraint satisfaction problem $\mathsf{CSP}(\Delta)$ (cf. (1)) which possibly involves cyclic dependencies among the penalty points, the constraint satisfaction problems of core c-representations are stratified, hence, can be solved successively.
- As being c-representations, core c-representations inherit many beneficial properties from c-representations including the satisfaction of syntax splitting and the solution of the drowning problem.
- Core c-representations provide a unique ranking model that is minimal in some respect while belief bases can have several pareto-minimal c-representations in general. Therewith, we obtain a natural model selection strategy for inductive reasoning based on so-called *minimal core c-representations*.

Definition 3 (Core c-Representation). *Let Δ be a consistent belief base. If $\eta \in \mathbb{N}_0^n$ is a solution of $\mathsf{CSP}_c^\psi(\Delta) = \{\hat{C}_1^\psi, \ldots, \hat{C}_n^\psi\}$ where*

$$\hat{C}_i^\psi: \quad \eta_i > \min\{\textstyle\sum_{\delta_j \in S} \eta_j \mid S \in V_i^\psi\}, \qquad i \in [n], \tag{4}$$

then we call $\kappa_\Delta^{\eta,c}(\omega) = \sum_{\delta_i \in \mathsf{fal}_\Delta(\omega)} \eta_i$, $\omega \in \Omega$, a core c-representation of Δ.

The constraint (4) corresponds to (2) without the negative part on the right-hand side. That is, like general c-representations, core c-representations penalize possible worlds for falsifying conditionals but put "higher" constraints on the penalty point vector η. In particular, we have the following first result.

Proposition 1. *Let Δ be a consistent belief base, and let $\kappa_\Delta^{\eta,c}$ be a core c-representation of Δ. Then, η is positive, i.e., for $i \in [n]$, $\eta_i \geq 1$ holds.*

Because of Proposition 1, core c-representations satisfy the property *inductive enforcement (Ind-Enf)* while general c-representations violate it (cf. [18]):

(Ind-Enf) For $\omega, \omega' \in \Omega$, $\mathsf{fal}_\Delta(\omega) \subsetneq \mathsf{fal}_\Delta(\omega')$ implies $\kappa(\omega) < \kappa(\omega')$.

Note that we use the reduced constraint inducing sets V_i^ψ in (4). While the application of the rewriting rules R1-R6 does not affect the solution set of $\mathsf{CSP}(\Delta)$, applying the rules R1-R6 makes a difference here, as the rewriting rules remove spurious dependencies between η_i and the set V_i which can no longer be resolved after cropping of the negative part of (2) as the next example illustrates.

Example 3. We continue Example 2. $\mathsf{CSP}_c^\psi(\Delta_{\mathsf{ex}})$ is given by

$$\eta_1 > \min\{\eta_3\}, \quad \eta_2 > \min\{0\}, \quad \eta_3 > \min\{0\}, \quad \eta_4 > \min\{\eta_3 + \eta_5\}, \quad \eta_5 > \min\{0\},$$

and has the unique component-wise minimal solution $(2,1,1,3,1)$. Note that if we had not applied the rewriting rules R1-R6, the constraint w.r.t. δ_5 would be $\eta_5 > \min\{\eta_3\}$ which takes no account of the fact that the positive and the negative part in C_5 (cf. Example 1) cancel each other out and, actually, η_5 does not depend on η_3.

Core c-representations are closely related to System Z which becomes clear when characterizing tolerance in terms of the constraint inducing sets V_i.

Proposition 2. *Let Δ be a consistent belief base, and let $T(\Delta) = (\Delta_1, \ldots, \Delta_m)$ be an ordered partition of Δ. Then, $T(\Delta)$ is a tolerance partition of Δ iff, for $k \in [m]$ and every conditional $\delta_i \in \Delta_k$, there is a set $S \in V_i$ with $S \subseteq \bigcup_{j=1}^{k-1} \Delta_j$. In particular, δ_i is tolerated by Δ iff $\emptyset \in V_i$.*

Analog to this, we can define ψ-*tolerance partitions* by replacing V_i by V_i^{ψ}.

Definition 4 (ψ-Tolerance Partition). *Let Δ be a consistent belief base. We call an ordered partition $(\Delta_1, \ldots, \Delta_m)$ of Δ a ψ-tolerance partition of Δ if, for $k \in [m]$ and every conditional $\delta_i \in \Delta_k$, there is $S \in V_i^{\psi}$ with $S \subseteq \bigcup_{j=1}^{k-1} \Delta_j$. If $V_i^{\psi} = \{\emptyset\}$, then we say that δ_i is ψ-tolerated by Δ.*

Tolerance partitions constitute a subclass of ψ-tolerance partitions. As a consequence, ψ-tolerance partitions of consistent belief bases always exist.

Proposition 3. *Let Δ be a consistent belief base. If $T(\Delta)$ is a tolerance partition of Δ, then $T(\Delta)$ is a ψ-tolerance partition of Δ.*

Based on ψ-tolerance partitions and the next lemma, we can formulate a construction method for core c-representations.

Lemma 1. *Let Δ be a non-empty consistent belief base. Then, there is $i \in [n]$ with $V_i^{\psi} = \{\emptyset\}$.*

The crucial point of the construction method for core c-representations is that the penalty points of conditionals in the i-th partitioning set of any ψ-tolerance partition of Δ may be specified solely based on the penalty points of conditionals in lower partitioning sets as captured in the concept of *base functions*.

Definition 5 (Base Function). *Let $T(\Delta) = (\Delta_1, \ldots, \Delta_m)$ be a ψ-tolerance partition of a consistent belief base Δ, and let $\eta \in \mathbb{N}^n$. We define the base function $\phi_{T(\Delta)}^{\eta} : \Delta \to \mathbb{N}_0$ w.r.t. η and $T(\Delta)$ by*

$$\phi_{T(\Delta)}^{\eta}(\delta_i) = \min\{\sum\nolimits_{\delta_j \in S} \eta_j \mid S \in V_i^{\psi} : S \subseteq \bigcup_{j=1}^{k-1} \Delta_j\}, \qquad i \in [n],$$

where k is the index of the partitioning set $\Delta_k \in T(\Delta)$ with $\delta_i \in \Delta_k$.

Proposition 4. *Let Δ be a consistent belief base, and let $T(\Delta) = (\Delta_1, \ldots, \Delta_m)$ be a ψ-tolerance partition of Δ. Further, let $\eta \in \mathbb{N}^n$ satisfy*

$$\eta_i > \phi_{T(\Delta)}^{\eta}(\delta_i), \qquad i \in [n]. \tag{5}$$

Then, $\kappa(\omega) = \sum_{\delta_i \in \mathsf{fal}_\Delta(\omega)} \eta_i$, $\omega \in \Omega$, is a core c-representation of Δ. In particular, this holds for $\eta_i = \phi_{T(\Delta)}^{\eta}(\delta_i) + 1$, $i \in [n]$.

In Proposition 8 we will show that for *every* core c-representation $\kappa_\Delta^{\eta,c}$ of Δ there is a ψ-tolerance partition $T(\Delta)$ such that η satisfies (5) which proves that core c-representations are *stratified*, i.e., the penalty points of core c-representations can be calculated layer by layer. This becomes clear when realizing that, actually, $\phi_{T(\Delta)}^\eta(\delta_i)$ does not depend on the whole vector η but only on its entries referring to the conditionals which occur in $T(\Delta)$ before δ_i.

Example 4. We continue Example 3. The ordered partition $T(\Delta_{\mathsf{ex}}) = (\Delta_1, \Delta_2)$ of Δ_{ex} with $\Delta_1 = \{\delta_2, \delta_3, \delta_5\}$ and $\Delta_2 = \{\delta_1, \delta_4\}$ is a ψ-tolerance partition of Δ_{ex} because $V_i^\psi = \{\emptyset\}$ for $i = 2, 3, 5$ and $\{\delta_3\} \in V_1^\psi \cap \Delta_1$ as well as $\{\delta_3, \delta_5\} \in V_4^\psi \cap \Delta_1$. According to Proposition 4, a penalty point vector which leads to a core c-representation of Δ_{ex} is $\eta = (2, 1, 1, 3, 1)$. This penalty point vector can be obtained as follows: First, we set $\eta_2 = \eta_3 = \eta_5 = 1$ for the conditionals in Δ_1 and then, based on these assignments, we set $\eta_1 = 2 > 1 = \eta_3$ and $\eta_4 = 3 > 1 + 1 = \eta_3 + \eta_5$ for $\delta_1, \delta_4 \in \Delta_2$.

A specific core c-representation that is already known from literature is the so-called *Z-c-representation*.

Definition 6 (Z-c-representation [16]). *Let Δ be consistent belief base, and let $Z(\Delta) = (\Delta_1, \ldots, \Delta_m)$ be the Z-partition of Δ. Further, let $\eta_\Delta^{Z,c} = (\eta_1, \ldots, \eta_n)$ be the penalty point vector with*

$$\eta_i = \phi_{Z(\Delta)}^{\eta_\Delta^{Z,c}}(\delta_i) + 1, \qquad i \in [n]. \tag{6}$$

Then, $\kappa_\Delta^{Z,c}(\omega) = \sum_{\delta_i \in \mathsf{fal}_\Delta(\omega)} \eta_i$, $\omega \in \Omega$, is called the Z-c-representation of Δ.

Proposition 5. *For every consistent belief base Δ, the Z-c-representation $\kappa_\Delta^{Z,c}$ of Δ exists and is unique. Further, $\kappa_\Delta^{Z,c}$ is a core c-representation of Δ.*

The Z-c-representation $\kappa_\Delta^{Z,c}$ illustrates the connection between the System Z ranking model and core c-representations well. Both κ_Δ^Z and $\kappa_\Delta^{Z,c}$ exploit the Z-partition of Δ, but while κ_Δ^Z is defined via a *maximum* of Z-ranks, $\kappa_\Delta^{Z,c}$ makes use of a *summation*. We make up for the obvious statement that core c-representations indeed are c-representations now.

Proposition 6. *Let Δ be a consistent belief base, and let $\kappa_\Delta^{\eta,c}$ be a core c-representation of Δ. Then, $\kappa_\Delta^{\eta,c}$ is also a c-representation of Δ.*

As a direct consequence of Proposition 6, core c-representations of a belief base Δ are ranking models of Δ. It follows that Δ is consistent iff Δ has a core c-representation which is due to the fact that the consistency of Δ concurs with the existence of a tolerance partition of Δ.

Proposition 7. *Let Δ be a belief base. Then, Δ is consistent iff there is a core c-representation of Δ.*

Next, we show that consistent belief bases have a unique minimal core c-representation and discuss this specific core c-representation in more detail.

4   Minimal Core c-Representation

The Z-c-representation $\kappa_{\Delta}^{Z,c}$ is a pragmatic way of defining a unique core c-representation of a consistent belief base Δ. However, $\kappa_{\Delta}^{Z,c}$ does not specify the penalty points in a minimal way. Nevertheless, consistent belief bases have a unique minimal core c-representation where we call a core c-representation $\kappa_{\Delta}^{\eta,c}$ of Δ *minimal* if there is no other core c-representation $\kappa_{\Delta}^{\eta',c}$ of Δ with $\eta_i' < \eta_i$ for some $i \in [n]$. Note that this concept of minimality necessitates a unique pareto-minimal solution $\boldsymbol{\eta}$ of $\mathsf{CSP}_c^{\psi}(\Delta)$ in general and implies $\kappa_{\Delta}^{\eta,c}(\omega) \leq \kappa_{\Delta}^{\eta',c}(\omega)$ for all other solutions $\boldsymbol{\eta}'$ and all $\omega \in \Omega$. That is, among all core c-representations, the minimal core c-representation assigns minimal ranks to possible worlds. The construction of the minimal core c-representation is based on a specific ψ-tolerance partition.

Definition 7 (Canonical ψ-Tolerance Partition). *Let Δ be a consistent belief base, and let $\kappa_{\Delta}^{\eta,c}$ be a core c-representation of Δ. Then, the canonical ψ-tolerance partition $\mathcal{Q}_{\eta}^{\psi}(\Delta) = (\Delta_1, \ldots, \Delta_m)$ of Δ w.r.t. $\boldsymbol{\eta}$ is defined as follows. For $k \in [m]$ and $\delta_i \in \Delta$, we have $\delta_i \in \Delta_k$ iff*

$$\delta_i \in \arg\min\{\phi_{\mathcal{Q}_{\eta}^{\psi}(\Delta)}^{\eta}(\delta_l) \mid \delta_l \in \Delta \setminus \bigcup_{j=1}^{k-1} \Delta_j : \exists S \in V_l^{\psi} \text{ s.t. } S \subseteq \bigcup_{j=1}^{k-1} \Delta_j\}. \quad (7)$$

$\mathcal{Q}_{\eta}^{\psi}(\Delta)$ is a ψ-tolerance partition of Δ because it includes δ_i into Δ_k only if there is $S \in V_i^{\psi}$ with $S \subseteq \bigcup_{j=1}^{k-1} \Delta_j$, and its existence follows from the consistency of Δ. By using $\mathcal{Q}_{\eta}^{\psi}(\Delta)$, we can show the reverse direction of Proposition 4, i.e., we can show that for every core c-representation $\kappa_{\Delta}^{\eta,c}$ of Δ there is a ψ-tolerance partition $\mathcal{T}(\Delta)$ of Δ such that $\eta_i > \phi_{\mathcal{T}(\Delta)}^{\eta}(\delta_i)$ for $i \in [n]$ holds.

Proposition 8. *Let Δ be a consistent belief base, $\kappa_{\Delta}^{\eta,c}$ a core c-representation of Δ, and let $\mathcal{Q}_{\eta}^{\psi}$ be the canonical ψ-tolerance partition of Δ w.r.t. $\boldsymbol{\eta}$. Then,*

$$\phi_{\mathcal{Q}_{\eta}^{\psi}(\Delta)}^{\eta}(\delta_i) = \min\{\sum_{\delta_j \in S} \eta_j \mid S \in V_i^{\psi}\}, \qquad i \in [n],$$

and, thus, $\eta_i > \phi_{\mathcal{Q}_{\eta}^{\psi}(\Delta)}^{\eta}(\delta_i)$ for $i \in [n]$ holds.

With regard to Proposition 7, the following corollary holds.

Corollary 1. *Let Δ be a belief base. Then, Δ is consistent iff there is a ψ-tolerance partition of Δ.*

An important consequence of Proposition 8 is that the computation of a penalty point η_i depends on the penalty points η_j w.r.t. conditionals in previous layers of $\mathcal{Q}_{\eta}^{\psi}(\Delta)$ only. Note that this holds for all core c-representations and, thus, allows for simplification and minimization in a natural way, so that we are now ready to define the minimal core c-representation of Δ.

Input:	Constraint satisfaction problem $\mathsf{CSP}_c^\psi(\Delta)$
Output:	Canonical ψ-tolerance partition $\mathcal{Q}^{mc}(\Delta)$, penalty point vector $\boldsymbol{\eta}_\Delta^{mc}$

```
1    m = 1
2    WHILE Δ ≠ ∅:
3        η_min = 0, Δ' = ∅
4        FOR δ_i ∈ Δ:
5            IF ∃ S ∈ V_i^ψ : S ⊆ ⋃_{j=1}^m Δ_j:
6                η_i = min{∑_{δ_j∈S} η_j | S ∈ V_i^ψ : S ⊆ ⋃_{j=1}^m Δ_j} + 1
7                IF η_min = 0:
8                    η_min = η_i, Δ' = Δ' ∪ {δ_i}
9                ELSE IF η_i = η_min:
10                   Δ' = Δ' ∪ {δ_i}
11               ELSE IF η_i < η_min:
12                   η_min = η_i, Δ' = {δ_i}
13       Δ_m = Δ', Δ = Δ \ Δ_m, m = m + 1
14   RETURN Q^{mc}(Δ) = (Δ_1, ..., Δ_m) and η_Δ^{mc} = (η_1, ..., η_n)
```

Algorithm 1. Computation of the canonical ψ-tolerance partition $\mathcal{Q}^{mc}(\Delta)$ and the penalty point vector $\boldsymbol{\eta}_\Delta^{mc}$ of a (non-empty) consistent belief base Δ.

Definition 8 (Minimal Core c-Representation). *Let Δ be a consistent belief base. We call $\kappa_\Delta^{mc}(\omega) = \sum_{\delta_i \in \mathsf{fal}_\Delta(\omega)} \eta_i$, $\omega \in \Omega$, where $\boldsymbol{\eta}_\Delta^{mc} = (\eta_1, \ldots, \eta_n)$ is defined w.r.t. the canonical ψ-tolerance partition $\mathcal{Q}^{mc}(\Delta) = \mathcal{Q}_{\boldsymbol{\eta}_\Delta^{mc}}^\psi(\Delta)$ by*

$$\eta_i = \phi_{\mathcal{Q}^{mc}(\Delta)}^{\boldsymbol{\eta}_\Delta^{mc}}(\delta_i) + 1, \qquad i \in [n],$$

the minimal core c-representation of Δ. We abbreviate $\phi_\Delta^{mc} = \phi_{\mathcal{Q}^{mc}(\Delta)}^{\boldsymbol{\eta}_\Delta^{mc}}$.

The canonical ψ-tolerance partition $\mathcal{Q}^{mc}(\Delta)$ and the penalty point vector $\boldsymbol{\eta}_\Delta^{mc}$ in Definition 8 can be determined in alternation, beginning with the lowest partitioning set in $\mathcal{Q}^{mc}(\Delta)$. For $k = 1$, (7) reduces to the claim that δ_i is ψ-tolerated by Δ and $\eta_i = 1$ follows. Afterwards, the conditionals δ_i in the second lowest partitioning set ($k = 2$) can be determined because $\phi_\Delta^{mc}(\delta_i)$ solely depends on the penalty points assigned to the conditionals in Δ_1, and so on. The basic idea is to include into the next partitioning set those of the remaining conditionals which are ψ-tolerated by the others and for which the base function makes the weakest possible restriction. Then, the penalty points of the included conditionals are specified in a minimal way among all core c-representations. The whole procedure is shown in pseudocode in Algorithm 1.

Proposition 9. *Let Δ be a consistent belief base. Then, the core c-representation κ_Δ^{mc} induced by the penalty point vector $\boldsymbol{\eta}_\Delta^{mc} = (\eta_1, \ldots, \eta_n)$ is the unique minimal core c-representation of Δ. That is, for all core c-representations $\kappa_\Delta^{\eta',c}$ of Δ, we have $\eta_i \leq \eta_i'$ for $i \in [n]$.*

We give an example.

Table 3. Verified and falsified conditionals from Δ_{ex2} in Example 6.

ω	$\mathrm{ver}_{\Delta_{\mathrm{ex2}}}(\omega)$	$\mathrm{fal}_{\Delta_{\mathrm{ex2}}}(\omega)$	ω	$\mathrm{ver}_{\Delta_{\mathrm{ex2}}}(\omega)$	$\mathrm{fal}_{\Delta_{\mathrm{ex2}}}(\omega)$
abc	$\{\delta_1\}$	$\emptyset$	$\bar{a}bc$	$\emptyset$	$\{\delta_5\}$
$ab\bar{c}$	$\{\delta_2\}$	$\{\delta_1\}$	$\bar{a}b\bar{c}$	$\emptyset$	$\{\delta_5\}$
$a\bar{b}c$	$\{\delta_1, \delta_4\}$	$\{\delta_2\}$	$\bar{a}\bar{b}c$	$\{\delta_5\}$	$\{\delta_4\}$
$a\bar{b}\bar{c}$	$\{\delta_3\}$	$\{\delta_1\}$	$\bar{a}\bar{b}\bar{c}$	$\{\delta_5\}$	$\{\delta_2, \delta_3\}$

Example 5. The vector $(2,1,1,3,1)$ calculated in Example 4 is the penalty point vector $\boldsymbol{\eta}_{\Delta_{\mathrm{ex}}}^{mc}$ of the minimal core c-representation $\kappa_{\Delta_{\mathrm{ex}}}^{mc}$ of Δ_{ex}. However, the ψ-tolerance partition $\mathcal{Q}^{mc}(\Delta_{\mathrm{ex}})$ differs from the ψ-tolerance partition $\mathcal{T}(\Delta_{\mathrm{ex}})$ calculated in Example 4. For $\mathcal{Q}^{mc}(\Delta_{\mathrm{ex}})$, we obtain $\Delta_1 = \{\delta_2, \delta_3, \delta_5\}$ as in $\mathcal{T}(\Delta_{\mathrm{ex}})$. But then, only δ_1 satisfies the minimization criterion in (7) because $\eta_3 < \eta_3 + \eta_5$ holds, which is why $\Delta_2 = \{\delta_1\}$ and $\Delta_3 = \{\delta_4\}$ in $\mathcal{Q}^{mc}(\Delta_{\mathrm{ex}})$. Although the merging of Δ_1 and Δ_2, which distinguishes $\mathcal{T}(\Delta_{\mathrm{ex}})$ from $\mathcal{Q}^{mc}(\Delta_{\mathrm{ex}})$, does not make a difference to the penalty point assignments here, there are examples in which it is necessary to take the minimization in (7) into account (cf. Example 6).

In a second example we show that the minimal core c-representation is different from the Z-c-representation in general. Note that this would also hold if no constraint reduction ψ was applied before.

Example 6. We consider the belief base $\Delta_{\mathrm{ex2}} = \{\delta_1, \ldots, \delta_5\}$ with

$$\delta_1 = (c|a), \quad \delta_2 = (ab\bar{c}|ab\bar{c} \vee a\bar{b}c \vee \bar{a}b\bar{c}), \quad \delta_3 = (a|\bar{b}\bar{c}), \quad \delta_4 = (a|\bar{b}c), \quad \delta_5 = (\bar{b}|\bar{a}).$$

The sets $\mathrm{ver}_{\Delta_{\mathrm{ex2}}}(\omega)$ and $\mathrm{fal}_{\Delta_{\mathrm{ex2}}}(\omega)$ are shown in Table 3, and $\mathrm{CSP}_c^{\psi}(\Delta_{\mathrm{ex2}})$ is

$$\eta_1 > \min\{0\}, \quad \eta_2, \eta_3 > \min\{\eta_1\}, \quad \eta_4 > \min\{\eta_2\}, \quad \eta_5 > \min\{\eta_2 + \eta_3, \eta_4\}.$$

While the Z-partition of Δ_{ex2} is $Z(\Delta_{\mathrm{ex2}}) = (\{\delta_1\}, \{\delta_2, \delta_3\}, \{\delta_4, \delta_5\})$ and, hence, the penalty point vector of the Z-c-representation of Δ_{ex2} is $\boldsymbol{\eta}_{\Delta_{\mathrm{ex2}}}^{Z,c} = (1,2,2,3,5)$, we have $\mathcal{Q}^{mc}(\Delta_{\mathrm{ex2}}) = (\{\delta_1\}, \{\delta_2, \delta_3\}, \{\delta_4\}, \{\delta_5\})$, and the minimal core c-representation $\kappa_{\Delta_{\mathrm{ex2}}}^{mc}$ of Δ_{ex2} is given by $\boldsymbol{\eta}_{\Delta_{\mathrm{ex2}}}^{mc} = (1,2,2,3,4)$. The difference here is that the Z-c-representation assigns the penalty points to δ_4 and δ_5 at the same time because they occur in the same partitioning set in $Z(\Delta_{\mathrm{ex2}})$. This means that we have to specify η_5 in a way that $\eta_5 > \eta_2 + \eta_3$ holds in order to satisfy the constraint $\eta_5 > \min\{\eta_2 + \eta_3, \eta_4\}$ because η_4 is not known when η_5 is specified. The minimal core c-representation assigns a penalty point to δ_4 before δ_5 instead, because η_4 is (potentially) smaller than η_5, so that it suffices for η_5 to satisfy $\eta_5 > \eta_4$ which leads to a smaller value of η_5 in this case. For comparison, the System Z ranking model of Δ_{ex2} is given by $(Z(\delta_1), \ldots, Z(\delta_5)) = (1,2,2,3,3)$ and assigns lower ranks than $\kappa_{\Delta_{\mathrm{ex2}}}^{mc}$ but it is not a c-representation.

Eventually, we note that $\mathcal{Q}^{mc}(\Delta)$ orders the conditionals from Δ w.r.t. their penalty point values that refer to the minimal core c-representation of Δ.

Table 4. Inference properties which are satisfied ($\checkmark$) or violated ($-$) by the inductive inference operators mentioned in this paper (System P inference $\mathcal{I}^P$, System Z inference $\mathcal{I}^Z$, skeptical c-inference $\mathcal{I}^c$, and c-core closure $\mathcal{I}^{mc}$).

	$\mathcal{I}^P$	$\mathcal{I}^Z$	$\mathcal{I}^c$	$\mathcal{I}^{mc}$
System P	$\checkmark$	$\checkmark$	$\checkmark$	$\checkmark$
(wSM)	$\checkmark$	$\checkmark$	$\checkmark$	$\checkmark$
(SM)	$\checkmark$	$-$	$-$	$-$
(Rel)	$\checkmark$	$\checkmark$	$\checkmark$	$\checkmark$
(Ind)	$-$	$-$	$\checkmark$	$\checkmark$
(SynSplit)	$-$	$-$	$\checkmark$	$\checkmark$
(CP)	$\checkmark$	$\checkmark$	$\checkmark$	$\checkmark$
(wRM)	$-$	$\checkmark$	$\checkmark$	$\checkmark$
(RM)	$-$	$\checkmark$	$-$	$\checkmark$

Proposition 10. *Let Δ be a consistent belief base, let κ_Δ^{mc} be the minimal core c-representation of Δ with $\boldsymbol{\eta}_\Delta^{mc} = (\eta_1, \ldots, \eta_n)$, and let $\mathcal{Q}^{mc}(\Delta) = (\Delta_1, \ldots, \Delta_m)$. Further, let $\delta_i \in \Delta_k$ and $\delta_j \in \Delta_l$ where $k, l \in [m]$. If $k = l$, then $\eta_i = \eta_j$, and if $k < l$, then $\eta_i < \eta_j$.*

In the next section we use the minimal core c-representation to define a novel inductive inference operation which we call *c-core closure*.

5   c-Core Closure Inference

We define an inference operator which selects for each consistent belief base Δ its unique minimal core c-representation κ_Δ^{mc}.

Definition 9 (c-Core Closure). *Let Δ be a consistent belief base, and let $A, B \in \mathcal{L}(\Sigma)$. We define the c-core closure inference operator $\mathcal{I}^{mc} \colon \Delta \mapsto \,\mid\!\sim_\Delta^{mc}$ by $A \mid\!\sim_\Delta^{mc} B$ if $A \mid\!\sim_{\kappa_\Delta^{mc}} B$ (cf. (3)) where κ_Δ^{mc} is the minimal core c-representation of Δ.*

c-Core closure inherits several inference properties which hold for arbitrary ranking models resp. c-representations[3] including System P and syntax splitting [17] and does not suffer from the drowning problem [15]. Like System Z and skeptical c-inference, c-core closure violates (SM) (cf. Example 7). With *weak semi-monotony (wSM)*, we propose a novel variant of (SM) which coincides with (SM) for the special case $A = \top$ and which is satisfied by c-core closure:

(wSM) $\top \mid\!\sim_\Delta^{\mathcal{I}} B$ and $\Delta \subseteq \Delta'$ implies $\top \mid\!\sim_{\Delta'}^{\mathcal{I}} B$.

---

[3] To be more precise, hereby we mean that $\mid\!\sim_\Delta^{mc}$ inherits the properties which hold for arbitrary $\mid\!\sim_\kappa$ (cf. (3)) where κ is a ranking model resp. c-representation of Δ.

Table 5. Minimal core c-representations of Δ_{ex3} and Δ'_{ex3} from Example 7.

ω	$\text{ver}_{\Delta'_{\text{ex3}}}(\omega)$	$\text{fal}_{\Delta'_{\text{ex3}}}(\omega)$	$\kappa^{mc}_{\Delta_{\text{ex3}}}(\omega)$	$\kappa^{mc}_{\Delta'_{\text{ex3}}}(\omega)$
abc	$\{\delta_1, \delta_2\}$	$\{\delta_3\}$	0	2
$ab\bar{c}$	$\{\delta_1, \delta_3\}$	$\{\delta_2\}$	1	1
$a\bar{b}c$	$\emptyset$	$\{\delta_1, \delta_3\}$	1	4
$a\bar{b}\bar{c}$	$\{\delta_3\}$	$\{\delta_1\}$	1	2
$\bar{a}bc$	$\{\delta_2\}$	$\emptyset$	0	0
$\bar{a}b\bar{c}$	$\emptyset$	$\{\delta_2\}$	1	1
$\bar{a}\bar{b}c$	$\emptyset$	$\emptyset$	0	0
$\bar{a}\bar{b}\bar{c}$	$\emptyset$	$\emptyset$	0	0

Proposition 11. *Like System P, System Z, and skeptical c-inference, c-core closure satisfies both (CP) (cf. Sect. 2) and (wSM).*

Proposition 11 states, among others, that the System Z ranking model and c-representations maintain most plausible beliefs, i.e., for instance in terms of the minimal core c-representation, if $\Delta \subseteq \Delta'$, then $\text{Bel}(\kappa^{mc}_\Delta) \subseteq \text{Bel}(\kappa^{mc}_{\Delta'})$.

Example 7. We consider the belief bases $\Delta_{\text{ex3}} = \{\delta_1, \delta_2\}$ and $\Delta'_{\text{ex3}} = \Delta_{\text{ex3}} \cup \{\delta_3\}$ with $\delta_1 = (b|a)$, $\delta_2 = (c|b)$, and $\delta_3 = (\bar{c}|a)$. Then, $\text{CSP}^\psi_c(\Delta_{\text{ex3}}) = \{\eta_1 > 0, \eta_2 > 0\}$ and $\text{CSP}^\psi_c(\Delta'_{\text{ex3}}) = \{\eta_1 > \min\{\eta_2, \eta_3\}, \eta_2 > 0, \eta_3 > \min\{\eta_1, \eta_2\}\}$ (cf. Table 5) so that the minimal core c-representations are given by $\boldsymbol{\eta}^{mc}_{\Delta_{\text{ex3}}} = (1, 1)$ respectively by $\boldsymbol{\eta}^{mc}_{\Delta'_{\text{ex3}}} = (2, 1, 2)$. The c-representations themselves are also shown in Table 5.

While $a \vdash\!\!\!\sim^{mc}_{\Delta_{\text{ex3}}} c$ holds because of $\kappa^{mc}_{\Delta_{\text{ex3}}}(ac) = 0 < 1 = \kappa^{mc}_{\Delta_{\text{ex3}}}(a\bar{c})$, we have $a \not\vdash\!\!\!\sim^{mc}_{\Delta'_{\text{ex3}}} c$ because of $\kappa^{mc}_{\Delta'_{\text{ex3}}}(ac) = 2 > 1 = \kappa^{mc}_{\Delta'_{\text{ex3}}}(a\bar{c})$ (even $a \vdash\!\!\!\sim^{mc}_{\Delta'_{\text{ex3}}} \bar{c}$) which proves that $\mathcal{I}^{mc}$ does not satisfy (SM) in general. However, for the most plausible beliefs, we have $\text{Bel}(\kappa^{mc}_{\Delta_{\text{ex3}}}) = \text{Cn}(abc \vee \bar{a}(\bar{b} \vee c)) \subseteq \text{Cn}(\bar{a}(\bar{b} \vee c)) = \text{Bel}(\kappa^{mc}_{\Delta'_{\text{ex3}}})$, where $\text{Cn}(A)$ is the deductive closure of $A \in \mathcal{L}(\Sigma)$, which is in compliance with (wSM).

Eventually, we note that c-core closure satisfies *weak rational monotony (wRM)* and also *rational monotony (RM)* (cf. [7]). This is worth mentioning because it distinguishes c-core closure from skeptical c-inference which satisfies (wRM) but violates (RM).

Proposition 12. *c-Core closure satisfies rational monotony (RM) and, therewith, also* weak rational monotony (wRM).

Table 4 gives an overview of the inference properties which are satisfied resp. violated by the inference formalisms mentioned in this paper. It shows that c-core closure differs from all the other inference formalisms in its properties.

In [11], inference relations which satisfy System P, (RM), and (CP) are called *basic defeasible entailment relations*. Therefore, c-core closure can be classified as a *basic defeasible entailment operator*. To sum up, c-core closure benefits from the

Table 6. Verified and falsified conditionals from Δ_{ex4} in Example 8.

ω	$\text{ver}_{\Delta_{ex4}}(\omega)$	$\text{fal}_{\Delta_{ex4}}(\omega)$	ω	$\text{ver}_{\Delta_{ex4}}(\omega)$	$\text{fal}_{\Delta_{ex4}}(\omega)$
abc	$\{\delta_1, \delta_2\}$	$\emptyset$	$\bar{a}bc$	$\emptyset$	$\emptyset$
$ab\bar{c}$	$\emptyset$	$\{\delta_1, \delta_2\}$	$\bar{a}b\bar{c}$	$\emptyset$	$\emptyset$
$a\bar{b}c$	$\{\delta_1, \delta_3\}$	$\emptyset$	$\bar{a}\bar{b}c$	$\emptyset$	$\emptyset$
$a\bar{b}\bar{c}$	$\emptyset$	$\{\delta_1, \delta_3\}$	$\bar{a}\bar{b}\bar{c}$	$\emptyset$	$\emptyset$

simple structure of the minimal core c-representations which are stratified like System Z while it inherits beneficial properties from the more complex framework of general c-reasoning.

6 Discussion and Related Work

Core c-representations $\kappa_\Delta^{\eta,c}$ are positive in the sense that $\eta_i > 0$ for $i \in [n]$ holds (cf. Proposition 1). This means that every conditional in Δ has an impact on $\kappa_\Delta^{\eta,c}$. However, there might be cases in which penalty points $\eta_i = 0$ are reasonable. This is the case when there are "redundant" conditionals in Δ where it appears to be debatable if they should increase implausibility ranks additionally, like in the next example.

Example 8. We consider $\Delta_{ex4} = \{(c|a), (c|ab), (c|a\bar{b})\}$. Then, $\text{CSP}(\Delta_{ex4})$ is

$$\eta_1 > -\min\{\eta_2, \eta_3\}, \qquad \eta_2, \eta_3 > -\eta_1,$$

and has the pareto-minimal solutions $(1, 0, 0)$ and $(0, 1, 1)$ (cf. Table 6). If we carefully look at Table 6, then we see that only the possible worlds $ab\bar{c}$ and $a\bar{b}\bar{c}$ are penalized, either by $\eta_1 + \eta_2$ or $\eta_1 + \eta_3$. This, and the fact that $(0, 1, 1)$ is a solution vector of $\text{CSP}(\Delta_{ex4})$, can be interpreted as δ_1 being redundant because the penalization by η_1 can be mimicked by the penalty points η_2 and η_3, so that δ_1 could be removed from Δ_{ex4} without altering the set of c-representations. The minimal core c-representation of Δ_{ex4} is characterized by $\eta_{\Delta_{ex4}}^{mc} = (1, 1, 1)$ which penalizes $ab\bar{c}$ and $a\bar{b}\bar{c}$ seemingly unnecessarily twice, though.

Example 8 suggests to remove redundant conditionals from belief bases before performing core c-reasoning. However, clarifying what "redundant" means is a hard problem in general. As an alternative, in [13] the authors define a subclass of belief bases, the so-called *minimal core sets*, which exclude belief bases Δ where $\eta_i = 0$ for conditionals $\delta_i \in \Delta$ is possible.

Definition 10 (Minimal Core Set [13]). *A consistent belief base Δ is a minimal core set if for every conditional $(B|A) \in \Delta$ its negation $(\overline{B}|A)$ is tolerated by $\Delta \setminus \{(B|A)\}$ or, equivalently, if for every $(B|A) \in \Delta$ there is a possible world which falsifies $(B|A)$ but no other conditional from Δ.*

In other words, Δ is a minimal core set iff $\emptyset \in F_i$ for $i \in [n]$. Consequently, (2) coincides with (4) and we have the following proposition.

Proposition 13. *Let Δ be a minimal core set. Then, κ_Δ^η is a c-representation of Δ iff it is a core c-representation of Δ. Consequently, Δ has a unique minimal c-representation, namely the minimal core c-representation κ_Δ^{mc}.*

Minimal core sets do not precisely characterize the belief bases which enforce the penalty points to be positive, though, and, conversely, not all belief bases which allow for non-positive penalty points automatically involve "redundant" conditionals (cf. Example 5 in [13]). Thus, a thorough investigation of this issue remains for future work.

The main topic of [13] is the derivation of a ranking model κ^* of a consistent belief base Δ from the ϵ-*semantics* [12] of conditionals and the *principle of maximum entropy* [23] from probability theory. The basic idea is to consider a set of parameterized probability distributions $\{\mathcal{P}_\epsilon^*\}$ over Ω with parameter $\epsilon > 0$ where each $\mathcal{P}_\epsilon^*$ is an ϵ-*model* of Δ, i.e., it satisfies $\mathcal{P}_\epsilon^*(B_i|A_i) \geq 1 - \epsilon$ for $i \in [n]$, and maximizes the entropy $\mathcal{H}(\mathcal{P}_\epsilon) = -\sum_{\omega \in \Omega} \mathcal{P}_\epsilon(\omega) \cdot \log \mathcal{P}_\epsilon(\omega)$ among all ϵ-models $\mathcal{P}_\epsilon$ of Δ. Then, κ^* is the ranking model of Δ which satisfies $A \mathrel{|\!\sim}_{\kappa^*} B$ iff $\lim_{\epsilon \to 0} \mathcal{P}_\epsilon^*(B|A) = 1$. The authors of [13] study this ranking model especially for minimal core sets Δ and it turns out that κ^* is given by $\kappa^*(\omega) = \sum_{\delta_i \in \mathsf{fal}_\Delta(\omega)} Z^*(\delta_i)$ where $Z^*(\delta_i) = \min_{\omega \in \mathsf{ver}(\delta_i)} \kappa^*(\omega) + 1$ in this case (cf. Equations (18) and (19) in [13]). This coincides with the definition of minimal core c-representations provided that no constraint reduction ψ is applied (cf. Definition 8). Hence, we generalize the ranking model κ^* from [13] to arbitrary consistent belief bases here and embed it into the theory of c-representations so that we provide a more convenient access to κ^* without the need to consider its probabilistic background.

7   Conclusion

In this paper, we identified with core c-representations a subclass of c-representations which constitute a family of ranking models of symbolic conditional belief bases with particularly good inference behavior. Core c-representations are easier to compute than general c-representations as the underlying constraint satisfaction problem is stratified while the constraint satisfaction problem for general c-representations may involve cyclic dependencies. As a consequence, core c-representations provide a unique minimal ranking model of a conditional belief base which makes it possible to define a novel, model-based inference operator that selects for each consistent belief base its minimal core c-representation. We proved that this c-core closure inference operation constitutes a basic defeasible entailment operator and differs from System P inference, System Z inference, as well as skeptical c-inference. Therefore, c-core closure inference synergizes all good properties of c-representations of a specific class while also satisfying rational monotony (RM) and a minimality constraint for the first time.

In future work, we want to investigate to what extent ideas from the construction of the minimal core c-representation can be transferred to the calculation of general c-representations. We would also like to investigate the question whether there is an axiomatization of c-core closure as well as complexity issues.

Acknowledgments. This work was supported by Grant KE 1413/14-1 of the German Research Foundation (DFG) awarded to Gabriele Kern-Isberner.

References

1. Adams, E.W.: Probability and the logic of conditionals. In: Hintikka, J., Suppes, P. (eds.) Aspects of Inductive Logic. Studies in Logic and the Foundations of Mathematics, vol. 43, pp. 265–316. Elsevier (1966)
2. Beierle, C., Eichhorn, C., Kern-Isberner, G.: Skeptical inference based on C-representations and its characterization as a constraint satisfaction problem. In: Gyssens, M., Simari, G. (eds.) FoIKS 2016. LNCS, vol. 9616, pp. 65–82. Springer, Cham (2016). https://doi.org/10.1007/978-3-319-30024-5_4
3. Beierle, C., Eichhorn, C., Kern-Isberner, G., Kutsch, S.: Properties of skeptical C-inference for conditional knowledge bases and its realization as a constraint satisfaction problem. Ann. Math. Artif. Intell. **83**(3–4), 247–275 (2018)
4. Beierle, C., Eichhorn, C., Kern-Isberner, G., Kutsch, S.: Properties and interrelationships of skeptical, weakly skeptical, and credulous inference induced by classes of minimal models. Artif. Intell. **297** (2021)
5. Beierle, C., Haldimann, J., Kern-Isberner, G.: Semantic splitting of conditional belief bases. In: Raschke, A., Riccobene, E., Schewe, K.-D. (eds.) Logic, Computation and Rigorous Methods. LNCS, vol. 12750, pp. 82–95. Springer, Cham (2021). https://doi.org/10.1007/978-3-030-76020-5_5
6. Beierle, C., Hermsen, R., Kern-Isberner, G.: Observations on the minimality of ranking functions for qualitative conditional knowledge bases and their computation. In: Eberle, W., Boonthum-Denecke, C. (eds.) Proceedings of the 27th International FLAIRS Conference, pp. 480–485. AAAI Press (2014)
7. Beierle, C., Kutsch, S., Breuers, H.: On rational monotony and weak rational monotony for inference relations induced by sets of minimal C-representations. In: Barták, R., Brawner, K.W. (eds.) Proceedings of the 32nd International FLAIRS Conference, pp. 458–463. AAAI Press (2019)
8. Beierle, C., Kutsch, S., Sauerwald, K.: Compilation of static and evolving conditional knowledge bases for computing induced nonmonotonic inference relations. Ann. Math. Artif. Intell. **87**(1–2), 5–41 (2019)
9. Benferhat, S., Dubois, D., Prade, H.: Possibilistic logic: from nonmonotonicity to logic programming. In: Clarke, M., Kruse, R., Moral, S. (eds.) ECSQARU 1993. LNCS, vol. 747, pp. 17–24. Springer, Heidelberg (1993). https://doi.org/10.1007/BFb0028177
10. Bochman, A.: A Logical Theory of Nonmonotonic Inference and Belief Change - Numerical Methods. Springer, Heidelberg (2001). https://doi.org/10.1007/978-3-662-04560-2
11. Casini, G., Meyer, T., Varzinczak, I.: Taking defeasible entailment beyond rational closure. In: Calimeri, F., Leone, N., Manna, M. (eds.) JELIA 2019. LNCS (LNAI), vol. 11468, pp. 182–197. Springer, Cham (2019). https://doi.org/10.1007/978-3-030-19570-0_12

12. Geffner, H., Pearl, J.: A framework for reasoning with defaults. In: Kyburg, H.E., Loui, R.P., Carlson, G.N. (eds.) Knowledge Representation and Defeasible Reasoning. Studies in Cognitive Systems, vol. 5, pp. 69–87. Springer, Dordrecht (1990). https://doi.org/10.1007/978-94-009-0553-5_3

13. Goldszmidt, M., Morris, P.H., Pearl, J.: A maximum entropy approach to nonmonotonic reasoning. In: Shrobe, H.E., Dietterich, T.G., Swartout, W.R. (eds.) Proceedings of the 8th National Conference on Artificial Intelligence, pp. 646–652. AAAI Press/MIT Press (1990)

14. Goldszmidt, M., Pearl, J.: On the Relation Between Rational Closure and System Z. CSD (Series). UCLA Computer Science Department (1991)

15. Heyninck, J., Kern-Isberner, G., Meyer, T.A., Haldimann, J.P., Beierle, C.: Conditional syntax splitting for non-monotonic inference operators. In: Williams, B., Chen, Y., Neville, J. (eds.) Proceedings of the 37th AAAI Conference on Artificial Intelligence, pp. 6416–6424. AAAI Press (2023)

16. Kern-Isberner, G.: A thorough axiomatization of a principle of conditional preservation in belief revision. Ann. Math. Artif. Intell. $40(1–2)$, 127–164 (2004)

17. Kern-Isberner, G., Beierle, C., Brewka, G.: Syntax splitting = relevance + independence: new postulates for nonmonotonic reasoning from conditional belief bases. In: Calvanese, D., Erdem, E., Thielscher, M. (eds.) Proceedings of the 17th International Conference on Principles of Knowledge Representation and Reasoning (KR 2020), pp. 560–571 (2020)

18. Kern-Isberner, G., Eichhorn, C.: Structural inference from conditional knowledge bases. Stud. Log. $102(4)$, 751–769 (2014)

19. Kraus, S., Lehmann, D., Magidor, M.: Nonmonotonic reasoning, preferential models and cumulative logics. Artif. Intell. $44(1–2)$, 167–207 (1990)

20. Lehmann, D., Magidor, M.: What does a conditional knowledge base entail? Artif. Intell. $55(1)$, 1–60 (1992)

21. Lukasiewicz, T.: Weak nonmonotonic probabilistic logics. Artif. Intell. $168(1–2)$, 119–161 (2005)

22. Parikh, R.: Beliefs, belief revision, and splitting languages, pp. 266–278. Center for the Study of Language and Information (1999)

23. Paris, J.B.: Common sense and maximum entropy. Synth $117(1)$, 75–93 (1998)

24. Pearl, J.: System Z: a natural ordering of defaults with tractable applications to nonmonotonic reasoning. In: Probabilistic and Causal Inference (1990)

25. Reiter, R.: A logic for default reasoning. Artif. Intell. $13(1–2)$, 81–132 (1980)

26. Schurz, G., Thorn, P.D.: Reward versus risk in uncertain inference: theorems and simulations. Rev. Symb. Log. $5(4)$, 574–612 (2012)

27. Spohn, W.: The Laws of Belief – Ranking Theory and its Philosophical Applications. Oxford University Press, Oxford (2014)

28. Wilhelm, M., Sezgin, M., Kern-Isberner, G., Haldimann, J., Beierle, C., Heyninck, J.: Splitting techniques for conditional belief bases in the context of c-representations. In: Gaggl, S.A., Martinez, M.V., Ortiz, M. (eds.) JELIA 2023. LNCS, vol. 14281, pp. 462–477. Springer, Cham (2023). https://doi.org/10.1007/978-3-031-43619-2_32

Knowledge Representation
and Reasoning

On Naive Labellings – Realizability, Construction and Patterns of Redundancy

Ringo Baumann[1,2] and Anne-Marie Heine[1,2(✉)]

[1] Leipzig University, Leipzig, Germany
{baumann,aheine}@informatik.uni-leipzig.de
[2] Center for Scalable Data Analytics and Artificial Intelligence (ScaDS.AI),
Dresden/Leipzig, Germany

Abstract. This paper is engaged with realizability in the realm of abstract argumentation. In particular, we deal with naive labellings forming the basis for a well-established family of semantics, namely the naivity-based semantics. Consequently, characterizing this semantics is a crucial step towards delineating further naivety-based semantics such as stable and stage semantics. We provide easily verifiable criteria deciding whether a certain set of labellings can be the naive outcome of a Dungean framework. Apart from this we also present a standard construction in the affirmative case. This means, constructing a witnessing framework for a realizable set of naive labelling is possible paving the way for applications. Finally, we offer insights into representational freedom and prove a kernel-based characterization for strong equivalence, which substantially differ from its extension-based counterpart.

Keywords: Knowledge Representation · Argumentation · Labellings

1 Introduction

Understanding the intrinsic properties of potential representation formalisms is crucial for making well-informed choices. For argumentation formalisms [3] several decisive properties including *complexity* of standard decision problems [19], *forgetting* [7,21], *enforcing* [8] or *realizability* [18] have already been studied, mainly in the context of so-called extension-based semantics [4]. The topic of realizability is important for several purposes such as revision tasks and dynamic evolvements in general [1,15,22]. In case of revision we are typically faced with the problem of modifying a given framework F in such a way that a revised version of it possesses a certain desired set of acceptable positions. Now, before trying to do this revision in a certain minimal way it is essential to know whether the desired set is realizable at all.

In this paper we consider the realizability of so-called *naive labellings* [2,14]. It's worth noting that having characterization theorems for extension-based semantics doesn't significantly aid in characterizing their labelling-based counterparts. This is mainly due to the fact that the latter provides one with strictly

A. Meier and M. Ortiz (Eds.): FoIKS 2024, LNCS 14589, pp. 125–143, 2024.
https://doi.org/10.1007/978-3-031-56940-1_7

more information. First of all, they are more restrictive as they assign a status to any argument. Thus, the possible number of realizing frameworks is inherently limited. Secondly, they are more fine-grained as they explicitly differentiate between two cases of non-acceptance, namely *rejected* and *undecided*. We provide easily verifiable criteria to determine whether a given set of labellings can be the naive outcome of a Dungean framework [16]. Additionally, in cases where this is affirmative, we offer a standard construction. This means, constructing a witnessing framework for a realizable set of naive labelling is possible paving the way for applications. Finally, we offer insights into representational freedom and establish a kernel-based characterization for strong equivalence, which substantially differ from its extension-based counterpart.

2   Formal Preliminaries

2.1   Argumentation Frameworks and Semantics

We start with the necessary background on abstract argumentation. An *argumentation framework* (AF) is a pair $F = (A, R)$ where A, the set of arguments, is a finite subset of a fixed infinite background set $\mathcal{U}$, and $R \subseteq A \times A$. The set of all finite AFs is denoted by $\mathcal{F}$ (cf. [11,12] for a treatment of infinite AFs). An *extension-based semantics* $\mathcal{E}_\sigma : \mathcal{F} \to 2^{2^{\mathcal{U}}}$ is a function which assigns to any AF $F = (A, R)$ a set of sets of arguments denoted by $\mathcal{E}_\sigma(F) \subseteq 2^A$. Each one of them, a so-called σ-*extension*, is considered to be acceptable with respect to F. The most basic criteria is *conflict-freeness* (*cf*) which guarantees no internal conflicts. Maximizing them w.r.t. subset inclusion yields the concept of *naive semantics* (*na*).

Definition 1. *Let $F = (A, R)$ be an AF and $E \subseteq A$.*

1. $E \in \mathcal{E}_{cf}(F)$ *iff there are no $a, b \in A$, s.t. $(a, b) \in R$ and*
2. $E \in \mathcal{E}_{na}(F)$ *iff E is $\subseteq$-maximal in $\mathcal{E}_{cf}(F)$.*

A *labelling-based semantics* $\mathcal{L}_\sigma : \mathcal{F} \to 2^{\left(2^{\mathcal{U}}\right)^3}$ is a function which assigns to any AF $F = (A, R)$ a set of triples of sets of arguments denoted by $\mathcal{L}_\sigma(F) \subseteq \left(2^A\right)^3$. Each one of them, a so-called σ-*labelling* of F, is a triple $L = (I, O, U)$ indicating that arguments in I, O or U are considered to be *accepted (in)*, *rejected (out)* or *undecided* with respect to F. We further assume pairwise disjointness and covering, i.e. $I \cap O = I \cap U = O \cap U = \emptyset$ and $I \cup O \cup U = A$. We use L^I (or $L^I(a)$) to refer to (*a* is an element of) the first component of the labelling L. Analogously for L^O and L^U. We proceed with the central notions of *conflict-free labellings* as well as *naive labellings* [2,14].

Definition 2. *A labelling L of $F = (A, R)$ is called conflict-free if we have:*

1. *If $a, b \in L^I$, then $(a, b) \notin R$, and*   (*no internal conflicts*)
2. *If $a \in L^O$, then there is a $b \in L^I$ with $(b, a) \in R$.*   (*reason for rejecting*)

We now introduce the labelling-based counterpart to conflict-free sets and naive extensions.

Definition 3. *Let $F = (A, R)$ be an AF and $L \in \left(2^A\right)^3$ a labelling of F.*

1. $L \in \mathcal{L}_{cf}(F)$ *iff L is a conflict-free labelling of F and*
2. $L \in \mathcal{L}_{na}(F)$ *iff $L \in \mathcal{L}_{cf}(F)$ and L^I is $\subseteq$-maximal in $\{M^I \mid M \in \mathcal{L}_{cf}(F)\}$.*

Consider the following illustrating example.

Example 1. Consider the following AF F. The introduced extension-based semantics together with its labelling-based counterparts are given below.

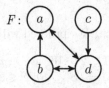

$$\mathcal{E}_{cf}(F) = \{\{a\}, \{b\}, \{c\}, \{d\}, \{a,c\}, \{b,c\}, \emptyset\}$$
$$\mathcal{L}_{cf}(F) = \{(\{a\}, \{d\}, \{b,c\}), (\{a\}, \emptyset, \{b,c,d\}), (\{b\}, \{a,d\}, \{c\}), (\{b\}, \{a\}, \{c,d\}),$$
$$(\{b\}, \{d\}, \{a,c\}), (\{b\}, \emptyset, \{a,c,d\}), (\{c\}, \{d\}, \{a,b\}), (\{c\}, \emptyset, \{a,b,d\}),$$
$$(\{d\}, \{a,b\}, \{c\}), (\{d\}, \{a\}, \{b,c\}), (\{d\}, \{b\}, \{a,c\}), (\{d\}, \emptyset, \{a,b,c\}),$$
$$(\{a,c\}, \{d\}, \{b\}), (\{a,c\}, \emptyset, \{d,b\}), (\{b,c\}, \{a,d\}, \emptyset), (\{b,c\}, \{a\}, \{d\}),$$
$$(\{b,c\}, \{d\}, \{a\}), (\{b,c\}, \emptyset, \{a,d\}), (\emptyset, \emptyset, \{a,b,c,d\})\}$$

$$\mathcal{E}_{na}(F) = \{\{d\}, \{a,c\}, \{b,c\}\}$$
$$\mathcal{L}_{na}(F) = \{(\{d\}, \{a,b\}, \{c\}), (\{d\}, \{a\}, \{b,c\}), (\{d\}, \{b\}, \{a,c\}), (\{d\}, \emptyset, \{a,b,c\}),$$
$$(\{a,c\}, \{d\}, \{b\}), (\{a,c\}, \emptyset, \{d,b\}), (\{b,c\}, \{a,d\}, \emptyset), (\{b,c\}, \{a\}, \{d\}),$$
$$(\{b,c\}, \{d\}, \{a\}), (\{b,c\}, \emptyset, \{a,d\})$$

Please observe that we do not have a match between the numbers of conflict-free/naive extensions and conflict-free/naive labellings. This observation is essential and one reason why realizability results for extension-based semantics do not directly carry over to their labelling-based counterparts.

The following properties relate the in-labels to extensions and vice versa. For more details and explanations please confer [4,5].

Proposition 1. *Given an AF $F = (A, R)$, a set $E \subseteq A$ and a semantics $\sigma \in \{cf, na\}$. In the following we use $E^{\mathcal{L}}$ as shorthand for $(E, E^+, A \setminus (E \cup E^+))$ where E^+ denotes the set $\{b|(a,b) \in R, a \in E\}$.*

1. *If $E \in \mathcal{E}_\sigma(F)$, then $E^{\mathcal{L}} \in \mathcal{L}_\sigma(F)$,*
2. *If $L \in \mathcal{L}_\sigma(F)$, then $L^I \in \mathcal{E}_\sigma(F)$.*

2.2   Realizability in Abstract Argumentation

The first formal consideration of realizability regarding Dungean frameworks was given by Dunne et al. [17,18]. For argumentation semantics we say that a certain set $\mathbb{S}$ is *realizable*, if there is an AF F such that its set of extensions/labellings coincides with $\mathbb{S}$. Collecting all realizable sets defines the concept of a *signature*. Consider the following definition. We mention that only $n = 1$ (extension-case) and $n = 3$ (labelling-case) will be relevant for this paper.

Definition 4. *Given a semantics $\sigma : \mathcal{F} \to 2^{\left(2^{\mathcal{U}}\right)^n}$. A set $\mathbb{S} \subseteq \left(2^{\mathcal{U}}\right)^n$ is σ-realizable if there is an AF $F \in \mathcal{F}$, s.t. $\sigma(F) = \mathbb{S}$. Moreover, the σ-signature is defined as $\Sigma_\sigma = \{\sigma(F) \mid F \in \mathcal{F}\}$.*

Extension-Based Semantics. We proceed with some further notation [18].

Definition 5. *Given a finite $\mathbb{S} \subseteq 2^{\mathcal{U}}$. We use $Args_{\mathbb{S}} = \bigcup_{S \in \mathbb{S}} S$, $Pairs_{\mathbb{S}} = \{(a,b) \mid \exists S \in \mathbb{S} : \{a,b\} \subseteq S\}$ and $dcl(\mathbb{S}) = \{S' \subseteq S \mid S \in \mathbb{S}\}$ (downward-closure of $\mathbb{S}$).*

Example 2. Let $\mathbb{S} = \{\{d\}, \{a,c\}, \{b,c\}\}$. Then $Args_{\mathbb{S}} = \{a,b,c,d\}$ and $Pairs_{\mathbb{S}} = \{(a,a), (b,b), (c,c), (d,d), (a,c), (b,c)\} \cup \{(c,a), (c,b)\}$ as well as $dcl(\mathbb{S}) = \{\emptyset, \{a\}, \{b\}, \{c\}, \{d\}, \{a,c\}, \{b,c\}\}$.

Definition 6. *Given a finite $\mathbb{S} \subseteq 2^{\mathcal{U}}$. It is called downward-closed if $\mathbb{S} = dcl(\mathbb{S})$ and incomparable if $\mathbb{S}$ is a $\subseteq$-antichain (i.e. for each pair of sets $S_1, S_2 \in \mathbb{S}$ holds $S_1 \not\subseteq S_2$ and $S_2 \not\subseteq S_1$). Additionally $\mathbb{S}$ is called tight whenever: for all $S \in \mathbb{S}$ and $x \in Args_{\mathbb{S}}$ we have: if $S \cup \{x\} \notin \mathbb{S}$, then there exists an $s \in S$ such that $(x,s) \notin Pairs_{\mathbb{S}}$.*

Example 3. Let $\mathbb{S} = \{\{d\}, \{a,c\}, \{b,c\}\}$. Then Obviously, $dcl(\mathbb{S}) \neq \mathbb{S}$. Hence, $\mathbb{S}$ is not downward-closed. However $\mathbb{S}$ is incomparable as there are no proper subset relations as well as tight. To exemplify this consider the set $\{a,c\} \in \mathbb{S}$. If $x \in \{a,c\}$ it follows $S \cup \{x\} = S \in \mathbb{S}$ and we have nothing to show. In the case $x \in \{b,d\}$ however $S \cup \{x\} \notin \mathbb{S}$ and we find $(b,a), (d,a) \notin Pairs_{\mathbb{S}}$.

Now, we present the already known characterization theorems [6,18].

Theorem 1. *Given a finite extension-set $\mathbb{S} \subseteq 2^{\mathcal{U}}$, then*

1. *$\mathbb{S} \in \Sigma_{\mathcal{E}_{cf}} \Leftrightarrow \mathbb{S}$ is a non-empty, downward-closed, and tight extension-set,*
2. *$\mathbb{S} \in \Sigma_{\mathcal{E}_{na}} \Leftrightarrow \mathbb{S}$ is a non-empty, incomparable extension-set and $dcl(\mathbb{S})$ is tight.*

Labelling-Based Semantics. Now let us turn to labelling-based semantics. Again, we start with some relevant notations and shorthands. Moreover, we introduce the central concept of a *labelling-set* and some labelling-properties later on used to characterized the realizabiliy. These concept were established in [9].

Definition 7. *Given a finite set* $\mathbb{L} \subseteq (2^{\mathcal{U}})^3$. *We use* $\mathbb{L}^I$, $\mathbb{L}^O$ *and* $\mathbb{L}^U$ *to denote* $\{L^I \mid L \in \mathbb{L}\}$, $\{L^O \mid L \in \mathbb{L}\}$ *or* $\{L^U \mid L \in \mathbb{L}\}$, *respectively and we set* $Args_{\mathbb{L}} = \bigcup_{L \in \mathbb{L}} (L^I \cup L^O \cup L^U)$. *Moreover, we say that* $\mathbb{L}$ *is a labelling-set if*

1. $L_1^I \cup L_1^O \cup L_1^U = L_2^I \cup L_2^O \cup L_2^U$ *for any* $L_1, L_2 \in \mathbb{L}$ *and,* *(same arguments)*
2. $L_1^I \cap L_1^O = L_1^I \cap L_1^U = L_1^O \cap L_1^U = \emptyset$ *for each* $L_1 \in \mathbb{L}$. *(disjointness)*

Finally for a fixed set of arguments $E \subseteq \mathcal{U}$ *we use*

- $\mathbb{L}_{I=E} = \{L \mid L \in \mathbb{L}, L^I = E\}$, *and* *(corresponding labellings)*
- $\mathbb{L}_{I=E}^O = \{L^O \mid L \in \mathbb{L}, L^I = E\}$. *(corresponding out-labels)*

as well as (in case it exists) $\overline{\mathbb{L}}_{I=E}^O$ *for the* $\subseteq$*-greatest element of* $\mathbb{L}_{I=E}^O$ *and* $\overline{\mathbb{L}}_{I=E}$ *for the associated labelling.*

Let us illustrate the introduced concepts with the following example.

Example 4. Consider $\mathbb{L} = \{(\{b,c\}, \{a,d\}, \emptyset), (\{d\}, \{a,b\}, \{c\}), (\{d\}, \{b\}, \{a,c\})\}$. First of all, we observe that $\mathbb{L}$ is indeed a labelling-set as all triples refer to the same arguments, namely a, b, c, d and moreover, for any triple we have that each argument occurs in one of the three sets only. We obtain the following sets:

- $\mathbb{L}^I = \{\{b,c\}, \{d\}\}$, $\mathbb{L}^O = \{\{a,d\}, \{a,b\}, \{b\}\}$ and $\mathbb{L}^U = \{\emptyset, \{c\}, \{a,c\}\}$,
- $\mathbb{L}_{I=\{b,c\}}^O = \{\{a,d\}\}$ and $\mathbb{L}_{I=\{d\}}^O = \{\{a,b\}, \{b\}\}$, and
- $\mathbb{L}_{I=\{b,c\}} = \{(\{b,c\}, \{a,d\}, \emptyset)\}$, $\mathbb{L}_{I=\{d\}} = \{(\{d\}, \{a,b\}, \{c\}), (\{d\}, \{b\}, \{a,c\})\}$,
- $\overline{\mathbb{L}}_{I=\{b,c\}}^O = \{\{a,d\}\}$ and $\overline{\mathbb{L}}_{I=\{d\}}^O = \{\{a,b\}\}$.

Conflict-Free Labellings. The question of realizability regarding conflict-free labellings was recently tackled in [9]. In the following we give a short review on introduced concepts and results as some of them will be relevant for the characterization of naive labellings.

We start with so-called *L-tightness*. A labelling-set $\mathbb{L}$ is L-tight if, first, the greatest out-sets exist, and secondly, the union of two in-sets I_1, I_2 is an in-set too if and only if the greatest out-set regarding I_1 does not share elements with I_2 and vice versa. Intuitively, L-tightness fulfills a similar purpose for labelling-sets as tightness for extensions since it gives a reason why certain sets are not in-labels.

Definition 8. *A labelling-set* $\mathbb{L}$ *is called L-tight, if*

1. *for each* $E \in \mathbb{L}^I$ *we have:* $\mathbb{L}_{I=E}^O$ *possesses a* $\subseteq$*-greatest element, and*
2. *for all* $I_1, I_2 \in \mathbb{L}^I$ *we have:* $I_1 \cup I_2 \in \mathbb{L}^I \Leftrightarrow (\overline{\mathbb{L}}_{I=I_1}^O \cap I_2) \cup (\overline{\mathbb{L}}_{I=I_2}^O \cap I_1) = \emptyset$.

The second relevant property is called *reject-compositionality*. In a nutshell, a labelling-set $\mathbb{L}$ is reject-compositional, if the out-labelled arguments for a given in-labelled set E can be found in the union of out-labels of single arguments in E.

Definition 9. *A labelling-set* $\mathbb{L}$ *is called reject-compositional, if for each* $E \in$ $\mathbb{L}^I$, *we have:*

$$\bigcup \mathbb{L}^O_{I=E} = \bigcup_{a \in E} \bigcup \mathbb{L}^O_{I=\{a\}}.$$

It is important to note that in case of L-tight labelling-sets the equation transforms to $\overline{\mathbb{L}}^O_{I=E} = \bigcup_{a \in E} \overline{\mathbb{L}}^O_{I=\{a\}}$.

Now we have everything at hand to present the main characterization theorem [9, Theorem 3].

Theorem 2. *Given a labelling-set* $\mathbb{L} \subseteq \left(2^{\mathcal{U}}\right)^3$ *we have*

$\mathbb{L} \in \Sigma_{\mathcal{L}_{cf}} \Leftrightarrow$ *1.* $\mathbb{L}^I$ *is downward-closed and non-empty,*

2. $\mathbb{L}^O_{I=E}$ *is downward-closed for all* $E \in \mathbb{L}^I$,

3. $\mathbb{L}$ *is L-tight, and*

4. $\mathbb{L}$ *is reject-compositional.*

We recall a proposition establishing a connection between tightness in terms of labellings and extensions [9, Proposition 4].

Proposition 2. *Let* $\mathbb{L}$ *be a labelling-set. If* $\mathbb{L}$ *satisfies L-tightness as well as reject-compositionality and* $\mathbb{L}^I$ *is downward-closed, then* $\mathbb{L}^I$ *is tight.*

We recall a construction witnessing realizability. Consider the following definition and the decisive witnessing property [9, Definition 10, Theorem 6].

Definition 10. *Given a labelling-set* $\mathbb{L}$. *We define* $F^{cf}_{\mathbb{L}} = (A_{\mathbb{L}}, R_{\mathbb{L}})$ *with* $A_{\mathbb{L}} = Args_{\mathbb{L}}$ *and*

1. $\forall a \in A_{\mathbb{L}}$: $(a, a) \in R_{\mathbb{L}}$ *if and only if* $\{a\} \notin \mathbb{L}^I$, *and*
2. $\forall a, b \in A_{\mathbb{L}}$: *If* $a \neq b$, *then* $(a, b) \in R_{\mathbb{L}}$ *iff* $\{a\} \in \mathbb{L}^I$ *and* $b \in \bigcup \mathbb{L}^O_{I=\{a\}}$.

Theorem 3. *For any labelling-set* $\mathbb{L}$, *we have:* $\mathbb{L} \in \Sigma_{\mathcal{L}_{cf}} \Leftrightarrow \mathbb{L} = \mathcal{L}_{cf}\left(F^{cf}_{\mathbb{L}}\right)$.

3   Realizability of Naive Labellings

Conflict-free sets and naive extensions have a close relationship to each other. They are connected via the so-called downward-closure, i.e. for any given AF F we have, $dcl(\mathcal{E}_{na}(F)) = \mathcal{E}_{cf}(F)$. The underlying idea in this paper is to transfer this connection to the realm of labellings. We will see that this works to a certain extent. However, further conditions are needed.

3.1 The Downward-Closure of a Labelling-Set

In the following we transfer the concept of a downward-closed set to the realm of labellings. Given a labelling-set $\mathbb{L}$ we first downward-close $\mathbb{L}^I$ and obtain any new in-label. In the next step we construct the corresponding out-labels for a given in-label E. This is done as follows: For each $a \in E$ we obtain a building block $O_{\{a\}}$. Such an $O_{\{a\}}$ contains an argument b if each former in-set I containing a possesses a witnessing out-label containing b. For a given in-label E the $\subseteq$-greatest out-label O_E is then defined as the union of all such $O_{\{a\}}$'s.

Definition 11. *For a labelling-set $\mathbb{L}$ we define the downward-closure of $\mathbb{L}$ as:*

$$^{\downarrow}\mathbb{L} := \left\{ (E, O, Args_{\mathbb{L}} \setminus (E \cup O)) \mid E \subseteq L^I, L^I \in \mathbb{L}^I, O \subseteq O_E \right\}$$

where

$$O_E = \bigcup_{a \in E} O_{\{a\}} \quad \text{with } O_{\{a\}} = \bigcap_{I' \in \mathbb{L}^I, \{a\} \subseteq I'} \bigcup \mathbb{L}^O_{I=I'}.$$

Please note that $\bigcup \mathbb{L}^O_{I=I'} = \overline{\mathbb{L}}^O_{I=I'}$ in case of $\mathbb{L}$-tight labelling-sets.

Example 5. Consider $\mathbb{L} := \mathcal{L}_{na}(F)$ from Example 1 given by the following table.

	I	O	U
L_1	$\{d\}$	$\{a,b\}$	$\{c\}$
L_2	$\{d\}$	$\{a\}$	$\{b,c\}$
L_3	$\{d\}$	$\{b\}$	$\{a,c\}$
L_4	$\{d\}$	$\{\}$	$\{a,b,c\}$
L_5	$\{a,c\}$	$\{d\}$	$\{b\}$
L_6	$\{a,c\}$	$\{\}$	$\{b,d\}$
L_7	$\{b,c\}$	$\{a,d\}$	$\{\}$
L_8	$\{b,c\}$	$\{a\}$	$\{d\}$
L_9	$\{b,c\}$	$\{d\}$	$\{a\}$
L_{10}	$\{b,c\}$	$\{\}$	$\{a,d\}$

We want to determine the associated downward-closure $^{\downarrow}\mathbb{L}$. In order to obtain the resulting labellings we first have to compute the set $O_{\{a\}}$ for each single $a \in Args_{\mathbb{L}^I}$. Note that the considered labelling-set $\mathbb{L}$ is $\mathbb{L}$-tight. Consequently, we may compute $O_{\{a\}}$ with the more convenient $\bigcap_{I' \in \mathbb{L}^I, \{a\} \subseteq I'} \overline{\mathbb{L}}^O_{I=I'}$.

1. We obtain:
   - $O_{\{a\}} = \displaystyle\bigcap_{I' \in \mathbb{L}^I, \{a\} \subseteq I'} \overline{\mathbb{L}}^O_{I=I'} = \overline{\mathbb{L}}^O_{I=\{a,c\}} = L_5^O = \{d\}.$
   - $O_{\{b\}} = \displaystyle\bigcap_{I' \in \mathbb{L}^I, \{b\} \subseteq I'} \overline{\mathbb{L}}^O_{I=I'} = \overline{\mathbb{L}}^O_{I=\{b,c\}} = L_7^O = \{a,d\}.$
   - $O_{\{c\}} = \displaystyle\bigcap_{I' \in \mathbb{L}^I, \{c\} \subseteq I'} \overline{\mathbb{L}}^O_{I=I'} = \overline{\mathbb{L}}^O_{I=\{a,c\}} \cap \overline{\mathbb{L}}^O_{I=\{b,c\}} = L_5^O \cap L_7^O = \{d\}.$

$$- O_{\{d\}} = \bigcap_{I' \in \mathbb{L}^I, \{d\} \subseteq I'} \overline{\mathbb{L}}^O_{I=I'} = \overline{\mathbb{L}}^O_{I=\{d\}} = L^O_1 = \{a, b\}.$$

2. The next step is to build O_E for a chosen $E \subseteq I' \in \mathbb{L}^I$. By definition O_E equals the union of the building blocks $O_{\{a\}}$ with $a \in E$. Three cases:

   - Let $E \subseteq \{d\}$. Hence, $E_1 = \{d\}$ and $E_2 = \emptyset$ is possible. We have $O_{E_1} = \bigcup_{x \in E_1} O_{\{x\}} = O_{\{d\}} = \{a, b\}$ and $O_{E_2} = \bigcup_{x \in E_2} O_{\{x\}} = \emptyset$.
   - Now, $E \subseteq \{a, c\}$. We obtain three new sets, namely $E_3 = \{a, c\}$, $E_4 = \{a\}$ and $E_5 = \{c\}$. Note that $E = \emptyset$ was already considered above. We have, $O_{E_3} = \bigcup_{x \in E_3} O_{\{x\}} = O_{\{a\}} \cup O_{\{c\}} = \{d\} \cup \{d\} = \{d\}$, $O_{E_4} = O_{\{a\}} = \{d\}$ and $O_{E_5} = O_{\{c\}} = \{d\}$.
   - Finally, $E \subseteq \{b, c\}$. We obtain $E_6 = \{b, c\}$ and $E_7 = \{b\}$. The sets $\{c\}(= E_5)$ and $\emptyset(= E_2)$ were already considered. We have, $O_{E_6} = O_{\{b\}} \cup O_{\{c\}} = \{d\} \cup \{a, d\} = \{a, d\}$ and $O_{E_7} = O_{\{b\}} = \{a, d\}$.

3. Finally, we construct the resulting labellings. Each single E_i induces several labellings manifested by the subsets $O \subseteq O_{E_i}$. Consider therefore the following table representing $^{\downarrow}\mathbb{L}$ in a compact way.

	I	O	U	
E_1	$\{d\}$	$\{a, b\}$	$\{c\}$	L_1
	$\{d\}$	$\{a\}$	$\{b, c\}$	L_2
	$\{d\}$	$\{b\}$	$\{a, c\}$	L_3
	$\{d\}$	$\{\}$	$\{a, b, c\}$	L_4
E_2	$\{\}$	$\{\}$	$\{a, b, c, d\}$	
E_3	$\{a, c\}$	$\{d\}$	$\{b\}$	L_5
	$\{a, c\}$	$\{\}$	$\{b, d\}$	L_6
E_4	$\{a\}$	$\{d\}$	$\{b, c\}$	
	$\{a\}$	$\{\}$	$\{b, c, d\}$	
E_5	$\{c\}$	$\{d\}$	$\{a, b\}$	
	$\{c\}$	$\{\}$	$\{a, b, d\}$	
E_6	$\{b, c\}$	$\{a, d\}$	$\{\}$	L_7
	$\{b, c\}$	$\{a\}$	$\{d\}$	L_8
	$\{b, c\}$	$\{d\}$	$\{a\}$	L_9
	$\{b, c\}$	$\{\}$	$\{a, d\}$	L_{10}
E_7	$\{b\}$	$\{a, d\}$	$\{c\}$	
	$\{b\}$	$\{a\}$	$\{c, d\}$	
	$\{b\}$	$\{d\}$	$\{a, c\}$	
	$\{b\}$	$\{\}$	$\{a, c, d\}$	

Please note that any conflict-free as well as naive labelling of F is reconstructed (cf. Example 1). This is no coincidence as we will see (Proposition 8).

We now prove the well-definedness of the construction.

Proposition 3. *If $\mathbb{L}$ is a labelling-set, then $^{\downarrow}\mathbb{L}$ is a labelling-set.*

Proof. We first have to show that any labelling $M \in {}^{\downarrow}\mathbb{L}$ considers the same arguments. Let $M = (E, O, U)$. Thus, by definition $M^I \cup M^O \cup M^U = E \cup O \cup (Args_{\mathbb{L}} \setminus (E \cup O)) = Args_{\mathbb{L}}$. The latter equals $Args_{\mathbb{L}}$ as $E, O \subseteq Args_{\mathbb{L}}$.

Secondly, disjointness, i.e. $M^I \cap M^O = M^I \cap M^U = M^O \cap M^U = \emptyset$. Towards a contradiction assume $M^I \cap M^O \neq \emptyset$, i.e. there is an element $a \in M^I \cap M^O$. Since $a \in M^I$ we deduce the existence of a labelling $L \in \mathbb{L}$ with $a \in M^I \subseteq L^I$. Moreover, since by assumption $a \in M^O$ and by definition $M^O \subseteq O_{M^I}$ we obtain the existence of an element $b \in M^I$ with $a \in O_{\{b\}}$. Since $O_{\{b\}} = \bigcap_{I' \in \mathbb{L}^I, \{b\} \subseteq I'} \bigcup \mathbb{L}^O_{I=I'}$ we infer $a \in \bigcup \mathbb{L}^O_{I=L^I}$. Thus, there has to be a labelling $L' \in \mathbb{L}$ with $a \in (L')^I = L^I$ and $a \in (L')^O$ contradicting disjointness and thus, the labelling-set property of $\mathbb{L}$. Hence $M^I \cap M^O = \emptyset$. The cases $M^I \cap M^U = \emptyset$ and $M^O \cap M^U = \emptyset$ follow immediately by construction as $U = Args_{\mathbb{L}} \setminus (E \cup O)$ concluding the proof.

We list some simple properties which will be frequently used throughout the paper.

Proposition 4. *Given a labelling-set $\mathbb{L}$. Then,*

1. *For $E \in \left(^{\downarrow}\mathbb{L}\right)^I$ we have: $\left(^{\downarrow}\mathbb{L}\right)^O_{I=E} = \{S \mid S \subseteq O_E\}$,*
2. *For $E \in \left(^{\downarrow}\mathbb{L}\right)^I$ we have: $\overline{\left(^{\downarrow}\mathbb{L}\right)}^O_{I=E} = O_E$,*
3. *$\mathbb{L} = \emptyset \Leftrightarrow {}^{\downarrow}\mathbb{L} = \emptyset$,*
4. *$\mathbb{L}^I \subseteq \left(^{\downarrow}\mathbb{L}\right)^I$,*
5. *$dcl(\mathbb{L}^I) = \left(^{\downarrow}\mathbb{L}\right)^I$.*

Proof. Items 1.-4. follow immediately by construction of $^{\downarrow}\mathbb{L}$. Let us prove the last assertion in more detail.

($\subseteq$) Let $E \in dcl(\mathbb{L}^I)$. Thus, by definition of the downward-closure of a set we obtain the existence of an $I' \in \mathbb{L}^I$ s.t. $E \subseteq I'$. Consequently, by definition of $\mathbb{L}^I$ there exists a labelling $L \in \mathbb{L}$ with $L^I = I'$. Hence, due to the construction of the downward-closure of a labelling-set we infer the existence of a labelling $M \in {}^{\downarrow}\mathbb{L}$ with $M^I = E$ implying $E \in \left(^{\downarrow}\mathbb{L}\right)^I$.

($\supseteq$) Let $E \in \left(^{\downarrow}\mathbb{L}\right)^I$. Thus, by definition of $\left(^{\downarrow}\mathbb{L}\right)^I$ we obtain the existence of an $I' \in \mathbb{L}^I$ s.t. $E \subseteq I'$. Hence, $E \in dcl(\mathbb{L}^I)$ by definition of the downward-closure of a set.

3.2   Inheritance of L-Tightness

The underlying idea in our approach is to reproduce (as far as possible) the relationship between conflict-free sets and naive extension sets in the realm of labellings. One important step towards a characterization is to show that naive realizability of a labelling-set implies conflict-free realizability of the associated downward-closure, i.e. the downward-closure satisfies any criteria listed in Theorem 2. While most of them can be shown quite easily, L-tightness requires a closer examination. The goal of this section is to show that L-tightness of a labelling-set conveys to the downward-closure under certain conditions. Before proving this important ingredient we have to show a few technical results first. To this end we now introduce *in-maximal labellings* of a given labelling-set. Applying this concept to a set of conflict-free labellings yields the naive ones of the AF in question.

Definition 12. *For any labelling-set* $\mathbb{L}$ *we define the set of in-maximal labellings as* $\{L \in \mathbb{L} \mid L^I \text{ is } \subseteq\text{-maximal in } \mathbb{L}^I\}$.

We now show that L-tightness inherits from the initial set to its in-maximal labellings.

Proposition 5. *Let* $\mathbb{L}$ *be an L-tight labelling-set and* $\mathbb{M}$ *the associated set of its in-maximal labellings. Then:*

1. $\overline{\mathbb{M}}_{I=E}^O$ *exists and* $\overline{\mathbb{M}}_{I=E}^O = \overline{\mathbb{L}}_{I=E}^O$ *for all* $E \in \mathbb{M}^I$.
2. $\mathbb{M}$ *is L-tight.*

Proof. 1. We first prove the existence of $\subseteq$-greatest elements regarding out-labels w.r.t. fixed in-sets. Consider $E \in \mathbb{M}^I$. By construction $\mathbb{M}$ and $\mathbb{L}$ share the same labellings with E as in-sets, i.e. $\mathbb{M}_{I=E} = \mathbb{L}_{I=E}$. Consequently, $\mathbb{M}_{I=E}^O = \mathbb{L}_{I=E}^O$. Now, due to L-tightness of $\mathbb{L}$ we deduce the existence of $\overline{\mathbb{L}}_{I=E}^O$, the $\subseteq$-greatest labelling regarding out-labels w.r.t. to the in-set E. Hence, $\overline{\mathbb{M}}_{I=E}^O$ is guarenteed and given as $\overline{\mathbb{L}}_{I=E}^O$.

2. Now, for the second property, consider $E_1, E_2 \in \mathbb{M}^I$. We immediately observe that $E_1 \cup E_2 \notin \mathbb{M}^I$ as $\mathbb{M}$ contains in-maximal labellings only. Hence, by definition of L-tightness we have to show $\left(\overline{\mathbb{M}}_{I=E_1}^O \cap E_2\right) \cup \left(\overline{\mathbb{M}}_{I=E_2}^O \cap E_1\right) \neq \emptyset$. Since $\mathbb{M} \subseteq \mathbb{L}$ we know that $E_1, E_2 \in \mathbb{L}^I$. Moreover, $E_1 \cup E_2 \notin \mathbb{L}^I$ as $E_1, E_2 \in \mathbb{M}^I$ is assumed. We may now apply L-tightness of $\mathbb{L}$ and derive $\left(\overline{\mathbb{L}}_{I=E_1}^O \cap E_2\right) \cup \left(\overline{\mathbb{L}}_{I=E_2}^O \cap E_1\right) \neq \emptyset$. Thus, using the equality $\overline{\mathbb{M}}_{I=E}^O = \overline{\mathbb{L}}_{I=E}^O$ for $E \in \mathbb{M}^I$ from above we obtain $\left(\overline{\mathbb{M}}_{I=E_1}^O \cap E_2\right) \cup \left(\overline{\mathbb{M}}_{I=E_2}^O \cap E_1\right) \neq \emptyset$ as required.

Now we are prepared to extend L-tightness to naive labelling-sets.

Proposition 6. *Given a labelling-set* $\mathbb{L}$. *If* $\mathbb{L} \in \Sigma_{\mathcal{L}_{na}}$, *then* $\mathbb{L}$ *is L-tight.*

Proof. Since $\mathbb{L}$ is naive-realizable we conclude the existence of an AF F with $\mathcal{L}_{na}(F) = \mathbb{L}$. By Definition 3 we have that $\mathbb{L}$ contains exactly the in-maximal labellings of $\mathcal{L}_{cf}(F)$. By Theorem 2 we know that $\mathcal{L}_{cf}(F)$ is L-tight. Thus, applying Proposition 5 yields L-tightness of $\mathbb{L}$.

Next we want show that L-tightness also conveys to the downward-closure (see Proposition 10). However, in order to do so, we have to show the following three non-trivial properties first.

Proposition 7. *Given a labelling-set* $\mathbb{L}$. *If* $\mathbb{L} \in \Sigma_{\mathcal{L}_{na}}$, *then for any* $E \in \mathbb{L}^I$ *we have:* $\overline{\mathbb{L}}_{I=E}^O = O_E$.

Proof. First of all, due to Proposition 6 we know that $\mathbb{L}$ is L-tight and thus, the existence of $\overline{\mathbb{L}}_{I=E}^O$ is guarenteed. Moreover, $O_E = \bigcup_{a \in E} O_{\{a\}}$ with $O_{\{a\}} = \bigcap_{I' \in \mathbb{L}^I, \{a\} \subseteq I'} \overline{\mathbb{L}}_{I=I'}^O$.

($\supseteq$) Let $x \in O_E$. Thus, there is an $a \in E$ with $x \in O_{\{a\}}$. Since $E \in \mathbb{L}^I$ and $\{a\} \subseteq E$ we obtain $x \in \overline{\mathbb{L}}^O_{I=E}$.

($\subseteq$) Let $x \in \overline{\mathbb{L}}^O_{I=E}$. Hence, there is an $L \in \mathbb{L}$ with $L^I = E$ and $x \in L^O$. Due to naive realizability we have the existence of an $F = (A, R)$, s.t. $\mathcal{L}_{na}(F) = \mathbb{L}$. Consequently, since L is a conflict-free labelling too, there has to be an $e \in L^I$ with $(e, x) \in R$ (Definition 2). Thus, due to reject-witness of $\mathcal{L}_{cf}(F)$ (Theorem 2), we have $(\{e\}, \{x\}, Args_{\mathbb{L}} \setminus \{e, x\}) \in \mathcal{L}_{cf}(F)$. Consequently, $x \in \overline{\mathcal{L}_{cf}(F)}^O_{I=\{e\}}$. Now, for each naive set $I' \in L^I = (\mathcal{L}_{na}(F))^I = \mathcal{E}_{na}(F)$ with $\{e\} \subseteq I'$ we have: $x \in \overline{\mathbb{L}}^O_{I=I'}$. This is due to fact that $\overline{\mathbb{L}}^O_{I=I'} = \overline{\mathcal{L}_{na}(F)}^O_{I=I'} = \overline{\mathcal{L}_{cf}(F)}^O_{I=I'} = \bigcup_{a \in I'} \overline{\mathcal{L}_{cf}(F)}^O_{I=\{a\}}$. The latter equation is justified by reject-compositionality and L-tightness of $\mathcal{L}_{cf}(F)$ (Theorem 2). This means, we have shown that $x \in O_{\{e\}} \subseteq O_E$ concluding the proof.

Proposition 8. *Given an AF $F = (A, R)$, then $\overline{(\mathcal{L}_{cf}(F))}^O_{I=E} \subseteq \overline{(^{\downarrow}\mathcal{L}_{na}(F))}^O_{I=E}$ for all $E \in (\mathcal{L}_{cf}(F))^I$.*

Proof. For the proof we set $\mathcal{L}_{na}(F) = \mathbb{L}$ and $\mathcal{L}_{cf}(F) = \mathbb{M}$.
Via the L-tightness of $\mathbb{M}$ (Theorem 2) the existence of the $\subseteq$-greatest element $\overline{\mathbb{M}}^O_{I=E}$ is ensured as well as the existence of $\overline{(^{\downarrow}\mathbb{L})}^O_{I=E} = O_E$ due to the construction of the downward-closure. This means, the desired subset relation coincides with $\overline{\mathbb{M}}^O_{I=E} \subseteq O_E$. Let $b \in \overline{\mathbb{M}}^O_{I=E}$. Due to reject-compositionality and L-tightness of $\mathbb{M}$ (Theorem 2) the existence of an $a \in E$, s.t. $b \in \overline{\mathbb{M}}^O_{I=\{a\}}$ is guaranteed. Consequently, for each $I' \in \mathbb{M}^I$ with $a \in I'$ we have $b \in \overline{\mathbb{M}}^O_{I=I'}$. This applies in particular to the in-maximal labellings of $\mathbb{M}$, i.e. to the labellings in $\mathbb{L}$. Moreover, in Proposition 5 we have shown that for such labellings $\overline{\mathbb{M}}^O_{I=I'} = \overline{\mathbb{L}}^O_{I=I'}$. Consequently, $b \in \bigcap_{I' \in \mathbb{L}^I, \{a\} \subseteq I'} \overline{\mathbb{L}}^O_{I=I'} = O_{\{a\}}$. Hence, $b \in \bigcup_{a \in E} O_{\{a\}} = O_E$ is shown concluding the proof.

Proposition 9. *Given an AF F, we have: $\mathcal{L}_{cf}(F)^I = (^{\downarrow}\mathcal{L}_{na}(F))^I$ as well as $\mathcal{L}_{cf}(F) \subseteq {}^{\downarrow}\mathcal{L}_{na}(F)$.*

Proof. For the proof we set $\mathcal{L}_{na}(F) = \mathbb{L}$ and $\mathcal{L}_{cf}(F) = \mathbb{M}$.
We first show $\mathbb{M}^I = {}^{\downarrow}\mathbb{L}^I$. By Item 5 of Proposition 4 we have $dcl(\mathbb{L}^I) = {}^{\downarrow}\mathbb{L}^I$ for any labelling-set $\mathbb{L}$. Furthermore, due to Definition 1 we have $dcl(\mathbb{L}^I) = \mathbb{M}^I$ which guarentees $\mathbb{M}^I = {}^{\downarrow}\mathbb{L}^I$ as required.
In order to show $\mathbb{M} \subseteq {}^{\downarrow}\mathbb{L}$ it suffices to prove that for each single $E \in \mathbb{M}^I$, $\mathbb{M}^O_{I=E} \subseteq (^{\downarrow}\mathbb{L})^O_{I=E}$ as $\mathbb{M}^I = {}^{\downarrow}\mathbb{L}^I$ is already known. Let us fix a certain $E \in \mathbb{M}^I$. According to Proposition 4, Items 1 and 2 we have downward-closedness of $(^{\downarrow}\mathbb{L})^O_{I=E}$ and the existence of a $\subseteq$-greatest element, namely $\overline{(^{\downarrow}\mathbb{L})}^O_{I=E} = O_E$. Furthermore, due to Definition 3 we have downward-closedness of $\mathbb{M}^O_{I=E}$ and via L-tightness of $\mathbb{M}$ (Theorem 2) we derive the existence of a $\subseteq$-greatest element

$\overline{M}^O_{I=E}$. Consequently, instead of showing $M^O_{I=E} \subseteq \left(^{\downarrow}\mathbb{L}\right)^O_{I=E}$ it suffices to prove $\overline{M}^O_{I=E} \subseteq O_E$, which was already shown in Proposition 8.

Proposition 10. *Given a labelling-set* $\mathbb{L}$. *If* $\mathbb{L} \in \Sigma_{\mathcal{L}_{na}}$, *then* $^{\downarrow}\mathbb{L}$ *is L-tight.*

Proof. First, the existence of a $\subseteq$-greatest element in $\left(^{\downarrow}\mathbb{L}\right)^O_{I=E}$ for a fixed $E \in \left(^{\downarrow}\mathbb{L}\right)^I$ was already shown (Item 2, Proposition 4). In particular, $\overline{\left(^{\downarrow}\mathbb{L}\right)}^O_{I=E} = O_E$.

For the second property let $E_1, E_2 \in \left(^{\downarrow}\mathbb{L}\right)^I$. We will show the following equivalence: $E_1 \cup E_2 \in \left(^{\downarrow}\mathbb{L}\right)^I \Leftrightarrow \left(\overline{\left(^{\downarrow}\mathbb{L}\right)}^O_{I=E_1} \cap E_2\right) \cup \left(\overline{\left(^{\downarrow}\mathbb{L}\right)}^O_{I=E_2} \cap E_1\right) = \emptyset$.

($\Rightarrow$) Given $E_1 \cup E_2 \in \left(^{\downarrow}\mathbb{L}\right)^I$. According to Definition 11 we deduce the existence of an $E \in \mathbb{L}^I$ with $E_1 \cup E_2 \subseteq E$. Note that $E \in \left(^{\downarrow}\mathbb{L}\right)^I$ (Item 4, Propostion 4). Due to L-tightness of $\mathbb{L}$ (Proposition 6) the existence of $\overline{\mathbb{L}}^O_{I=E}$ is guaranteed. Please note that $E \cap \overline{\mathbb{L}}^O_{I=E} = \emptyset$ as $\mathbb{L}$ is a labelling-set. Thus, showing $\overline{\left(^{\downarrow}\mathbb{L}\right)}^O_{I=E_i} \subseteq \overline{\mathbb{L}}^O_{I=E}$ for $i \in \{1,2\}$ would yield $\left(\overline{\left(^{\downarrow}\mathbb{L}\right)}^O_{I=E_1} \cap E_2\right) \cup \left(\overline{\left(^{\downarrow}\mathbb{L}\right)}^O_{I=E_2} \cap E_1\right) = \emptyset$ as required. This can be seen as follows:

$$\overline{\left(^{\downarrow}\mathbb{L}\right)}^O_{I=E_i} = O_{E_i} = \bigcup_{a \in E_i} O_{\{a\}} \subseteq \bigcup_{a \in E} O_{\{a\}} = O_E = \overline{\mathbb{L}}^O_{I=E}$$

The last equality is due to Proposition 7.

($\Leftarrow$) Given $\left(\overline{\left(^{\downarrow}\mathbb{L}\right)}^O_{I=E_1} \cap E_2\right) \cup \left(\overline{\left(^{\downarrow}\mathbb{L}\right)}^O_{I=E_2} \cap E_1\right) = \emptyset$. Hence, $(O_{E_1} \cap E_2) \cup (O_{E_2} \cap E_1) = \emptyset$. Since $\mathbb{L}$ is *na*-realizable there is an AF $F = (A, R)$ with $\mathcal{L}_{na}(F) = \mathbb{L}$. We set $\mathcal{L}_{cf}(F) = M$. As $E_1, E_2 \in {^{\downarrow}\mathbb{L}}^I$ we derive the existence of $I_1, I_2 \in \mathbb{L}^I$ with $E_1 \subseteq I_1$ and $E_2 \subseteq I_2$. Moreover, $E_1, E_2 \in M^I$ since $M^I = {^{\downarrow}\mathbb{L}}^I$ by Proposition 9. Applying Proposition 8 we obtain $\overline{M}^O_{I=E_1} \subseteq O_{E_1}$ as well as $\overline{M}^O_{I=E_2} \subseteq O_{E_2}$. Consequently, $(E_1 \cap \overline{M}^O_{I=E_2}) \cup (E_2 \cap \overline{M}^O_{I=E_1}) = \emptyset$. Since M is itself L-tight (Theorem 2) we deduce $E_1 \cup E_2 \in M^I$ and finally, applying Proposition 9 $E_1 \cup E_2 \in \left(^{\downarrow}\mathbb{L}\right)^I$ concluding the proof.

3.3 Characterization Theorem

Now, we proceed with the central realizability result for naive labellings. In total, five properties have to be checked for naive realizability. Beside properties induced by extension-based realizability (Item 1) and further technical properties (Items 2–4), the decisive point is the conflict-free realizability of the associated downward-closure (Item 5).

To mention a subtle difference: In contrast to naive extensions and conflict-free sets where each one of them precisely determines the other we have that naive labellings may be induced by different conflict-free labelling-sets (cf. Example 6). This means, the introduced downward-closure of labelling-sets is only one possibility. However, the characterization theorem shows that it can be used to decide naive realizability. Please note that each property can be verified by examining the given labelling-set only.

Theorem 4. *Given a labelling-set $\mathbb{L}$ we have*

$$\mathbb{L} \in \Sigma_{\mathcal{L}_{na}} \;\Leftrightarrow\; \begin{array}{l} \textit{1. } \mathbb{L}^I \textit{ is incomparable and non-empty,} \\[4pt] \textit{2. } \mathbb{L}^O_{I=E} \textit{ is downward-closed for each } E \in \mathbb{L}^I, \\[4pt] \textit{3. } \overline{\mathbb{L}}^O_{I=E} \textit{ exists for each } E \in \mathbb{L}^I, \\[4pt] \textit{4. } \overline{\mathbb{L}}^O_{I=E} \subseteq \bigcup_{a \in E} \bigcap_{I' \in \mathbb{L}^I, \{a\} \subseteq I'} \overline{\mathbb{L}}^O_{I=I'} \textit{ for each } E \in \mathbb{L}^I, \\[4pt] \textit{5. } {}^{\downarrow}\mathbb{L} \in \Sigma_{\mathcal{L}_{cf}}. \end{array}$$

Proof. We will split the prove in if- and only-if-direction as usual.

($\Rightarrow$) Let $\mathbb{L} \in \Sigma_{\mathcal{L}_{na}}$ be given. Hence, there is an AF $F = (A, R)$ with $\mathcal{L}_{na}(F) = \mathbb{L}$. Applying Items 3 and 4 of Proposition 1 we deduce $\mathbb{L}^I = \mathcal{E}_{na}(F)$. Moreover, Theorem 1 yields the incomparability and non-emptiness of $\mathbb{L}^I$.

Let $\mathbb{M} = \mathcal{L}_{cf}(F)$. We have $\mathbb{M}^O_{I=E}$ is downward-closed for all $E \in \mathbb{M}^I$ (Item 2, Theorem 2). In light of Definition 3 we obtain: $\mathbb{L} = \mathcal{L}_{na}(F) = \{L \in \mathbb{M} \mid L^I \text{ is } \subseteq -\text{maximal in } \{M^I \mid M \in \mathbb{M}\}\}$. Thus, $\mathbb{L}^O_{I=E}$ is downward-closed for each $E \in \mathbb{L}^I$.

The existence of a $\subseteq$-greatest element $\overline{\mathbb{L}}^O_{I=E}$ for each single $E \in \mathbb{L}^I$ follows by the L-tightness (Item 1, Definition 8) of any naive realizable labelling-set (Proposition 6).

By Proposition 7 we have $\overline{\mathbb{L}}^O_{I=E} = O_E$. Moreover, $O_E = \bigcup_{a \in E} \bigcap_{I' \in \mathbb{L}^I, \{a\} \subseteq I'} \overline{\mathbb{L}}^O_{I=I'}$ (Definition 11). Consequently, $\overline{\mathbb{L}}^O_{I=E} \subseteq \bigcup_{a \in E} \bigcap_{I' \in \mathbb{L}^I, \{a\} \subseteq I'} \overline{\mathbb{L}}^O_{I=I'}$ for each $E \in \mathbb{L}^I$ as required.

Finally, in order to show the fifth item, i.e. ${}^{\downarrow}\mathbb{L} \in \Sigma_{\mathcal{L}_{cf}}$ it suffices to prove the following four properties (Theorem 2).

i) $({}^{\downarrow}\mathbb{L})^I$ is downward-closed and non-empty.
Downward-closedness is due to Item 5 of Proposition 4. Since naive semantics is universally defined we have $\mathcal{L}_{na}(F) = \mathbb{L} \neq \emptyset$. Thus, ${}^{\downarrow}\mathbb{L} \neq \emptyset$ and therefore $({}^{\downarrow}\mathbb{L})^I \neq \emptyset$ (Item 3, Proposition 4).

ii) $({}^{\downarrow}\mathbb{L})^O_{I=E}$ is downward-closed for all $E \in ({}^{\downarrow}\mathbb{L})^I$ (Item 1, Proposition 4).

iii) ${}^{\downarrow}\mathbb{L}$ is L-tight (Proposition 10).

iv) ${}^{\downarrow}\mathbb{L}$ is reject-compositional.
Since L-tightness of ${}^{\downarrow}\mathbb{L}$ is already shown we have to prove: for any $E \in ({}^{\downarrow}\mathbb{L})^I$ we have, $\overline{({}^{\downarrow}\mathbb{L})}^O_{I=E} = \bigcup_{a \in E} \overline{({}^{\downarrow}\mathbb{L})}^O_{I=\{a\}}$. As $({}^{\downarrow}\mathbb{L})^I$ is shown to be downward-closed we infer that $E \in ({}^{\downarrow}\mathbb{L})^I$ implies $\{a\} \in ({}^{\downarrow}\mathbb{L})^I$ for each $a \in E$. Consequently, the equality transforms to $O_E = \bigcup_{a \in E} O_{\{a\}}$ (Item 2,

Proposition 4). There is nothing further to show as this equality holds by construction (Definition 11).

($\Leftarrow$) By assumption $^{\downarrow}\mathbb{L}$ is cf-realizable (Item 5). Hence, applying Theorem 3 we immediately obtain $^{\downarrow}\mathbb{L} = \mathcal{L}_{cf}\left(F^{cf}_{\downarrow\mathbb{L}}\right)$. Given incomparability and non-emptiness of $\mathbb{L}^I$ (Item 1) as well as the way of constructing $^{\downarrow}\mathbb{L}$ (Definition 11) we may conclude that $\mathbb{L}^I$ represents the $\subseteq$-maximal sets of $(^{\downarrow}\mathbb{L})^I$ being the naive sets of $F^{cf}_{\downarrow\mathbb{L}}$. Now consider a certain set $E \in \mathbb{L}^I$ and an argument $b \in O_E$. By Definition 11 we may replace O_E with $b \in \bigcup_{a \in E} \bigcap_{I' \in \mathbb{L}^I, \{a\} \subseteq I'} \overline{\mathbb{L}}^O_{I=I'}$.

Note that the existence of $\overline{\mathbb{L}}^O_{I=E}$ is assured by assumption (Item 3). By $b \in \bigcup_{a \in E} \bigcap_{I' \in \mathbb{L}^I, \{a\} \subseteq I'} \overline{\mathbb{L}}^O_{I=I'}$ we derive the existence of an $a \in E$ s.t. $b \in \overline{\mathbb{L}}^O_{I=I'}$ for all $I' \in \mathbb{L}^I$ where $a \in I'$. In particular, $b \in \overline{\mathbb{L}}^O_{I=E}$. Consequently, $O_E \subseteq \overline{\mathbb{L}}^O_{I=E}$. Combining this subset relation with the assumed superset relation (Item 4) yields $\overline{\mathbb{L}}^O_{I=E} = O_E$ for each $E \in \mathbb{L}^I$. Finally, since $\mathbb{L}^O_{I=E}$ is downward-closed for each $E \in \mathbb{L}^I$ (Item 2) we deduce that $\mathbb{L}$ represents the in-maximal labellings of $^{\downarrow}\mathbb{L}$. Thus, $\mathbb{L} = \mathcal{L}_{na}\left(F^{cf}_{\downarrow\mathbb{L}}\right)$ concluding the proof.

Finally, we compare the achieved characterization theorem with the already existing one regarding naive extensions (Theorem 1). Due to Proposition 1 we have that labelling-based na-realizability of $\mathbb{L}$ requires extension-based na-realizability of $\mathbb{L}^I$. This means, $\mathbb{L}^I$ has to be non-empty and incomparable, and $dcl(\mathbb{L}^I)$ has to be tight. The first two properties are explicitly given in Theorem 4. The tightness of the downward-closure of $\mathbb{L}^I$ is implicit as shown next.

Proposition 11. *Given a labelling-set* $\mathbb{L}$. *If* $^{\downarrow}\mathbb{L} \in \Sigma_{\mathcal{L}_{cf}}$, *then* $dcl(\mathbb{L}^I)$ *is tight.*

Proof. It suffices to show that $(^{\downarrow}\mathbb{L})^I$ is tight as $dcl(\mathbb{L}^I) = (^{\downarrow}\mathbb{L})^I$ (Proposition 4, Item 5). Moreover, the equality implies that $(^{\downarrow}\mathbb{L})^I$ is downward-closed. The assumption $^{\downarrow}\mathbb{L} \in \Sigma_{\mathcal{L}_{cf}}$ gives us L-tightness and reject-compositionality of $^{\downarrow}\mathbb{L}$ (Theorem 2). Thus, applying Proposition 2 yields tightness of $(^{\downarrow}\mathbb{L})^I$ concluding the proof.

3.4   Representational Freedom and Patterns of Redundancy

Standard Construction and Maximality. In case of conflict-free labellings it has been surprisingly discovered that the standard construction (cf. Definition 10) represents the uniquely determined witnessing AF in case of selfloop-free AFs ([9, Proposition 7]). This means, for selfloop-free AFs we do not have any representational freedom. The following example shows that this property does not carry over to naive labellings.

Example 6. Consider the following two selfloop-free AFs F and G.

The tables in Fig. 1 show conflict-free labellings of the selfloop-free AFs F and G. Although F and G are syntactically different, they possess matching naive labellings which can be found above the separating line $(L_1, \ldots, L_{10})$. According to [9, Proposition 7] they have to disagree on their conflict-free labellings illustrated, for example, by $L_{13} \in \mathcal{L}_{cf}(F) \setminus \mathcal{L}_{cf}(G)$.

$\mathcal{L}_{cf}(F)$	I	O	U
L_1	$\{d\}$	$\{a,b\}$	$\{c\}$
L_2	$\{d\}$	$\{a\}$	$\{b,c\}$
L_3	$\{d\}$	$\{b\}$	$\{a,c\}$
L_4	$\{d\}$	$\{\}$	$\{a,b,c\}$
L_5	$\{a,c\}$	$\{d\}$	$\{b\}$
L_6	$\{a,c\}$	$\{\}$	$\{d,b\}$
L_7	$\{b,c\}$	$\{a,d\}$	$\{\}$
L_8	$\{b,c\}$	$\{a\}$	$\{d\}$
L_9	$\{b,c\}$	$\{d\}$	$\{a\}$
L_{10}	$\{b,c\}$	$\{\}$	$\{a,d\}$
L_{11}	$\{a\}$	$\{d\}$	$\{b,c\}$
L_{12}	$\{a\}$	$\{\}$	$\{b,c,d\}$
L_{13}	$\{b\}$	$\{a,d\}$	$\{c\}$
L_{14}	$\{b\}$	$\{a\}$	$\{a,c\}$
L_{15}	$\{b\}$	$\{d\}$	$\{c,d\}$
L_{16}	$\{b\}$	$\{\}$	$\{a,c,d\}$
L_{17}	$\{c\}$	$\{d\}$	$\{a,b\}$
L_{18}	$\{c\}$	$\{\}$	$\{a,b,d\}$

$\mathcal{L}_{cf}(G)$	I	O	U
L_1	$\{d\}$	$\{a,b\}$	$\{c\}$
L_2	$\{d\}$	$\{a\}$	$\{b,c\}$
L_3	$\{d\}$	$\{b\}$	$\{a,c\}$
L_4	$\{d\}$	$\{\}$	$\{a,b,c\}$
L_5	$\{a,c\}$	$\{d\}$	$\{b\}$
L_6	$\{a,c\}$	$\{\}$	$\{d,b\}$
L_7	$\{b,c\}$	$\{a,d\}$	$\{\}$
L_8	$\{b,c\}$	$\{a\}$	$\{d\}$
L_9	$\{b,c\}$	$\{d\}$	$\{a\}$
L_{10}	$\{b,c\}$	$\{\}$	$\{a,d\}$
L_{11}	$\{a\}$	$\{d\}$	$\{b,c\}$
L_{12}	$\{a\}$	$\{\}$	$\{b,c,d\}$
L_{14}	$\{b\}$	$\{a\}$	$\{a,c\}$
L_{16}	$\{b\}$	$\{\}$	$\{a,c,d\}$
L_{17}	$\{c\}$	$\{d\}$	$\{a,b\}$
L_{18}	$\{c\}$	$\{\}$	$\{a,b,d\}$

Fig. 1. Tables Example 6

However, instead of a uniqueness result as in case of conflict-free labellings, we may show a maximality result. More precisely, in the realm of selfloop-free AFs, the standard construction (applied to the downward closure) contains any possible attack, i.e. it represents the greatest witness w.r.t. subgraph relation.

Proposition 12. *Given a labelling-set $\mathbb{L}$ and the AF $F_{\downarrow\mathbb{L}}^{cf} = (A_{\downarrow\mathbb{L}}, R_{\downarrow\mathbb{L}})$. For any selfloop-free AF $F = (A, R)$ with $\mathcal{L}_{na}(F) = \mathbb{L}$ we have:*

$$A = A_{\downarrow\mathbb{L}} \quad and \quad R \subseteq R_{\downarrow\mathbb{L}}.$$

Proof. Given a selfloop-free $F = (A, R)$ with $\mathcal{L}_{na}(F) = \mathbb{L}$ and let $\mathcal{L}_{cf}(F) = \mathbb{M}$.

1. Arguments: Since $\mathcal{L}_{na}(F) = \mathbb{L}$ we have $A = Args_{\mathbb{L}}$. Moreover, by Definition 11 we deduce $Args_{\mathbb{L}} = Args_{\downarrow \mathbb{L}}$. Finally, in light of the standard construction (Definition 10) we get $Args_{\downarrow \mathbb{L}} = A_{\downarrow \mathbb{L}}$ proving $A = A_{\downarrow \mathbb{L}}$.

2. Attacks: Let $(a, b) \in R$. As F is assumed to be selfloop-free we deduce $a \neq b$. In order to prove $(a, b) \in R_{\downarrow \mathbb{L}}$ we have to show 1. $\{a\} \in (\downarrow \mathbb{L})^I$ and 2. $b \in \bigcup (\downarrow \mathbb{L})^O_{I=\{a\}}$ (Item 2, Definition 10). The latter can be replaced by $b \in \overline{\downarrow \mathbb{L}}^O_{I=\{a\}}$ as $\mathbb{L}$-tightness of $\downarrow \mathbb{L}$ (and thus, the existence of a $\subseteq$-greatest element) is given via *na*-realizability of $\mathbb{L}$ (Proposition 10). Regarding the first requirement. Since F is selfloop-free we obtain $\{a\} \in \mathbb{M}^I$. Consequently, $\{a\} \in (\downarrow \mathbb{L})^I$ as $\mathbb{M}^I = (\downarrow \mathbb{L})^I$ (Proposition 9). Regarding the second condition. Since $\{a\} \in \mathbb{M}^I$ and $(a, b) \in R$ we deduce $b \in \overline{\mathbb{M}}^O_{I=\{a\}}$. By Proposition 8 we know $\overline{\mathbb{M}}^O_{I=\{a\}} \subseteq \overline{\downarrow \mathbb{L}}^O_{I=\{a\}}$ for any $\{a\} \in \mathbb{M}^I$. Thus, $b \in \overline{\downarrow \mathbb{L}}^O_{I=\{a\}}$ concluding the proof.

3.5   Strong Equivalence

Now let us turn to strong equivalence [13, 25], i.e. how to decide whether two AFs are interchangeable in any given context without changing the semantics. More formally, in case of a labelling-based semantics $\mathcal{L}_\sigma$, two AFs F and G are *strongly equivalent* (denoted as $F \equiv_s^{\mathcal{L}_\sigma} G$) if and only if $\mathcal{L}_\sigma(F \sqcup H) = \mathcal{L}_\sigma(G \sqcup H)$ for any further AF H. In case of naive extensions, the so-called naive kernel characterizes strong equivalence [10]. The following result shows that its characterizing potential does not carry over to naive labellings. In contrast, for naive labellings the classical stable kernel has to be used [5, 24].

Definition 13. *For a given AF $F = (A, R)$ the stable kernel is defined as $F^{sk} = (A, R \setminus \{(a, b) \in R \mid a \neq b, (a, a) \in R\})$.*

Theorem 5. *Given two AFs F and G. We have:*

$$F \equiv_s^{\mathcal{L}_{na}} G \Leftrightarrow F^{sk} = G^{sk}.$$

Proof. Given AFs F and G. The associated stable kernels are $F^{sk} = (A, R^{sk})$ and $G^{sk} = (B, S^{sk})$. We split the proof into two directions.

($\Rightarrow$) We show the contrapositive. Let $F^{sk} \neq G^{sk}$. We first show that $A(F) \neq A(G)$ immediately yields $F \not\equiv_s^{\mathcal{L}_{na}} G$. W.l.o.g. let $a \in A(F) \setminus A(G)$. Case distinction. If $(a, a) \notin R(F)$ we have nothing to show as there has to be a naive extension $E \in \mathcal{E}_{na}(F)$ with $a \in E$. Consequently, $E^{\mathcal{L}} \in \mathcal{L}_{na}(F)$ (Proposition 1) and obviously, $E^{\mathcal{L}} \notin \mathcal{L}_{na}(G)$ as $a \notin A(G)$. In case of $(a, a) \in R(F)$ we consider $H = (\{a\}, \emptyset)$. In the same fashion as above we conclude there has to be an E with $a \in E$ and $E^{\mathcal{L}} \in \mathcal{L}_{na}(G \sqcup H)$. Moreover, $E^{\mathcal{L}} \notin \mathcal{L}_{na}(F \sqcup H)$ as $(a, a) \in R(F \sqcup H)$. Let us now assume that

$A(F) = A(G)$. As $F^{sk} \neq G^{sk}$ is given, we deduce $F \not\equiv^{\mathcal{L}_{cf}} G$ [9, Theorem 8]. Consequently, w.l.o.g. there is a labelling $L \in \mathcal{L}_{cf}(F) \setminus \mathcal{L}_{cf}(G)$. Consider the AF $H = (A(F), \{(a,a) \mid a \in A(F) \setminus L^I\})$. Obviously, $L \in \mathcal{L}_{cf}(F \sqcup H)$ as regarding L^I, no internal conflicts are added and secondly, regarding L^O, the reason for rejection still holds in $F \sqcup H$ (cf. Definition 3). Moreover, by construction, $L \in \mathcal{L}_{na}(F \sqcup H)$ as L^I is even the $\subseteq$-greatest conflict-free in-label. On the other hand, the assumption $L \notin \mathcal{L}_{cf}(G)$ implies two possible reasons: 1. L^I is conflicting in G or 2. there is an element in L^O not attacked by an element in L^I. Please observe that both reasons still hold in $G \sqcup H$. Consequently, $L \notin \mathcal{L}_{cf}(G \sqcup H)$ and thus, $L \notin \mathcal{L}_{na}(G \sqcup H)$.

($\Leftarrow$) Given $F^{sk} = G^{sk}$. Consequently, for any AF H, $(F \sqcup H)^{sk} = (G \sqcup H)^{sk}$ [24, Lemma 2] and thus, $\mathcal{L}_{cf}(F \sqcup H) = \mathcal{L}_{cf}(G \sqcup H)$ [9, Theorem 8]. Hence, $\mathcal{L}_{cf}(F \sqcup H) = \mathcal{L}_{cf}(G \sqcup H)$ implying $F \equiv_s^{\mathcal{L}_{na}} G$ concluding the proof.

4   Conclusion and Related Works

For knowledge representation formalisms the issue of expressibility is essential. In the realm of abstract argumentation this question was mostly studied for extension-based semantics. In this paper we considered naive labellings which form the basis for a well-established family of semantics, namely the naivity-based semantics. We provided a characterization theorem which is a crucial step towards characterizing further naivety-based semantics such as stable and stage semantics. Moreover, we clarified the question of representational freedom and patterns of redundancy. There is only few related work. One important one is *realizibility under projection* [20]. In this setup, it suffices to come up with an AF F, s.t. its set of labellings restricted to the desired arguments coincide with $\mathbb{L}$. A second related work deals with the standard notion of realizability and presents a *propagate-and-guess algorithm* which returns either "No" in case of non-realizability or a witnessing AF [23]. The mentioned papers do not consider naive labellings, nor do they provide simple criteria for realizability.

Acknowledgments.. This work was supported by the German Research Foundation (DFG, BA 6170/3-1) and by the German Federal Ministry of Education and Research (BMBF, 01/S18026A-F) by funding the competence center for Big Data and AI "ScaDS.AI" Dresden/Leipzig.

Disclosure of Interests. The authors have no competing interests to declare that are relevant to the content of this article.

References

1. Alchourrón, C.E., Gärdenfors, P., Makinson, D.: On the logic of theory change: partial meet contraction and revision functions. J. Symb. Log. **50**(2), 510–530 (1985). https://doi.org/10.2307/2274239

2. Arieli, O.: Conflict-tolerant semantics for argumentation frameworks. In: del Cerro, L.F., Herzig, A., Mengin, J. (eds.) JELIA 2012. LNCS (LNAI), vol. 7519, pp. 28–40. Springer, Heidelberg (2012). https://doi.org/10.1007/978-3-642-33353-8_3

3. Atkinson, K., Baroni, P., Giacomin, M., Hunter, A., Prakken, H., Reed, C., Simari, G.R., Thimm, M., Villata, S.: Towards artificial argumentation. AI Mag. **38**(3), 25–36 (2017). https://doi.org/10.1609/aimag.v38i3.2704

4. Baroni, P., Caminada, M., Giacomin, M.: Abstract argumentation frameworks and their semantics. In: Baroni, P., Gabbay, D., Giacomin, M., van der Torre, L. (eds.) Handbook of Formal Argumentation, chap. 4. College Publications (2018)

5. Baumann, R.: Characterizing equivalence notions for labelling-based semantics. In: Principles of Knowledge Representation and Reasoning: Proceedings of the Fifteenth International Conference, KR 2016, Cape Town, South Africa, 25–29 April 2016, pp. 22–32 (2016). http://www.aaai.org/ocs/index.php/KR/KR16/paper/view/12836

6. Baumann, R.: On the nature of argumentation semantics: existence and uniqueness, expressibility, and replaceability. In: Handbook of Formal Argumentation, chap. 14. College Publications (2018)

7. Baumann, R., Berthold, M.: Limits and possibilities of forgetting in abstract argumentation. In: Raedt, L.D. (ed.) Proceedings of the Thirty-First International Joint Conference on Artificial Intelligence, IJCAI 2022, Vienna, Austria, 23–29 July 2022, pp. 2539–2545. ijcai.org (2022). https://doi.org/10.24963/ijcai.2022/352

8. Baumann, R., Doutre, S., Mailly, J., Wallner, J.P.: Enforcement in formal argumentation. FLAP **8**(6), 1623–1678 (2021). https://collegepublications.co.uk/ifcolog/?00048

9. Baumann, R., Heine, A.: On conflict-free labellings - realizability, construction and patterns of redundancy. In: Marquis, P., Son, T.C., Kern-Isberner, G. (eds.) Proceedings of the 20th International Conference on Principles of Knowledge Representation and Reasoning, KR 2023, Rhodes, Greece, 2–8 September 2023, pp. 720–725 (2023). https://doi.org/10.24963/kr.2023/70

10. Baumann, R., Linsbichler, T., Woltran, S.: Verifiability of argumentation semantics. In: Baroni, P., Gordon, T.F., Scheffler, T., Stede, M. (eds.) Computational Models of Argument - Proceedings of COMMA 2016, Potsdam, Germany, 12–16 September 2016. Frontiers in Artificial Intelligence and Applications, vol. 287, pp. 83–94. IOS Press (2016). https://doi.org/10.3233/978-1-61499-686-6-83

11. Baumann, R., Spanring, C.: Infinite argumentation frameworks - On the existence and uniqueness of extensions. In: Eiter, T., Strass, H., Truszczyński, M., Woltran, S. (eds.) Advances in Knowledge Representation, Logic Programming, and Abstract Argumentation. LNCS (LNAI), vol. 9060, pp. 281–295. Springer, Cham (2015). https://doi.org/10.1007/978-3-319-14726-0_19

12. Baumann, R., Spanring, C.: Infinite argumentation frameworks - on the existence and uniqueness of extensions. In: Eiter, T., Strass, H., Truszczyński, M., Woltran, S. (eds.) Advances in Knowledge Representation, Logic Programming, and Abstract Argumentation. LNCS (LNAI), vol. 9060, pp. 281–295. Springer, Cham (2015). https://doi.org/10.1007/978-3-319-14726-0_19

13. Baumann, R., Strass, H.: An abstract, logical approach to characterizing strong equivalence in non-monotonic knowledge representation formalisms. Artif. Intell. **305**, 103680 (2022). https://doi.org/10.1016/j.artint.2022.103680

14. Caminada, M.: A labelling approach for ideal and stage semantics. Argument Comput. **2**(1), 1–21 (2011). https://doi.org/10.1080/19462166.2010.515036

15. Diller, M., Haret, A., Linsbichler, T., Rümmele, S., Woltran, S.: An extension-based approach to belief revision in abstract argumentation. In: Proceedings of the Twenty-Fourth International Joint Conference on Artificial Intelligence, IJCAI 2015, Buenos Aires, Argentina, 25–31 July 2015, pp. 2926–2932 (2015). http://ijcai.org/Abstract/15/414

16. Dung, P.M.: On the acceptability of arguments and its fundamental role in non-monotonic reasoning, logic programming and n-person games. Artif. Intell. **77**(2), 321–358 (1995). https://doi.org/10.1016/0004-3702(94)00041-X

17. Dunne, P.E., Dvorák, W., Linsbichler, T., Woltran, S.: Characteristics of multiple viewpoints in abstract argumentation. In: Baral, C., Giacomo, G.D., Eiter, T. (eds.) Principles of Knowledge Representation and Reasoning: Proceedings of the Fourteenth International Conference, KR 2014, Vienna, Austria, 20–24 July 2014. AAAI Press (2014). http://www.aaai.org/ocs/index.php/KR/KR14/paper/view/7871

18. Dunne, P.E., Dvorák, W., Linsbichler, T., Woltran, S.: Characteristics of multiple viewpoints in abstract argumentation. Artif. Intell. **228**, 153–178 (2015). https://doi.org/10.1016/j.artint.2015.07.006

19. Dvorák, W., Dunne, P.E.: Computational problems in formal argumentation and their complexity. In: Baroni, P., Gabbay, D., Giacomin, M., van der Torre, L. (eds.) Handbook of Formal Argumentation. College Publications (2018). Also appears in IfCoLog Journal of Logics and their Applications **4**(8), 2623–2706

20. Dyrkolbotn, S.K.: How to argue for anything: enforcing arbitrary sets of labellings using AFS. In: Baral, C., Giacomo, G.D., Eiter, T. (eds.) Principles of Knowledge Representation and Reasoning: Proceedings of the Fourteenth International Conference, KR 2014, Vienna, Austria, 20–24 July 2014. AAAI Press (2014). http://www.aaai.org/ocs/index.php/KR/KR14/paper/view/8018

21. Eiter, T., Kern-Isberner, G.: A brief survey on forgetting from a knowledge representation and reasoning perspective. Künstliche Intell. **33**(1), 9–33 (2019). https://doi.org/10.1007/s13218-018-0564-6

22. Haret, A., Wallner, J.P., Woltran, S.: Two sides of the same coin: Belief revision and enforcing arguments. In: Lang, J. (ed.) Proceedings of the Twenty-Seventh International Joint Conference on Artificial Intelligence, IJCAI 2018, 13–19 July 2018, Stockholm, Sweden, pp. 1854–1860. ijcai.org (2018). https://doi.org/10.24963/ijcai.2018/256

23. Linsbichler, T., Pührer, J., Strass, H.: A uniform account of realizability in abstract argumentation. In: Kaminka, G.A., et al. (eds.) ECAI 2016 - 22nd European Conference on Artificial Intelligence, 29 August–2 September 2016, The Hague, The Netherlands - Including Prestigious Applications of Artificial Intelligence (PAIS 2016). Frontiers in Artificial Intelligence and Applications, vol. 285, pp. 252–260. IOS Press (2016). https://doi.org/10.3233/978-1-61499-672-9-252

24. Oikarinen, E., Woltran, S.: Characterizing strong equivalence for argumentation frameworks. Artif. Intell. **175**(14–15), 1985–2009 (2011). https://doi.org/10.1016/j.artint.2011.06.003

25. Truszczynski, M.: Strong and uniform equivalence of nonmonotonic theories - an algebraic approach. Ann. Math. Artif. Intell. **48**(3–4), 245–265 (2006). https://doi.org/10.1007/s10472-007-9049-2

Propositional Variable Forgetting and Marginalization: Semantically, Two Sides of the Same Coin

Kai Sauerwald[1]([✉])[iD], Christoph Beierle[1][iD], and Gabriele Kern-Isberner[2][iD]

[1] FernUniversität in Hagen, 58084 Hagen, Germany
{kai.sauerwald,christoph.beierle}@fernuni-hagen.de
[2] Technische Universität Dortmund, 44227 Dortmund, Germany
gabriele.kern-isberner@cs.tu-dortmund.de

Abstract. This paper investigates variable forgetting and marginalization in propositional logic. We show that for finite signatures and infinite signatures, variable forgetting and marginalization are corresponding operations, i.e., they yield semantically equivalent outputs for respective complementary inputs. This observation holds for formulas and also for sets of formulas. For formulas, both operations, variable forgetting and marginalization, are shown to be compatible with disjunctions, but not with conjunction, implication and negation. For general sets of formulas, a consequence is that the element-wise application of these operations to a set of formulas and the application to a formula equivalent to this set are not equivalent in general. However, for every deductively closed set X, we show that the element-wise application of variable forgetting or marginalization, respectively, and the application to any formula equivalent to X are equivalent. This latter observation is important because deductively closed sets play an important role in many areas, e.g., in logic-based approaches to knowledge representation and databases.

1 Introduction

Focusing on relevant information is a key ability of intelligent agents to reason and thus an important concern of artificial intelligence, in particular in the field of knowledge representation (KR) where research deals with representing knowledge and belief most adequately in a formal way. Whenever we set up a toy example or a large model for an application in KR, we expect that all variables that we deem to be irrelevant to our model and thus are left out, do not have any influence on reasoning processes and outcomes. For example, when we write an answer set program to provide medical knowledge for finding a best cancer therapy for a patient [25], we would like to safely *forget* variables that speak about, e.g., the weather. More precisely, we expect that the recommended therapy would be the same even if we had taken those variables into account. Similarly, in the well-known Tweety example, we expect the penguin Tweety not to fly even if we had taken dozens of other animal species into account. Such expectations might be justified by a principle analogous to what is known as the *principle of irrelevant alternatives* in social choice theory [22] – adding irrelevant variables should not change the inferences. This is also the basic idea of syntax splitting in nonmonotonic inductive reasoning and belief revision [10,13,19].

For logic-based artificial intelligence, many such forgetting approaches are known, for an overview see [6]. Several approaches considered here fall into the tradition of *variable forgetting* [17], i.e., approaches that remove signature elements from a given logical representation. Variable forgetting is also known as *variable elimination* [15] and has been studied for many formalisms like propositional logic [15], first-order logic [17], description logics [14,18], modal logic [5,24,27], etc. [8,16,26]. Closely related to variable forgetting is also the computation of the uniform interpolant [18].

Technically, in the most basic case where a variable a is to be forgotten from a propositional formula A, *variable forgetting* is implemented by the disjunction of the two modifications of A that arise if a is set to $\top$ resp. $\bot$ [15]. The resulting formula in which a does not occur anymore thus takes both possibilities of a being true or false into account, but abstracts from the specific outcome.

In probability theory, there is a similar (semantic) operation called *marginalization* [20]: the marginal probability of a formula A defined over a signature $\Sigma \backslash \{a\}$ is the sum of the probabilities of all worlds ω whose $\Sigma \backslash \{a\}$-part is a model of A and whose a-part can be positive or negative. This means that semantic marginalization executes the modifications regarding the truth values of a on the models. Marginalization can be defined in a straightforward way also for Spohn's ranking functions [23] and for total preorders [13] that both play a major role for nonmonotonic reasoning and belief revision. The question arises whether there are formal relationships between these two operations of forgetting variables in the syntax resp. semantics, and how exactly they can be made explicit. In particular, in the context of nonmonotonic reasoning resp. belief revision and syntax splitting [10,13], a most relevant question would be if the belief set induced by a marginalized ranking function or a total preorder, respectively, coincides with the result of applying the syntactic operation of variable forgetting to the belief set of the original function. Since belief sets are deductively closed, this leads us naturally to investigations of variable forgetting on sets of formulas, its interactions with Boolean connectives, and its behaviour under deductive closure.

In this paper, we elaborate on the correspondences between variable forgetting and marginalization in propositional logic for finite and infinite signatures. Our main contributions are summarized in the following[1]:

(1) *Variable forgetting and marginalization are two sides of the same coin, semantically.* We show that for a formula φ over Σ, the marginalization of $Mod(\varphi)$ to Γ yields the same as the models of forgetting variables $\Sigma \setminus \Gamma$ in φ. This give reason to define the novel notion of *syntactic marginalization of Γ*, defined as forgetting variables $\Sigma \setminus \Gamma$ in φ. Our results carry over to sets.

(2) *Determine the compatibility of syntactic marginalization with Boolean connectives.* We consider whether marginalization of a complex formula is equiv-

---

[1] The proofs are available at: https://kai-sauerwald.de/pub/FoIKS2024.pdf.

alent to performing marginalization of the sub-formulas instead. Our investigations show that syntactic marginalization, and thus also variable forgetting, are compatible with disjunction, but incompatible with conjunction, negation and implication.

(3) *Syntactic marginalizing of a set of formulas **does not** commute with marginalization of a formula that is equivalent to that set.* In general, performing syntactic marginalizing on each element of a set of formulas Γ does not yield a result equivalent to the syntactic marginalization of φ with $\varphi \equiv \Gamma$.

(4) *Syntactic marginalizing of a deductively closed set of formulas **does** commute with marginalization of a formula that is equivalent to that set.* Syntactic marginalizing of each element from a deductively closed set of formulas Γ does yield a result equivalent to the syntactic marginalization of φ with $\varphi \equiv \Gamma$.

We also show that syntactic marginalization is related to the minimal set of syntax elements required for representing a formula. Note that (3) and (4) provide insights on the marginalization-compatibility of different representations for sets of formulas. Because of (3), for knowledge-based systems that execute marginalizations, representation does matter, and one has to be careful when invoking classical equivalences between representations. Furthermore, (4) guarantees that when representing a deductive closed set of formulas K, typically also called a belief set, by an equivalent formula A, i.e., $A \equiv K$, then marginalization can be safely applied.

Note that for the formulation of properties and theorems we establish in this paper we focus on viewpoint of syntactic marginalization. Due to (1), all these properties, theorems and the contributions mentioned above also apply to variable forgetting and (model)-marginalization.

This paper is organized as follows. The next section provides the background on logic and further preliminaries. In Sect. 3, we establish that, semantically, variable forgetting and (model)-marginalization are dual operations. Furthermore, we define syntactic marginalization. Section 4 considers the connection between syntactic marginalization of a formula A and the minimal set of signature elements required for a formula to be equivalent to A. In Sect. 5, we determine the compatibility of connectives with syntactic marginalization. The general case of marginalization of arbitrary sets of formulas is considered in Sect. 6. The case of deductively closed sets is considered in Sect. 7. Section 8 discusses representational aspects and further results on the marginalization of deductively closed sets of formulas. In Sect. 9, we conclude and point out future work.

2   Preliminaries and Background

Let $\Sigma = \{a, b, c, \ldots\}$ be a (possible infinite) signature, whose elements are called atoms or variables, and let $\mathcal{L}_\Sigma = \{A, B, C, \ldots\}$ denote the finitely generated propositional language over Σ. For conciseness of notation, we sometimes omit the logical *and*-connector, writing AB instead of $A \wedge B$, and overlining formulas will indicate negation, i.e., $\overline{A}$ means $\neg A$. Furthermore, we require $\mathcal{L}$ to contain $\top$

and $\bot$, where $\top$ is interpreted, as usually, as a tautology, and $\bot$ as a contradiction. Let Ω_Σ denote the set of all possible worlds (propositional interpretations) over Σ. As usual, $\omega \models_\Sigma A$ means that the propositional formula $A \in \mathcal{L}_\Sigma$ holds in the possible world $\omega \in \Omega_\Sigma$, and $Mod_\Sigma(A) = \{\omega \mid \omega \models_\Sigma A\}$ denotes the set of all such possible worlds. With $A \equiv_\Sigma B$ we denote semantic equivalence defined as usually, i.e. $Mod_\Sigma(A) = Mod_\Sigma(B)$. With $Cn_\Sigma(A) = \{F \in \mathcal{L}_\Sigma \mid A \models_\Sigma F\}$ we denote the set of all logical consequences of A and say that $L \subseteq \mathcal{L}_\Sigma$ is *deductively closed* if $Cn_\Sigma(L) = L$. To simplify notation in the following, if Σ is finite, we will use ω both for the model and the corresponding complete conjunction containing all atoms either in positive or negative form. We say a formula A is *contingent* if $A \not\equiv \top$ and $A \not\equiv \bot$. For a set $X \subseteq \mathcal{L}_\Sigma$ of formulas, we lift the models relation to X by defining $\omega \models_\Sigma X$ if $\omega \models_\Sigma A$ for all $A \in X$. The above-mentioned notions carry over to sets of formulas in the usual way, e.g., the set of models of X is $Mod_\Sigma(X) = \{\omega \mid \omega \models_\Sigma X\}$, semantical equivalence of $A \in \mathcal{L}_\Sigma$ and X is $X \equiv_\Sigma A$ if $Mod_\Sigma(A) = Mod_\Sigma(X)$, and so forth. We assume that signatures are always non-empty sets, which applies especially to subsignatures $\Gamma \subseteq \Sigma$. If $A \in \mathcal{L}_\Sigma$ is a formula, then $Sig(A)$ denotes the atoms that appear in A. Furthermore, the minimal set of signature elements (in terms of set inclusion) of a formula that is equivalent to A is denoted by $Sig_{min}(A)$. Parikh showed that $Sig_{min}(A)$ is unique and hence well-defined [19, Lem. 2]. Note that $Sig_{min}(A) = \varnothing$ holds if and only if $A \equiv \bot$ or $A \equiv \top$ holds. Moreover, negation is a neutral operation regarding minimal signatures, i.e., $Sig_{min}(A) = Sig_{min}(\neg A)$. For a deductively closed set of formulas $Cn_\Sigma(X)$ we denote its signature with $Sig(Cn_\Sigma(X)) = \Sigma$.

3   Marginalization and Variable Forgetting for Formulas

In this section, we start by introducing the basic notions of variable forgetting and marginalization. Then, we will define a syntactic version of marginalization and establish the connection between these three operations.

Variable Forgetting. Forgetting in a logical setting is sometimes understood as removing a variable by an syntactic operation. The approach is rooted in the work of Lin and Reiter [17], which established a whole line of research on that topic, e.g., [4,15]. However, the technical notion but was introduced by Boole [3].

Definition 3.1 (variable forgetting [15]). *Let $A \in \mathcal{L}_\Sigma$ be a formula, let $a \in \Sigma$ be an atom, and let $\Gamma \subseteq \Sigma$ be a subsignature. The* variable forgetting of a in A,

$$\mathrm{VarForget}(A, a) = A[a/\top] \vee A[a/\bot] \,,$$

arises from A by replacing all occurrences of a by $\top$, yielding $A[a/\top]$, and by replacing all occurrences of a by $\bot$, yielding $A[a/\bot]$. The variable forgetting of Γ in A, denoted by $\mathrm{VarForget}(A, \Gamma)$, *is the result of successively eliminating all variables of Γ in A that appear in $Sig(A)$.*

Note that $\mathrm{VarForget}(A, \Gamma)$ is a proper propositional formula; as $Sig(A)$ is always finite, also $\mathrm{VarForget}(A, \Gamma)$ is finite. It has been shown that $\mathrm{VarForget}(A, \Gamma)$ yields a syntactically equivalent formula (up to associativity of disjunction) for every order on Γ [15]. Clearly, when one is interested in the exact syntactic result of VarForget(A, Γ), order of execution matters. However, as we consider here semantic equivalences, we not investigate this further.

Example 3.2. Let $\Sigma = \{t, b, c\}$ be a signature where the atoms have following intended meaning: t stands for "tea is served", and b stands for "biscuits are served", and c stands for "coffee is served". We consider the formulas $A = (t \vee c) \to b$ ("When tea or coffee are served, then biscuits are served") and $B = (t \vee c) \wedge b$ ("tea or coffee are served, and also biscuits are served"). Various different variable eliminations in A and B are:

$$\text{VarForget}(A, t) = ((\top \vee c) \to b) \vee ((\bot \vee c) \to b) \equiv_{\{c,b\}} c \to b$$
$$\text{VarForget}(A, c) = ((t \vee \top) \to b) \vee ((t \vee \bot) \to b) \equiv_{\{t,b\}} t \to b$$
$$\text{VarForget}(A, b) = ((t \vee c) \to \top) \vee ((t \vee c) \to \bot) \equiv_{\{t,c\}} \top$$
$$\text{VarForget}(B, t) = ((\top \vee c) \wedge b) \vee ((\bot \vee c) \wedge b) \equiv_{\{c,b\}} b$$
$$\text{VarForget}(B, c) = ((t \vee \top) \wedge b) \vee ((t \vee \bot) \wedge b) \equiv_{\{t,b\}} b$$
$$\text{VarForget}(B, b) = ((t \vee c) \wedge \top) \vee ((t \vee c) \wedge \bot) \equiv_{\{t,c\}} t \vee c$$

Variable forgetting of the signature $\Gamma = \{t, c\}$ in A and B yields the following:

$$\text{VarForget}(A, \Gamma) = \text{VarForget}(A, t)[c/\top] \vee \text{VarForget}(A, t)[c/\bot]$$
$$= (A[t/\top] \vee A[t/\bot])[c/\top] \vee (A[t/\top] \vee A[t/\bot])[c/\bot]$$
$$= (((\top \vee \top) \to b) \vee ((\bot \vee \top) \to b)) \vee (((\top \vee \bot) \to b) \vee ((\bot \vee \bot) \to b)) \equiv_\Gamma \top$$
$$\text{VarForget}(B, \Gamma) = \text{VarForget}(B, t)[c/\top] \vee \text{VarForget}(B, t)[t/\bot]$$
$$= (B[t/\top] \vee B[t/\bot])[c/\top] \vee (B[t/\top] \vee B[t/\bot])[c/\bot]$$
$$= (((\top \vee \top) \wedge b) \vee ((\bot \vee \top) \wedge b)) \vee (((\top \vee \bot) \wedge b) \vee ((\bot \vee \bot) \wedge b)) \equiv_\Gamma b$$

A and B could be viewed as general knowledge about different serving practices. However, when being in a specific context, e.g., in a tearoom, it's sufficient (or even rational) to reason and discuss only tea and biscuits as in VarForget(A, Γ) and VarForget(B, Γ) because there will be no coffee at all.

Model Marginalization. Another approach to forgetting is marginalization, which is rooted in probability theory [20]. In contrast to variable forgetting, marginalization is defined on interpretations, using the idea of Γ-parts of interpretations. For a subsignature $\Gamma \subseteq \Sigma$ and an interpretation $\omega \in \Omega_\Sigma$ we denote the Γ-part of ω with $\omega^\Gamma \in \Omega_\Gamma$, mentioning exactly the atoms from Γ, i.e., $\omega^\Gamma : \Gamma \to \{0, 1\}$ with $\omega^\Gamma(a) = \omega(a)$ for all $a \in \Gamma$. Marginalization is then the reduction to the Γ-part of an interpretation.

Definition 3.3 (model marginalization, $\text{ModMg}_\Sigma(\omega, \Gamma)$, $\text{ModMg}_\Sigma(M, \Gamma)$). *Let $\omega \in \Omega_\Sigma$, let $M \subseteq \Omega_\Sigma$, and let $\Gamma \subseteq \Sigma$. We say $\text{ModMg}_\Sigma(\omega, \Gamma) = \omega^\Gamma$ is the (model) marginalization of ω from Σ to Γ. The element-wise marginalization of all $\omega \in M$ from Σ to Γ is called (model) marginalization of M from Σ to Γ, denoted by $\text{ModMg}_\Sigma(M, \Gamma) = \{\text{ModMg}_\Sigma(\omega, \Gamma) \mid \omega \in M\}$.*

When viewing a logic as an institution [7], the marginalization of models to a subsignature as given in Definition 3.3 is just a special case of the general forgetful functor $Mod(\varphi)$ from Σ-models to Γ-models induced by any signature morphism φ from Γ to Σ. The special case of Definition 3.3 is given by the forgetful functor $Mod(\iota)$ induced by the signature inclusion $\iota : \Gamma \to \Sigma$ (cf. also [1]). In the following, we consider an example on model marginalization:

Example 3.4. Consider again $\Sigma = \{t, b, c\}$ from Example 3.2. For illustration of the model marginalization of individual interpretations, consider $\omega_1 = \bar{t}cb$ ("coffee and biscuits are served, but no tea") and $\omega_2 = \bar{t}\bar{c}b$ ("coffee is served, but no tea and biscuits") and the subsignature $\Gamma = \{t, b\}$. The Γ-part of ω_1 is $\omega_1^\Gamma = \bar{t}b$. Likewise, the Γ-part of ω_2 is the same, i.e., $\omega_2^\Gamma = \bar{t}b$. Consequently, the marginalization of these interpretations is as follows ("biscuits are served, but no tea"):

$$\mathrm{ModMg}_\Sigma(\omega_1, \Gamma) = \omega_1^\Gamma \quad \mathrm{ModMg}_\Sigma(\omega_2, \Gamma) = \omega_2^\Gamma = \bar{t}b$$

The models $A = (t \lor c) \to b$ and $B = (t \lor c) \land b$ from Example 3.2 are:

$$Mod_\Sigma(A) = \{\, tcb,\ t\bar{c}b,\ \bar{t}cb,\ \bar{t}\bar{c}b,\ \bar{t}\bar{c}\bar{b} \,\} \qquad Mod_\Sigma(B) = \{\, tcb,\ t\bar{c}b,\ \bar{t}cb \,\}$$

Several model marginalizations of $Mod_\Sigma(A)$ and $Mod_\Sigma(B)$ are:

$$\mathrm{ModMg}_\Sigma(Mod_\Sigma(A), \{c, b\}) = \{\, cb,\ \bar{c}b,\ \bar{c}\bar{b} \,\}$$
$$\mathrm{ModMg}_\Sigma(Mod_\Sigma(A), \{t, b\}) = \{\, tb,\ \bar{t}b,\ \bar{t}\bar{b} \,\}$$
$$\mathrm{ModMg}_\Sigma(Mod_\Sigma(A), \{t, c\}) = \{\, tc,\ t\bar{c},\ \bar{t}c,\ \bar{t}\bar{c} \,\}$$
$$\mathrm{ModMg}_\Sigma(Mod_\Sigma(A), \{b\}) = \{\, b,\ \bar{b} \,\}$$
$$\mathrm{ModMg}_\Sigma(Mod_\Sigma(B), \{c, b\}) = \{\, cb,\ \bar{c}b \,\}$$
$$\mathrm{ModMg}_\Sigma(Mod_\Sigma(B), \{t, b\}) = \{\, tb,\ \bar{t}b \,\}$$
$$\mathrm{ModMg}_\Sigma(Mod_\Sigma(B), \{t, c\}) = \{\, tc,\ t\bar{c},\ \bar{t}c \,\}$$
$$\mathrm{ModMg}_\Sigma(Mod_\Sigma(B), \{b\}) = \{\, b \,\}$$

One can observe easily that $\mathrm{ModMg}_\Sigma(Mod_\Sigma(A), \{b\})$ is the same as the set of models of $\Sigma \setminus \mathrm{VarForget}(A, b)$, and analogously for $\mathrm{ModMg}_\Sigma(Mod_\Sigma(B), \{b\})$ and $\Sigma \setminus \mathrm{VarForget}(B, b)$ (cf. Example 3.2). We will see that this is no coincidence, as both operations are two sides of the same coin.

Syntactic Marginalization. Note that variable forgetting is a syntactic operation on formulas and model marginalization is a semantic operation on interpretations. Moreover, variable forgetting takes the signature elements to be removed as a parameter, while for marginalization the posterior sub-signature is a parameter. To avoid this duality, we define syntactic marginalization as the dual of variable forgetting.

Definition 3.5 (syntactic marginalization). *Let $A \in \mathcal{L}_\Sigma$ and let $\Gamma \subseteq \Sigma$. The syntactic marginalization of A (from Σ) to Γ, written $\mathrm{SynMg}_\Sigma(A, \Gamma)$, is $\mathrm{VarForget}(A, \Sigma \setminus \Gamma)$.*

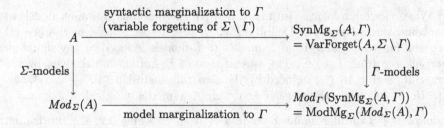

Fig. 1. Semantic compatibility between marginalization and variable forgetting.

The syntactic marginalization of a formula to a reduced signature is equivalent to the formula obtained by forgetting all variables that are not in the subsignature[2].

Interrelation. We obtain the following compatibility result for variable forgetting and marginalization which is closely related to known results on variable forgetting [15]. Figure 1 provides an illustration of these interrelations.

Theorem 3.6. *For every $A \in \mathcal{L}_\Sigma$ and $\Gamma \subseteq \Sigma$ the following holds:*

$$\mathrm{ModMg}_\Sigma(Mod_\Sigma(A), \Gamma) = Mod_\Gamma(\mathrm{SynMg}_\Sigma(A, \Gamma))$$
$$= Mod_\Gamma(\mathrm{VarForget}(A, \Sigma \setminus \Gamma))$$

As a first consequence of Theorem 3.6, we obtain that despite syntactic marginalization being a pure syntactic operation, syntactic marginalization yields semantic equivalent results for semantic equivalent formulas and complies with entailment.

Corollary 3.7. *Let $A, B \in \mathcal{L}_\Sigma$ and let $\Gamma \subseteq \Sigma$. The following statements hold:*

(a) If $A \equiv_\Sigma B$, then we have $\mathrm{SynMg}_\Sigma(A, \Gamma) \equiv_\Gamma \mathrm{SynMg}_\Sigma(B, \Gamma)$.
(b) If $A \models_\Sigma B$, then we have $\mathrm{SynMg}_\Sigma(A, \Gamma) \models_\Gamma \mathrm{SynMg}_\Sigma(B, \Gamma)$.

Because (model and syntactic) marginalization and variable forgetting comply with each other semantically, in the following sections we continue to present results from the viewpoint of syntactic marginalization. Cleary, due to Theorem 3.6 these results also carry over to variable forgetting and model marginalization.

4   Marginalization and Minimal Sets of Atoms

Before investigating syntactic marginalization in more detail, we show that $\mathrm{Sig}_{\min}(A)$ is the set of those atoms that distinguish models of A from non-models of A by exactly one signature element.

Proposition 4.1. *For each propositional formula $A \in \mathcal{L}_\Sigma$ we have:*

$$\mathrm{Sig}_{\min}(A) = \{a \in \Sigma \mid \exists \omega_1, \omega_2 \in \Omega. \ \omega_1 \models_\Sigma A \text{ and } \omega_2 \not\models_\Sigma A \text{ and } \omega_1^{\Sigma \setminus \{a\}} = \omega_2^{\Sigma \setminus \{a\}}\}$$

---

[2] We thank the anonymous reviewer for phrasing this interrelation so nicely.

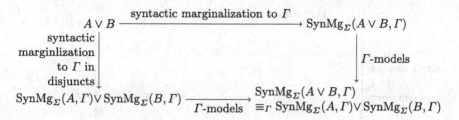

Fig. 2. Semantic compatibility between disjunction and syntactic marginalization.

Proposition 4.1 formally underpins the intuition that a minimal formula (in terms of different atoms) is required to make use of exactly those atoms which can be distinguished semantically.

From Theorem 3.6 and Proposition 4.1, we obtain the following connection between syntactic marginalization and $\mathrm{Sig}_{\min}(A)$.

Proposition 4.2. *Let Σ and Γ be signatures with $\Gamma \subseteq \Sigma$ and let $A \in \mathcal{L}_\Sigma$. The following statements hold:*

(a) *We have that $\mathrm{Sig}_{\min}(\mathrm{SynMg}_\Sigma(A, \Gamma)) \subseteq \mathrm{Sig}_{\min}(A) \cap \Gamma$ holds.*
(b) *We have that $a \in \mathrm{Sig}_{\min}(A)$ iff $A \not\equiv_\Sigma \mathrm{SynMg}_\Sigma(A, \Sigma \setminus \{a\})$ holds.*
(c) *If A is consistent, then $\Gamma \cap \mathrm{Sig}_{\min}(A) = \varnothing$ iff $\mathrm{SynMg}_\Sigma(A, \Gamma) \equiv_\Sigma \top$.*

5 Compatibility of Syntactic Marginalization with Connectives

We now investigate the compatibility of syntactic marginalization with the standard connectives of propositional logic. The compatibility with disjunction and conjunction over finite signatures was investigated for propositional logic from the perspective for variable forgetting by Zhang and Zhou [27]. We show that syntactic marginalization is fully compatible with disjunctions and only partially compatible with the $\wedge$ connective and also with the $\neg$ connective of propositional logic both for finite and infinite signatures.

We start with the compatibility of syntactic marginalization with disjunction (Fig. 2).

Proposition 5.1. *For each $A \equiv_\Sigma A_1 \vee \ldots \vee A_n$ with $A, A_1, \ldots A_n \in \mathcal{L}_\Sigma$ and each $\Gamma \subseteq \Sigma$ the following holds:*

$$\mathrm{SynMg}_\Sigma(A, \Gamma) \equiv_\Gamma \mathrm{SynMg}_\Sigma(A_1, \Gamma) \vee \ldots \vee \mathrm{SynMg}_\Sigma(A_n, \Gamma)$$

For conjunction we consider both directions of semantic equivalence separately. In general syntactic marginalization and conjuncts are not compatible; however, the following proposition shows that one direction of semantic equivalence holds.

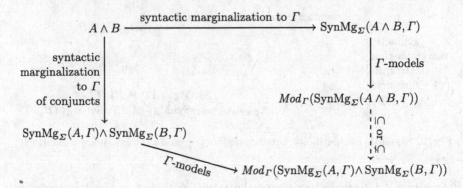

Fig. 3. Semantic relations between conjunction and syntactic marginalization with respect to Γ. The relation between Γ-models of $\mathrm{SynMg}_\Sigma(A \wedge B, \Gamma)$ and of $\mathrm{SynMg}_\Sigma(A, \Gamma) \wedge \mathrm{SynMg}_\Sigma(B, \Gamma)$ is a subset-relation (represented by the dashed arrow); in certain cases this subset-relation is strict.

Proposition 5.2. *For each $A, A_1, \ldots A_n \in \mathcal{L}_\Sigma$ with $A \equiv_\Sigma A_1 \wedge \ldots \wedge A_n$ and for each $\Gamma \subseteq \Sigma$ the following holds:*

$$Mod_\Gamma(\mathrm{SynMg}_\Sigma(A, \Gamma)) \subseteq Mod_\Gamma(\mathrm{SynMg}_\Sigma(A_1, \Gamma) \wedge \ldots \wedge \mathrm{SynMg}_\Sigma(A_n, \Gamma)) \quad (1)$$

The converse direction of Eq. (1) in Proposition 5.2 does not hold in general. In the following proposition, we present this claim formally.

Proposition 5.3. *Let Σ be a signature with three or more elements. There exist $A, A_1, \ldots A_n \in \mathcal{L}_\Sigma$ with $A \equiv_\Sigma A_1 \wedge \ldots \wedge A_n$ and $\Gamma \subseteq \Sigma$ such that:*

$$Mod_\Gamma(\mathrm{SynMg}_\Sigma(A_1, \Gamma) \wedge \ldots \wedge \mathrm{SynMg}_\Sigma(A_n, \Gamma)) \not\subseteq Mod_\Gamma(\mathrm{SynMg}_\Sigma(A, \Gamma))$$

Figure 3 illustrates and summarizes our observations on the compatibility between conjunction and syntactic marginalization. Next, we consider an example on Proposition 5.3.

Example 5.4. Suppose that $\Sigma = \{a, s, f\}$ is a signature, where a has the intended meaning "is an animal", and s stands for "can swim", and f stands for "has fins". We consider the formulas $A = a \wedge s \wedge f$ ("It is an animal that can swim and has fins."), $A_1 = a \wedge (s \leftrightarrow f)$ ("It is an animal and it can swim if and only if it has fins.") and $A_2 = a \wedge f$ ("It is an animal with fins."). The syntactic marginalizations of these formulas to $\Gamma = \{a, s\}$ are:

$$\mathrm{SynMg}_\Sigma(A, \Gamma) = (a \wedge s \wedge \top) \vee (a \wedge s \wedge \bot) \qquad \equiv a \wedge s$$
$$\text{("It is an animal that can swim.")}$$
$$\mathrm{SynMg}_\Sigma(A_1, \Gamma) = (a \wedge (s \leftrightarrow \top)) \vee (a \wedge (s \leftrightarrow \bot)) \quad \equiv a \quad \text{("It is an animal.")}$$
$$\mathrm{SynMg}_\Sigma(A_2, \Gamma) = (a \wedge \top) \vee (a \wedge \bot) \qquad\qquad \equiv a \quad \text{("It is an animal.")}$$

We observe that $A \equiv A_1 \wedge A_2$ holds, yet $\mathrm{SynMg}_\Sigma(A, \Gamma)$ differs semantically from $\mathrm{SynMg}_\Sigma(A_1, \Gamma) \wedge \mathrm{SynMg}_\Sigma(A_2, \Gamma)$. More intuitively speaking, the information

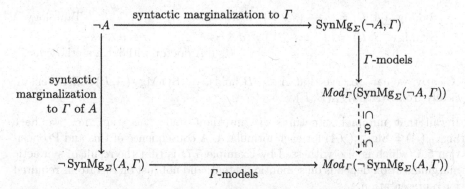

Fig. 4. Semantic relations between negation and syntactic marginalization with respect to Γ. The relation between Γ-models of $\mathrm{SynMg}_\Sigma(A, \Gamma)$ and of $\neg\,\mathrm{SynMg}_\Sigma(A, \Gamma)$ is a subset-relation (represented by the dashed arrow); in certain cases this subset-relation is strict.

about s, which is clearly stated in A, has got lost in the forgetting of f from $A_1 \wedge A_2$. This is because the conjunction $A_1 \wedge A_2$ encodes the truth of s via a dependence of s from f, which is forgotten.

For the case of negation we obtain results analogue to the case of conjunction. Syntactic marginalization is in general not fully compatible with negation; however, the following proposition attests that one direction of semantic equivalence holds.

Proposition 5.5. *For all $A, B \in \mathcal{L}_\Sigma$ with $A \equiv_\Sigma \neg B$ and for all $\Gamma \subseteq \Sigma$ we have:*
$$Mod_\Gamma(\neg(\mathrm{SynMg}_\Sigma(B, \Gamma))) \subseteq Mod_\Gamma(\mathrm{SynMg}_\Sigma(A, \Gamma))$$

The next proposition states that the inclusion (5.5) in Proposition 5.5 is sometimes strict. In contrast to conjunction, the incompatibility arizes already for signatures of size two.

Proposition 5.6. *Let Σ be a signature with two or more elements and let $\Gamma \subsetneq \Sigma$ be a strict subsignature. There are formulas $A, B \in \mathcal{L}_\Sigma$ with $A \equiv_\Sigma \neg B$ such that:*
$$Mod_\Gamma(\mathrm{SynMg}_\Sigma(A, \Gamma)) \nsubseteq Mod_\Gamma(\neg\,\mathrm{SynMg}_\Sigma(B, \Gamma))$$

Figure 4 summarizes the results presented here on the compatibility of marginalization and Boolean negation.

Example 5.7. Suppose that $\Sigma = \{d, s, c\}$ is a signature, where d has the intended meaning "is a doctor", and s stands for "wears a stethoscope", and c stands for "wears a doctor's coat". We consider the formulas $A = d \rightarrow (s \vee c)$ ("A doctor wears a stethoscope or a coat.") and $B = d \wedge \neg s \wedge \neg c$ ("A doctor without a stethoscope who wears no coat."). The syntactic marginalizations to $\Gamma = \{d, s\}$ of these formulas are:

$$\mathrm{SynMg}_\Sigma(A, \Gamma) = (d \to (s \lor \top)) \lor (d \to (s \lor \bot)) \qquad \equiv \top \qquad (\text{``Tautology.''})$$
$$\mathrm{SynMg}_\Sigma(B, \Gamma) = (d \land \neg s \land \top) \lor (d \land \neg s \land \bot) \qquad \equiv d \land \neg s$$
$$(\text{``A doctor without a stethoscope.''})$$

Clearly, we can observe that $A \equiv \neg B$ holds, yet $\mathrm{SynMg}_\Sigma(A, \Gamma)$ differs semantically from $\neg\,\mathrm{SynMg}_\Sigma(B, \Gamma)$.

Recall that minimal signatures are invariant under negation, i.e., we have $\mathrm{Sig}_{\min}(A) = \mathrm{Sig}_{\min}(\neg A)$ for each formula A. A consequence of this and Proposition 5.6 (which is also witnessed by Example 5.7) is that the result of syntactic marginalization depends on semantic content, and not just on the atoms required for representation.

Corollary 5.8. *For each signature Σ with two or more elements, there exist formulas $A, B \in \mathcal{L}_\Sigma$ with $\mathrm{Sig}_{\min}(A) = \mathrm{Sig}_{\min}(B)$ such that $\mathrm{SynMg}_\Sigma(A, \Gamma) \neq \mathrm{SynMg}_\Sigma(B, \Gamma)$.*

Another consequence of the results given above is the following result on syntactic marginalization and implication.

Proposition 5.9. *For each $A, B, C \in \mathcal{L}_\Sigma$ with $A \equiv_\Sigma B \to C$ and for each $\Gamma \subseteq \Sigma$ the following holds:*

$$Mod_\Gamma(\mathrm{SynMg}_\Sigma(B, \Gamma) \to \mathrm{SynMg}_\Sigma(C, \Gamma)) \subseteq Mod_\Gamma(\mathrm{SynMg}_\Sigma(A, \Gamma))$$

However, as in the case of conjunction and negation, syntactic marginalization does not comply with implication.

Example 5.10. Let $\Sigma = \{a, b, \ldots\}$ and let $\Gamma \subseteq \Sigma$ be a subsignature such that $a \notin \Gamma$ and $b \in \Gamma$. We choose the formulas $A = a \land b$ and $B = \neg a \lor \neg b$ and $C = \bot$. One can observe easily that $A \equiv_\Sigma B \to C = \neg B \lor C$ holds.

$$\mathrm{SynMg}_\Sigma(A, \Gamma) = (\top \land b) \lor (\bot \land b) \equiv_\Gamma b$$
$$\mathrm{SynMg}_\Sigma(B, \Gamma) = (\neg\top \lor \neg b) \lor (\neg\bot \lor \neg b) \equiv_\Gamma \top$$
$$\mathrm{SynMg}_\Sigma(C, \Gamma) = \bot$$
$$\mathrm{SynMg}_\Sigma(A, \Gamma) \equiv_\Gamma b \not\equiv_\Gamma \mathrm{SynMg}_\Sigma(B, \Gamma) \to \mathrm{SynMg}_\Sigma(C, \Gamma) \equiv_\Gamma \bot$$

Thus, we obtain $Mod_\Gamma(\mathrm{SynMg}_\Sigma(A, \Gamma)) \not\subseteq Mod_\Gamma(\neg\,\mathrm{SynMg}_\Sigma(B, \Gamma))$.

Proposition 5.11. *Let Σ be a signature with two or more elements and let $\Gamma \subsetneq \Sigma$ be a strict subsignature. There are formulas $A, B, C \in \mathcal{L}_\Sigma$ with $A \equiv B \to C$ such that:*

$$\mathrm{SynMg}_\Sigma(A, \Gamma) \not\equiv \mathrm{SynMg}_\Sigma(B, \Gamma) \to \mathrm{SynMg}_\Sigma(C, \Gamma)$$

In summary, we showed that marginalization is not fully compatible with standard connectives of propositional logic both for finite and infinite signatures, whereby disjunction can be listed as the only mentionable exception (see Table 1).

Table 1. Overview of the compatibility of syntactic marginalization, respectively variable forgetting, with connectives of propositional logic. Here, $\equiv$ stands for full compatibility; $\models$ expresses that marginalization of the full formula implies the formula obtained by marginalizing the components of the connective; analogously, $\dashv$ expresses that marginalization of the components of the connectives implies the marginalized formula.

Connective	Compatibility	Counterexample
$\vee$	$\equiv$ (Proposition 5.1)	fully compatible
$\wedge$	$\models$ (Proposition 5.2)	Proposition 5.3/Example 5.4
$\neg$	$\dashv$ (Proposition 5.5)	Proposition 5.6/Example 4
$\rightarrow$	$\dashv$ (Proposition 5.9)	Proposition 5.11/Example 5.10

6   Marginalization and Variable Forgetting for Sets of Formulas

In this section, we investigate and discuss marginalization and variable forgetting for finite and infinite sets of formulas and for finite and infinite signatures. For that, we will use results obtained in Sect. 5. While some results seem rather straightforward to obtain technically, these results are not trivial because one might fall quickly into the trap of thinking that marginalization behaves very intuitively for sets of propositional formulas. In particular, we will see that one has to be careful about representation, e.g., syntactic structure, when performing marginalization or variable forgetting, respectively.

Element-Wise Marginalization for Sets. In order to lift syntactic marginalization of a formula to sets of formulas a natural choice is element-wise marginalization of each single formula.

Definition 6.1 (element-wise marginalization). *Let $X \subseteq \mathcal{L}_\Sigma$ be a set of formula and $\Gamma \subseteq \Sigma$. The* element-wise marginalization *of X (from Σ) to Γ, written $\mathrm{EWSynMg}_\Sigma(X, \Gamma)$, is given by $\mathrm{EWSynMg}_\Sigma(X, \Gamma) = \{\mathrm{SynMg}_\Sigma(B, \Gamma) \mid B \in X\}$.*

One can see that $\mathrm{EWSynMg}_\Sigma(X, \Gamma)$ is always well-defined, even for those cases where X, Σ or Γ are infinite. This is mainly due to the fact that $\mathrm{SynMg}_\Sigma(B, \Gamma)$ is a well-defined propositional formula for any formula B (cf. Sect. 3).

Similarly to Definition 6.1, we define a notion of element-wise variable forgetting for a set of formulas as $\mathrm{EWVarForget}(X, \Gamma) = \{\mathrm{VarForget}(B, \Gamma) \mid B \in X\}$. In Sect. 3, we have seen that variable forgetting and marginalization are corresponding operations on formulas, and from this correspondence we easily obtain that $\mathrm{EWSynMg}_\Sigma(X, \Gamma) = \mathrm{EWVarForget}(X, \Sigma \setminus \Gamma)$ holds. Because of this, in this section and in the following sections, we will take the viewpoint of (syntactic) marginalization.

Recall that the semantics for a set of formulas is given by intersection, which corresponds to conjunction in the case of finite sets of formulas. We will see in the following that due to Proposition 5.3 the notion of element-wise marginalization behaves already very unexpectedly on finite sets and does not seem to be an adequate way to define syntactic marginalization of sets of formulas.

Proposition 6.2. *Let Σ be a signature with three or more elements. There is a finite set of formulas $X \subseteq \mathcal{L}_\Sigma$ and a signature $\Gamma \subseteq \Sigma$ such that for every formula $A \in \mathcal{L}_\Sigma$ with $A \equiv_\Sigma X$ we obtain:*

$$\text{EWSynMg}_\Sigma(X, \Gamma) \not\models_\Gamma \text{SynMg}_\Sigma(A, \Gamma)$$

Proposition 6.2 shows that element-wise marginalization of sets of formulas is not reducible to syntactic marginalization of an equivalent formula. However, the syntactic marginalization of a formula equivalent to a set of formulas is complete, in the sense that every logical consequence of the element-wise marginalization is also a logical consequence of the syntactic marginalization of a corresponding formula. The following proposition attests this observation.

Proposition 6.3. *Let $X \subseteq \mathcal{L}_\Sigma$ be an arbitrary set of formulas, $A \in \mathcal{L}_\Sigma$ be a formula and $\Gamma \subseteq \Sigma$. If $A \equiv_\Sigma X$, then $\text{SynMg}_\Sigma(A, \Gamma) \models_\Gamma \text{EWSynMg}_\Sigma(X, \Gamma)$.*

We continue by demonstrating how the incompatibility of conjunction with syntactic marginalization carries over to sets of formulas.

Example 6.4. Let $\Sigma = \{a, s, f\}$ be the signature from Example 5.4 and let $A = a \wedge s \wedge f$ and $A_1 = a \wedge (s \leftrightarrow f)$ and $A_2 = a \wedge f$ be the formulas from the same example. As shown before, for $\Gamma = \{a, s\}$ we have $\text{SynMg}_\Sigma(A, \Gamma) \equiv_\Gamma a \wedge s$ and $\text{SynMg}_\Sigma(A_1, \Gamma) \equiv_\Gamma \text{SynMg}_\Sigma(A_2, \Gamma) \equiv_\Gamma a$. This renders $\text{SynMg}_\Sigma(A, \Gamma)$ to be semantically different to $\text{SynMg}_\Sigma(A_1, \Gamma) \wedge \text{SynMg}_\Sigma(A_2, \Gamma)$. We reproduce this result by using sets of formulas. Let $X = \{A_1, A_2\}$ be the set containing A_1 and A_2, which is equivalent to A, i.e., $X \equiv_\Sigma A$. Applying element-wise marginalization to X yields $\text{EWSynMg}_\Sigma(X, \Gamma) = \{\text{SynMg}_\Sigma(A_1, \Gamma), \text{SynMg}_\Sigma(A_2, \Gamma)\} \equiv_\Gamma \{a\}$, which is semantically different from $\text{SynMg}_\Sigma(A, \Gamma)$.

Infinite Signatures. For a set of formulas $X \subseteq \mathcal{L}_\Sigma$, we say that X *is finitely representable over Σ* if there is a formulas $A \in \mathcal{L}_\Sigma$ such that $X \equiv_\Sigma A$. Clearly, if Σ is finite, we have that X is finitely representable. But in general, not every set of formulas is finitely representable when the signature is infinite. This give rise to representational problems that carry over to syntactic marginalization as well.

Example 6.5. Let $\Sigma = \{a, a_1, a_2, a_3, \ldots\}$ be an infinite signature. We consider the set of formulas $X = \{a, \bar{a}a_1, \bar{a}a_2, , \bar{a}a_3, , \bar{a}a_4 \ldots\}$. First, note that X is inconsistent, i.e., $Mod_\Sigma(X) = \varnothing$. This is because the formula a is inconsistent with all other formulas $\bar{a} \wedge a_i$ in X. Clearly, X is finitely representable, e.g., by employing the formula $\bot$. Now let $\Gamma = \{a_1, a_2, \ldots\}$ be the subsignature of Σ which contains every atom of Σ except a. The syntactic marginalization of a to Γ is $\text{SynMg}_\Sigma(a, \Gamma) = \top \vee \bot$ and the syntactic marginalization of each $\bar{a} \wedge a_i \in X$ to Γ is $\text{SynMg}_\Sigma(\bar{a} \wedge a_i, \Gamma) = (\top \wedge a_i) \vee (\bot \wedge a_i)$. Consequently, we have $\text{SynMg}_\Sigma(a, \Gamma) \equiv_\Gamma \top$ and $\text{SynMg}_\Sigma(\overline{a}a_i, \Gamma) \equiv_\Gamma a_i$. Hence, we have $\text{SynMg}_\Sigma(X, \Gamma) \equiv_\Gamma \{a_1, a_2, \ldots\}$, implying that $\text{SynMg}_\Sigma(X, \Gamma) \equiv_\Gamma \{a_1, a_2, \ldots\}$ is not finitely representable over Γ.

The following proposition is an implication of the observation made in Example 6.5.

Proposition 6.6. *If Σ is infinite, then there is a set of formulas $X \subseteq \mathcal{L}_\Sigma$ and a subsignature Γ such that $\text{EWSynMg}_\Sigma(X, \Gamma)$ is not not finitely representable, even when X is finitely representable.*

Nevertheless, note that even for sets of formulas that are not finitely representable, we can always obtain a finite representation for marginalizations to finite signatures.

Proposition 6.7. *Let $X \subseteq \mathcal{L}_\Sigma$ be a set of formulas and let $\Gamma \subseteq \Sigma$ be a subsignature. If Γ is finite, then $\text{EWSynMg}_\Sigma(X, \Gamma)$ is finitely representable over Γ.*

This section provides evidence that it is not obvious how marginalization and variable forgetting can be implemented on representations of sets of formulas. For infinite signatures, we showed that in the basic case, where the target subsignature is finite, the existence of representations of the marginalization of sets of formulas is guaranteed.

7   Marginalization for Deductively Closed Sets of Formulas

We will now review syntactic marginalization for deductively closed sets of formulas. In particular, Proposition 6.2 does not apply to deductively closed sets, and we can show that marginalization is indeed a useful and adequate notion for deductively closed sets.

Proposition 7.1. *Let $X \subseteq \mathcal{L}_\Sigma$ be a deductive closed set of formulas, let $A \in \mathcal{L}_\Sigma$ be a formula and $\Gamma \subseteq \Sigma$. If $A \equiv_\Sigma X$, then $\text{EWSynMg}_\Sigma(X, \Gamma) \models_\Gamma \text{SynMg}_\Sigma(A, \Gamma)$.*

From Propositions 6.3 and 7.1 we obtain the following central observation.

Corollary 7.2. *Let $X \subseteq \mathcal{L}_\Sigma$ be a deductively closed set of formulas and let $A \in \mathcal{L}_\Sigma$ be a formula. If $A \equiv_\Sigma X$, then for every $\Gamma \subseteq \Sigma$, we have:*

$$\text{EWSynMg}_\Sigma(X, \Gamma) \equiv_\Gamma \text{SynMg}_\Sigma(A, \Gamma)$$

Clearly, Corollary 7.2 implies that the deductive closures of $\text{EWSynMg}_\Sigma(X, \Gamma)$ and $\text{SynMg}_\Sigma(A, \Gamma)$ are the same, i.e.

$$Cn_\Gamma(\text{EWSynMg}_\Sigma(X, \Gamma)) = Cn_\Gamma(\text{SynMg}_\Sigma(A, \Gamma)).$$

However, in general, element-wise marginalization of a deductively closed set to Γ does not yield a deductively closed set. This is because $\text{EWSynMg}_\Sigma(X, \Gamma)$ does

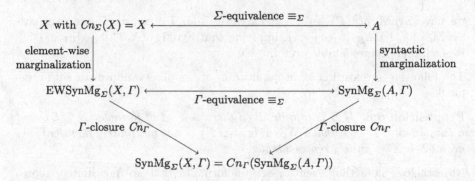

Fig. 5. Relations for a deductively closed set X and an equivalent formula A between element-wise marginalization, syntactic marginalization for a deductively closed set and syntactic marginalization for formula.

not contain all syntactic equivalent formulas. Thus, after element-wise application of marginalization we have to apply deductive closure to obtain a deductively closed set. This gives the rationale for the following notion of syntactic marginalization of deductively closed sets.

Definition 7.3. *Let $X \subseteq \mathcal{L}_\Sigma$ be a deductively closed set and $\Gamma \subseteq \Sigma$. The syntactic marginalization of X from Σ to Γ, written $\mathrm{SynMg}_\Sigma(X, \Gamma)$, is*

$$\mathrm{SynMg}_\Sigma(X, \Gamma) = Cn_\Gamma(\mathrm{EWSynMg}_\Sigma(X, \Gamma)) \,,$$

the deductive closure of the element-wise marginalization of X to Γ.

The following theorem describes that for a deductively closed set X, the syntactic marginalization of a representation of X and the syntactic marginalization of X comply with each other, semantically.

Theorem 7.4 (Representation Theorem for Marginalization). *For every deductively closed set $X \subseteq \mathcal{L}_\Sigma$ and every formula $A \in \mathcal{L}_\Sigma$ representing X, i.e., $X \equiv_\Sigma A$, and every $\Gamma \subseteq \Sigma$, we have:*

$$\mathrm{SynMg}_\Sigma(X, \Gamma) = Cn_\Gamma(\mathrm{SynMg}_\Sigma(A, \Gamma))$$

Figure 5 illustrates the compatibility between syntactic marginalization for formulas and syntactic marginalization for deductively closed sets. We continue with an example of syntactic marginalisation of deductively closed sets.

Example 7.5. Consider the signature $\Sigma = \{a, s, f\}$ from Example 5.4, and let A, A_1, A_2 as in Example 5.4. As explained in Example 6.4, we have that $X = \{A_1, A_2\}$ is semantically equivalent to A, i.e., we have $X \equiv_\Sigma A$. Furthermore, we already observed that of $\Gamma = \{a, s\}$ the element-wise marginalzation of X differs semantically from the syntactic marginalization of A, i.e., we have $\mathrm{EWSynMg}_\Sigma(X, \Gamma) \not\equiv_\Gamma \mathrm{SynMg}_\Sigma(A, \Gamma)$. However, when considering $Cn(X)$, the situation is different. Theorem 7.4 guarantees that we have

$\mathrm{SynMg}_{\Sigma}(Cn(X), \Gamma) \equiv_{\Gamma} \mathrm{SynMg}_{\Sigma}(A, \Gamma)$. One reason for this last observation is that $Cn(X)$ does also contain A, consequently, $\mathrm{SynMg}_{\Sigma}(Cn(X), \Gamma)$ contains also $\mathrm{SynMg}_{\Sigma}(A, \Gamma)$.

Note that the concept introduced in Definition 7.3 and the result of Theorem 7.4 is of importance for potential application in many areas of knowledge representation. For instance, in syntax-splitting, belief revision and non-monotonic reasoning, deductively closed sets are often used to model agents' beliefs (also called belief sets). The incompatibility results from Sect. 5 and Sect. 6 indicate that marginalization and variable forgetting are not easily applicable techniques in the areas mentioned above, yet the results obtained in this section point out that this is not the case. Theorem 7.4 shows that formulas are an *adequate finite representation* for an agent's belief set when one wants to perform marginalization or variable forgetting on the agent's beliefs. Clearly, while this is always true in the case of finite signatures, for infinite signatures, this statement applies only to those belief sets that are finitely representable.

8   Applications of the Marginalization of Deductively Closed Sets

We consider some basic applications of the notion of syntactic marginalization.

Notions of Forgetting. Another approach to forgetting is due to Delgrande [4] in which he proposes to understand forgetting of variables as a reduction to a sublanguage, i.e. $forget(X, \Gamma) = X \cap \mathcal{L}_{\Sigma \setminus \Gamma}$. We show that the approach by Delgrande complies with the notion of syntactic marginalization developed here.

Theorem 8.1 (Extended Representation Theorem for Marginalization). *Let $X \subseteq \mathcal{L}_{\Sigma}$ be a deductively closed set and $A \in \mathcal{L}_{\Sigma}$ be a formula representing X, i.e. $X \equiv_{\Sigma} A$, then the following holds:*

$$\mathrm{SynMg}_{\Sigma}(X, \Gamma) = Cn_{\Gamma}(\mathrm{SynMg}_{\Sigma}(A, \Gamma)) = X \cap \mathcal{L}_{\Gamma}$$

By Theorem 8.1, the extended representation theorem for deductively closed sets, we obtain different characterizations for syntactic marginalization for deductively closed sets and formulas equivalent to them.

Properties for Syntactic Marginalization. The following proposition summarizes useful properties of syntactic marginalization of deductively closed sets.

Proposition 8.2. *Let $X \subseteq \mathcal{L}_{\Sigma}$ be a deductively closed set and let $\Gamma \subseteq \Sigma$ and $\Gamma' \subseteq \Sigma$ be subsignatures of Σ. Syntactic marginalization satisfies the following properties:*

(Reduction)	$\mathrm{SynMg}_{\Sigma}(X, \Gamma) \subseteq \mathcal{L}_{\Gamma}$
(Inclusion)	$\mathrm{SynMg}_{\Sigma}(X, \Gamma) \subseteq X$
(Idempotency)	$\mathrm{SynMg}_{\Sigma}(X, \Gamma) = \mathrm{SynMg}_{\Sigma}(\mathrm{SynMg}_{\Sigma}(X, \Gamma), \Gamma)$
(Monotonicity)	*If* $\Gamma \subseteq \Gamma'$ *holds, then* $\mathrm{SynMg}_{\Sigma}(X, \Gamma) \subseteq \mathrm{SynMg}_{\Sigma}(X, \Gamma')$

Observe that (Inclusion), (Idempotency) and (Monotonicity) from Proposition 8.2 are properties that are similar to the properties of an interior operator, which are dual to closure operators, i.e., Tarskian consequence relations[3].

Marginalization for Ordinal Conditional Functions. In knowledge representation and reasoning, the representation of an agent's epistemic state is often realized by ordinal conditional functions [23], also called ranking functions. A ranking function is a function $\kappa : \Omega_\Sigma \to \mathbb{N}_0$ such that there is at least one interpretation ω with $\kappa(\omega) = 0$. The ranks assigned by such a κ are understood as degrees of implausibility, where the rank 0 stands for the most plausible rank. The belief set induced by a ranking function κ is the set of formulas $\mathrm{Bel}(\kappa) = \{\alpha \in \mathcal{L}_\Sigma \mid \{\omega \mid \kappa(\omega) = 0\} \subseteq Mod_\Sigma(\alpha)\}$, i.e., all Σ-formulas whose models are a superset of the most plausible models according to κ. The marginalization of κ to a subsignature Γ is defined as $\kappa|_\Gamma : \Omega_\Gamma \to \mathbb{N}_0$ with $\kappa|_\Gamma(\omega) = \min\{\kappa(\omega_\Sigma) \mid \omega_\Sigma \in \Omega_\Sigma, \omega_\Sigma^\Gamma = \omega\}$. Using Theorem 3.6 and Theorem 7.4, the following proposition relates $\mathrm{Bel}(\kappa)$ and $\mathrm{Bel}(\kappa|_\Gamma)$.

Proposition 8.3. *For every ranking function* $\kappa : \Omega_\Sigma \to \mathbb{N}_0$ *and every subsignature* $\Gamma \subseteq \Omega$ *we have:*

$$\mathrm{SynMg}_\Sigma(\mathrm{Bel}(\kappa), \Gamma) = \mathrm{Bel}(\kappa|_\Gamma)$$

Proposition 8.3 shows that the belief set of the marginalized ranking function coincides with the syntactically marginalized belief set of the original function. This nicely established relationship between the belief sets $\mathrm{Bel}(\kappa)$ and $\mathrm{Bel}(\kappa|_\Gamma)$ in Proposition 8.3 relies on the property that belief sets are deductively closed.

9   Conclusion

In this paper, we show that syntactic variable forgetting and semantic marginalization share the same basic technique, namely, aggregating the truth value of formulas over all possible interpretations of the atoms to be forgotten respectively to be suppressed. Semantically, marginalizing a possible world over an atom is the same as forgetting this variable from the complete conjunction that has this world as its only model. This can be successfully lifted to single formulas. Due to this close correspondence, we interpret variable forgetting as a syntactic marginalization operation.

However, we also point out clearly that one has to be careful when considering sets of formulas because variable forgetting applied to each of the formulas does not yield a result which is semantically equivalent to what one obtains after applying variable forgetting to the conjunction of the formulas. This is due to the fact that variable forgetting is not fully compatible with conjunction (and negation). Luckily for many scenarios considered in knowledge representation, semantic equivalence can be guaranteed here for deductively closed sets of formulas. In particular, this provides a justification for using formulas as a

---

[3] Closure operators satisfy (Monotonicity), (Idempotency) and (Extensivity), i.e., $X \subseteq Cl(X)$.

marginalization-compatible representation for deductively closed sets of formulas, as it is common, e.g., in belief revision theory [9]. Furthermore, we show that syntactic marginalization also complies with Delgrands' forgetting approach [4], and we provide some basic properties for syntactic marginalization.

We like to remark again that most properties and theorems for syntactic marginalization in this paper carry over to variable forgetting and model marginalization, as we showed that all these three operators yield semantically the same results (in a dual way). In future work, we will consider the compatibility of syntactic marginalization to different formalisms, like conditional logics or predicate logics, other kinds of forgetting, see, e.g., [2], and their axiomatics [11,12,21].

Acknowledgements. We thank the reviewers for their constructive and helpful comments. This work was funded by the Deutsche Forschungsgemeinschaft (DFG, German Research Foundation) within the Priority Research Program "Intentional Forgetting in Organizations" (SPP 1921; grant BE 1700/10-1 awarded to Christoph Beierle and grant KE 1413/10-1 awarded to Gabriele Kern-Isberner).

References

1. Beierle, C., Kern-Isberner, G.: Semantical investigations into nonmonotonic and probabilistic logics. Ann. Math. Artif. Intell. **65**(2–3), 123–158 (2012)
2. Beierle, C., Kern-Isberner, G., Sauerwald, K., Bock, T., Ragni, M.: Towards a general framework for kinds of forgetting in common-sense belief management. KI - Künstliche Intelligenz **33**(1), 57–68 (2019)
3. Boole, G.: An Investigation of the Laws of Thought, on Which are Founded the Mathematical Theories of Logic and Probabilities. Walton and Maberly, London (1854)
4. Delgrande, J.P.: A knowledge level account of forgetting. J. Artif. Intell. Res. **60**, 1165–1213 (2017)
5. van Ditmarsch, H., Herzig, A., Lang, J., Marquis, P.: Introspective forgetting. Synthese **169**(2), 405–423 (2009)
6. Eiter, T., Kern-Isberner, G.: A brief survey on forgetting from a knowledge representation and reasoning perspective. KI - Künstliche Intelligenz **33**(1), 9–33 (2019)
7. Goguen, J., Burstall, R.: Institutions: abstract model theory for specification and programming. J. ACM **39**(1), 95–146 (1992)
8. Gonçalves, R., Knorr, M., Leite, J.: Forgetting in answer set programming - a survey. Theory Pract. Log. Program. **23**(1), 111–156 (2023)
9. Katsuno, H., Mendelzon, A.: Propositional knowledge base revision and minimal change. Artif. Intell. **52**, 263–294 (1991)
10. Kern-Isberner, G., Beierle, C., Brewka, G.: Syntax splitting = relevance + independence: New postulates for nonmonotonic reasoning from conditional belief bases. In: Calvanese, D., Erdem, E. (eds.) Proceedings of the 17th International Conference on Principles of Knowledge Representation and Reasoning, KR 2020, pp. 560–571. IJCAI.org (2020)
11. Kern-Isberner, G., Bock, T., Beierle, C., Sauerwald, K.: Axiomatic evaluation of epistemic forgetting operators. In: Barták, R., Brawner, K.W. (eds.) Proceedings of the Thirty-Second International Florida Artificial Intelligence Research Society Conference, Sarasota, Florida, USA, 19–22 May 2019, pp. 470–475. AAAI Press (2019)

12. Kern-Isberner, G., Bock, T., Sauerwald, K., Beierle, C.: Belief change properties of forgetting operations over ranking functions. In: Nayak, A., Sharma, A. (eds.) PRICAI 2019. LNCS, vol. 11670, pp. 459–472. Springer, Cham (2019). https://doi.org/10.1007/978-3-030-29908-8_37

13. Kern-Isberner, G., Brewka, G.: Strong syntax splitting for iterated belief revision. In: Sierra, C. (ed.) Proceedings International Joint Conference on Artificial Intelligence, IJCAI 2017, pp. 1131–1137. ijcai.org (2017)

14. Konev, B., Walther, D., Wolter, F.: Forgetting and uniform interpolation in extensions of the description logic EL. In: Grau, B.C., Horrocks, I., Motik, B., Sattler, U. (eds.) Proceedings of the 22nd International Workshop on Description Logics (DL 2009), Oxford, UK, 27–30 July 2009. CEUR Workshop Proceedings, vol. 477. CEUR-WS.org (2009)

15. Lang, J., Liberatore, P., Marquis, P.: Propositional independence: formula-variable independence and forgetting. J. Artif. Intell. Res. **18**, 391–443 (2003)

16. Lang, J., Marquis, P.: Reasoning under inconsistency: a forgetting-based approach. Artif. Intell. **174**(12–13), 799–823 (2010)

17. Lin, F., Reiter, R.: Forget it! In: Proceedings of the AAAI Fall Symposium on Relevance, pp. 154–159. AAAI Press, Menlo Park (1994)

18. Nikitina, N., Rudolph, S.: Expexpexplosion: uniform interpolation in general EL terminologies. In: Raedt, L.D., et al. (eds.) 20th European Conference on Artificial Intelligence. Including Prestigious Applications of Artificial Intelligence, ECAI 2012 (PAIS-2012) System Demonstrations Track, Montpellier, France, 27–31 August 2012, Frontiers in Artificial Intelligence and Applications, vol. 242, pp. 618–623. IOS Press (2012)

19. Parikh, R.: Beliefs, Belief Revision, and Splitting Languages, pp. 266–278. Center for the Study of Language and Information, USA (1999)

20. Pearl, J.: Probabilistic Reasoning in Intelligent Systems. Morgan Kaufmann, San Mateo (1988)

21. Sauerwald, K., Kern-Isberner, G., Becker, A., Beierle, C.: From forgetting signature elements to forgetting formulas in epistemic states. In: de Saint-Cyr, F.D., Öztürk-Escoffier, M., Potyka, N. (eds.) SUM 2022. LNCS, vol. 13562, pp. 92–106. Springer, Cham (2022). https://doi.org/10.1007/978-3-031-18843-5_7

22. Sen, A.: Social choice theory. In: Arrow, K., Intriligator, M. (eds.) Handbook of Mathematical Economics, vol. III, pp. 1073–1181. Elsevier Science Publishers (1986)

23. Spohn, W.: Ordinal conditional functions: a dynamic theory of epistemic states. In: Harper, W., Skyrms, B. (eds.) Causation in Decision, Belief Change, and Statistics, II, pp. 105–134. Kluwer Academic Publishers (1988)

24. Su, K., Sattar, A., Lv, G., Zhang, Y.: Variable forgetting in reasoning about knowledge. J. Artif. Intell. Res. **35**, 677–716 (2009)

25. Thevapalan, A., Kern-Isberner, G., Howey, D., Beierle, C., Meyer, R.G., Nietzke, M.: Decision support core system for cancer therapies using ASP-HEX. In: Brawner, K., Rus, V. (eds.) Proceedings of the Thirty-First International Florida Artificial Intelligence Research Society Conference, FLAIRS 2018, Melbourne, Florida, USA, 21–23 May 2018, pp. 531–536. AAAI Press (2018)

26. Wijs, A.: Forgetting the time in timed process algebra. In: Hatcliff, J., Zucca, E. (eds.) FMOODS FORTE 2010. LNCS, vol. 6117, pp. 110–124. Springer, Heidelberg (2010). https://doi.org/10.1007/978-3-642-13464-7_10

27. Zhang, Y., Zhou, Y.: Knowledge forgetting: properties and applications. Artif. Intell. **173**(16), 1525–1537 (2009)

Nonmonotonicity

Minimizing Agents' State Corruption Resulting from Leak-Free Epistemic Communication Modeling

Giorgio Cignarale[ID], Roman Kuznets[ID], and Thomas Schlögl[(✉)][ID]

TU Wien, Vienna, Austria

{giorgio.cignarale,roman.kuznets,thomas.e191-02.schloegl}@tuwien.ac.at

Abstract. *Epistemic Logic* (EL) successfully models epistemic and dox-astic attitudes of agents and groups in multi-agent systems, including distributed systems, via relational structures called Kripke models. *Dynamic Epistemic Logic* (DEL) adds communication in the form of model-transforming updates. Private communication is key in distributed systems as processes exchanging (potentially corrupted) information about their private local state may not be detectable by any other process. This focus on privacy clashes with the fact that updates are applied to the whole Kripke model, which is usually commonly known by all agents, potentially leading to information leakage. To avoid information leakage and to minimize the corruption of local states resulting from faulty information, we introduce a special stratified structure for Kripke models using a *privatization* operation that explicitly breaks the common knowledge of the model. To represent agent-to-agent communication we introduce a novel leakage-free update mechanism for solving the *consistent update synthesis* task: design an update that makes a given goal formula true while maintaining the consistency of agents' beliefs, if possible.

Keywords: Dynamic epistemic logic · Update synthesis · Distributed systems

1 Introduction

Epistemic Logic (EL) [10] has been successfully applied in the modeling of epistemic and doxastic attitudes of agents and groups in multi-agent systems, including distributed systems [6]. *Dynamic Epistemic Logic* (DEL) [4,12] upgrades EL by introducing model transforming modalities called *updates*. Relational structures, e.g., *action models* in Action Model Logic (AML) and *arrow update models* in the Generalized Arrow Update Logic (GAUL) [11], are used to represent the evolution of agents' uncertainty under information change in complex

Supported by the Austrian Science Fund (FWF) projects ByzDEL (P33600) and Digital Modeling of Asynchronous Integrated Circuits (P32431-N30).

A. Meier and M. Ortiz (Eds.): FoIKS 2024, LNCS 14589, pp. 165–181, 2024.
https://doi.org/10.1007/978-3-031-56940-1_9

communication scenarios. GAUL and AML have proved to be equally *update expressive* [5]: for this reason, we will apply the term "update models" to both AML action models and GAUL arrow update models. In the update *synthesis* task, the aim is to construct an update model that makes a given goal formula φ true if such an update model exists [5]. Existing synthesis algorithms typically work in very expressive languages with quantifiers over updates, such as the Arbitrary Action Model Logic (AAML) [8] or Arbitrary Arrow Update Model Logic (AAUML) [5], and make no attempt to preserve the consistency of agents.

Apart from the natural desire to model updates that keep agents' beliefs consistent, i.e., preventing corrupted local states of agents, our method, which operates in the simpler basic epistemic language, is motivated by the following considerations. As noted by Artemov [1], in order to reason about higher-order beliefs of other agents, it is typical to assume the common knowledge of the (Kripke) model (CKM) by all agents (this assumption is, in fact, necessary in case of factive beliefs). This common knowledge assumption is then naturally extended to the common knowledge of the update model, resulting in the common knowledge of the Kripke model obtained after the update. Apart from creating difficulties for modeling fully private communication where some agents should not even be aware of the fact that an update took place, this view has another weakness.

Kripke models are based on the idea of possible worlds and of agents being uncertain about which of these worlds is the actual world. The CKM assumption (whether explicit or implicit) often leads to all worlds considered by any of the agents being commonly conceived as possible by all agents. Thus, any update model is applied to all these worlds homogeneously, preventing the agents from processing information differently. Byzantine agents in fault-tolerant systems, on the other hand, may have a corrupted local state. One of the primary goals in distributed systems is to prevent the corruption of few agents from spreading to the whole system. Thus, ideally, messages from, say, one faulty agent, no matter how contradictory, should not lead to their recipients becoming faulty.

Unfortunately, update models neither naturally represent private agent-to-agent communication nor are equipped to distinguish messages from different agents, prompting Herzig to note that "it is not easy to come up with a meaningful notion of a speaker" using typical DEL updates [9]. As a result, instead of taking it to be a sign of sender's fault, recipients treat contradictory information as objective truth and become faulty themselves.

In order to avoid such cross-contamination, we stratify the model creating disjoint individual private spaces for each agent and, if need be, recursively stratifying those private spaces further to imbue the agents themselves with this useful device. In these stratified models, the CKM assumption is dropped and each agent is assumed to be aware only of its own private part of the model.[1] If this private part is further stratified, then it is possible for a particular world w to be conceived only by agent a, and conceived not as a possibility at that, but

---

[1] A formal definition of privatization is provided in Sect. 3.3, while the notion of accessible part of a model for a given agent is described in Remark 24.

rather as something another agent b considers. In this setting, if a learns that b's beliefs are different from what a expected, a can simply adjust b's part of a's private submodel without touching any of the worlds a itself considers possible and, hence, without risking a's own consistency.

Leaving the broader issue of agency and agent-to-agent interaction, as identified by Herzig, for future work, in this paper we show how to use stratification to avoid inconsistent states in case of objective, trusted updates. We apply model stratification to solve the consistent update synthesis problem. Given a goal formula φ about (higher-order) beliefs of multiple agents, we first extract from φ the stratification sufficient to separate all the beliefs to be updated in the form of a *belief privatization graph*. This stratification is then applied to the initial Kripke model, after which all beliefs can be updated independently of each other. Since these updates represent mental changes of the agent, the actual world is taken out of the equation by placing it outside of agents' private submodels. The isolation of the actual world does not make it impossible for an agent's beliefs to be factual but rather makes it unnecessary: for example, the agent's beliefs would be factual if it considers possible an "exact copy" of the actual world (e.g., a bisimilar world).

Our Contributions. The aim of this paper is to provide an algorithmic way to enforce private beliefs specified by a quantifier-free goal formula while preserving the consistency of agents' beliefs whenever possible. To this extent, we solve the consistent update synthesis task, i.e., we provide algorithms that take a Kripke model and the goal formula as inputs and output a privatized Kripke model where the goal formula holds. The privatization operation makes sure that:

(i) only the local states of the agents in the goal formula (which is meant to represent fallible communication) are updated, validating our claim of minimal side effects and of information-leak-freeness, i.e., the other agents' local states are unchanged, meaning that they are not even aware that something happened;

(ii) agents' state corruption (e.g., agent believing falsum resulting from receiving contradictory information) is limited to some specific (iterated) submodels, without unnecessarily propagating to submodels of other agents, validating our consistency-preserving claim.

Related Work. As mentioned before, the update model synthesis problem has been considered both for AAML [8] and AAUML [5]. Given our specific application domain, our approach differs from those methods for three main reasons:

(i) While it is possible to construct AML or GAUL update models that represent completely private communication [3], there is no standardized update synthesis procedure for it. By contrast, we provide an algorithm that privatizes Kripke models, so that local updates can be enforced without information leakage and with minimal side effects, which is usually not addressed by existing synthesis algorithms.

(ii) Most existing synthesis methods do not address belief consistency preservation [5]: if a goal formula can be made true by making an agent inconsistent, the algorithm will do so. Our algorithm, by contrast, preserves agents' consistency whenever possible, limiting the state corruption originating from false information exchange.

(iii) The proposed update mechanism is generally more efficient w.r.t. AML and GAUL updates as it deletes all states not reachable from the actual world, making the growth in size of the model at worst linear in the size of the goal formula after one update and decreasing starting from the second update based on the same modal syntactic tree. By contrast, it is well known that repeated applications of AML or GAUL updates lead to the exponential growth of the model [2].

Paper Organization. We start by giving a motivating example in Sect. 2. In Sect. 3 we describe the steps of the proposed update mechanism: Sect. 3.1 provides some background definitions, Sect. 3.2 introduces belief privatization graphs and their construction from goal formulas, Sect. 3.3 shows how to privatize a Kripke model given a belief privatization graph, and the algorithms performing the update on the already privatized model are given in Sect. 3.4. Some simple lemmas and corollaries are left without a proof. We provide conclusions and directions of further research in Sect. 4.

2 Motivating Example

We consider a finite set of agents $\mathcal{A}$, a set of propositions *Prop*, and the standard doxastic multimodal language $\varphi ::= p \mid \neg\varphi \mid (\varphi \wedge \varphi) \mid B_i\varphi$ where $i \in \mathcal{A}$ and $p \in Prop$. The other boolean connectives are defined as usual. Formula $B_i\varphi$ means "agent i believes φ to be true"; note that we generally do not assume the factivity of beliefs. We generally assume w.l.o.g. that $\mathcal{A} = \{1, \ldots, n\}$, unless more personalized agent names are warranted.

Definition 1 (Kripke model). *For a set of agents $\mathcal{A}$, a* pointed *KD45 Kripke model is $(\mathcal{M}, v) = (\langle S, R, V \rangle, v)^2$, where the* domain *(set of* possible *worlds) $S \neq \varnothing$, the accessibility relation $R = (R_1, \ldots, R_n)$ consists of binary relations $R_i \subseteq S \times S$ on S that satisfy transitivity[3], euclideanity[4], and seriality[5], the valuation function $V : Prop \to 2^S$, and $v \in S$ represents the real (actual) world. Truth at world w of model $\mathcal{M}$ is determined by $\mathcal{M}, w \models p$ iff $w \in V(p)$, the classical behavior of the boolean connectives, and $\mathcal{M}, w \models B_i\varphi$ iff $\mathcal{M}, w' \models \varphi$ for all $w' \in S$ such that wR_iw'. A formula φ is false at world w, written $\mathcal{M}, w \not\models \varphi$, iff it is not true at w. Formula φ is valid in model $\mathcal{M}$, written $\mathcal{M} \models \varphi$, iff $\mathcal{M}, w \models \varphi$ for all $w \in S$. Formula φ is KD45-valid, written $KD45 \models \varphi$, iff it is true in all pointed KD45 Kripke models.*

---

[2] A Kripke model (without an explicit point) is simply defined as $\mathcal{M} = \langle S, R, V \rangle$.

[3] If vR_iu and uR_iw, then vR_iw.

[4] If vR_iu and vR_iw, then uR_iw.

[5] For every state v and agent i, there exists a state v' such that vR_iv'.

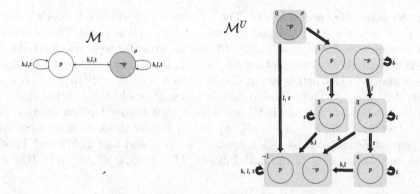

Fig. 1. In both pointed models, the actual world is dark gray. Left: Initial pointed Kripke model $\mathcal{M}$. Right: Updated model $\mathcal{M}^U$. A formula φ within a circle representing a world means that φ is true in this world. A light-gray rectangle with n in the top left corner is the cluster that is numbered n. A double arrow from such cluster n to cluster m represents a set of accessibility arrows with the same agent's label from every world of cluster n to every world of cluster m. (Color figure online)

Example 2 (Balder–Loki–Thor example). Teenage brothers Balder, Loki, and Thor prepare for an exam that, as is commonly known among them, contains one question asking to decide whether p or $\neg p$ is the case. Suppose the correct answer is $\neg p$. The initial Kripke model $\mathcal{M}$ is the left model of Fig. 1. While the three are studying, Loki, unbeknownst to Thor, tries to trick Balder, telling him that he, Loki, has overheard Thor boasting to Lady Sif that he knew the correct answer to be p. Balder seems to dismiss Loki's claim as a ruse, leaving Loki thinking his trick had no effect. In truth, however, Balder does believe Loki and is now under the impression that Loki agrees with Thor that the answer is p. Balder himself, on the other hand, is not going to take Thor's word on it, given Thor's propensity to boast and act rashly. Thus, using b, l, and t for the brothers, Loki's trick should change their beliefs to achieve the *goal formula* $\varphi = B_b B_t p \wedge B_b B_l B_t p \wedge B_b B_l p$ without affecting Loki's or Thor's beliefs.

Since ignorance of the correct answer is common belief in the initial Kripke model $\mathcal{M}$, the public announcement of φ would cause everybody's beliefs to become inconsistent, whereas a private message $B_t p \wedge B_l B_t p \wedge B_l p$ to Balder would do the same to Balder's beliefs only. This happens whether one uses the world-removing or arrow-removing updates.

Instead, we propose a method of stratifying the initial Kripke model $\mathcal{M}$ into several clusters representing individual beliefs and updating only some of these clusters, depending on the modal structure of the goal formula, resulting in pointed Kripke model $\mathcal{M}^U$, the right model in Fig. 1, where updated clusters are represented by gray rectangles. Cluster 0 represents the real world ρ, which no agent considers possible. Cluster -1 (the *sink*) is the copy of the initial model representing beliefs of agents unaffected by the message, including Loki's and Thor's beliefs. In particular, the ignorance of the correct answer is still common belief between Loki and Thor. Cluster 1 represents Balder's beliefs, so $\mathcal{M}^U, \rho \not\models B_b p \vee B_b \neg p$. Cluster 2 is for Balder's beliefs about Thor's beliefs, which ensures that $\mathcal{M}^U, \rho \models B_b B_t p$. Cluster 3 plays the same role for Balder's beliefs about Loki's beliefs, making $\mathcal{M}^U, \rho \models B_b B_l p$. Finally, cluster 4 is Balder's beliefs about Loki's beliefs about Thor's beliefs so that $\mathcal{M}^U, \rho \models B_b B_l B_t p$. Thus, $\mathcal{M}^U, \rho \models \varphi$. The b-labeled double arrow from cluster 4 to the sink -1 means that Balder believes that Loki believes that Balder has not changed his beliefs, $\mathcal{M}^U, \rho \models B_b B_l(\neg B_b p \wedge \neg B_b \neg p)$, etc. It is easy to see that no agent has inconsistent beliefs, $\mathcal{M}^U \models \neg B_b \bot \wedge \neg B_l \bot \wedge \neg B_t \bot$, and that Loki's and Thor's beliefs are the same as in the initial model, $M, \rho \models B_a \psi$ iff $\mathcal{M}^U, \rho \models B_a \psi$ for $a \in \{l, t\}$.

The goal of this paper is to provide algorithms to compute such a Kripke model based on a goal formula that would apply to any given initial model.

3   Private Belief-Increasing Announcements

An announcement is characterized by a *goal formula* specifying a change in agents' beliefs. In this paper, we consider only deterministic belief-increasing goal formulas, i.e., disallow negations in front of belief operators and disjunctions of belief operators[6]. An announcement may simultaneously increase beliefs (including higher-order beliefs) of several agents. Thus, goal formulas are combinations of doxastic operators. The novelty of this approach is that we try to preserve consistency whenever possible. We limit the set of allowed goal formulas and we characterize their structure using modal syntactic trees in the following definition:

Definition 3 (Goal formula, normal form, modal syntactic tree). Goal formulas φ are defined by the following BNF:

$$\varphi ::= B_i \xi \mid B_i(\xi \wedge \varphi) \mid (\varphi \wedge \varphi) \mid B_i \varphi \tag{1}$$

where ξ is any purely propositional formula. Thus, each goal formula is a non-empty conjunction of belief operators (possibly of a single belief operator). We define the set of target agents of a goal formula as follows:

$$\begin{aligned} \mathsf{ta}(B_i \xi) &:= \{i\}, & \mathsf{ta}(B_i(\xi \wedge \varphi)) &:= \{i\}, \\ \mathsf{ta}(B_i \varphi) &:= \{i\}, & \mathsf{ta}(\varphi \wedge \psi) &:= \mathsf{ta}(\varphi) \cup \mathsf{ta}(\psi). \end{aligned}$$

Formulas in goal-normal form *are goal formulas φ obtained by restricting the construction as follows: $B_i \xi$ is always goal-normal; $B_i \varphi$ and $B_i(\xi \wedge \varphi)$ are goal-normal iff φ is goal-normal and $i \notin \mathsf{ta}(\varphi)$; $\varphi \wedge \psi$ is goal-normal if φ and ψ are goal-normal and $\mathsf{ta}(\varphi) \cap \mathsf{ta}(\psi) = \varnothing$.*

---

[6] This restriction on the kind of allowed goal formulas is very natural for full-information protocols, wherein agents communicate all the beliefs they have accumulated.

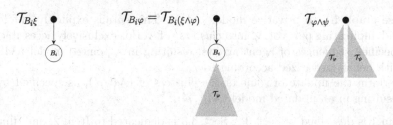

Fig. 2. Modal syntactic trees

The modal syntactic tree $\mathcal{T}_\varphi$ *of a goal formula φ is roughly the syntactic tree of φ with all non-modal-operator nodes omitted. To unify how the root is treated, we provide a precise definition. It is a tree with all non-root nodes labeled with modal operators. The root remains unlabeled. It is defined as follows. In $\mathcal{T}_{B_i\xi}$, the root has one child-leaf labeled B_i. Both $\mathcal{T}_{B_i\varphi}$ and $\mathcal{T}_{B_i(\xi\wedge\varphi)}$ are obtained by labeling the root of $\mathcal{T}_\varphi$ with B_i and making it the only child of the new root. Finally, $\mathcal{T}_{\varphi\wedge\psi}$ is obtained by taking the disjoint union of $\mathcal{T}_\varphi$ and $\mathcal{T}_\psi$ and identifying their roots (see Fig. 2).*

Formulas in goal-normal form are, in fact, sufficient to succinctly represent all updates encoded by goal formulas, as the following lemma shows:

Lemma 4. *For any goal formula φ, there exists a formula φ^n in goal-normal form such that $KD45 \models \varphi \leftrightarrow \varphi^n$.*

Intuitively, the modal syntactic tree of a formula represents its modal structure. The following lemma directly follows from the preceding definition:

Lemma 5. *Let φ be a formula in goal-normal form and $\mathcal{T}_\varphi$ be its modal syntactic tree. Then*

- *all children of the root are labeled with pairwise distinct modal operators;*
- *for any internal node (neither a leaf nor the root), the node and all its children are labeled with pairwise distinct modal operators.*

Thus, from now on, we only consider formulas in goal-normal form.

Given a goal formula φ we conduct an update of a given pointed model $(\mathcal{M}, \rho)$ with "minimal side effects" to ensure that $\mathcal{M}_\varphi^U, \rho' \models \varphi$ in the updated model. Informally, by minimal side effects we mean that an update should not influence any beliefs other than those explicitly stated in the goal formula (unless it follows from the goal formula combined with the agent's pre-update beliefs, e.g., an agent originally believing p who is now led to believe q would have to also believe $p \wedge q$ after the update). In particular, an update of i's beliefs should not affect j's views on what i believes, unless explicitly specified.

Given an initial pointed Kripke model $(\mathcal{M}, \rho)$ and a goal formula φ, we achieve a private update of φ on $(\mathcal{M}, \rho)$ in three steps:

1. Construct/extract a *belief privatization graph* $\mathbb{G}_\varphi$ from goal formula φ.

2. Use graph $\mathbb{G}_\varphi$ to privatize model $(\mathcal{M}, \rho)$. This entails explicitly unfolding and duplicating parts of $\mathcal{M}$ into *clusters*[7] of worlds exclusively accessible via specified sequences of agent arrows, resulting in a pointed model $(\mathcal{M}', \rho')$ with beliefs privatized according to φ.
3. Perform the update of some of the clusters of $(\mathcal{M}', \rho')$, as specified by φ, resulting in an updated model $(\mathcal{M}^U, \rho')$.

Item 1 is described in Sect. 3.2; Sect. 3.3 is dedicated to Item 2, and, finally, Item 3 is outlined in Sect. 3.4.

3.1 Formal Preliminaries

In this section, we provide some basic definitions that will be used later for proving the properties of the privatization operation.

Definition 6 (Path in a graph). *A path in $\mathbb{G}$ is a (possibly empty) sequence of edges $(e_1, \ldots, e_l)$ with $l \geq 0$ such that $\pi_2 e_i = \pi_1 e_{i+1}$ for each $1 \leq i \leq l - 1$, where for an edge $e = (\alpha_1, \alpha_2, j)$ we use the projection function π such that $\pi_1 e = \alpha_1$ and $\pi_2 e = \alpha_2$. For a DAG[8] $\mathbb{G}$ with a single source (i.e., a node with no incoming edges) labeled 0 and a single sink (i.e., a node with no outgoing edges) labeled -1, we consider the following sets of paths:*

- *$Path(\mathbb{G})$ is the set of all paths in $\mathbb{G}$;*
- *$SourceP(\mathbb{G}) \subseteq Path(\mathbb{G})$ is the set of all (possibly empty) paths starting from the source, i.e., a non-empty path $(e_1, \ldots, e_l) \in SourceP(\mathbb{G})$ iff $\pi_1 e_1 = 0$;*
- *$SourcePSink(\mathbb{G}) \subseteq SourceP(\mathbb{G})$ is the set of all paths that start from 0 and end in the sink, i.e., $(e_1, \ldots, e_l) \in SourceP(\mathbb{G})$ is in $SourcePSink(\mathbb{G})$ iff $l > 0$ and $\pi_2 e_l = -1$;*
- *$SourcePNoSink(\mathbb{G}) \subseteq SourceP(\mathbb{G})$ is the set of all paths that start from 0 and do <u>not</u> end in -1, i.e., $SourcePNoSink(\mathbb{G}) := SourceP(\mathbb{G}) \setminus SourcePSink(\mathbb{G})$. In particular, the empty path $\varepsilon \in SourcePNoSink(\mathbb{G})$.*

We introduce an unravelling similar to [7] of a Kripke model based on clusters of agents. This variation is motivated by the fact that we consider epistemic models, and the intended result is to have each cluster representing the nth higher-order belief of that agent w.r.t. other agents:

Definition 7 (Cluster and reachable state). *For a Kripke model $\mathcal{M} = \langle S, R, V \rangle$, world $v \in S$, and sequence $(i_1, \ldots, i_l) \in \mathcal{A}^l$ of agents, we introduce the cluster of path-accessible worlds*

$$C_{\mathcal{M}, v}^{i_1, i_2, \ldots, i_l} := \{ u \in S \mid (\exists u_2, \ldots, u_l \in S) \ v R_{i_1} u_2 R_{i_2} \ldots u_l R_{i_l} u \}. \tag{2}$$

In particular, for the empty sequence, $C_{\mathcal{M}, v}^{\varepsilon} = \{v\}$. We also define the reachability operator

$$\mathscr{R}(\mathcal{M}, v) := \bigcup_{l=0}^{\infty} \bigcup_{seq \in \mathcal{A}^l} C_{\mathcal{M}, v}^{seq}. \tag{3}$$

---

[7] A cluster is a totally connected subset of worlds.
[8] Directed acyclic graph.

For a set $W \subseteq S$, we define $\mathscr{R}(\mathcal{M}, W) := \bigcup_{v \in W} \mathscr{R}(\mathcal{M}, v)$.

Definition 8 (Agent sequence). *Given a DAG* $\mathbb{G}$ *with a single source* 0 *and a single sink* -1, *for a path* $= ((\alpha_1, \alpha_2, i_1), \ldots, (\alpha_l, \alpha_{l+1}, i_l)) \in Path(\mathbb{G})$ *we define* $AgSeq(path) := (i_1, \ldots, i_l)$. *In particular,* $AgSeq(\varepsilon) := \varepsilon$.

Definition 9 (Appending a sequence). *Let* $sq = (x_1, \ldots, x_n)$ *be a sequence of* $n \geq 0$ *elements (of any nature). We write* $sq \circ y$ *to denote the sequence* $(x_1, \ldots, x_n, y)$.

Definition 10 (Bisimulation). *A* bisimulation *between Kripke models* $\mathcal{M} = \langle S, R, V \rangle$ *and* $\mathcal{M}' = \langle S', R', V' \rangle$ *is a non-empty binary relation* $\mathscr{B} \subseteq S \times S'$, *such that for every* $v \mathscr{B} v'$, *for every* $i \in \mathcal{A}$ *and* $p \in Prop$:

- **Atoms:** $v \in V(p)$ *iff* $v' \in V'(p)$;
- **Forth:** *if* $v R_i u$, *then there is* $u' \in S'$ *such that* $v' R'_i u'$ *and* $u \mathscr{B} u'$;
- **Back:** *if* $v' R'_i u'$, *then there is* $u \in S$ *such that* $v R_i u$ *and* $u \mathscr{B} u'$.

Pointed models $(\mathcal{M}, v)$ *and* $(\mathcal{M}', v')$ *are bisimilar, notation* $(\mathcal{M}, v) \leftrightarrow (\mathcal{M}', v')$, *iff there is a bisimulation* $\mathscr{B}$ *between* $\mathcal{M}$ *and* $\mathcal{M}'$ *such that* $v \mathscr{B} v'$.

We write $(\mathcal{M}, v) \equiv (\mathcal{M}', v')$ if and only if $\mathcal{M}, v \models \varphi$ iff $\mathcal{M}', v' \models \varphi$ for all φ.

Theorem 11 ([4]). $(\mathcal{M}, v) \leftrightarrow (\mathcal{M}', v')$ *implies* $(\mathcal{M}, v) \equiv (\mathcal{M}', v')$ *for arbitrary pointed Kripke models* $(\mathcal{M}, v)$ *and* $(\mathcal{M}', v')$.

In other words, if two pointed Kripke models are bisimilar, then they are modally equivalent.

3.2 Belief Privatization Graphs and Their Construction from a Goal Formula

In this section, we illustrate the role of belief privatization graphs and how to compute them from a given goal formula. Belief privatization graphs are an auxiliary tool extracting the structure sufficient to achieve consistent synthesis based on the target goal formula. Their role is akin to that of action models in AML[9] Intuitively, belief privatization graphs represent goal formulas while maintaining their tree-structure, wherein each node represents a modal operator of the goal formula:

Definition 12 (Belief privatization graph). *Let* $\mathbb{G} = (V, E)$ *be a finite DAG with vertices* $\{0, -1\} \subseteq V \subseteq \mathbb{N} \cup \{-1\}$ *that include two special nodes, a single source* 0 *with no incoming edges and a single sink* -1 *with no outgoing edges. The edges* $E \subseteq \{(\alpha_1, \alpha_2, i) \mid \alpha_1 \neq \alpha_2 \in V \text{ and } i \in \mathcal{A}\}$ *are labeled with agents.*

---

[9] Indeed, belief privatization graphs act as action models with additional privatization properties, and Algorithm 1 ensures that these properties are transferred into the resulting Kripke model. An approach using only action models, while possible, is not necessarily simpler, especially for planned future work with more complex goal formulas.

For $\alpha \in V$, the set $\mathscr{I}(\mathbb{G}, \alpha) := \{i \in \mathcal{A} \mid (\exists \beta)(\beta, \alpha, i) \in E\}$ consists of all agents who have an incoming edge into node α in $\mathbb{G}$ and the set $\mathscr{O}(\mathbb{G}, \alpha) := \{i \in \mathcal{A} \mid (\exists \beta)(\alpha, \beta, i) \in E\}$ of all agents who have an outgoing edge from α. In particular, $\mathscr{I}(\mathbb{G}, \alpha) = \varnothing$ iff $\alpha = 0$ and $\mathscr{O}(\mathbb{G}, \alpha) = \varnothing$ iff $\alpha = -1$.

Graph $\mathbb{G}$ is called a belief privatization graph iff it satisfies the following condition: all non-sink nodes in $\mathbb{G}$ have exactly one edge (incoming or outgoing) for each agent and at most one incoming edge. In other words, if $\alpha \neq -1$, then

- $\mathscr{I}(\mathbb{G}, \alpha) \cup \mathscr{O}(\mathbb{G}, \alpha) = \mathcal{A}$,
- $\mathscr{I}(\mathbb{G}, \alpha) \cap \mathscr{O}(\mathbb{G}, \alpha) = \varnothing$,
- $i \neq j$ whenever $(\alpha, \beta, i) \neq (\alpha, \gamma, j) \in E$ for any $\beta, \gamma \in V$,   and
- $(\beta, \alpha, i) \in E$ implies $(\gamma, \alpha, j) \notin E$ for any $j \neq i$ and $(\gamma, \alpha, i) \notin E$ for any $\gamma \neq \beta$.

Accordingly, the construction of a belief privatization graph from a formula φ corresponds to a stratification of those beliefs that φ requires changing:

Definition 13 (Belief privatization graph construction). *Given a formula φ in goal-normal form, its belief privatization graph $\mathbb{G}_\varphi$ is constructed from its modal syntactic tree $\mathcal{T}_\varphi$ as follows:*

- *the nodes are numbered by non-negative integers with 0 used for the root of $\mathcal{T}_\varphi$, which becomes the source of $\mathbb{G}_\varphi$;*
- *whenever an edge leads to a node with B_i, this edge is labeled i;*
- *a new sink node -1 is added;*
- *whenever a non-sink node has neither an incoming nor an outgoing edge labeled with i, add an i-labeled edge from this node to the sink.*

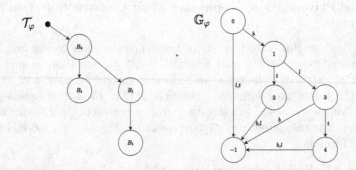

Fig. 3. Modal syntactic tree $\mathcal{T}_\varphi$ (Left) and belief privatization graph $\mathbb{G}_\varphi$ (Right) for the goal formula from Example 2 obtained from the goal-normal form $\varphi = B_b(B_t p \land B_l(p \land B_t p))$.

Example 14. For the goal formula $B_b B_t p \land B_b B_l B_t p \land B_b B_l p$ from Example 2, its goal-normal form is $\varphi = B_b(B_t p \land B_l(p \land B_t p))$. The corresponding modal syntactic tree $\mathcal{T}_\varphi$ and belief privatization graph $\mathbb{G}_\varphi$ can be found in Fig. 3.

Theorem 15. *For a formula φ in goal-normal form, the graph $\mathbb{G}_\varphi$ constructed in Definition 13 is a belief privatization graph.*

In the synthesis approach, the easiest way to impose beliefs on an agent is to corrupt its local state by removing all accessible worlds for this agent: no accessible worlds means that the agent believes falsum, i.e., $B_a\bot$, and since everything follows from falsum the agent suddenly believes everything (including the beliefs prescribed by the goal formula). Clearly, this approach does not ensure minimal change and does not avoid state corruption of agents. The tree structure of our belief privatization graph favors a more conservative approach, for which an agent would rather make its higher-order beliefs inconsistent, before making its own beliefs so, whenever possible.

3.3 Privatization

We can now introduce the privatization operation of a pointed Kripke model based on a belief privatization graph, which turns the starting pointed Kripke model into a privatized Kripke model:

Definition 16 (Privatization). *The* privatization *of a pointed Kripke model* $(\mathcal{M}, v)$ *according to a belief privatization graph* $\mathbb{G} = (V, E)$ *is a pointed model* $\left(\mathcal{M}_{v,\mathbb{G}}^{P}, (v, \varepsilon)\right)$*, with* $\mathcal{M}_{v,\mathbb{G}}^{P} := \langle \widetilde{S}, \widetilde{R}, \widetilde{V} \rangle$ *where*

$$
\begin{aligned}
\widetilde{S} := &\left\{ (u, p) \mid p \in SourcePNoSink(\mathbb{G}) \text{ and } u \in C_{\mathcal{M},v}^{AgSeq(p)} \right\} \sqcup \\
&\left\{ (w, -1) \mid (\exists p \in SourcePSink(\mathbb{G}))\ w \in \mathscr{R}\left(\mathcal{M}, C_{\mathcal{M},v}^{AgSeq(p)} \right) \right\}
\end{aligned}
\tag{4}
$$

$\widetilde{R} := (\widetilde{R}_1, \ldots, \widetilde{R}_n)$ *where for each* $i \in \mathcal{A}$, $\widetilde{R}_i \subseteq \widetilde{S} \times \widetilde{S}$ *such that*

$$
\begin{aligned}
\widetilde{R}_i := &\left\{ ((u_1, p),\ (u_2, p \circ (\alpha_1, \alpha_2, i))) \mid u_1 R_i u_2 \right\} \sqcup \\
&\left\{ ((u_1, p \circ (\alpha_1, \alpha_2, i)),\ (u_2, p \circ (\alpha_1, \alpha_2, i))) \mid u_1 R_i u_2 \right\} \sqcup \\
&\left\{ ((u_1, p), (u_2, -1)) \mid ((\exists (\alpha_1, -1, i) \in E)\ p \circ (\alpha_1, -1, i) \in SourcePSink(\mathbb{G})) \right. \\
&\left. \text{and } u_1 R_i u_2 \right\} \sqcup \\
&\left\{ ((u_1, -1), (u_2, -1)) \mid u_1 R_i u_2 \right\},
\end{aligned}
\tag{5}
$$

and $\widetilde{V}(q) \subseteq \widetilde{S}$ *such that*

$$
\widetilde{V}(q) := \{ (u, p) \mid u \in V(q) \} \sqcup \{ (u, -1) \mid u \in V(q) \}.
\tag{6}
$$

We will use the notations $\mathcal{M}_{v,\varphi}^{P} := \mathcal{M}_{v,\mathbb{G}_\varphi}^{P}$ *and* $\left(\mathcal{M}_{\varphi}^{P}, (v, \varepsilon)\right) := \left(\mathcal{M}_{v,\mathbb{G}_\varphi}^{P}, (v, \varepsilon)\right)$. *We partition* $\widetilde{S}$ *into the source* (v, ε)*, sink cluster that consists of all states* $(u, -1)$ *from* $\widetilde{S}$*, and p-clusters for each path* $p \in SourcePNoSink(\mathbb{G})$ *that consist of all states* (u, p) *from* $\widetilde{S}$.

Algorithm 1. `PerformUpdateAlg`$(\varphi, v, \langle S, R, V \rangle)$

1: **if** $\varphi = \varphi_1 \wedge \varphi_2$ where φ_1 and φ_2 are in goal-normal form **then**
2:     `PerformUpdateAlg`$(\varphi_1, v, \langle S, R, V \rangle)$
3:     `PerformUpdateAlg`$(\varphi_2, v, \langle S, R, V \rangle)$
4: **else if** $\varphi = B_i \varphi'$ where φ' is in goal-normal form **then**
5:     **for all** $v' \in S$ such that $v R_i v'$ **do**
6:         `PerformUpdateAlg`$(\varphi', v', \langle S, R, V \rangle)$
7: **else if** $\varphi = B_i \xi$ where ξ is propositional **then**
8:     **for all** $v' \in S$ such that $v R_i v'$ **do**
9:         **if** $\langle S, R, V \rangle, v' \not\models \xi$ **then**
10:             `RemoveState`$(v', \langle S, R, V \rangle)$
11: **else if** $\varphi = B_i(\xi \wedge \varphi')$ where φ' is in goal-normal form and ξ is propositional **then**
12:     **for all** $v' \in S$ such that $v R_i v'$ **do**
13:         **if** $\langle S, R, V \rangle, v' \not\models \xi$ **then**
14:             `RemoveState`$(v', \langle S, R, V \rangle)$
15:         **else**
16:             `PerformUpdateAlg`$(\varphi', v', \langle S, R, V \rangle)$

Algorithm 2. `RemoveState`$(v, \langle S, R, V \rangle)$

1: **for all** $i \in \mathcal{A}$ **do**
2:     $R_i := (R_i \setminus (S \times \{v\})) \setminus (\{v\} \times S)$
3: **for all** propositional variables q **do**
4:     $V(q) := V(q) \setminus \{v\}$
5: $S := S \setminus \{v\}$

Applying a belief privatization graph to a pointed Kripke model determines the shape of the resulting model, so that each of the (higher-order) beliefs specified in the goal formula can be updated independently and without information leakage, i.e., without affecting beliefs of agents not specified in the goal formula.

The following theorem states that a privatized pointed Kripke model is bisimilar to the original pointed Kripke model before privatization. A proof of a similar statement can be found in [7]:

Theorem 17 (Bisimulation). *For a belief privatization graph* $\mathbb{G} = (V, E)$, *the privatization* $\mathcal{M}^P_{v,\mathbb{G}}$ *of a pointed KD45 Kripke model* $(\mathcal{M}, v)$ *is itself a pointed KD45 Kripke model such that* $\left(\mathcal{M}^P_{v,\mathbb{G}}, (v, \varepsilon)\right) \Leftrightarrow (\mathcal{M}, v)$. *Hence, for any formula* φ

$$\mathcal{M}, v \models \varphi \quad \Leftrightarrow \quad \mathcal{M}^P_{v,\mathbb{G}}, (v, \varepsilon) \models \varphi.$$

3.4 Performing an Update

This section describes the algorithms that are used to perform updates on privatized Kripke models, preserving their clustered structure and thus simulating agent-to-agent communication.

`PerformUpdateAlg`$(\varphi, (v, \varepsilon), \mathcal{M}^P_{v,\varphi})$ in Algorithm 1 is called for the privatized model $\mathcal{M}^P_{v,\varphi}$, its point (v, ε), and formula φ in goal-normal form. It performs the update by removing all worlds (u, p) from the already privatized model $\mathcal{M}^P_{v,\varphi}$ that do not satisfy the propositional part in the goal formula corresponding to the path p. For $\varphi = \varphi_1 \wedge \varphi_2$ the algorithm is called for each conjunct, but the calls do not interfere with each other because they apply to disjoint parts of $\mathcal{M}^P_{v,\varphi}$ due to the formulas in goal-normal form not having $B_i\varphi \wedge B_i\psi$ subformulas. For $\varphi = B_i\varphi'$ the algorithm is called recursively for φ' in each state $v' \in S$ such that vR_iv' without removing any of these worlds because there is no restriction on v' themselves, only on their descendants. For $\varphi = B_i\xi$, the algorithm removes all R_i-accessible worlds where ξ does not hold using Algorithm 2. The case of $\varphi = B_i(\xi \wedge \varphi')$ is a combination of the preceding two cases.

After `PerformUpdateAlg`$(\varphi, (v, \varepsilon), \mathcal{M}^P_{v,\varphi})$ yields $\mathcal{M}^{U'}_{v,\varphi}$, we restrict the resulting model to $\mathscr{R}(\mathcal{M}^{U'}_{v,\varphi}, (v, \varepsilon))$ to get rid of unreachable states and call the resulting model $\mathcal{M}^U_{v,\varphi}$ with source (v, ε).

The correctness of Algorithm 1 is due to the fact that truth of goal formulas is stable with respect to state removals.

Lemma 18 (Goal formula update invariance). *Let φ be a goal formula such that $\mathcal{M}, v \models \varphi$ and let model $\mathcal{M}' = \langle S', R', V' \rangle$ be the restriction of $\mathcal{M} = \langle S, R, V \rangle$ to $S' \subseteq S$ such that $v \in S'$, e.g., obtained by iterative use of Algorithm 2. Then $\mathcal{M}', v \models \varphi$.*

Theorem 19 (Correctness). *Let a call of* `PerformUpdateAlg`$(\varphi, v, \langle S, R, V \rangle)$ *(see Algorithm 1) return $\mathcal{M}' = \langle S', R', V' \rangle$. Then $\mathcal{M}'$ is the restriction of $\mathcal{M}$ to some $S' \subseteq S$, and $\mathcal{M}', v \models \varphi$ whenever $v \in S'$. Moreover, if $\mathcal{M}$ was a KD45 model, then $\mathcal{M}'$ is a K45 model, i.e., satisfies transitivity and euclideanity. In addition, if v has no incoming arrows, i.e., if $(u, v) \notin R_i$ for any $i \in \mathcal{A}$ and $u \in S$, then v survives the update.*

From the previous theorem it follows that Algorithm 1 is successful in the synthesis task:

Corollary 20 (Update synthesis success). *Let $\mathcal{M}$ be a KD45 Kripke model with state v and φ be a formula in goal-normal form. Since state (v, ε) of the privatized model $\mathcal{M}^P_{v,\varphi}$ has no incoming arrows, the model $\mathcal{M}^U_{v,\varphi}$ returned by* `PerformUpdateAlg`$(\varphi, (v, \varepsilon), \mathcal{M}^P_{v,\varphi})$ *is a K45 model that still contains state (v, ε) and $\mathcal{M}^U_{v,\varphi}, (v, \varepsilon) \models \varphi$.*

We show that beliefs of agents not specified by the goal formula remain unchanged in several minimality results:

Theorem 21 (Minimal change: beliefs of unaffected agents). *Let $(\mathcal{M}, v)$ be a pointed Kripke model and $\varphi = \bigwedge_{j \in G} B_j\theta_j$ for some $\varnothing \neq G \subseteq \mathcal{A}$ be a formula in goal-normal form. Let $\mathcal{M}^U_{v,\varphi}$ be returned by* `PerformUpdateAlg`$(\varphi, (v, \varepsilon), \mathcal{M}^P_{v,\varphi})$. *If $i \notin G$, then for any formula ψ*

$$\mathcal{M}, v \models B_i\psi \quad \Longleftrightarrow \quad \mathcal{M}^U_{v,\varphi}, (v, \varepsilon) \models B_i\psi. \tag{7}$$

Using similar reasoning, the above theorem can be generalized to state that any higher-order beliefs not explicitly mentioned in the goal formula remain unaffected by the update:

Theorem 22 (Minimal change: higher-order beliefs). *Let $(\mathcal{M}, v)$ be a pointed Kripke model, $\sigma \in \mathcal{A}_{seq}$ be an agent sequence, and φ be a formula in goal-normal form such that there doesn't exist a path $p \in SourcePNoSink(\mathbb{G}_\varphi)$, where $AgSeq(p) = \sigma$. Let $\mathcal{M}_{v,\varphi}^U$ be returned by* `PerformUpdateAlg`$(\varphi, (v, \varepsilon), \mathcal{M}_{v,\varphi}^P)$. *For any formula ψ*

$$\mathcal{M}, v \models B_{\pi_1 \sigma} \cdots B_{\pi_{|\sigma|} \sigma} \psi \iff \mathcal{M}_{v,\varphi}^U, (v, \varepsilon) \models B_{\pi_1 \sigma} \cdots B_{\pi_{|\sigma|} \sigma} \psi. \qquad (8)$$

Finally, there is a special case when the goal formula specifies only higher-order beliefs of agent i. Minimality in this case means that the change in i's higher-order beliefs should not have any effect on i's views of the world:

Theorem 23 (Minimal change: propositional beliefs). *Let $(\mathcal{M}, v)$ be a pointed Kripke model and*

$$\varphi = \bigwedge\nolimits_{k \in G'} B_k \eta_k \wedge B_i \left(\bigwedge\nolimits_{j \in G} B_j \theta_j \right)$$

for some $\varnothing \neq G, G' \subseteq \mathcal{A} \setminus \{i\}$ be a formula in goal-normal form. Let $\mathcal{M}_{v,\varphi}^U$ be returned by `PerformUpdateAlg`$(\varphi, (v, \varepsilon), \mathcal{M}_{v,\varphi}^P)$. *Then for any propositional formula ξ*

$$\mathcal{M}, v \models B_i \xi \iff \mathcal{M}_{v,\varphi}^U, (v, \varepsilon) \models B_i \xi. \qquad (9)$$

Proof. This follows from the fact that truth values of propositional formulas are not affected by state removals and from the fact that no worlds i-accessible from (v, ε) will be removed by the algorithm. $\qquad \square$

Similar to Theorem 22, the same minimal change holds for propositional higher-order beliefs, provided the goal formula does not use the $B_i(\xi \wedge \varphi)$ clause for this particular higher-order belief. The following remark emphasizes that the agents have access to a limited portion of the model and the fact that other agents cannot access that part is what makes such local view private:

Remark 24. We argued earlier that common knowledge of the model is too strong an assumption for private announcements. We are now ready to state the exact extent of every agent's knowledge of the updated privatized model $\mathcal{M}^U$ sufficient for this agent to compute its own beliefs, including all higher-order beliefs. Agent i should know $\mathcal{R}\left(\mathcal{M}_{v,\varphi}^U, C_{\mathcal{M}_{v,\varphi}^U, (v,\varepsilon)}^{(i)} \right)$. In this case, no agent is aware of the real world (v, ε), which enables having false beliefs, and the only part of the privatized model that is commonly known is contained within the sink cluster. How much of the sink is commonly known depends on how much of the given model was commonly known before the privatization, e.g., in case of repeated updates.

Lemma 25. *For pointed Kripke model $(\mathcal{M}, v)$, goal formula φ, belief privatization graph $\mathbb{G}_\varphi = (V, E)$, for $\mathcal{M}_{v,\mathbb{G}_\varphi}^P = \langle S^P, R^P, V^P \rangle$ with point (v, ε) let $(\mathcal{M}', (v, \varepsilon)) = (\langle S', R', V' \rangle, (v, \epsilon))$ be a submodel of $(\mathcal{M}_{v,\mathbb{G}_\varphi}^P, (v, \varepsilon))$ meaning $S' \subseteq S^P$, $R' = R^P \cap S' \times S'$, $V' = V^P \cap S'$, then the privatized model $\mathcal{M}_{v,\mathbb{G}_\varphi}'^P$ of $\mathcal{M}'$ is the same as $\mathcal{M}'$, but restricted to states, which are reachable from its point.*

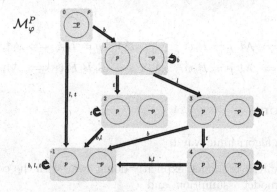

Fig. 4. Privatized Kripke model $\mathcal{M}_\varphi^P$ for $\varphi = B_b(B_t p \wedge B_l(p \wedge B_t p))$ with the real world ρ underlined. A gray rectangle with n in the top left corner is cluster numbered n. A double arrow from cluster n to cluster m represents a set of accessibility arrows with the same agent's label from every world of n to every world of m. (Color figure online)

Unlike DEL-style updates, where repeating the same update may result in an exponential increase of the model size, our updates do not result in a blow up.

Theorem 26. *Repeated updates with the same goal formula do not increase the model size, except for the first update.*

Proof. Follows from Lemma 25 since Algorithm 1 only removes states.

Example 27 (Balder–Loki–Thor example constructively). To illustrate how the update mechanism works, we return to Example 2. Recall that initial model $\mathcal{M}$ is depicted in Example 1, and that the goal formula $B_b B_t p \wedge B_b B_l B_t p \wedge B_b B_l p$ can be transformed to the goal-normal form $\varphi = B_b(B_t p \wedge B_l(p \wedge B_t p))$.

The belief privatization graph $\mathbb{G}_\varphi$ computed from goal formula φ is depicted in Fig. 3, and is constructed according to Definition 13. The privatized Kripke model $\mathcal{M}_\varphi^P$ depicted in Def. 4 is constructed according to the privatization operation described in Definition 16: in this case, each node in the belief privatization graph is replaced by a copy of the whole initial model, forming the corresponding clusters. Each edge (α, β, i) in the privatization graph results in i-labeled edges from states of the cluster corresponding to α to states of the cluster corresponding to β. Also i-labeled edges between states of the cluster corresponding to β are added as needed, which in this example means for all possible pairs. The resulting Kripke model $\mathcal{M}^U$ in Fig. 1 is obtained by updating the privatized Kripke model $\mathcal{M}_\varphi^P$, using Algorithm 1. The arrows pointing to states that would make the goal formula false are eliminated, and the states that become unreachable from ρ as a result are dropped from the model. In our example, only clusters 2, 3, and 4 are updated by deleting incoming arrows pointing to $\neg p$ states. As a result, $\mathcal{M}^U, \rho \models \varphi$. It is also easy to see that, for any formula ψ

and a propositional ξ

$$\mathcal{M}^U, \rho \models B_l\psi \iff \mathcal{M}, \rho \models B_l\psi \qquad \mathcal{M}^U, \rho \models B_b\xi \iff \mathcal{M}, \rho \models B_b\xi$$

$$\mathcal{M}^U, \rho \models B_t\psi \iff \mathcal{M}, \rho \models B_t\psi \qquad \mathcal{M}^U, \rho \models B_bB_tB_l\psi \iff \mathcal{M}, \rho \models B_bB_tB_l\psi$$

4   Conclusions

We presented an algorithmic way to

(i) privatize any Kripke model, explicitly doing away with the common knowledge of the model assumption, and

(ii) perform the consistent update synthesis task on privatized Kripke models.

The privatization is obtained according to a goal formula, based on which the corresponding belief privatization graph is constructed. The goal formulas are of a restricted form suitable for updates originating from agent-to-agent communication as the communicated message should be viewed as the speaker's subjective and fallible opinion (belief) rather than the objective truth. We also restrict goal formulas to exclude non-determinism or creating ignorance, which in belief revision terms corresponds to dealing with belief revision but not with belief contraction. The proposed update mechanism is quite efficient: only the initial update increases the size of the model at worst linearly in the size of the goal formula, while all subsequent updates via goal formulas with the same belief structure (or substructure thereof) only decrease the model size. Compare this with the exponential blow up after iterated AML or GAUL updates [2]. While it is impossible to always guarantee consistent updates (cf., e.g., goal formula B_ip applied to a model where $\neg p$ is valid), our synthesis method preserves consistency of beliefs, including higher-order beliefs, if possible, marking a difference from, e.g., [5].

Future Work. We aim at extending the update mechanism to arbitrary goal formulas, incorporating the non-determinism embedded in the $\hat{B}_i$ operator, dual to modality B_i, and in disjunctions of B_i operators, as well as at enabling the formalization of the conditions of consistency for each level of iterated beliefs and outlining the exact set of beliefs unaffected by the update based on a given goal formula. We also plan to provide algorithms to simulate the effects of public announcements and of other (less restrictive) kinds of updates in our framework, providing full granularity in the update design. Finally, while the suggested update mechanism is more efficient w.r.t. AML and GAUL, we leave the inquiry of the complexity of the synthesis procedure for future work.

Acknowledgments. We are grateful to Hans van Ditmarsch, Stephan Felber, Kristina Fruzsa, Rojo Randrianomentsoa, Hugo Rincón Galeana for multiple illuminating and inspiring discussions and additionally to Ulrich Schmid for his encouragement and inexhaustible optimism. We also thank the anonymous reviewers for their helpful comments and suggestions.

References

1. Artemov, S.: Observable models. In: Artemov, S., Nerode, A. (eds.) LFCS 2020. LNCS, vol. 11972, pp. 12–26. Springer, Cham (2020). https://doi.org/10.1007/978-3-030-36755-8_2

2. Aucher, G., Schwarzentruber, F.: On the complexity of dynamic epistemic logic. In: Schipper, B.C. (ed.) TARK 2013: Theoretical Aspects of Rationality and Knowledge, Proceedings of the 14th Conference, Chennai, India, pp. 19–28. University of California, Davis (2013). https://doi.org/10.48550/arXiv.1310.6406

3. Baltag, A., Renne, B.: Dynamic epistemic logic. In: Zalta, E.N. (ed.) The Stanford Encyclopedia of Philosophy. Metaphysics Research Lab, Stanford University, Winter 2016 edn. (2016). https://plato.stanford.edu/archives/win2016/entries/dynamic-epistemic/

4. van Ditmarsch, H., van der Hoek, W., Kooi, B.: Dynamic Epistemic Logic. Synthese Library, vol. 337. Springer, Heidelberg (2007). https://doi.org/10.1007/978-1-4020-5839-4

5. van Ditmarsch, H., van der Hoek, W., Kooi, B., Kuijer, L.B.: Arrow update synthesis. Inf. Comput. **275**(Article 104544) (2020). https://doi.org/10.1016/j.ic.2020.104544

6. Fagin, R., Halpern, J.Y., Moses, Y., Vardi, M.Y.: Reasoning About Knowledge. MIT Press, Cambridge (1995). https://doi.org/10.7551/mitpress/5803.001.0001

7. Goranko, V., Otto, M.: Model theory of modal logic. In: Blackburn, P., van Benthem, J., Wolter, F. (eds.) Handbook of Modal Logic. Studies in Logic and Practical Reasoning, vol. 3, pp. 249–329. Elsevier (2007). https://doi.org/10.1016/S1570-2464(07)80008-5

8. Hales, J.: Arbitrary action model logic and action model synthesis. In: 2013 28th Annual ACM/IEEE Symposium on Logic and Computer Science (LICS), 25–28 June 2013, New Orleans, Louisiana, pp. 253–262. IEEE (2013). https://doi.org/10.1109/LICS.2013.31

9. Herzig, A.: Dynamic epistemic logics: promises, problems, shortcomings, and perspectives. J. Appl. Non-Classical Log. **27**(3–4), 328–341 (2017). https://doi.org/10.1080/11663081.2017.1416036

10. Hintikka, J.: Knowledge and Belief: An Introduction to the Logic of the Two Notions. Cornell University Press (1962)

11. Kooi, B., Renne, B.: Generalized arrow update logic. In: Apt, K.R. (eds.) TARK XIII, Theoretical Aspects of Rationality and Knowledge: Proceedings of the Thirteenth Conference (TARK 2011), pp. 205–211. Association for Computing Machinery (2011). https://doi.org/10.1145/2000378.2000403

12. Plaza, J.: Logics of public communications. Synthese **158**(2), 165–179 (2007). https://doi.org/10.1007/s11229-007-9168-7. Originally published in 1989

Scaling up Nonmonotonic c-Inference
via Partial MaxSAT Problems

Martin von Berg, Arthur Sanin, and Christoph Beierle[✉][iD]

Knowledge-Based Systems, Faculty of Mathematics and Computer Science,
FernUniversität in Hagen, 58084 Hagen, Germany
christoph.beierle@fernuni-hagen.de

Abstract. Ranking functions, also called ordinal conditional functions
(OCF), provide a semantics for conditionals by assigning a degree of
implausibility to the underlying possible worlds. The entailment relation c-inference takes all c-representations, which are special ranking
functions, into account, and exhibits excellent properties put forward
for nonmonotonic reasoning. However, for realizing c-inference, showing the unsolvability of a complex constraint satisfaction problem (CSP)
is required, involving in particular satisfaction conditions affecting all
possible worlds. All previous implementations of c-inference are severely
limited by this requirement, making inferences from conditional belief
bases involving more than about 25 signature elements, and thus 2^{25}
possible worlds, practically infeasible. In this paper, we present an approach for reducing the size of the CSP underlying c-inference significantly
by using partial maximum satisfiability problems (PMaxSAT) and the
power of current PMaxSAT solvers. In particular, we introduce the dual
notion of minimum satisfiability problems for simplifying the minimum
expressions in the CSP. We prove the soundness of our CSP optimization
and develop an implementation for it. An evaluation demonstrates that
it outperforms all previous implementations and that it, while still having to cope with the exponentially increasing number of possible worlds,
scales up c-inference to a new dimension, allowing for c-inference from
belief bases with up to 100 signature elements and thus involving 2^{100}
possible worlds.

Keywords: Conditional · Belief Base · Nonmonotonic Reasoning ·
c-Inference · Partial MaxSAT

1 Introduction

In knowledge representation and reasoning, the subfield of Artificial Intelligence
research dealing with the formalization of, inter alia, commonsense and human-
like reasoning, nonmonotonic inference relations play an important role for capturing, e.g., dynamically interrelated knowledge, defaults and uncertainty. Conditional logics constitute a main approach for nonmonotonic reasoning. Semantical frameworks for conditionals range from quantitative probability distributions

A. Meier and M. Ortiz (Eds.): FoIKS 2024, LNCS 14589, pp. 182–200, 2024.
https://doi.org/10.1007/978-3-031-56940-1_10

to purely qualitative approaches which make use of total preorders over possible worlds. Here, we make use of the semi-qualitative framework of ranking functions, also called ordinal conditional functions (OCF) [30], which assign natural numbers as degrees of implausibility of possible worlds. More specifically, our work uses c-representations as a special type of such ranking functions exhibiting desirable inference properties [26,27]. Taking the set of all c-representations of a conditional knowledge base into account yields the nonmonotonic entailment relation *c-inference* [4,7], again exhibiting excellent inference properties like fulfilling the standard axioms of system P [1,25], not suffering from the well-known drowning problem [9,17] and fully satisfying syntax splitting [21,29].

However, for realizing c-inference, solving a complex constraint satisfaction problem (CSP) is required [4,7], involving in particular satisfaction conditions affecting all possible worlds. For all previously existing implementations of c-inference, this is a severe limiting factor, making inferences from conditional belief bases involving more than about 25 conditionals and 25 signature elements, and thus 2^{25} possible worlds, practically infeasible [3,5,10,26].

In this paper, we present an approach for scaling up c-inference to new orders of magnitude, allowing for c-inference from belief bases with up to 100 conditionals and 100 signature elements and thus involving 2^{100} worlds. For this, we employ partial maximum satisfiability problems (*PMaxSAT*) [28] and the power of modern *PMaxSAT* solvers [18] for reducing the complexity of the CSP characterizing c-inference. Specifically, we introduce a dual minimum satisfiability problem for simplifying the minimum expressions occurring in that CSP. We formally develop all steps required for this CSP optimization and prove its soundness. Furthermore, we present an implementation of our approach and evaluate it w.r.t. previous implementations, demonstrating its superiority and how it scales up c-inference to new dimensions.

After briefly recalling the required background on conditional logic and c-inference in Sect. 2, we develop the approach of the CSP optimization via *PMaxSAT* in Sect. 3, prove its soundness, and illustrate it with a running example. The optimized CSP is transformed into a satisfiability-modulo-theories (SMT) problem in Sect. 4, and Sect. 5 presents an implementation and evaluation. Section 6 concludes and points out further work.

2   Background: Conditionals and c-Inference

2.1   Conditional Logic and OCFs

Let $\mathcal{L}$ be a propositional language over a finite signature Σ. We write AB for $A \wedge B$ and $\overline{A}$ for $\neg A$ for formulas $A, B \in \mathcal{L}$. We denote the set of all interpretations over $\mathcal{L}$, also called *worlds*, as Ω. For $\omega \in \Omega$, $\omega \models A$ means that $A \in \mathcal{L}$ holds in ω. We define the set $(\mathcal{L} \mid \mathcal{L}) = \{(B|A) \mid A, B \in \mathcal{L}\}$ of *conditionals* over $\mathcal{L}$. The intuition of $(B|A)$ is that if A holds, then usually B holds, too. As semantics for conditionals, we use functions $\kappa : \Omega \to \mathbb{N}$ such that $\kappa(\omega) = 0$ for at least one $\omega \in \Omega$, called *ordinal conditional functions (OCF)*, introduced (in a more general form) in [30]. They express degrees of plausibility of possible worlds where a lower degree denotes "less surprising". Each κ uniquely extends to a function mapping sentences to $\mathbb{N} \cup \{\infty\}$ given by $\kappa(A) = \min\{\kappa(\omega) \mid \omega \models A\}$ where $\min \emptyset = \infty$. An OCF κ *accepts* a conditional $(B|A)$, written $\kappa \models (B|A)$, if $\kappa(AB) < \kappa(A\overline{B})$. This can also be understood as a nonmonotonic inference relation where A κ-*entails* B, written $A \vdash^\kappa B$, if κ accepts $(B|A)$; formally, this is given by $A \vdash^\kappa B$ iff $A \equiv \bot$ or $\kappa(AB) < \kappa(A\overline{B})$. A finite set $\mathcal{R} \subseteq (\mathcal{L}|\mathcal{L})$ of conditionals is called a *knowledge base*. An OCF κ accepts $\mathcal{R}$, written $\kappa \models \mathcal{R}$, if κ accepts all conditionals in $\mathcal{R}$, see e.g. [15].

2.2   C-Representations and C-Inference

Among the models of $\mathcal{R}$, c-representations are special ranking models obtained by assigning individual integer impacts to the conditionals in $\mathcal{R}$. For an in-depth introduction to c-representations and their use of the principle of conditional preservation we refer to [19,20].

Definition 1 (c-representation [19,20]). *A c-representation of a knowledge base* $\mathcal{R} = \{(B_1|A_1), \ldots, (B_n|A_n)\}$ *is a ranking function* κ *constructed from integer impacts* $\eta_i \in \mathbb{N}_0$ *assigned to each conditional* $(B_i|A_i)$ *such that* κ *accepts* $\mathcal{R}$ *and is given by:*

$$\kappa(\omega) = \sum_{1 \leqslant i \leqslant n, \, \omega \models A_i \overline{B}_i} \eta_i \tag{1}$$

C-inference takes all c-representations of $\mathcal{R}$ into account.

Definition 2 (c-inference, $\vdash^c_\mathcal{R}$ [4]). *Let* $\mathcal{R}$ *be a knowledge base and let* A, B *be formulas.* B *is a (skeptical) c-inference from* A *in the context of* $\mathcal{R}$, *denoted by* $A \vdash^c_\mathcal{R} B$, *iff* $A \vdash^\kappa B$ *holds for all c-representations* κ *for* $\mathcal{R}$.

Definition 3 ($CR(\mathcal{R})$). *Let* $\mathcal{R} = \{(B_1|A_1), \ldots, (B_n|A_n)\}$. *The constraint satisfaction problem* $CR(\mathcal{R})$ *on the constraint variables* $\{\eta_1, \ldots, \eta_n\}$ *ranging over* $\mathbb{N}_0$ *is given by the constraints, for all* $i \in \{1, \ldots, n\}$:

$$\eta_i \geqslant 0 \tag{2}$$

$$\eta_i > \underbrace{\min_{\omega \models A_i B_i} \sum_{\substack{j \neq i \\ \omega \models A_j \overline{B}_j}} \eta_j}_{V_{min_i}} - \underbrace{\min_{\omega \models A_i \overline{B}_i} \sum_{\substack{j \neq i \\ \omega \models A_j \overline{B}_j}} \eta_j}_{F_{min_i}} \tag{3}$$

Example 1 ($\mathcal{R}_{bird}$ [8]). Let $\Sigma = \{b, p, f, w\}$ representing birds, penguins, flying things and winged things, and let $\mathcal{R}_{bird}$ contain $r_1 = (B_1|A_1) = (f|b)$, $r_2 = (B_2|A_2) = (\overline{f}|p)$, $r_3 = (B_3|A_3) = (b|p)$, and $r_4 = (B_4|A_4) = (w|b)$. For instance, r_1 expresses "*birds usually fly*". Verification and falsification of these conditionals are given in Table 1, along with the three vectors $\vec{\eta}_1, \vec{\eta}_2, \vec{\eta}_3$ which are some solutions of $CR(\mathcal{R}_{bird})$ and their induced ranking functions $\kappa_{\vec{\eta}_1}, \kappa_{\vec{\eta}_2}, \kappa_{\vec{\eta}_3}$.

Table 1. Verification (v) and falsification (f) with induced impacts for $\mathcal{R}_{bird}$ in Example 1.

ω	r_1: $(f\|b)$	r_2: $(\overline{f}\|p)$	r_3: $(b\|p)$	r_4: $(w\|b)$	impact on ω	$\kappa_{\vec{\eta}_1}(\omega)$	$\kappa_{\vec{\eta}_2}(\omega)$	$\kappa_{\vec{\eta}_3}(\omega)$
$bpfw$	v	f	v	v	η_2	2	4	5
$bpf\overline{w}$	v	f	v	f	$\eta_2+\eta_4$	3	7	12
$bp\overline{f}w$	f	v	v	v	η_1	1	3	4
$bp\overline{f}\,\overline{w}$	f	v	v	f	$\eta_1+\eta_4$	2	6	11
$b\overline{p}fw$	v	−	−	v	0	0	0	0
$b\overline{p}f\overline{w}$	v	−	−	f	η_4	1	3	7
$b\overline{p}\,\overline{f}w$	f	−	−	v	η_1	1	3	4
$b\overline{p}\,\overline{f}\,\overline{w}$	f	−	−	f	$\eta_1+\eta_4$	2	6	11
$\overline{b}pfw$	−	f	f	−	$\eta_2+\eta_3$	4	8	11
$\overline{b}pf\overline{w}$	−	f	f	−	$\eta_2+\eta_3$	4	8	11
$\overline{b}p\overline{f}w$	−	v	f	−	η_3	2	4	6
$\overline{b}p\overline{f}\,\overline{w}$	−	v	f	−	η_3	2	4	6
$\overline{b}\,\overline{p}fw$	−	−	−	−	0	0	0	0
$\overline{b}\,\overline{p}f\overline{w}$	−	−	−	−	0	0	0	0
$\overline{b}\,\overline{p}\,\overline{f}w$	−	−	−	−	0	0	0	0
$\overline{b}\,\overline{p}\,\overline{f}\,\overline{w}$	−	−	−	−	0	0	0	0

impacts:	η_1	η_2	η_3	η_4
$\vec{\eta}_1$	1	2	2	1
$\vec{\eta}_2$	3	4	4	3
$\vec{\eta}_3$	4	5	6	7

Using Table 1, we can check that $\vec{\eta}_i \models \mathcal{R}_{bird}$ holds for $i = 1, 2, 3$. More generally, $CR(\mathcal{R})$ is a sound and complete characterization of the set of all c-representations of $\mathcal{R}$. The key idea for proving this is to employ the definition of κ as given in Eq. (1) and its extension to formulas and to transform the acceptance condition $\kappa(A_iB_i) < \kappa(A_i\overline{B_i})$ for the conditional $(B_i|A_i)$ stepwise into the constraint (3) [4,20].

C-inference can be characterized by a CSP, too.

Theorem 4 ($CR(\mathcal{R}, A, B)$ [4]). *Let* $\mathcal{R} = \{(B_1|A_1), \ldots, (B_n|A_n)\}$ *and* A, B *formulas. Then for*

$$CR(\mathcal{R}, A, B) = CR(\mathcal{R}) \cup \{\neg CR_{\mathcal{R}}(B|A)\} \tag{4}$$

with $\neg CR_{\mathcal{R}}(B|A)$ *being the constraint*

$$\underbrace{\min_{\omega \models AB} \sum_{\substack{1 \leqslant i \leqslant n \\ \omega \models A_i\overline{B}_i}} \eta_i}_{V_{min_q}} \geqslant \underbrace{\min_{\omega \models A\overline{B}} \sum_{\substack{1 \leqslant i \leqslant n \\ \omega \models A_i\overline{B}_i}} \eta_i}_{F_{min_q}} \tag{5}$$

we have $A \hspace{0.1em}\vdash\hspace{-0.5em}\sim_{\mathcal{R}}^{c} B$ iff $CR(\mathcal{R}, A, B)$ is not solvable.

Example 2. In addition to the constraints $\eta_i \geqslant 0$, $CR(\mathcal{R}_{bird}, p, w)$ is:

$$\eta_1 > \min_{\substack{\omega \in \Omega_\Sigma \\ \omega \models bf}} \sum_{\substack{j \neq 1 \\ \omega \models A_j \overline{B}_j}} \eta_j - \min_{\substack{\omega \in \Omega_\Sigma \\ \omega \models b\overline{f}}} \sum_{\substack{j \neq 1 \\ \omega \models A_j \overline{B}_j}} \eta_j$$

$$\eta_2 > \min_{\substack{\omega \in \Omega_\Sigma \\ \omega \models p\overline{f}}} \sum_{\substack{j \neq 2 \\ \omega \models A_j \overline{B}_j}} \eta_j - \min_{\substack{\omega \in \Omega_\Sigma \\ \omega \models pf}} \sum_{\substack{j \neq 2 \\ \omega \models A_j \overline{B}_j}} \eta_j$$

$$\eta_3 > \min_{\substack{\omega \in \Omega_\Sigma \\ \omega \models pb}} \sum_{\substack{j \neq 3 \\ \omega \models A_j \overline{B}_j}} \eta_j - \min_{\substack{\omega \in \Omega_\Sigma \\ \omega \models p\overline{b}}} \sum_{\substack{j \neq 3 \\ \omega \models A_j \overline{B}_j}} \eta_j$$

$$\eta_4 > \min_{\substack{\omega \in \Omega_\Sigma \\ \omega \models bw}} \sum_{\substack{j \neq 4 \\ \omega \models A_j \overline{B}_j}} \eta_j - \min_{\substack{\omega \in \Omega_\Sigma \\ \omega \models b\overline{w}}} \sum_{\substack{j \neq 4 \\ \omega \models A_j \overline{B}_j}} \eta_j$$

$$\min_{\substack{\omega \in \Omega_\Sigma \\ \omega \models pw}} \sum_{\substack{1 \leqslant i \leqslant 4 \\ \omega \models A_i \overline{B}_i}} \eta_i \geqslant \min_{\substack{\omega \in \Omega_\Sigma \\ \omega \models p\overline{w}}} \sum_{\substack{1 \leqslant i \leqslant 4 \\ \omega \models A_i \overline{B}_i}} \eta_i$$

Since $CR(\mathcal{R}_{bird}, p, w)$ is unsolvable, we conclude that $p \hspace{0.1em}\vdash\hspace{-0.5em}\sim_{\mathcal{R}_{bird}}^{c} w$ (it follows by c-inference from $\mathcal{R}_{bird}$ that penguins usually have wings).

3   Optimizing $CR(\mathcal{R}, A, B)$ Using Partial MaxSAT

3.1   Partial MaxSAT Problems

While a Boolean satisfiability problem (SAT) is a decision problem that asks for the satisfiability of a propositional formula in clausal normal form [2], a maximum satisfiability problem $(MaxSAT)$ is an optimization problem seeking to maximize the number of satisfied clauses in a propositional formula in clausal normal form [18]. Here, we use a more general form by taking arbitrary formulas into account.

Definition 5 (Maximum Satisfiability Problem, $MaxSAT(A)$). *Let $A = \{A_i, \ldots, A_n\} \subseteq \mathcal{L}$ be a set of formulas called "soft constraints". The maximum satisfiability problem $MaxSAT(A)$ is the optimization problem of maximizing the number of satisfied soft constraints over all interpretations $\omega \in \Omega$.*

Thus, the solution of $MaxSAT(A)$ is the maximum number of formulas from A that can be satisfied simultaneously. We will now generalize $MaxSAT$ problems by asking for *all sets* of simultaneously satisfiable formulas that are maximal in the sense that no superset of formulas can be satisfied.

Definition 6 (Extended   Maximum   Satisfiability   Problem, $EMaxSAT(A)$). *Let $A = \{A_1, \ldots, A_n\} \subseteq \mathcal{L}$. The extended maximum satisfiability problem $EMaxSAT(A)$ is the problem of determining all subsets $M \subseteq A$ for which there is an $\omega \in \Omega$ with $\omega \models M$ such that for every $M' \subseteq A$ with $M \subsetneq M'$ there is no $\omega' \in \Omega$ with $\omega' \models M'$.*

Note that the subsets M mentioned in Definition 6 are the so-called *maximal satisfiable subsets (MSS)*. Hence, solving $EMaxSAT(A)$ requires the computation of all MSS, and hence the computation of a set of sets of formulas. The following definition provides a compact representation for such solution sets that will be convenient in the sequel.

Definition 7 (Satisfaction vectors w.r.t. $EMaxSAT(A)$, $SV(A)$). *Let $A = \{A_1, \ldots, A_n\} \subseteq \mathcal{L}$ be a set of formulas. For an interpretation $\omega \in \Omega$, the vector $\vec{s}_\omega = (s_1, \ldots, s_n)$ with $s_i = 0$ if $\omega \models A_i$ and $s_i = 1$ if $\omega \not\models A_i$ is the* satisfaction *vector of ω (w.r.t. $EMaxSAT(A)$). The set*

$$SV(A) = \{\vec{s}_\omega \mid \omega \in \Omega\}$$

is the set of all satisfaction vectors w.r.t. $EMaxSAT(A)$ and

$$SV_{pm}(A) = \{\vec{s} \mid \vec{s} \text{ is Pareto-minimal in } SV(A)\}$$

is the set of Pareto-minimal satisfaction vectors w.r.t. $EMaxSAT(A)$.

It is straightforward to check that the Pareto-minimal satisfaction vectors identify the solution elements of $EMaxSAT(A)$.

Proposition 8 (Solution set of $EMaxSAT(A)$). *Let $A = \{A_i, \ldots, A_n\} \subseteq \mathcal{L}$. A set $M \subseteq A$ is in the solution set for $EMaxSAT(A)$ iff there is $(s_1, \ldots, s_n) \in SV_{pm}(A)$ such that $M = \{A_i \mid i \in \{1, \ldots, n\}$ and $s_i = 0\}$.*

Example 3. Consider our knowledge base $\mathcal{R}_{bird} = \{(f|b), (\overline{f}|p), (b|p), (w|b)\}$ from Example 1. For determining how many and which of these conditionals can be simultaneously verified by a world, we consider the set $S = \{bf, p\overline{f}, pb, bw\}$ of verifications of the four conditionals as constraints. Then the satisfaction vectors $SV(S)$ and $SV_{pm}(S)$ w.r.t. $EMaxSAT(S)$ are:

$$SV(S) = \{(0,1,0,0), (0,1,0,1), (1,0,0,0), (1,0,0,1), (0,1,1,0),$$
$$(0,1,1,1), (1,1,1,0), (1,1,1,1), (1,0,1,1)\}$$
$$SV_{pm}(S) = \{(0,1,0,0), (1,0,0,0)\}$$

For instance, for $\omega_e = bp f \overline{w}$, we have $\vec{s}_{\omega_e} = (0,1,0,1)$, and the solution set for $EMaxSAT(S)$ is $M_S = \{\{bf, pb, bw\}, \{p\overline{f}, pb, bw\}\}$.

The next proposition makes explicit how $EMaxSAT(A)$ generalizes $MaxSAT(A)$.

Proposition 9 (Relation between $MaxSAT(A)$ and $EMaxSAT(A)$). *Let $A = \{A_1, \ldots, A_n\} \subseteq \mathcal{L}$, let $SV_{pm}(A) = \{\vec{s}_1, \ldots, \vec{s}_m\}$ with vectors $\vec{s}_j = (s_{j,1}, \ldots, s_{j,n})$ be the set of satisfaction vectors identifying the solution of $EMaxSAT(A)$. Then,*

$$MS_{sol}(A) = n - \min_{1 \leqslant j \leqslant m} \sum_{k=1}^{n} s_{j,k}$$

is the solution of $MaxSAT(A)$.

Proposition 10 (Relation between $MS_{sol}(A)$, $SV_{pm}(A)$ and $SV(A)$).
Let A and $SV_{pm}(A)$ be as in Proposition 9, let $SV_{sum}(A) = \{\vec{s}_j = (s_{j,1}, \ldots, s_{j,n}) | \vec{s}_j \in SV_{pm}(A), n - \sum_{k=1}^{n} s_{j,k} = MS_{sol}(A)\}$. Then,

$$SV_{sum}(A) \subseteq SV_{pm}(A) \subseteq SV(A).$$

Example 4. Continuing Example 3, it is obvious that $SV_{pm}(S) \subseteq SV(S)$, and as $MS_{sol}(S) = 3$ (which can be verified by inspection of $SV_{pm}(S)$, because maximally three formulas can be satisfied simultaneously), we also have $SV_{sum}(S) \subseteq SV_{pm}(S)$, in this particular example even $SV_{sum}(S) = SV_{pm}(S)$.

A partial maximum satisfiability problem is obtained from $MaxSAT(A)$ by taking additionally a formula B as a hard constraint into account [28]. Instead of using two parameters denoting the set of soft constraints and the hard constraint, respectively, we will use a set $A = \{A_1, \ldots, A_n\}$ denoting the set of all constraints and an index h into A pointing out the single hard constraint A_h in A.

Definition 11 (Partial Maximum Satisfiability Problem, $PMaxSAT(A, h)$). *Let $A = \{A_1, \ldots, A_n\} \subseteq \mathcal{L}$ be a set of constraints and let $h \in \{1, \ldots, n\}$. A_h is called a hard constraint, while the other A_i are soft constraints. The partial maximum satisfiability problem $PMaxSAT(A, h)$ is the optimization problem of maximizing the number of satisfied soft constraints over all interpretations $\omega \in \Omega_{A_h}$.*

Analogously to the extended $MaxSAT$ problem that we have introduced above, we will also extend the $PMaxSAT$ problem.

Definition 12 (Extended Partial Maximum Satisfiability Problem, $EPMaxSAT(A, h)$). *Let $A = \{A_1, \ldots, A_n\} \subseteq \mathcal{L}$ be a set of constraints. A_h is called a hard constraint, while the other A_i are soft constraints. The extended partial maximum satisfiability problem $EPMaxSAT(A, h)$ is the problem of determining all subsets $M \subseteq A$ with $A_h \in M$ for which there is an $\omega \in \Omega_{A_h}$ with $\omega \models M$ such that for every $M' \subseteq A$ with $A_h \in M'$ and $M \subsetneq M'$ there is no $\omega' \in \Omega_{A_h}$ with $\omega' \models M'$.*

The notion of satisfaction vector carries over directly to $EPMaxSAT$ problems by considering only interpretations $\omega \in \Omega_{A_h}$ instead of $\omega \in \Omega$. With

$$SV(A, h) = \{\vec{s}_\omega \mid \omega \in \Omega_{A_h}\}$$

we denote the set of all satisfaction vectors w.r.t. $EPMaxSAT(A, h)$, and

$$SV_{pm}(A, h) = \{\vec{s} \mid \vec{s} \text{ is Pareto-minimal in } SV(A, h)\}$$

is the set of Pareto-minimal satisfaction vectors w.r.t. $EPMaxSAT(A, h)$.

Note that due to the hard constraint A_h holding in every $\omega \in \Omega_{A_h}$, for every vector $\vec{s} = (s_1, \ldots, s_n) \in SV(A, h)$, we have $s_h = 0$.

Example 5. As in Example 3, consider the set $S = \{bf, p\overline{f}, pb, bw\}$ of verifications for the four conditionals in $\mathcal{R}_{bird}$ as constraints, and let the third element pb be a hard constraint. Then, the sets of satisfaction vectors $SV(S, 3)$ and $SV_{pm}(S, 3)$ w.r.t. $EPMaxSAT(S, 3)$ are:

$$SV(S, 3) = \{(0, 1, 0, 0), (0, 1, 0, 1), (1, 0, 0, 0), (1, 0, 0, 1)\}$$
$$SV_{pm}(S, 3) = \{(0, 1, 0, 0), (1, 0, 0, 0)\}$$

3.2 Modelling Minimum Expressions by *EPMaxSAT* Problems

The following definition connects our notion of a set containing various soft constraints and one hard constraint specified by an index with the type of minimum expressions occurring in $CR(\mathcal{R}, A, B)$.

Definition 13 (*Min(A, h)*). *Let $A = \{A_1, \ldots, A_n\} \subseteq \mathcal{L}$ and let $h \in \{1, \ldots, n\}$. The (A, h)-guarded minimum expression, denoted by $Min(A, h)$, is given by*

$$\min_{\omega \models A_h} \sum_{\substack{i \neq h \\ \omega \models A_i}} v_i$$

where $V = \{v_1, \ldots, v_n\}$ are variables over the non-negative numbers attached to the elements of A.

Example 6. Again, consider our knowledge base $\mathcal{R}_{bird}$ from Example 1. Considering the verification of the third conditional and the falsifications of the other three conditionals, we get the set of constraints $C = \{C_1, C_2, C_3, C_4\} = \{b\overline{f}, pf, pb, b\overline{w}\}$ with associated constraint variables $\{\eta_1, \eta_2, \eta_3, \eta_4\}$. Taking the verification pb of the third conditional as a hard constraint, we get:

$$Min(C, 3) = \min_{\omega \models pb} \sum_{\substack{1 \leqslant i \leqslant 4 \\ i \neq 3 \\ \omega \models A_i \overline{B}_i}} \eta_i$$

Note that in Example 6, the expression $Min(C, 3)$ corresponds exactly to V_{min_3} in $CR(\mathcal{R}_{bird})$, where the $\eta_1, \ldots, \eta_4$ are the variables attached to the constraints $C_1, \ldots, C_4$, cf. Example 1 and Eq. (3) in Definition 3. More generally, we can write all minimum expressions in $CR(\mathcal{R})$ and in $CR(\mathcal{R}, A, B)$ as (A, h)-guarded minimum expressions.

Proposition 14 ((A, h)-**guarded minimum expressions for** $CR(\mathcal{R}, A, B)$). *Let $\mathcal{R} = \{(B_1|A_1), \ldots, (B_n|A_n)\}$ and $A, B \in \mathcal{L}$. For $i \in \{1, \ldots, n\}$, the constraints associated to the conditional $(B_i|A_i)$ and to the query $(B|A)$, respectively, are given by:*

$$C_{\mathcal{R}}^{i,v} = \{A_1\overline{B}_1, \ldots, A_{i-1}\overline{B}_{i-1}, A_iB_i, A_{i+1}\overline{B}_{i+1}, \ldots, A_n\overline{B}_n\}$$
$$C_{\mathcal{R}}^{i,f} = \{A_1\overline{B}_1, \ldots, A_{i-1}\overline{B}_{i-1}, A_i\overline{B}_i, A_{i+1}\overline{B}_{i+1}, \ldots, A_n\overline{B}_n\}$$
$$C_{A,B}^{q,v} = \{A_1\overline{B}_1, \ldots, A_n\overline{B}_n, AB\}$$
$$C_{A,B}^{q,f} = \{A_1\overline{B}_1, \ldots, A_n\overline{B}_n, A\overline{B}\}$$

Then, by using $V = \{\eta_1, \ldots, \eta_n\}$ as variables, the minimum expressions in $CR(\mathcal{R}, A, B)$ can be written as:

$$V_{min_i} = Min(C_{\mathcal{R}}^{i,v}, i)$$
$$F_{min_i} = Min(C_{\mathcal{R}}^{i,f}, i)$$
$$V_{min_q} = Min(C_{A,B}^{q,v}, n+1)$$
$$F_{min_q} = Min(C_{A,B}^{q,f}, n+1)$$

We say that two minimum expressions M, M' over V as in Definition 13 are equivalent, denoted by $M \equiv M'$, if $\rho(M) = \rho(M')$ for every ρ assigning values to V. Furthermore, for optimizing such minimum expressions, we introduce the following notation. If $M_1, \ldots, M_m$ are sets, $Min_{\subseteq}\{M_1, \ldots, M_m\} \subseteq \{M_1, \ldots, M_m\}$ denotes the set of subsetwise minimal elements in $\{M_1, \ldots, M_m\}$. Thus, for $i \in \{1, \ldots, m\}$, we have $M_i \in Min_{\subseteq}\{M_1, \ldots, M_m\}$ iff $M_i \in \{M_1, \ldots, M_m\}$ and there is no $M_j \in \{M_1, \ldots, M_m\}$ with $M_j \subsetneq M_i$.

Proposition 15. *Let $\mathcal{I} = \{1, \ldots, n\}$ and $\mathcal{I}_1, \ldots, \mathcal{I}_k \subseteq \mathcal{I}$ be subsets of $\mathcal{I}$. If $\{v_1, \ldots, v_n\}$ is a set of variables over the non-negative numbers, then:*

$$\underbrace{\min \sum_{\substack{S \in \{\mathcal{I}_1, \ldots, \mathcal{I}_k\} \\ j \in S}} v_j}_{M} \equiv \underbrace{\min \sum_{\substack{S \in Min_{\subseteq}\{\mathcal{I}_1, \ldots, \mathcal{I}_k\} \\ j \in S}} v_j}_{M'}$$

Proof. Let ρ be an assignment of non-negative numbers to $\{v_1, \ldots, v_n\}$. Because $Min_{\subseteq}\{\mathcal{I}_1, \ldots, \mathcal{I}_k\} \subseteq \{\mathcal{I}_1, \ldots, \mathcal{I}_k\}$, the minimum in M' is taken over a subset of sum-expressions compared to M, implying $\rho(M) \leqslant \rho(M')$ since $\rho(v_i) \geqslant 0$ for every v_i. Furthermore, every sum-expression occurring in M but not in M' has one or more additional summands than some other sum-expression in M'. Thus, $\rho(M) \geqslant \rho(M')$ because $\rho(v_i) \geqslant 0$ for every v_i. □

Proposition 15 states that we can reduce the problem size of determining the minimum of a set of sum-expressions by ignoring sum-expressions which are, because of additional summands, necessarily equal or greater than some other sum-expression.

Example 7. As in Example 6, consider the set of constraints $C = \{C_1, C_2, C_3, C_4\} = \{b\overline{f}, pf, pb, b\overline{w}\}$ with associated constraint variables $\{\eta_1, \eta_2, \eta_3, \eta_4\}$ and the minimum expression

$$Min(C, 3) = V_{min_3} = \min_{\omega \models pb} \sum_{\substack{1 \leqslant i \leqslant 4 \\ i \neq 3 \\ \omega \models A_i \overline{B}_i}} \eta_i$$

Then, $\mathcal{I}^3 = \{1, 2, 4\}$, $\{\mathcal{I}_1^3, \mathcal{I}_2^3, \mathcal{I}_3^3, \mathcal{I}_4^3\} = \{\{2\}, \{2, 4\}, \{1\}, \{1, 2\}\}$, and $Min_{\subseteq}\{\{\mathcal{I}_1^3, \mathcal{I}_2^3, \mathcal{I}_3^3, \mathcal{I}_4^3\}\} = \{\{2\}, \{1\}\}$. We get, as stated in Proposition 15,

$$M = \min\{\eta_2, \eta_2 + \eta_4, \eta_1, \eta_1 + \eta_4\} \equiv \min\{\eta_2, \eta_1\} = M'.$$

The next definition provides the link between satisfaction vectors as solutions of *EPMaxSAT* problems and our minimum expressions.

Definition 16 ($\mathcal{M}(S)$). *Let $A = \{A_1, \ldots, A_n\} \subseteq \mathcal{L}$, let $h \in \{1, \ldots, n\}$ and let $S \subseteq SV(A, h)$ be a set of satisfaction vectors for EPMaxSAT(A, h). The minimum expression associated to S, denoted by $\mathcal{M}(S)$, is*

$$\min_{\omega \models A_h} \sum_{\substack{(s_1, \ldots, s_n) \in S \\ s_i = 1}} v_i$$

where $\{v_1, \ldots, v_n\}$ are variables over the non-negative numbers as in Definition 13.

Note that the condition $\omega \models A_h$ in Definition 16 is not needed because s_h will always be equal to 0 in any satisfaction vector for *EPMaxSAT(A, h)*. The condition is only added for underlining the relationship to the notation in Definition 13.

Example 8. Let $C = \{C_1, C_2, C_3, C_4\} = \{b\overline{f}, pf, pb, b\overline{w}\}$ be as in Example 6. Then $SV_{pm}(C, 3) = \{(0, 1, 0, 0), (1, 0, 0, 0)\}$ is the set of Pareto-minimal satisfaction vectors for *EPMaxSAT$(C, 3)$* and

$$\mathcal{M}(SV_{pm}(C, 3)) = \min_{\omega \models pb} \sum_{\substack{(s_1, \ldots, s_4) \in SV_{pm}(C, 3) \\ s_i = 1}} \eta_i = \min\{\eta_2, \eta_1\}.$$

For employing *MaxSAT* techniques for computations involving minimum expressions, we introduce the concept of an extended partial minimum satisfiability problem analogously to *EPMaxSAT*.

Definition 17 (*EPMinSAT(A, h)*). *Let $A = \{A_1, \ldots, A_n\} \subseteq \mathcal{L}$ and let $h \in \{1, \ldots, n\}$. EPMinSAT(A, h), called the* extended partial minimum satisfiability problem, *is the problem of determining all subsetwise smallest subsets $M \subseteq A$ with $A_h \in M$ for which there is an $\omega \in \Omega_{A_h}$ with $\omega \models M$ and $\omega \nvDash A_i$ for all $A_i \in A \setminus M$.*

The notions of satisfaction vectors SV and SV_{pm} carry over to *EPMinSAT(A, h)*, modified as follows:

Definition 18 (Satisfaction vectors w.r.t. *EPMinSAT(A, h)*, $SV^{min}(A, h)$). *Let $A = \{A_1, \ldots, A_n\} \subseteq \mathcal{L}$ be a set of formulas and let $h \in \{1, \ldots, n\}$. For an interpretation $\omega \in \Omega$, the vector $\vec{s}_\omega = (s_1, \ldots, s_n)$ with $s_h = 0$, $s_i = 0$ if $\omega \nvDash A_i$ and $s_i = 1$ if $\omega \models A_i$ is the satisfaction vector of ω w.r.t. EPMinSAT(A, h). The set*

$$SV^{min}(A, h) = \{\vec{s}_\omega \mid \omega \in \Omega_{A_h}\}$$

is the set of all satisfaction vectors w.r.t. EPMinSAT(A, h) and

$$SV_{pm}^{min}(A) = \{\vec{s} \mid \vec{s} \text{ is Pareto-minimal in } SV^{min}(A, h)\}$$

is the set of Pareto-minimal satisfaction vectors w.r.t. EPMinSAT(A, h).

The following proposition shows that the solutions of $EPMinSAT(A, h)$ coincide with the dual $EPMaxSAT$ problem obtained by negating all soft constraints but keeping the hard constraint as is.

Proposition 19. *Let $A = \{A_1, \ldots, A_n\} \subseteq \mathcal{L}$ and let $h \in \{1, \ldots, n\}$. Then*

$$SV_{pm}^{min}(EPMinSAT(A, h)) = SV_{pm}(EPMaxSAT(\widetilde{A}, h))$$

where $\widetilde{A} = \{\overline{A}_1, \ldots, \overline{A}_{h-1}, A_h, \overline{A}_{h+1}, \ldots, \overline{A}_n\}$.

Proof. If $\widetilde{M} = \{\overline{A}_{k_1}, \ldots, \overline{A}_{k_m}, A_h\}$ is a solution of $EPMaxSAT(\widetilde{A}, h)$, then $\widetilde{M}$ can not be enlarged by an additionally satisfied $\overline{A}_i \in \widetilde{A} \setminus \widetilde{M}$. Thus, $M = \{A_{k_1}, \ldots, A_{k_m}, A_h\}$ is a solution of $EPMinSAT(A, h)$. For the other direction, the claim holds due to a dual observation. $\qquad\square$

Example 9. Let $C = \{b\overline{f}, pf, pb, b\overline{w}\}$, as in Example 6, and $\widetilde{C} = \{\overline{b} \vee f, \overline{p} \vee \overline{f}, pb, \overline{b} \vee w\}$. Then

$$SV_{pm}^{min}(EPMinSAT(C, 3)) = SV_{pm}(EPMaxSAT(\widetilde{C}, 3))$$
$$= \{(0, 1, 0, 0), (1, 0, 0, 0)\}.$$

Proposition 19 provides the key for using $EPMaxSAT$ for optimizing (A, h)-guarded minimum-expressions:

(1) Construct $EPMaxSAT(\widetilde{A}, h)$,
(2) determine its Pareto-minimal solutions, and
(3) then take the minimum expressions associated to these solutions.

Proposition 20. *Let $A = \{A_1, \ldots, A_n\} \subseteq \mathcal{L}$ and let $h \in \{1, \ldots, n\}$. Then*

$$Min(A, h) \equiv \mathcal{M}(SV_{pm}(EPMaxSAT(\widetilde{A}, h))).$$

Proof. According to Proposition 19, $EPMaxSAT(\widetilde{A}, h)$ computes the subsetwise minimal index sets determining the sum-expressions in $Min(A, h)$. Therefore, according to Proposition 15, the minimum expression associated with the Pareto-minimal satisfaction vectors of $EPMaxSAT(\widetilde{A}, h)$ is equivalent to $Min(A, h)$. $\square$

Example 10. Let $Min(C, 3)$ be the minimum expression considered in Examples 6 and 7. According to Proposition 20, $Min(C, 3)$ is equivalent to

$$\mathcal{M}(SV_{pm}(EPMaxSAT(\widetilde{C}, 3))) = \min\{\eta_2, \eta_1\}.$$

In the course of this subsection, we have demonstrated how minimum expressions over sums of constraint variables ranging over the non-negative numbers, as they appear in the constraint satisfaction problem for c-inference $CR(\mathcal{R}, A, B)$, can be reduced in size while still guaranteeing the correct evaluation of the optimized minimum expressions.

3.3   Instances of *EPMaxSAT* for C-Inference

With the prerequisites defined, we now develop specific *EPMaxSAT* problems corresponding to the optimization of minimum expressions in $CR(\mathcal{R}, A, B)$.

Definition 21 (*EPMaxSAT* for $CR(\mathcal{R}, A, B)$, $\mathcal{E}_x^i(\mathcal{R}, A, B)$). *Let* $\mathcal{R} = \{(B_1|A_1), \ldots, (B_n|A_n)\}$, *let* $A, B \in \mathcal{L}$ *and* $C_\mathcal{R}^{i,v}$, $C_\mathcal{R}^{i,f}$, $C_{A,B}^{q,v}$ *and* $C_{A,B}^{q,f}$ *be as in Proposition 14. Then, the EPMaxSAT problems associated to the min-expressions* V_{min_i}, F_{min_i}, V_{min_q}, *and* F_{min_q}, *respectively, are:*

$$\mathcal{E}_v^i(\mathcal{R}, A, B) = EPMaxSAT(\widetilde{C_\mathcal{R}^{i,v}}, i) \tag{6}$$

$$\mathcal{E}_f^i(\mathcal{R}, A, B) = EPMaxSAT(\widetilde{C_\mathcal{R}^{i,f}}, i) \tag{7}$$

$$\mathcal{E}_v^q(\mathcal{R}, A, B) = EPMaxSAT(\widetilde{C_{A,B}^{q,v}}, n+1) \tag{8}$$

$$\mathcal{E}_f^q(\mathcal{R}, A, B) = EPMaxSAT(\widetilde{C_{A,B}^{q,f}}, n+1) \tag{9}$$

The minimum expressions constructed from the Pareto-minimal solutions of (6),..., (9) *are denoted by:*

$$V_{min_i}^{opt} = \mathcal{M}(SV_{pm}(\mathcal{E}_v^i(\mathcal{R}, A, B))) \tag{10}$$

$$F_{min_i}^{opt} = \mathcal{M}(SV_{pm}(\mathcal{E}_f^i(\mathcal{R}, A, B))) \tag{11}$$

$$V_{min_q}^{opt} = \mathcal{M}(SV_{pm}(\mathcal{E}_v^q(\mathcal{R}, A, B))) \tag{12}$$

$$F_{min_q}^{opt} = \mathcal{M}(SV_{pm}(\mathcal{E}_f^q(\mathcal{R}, A, B))) \tag{13}$$

Note that for our purpose of reducing the size of the minimum expressions, we compute the maximally satisfiable subsets of the set of negations of the falsifications of the conditionals in a given knowledge base according to the duality between minimum expressions and maximally satisfiable subsets as expressed in Proposition 20.

Example 11. Consider $\mathcal{R}_{bird} = \{(f|b), (\overline{f}|p), (b|p), (w|b)\}$ from Example 1. With the sets of constraints

$$\widetilde{C_{\mathcal{R}_{bird}}^{3,v}} = \{\overline{b} \vee f, \overline{p} \vee \overline{f}, pb, \overline{b} \vee w\}$$

$$\widetilde{C_{\mathcal{R}_{bird}}^{3,f}} = \{\overline{b} \vee f, \overline{p} \vee \overline{f}, p\overline{b}, \overline{b} \vee w\}$$

the *EPMaxSAT* problems for V_{min_3} and F_{min_3} for the conditional $r_3 = (b|p)$ are given by:

$$\mathcal{E}_v^3(\mathcal{R}_{bird}, A, B) = EPMaxSAT(\widetilde{C_{\mathcal{R}_{bird}}^{3,v}}, 3)$$

$$\mathcal{E}_f^3(\mathcal{R}_{bird}, A, B) = EPMaxSAT(\widetilde{C_{\mathcal{R}_{bird}}^{3,f}}, 3)$$

The respective Pareto-minimal satisfaction vectors are:

$$SV_{pm}(\mathcal{E}_v^3(\mathcal{R}_{bird}, A, B)) = \{(0, 1, 0, 0), (1, 0, 0, 0)\}$$
$$SV_{pm}(\mathcal{E}_f^3(\mathcal{R}_{bird}, A, B)) = \{(0, 0, 0, 0)\}$$

Thus, for the optimized minimum expressions for r_3, we get:

$$V_{min_3}^{opt} = \mathcal{M}(SV_{pm}(\mathcal{E}_v^3(\mathcal{R}_{bird}, A, B))) = \min\{\eta_2, \eta_1\}$$
$$F_{min_3}^{opt} = \mathcal{M}(SV_{pm}(\mathcal{E}_f^3(\mathcal{R}_{bird}, A, B))) = 0$$

By utilizing Definition 21, we have obtained an associated *EPMaxSAT* problem for every minimum expression in $CR(\mathcal{R})$ and $\neg CR_{\mathcal{R}}(B|A)$, and thus for the whole of $CR(\mathcal{R}, A, B)$.

3.4   Soundness of $CR(\mathcal{R}, A, B)$ Optimization via *EPMaxSAT*

In the following, an optimized constraint satisfaction problem for c-inference is introduced.

Definition 22 ($CR_{opt}(\mathcal{R}, A, B)$). *Let* $\mathcal{R} = \{(B_1|A_1), \ldots, (B_n|A_n)\}$ *and* A, B *formulas. The* optimized constraint satisfaction problem $CR_{opt}(\mathcal{R}, A, B)$ *is obtained from* $CR(\mathcal{R}, A, B)$ *by replacing* V_{min_i} *by* $V_{min_i}^{opt}$ *and* F_{min_i} *by* $F_{min_i}^{opt}$ *for every* $i \in \{1, \ldots, n\}$, *and replacing* V_{min_q} *by* $V_{min_q}^{opt}$ *and* F_{min_q} *by* $F_{min_q}^{opt}$.

Example 12. Together with $\eta_i \geq 0$ as in Example 2, $CR_{opt}(\mathcal{R}_{bird}, p, w)$ is:

$$\eta_1 > 0 - 0$$
$$\eta_2 > \min\{\eta_1, \eta_3\} - 0$$
$$\eta_3 > \min\{\eta_2, \eta_1\} - 0$$
$$\eta_4 > 0 - 0$$
$$\min\{\eta_1, \eta_2, \eta_3\} \geq \min\{\eta_3, \eta_1 + \eta_4, \eta_2 + \eta_4\}$$

We denote the sets of solutions of $CR(\mathcal{R}, A, B)$ and $CR_{opt}(\mathcal{R}, A, B)$, which are assignments of values from $\mathbb{N}_0$ to the variables $\eta_1, \ldots, \eta_n$, with $Sol(CR(\mathcal{R}, A, B))$ and $Sol(CR_{opt}(\mathcal{R}, A, B))$, respectively.

Proposition 23 (Equality of $Sol(CR(\mathcal{R}, A, B))$ and $Sol(CR_{opt}(\mathcal{R}, A, B))$). *Let* $\mathcal{R} = \{(B_1|A_1), \ldots, (B_i|A_i), \ldots (B_n|A_n)\}$ *and let* A, B *formulas. Then*

$$Sol(CR(\mathcal{R}, A, B)) = Sol(CR_{opt}(\mathcal{R}, A, B)). \tag{14}$$

Proof. For $i \in \{1, \ldots, n\}$ *let* V_{min_i} *as in Eq. (3). According to Proposition 14 and Definition 21,*

$$V_{min_i} = Min(C_{\mathcal{R}}^{i,v}, i)$$
$$V_{min_i}^{opt} = \mathcal{M}(SV_{pm}(EPMaxSAT(\widetilde{C_{\mathcal{R}}^{i,v}}, i)))$$

and applying Proposition 20 yields:

$$V_{min_i} \equiv V_{min_i}^{opt} \tag{15}$$

The same reasoning applies analogously to F_{min_i}, V_{min_q} and F_{min_q}. Thus, the minimum expressions V_{min_i}, F_{min_i}, V_{min_q} and F_{min_q} from Eq. (3) and (5) in $CR(\mathcal{R}, A, B)$ are equivalent to the minimum expressions $V_{min_i}^{opt}$, $F_{min_i}^{opt}$, $V_{min_q}^{opt}$ and $F_{min_q}^{opt}$ in $CR_{opt}(\mathcal{R}, A, B)$, respectively. Therefore, an assignment ρ to the variables η_i is a solution of $CR(\mathcal{R}, A, B)$ iff ρ is a solution of $CR_{opt}(\mathcal{R}, A, B)$. $\qquad\square$

Theorem 24 ($CR_{opt}(\mathcal{R}, A, B)$ models c-inference). *Let $\mathcal{R} = \{(B_1|A_1), \ldots, (B_n|A_n)\}$ and A, B formulas. Then*

$$A \mathrel{\vdash^c_{\mathcal{R}}} B \text{ iff } CR_{opt}(\mathcal{R}, A, B) \text{ is not solvable.} \tag{16}$$

Proof. This is a direct consequence of Theorem 4 and Proposition 23. $\qquad\square$

For our running example, $CR_{opt}(\mathcal{R}_{bird}, p, w)$ is unsolvable, as is $CR(\mathcal{R}_{bird}, p, w)$ from Example 2, which it originates from, and therefore $p \mathrel{\vdash^c_{\mathcal{R}_{bird}}} w$.

4   Modelling C-Inference as an SMT Problem

It has been shown that c-inference can be modelled as a satisfiability modulo theories (SMT) problem [10]. The characterization of c-inference in [10] is obtained by transforming $CR(\mathcal{R}, A, B)$ into an SMT problem with linear arithmetic (SMT_{LIA}, [14]), denoted by $SMT(\mathcal{R}, A, B)$. One of the key ideas of the transformation from $CR(\mathcal{R}, A, B)$ to $SMT(\mathcal{R}, A, B)$ is the replacement of minimum expressions according to the following principle: For integers m, a, b, c, the equation $m = min\{a, b, c\}$ is equivalent to $(m \leqslant a) \wedge (m \leqslant b) \wedge (m \leqslant c) \wedge \neg((m < a) \wedge (m < b) \wedge (m < c))$. This translation carries over to minima of sum terms. The SMT_{LIA} formula representing $CR(\mathcal{R}, A, B)$ is then constructed as a conjunctive connection of all constraints in $CR(\mathcal{R}, A, B)$ with all minimum expressions replaced by placeholder variables, which is in turn conjunctively connected with the additional constraints modelling the minimum expressions by imposing the relevant bounds on the placeholder variables.

Because the albeit important, but only difference between $CR(\mathcal{R}, A, B)$ and $CR_{opt}(\mathcal{R}, A, B)$ is the simplification of minimum-expressions (cf. Definition 22), the transformation process of $CR(\mathcal{R}, A, B)$ developed in [10] can be also applied directly to $CR_{opt}(\mathcal{R}, A, B)$, yielding the SMT_{LIA} problem $SMT_{opt}(\mathcal{R}, A, B)$.

Theorem 25 ($SMT_{opt}(\mathcal{R}, A, B)$ models c-inference).

$$A \mathrel{\vdash^c_{\mathcal{R}}} B \text{ iff } SMT_{opt}(\mathcal{R}, A, B) \text{ is not solvable.} \tag{17}$$

Proof. This is a direct consequence of [10, Theorem 4] and Proposition 23. $\quad\square$

5   Implementation and Evaluation

In our implementation, the optimization of the underlying CSP from $CR(\mathcal{R}, A, B)$ to $CR_{opt}(\mathcal{R}, A, B)$ is performed with the help of the partial maximum satisfiability solver RC2 [18]. From $CR_{opt}(\mathcal{R}, A, B)$, we construct the SMT_{LIA} problem $SMT_{opt}(\mathcal{R}, A, B)$ as described in Sect. 4 and represent it as a Python program. For solving $SMT_{opt}(\mathcal{R}, A, B)$, we use the satisfiability-modulo-theories (SMT) solver Z3 [11].

Table 2. Evaluation comparing different implementations of c-inference, time in seconds. Timeout was set at 300 s.

$|\mathcal{R}|$	$|\Sigma|$	CSP^u	SAT^u	SMT^u	SMT^e	SMT	SMT_{opt}
4	4	0.773	0.441	**0.007**	**0.007**	0.009	0.008
6	6	3.005	0.512	**0.009**	0.010	0.011	0.013
8	8	79.290	0.851	**0.020**	0.022	0.023	**0.020**
10	10	timeout	1.147	0.048	0.050	0.044	**0.030**
12	12	timeout	1.750	0.071	0.071	0.073	**0.053**
14	14	timeout	162.436	2.153	1.818	2.005	**0.076**
16	16	timeout	timeout	6.227	5.447	7.696	**0.106**
18	18	timeout	timeout	10.719	12.618	12.636	**0.146**
20	20	timeout	timeout	106.975	145.477	94.183	**0.207**
22	22	timeout	timeout	205.701	209.209	225.539	**0.284**
30	30	timeout	timeout	timeout	timeout	timeout	**0.197**
40	40	timeout	timeout	timeout	timeout	timeout	**0.449**
50	50	timeout	timeout	timeout	timeout	timeout	**0.730**
60	60	timeout	timeout	timeout	timeout	timeout	**6.140**
70	70	timeout	timeout	timeout	timeout	timeout	**10.993**
80	80	timeout	timeout	timeout	timeout	timeout	**22.387**
90	90	timeout	timeout	timeout	timeout	timeout	**24.414**
100	100	timeout	timeout	timeout	timeout	timeout	**30.770**

We have built a set of 1.300 benchmark knowledge bases and 26.000 associated queries with signature size $|\Sigma|$ of as many propositional variables as the number of conditionals $n = |\mathcal{R}|$ by employing a randomized scheme for generating knowledge bases and queries; the knowledge bases and queries are available in the CLKR repository at https://www.fernuni-hagen.de/wbs/clkr/. Only consistent knowledge bases are taken into account because every c-inference from an inconsistent knowledge base holds trivially. Note that the number of worlds is exponential with respect to the signature size, leading to, for instance, $2^{22} = 4.194.304$ possible worlds, and for the biggest knowledge bases examined in our evaluation to 2^{100} worlds.

All implementations of c-inference rely on its characterization as the unsolvability of a constraint satisfaction problem [4, 8], cf. Therorem 4. The first implementations of c-inference had to make use of an approximation of c-inference by setting an upper bound u for the impact values η_i, called *maximal impact*, because they modelled c-inference as a problem over finite domains [5]. As an initial assumption and supported by empirical observations [7], the maximal impact was set to be equal to the number of conditionals in a knowledge base $\mathcal{R}$, but it has been subsequently shown that at least a maximal impact of $u = 2^{|\mathcal{R}|-1}$ is needed to guarantee a sound modelling of c-inference, because some c-representations which are not inferentially equivalent to any of the ones considered would otherwise be omitted in the inference [23, 24].

In our evaluation, we compared all available implementations of c-inference, denoted by the names used in the first row in Table 2:

- CSP^u denotes the results of the first implementation of c-inference [5, 27]. It uses a Prolog-based approach and employs the constraint logic programming solver over finite domains of SICStus Prolog [12, 13] and the Java library InfOCF-Lib [26]. As an upper limit for the impact values, we used $u = |\mathcal{R}|$, the number of conditionals in $\mathcal{R}$.
- SAT^u denotes the results using the implementation of c-inference as an instance of a Boolean satisfiability problem [3]. As maximal impact value, $u = |\mathcal{R}|$ is used.
- SMT^u denotes the results of an implementation of c-inference as an SMT_{LIA} problem [10]. Also here, a maximal impact value of $u = |\mathcal{R}|$ is used.
- SMT^e denotes the results of the same implementation as SMT^u, except that a maximal impact value of $u = 2^{|\mathcal{R}|-1}$ is used.
- SMT denotes the results of an implementation of c-inference as an SMT_{LIA} problem, being the first implementation not requiring a maximal impact value [10].
- SMT_{opt} denotes the results of the implementation of the approach developed in this paper.

All computations for the results in Table 2 were performed on a machine with an Intel Core i9-11950H Octa-Core CPU (up to 5 GHz) and 128 GB DDR4-3200 working memory. We observe an increase of feasible problem size w.r.t. $|\mathcal{R}|$ and $|\Sigma|$ of about the factor 2 from the CSP^u implementation to the SAT^u representation, and a corresponding exponential increase w.r.t. the number of worlds. A comparable increase was achieved by the three implementations SMT^u, SMT^u and SMT. Among these three previous SMT_{LIA} implementations, only small differences are observable, leading to the conclusion that the implementation without maximal impact (SMT) should indeed be preferred in order to reach not only an approximation, but a full modelling of c-inference.

Our new implementation SMT_{opt} outperforms all other implementations while still not needing a maximal impact. While the first five result columns display only the mean of the time needed for solving the constraint satisfaction problems (not taking into account the time to build them), the last column showing our new results for SMT_{opt} displays the mean of the combined time needed for optimizing the problem via *EPMaxSAT* problems and for solving it. If the time for building the SMT_{LIA} problem $SMT_{opt}(\mathcal{R}, A, B)$ were subtracted, the last column would show even faster results and consistently dominate the others, even for small $|\mathcal{R}|$, $|\Sigma|$. In particular, our *EPMaxSAT* approach scales up c-inference and opens up a new order of magnitude in problem size for non-monotonic reasoning from conditional belief bases with c-inference.

6   Conclusions and Further Work

In this paper, we have developed a method for optimizing c-inference by employing *PMaxSAT* problems and current *PMaxSAT* solvers. The optimization process significantly reduces the number and the size of the minimum expressions occurring in the CSP underlying the required characterization of c-inference. We have proven the soundness of the transformation process and also implemented it. Its empirical evaluation shows that it not only outperforms all previous implementations, but that it also scales up c-inference to formerly intractable problem sizes.

Future work includes studying the formal complexity of c-inference and its implementation. Furthermore, we will extend our implementation approach to c-inference dealing also with weakly consistent belief bases [16] and to other operations on conditional belief bases involving c-representations, including belief change operations like revision or forgetting [6,22], and to conditionals over a first-order language.

Acknowledgments. We are grateful to the anonymous reviewers for their constructive and helpful comments. This work was supported by the Deutsche Forschungsgemeinschaft (DFG, German Research Foundation), grant BE 1700/10-1 awarded to Christoph Beierle as part of the priority program "Intentional Forgetting in Organizations" (SPP 1921).

References

1. Adams, E.: Probability and the logic of conditionals. In: Hintikka, J., Suppes, P. (eds.) Aspects of Inductive Logic, pp. 265–316. North-Holland, Amsterdam (1966)
2. Al-Yahya, T.N., Menai, M.E.B., Mathkour, H.: On the structure of the Boolean satisfiability problem: a survey. ACM Comput. Surv. **55**(3), 46:1–46:34 (2023). https://doi.org/10.1145/3491210
3. Beierle, C., von Berg, M., Sanin, A.: Realization of c-inference as a SAT problem. In: Keshtkar, F., Franklin, M. (eds.) Proceedings of the Thirty-Fifth International Florida Artificial Intelligence Research Society Conference (FLAIRS), Hutchinson Island, Florida, USA, 15–18 May 2022. https://doi.org/10.32473/flairs.v35i.130663
4. Beierle, C., Eichhorn, C., Kern-Isberner, G.: Skeptical inference based on C-representations and its characterization as a constraint satisfaction problem. In: Gyssens, M., Simari, G. (eds.) FoIKS 2016. LNCS, vol. 9616, pp. 65–82. Springer, Cham (2016). https://doi.org/10.1007/978-3-319-30024-5_4

5. Beierle, C., Eichhorn, C., Kutsch, S.: A practical comparison of qualitative inferences with preferred ranking models. KI - Künstliche Intelligenz **31**(1), 41–52 (2017). https://doi.org/10.1007/s13218-016-0453-9

6. Beierle, C., Kern-Isberner, G., Sauerwald, K., Bock, T., Ragni, M.: Towards a general framework for kinds of forgetting in common-sense belief management. KI - Künstliche Intelligenz **33**(1), 57–68 (2019). https://doi.org/10.1007/s13218-018-0567-3

7. Beierle, C., Kutsch, S.: Computation and comparison of nonmonotonic skeptical inference relations induced by sets of ranking models for the realization of intelligent agents. Appl. Intell. **49**(1), 28–43 (2019)

8. Beierle, C., Kutsch, S., Sauerwald, K.: Compilation of static and evolving conditional knowledge bases for computing induced nonmonotonic inference relations. Ann. Math. Artif. Intell. **87**(1–2), 5–41 (2019)

9. Benferhat, S., Cayrol, C., Dubois, D., Lang, J., Prade, H.: Inconsistency management and prioritized syntax-based entailment. In: Proceedings of the IJCAI'93, vol. 1, pp. 640–647. Morgan Kaufmann Publishers, San Francisco, CA, USA (1993)

10. von Berg, M., Sanin, A., Beierle, C.: Representing nonmonotonic inference based on c-representations as an SMT problem. In: Bouraoui, Z., Vesic, S. (eds.) Symbolic and Quantitative Approaches to Reasoning with Uncertainty. ECSQARU 2023. LNCS, vol. 14294, pp. 210–223. Springer, Cham (2023). https://doi.org/10.1007/978-3-031-45608-4_17

11. Bjørner, N., de Moura, L., Nachmanson, L., Wintersteiger, C.M.: Programming z3. Engineering Trustworthy Software Systems: 4th International School, SETSS 2018, Chongqing, China, 7–12 April 2018, Tutorial Lectures 4, pp. 148–201 (2019)

12. Carlsson, M., Ottosson, G.: Finite domain constraints in SICStus Prolog. Technical report, Swedish Institute of Computer Science, Kista, Sweden (1996)

13. Carlsson, M., Ottosson, G., Carlson, B.: An open-ended finite domain constraint solver. In: Glaser, H., Hartel, P., Kuchen, H. (eds.) PLILP 1997. LNCS, vol. 1292, pp. 191–206. Springer, Heidelberg (1997). https://doi.org/10.1007/BFb0033845

14. Dutertre, B., de Moura, L.: A fast linear-arithmetic solver for DPLL(T). In: Ball, T., Jones, R.B. (eds.) CAV 2006. LNCS, vol. 4144, pp. 81–94. Springer, Heidelberg (2006). https://doi.org/10.1007/11817963_11

15. Goldszmidt, M., Pearl, J.: Qualitative probabilities for default reasoning, belief revision, and causal modeling. Artif. Intell. **84**(1–2), 57–112 (1996)

16. Haldimann, J., Beierle, C., Kern-Isberner, G.: Syntax splitting and reasoning from weakly consistent conditional belief bases with c-inference. In: Meier, A., Ortiz, M. (eds.) Foundations of Information and Knowledge Systems - 13th International Symposium, FoIKS 2024, UK, Sheffield, 8–11 April 2024, Proceedings. LNCS, vol. 14589. Springer, Berlin, Heidelberg (2024). https://doi.org/10.1007/978-3-031-56940-1_5

17. Heyninck, J., Kern-Isberner, G., Meyer, T.A., Haldimann, J.P., Beierle, C.: Conditional syntax splitting for non-monotonic inference operators. In: Williams, B., Chen, Y., Neville, J. (eds.) Thirty-Seventh AAAI Conference on Artificial Intelligence, AAAI 2023, Thirty-Fifth Conference on Innovative Applications of Artificial Intelligence, IAAI 2023, Thirteenth Symposium on Educational Advances in Artificial Intelligence, EAAI 2023, Washington, DC, USA, 7–14 February 2023, pp. 6416–6424. AAAI Press (2023). https://doi.org/10.1609/aaai.v37i5.25789

18. Ignatiev, A., Morgado, A., Marques-Silva, J.: RC2: an efficient maxsat solver. J. Satisf. Boolean Model. Comput. **11**(1), 53–64 (2019). https://doi.org/10.3233/SAT190116

19. Kern-Isberner, G.: Conditionals in Nonmonotonic Reasoning and Belief Revision. LNCS (LNAI), vol. 2087. Springer, Heidelberg (2001). https://doi.org/10.1007/3-540-44600-1

20. Kern-Isberner, G.: A thorough axiomatization of a principle of conditional preservation in belief revision. Ann. Math. Artif. Intell. **40**(1–2), 127–164 (2004)

21. Kern-Isberner, G., Beierle, C., Brewka, G.: Syntax splitting = relevance + independence: new postulates for nonmonotonic reasoning from conditional belief bases. In: Calvanese, D., Erdem, E., Thielscher, M. (eds.) Principles of Knowledge Representation and Reasoning: Proceedings of the 17th International Conference, KR 2020, pp. 560–571. IJCAI Organization (2020). https://doi.org/10.24963/kr.2020/56

22. Kern-Isberner, G., Bock, T., Sauerwald, K., Beierle, C.: Iterated contraction of propositions and conditionals under the principle of conditional preservation. In: Benzmüller, C., Lisetti, C.L., Theobald, M. (eds.) GCAI 2017, 3rd Global Conference on Artificial Intelligence, Miami, FL, USA, 18–22 October 2017. EPiC Series in Computing, vol. 50, pp. 78–92. EasyChair (2017). http://www.easychair.org/publications/volume/GCAI_2017

23. Komo, C., Beierle, C.: Upper and lower bounds for finite domain constraints to realize skeptical c-inference over conditional knowledge bases. In: International Symposium on Artificial Intelligence and Mathematics (ISAIM 2020), Fort Lauderdale, FL, USA, 6–8 January 2020

24. Komo, C., Beierle, C.: Nonmonotonic reasoning from conditional knowledge bases with system W. Ann. Math. Artif. Intell. **90**(1), 107–144 (2022)

25. Kraus, S., Lehmann, D.J., Magidor, M.: Nonmonotonic reasoning, preferential models and cumulative logics. Artif. Intell. **44**(1–2), 167–207 (1990)

26. Kutsch, S.: InfOCF-Lib: a Java library for OCF-based conditional inference. In: Beierle, C., Ragni, M., Stolzenburg, F., Thimm, M. (eds.) Proceedings of the 8th Workshop on Dynamics of Knowledge and Belief (DKB-2019) and the 7th Workshop KI & Kognition (KIK-2019) co-located with 44nd German Conference on Artificial Intelligence (KI 2019), Kassel, Germany, September 23, 2019. CEUR Workshop Proceedings, vol. 2445, pp. 47–58. CEUR-WS.org (2019)

27. Kutsch, S., Beierle, C.: InfOCF-Web: an online tool for nonmonotonic reasoning with conditionals and ranking functions. In: Zhou, Z. (ed.) Proceedings of the Thirtieth International Joint Conference on Artificial Intelligence, IJCAI 2021, Virtual Event/Montreal, Canada, 19–27 August 2021, pp. 4996–4999. ijcai.org (2021). https://doi.org/10.24963/ijcai.2021/711

28. Larrosa, J., Rollon, E.: Towards a better understanding of (partial weighted) MaxSAT proof systems. In: Pulina, L., Seidl, M. (eds.) SAT 2020. LNCS, vol. 12178, pp. 218–232. Springer, Cham (2020). https://doi.org/10.1007/978-3-030-51825-7_16

29. Parikh, R.: Beliefs, belief revision, and splitting languages. Log. Lang. Comput. **2**, 266–278 (1999)

30. Spohn, W.: Ordinal conditional functions: a dynamic theory of epistemic states. In: Harper, W., Skyrms, B. (eds.) Causation in Decision, Belief Change, and Statistics, II, pp. 105–134. Kluwer Academic Publishers (1988)

Axiomatizations

On the Logic of Interventionist Counterfactuals Under Indeterministic Causal Laws

Fausto Barbero(✉) iD

University of Helsinki, Helsinki, Finland
fausto.barbero@helsinki.fi

Abstract. We investigate the generalization of causal models to the case of indeterministic causal laws that was suggested in Halpern (2000). We give an overview of what differences in modeling are enforced by this more general perspective, and propose an implementation of generalized models in the style of the causal team semantics of Barbero & Sandu (2020). In these models, the laws are not represented by functions (as in the deterministic case), but more generally by relations.

We analyze significant differences in the axiomatization of interventionist counterfactuals in the indeterministic vs. the deterministic case, and provide strongly complete axiomatizations over the full class of indeterministic models and over its recursive subclass.

Keywords: Interventionist counterfactuals · Causal models · Indeterministic laws · Axiom systems · Completeness · Team semantics

1 Introduction

When the existence of causal laws is considered at all, the discussion of causality in the philosophy of science tends to focus on *deterministic* causal mechanisms, which uniquely determine an effect given full knowledge of the causes. The restriction to deterministic laws is in some case a deliberate choice to avoid technical complications (see e.g. [21], sec. 4.3), as many important and sometimes puzzling aspects of causation already emerge at this level. However, often the laws considered in applied sciences are not of this kind. A physical law may allow us to predict, for example, that

A cannonball shot at a certain angle will fall *within a certain range*.

In contrast to more idealized laws of mechanics, this kind of law tells us that, *even without taking into account some factor that is not mentioned by the law* (such as the direction or intensity of the wind), we can predict that the effect will (quite literally) fall within a certain range of possible values. These kinds of causal dependencies are discussed at length e.g. by Bohm in [7] (chapter I.7), under the name of *one-to-many causal relationships*.

The author's work was supported by the Academy of Finland Research Fellowship grant n. 349803.

A. Meier and M. Ortiz (Eds.): FoIKS 2024, LNCS 14589, pp. 203–221, 2024.
https://doi.org/10.1007/978-3-031-56940-1_11

Note that in the cannonball example the law is indeterministic due to the impossibility of taking into account all factors, i.e. it accounts for *epistemic* limitations. On the other hand, many physicists would think that the following statement expresses a *metaphysical* statement about the behaviour of a particle:

If an atom of silver passes through a Stern-Gerlach apparatus, it will either go up or down.

In other words, a physical law may tell us that the outcome of a certain experiment is unpredictable in principle – even if we had a complete knowledge of the initial conditions of a physical system. Indeterministic laws do not just arise within scientific theories, but also justify everyday statements such as

If I toss the coin, it will land on heads or tails.

Far from being a platitude, such a statement implicitly assumes an indeterministic causal law, which allows two values for the future state of the coin, while excluding other alternatives (such as the coin staying in my pocket or breaking into pieces). Notice also that all these examples do not *require* probabilities for their formulation and justification. We might not know what the probabilistic distributions involved are, or in some context it might even be mathematically impossible to associate a probability distribution to a given phenomenon (see e.g. [28] for some examples of this kind). Thus, probabilistic laws are only a special case of indeterministic laws.

In the last decades, causal reasoning has been mathematically formalized in the fields of statistics and computer science known as *causal discovery* [27] and *causal inference* [22], which have found applications e.g. in machine learning [24,26], epidemiology [16], econometrics [15] and social sciences [19]. Do indeterministic laws feature in these approaches? There are two main types of models considered in this context. The first are the *Bayesian networks*; these consist of probabilistic distributions paired with graphs, and are intrinsically indeterministic models; but laws or mechanisms are not specified in any way by such models. Instead, *structural equation models* (or *causal models*) use systems of equations to encode the causal laws that link together the relevant variables of the scenario under examination. The equations take the form:

$$Y := f(X_1, \ldots, X_n)$$

where the term $f(X_1, \ldots, X_n)$ stands for a *function* of the variables $X_1, \ldots, X_n$. The equations, together with some information about the state of the variables, allow one to formulate and often answer queries about the deterministic and probabilistic behaviour of the variables. A significant example of such a query is establishing the truth or falsity of an *interventionist counterfactual* [10]:

If variables $Z_1, \ldots Z_m$ were set to values $z_1, \ldots z_m$, then condition ψ would hold.

These kinds of expressions can be studied with the methods of logic. The classic work of Halpern [11,13] provided a wealth of complete deduction systems for classes of causal models, and the idea has since been extended in various directions (e.g. [3–6,8,9,14,17,29]). Now, the very fact that causal laws are represented by functions amounts to a restriction to deterministic laws. The natural way to extend these kinds of models to the indeterministic case is to replace these functional constraints with *relational* constraints. If we write R_Y for the causal law describing the behaviour of variable Y, we shall interpret the statement that $(x_1, \ldots, x_n, y) \in R_Y$ as expressing the fact that, if variables $X_1, \ldots, X_n$ are set to values $x_1, \ldots, x_n$, then Y *might* take value y (but it might also take any other value y' such that $(x_1, \ldots, x_n, y') \in R_Y$). Equivalently, we might recover the equational form by encoding the causal law as a *multivalued function* $\mathcal{F}_Y$ that associates to each tuple of values for $X_1, \ldots X_n$ a *set* of possible values for Y.

The possibility of such an extension is hinted at by Halpern in the very conclusions of his paper on the axiomatization of interventionist counterfactuals:

> (...) a more general approach to modeling causality would allow there to be more than one value of X once we have set all other variables. This would be appropriate if we model things at a somewhat coarser level of granularity, where the values of all the variables other than X do not suffice to completely determine the value of X. I believe the results of this paper can be extended in a straightforward way to deal with this generalization, although I have not checked the details. [11]

Perhaps stating that this generalization is "straightforward" discouraged researchers from pursuing this direction: or was it the discovery that, after all, the details are not so straightforward? To the best of our knowledge, the idea has been taken up again only in 2021, when Peters and Halpern [14,25] modeled indeterministic causal laws within the more complex framework of *generalized structural equation models*. More recently, a simpler framework, closer to Halpern's original idea for extending causal models was considered by Wysocki [28], who provided a cursory examination of differences between deterministic and indeterministic counterfactuals. The purpose of the present paper is to sharpen the understanding of the logic of interventionist counterfactuals in the indeterministic (but not probabilistic) context and ultimately provide complete axiomatizations for significant classes of indeterministic causal models. The models we use (*relational causal teams*) are a generalization of the *causal teams* proposed in [2] and are somewhat more general than Wysocki's (one key difference being that our models – like structural equation models – do not necessarily obey the Markov condition[1]). In Sect. 2 we will describe, in general terms, some key differences between deterministic and indeterministic frameworks, and how they will affect our modeling choices. We then use the insights just gained to provide (Sect. 3) a precise definition of relational causal teams. We then introduce (Sect. 4) a language similar to those considered in Halpern's [11] paper, and describe the most significant differences that arise in its logic when we switch from deterministic to indeterministic models. Finally, we

---

[1] Which, in the context of non-probabilistic models, amounts to the fact that there may be data dependencies among exogenous variables.

provide strongly complete axiomatizations over the class of all relational causal teams (Sect. 5.1) and on the *recursive* subclass (Sect. 5.2), where cyclic causal relationships are forbidden.

2   Differences with the Deterministic Case

We describe here a few differences and challenges that arise when trying to describe models that are not limited to deterministic causal laws.

We need to introduce some notation, for which we follow usage from the field of causal inference. We use capital letters $X, Y, \ldots$ to denote **variables**; the **values** that a variable X may take will be denoted by small letters such as x, x', x''. We use basic formulas of the form $X = x$ to assert that (in a given context) X takes value x. We assume that the variables come from a finite set Dom, and that there is a function Ran that associates to each variable X a finite set $\mathrm{Ran}(X)$ of possible values. The pair (Dom, Ran) is called a **signature**. An **assignment** of signature $\sigma = (\mathrm{Dom}, \mathrm{Ran})$ is a function that assigns to each variable an allowed value (i.e., a function $f : \mathrm{Dom} \to \bigcup_{V \in \mathrm{Dom}} \mathrm{Ran}(V)$ such that, for all $V \in \mathrm{Dom}$, $s(V) \in \mathrm{Ran}(V)$). We call $\mathbb{A}_\sigma$ the set of all such assignments.

Boldface letters such as $\mathbf{X}, \mathbf{x}$ denote (depending on context) either finite sets or finite tuples of variables, resp. of values. If $\mathbf{X} = (X_1, \ldots, X_n)$, then $\mathrm{Ran}(\mathbf{X})$ abbreviates $\mathrm{Ran}(X_1) \times \cdots \times \mathrm{Ran}(X_n)$. If furthermore $\mathbf{x} = (x_1, \ldots, x_n)$, we abbreviate as $\mathbf{X} = \mathbf{x}$ either a multiset of basic formulas $X_1 = x_1, \ldots, X_n = x_n$ or their conjunction.

We use $\mathbf{W}$, resp. $\mathbf{W}_X, \mathbf{W}_{XY}$ to denote tuples listing without repetitions the variables in Dom, resp. Dom $\setminus \{X\}$, Dom $\setminus \{X, Y\}$.

2.1   Uncertainty

While working with deterministic causal laws, it has been customary to describe a scenario by means of an assignment of values to the variables of the system. This may be appropriate, in some case, also in the presence of indeterministic laws. Consider the scenario "Alice tosses a coin, and it comes out heads"; we would model it by one causal law (saying that the coin tossing will lead either to a "heads" or a "tails" outcome) together with the following assignment:

A ⊰ C
1	heads

where the Boolean variable A tells us whether Alice tossed the coin ($A = 1$) or not ($A = 0$), and C records the outcome of the toss; we drew the symbol ⊰ to emphasize that A is an indeterministic cause of C. However, one might want also to model the scenario "Alice tossed a coin". The indeterministic law does not allow us to infer the outcome of the toss; thus, to represent this kind of scenario, we need *two* assignments, describing the two alternative situations that are not excluded by the description of the scenario:

A	⊰ C
1	heads
1	tails

These kinds of considerations lead us to shift attention from causal models to the more general *causal teams* [2], models which allow a multiplicity of variable assignments (*team*) compatible with the causal laws. This perspective is not alien to the previous literature on causal inference: it is implicit e.g. in the treatment of interventions in the presence of cyclic causal laws. Even when considering a full description of a scenario (i.e. a single assignment), such an intervention may produce a multiplicity of possible new scenarios [10, 11].

In a similar way, the need for teams emerges also when asking counterfactual queries about the first scenario. If we want to know what would happen if Alice tossed the coin again, we will need to consider an intervention that sets A to 1 ($do(A = 1)$), which produces the same model that we considered in the second scenario. We thus see that the class of causal models is not closed under interventions: intervenining on an (indeterministic) causal model produces an (indeterministic) causal team. Our definitions will ensure that the class of indeterministic causal teams is closed under interventions.

2.2 Specifying the Causal Laws

In the deterministic case, the causal laws can be specified in at least two different ways, which are, for most purposes, equivalent:

1. First pick out some variables, which will be considered *endogenous*. For each endogenous variable V, we specify which other variables are *direct causes* or *parents* of V; call this set PA_V. We then specify the law for V as a function $\mathcal{F}_V : \text{Ran}(PA_V) \to \text{Ran}(V)$.
2. Assign to each variable V a function $\mathcal{F}_V : \text{Ran}(\mathbf{W}_V) \to \text{Ran}(V)$. Observe that some of the variables of $\mathbf{W}_V$ are dummy arguments of $\mathcal{F}_V$; *define* PA_V as the set of variables of $\mathbf{W}_V$ that are *not* dummy for $\mathcal{F}_V$. *Define* the set of endogenous variables as those whose parent set is nonempty.

The first approach is more natural and direct, but it has technical disadvantages, prominently the fact that it allows a proliferation of essentially equivalent models (for example, we might have two models that differ only in that, in the former, variable Z is generated by the law $\mathcal{F}_Z(X, Y) = X + Y$, while in the latter the law is $\mathcal{F}_Z(X, Y, U, V, W) = X + Y$, i.e., the same function with three dummy arguments). For this reason, in technical papers the second approach is usually preferred.

Analogously, in the indeterministic case we might want to encode the laws as relations in $\text{Ran}(PA_V) \times \text{Ran}(V)$ or rather in $\text{Ran}(\mathbf{W}_V) \times \text{Ran}(V)$. Unfortunately, in the indeterministic case approach 2. seems not to be viable. We consider two examples that raise problems for this approach.

Example 1. In this scenario we have Boolean variables A (whether Alice jumps), B (whether Bob tosses a coin) and C representing three possible states of the coin (whether it is on heads, tails, or stays in Bob's pocket). Suppose we represent the causal law determining the state of the coin by the relation $\mathcal{F}_C \subseteq \text{Ran}(A) \times \text{Ran}(B) \times \text{Ran}(C)$, $\mathcal{F}_C = \{(0, 0, \textit{in-pocket}), (1, 0, \textit{in-pocket}), (0, 1, \textit{heads}), (0, 1, \textit{tails}), (1, 1, \textit{heads}), (1, 1, \textit{tails})\}$. Suppose also that we know that Ann did not jump, B tossed the coin and it came heads:

A	B	C
0	1	heads

Suppose we intervene on the system by forcing Ann to jump. According to Halpern's [11] definition of intervention, the possibile scenarios after such an intervention are those that agree 1) with the law, 2) with the condition $A = 1$, 3) with the current state of the exogenous variables[2] (different from A), i.e. $B = 1$. There are two assignments consistent with these conditions, namely:

A	B	C
1	1	heads
1	1	tails

In other words, forcing Ann to jump makes us lose information about the outcome of a (past) coin toss. This is clearly unwanted.

There seems to be a straightforward way to repair this problem. A is obviously not a direct cause of C, i.e., it is a "dummy argument" of the law $\mathcal{F}_C$ (changing the value of A does not change the range of allowed values for C, when B is held fixed). Now, it seems to be reasonable that an intervention on a variable A should only affect variables that are (directly or indirectly) causally dependent on A. Then, we should reject the second assignment in the table, which modifies the value of C, non-descendant of A. To this end, we will adopt a definition of intervention in the style of [1], which, differently from Halpern's, does not violate this constraint on cyclic models.

There is more. As the following example shows, and contrarily to what happens in the deterministic case, identifying the dummy arguments of the relational laws is not sufficient for identifying the parents of a variable.

Example 2. In this scenario Bob has two coins, say coin 1 and coin 2, and may toss one of the two ($B = 1$ or $B = 2$). Variable O represents the outcome of the toss (heads or tails), and its behaviour is described by the relational law $\mathcal{F}_O = \{(1, \textit{heads}), (1, \textit{tails}), (2, \textit{heads}), (2, \textit{tails})\}$. Furthermore, we know that Bob has tossed coin 1 and got heads:

---

[2] Roughly speaking, a variable is exogenous if causally unaffected by any other variable in the model. Later we will have a formal definition.

B	O
1	heads

Now, B is a dummy argument of the law $\mathcal{F}_O$: changing the value of B does not change the range of values that O may attain ($\mathcal{F}_O(1) = \mathcal{F}_O(2) = \{heads, tails\}$). Seen as a multivalued function, $\mathcal{F}_O$ is a constant-valued law. But our intuition about the real world seems to disagree with the idea that B is not a cause of O, and that O should be considered exogenous (uncaused) in this context (indeed, we presume that, if we force Bob to make another toss, the outcome may change). B should be considered a direct cause of O, even if it is a dummy argument of $\mathcal{F}_O$. And indeed, we shall see that the intervention $do(B = 1)$, forcing Bob to repeat the toss, will produce two alternative scenarios where

B	O
1	heads
1	tails

the range of possible values for O has changed from $\{heads\}$ to $\{heads, tails\}$.

This second example should clarify that a relational causal law $\mathcal{F}_V$, by itself, determines the set of its own non-dummy arguments, but does not determine the (possibly larger) set of direct causes of V. Learning the set of direct causes is possible once we have a notion of intervention – we may then check whether intervening on a given argument Z may change the range of allowed values for V in some model. But on the other hand, to know whether intervening on Z may affect V we need to know whether Z is a direct cause of V. We can escape this vicious circle by declaring explicitly the set of parents of a variable as part of a specification of model, i.e. follow the approach 1. delineated at the beginning of this section (the set of direct causes of Y will then be a subset of PA_Y).

3 Models: Relational Causal Teams

The considerations from the previous section lead us to the following definition of a model. A **team** of signature σ is a set of assignments of signature σ.

Definition 1. *A **relational causal team** (of signature σ and **internal** variables* Int(T)*) is a pair $T = (T^-, \mathcal{F})$, where:*

- *T^- is a team of signature σ (team component)*
- *$\mathcal{F}$ (law component) is a function that associates to each $V \in$ Int(T):*
    - *a set of variables $PA_V \subseteq$ Dom $\setminus \{V\}$ (parents of V)*
    - *a relation $\mathcal{F}_V \subseteq$ Ran(PA_V) $\times$ Ran(V) (V-generating law)*
- *For all $V \in$ Int(T), for all $s \in T^-$, ($s(PA_V), s(V)$) $\in \mathcal{F}_V$.*

For brevity, we will sometimes simply call it a **model**. The last condition (*compatibility constraint*) can be thought of as admitting in the team only "solutions" of the system of causal laws. The variables in the domain that are not internal (and thus have no associated causal laws) will be called **external**, and the set of such variables will be denoted by $\mathrm{Ext}(T)$.

We remark that the causal law for an internal variable V can also be, equivalently, represented by showing what set of values is associated by $\mathcal{F}_V$ to each tuple pa in PA_V; we may denote such set as $\mathcal{F}_V(pa)$, thus treating the relation as a multivalued function.

We will say that a relational causal team is **total** if all causal laws are total multi-valued functions, i.e., for each $V \in \mathrm{Int}(T)$ and for each $pa \in \mathrm{Ran}(PA_V)$, $\mathcal{F}_V(pa) \neq \emptyset$. We will say it is **deterministic** if, for each $V \in \mathrm{Int}(T)$ and for each $pa \in \mathrm{Ran}(PA_V)$, $|\mathcal{F}_V(pa)| \leq 1$. The total deterministic models essentially coincide with the causal teams introduced in [2].

We define the **weak causal graph** of T to be the graph whose vertices are the variables of the system, and where an arrow (directed edge) connects X to Y if and only if X is a parent of Y. The weak causal graph allows us to apply some graph theoretic terminology to the variables; for example, we will say that Y is a *descendant* of X if either Y and X are the same variable, or there is a path $X \rightarrow Z \rightarrow \cdots \rightarrow Z_n \rightarrow Y$ in the weak causal graph. We will see later (Sect. 4.2) how to define a notion of *causal graph* closer to that used for the deterministic case (and related notions of endogeneity, exogeneity, recursivity).

Interventions can be defined similarly as in the deterministic case, using the weak causal graph as a guide. It was however argued in [1] that Halpern's general defining clause (from [11]) leads to paradoxical outcomes: if the causal graph has cycles, intervening on a variable X may affect a variable Y that is not its descendant. We then adopt the modifications suggested in [1].[3] Given a finite multiset of basic clauses, say $X_1 = x_1, \ldots X_n = x_n$, we say it is **consistent** if, whenever X_i and X_j are the same variable, then x_i and x_j also coincide. Given a consistent $\mathbf{X} = \mathbf{x}$, and a relational causal team T, the effect of an intervention $do(\mathbf{X} = \mathbf{x})$ on T is to produce a new model $T_{\mathbf{X}=\mathbf{x}} = ((T_{\mathbf{X}=\mathbf{x}})^-, \mathcal{F}_{\mathbf{X}=\mathbf{x}})$ with components:

- $\mathcal{F}_{\mathbf{X}=\mathbf{x}} := \mathcal{F}_{\restriction \mathrm{Int}(T) \setminus \mathbf{X}}$ (the restriction of $\mathcal{F}$ to $\mathrm{Int}(T) \setminus \mathbf{X}$)
- $(T_{\mathbf{X}=\mathbf{x}})^- := \{s \in \mathbb{A}_\sigma \text{ compatible with } \mathcal{F}_{\mathbf{X}=\mathbf{x}} \mid s(\mathbf{X}) = \mathbf{x} \text{ and } s(\mathbf{N_X}) \in T^-\}$

where $\mathbf{N_X}$ is the set of nondescendants of $\mathbf{X}$ in the weak causal graph. The definition above includes as a special case the empty intervention $do()$ corresponding to the empty multiset of basic clauses. Such an intervention leaves both components of the causal team unchanged.[4]

In case the weak causal graph is acyclic, the team component of intervened teams can be presented more concretely as the union $(T_{\mathbf{X}=\mathbf{x}})^- = \bigcup_{s \in T^-} s^{\mathcal{F}}_{\mathbf{X}=\mathbf{x}}$, where each $s^{\mathcal{F}}_{\mathbf{X}=\mathbf{x}}$

---

[3] Judea Pearl seems to have been aware of this problem, as he adopts in [23] a definition of intervention close to ours.

[4] This is in contrast with Halpern's semantics, according to which new assignments may appear after an empty intervention. In our case, this does not happen because our interventions fix the values of all nondescendants of the intervened variables, and in the case of empty interventions this set of variables is the whole variable domain.

is the outcome of the intervention applied to the single assignment s, which can be described recursively:

$$s_{\mathbf{X}=x}^{\mathcal{F}} := \{t \in \mathbb{A}_\sigma \mid \forall X \in \mathbf{X} : t(X) = x$$
$$\forall V \in \mathrm{Ext}(T) \setminus \mathbf{X} : t(V) = s(V)$$
$$\forall V \in \mathrm{Int}(T) \setminus \mathbf{X} : (t(PA_V), t(V)) \in \mathcal{F}_V\}.$$

Example 3. Consider the following game. I can toss, or not, a coin with my left hand ($L = 0$ or 1); the outcome is recorded by a variable C_L with 3 possible values: heads (h), tails (t) or none (n) in case I do not toss. If I toss and get heads, then I will toss the coin that I hold in my right hand ($R = 1$) whose outcome is recorded analogously in C_R. The parent sets and causal laws are then as follows: $PA_{C_L} = \{L\}$, $PA_R = \{C_L\}$, $PA_{C_R} = \{R\}$; $\mathcal{F}_{C_L} = \{(0, n), (1, h)(1, t)\}$; $\mathcal{F}_R = \{(n, 0), (h, 1), (t, 0)\}$, $\mathcal{F}_{C_R} = \{(0, n), (1, h), (1, t)\}$. The current situation is that neither coin has been tossed, which can be represented by a single assignment s:

L	⊰ C_L	→	R	⊰	C_R
0	n		0		n

(the arrow $\to$ emphasizes that the law for R is deterministic). Let $T = (\{s\}, \mathcal{F})$. If now I decide to toss with my left hand (intervention $do(L = 1)$), then we need to update all columns (since all variables are descendants of L):

L	⊰ C_L	→	R	⊰	C_R
1	...		...		...

$\rightsquigarrow$

L	⊰ C_L	→	R	⊰	C_R
1	h		...		...
1	t		...		...

$\rightsquigarrow$

L	⊰ C_L	→	R	⊰	C_R
1	h	1			...
1	t	0			...

$\rightsquigarrow$

$T_{L=1}$:

L	⊰ C_L	→	R	⊰	C_R
1	h	1			h
1	h	1			t
1	t	0			n

4 Causal Reasoning: General Remarks on Axiomatization

We consider a family of languages that is close to Halpern's languages in [11]. Given a consistent multiset $\mathbf{X} = \mathbf{x}$, we call the expression $[\mathbf{X} = \mathbf{x}]$ a *modal operator*.[5] We also allow the empty multiset, in which case the operator will be just written as □. For any

---

[5] We identify strings of symbols that represent the same multiset. This saves us the somewhat trivial issue of axiomatizing this form of equivalence. See [2] for a complete list of axioms for the antecedents of counterfactuals.

given signature $\sigma = (\text{Dom}, \text{Ran})$, we define a corresponding language $\mathcal{H}_\sigma$. The suffix σ will be omitted when the signature is clear.

$$\text{Language } \mathcal{H}_\sigma : \qquad X = x \mid \sim\psi \mid \psi \& \chi \mid [\mathbf{X} = \mathbf{x}]\eta$$

where $\mathbf{X} \cup \{X\} \subseteq \text{Dom}$, $x \in \text{Ran}(X)$, $\mathbf{x} \in \text{Ran}(\mathbf{X})$, and η has no occurrences of modal operators (i.e., it is a Boolean combination of atoms like $X = x$). This language differs from Halpern's in some minor respects: 1) we allow for atomic formulas not prefixed by modal operators (as in [2,4,5]); 2) we allow interventions on any variable (the signature does not specify a distinction between exogenous and endogenous variables, as e.g. in [8]). The semantics is:

- $T \models X = x$ iff $s(X) = x$ for each $s \in T^-$.
- $T \models \sim\psi$ iff $T \not\models \psi$.
- $T \models \psi \& \chi$ iff $T \models \psi$ and $T \models \chi$.
- $T \models [\mathbf{X} = \mathbf{x}]\eta$ iff for all $s \in T^-_{\mathbf{X}=\mathbf{x}}$, $(\{s\}, \mathcal{F}) \models \eta$.

Formulas of the form $[\mathbf{X} = \mathbf{x}]\eta$ will be called *counterfactuals*. We can also define the *might-counterfactual* $\langle \mathbf{X} = \mathbf{x}\rangle\eta$ as an abbreviation for $\sim[\mathbf{X} = \mathbf{x}]\sim\eta$; it is easy then to see that the semantics of such formulas is:

- $T \models \langle \mathbf{X} = \mathbf{x}\rangle\eta$ iff there is $s \in T^-_{\mathbf{X}=\mathbf{x}}$ such that $(\{s\}, \mathcal{F}) \models \eta$.

As a special case, we write $\Diamond$ for $\sim\Box\sim$. Our definition of intervention yields the following derived semantic clauses:

- $T \models \Box\eta$ iff for all $s \in T^-$, $(\{s\}, \mathcal{F}) \models \eta$.
- $T \models \Diamond\eta$ iff for some $s \in T^-$, $(\{s\}, \mathcal{F}) \models \eta$.

We can then define a few additional operators:

- $\psi \sqcup \chi$ as $\sim(\sim\psi \& \sim\chi)$
- $\psi \to \chi$ as $\sim\psi \sqcup \chi$
- $\psi \leftrightarrow \chi$ as $(\psi \to \chi) \& (\chi \to \psi)$
- $\bot$ as $X = x \& \sim X = x$
- $\top$ as $\sim\bot$
- $X \neq x$ as $\sim X = x$

We will use index sets for iterated conjunctions and disjunction; conventionally, if $I = \emptyset$, $\&_{i \in I}\psi_i$ stands for $\top$ and $\bigsqcup_{i \in I}\psi_i$ stands for $\bot$.

4.1 Axiomatizing the General Class

We will see that the general class of relational causal teams (which also allows for cyclic causation) obeys a set of laws that is quite similar to that given by Halpern for the general class of *deterministic* causal models [11]. There is a significant omission: Halpern had an axiom stating that, if you intervene on all variables except one, say Y, then Y will take a single value in the resulting model. This is false in our context: first, because if Y is internal, an indeterministic law for Y may produce multiple values upon intervention; and secondly, if Y is external, a causal team may record more than one value for it, in distinct assignments. The role of this unicity axiom is taken by a principle that describes the fact that exogenous variables (to be defined in Sect. 4.2) are not affected by interventions on *all* other variables. It does so by saying that, if the variable Y is exogenous (which, as we shall see, is a definable concept in $\mathcal{H}$), then the available values for Y are the same either before or after an intervention:

$$\langle \mathbf{W}_Y = \mathbf{w} \rangle Y = y \leftrightarrow \Diamond Y = y.$$

A second new axiom (*Flatness*) needs to be added to account for the fact that in $\mathcal{H}$ we also have non-modal formulas; it tells us that (over nonempty models) conjunctions of basic formulas, say $\mathbf{Y} = \mathbf{y}$, can be converted into modal statements $\Box \mathbf{Y} = \mathbf{y}$; i.e., formula $\mathbf{Y} = \mathbf{y}$ just states that $\mathbf{Y}$ take values $\mathbf{y}$ *in all assignments*. A third new axiom (*Nonemptyness*) states that a model is nonempty if and only if intervening on all variables produces a nonempty model.

4.2 The Recursive Case

Besides the full class of models, we want to characterize axiomatically the class of models in which the causal laws are acyclic (recursive case). It is not straightforward to identify the analogue of this notion in the indeterministic context; it seems to us that lack of cycles in the weak causal graph is not the proper analogue of deterministic recursivity. Arguably, we have to look at a graph induced by a notion of direct cause rather than parenthood. What is a direct cause in an indeterministic model? Roughly, as in [28], X being a direct cause of Y will mean that, once we set all variables in Dom $\setminus \{X, Y\}$ in some appropriate way, some intervention on X may change *the range of values* that Y attains in the model. We can formalize this idea as follows: X is a direct cause of Y ($X \leadsto Y$) if and only if the following holds (writing $\mathbf{Z}$ for Dom $\setminus \{XY\}$):

$$\bigsqcup_{(\mathbf{z},x,y) \in \mathrm{Ran}(\mathbf{Z}XY)} \sim(\langle \mathbf{Z}X = \mathbf{z}x \rangle Y = y \leftrightarrow \langle \mathbf{Z} = \mathbf{z} \rangle Y = y)$$

It is easy to see that, with our definitions, we have:

$$PA_V \supseteq \{\text{direct causes of } V\} \supseteq \{\text{non-dummy arguments of } V\}.$$

We can then define a **causal graph** whose vertices are the variables in the domain, and where there is an arrow from X to Y iff X is a direct cause of Y; it will be, in general, smaller than the weak causal graph defined in Sect. 3. We will call **exogenous** the variables that have indegree 0 in the causal graph (i.e. no arrows point at them) and **endogenous** the remaining ones. These notions are definable in $\mathcal{H}$:

– $\varphi_{\mathrm{Exo}(V)} : \&_{X \in \mathrm{Dom}\setminus\{V\}} \sim X \leadsto V$ \qquad – $\varphi_{\mathrm{End}(V)} : \sim\varphi_{\mathrm{Exo}(V)}.$

A model whose causal graph is acyclic will be called **recursive**. In the deterministic case, the recursive models play a special role: their causal interpretation is generally considered less controversial, their theory is better understood, and counterfactuals over deterministic recursive models admit a significantly simpler axiomatization [11], closer to axiomatizations for Stalnaker-Lewis counterfactuals [12]. The recursive models seem to be special also in the indeterministic case. For example, they share with their deterministic counterparts the fact that the effect of an intervention is fully determined, via a recursive procedure, by the modified variables together with the values of the exogenous variables.

In order to turn an axiomatization of the general class of models into one for the recursive class, it will suffice to add a *Recursivity axiom* of the form

$$R: (X_1 \leadsto X_2 \& \ldots \& X_{n-1} \leadsto X_n) \to \sim X_n \leadsto X_1$$

which forbids cycles in the causal graph. Axioms of this form, using different notions of causal dependence in place of $X \leadsto Y$, are common in the literature; e.g., [3] uses the deterministic notion of direct cause, while [11] uses a weaker dependence called "causally affecting".

4.3 Failure of Composition

There are further significant differences between the deterministic and indeterministic recursive cases that are not evident from the proposed axiomatization. In the deterministic case, intervening on a single state of affairs produces again a single state of affairs (the unique solution of a certain system of equations). It then follows that counterfactuals $[\mathbf{X} = \mathbf{x}]\psi$ and *might*-counterfactuals $\langle \mathbf{X} = \mathbf{x} \rangle \psi$ are equivalent, and so the latter are redundant. If indeterministic laws are involved, instead, interventions on a single state of affairs may produce multiple possible states of affairs even if there are no cyclic causal laws. The operator $\langle \mathbf{X} = \mathbf{x} \rangle$, then, albeit definable as $\sim[\mathbf{X} = \mathbf{x}]\sim$, seems to be vital for expressing properties of the solution sets in a natural way.

Another important difference is the failure of one of Galles and Pearl's principles for recursive models, the law of *Composition*. This can be expressed as

$$([\mathbf{X} = \mathbf{x}]W = w \& [\mathbf{X} = \mathbf{x}]Y = y) \to [\mathbf{X} = \mathbf{x}, W = w]Y = y$$

which can usually be replaced, in axiomatizations for recursive models, by the more intuitive *Conjunction conditionalization*

$$(\mathbf{X} = \mathbf{x} \& \eta) \to [\mathbf{X} = \mathbf{x}]\eta$$

where, crucially, η is a formula without counterfactuals. The example given in Sect. 2.1 shows that both laws fail for indeterministic recursive models. Indeed, in it $A = 1$ and $C = heads$ hold, but $[A = 1]C = heads$ does not.

It turns out that the weakened form of *Composition*,

$$\langle \mathbf{X} = \mathbf{x} \rangle (W = w \& Y = y) \to \langle \mathbf{X} = \mathbf{x}, W = w \rangle Y = y$$

which was proposed in [11] for the axiomatization of the (possibly) *cyclic* case, is sound for indeterministic models (both in the recursive and nonrecursive case). This law illustrates the importance of *might*-counterfactuals in the indeterministic context.

4.4 Strong Reversibility

Besides *Recursivity* and *Composition*, the third principle proposed by Galles and Pearl [10] for recursive models is the (strong) *Reversibility* axiom:

$$([\mathbf{X} = \mathbf{x}, W = w]Y = y \,\&\, [\mathbf{X} = \mathbf{x}, Y = y]W = w) \rightarrow [\mathbf{X} = \mathbf{x}]Y = y.$$

In [10], this axiom was thought of as a characterization of the *unique solution* property[6], which (in the deterministic case) is more general than recursivity. It is indeed part of Halpern's axiomatization of unique solution causal models in [11]; it does not feature in the axiomatization of recursive causal models because it is derivable from the other axioms including *Recursivity*.

It turns out, however, that strong *Reversibility* is valid also on *indeterministic* recursive models (provided the causal laws are *total* multivalued functions). But multiplicity of solutions is the norm when the laws are indeterministic, even under the assumptions of recursivity and totality; thus, in our broader class of models, *Reversibility* has no clear ties with the concept of unicity of solutions.

Theorem 1 (Strong reversibility). *Let* $T = (T^-, \mathcal{F})$ *be a total and recursive model. Then,* $T \models ([\mathbf{X} = \mathbf{x}, W = w]Y = y \,\&\, [\mathbf{X} = \mathbf{x}, Y = y]W = w) \rightarrow [\mathbf{X} = \mathbf{x}]Y = y$.

Proof. Suppose $T \models [\mathbf{X} = \mathbf{x}, W = w]Y = y$ and $T \models [\mathbf{X} = \mathbf{x}, Y = y]W = w$. Since T is recursive, either W is not an ancestor of Y or Y is not an ancestor of W.

Case 1: W is not an ancestor of Y. Then, by the characterization of interventions on (total) recursive models, intervening on W does not affect Y (without the totality assumption, the intervention $do(\mathbf{X} = \mathbf{x}, W = w)$ might erase some assignments that instead occur in $T_{\mathbf{X}=\mathbf{x}}$). Thus, from the assumption $T \models [\mathbf{X} = \mathbf{x}, W = w]Y = y$ we immediately obtain $T \models [\mathbf{X} = \mathbf{x}]Y = y$.

Case 2: Y is not an ancestor of W. By the assumption that $T \models [\mathbf{X} = \mathbf{x}, Y = y]W = w$, we get that $T_{\mathbf{X}=\mathbf{x}, Y=y} \models W = w$. Since Y is not an ancestor of W, we get $T_{\mathbf{X}=\mathbf{x}} \models W = w$. But then the intervention $do(W = w)$ does not modify the team component of $T_{\mathbf{X}=\mathbf{x}}$, i.e. $T_{\mathbf{X}=\mathbf{x}}^- = T_{\mathbf{X}=\mathbf{x}, W=w}^-$. Now, for each $s \in T_{\mathbf{X}=\mathbf{x}, W=w}^-$ we have $s(Y) = y$ by the assumption that $T \models [\mathbf{X} = \mathbf{x}, W = w]Y = y$; so, $T \models [\mathbf{X} = \mathbf{x}]Y = y$.

5 Completeness Results

5.1 Axiomatization for the General Case

We will denote as A the following set of rules and axioms:

$$\text{Rule MP.} \quad \frac{\psi \qquad \psi \rightarrow \chi}{\chi} \qquad\qquad \text{Rule NEC.} \quad \frac{\vdash \psi}{\vdash [\mathbf{X} = \mathbf{x}]\psi}$$

---

[6] A structural equation model has this property if 1) its system of equations is satisfied by a unique assignment once values for the exogenous variables are fixed, and 2) the same holds after any intervention.

I0. Instances of classical tautologies in $\sim, \&$.

I1°. $[\mathbf{X} = \mathbf{x}]Y = y \rightarrow [\mathbf{X} = \mathbf{x}]Y \neq y'$ (when $y \neq y'$)   [Uniqueness]

I2°. $[\mathbf{X} = \mathbf{x}] \bigsqcup_{y \in \mathrm{Ran}(Y)} Y = y$ [Definiteness]

I3•. $\langle \mathbf{X} = \mathbf{x} \rangle (Z = z \,\&\, \mathbf{Y} = \mathbf{y}) \rightarrow \langle \mathbf{X} = \mathbf{x}, Z = z \rangle \mathbf{Y} = \mathbf{y}$ [Weak composition]

I4°. $[\mathbf{X} = \mathbf{x}, Y = y]Y = y$ [Effectiveness]

I5•. $[\mathbf{X} = \mathbf{x}]\psi \,\&\, [\mathbf{X} = \mathbf{x}](\psi \rightarrow \chi) \rightarrow [\mathbf{X} = \mathbf{x}]\chi$ [K-axiom]

I6°. $(\langle \mathbf{X} = \mathbf{x}, V = v \rangle (Y = y \,\&\, \mathbf{Z} = \mathbf{z}) \,\&\, \langle \mathbf{X} = \mathbf{x}, Y = y \rangle (V = v \,\&\, \mathbf{Z} = \mathbf{z})) \rightarrow$

                $\langle \mathbf{X} = \mathbf{x} \rangle (V = v \,\&\, Y = y \,\&\, \mathbf{Z} = \mathbf{z})$

                (for $V \neq Y$, and $\mathbf{Z} = \mathrm{Dom} \setminus (\mathbf{X} \cup \{V, Y\})$)   [Weak reversibility]

I7. $Y = y \leftrightarrow \Box Y = y$.   [Flatness]

I8. $\varphi_{\mathrm{Exo}(Y)} \rightarrow (\langle \mathbf{W}_Y = \mathbf{w} \rangle Y = y \leftrightarrow \Diamond Y = y)$ [Exogenous variables]

I9. $\Diamond \top \leftrightarrow \langle \mathbf{W} = \mathbf{w} \rangle \top$.   [Nonemptyness]

The axioms marked with a black dot • include as special cases versions in which the intervention operator is empty ($\Box/\Diamond$) or is absent. Those marked with a white dot ° admit empty interventions but not their absence. Notice e.g. that $\bigsqcup_{y \in \mathrm{Ran}(Y)} Y = y$ is not valid (it asserts that Y takes the same value in all the assignments of the team), so it cannot be included in I2; and $Y = y \rightarrow Y \neq y'$ is false on empty models, so it is not featured in I1. Axioms I0-I6 essentially coincide with the part of Halpern's axiomatization (for the general class of causal models) that is meaningful for our language and sound on indeterministic models.

We shall write $\vdash$ for derivability in axiom system A. By $A_\sigma, \vdash_\sigma$ we denote the restrictions of $A, \vdash$ to formulas of signature σ. We will show, by a Henkin construction, that system A_σ is sound and complete over the class of all models of signature σ. The following lemma lists basic properties of A.

Lemma 1. *1. (Deduction theorem) If $\Gamma, \psi \vdash \chi$, then $\Gamma \vdash \psi \rightarrow \chi$.*

2. (Monotonicity) If $\Gamma \vdash [\mathbf{X} = \mathbf{x}]\psi$ and $\vdash \psi \rightarrow \psi'$, then $\Gamma \vdash [\mathbf{X} = \mathbf{x}]\psi'$.

    If $\Gamma \vdash \langle \mathbf{X} = \mathbf{x} \rangle \psi$ and $\vdash \psi \rightarrow \psi'$, then $\Gamma \vdash \langle \mathbf{X} = \mathbf{x} \rangle \psi'$.

3. $([\mathbf{X} = \mathbf{x}]\psi \,\&\, [\mathbf{X} = \mathbf{x}]\chi) \leftrightarrow [\mathbf{X} = \mathbf{x}](\psi \,\&\, \chi)$.

4. (Replacement) Suppose $\vdash \theta \leftrightarrow \theta'$. Then $\vdash \varphi \leftrightarrow \varphi[\theta'/\theta]$.

5. $\vdash \sim[\mathbf{X} = \mathbf{x}]\psi \leftrightarrow \langle \mathbf{X} = \mathbf{x} \rangle \sim\psi$

6. $\vdash \sim\langle \mathbf{X} = \mathbf{x} \rangle \psi \leftrightarrow [\mathbf{X} = \mathbf{x}]\sim\psi$

7. $\vdash (\langle \mathbf{X} = \mathbf{x} \rangle \psi \sqcup \langle \mathbf{X} = \mathbf{x} \rangle \chi) \leftrightarrow \langle \mathbf{X} = \mathbf{x} \rangle (\psi \sqcup \chi)$.

8. $\vdash ([\mathbf{X} = \mathbf{x}]\psi \,\&\, \langle \mathbf{X} = \mathbf{x} \rangle \top) \rightarrow \langle \mathbf{X} = \mathbf{x} \rangle \psi$.

We say that a set of $\mathcal{H}_\sigma$ formulas is **consistent** if it does not contain any pair of formulas of the forms $\psi, \sim\psi$. Γ is **maximally consistent** if it is consistent and, furthermore, if $\Gamma' \supseteq \Gamma$ is consistent, then $\Gamma' = \Gamma$.

Lemma 2 (Lindenbaum). *Any consistent set Δ of $\mathcal{H}_\sigma$ formulas can be extended to a maximal consistent set.*

Lemma 3. *Let Γ be a maximally consistent set of $\mathcal{H}_\sigma$ formulas. Then:*

1. Completeness: for every formula ψ, either ψ or $\sim\psi$ is in Γ.

2. Closure under $\vdash$: if $\Gamma \vdash \psi$, then $\psi \in \Gamma$.

3. Closure under $\&$: if $\psi, \chi \in \Gamma$, then $\psi \,\&\, \chi \in \Gamma$.

4. *Primality: if $\psi \sqcup \chi \in \Gamma$, then $\psi \in \Gamma$ or $\chi \in \Gamma$.*

The canonical relational causal team associated to a maximal consistent set Γ, which we shall denote as $\mathbb{T}^\Gamma = ((\mathbb{T}^\Gamma)^-, \mathcal{F}^\Gamma)$ is defined as follows:

- We define $(\mathbb{T}^\Gamma)^- := \{s \in \mathbb{A}_\sigma \mid \Diamond\mathbf{W} = s(\mathbf{W}) \in \Gamma\}$.
- For each pair of variables X, Y we let $X \in PA_Y$ if and only if there are $\mathbf{w}, y \in \text{Ran}(\mathbf{W}_{XY}Y)$, $x, x' \in \text{Ran}(X)$ such that either of the following hold:
  1. $\langle\mathbf{W}_{XY} = \mathbf{w}\rangle Y = y \, \& \sim\langle\mathbf{W}_{XY} = \mathbf{w}, X = x\rangle Y = y \in \Gamma$
  2. $\langle\mathbf{W}_{XY} = \mathbf{w}, X = x\rangle Y = y \, \& \sim\langle\mathbf{W}_{XY} = \mathbf{w}\rangle Y = y \in \Gamma$
- If $PA_Y \neq \emptyset$, we declare that $Y \in \text{Int}(\mathbb{T}^\Gamma)$
- If $Y \in \text{Int}(\mathbb{T}^\Gamma)$, we let $(pa, y) \in \mathcal{F}_Y^\Gamma$ if and only if, for any $\mathbf{w} \in \text{Ran}(\mathbf{W}_Y)$ such that $\mathbf{w}_{\restriction PA_Y} = pa$, $\langle\mathbf{W}_Y = \mathbf{w}\rangle Y = y \in \Gamma$.

Lemma 4 (Canonical team). *Let Γ be a maximal consistent set of $\mathcal{H}_\sigma$ formulas that contains all axioms of A_σ. Then $\mathbb{T}^\Gamma$ is a relational causal team, i.e.:*

1. *For all $Y \in \text{Int}(\mathbb{T}^\Gamma)$, $\mathcal{F}_Y^\Gamma$ is well-defined.*
2. *For all $Y \in \text{Int}(\mathbb{T}^\Gamma)$ and $s \in (\mathbb{T}^\Gamma)^-$, $(s(PA_Y), s(Y)) \in \mathcal{F}_Y^\Gamma$.*

Proof. 1) We need to show that the specific choice of a $\mathbf{w}$ extending pa does not matter for the definition of $\mathcal{F}_Y^\Gamma$. In other words, we need to prove that, if $\mathbf{w}, \mathbf{w}' \in \text{Ran}(\mathbf{W}_Y)$ are such that $\mathbf{w}_{\restriction PA_Y} = \mathbf{w}'_{\restriction PA_Y} = pa$, then

$$\langle\mathbf{W}_Y = \mathbf{w}\rangle Y = y \in \Gamma \text{ if and only if } \langle\mathbf{W}_Y = \mathbf{w}'\rangle Y = y \in \Gamma.$$

We prove this by induction on the number n of variables on which $\mathbf{w}, \mathbf{w}'$ differ. If $n = 0$, the statement is trivial. If $n = 1$, $\mathbf{w}, \mathbf{w}'$ differ over a single variable $X \notin PA_Y$. Write w^* for $\mathbf{w}_{\restriction W_{XY}} = \mathbf{w}'_{\restriction W_{XY}}$. Assume $\langle\mathbf{W}_Y = \mathbf{w}\rangle Y = y \in \Gamma$. Since $X \notin PA_Y$, by the definition of PA_Y in the canonical model, clause 2., we have then that $\sim\langle\mathbf{W}_{XY} = \mathbf{w}^*\rangle Y = y \notin \Gamma$. But then, by lemma 3, 1., and I0, $\langle\mathbf{W}_{XY} = \mathbf{w}^*\rangle Y = y \in \Gamma$. Again, since $X \notin PA_Y$, by clause 1., $\sim\langle\mathbf{W}_Y = \mathbf{w}'\rangle Y = y \notin \Gamma$; so, similarly as before, we conclude $\langle\mathbf{W}_Y = \mathbf{w}'\rangle Y = y \in \Gamma$. The converse is analogous.

Now let $n \geq 1$, and suppose $\mathbf{w}, \mathbf{w}'$ differ on $n + 1$ variables $X_1, \ldots, X_{n+1}$ (which take values $x_1, \ldots, x_{n+1}$ in $\mathbf{w}$ and values $x'_1, \ldots, x'_{n+1}$ in $\mathbf{w}'$). Write $\mathbf{Z}$ for $\mathbf{W}_Y \setminus \{X_1, \ldots, X_{n+1}\}$ and $\mathbf{z}$ for $\mathbf{w}_{\restriction \mathbf{Z}}$. By the inductive hypothesis (for case n) we have:

$$\langle\mathbf{W}_Y = \mathbf{w}\rangle Y = y \in \Gamma \text{ if and only if } \langle\mathbf{Z}X_1 \ldots X_n X_{n+1} = \mathbf{z}x'_1 \ldots x'_n x_{n+1}\rangle Y = y \in \Gamma$$

Since $\mathbf{z}x'_1 \ldots x'_n x_{n+1}$ and $\mathbf{w}'$ differ only on one variable (X_{n+1}), we can apply again the inductive hypothesis (case for 1) to obtain that $\langle\mathbf{Z}X_1 \ldots X_n X_{n+1} = \mathbf{z}x'_1 \ldots x'_n x_{n+1}\rangle Y = y \in \Gamma$ if and only if $\langle\mathbf{W}_Y = \mathbf{w}'\rangle Y = y \in \Gamma$.

2) Let $s \in (\mathbb{T}^\Gamma)^-$. By definition of $(\mathbb{T}^\Gamma)^-$, $\Diamond\mathbf{W} = s(\mathbf{W}) \in \Gamma$. Thus, by axiom I3, $\langle\mathbf{W}_Y = s(\mathbf{W}_Y)\rangle Y = s(Y) \in \Gamma$. Since the restriction of $s(\mathbf{W}_Y)$ to PA_Y is $s(PA_Y)$, then, by definition of $\mathcal{F}^\Gamma$ we have $(s(PA_Y), s(Y)) \in \mathcal{F}_Y^\Gamma$.

Lemma 5 (Normal form). *Every $\mathcal{H}_\sigma$ formula φ is provably equivalent to a Boolean combination of formulas $\langle\mathbf{X} = \mathbf{x}\rangle\mathbf{Y} = \mathbf{y}$, where $\mathbf{X} \cap \mathbf{Y} = \emptyset$ and $\mathbf{X} \cup \mathbf{Y} = \text{Dom}$.*

The proof of the normal form (which uses axiom I7) is omitted for lack of space.

Lemma 6 (Truth lemma). *Let $\Gamma \supseteq A$ be a maximally consistent set of $\mathcal{H}_\sigma$ formulas, and φ an $\mathcal{H}_\sigma$ formula. Then, $\varphi \in \Gamma \iff \mathbb{T}^\Gamma \models \varphi$.*

Proof. We can assume φ is in the normal form described in lemma 5. The proof proceeds as in [11], theorem 3.3, by induction on φ; the case for $\varphi = \langle \mathbf{X} = \mathbf{x} \rangle \mathbf{Y} = \mathbf{y}$ requires a subinduction on $n = |\text{Dom} \setminus \mathbf{X}|$. The proof of the inductive step (which uses I6) is identical as in [11]; we include the base cases $n = 0$ and $n = 1$ (the latter is required to prove the inductive step).

Case $n = 0$. In this case φ is simply $\langle \mathbf{X} = \mathbf{x} \rangle \top$. If $\langle \mathbf{X} = \mathbf{x} \rangle \top \in \Gamma$, by axiom I9 $\Diamond \top \in \Gamma$. By I2, I0 and replacement, $\Diamond \bigsqcup_{\mathbf{x}' \in \text{Ran}(\mathbf{X})} \mathbf{X} = \mathbf{x}' \in \Gamma$. By Lemma 1, 7., $\bigsqcup_{\mathbf{x}' \in \text{Ran}(\mathbf{X})} \Diamond \mathbf{X} = \mathbf{x}' \in \Gamma$. Thus, by Lemma 3, 4., there is an $\mathbf{x}^* \in \text{Ran}(\mathbf{X})$ such that $\Diamond \mathbf{X} = \mathbf{x}^* \in \Gamma$. Thus, by definition of $(\mathbb{T}^\Gamma)^-$ there is an $s \in (\mathbb{T}^\Gamma)^-$ (namely, $s(\mathbf{X}) = \mathbf{x}^*$), i.e. $(\mathbb{T}^\Gamma)^- \neq \emptyset$. But then (by definition of intervention) $(\mathbb{T}^\Gamma_{\mathbf{X}=\mathbf{x}})^-$ contains the assignment $t(\mathbf{X}) = \mathbf{x}$ and is therefore nonempty. Thus $\mathbb{T}^\Gamma \models \langle \mathbf{X} = \mathbf{x} \rangle \top$.

Vice versa, assume $\mathbb{T}^\Gamma \models \langle \mathbf{X} = \mathbf{x} \rangle \top$, i.e. $(\mathbb{T}^\Gamma_{\mathbf{X}=\mathbf{x}})^- \neq \emptyset$. Thus, $(\mathbb{T}^\Gamma)^- \neq \emptyset$. Let $s \in (\mathbb{T}^\Gamma)^-$; write $\mathbf{x}^*$ for $s(\mathbf{X})$. By definition of $(\mathbb{T}^\Gamma)^-$, $\Diamond \mathbf{X} = \mathbf{x}^* \in \Gamma$. Thus, by I3, $\langle \mathbf{X} = \mathbf{x}^* \rangle \top \in \Gamma$. By I9, $\Diamond \top \in \Gamma$. By I9 again, $\langle \mathbf{X} = \mathbf{x} \rangle \top \in \Gamma$.

Case $n = 1$. Suppose $\langle \mathbf{X} = \mathbf{x} \rangle Y = y \in \Gamma$. If Y is endogenous in $\mathbb{T}^\Gamma$, by the definition of $\mathcal{F}^\Gamma_Y$, we have $(\mathbf{x}_{\restriction PA_Y}, y) \in \mathcal{F}^\Gamma_Y$. Thus, by definition of intervention, $\mathbb{T}^\Gamma \models \langle \mathbf{X} = \mathbf{x} \rangle Y = y$.

If instead Y is exogenous in $\mathbb{T}^\Gamma$, by definition of PA_Y in $\mathbb{T}^\Gamma$ we have $\varphi_{\text{Exo}(Y)} \in \Gamma$. Together with $\langle \mathbf{X} = \mathbf{x} \rangle Y = y \in \Gamma$, by axiom I8 this yields $\Diamond Y = y \in \Gamma$. By I2, I0 and replacement we obtain $\Diamond((\bigsqcup_{\mathbf{x}' \in \text{Ran}(\mathbf{X})} \mathbf{X} = \mathbf{x}') \& Y = y) \in \Gamma$. By I0 and replacement, $\Diamond \bigsqcup_{\mathbf{x}' \in \text{Ran}(\mathbf{X})}(\mathbf{X} = \mathbf{x}' \& Y = y) \in \Gamma$. By Lemma 1, 7., $\bigsqcup_{\mathbf{x}' \in \text{Ran}(\mathbf{X})} \Diamond(\mathbf{X} = \mathbf{x}' \& Y = y) \in \Gamma$. By Lemma 3, 4., there is an $\mathbf{x}^* \in \text{Ran}(\mathbf{X})$ such that $\Diamond(\mathbf{X} = \mathbf{x}^* \& Y = y) \in \Gamma$. By definition of $\mathbb{T}^\Gamma$, there is an $s \in (\mathbb{T}^\Gamma)^-$ (namely $s(\mathbf{X}Y) = \mathbf{x}^* y$). Since Y is exogenous, it is not affected by interventions; thus, there is a $t \in s^{\mathcal{F}}_{\mathbf{X}=\mathbf{x}}$ with $t(Y) = y$. Thus, $\mathbb{T}^\Gamma \models \langle \mathbf{X} = \mathbf{x} \rangle Y = y$.

Vice versa, suppose $\mathbb{T}^\Gamma \models \langle \mathbf{X} = \mathbf{x} \rangle Y = y$. Then, again, we have two cases: Y is exogenous or endogenous. In the latter case, by definition of intervention, $(\mathbf{x}_{\restriction PA_Y}, y) \in \mathcal{F}^\Gamma_Y$. But then, by definition of $\mathcal{F}^\Gamma_Y$, this means that $\langle \mathbf{X} = \mathbf{x} \rangle Y = y \in \Gamma$.

Suppose Y is exogenous; then $\mathbb{T}^\Gamma \models \langle \mathbf{X} = \mathbf{x} \rangle Y = y$ entails $\mathbb{T}^\Gamma \models \Diamond Y = y$. Let then $s \in (\mathbb{T}^\Gamma)^-$ such that $s(Y) = y$. Write $\mathbf{x}^*$ for $s(\mathbf{X})$. Then $\mathbb{T}^\Gamma \models \Diamond(\mathbf{X} = \mathbf{x}^* \& Y = y)$. By definition of $(\mathbb{T}^\Gamma)^-$, $\Diamond(\mathbf{X} = \mathbf{x}^* \& Y = y) \in \Gamma$. By I0 and monotonicity, it is then easy to show that $\Diamond Y = y \in \Gamma$. (Suppose $\Diamond Y = y \notin \Gamma$, i.e. $\sim \Box \sim Y = y \notin \Gamma$; by Lemma 3, 1., $\sim\sim\Box\sim Y = y \in \Gamma$; by I0, $\Box \sim Y = y \in \Gamma$; by monotonicity, $\Box \sim(\mathbf{X} = \mathbf{x}^* \& Y = y) \in \Gamma$; by Lemma 1, 6., $\sim\Diamond(\mathbf{X} = \mathbf{x}^* \& Y = y) \in \Gamma$.) Thus, by axiom I8, $\langle \mathbf{X} = \mathbf{x} \rangle Y = y \in \Gamma$.

We write $\Gamma \models_\sigma \varphi$ (resp. $\Gamma \models^R_\sigma \varphi$) if every model (resp. recursive model) of signature σ that satisfies Γ also satisfies φ.

Theorem 2 (Strong completeness for A). *For $\Gamma \cup \{\varphi\} \subseteq \mathcal{H}_\sigma$,*

$$\Gamma \models_\sigma \varphi \iff \Gamma \vdash_\sigma \varphi.$$

Proof. The soundness direction is left to the reader. For completeness, suppose $\Gamma \nvdash \varphi$. Then, by routine reasoning $\Gamma \cup A \cup \{\sim\varphi\}$ is consistent, so by Lemma 2 there is a maximally consistent $\Delta \supseteq \Gamma \cup A \cup \{\sim\varphi\}$. Now, $\mathbb{T}^\Delta$ is a model (Lemma 4), and by Lemma 6, $\mathbb{T}^\Delta \models \Gamma \cup \{\sim\varphi\}$. Thus, $\Gamma \nvDash \varphi$.

5.2 Axiomatizing the Recursive Class

We write A^R for the axiom system A enriched with the following axiom:

R. $(X_1 \rightsquigarrow X_2 \& \dots \& X_{n-1} \rightsquigarrow X_n) \rightarrow \sim X_n \rightsquigarrow X_1$.   [Generalized recursivity]

where $X \rightsquigarrow Y$ abbreviates the formula for direct cause defined in Sect. 4.2. We shall write $\vdash^R$ for derivability in A^R.

Lemma 7. *Suppose $\Gamma \supseteq A^R$ is maximally consistent. Then, $\mathbb{T}^\Gamma$ is recursive.*

Proof. Suppose the causal graph of $\mathbb{T}^\Gamma$ has a cycle $X_1, \dots X_n$. Since $PA_{X_i} \subseteq$ {direct causes of X_i}, by the definition of PA_{X_i} in $\mathbb{T}^\Gamma$ we have $X_1 \rightsquigarrow X_2, \dots, X_{n-1} \rightsquigarrow X_n, X_n \rightsquigarrow X_1 \in \Gamma$. But, since Γ contains all the instances of axiom R, we also obtain $\sim X_n \rightsquigarrow X_1 \in \Gamma$. This contradicts the consistency of Γ.

Theorem 3 (Strong completeness for A^R). *For $\Gamma \cup \{\varphi\} \subseteq \mathcal{H}_\sigma$,*

$$\Gamma \vDash_\sigma^R \varphi \iff \Gamma \vdash_\sigma^R \varphi.$$

Proof. As for theorem 2, using the fact that $\mathbb{T}^\Delta$ is recursive if $A^R \subseteq \Delta$ (Lemma 7).

6 Conclusions

We have shown that extending causal models to the case of indeterministic causal laws, as suggested in [11], is doable but not as straightforward as Halpern suggested. We have seen that the notions of direct cause and causal parenthood are more complex than in the deterministic case, and even more complicated than what suggested in [28], since it turns out that even the dummy arguments of causal laws can be direct causes. These insights lead us to the definition of appropriate models (relational causal teams).

We then produced strongly complete axiomatizations for the logic of interventionist counterfactuals over this new class of models and over its recursive subclass. These differ from their deterministic counterparts in a few respects, among which we may remark the failure of the *Composition* law, already in the recursive case. We also observed that the *Reversibility* law holds in the total recursive case, showing that its traditional connection to the property of uniqueness of solutions breaks in indeterministic frameworks.

We limited ourselves to a simple counterfactual language in the style of [11]; it is to be seen if good axiomatizations can be obtained also if we allow for nested counterfactuals. Furthermore, in [5] we suggested a strategy for allowing complex, disjunctive antecedents, by assigning them a semantics by means of *indeterminate interventions*.

This venue requires a further generalization of the models and is not explored in the present paper.

A number of natural directions of investigation opens ahead, among which is the axiomatic characterization of the properties of determinism and totality of the causal laws; a systematical comparison with the logic of Stalnaker-Lewis counterfactuals [18] in the spirit of [9,12,29]; and the analysis of the computational and descriptive complexity of the formalism (cf. [13], Chap. 5, and [20] for the deterministic case).

References

1. Barbero, F., Galliani, P.: Embedding causal team languages into predicate logic. Ann. Pure Appl. Log. 103–159 (2022)
2. Barbero, F., Sandu, G.: Team semantics for interventionist counterfactuals: observations vs. interventions. J. Philos. Log. **50**, 471–521 (2021)
3. Barbero, F., Schulz, K., Velazquez-Quesada, F.R., Xie, K.: Observing interventions: a logic for thinking about experiments. J. Log. Comput. (2022)
4. Barbero, F., Virtema, J.: Strongly complete axiomatization for a logic with probabilistic interventionist counterfactuals. In: Gaggl, S., Martinez, M.V., Ortiz, M. (eds.) Logics in Artificial Intelligence. JELIA 2023. LNCS, vol. 14281, pp. 649–664. Springer, Cham (2023). https://doi.org/10.1007/978-3-031-43619-2_44
5. Barbero, F., Yang, F.: Characterizing counterfactuals and dependencies over (generalized) causal teams. Notre Dame J. Form. Log. **63**(3) (2022)
6. Beckers, S., Halpern, J., Hitchcock, C.: Causal models with constraints. In: Conference on Causal Learning and Reasoning, pp. 866–879. PMLR (2023)
7. Bohm, D.: Causality and Chance in Modern Physics. Van Nostrand Company Inc., Princeton, NJ (1957)
8. Briggs, R.: Interventionist counterfactuals. Philos. Stud. Int. J. Philos. Anal. Tradit. **160**(1), 139–166 (2012)
9. Fang, J., Zhang, J.: A characterization of Lewisian causal models. In: Alechina, N., Herzig, A., Liang, F. (eds.) Logic, Rationality, and Interaction. LORI 2023. LNCS, vol. 14329, pp. 94–108. Springer, Cham (2023). https://doi.org/10.1007/978-3-031-45558-2_8
10. Galles, D., Pearl, J.: An axiomatic characterization of causal counterfactuals. Found. Sci. **3**(1), 151–182 (1998)
11. Halpern, J.Y.: Axiomatizing causal reasoning. J. Artif. Int. Res. **12**(1), 317–337 (2000)
12. Halpern, J.Y.: From causal models to counterfactual structures. Rev. Symb. Log. **6**(2), 305–322 (2013)
13. Halpern, J.Y.: Actual Causality. MIT Press, Cambridge (2016)
14. Halpern, J.Y., Peters, S.: Reasoning about causal models with infinitely many variables. In: Proceedings of the AAAI Conference on Artificial Intelligence, vol. 36, pp. 5668–5675 (2022)
15. Heckman, J.J., Vytlacil, E.J.: Econometric evaluation of social programs, part i: causal models, structural models and econometric policy evaluation. Handb. Econ. **6**, 4779–4874 (2007)
16. Hernan, M.A., Robins, J.: Causal Inference: What if. Chapman & Hill/CRC, Boca Raton. forthcoming
17. Ibeling, D., Icard, T.: Probabilistic reasoning across the causal hierarchy. In: Proceedings of the AAAI Conference on Artificial Intelligence, vol. 34, pp. 10170–10177 (2020)
18. Lewis, D.: Counterfactuals. Blackwell Publishers, Oxford (1973)
19. Morgan, S.L., Winship, C.: Counterfactuals and Causal Inference. Cambridge University Press, Cambridge (2015)

20. Mosse, M., Ibeling, D., Icard, T.: Is causal reasoning harder than probabilistic reasoning? Rev. Symb. Log. 1–26 (2022)
21. Paul, L.A., Hall, E.J.: Causation: A User's Guide. Oxford University Press, Oxford (2013)
22. Pearl, J.: Causality: Models, Reasoning, and Inference. Cambridge University Press, New York, NY, USA (2000)
23. Pearl, J.: Physical and metaphysical counterfactuals: evaluating disjunctive actions. J. Causal Inference 5(2), 20170018 (2017)
24. Peters, J., Janzing, D., Scholkopf, B.: Elements of Causal Inference: Foundations and Learning Algorithms. MIT Press, Cambridge (2017)
25. Peters, S., Halpern, J.Y.: Causal modeling with infinitely many variables. arXiv preprint arXiv:2112.09171 (2021)
26. Schölkopf, B.: Causality for machine learning. In: Probabilistic and Causal Inference: The Works of Judea Pearl, pp. 765–804. Association for Computing Machinery (2022)
27. Spirtes, P., Glymour, C.N., Scheines, R.: Causation, Prediction, and Search, vol. 81 of LNS. Springer, New York (1993). https://doi.org/10.1007/978-1-4612-2748-9
28. Wysocki, T.: The underdeterministic framework. Br. J. Philos. Sci. forthcoming
29. Zhang, J.: A Lewisian logic of causal counterfactuals. Minds Mach. 23(1), 77–93 (2013)

Axiomatization of Implication for Probabilistic Independence and Unary Variants of Marginal Identity and Marginal Distribution Equivalence

Minna Hirvonen$^{(\boxtimes)}$ [ID]

Department of Mathematics and Statistics, University of Helsinki, Helsinki, Finland
minna.hirvonen@helsinki.fi

Abstract. We consider probabilistic independence and unary variants of marginal identity and marginal distribution equivalence over finite probability distributions. Two variables x and y satisfy a unary marginal identity when they are identically distributed. If the multisets of the marginal probabilities of all possible values for variables x and y are equal, the variables satisfy a unary marginal distribution equivalence. This paper offers a sound and complete finite axiomatization and a polynomial-time algorithm for the implication problem for probabilistic independence, unary marginal identity, and unary marginal distribution equivalence.

Keywords: Complete axiomatization · Probabilistic independence · Marginal distribution equivalence · Marginal identity · Polynomial-time algorithm · Probabilistic team semantics

1 Introduction

Suppose that one does research, e.g. statistical analysis, on a probabilistic phenomenon and obtains information that some variables are independent or in some sense equivalently distributed. It would then be useful to be able to deduce new independencies and equivalences of distributions without further measurements and (numerical) analysis. This idea can be formalized as the so-called *implication problem* of probabilistic independencies, unary marginal identities, and unary marginal distribution equivalences.

We consider finite random variables, i.e., random variables with a finite support. Independence of two sequences of variables $\bar{x}$ and $\bar{y}$ can be expressed by the *probabilistic independence* atom, written as $\bar{x} \perp\!\!\!\perp \bar{y}$. We also have two different notions for equivalence of distributions. A *marginal identity* atom $x \approx y$, introduced in [4][1], states that the distributions of x and y are identical. A *marginal*

---

[1] In [4], the marginal identity was called the probabilistic inclusion atom with slightly different, but equivalent semantics [11].

© The Author(s), under exclusive license to Springer Nature Switzerland AG 2024
A. Meier and M. Ortiz (Eds.): FoIKS 2024, LNCS 14589, pp. 222–234, 2024.
https://doi.org/10.1007/978-3-031-56940-1_12

distribution equivalence atom $x \approx^* y$, introduced in [11], states that the multi-sets of the marginal probabilities of all possible values for variables x and y are equal.

For any set of these atoms $\Sigma \cup \{\sigma\}$, we say that σ is logically implied by Σ if and only if every finite distribution that satisfies all the atoms in Σ also satisfies σ. The task of determining whether Σ logically implies σ is called the *implication problem* for probabilistic independence, unary marginal identity, and unary marginal distribution equivalence. Our goal is to give an axiomatic characterization and a polynomial-time algorithm for this problem that combines all these three different kinds of atoms.

The implication problem studied in this article is closely connected to the disjoint probabilistic independence implication. A probabilistic independence atom $\bar{x} \perp\!\!\!\perp \bar{y}$ is *disjoint* if the tuples $\bar{x}$ and $\bar{y}$ do not share any variables, i.e., the sets of variables that appear in $\bar{x}$ and $\bar{y}$ are disjoint. The implication problem of disjoint probabilistic independence has a finite axiomatization and polynomial-time algorithm [8]. Note that the disjoint and the non-disjoint cases of probabilistic independence implication are reducible to each other: the disjoint case is clearly a subproblem of the non-disjoint case, and the proof of Theorem 4 implicitly shows that the non-disjoint case is reducible to the disjoint case.

Although there is already an axiomatization for disjoint probabilistic independence, we want to study probabilistic independence together with other kinds of dependency and independency notions, because in practice these different notions can appear at the same time. For example, in probability theory, collections of random variables are often assumed to be independent and identically distributed (i.i.d.). This is essentially the same as the random sample assumption in statistics. We can express this for finite random variables using probabilistic independence and unary marginal identity atoms: for $n \in \mathbb{N}$, we have that finite random variables $x_1, \ldots, x_n$ are i.i.d. if and only if $x_1 \approx x_i$ and $x_1 \ldots x_i \perp\!\!\!\perp x_{i+1}$ for all $i \in \{1, \ldots, n\}$.

Besides the atoms studied in this paper, examples of interesting probabilistic dependency and independency notions include *probabilistic conditional independence* $\bar{y} \perp\!\!\!\perp_{\bar{x}} \bar{z}$ (stating that $\bar{y}$ and $\bar{z}$ are independent given $\bar{x}$) and general versions of marginal identity $\bar{x} \approx \bar{y}$ and marginal distribution equivalence $\bar{x} \approx^* \bar{y}$, which compare distributions of tuples instead of just single variables [4,5,11]. Conditional independence and marginal identity can be used, e.g., to formalize the derivation of non-Shannon information inequalities via copy lemma in positive semirings [10]. Probabilistic conditional independence implication is known to be undecidable [17] and marginal identity implication has a finite axiomatization [13]. It may also be useful to study problems that combine suitable fragments of probabilistic conditional independencies and general marginal identities and marginal distribution equivalences.

Probabilistic notions can also be studied with qualitative (non-probabilistic) dependencies. This kind of dependencies include, e.g., functional dependencies (primary keys) and inclusion dependencies (foreign keys) that have been studied extensively in database theory since they can be used as logical integrity constraints in various data management tasks. The implication problem for functional dependencies has the so-called Armstrong axiomatization [1] and a linear-time algorithm [2]. On the other hand, the implication problem for inclusion dependencies also has an axiomatization, but it is PSPACE-complete [3].

An example of an implication problem that combines both qualitative and probabilistic notions is the implication for functional dependencies, unary marginal identities, and unary marginal distribution equivalences[2]. It has an axiomatization and a polynomial-time algorithm [14]. The axiomatization was formalized in the setting of probabilistic team semantics, which was originally developed as a semantical framework for logics with atomic formulas that express various qualitative and quantitative dependencies and independencies, including functional dependency, probabilistic independence, marginal identity and marginal distribution equivalence. Much of the terminology used in this paper comes from logics with team semantics. Since using the framework of team semantics in the formulation of the implication problem makes the connection to these logics explicit, we continue working in this setting.

The framework of team semantics (without probabilities) was introduced by Hodges [15] and popularized by Väänänen [18] via *dependence logic*, which extends first-order logic with dependence atoms, i.e., functional dependencies. In team semantics, satisfaction of formulas is defined with respect to sets of assignments, called *teams*, instead of single assignments. This is the essential feature which allows us to combine dependency notions with first-order logic. There is a close connection to databases: a team can be viewed as a relation or a table in a database. Other examples of logics with team semantics include *inclusion logic* (extension with inclusion dependencies) [7] and *independence logic* (extension with embedded multivalued dependencies) [9].

Probabilistic team semantics generalizes team semantics by introducing the notion of a *probabilistic team*, which is a probability distribution over a set of assignments. One may also think of it as a team where each assignment is associated with some non-negative real number called the *weight* of the assignment. Each of these so-called *weighted teams* corresponds to a probability distribution that can be obtained by scaling the weights such that the sum of all the weights is one. The generalization of team semantics to the probabilistic setting began with Galliani [6], Hyttinen et al. [16], and a systematic study of probabilistic team semantics started with Durand et al. [4,5].

The paper is structured as follows: Sect. 2 introduces the basic definitions needed for the paper. Section 3 contains the axiomatization for the implication problem. In Sect. 4, we show that the axiomatization is complete and in Sect. 5, that the implication problem has a polynomial-time algorithm. Section 6 concludes the paper with some related open questions.

---

[2] Since a functional dependency $=(\bar{x}, \bar{y})$ (i.e. $\bar{x}$ determines $\bar{y}$) and probabilistic independence $\bar{x}\perp\bar{y}$ can be expressed with probabilistic conditional independencies $\bar{y} \perp_{\bar{x}} \bar{y}$ and $\bar{x} \perp_{\emptyset} \bar{y}$, respectively, this problem and the one considered in this paper are both examples of implication problems for a fragment of probabilistic conditional independencies together with unary marginal identities and marginal distribution equivalences.

2   Preliminaries

Let D and A be two finite sets. We call the elements of D variables and the elements of A values. We use the letters at the end of the alphabet x, y, z for variables and the letters at the beginning of the alphabet a, b, c for values (both with or without indices). Tuples of variables and tuples of values are denoted by $\bar{x}, \bar{y}, \bar{z}$ and $\bar{a}, \bar{b}, \bar{c}$, respectively, and $\mathsf{var}(\bar{x})$ is the set of variables that appear in the tuple $\bar{x}$. The notation $|\bar{x}|$ refers to the length of the tuple $\bar{x}$.

An *assignment* of values from A for the set D is a function $s \colon D \to A$ and a *team* X of A over D is a finite set of assignments $s \colon D \to A$. Let $D = \{x_1, \ldots, x_n\}$. Then an assignment s can be viewed as the tuple $s(x_1, \ldots, x_n) = (s(x_1), \ldots, s(x_n)) \in A^n$ and a team X over $D = \{x_1, \ldots, x_n\}$ as a table whose columns are the variables $x_1, \ldots, x_n$, and rows are the tuples $s \in X$. For a tuple of variables $\bar{x}$ from D, let

$$X(\bar{x}) := \{s(\bar{x}) \in A^{|\bar{x}|} \mid s \in X\}.$$

A probabilistic team $\mathbb{X}$ is a function $\mathbb{X} \colon X \to (0,1]$ such that $\sum_{s \in X} \mathbb{X}(s) = 1$. For a tuple of variables $\bar{x}$ from D and a tuple of values $\bar{a}$ from A, let

$$|\mathbb{X}_{\bar{x}=\bar{a}}| := \sum_{\substack{s(\bar{x})=\bar{a} \\ s \in X}} \mathbb{X}(s).$$

A multiset is a pair (B, m) where B is a set, and $m \colon B \to \mathbb{N}$ is a multiplicity function. The function m determines for each element $b \in B$ how many copies of b the multiset (B, m) contains. We denote multisets using double wave brackets, e.g., $(B, m) = \{\{0, 1, 1\}\}$ when $B = \{0, 1\}$ and m is such that $m(0) = 1$ and $m(1) = 2$.

Let $\bar{x}, \bar{y}$ be tuples of variables from D. Then $\bar{x} \perp\!\!\!\perp \bar{y}$ and $\bar{x} \approx^* \bar{y}$ are called *probabilistic independence* (PIA) and *marginal distribution equivalence atoms* (MDE), respectively. If the tuples $\bar{x}, \bar{y}$ are of the same length, then $\bar{x} \approx \bar{y}$ is called a *marginal identity atom* (MI). If both tuples in a PIA, MDE, or MI are unary, i.e. $|\bar{x}| = |\bar{y}| = 1$, an atom is called *unary*. We use the abbreviations UPIA, UMDE, and UMI for unary atoms.

Define the satisfaction relation $\mathbb{X} \models \sigma$ for probabilistic teams $\mathbb{X}$ and atoms σ as follows:

(i) $\mathbb{X} \models \bar{x} \perp\!\!\!\perp \bar{y}$ iff $|\mathbb{X}_{\bar{x}=\bar{a}}| \cdot |\mathbb{X}_{\bar{y}=\bar{b}}| = |\mathbb{X}_{\bar{x}\bar{y}=\bar{a}\bar{b}}|$ for all $\bar{a}\bar{b} \in A^{|\bar{x}\bar{y}|}$.
(ii) $\mathbb{X} \models \bar{x} \approx^* \bar{y}$ iff $\{\{|\mathbb{X}_{\bar{x}=\bar{a}}| \mid \bar{a} \in X(\bar{x})\}\} = \{\{|\mathbb{X}_{\bar{y}=\bar{a}}| \mid \bar{a} \in X(\bar{y})\}\}$.
(iii) $\mathbb{X} \models \bar{x} \approx \bar{y}$ iff $|\mathbb{X}_{\bar{x}=\bar{a}}| = |\mathbb{X}_{\bar{y}=\bar{a}}|$ for all $\bar{a} \in A^{|\bar{x}|}$.

If $\mathbb{X} \models \sigma$, we say that a probabilistic team $\mathbb{X}$ satisfies the atom σ.

Example 1. Table 1 depicts a probabilistic team $\mathbb{X}$. The following are some examples and nonexamples of atoms satisfied in $\mathbb{X}$. Probabilistic independencies: $\mathbb{X} \models x \perp\!\!\!\perp y$, $\mathbb{X} \models u \perp\!\!\!\perp u$, $\mathbb{X} \not\models w \perp\!\!\!\perp w$, and $\mathbb{X} \not\models x \perp\!\!\!\perp z$. Marginal distribution equivalences: $\mathbb{X} \models x \approx^* y$, $\mathbb{X} \models z \approx^* w$, and $\mathbb{X} \not\models x \approx^* z$. Marginal identities: $\mathbb{X} \models x \approx y$ and $\mathbb{X} \not\models z \approx w$.

Table 1. An example of a probabilistic team X.

x	y	z	w	u	X
0	0	0	1	0	1/4
0	1	0	1	0	1/4
1	0	0	1	0	1/4
1	1	1	0	0	1/4

We can also generalize satisfaction relation to sets of atoms. For a set of atoms $\Sigma \cup \{\sigma\}$, we write

(i) $\mathbb{X} \models \Sigma$ iff $\mathbb{X} \models \sigma'$ for all $\sigma' \in \Sigma$,
(ii) $\Sigma \models \sigma$ iff $\mathbb{X} \models \Sigma$ implies $\mathbb{X} \models \sigma$ for all $\mathbb{X}$.

A decision problem of checking whether $\Sigma \models \sigma$ is called an *implication problem* (for PIAs+UMIs+UMDEs).

3 Axioms

In this section, we present a sound axiomatization for PIA+UMI+UMDE implication. The axiomatization is finite and consists of the following axioms[3] PIA1–PIA5, UMI1–UMI3, UMDE1–UMDE3, UMI & UMDE, and PIA & UMDE 1–PIA & UMDE 2 listed below.

For probabilistic independence we have trivial independence, symmetry, decomposition, exchange, and constancy:

PIA1: $\emptyset \perp\!\!\!\perp \bar{x}$
PIA2: If $\bar{x} \perp\!\!\!\perp \bar{y}$, then $\bar{y} \perp\!\!\!\perp \bar{x}$.
PIA3: If $\bar{x} \perp\!\!\!\perp \bar{y}$, then $\bar{x}' \perp\!\!\!\perp \bar{y}'$ for all $\mathrm{var}(\bar{x}') \subseteq \mathrm{var}(\bar{x})$, $\mathrm{var}(\bar{y}') \subseteq \mathrm{var}(\bar{y})$.
PIA4: If $\bar{x} \perp\!\!\!\perp \bar{y}$ and $\bar{x}\bar{y} \perp\!\!\!\perp \bar{z}$, then $\bar{x} \perp\!\!\!\perp \bar{y}\bar{z}$.
PIA5: If $\bar{x} \perp\!\!\!\perp \bar{y}$ and $\bar{z} \perp\!\!\!\perp \bar{z}$, then $\bar{x} \perp\!\!\!\perp \bar{y}\bar{z}$.

Note that the decomposition axiom is written in the form that considers subsets, because we want to be able to permute the variables within the tuples.

For unary marginal identity and unary marginal distribution equivalence, we have the equivalence axioms, i.e., reflexivity, symmetry, and transitivity:

UMI1: $x \approx x$
UMI2: If $x \approx y$, then $y \approx x$.
UMI3: If $x \approx y$ and $y \approx z$, then $x \approx z$.

UMDE1: $x \approx^* x$
UMDE2: If $x \approx^* y$, then $y \approx^* x$.
UMDE3: If $x \approx^* y$ and $y \approx^* z$, then $x \approx^* z$.

---

[3] Note that we do not make a distinction between axioms and inference rules; in this paper they are both called "axioms".

As marginal identity implies marginal distribution equivalence, we add the following axiom:

UMI & UMDE 1: If $x \approx y$, then $x \approx^* y$.

For the interaction of PIAs and UMDEs, we have the two following axioms:

PIA & UMDE 1: If $x \approx^* y$ and $y \perp y$, then $x \perp x$.
PIA & UMDE 2: If $x \perp x$ and $y \perp y$, then $x \approx^* y$.

We write $\Sigma \vdash \sigma$ if and only if an atom σ can be derived from a set of atoms Σ by using the rules of the axiomatization defined above. We say that an axiomatization is sound if $\Sigma \vdash \sigma$ implies $\Sigma \models \sigma$ for every set $\Sigma \cup \{\sigma\}$ of PIA, UMI, and UMDE atoms. Since it is straightforward to check the soundness of the axioms, our axiomatization for PIA+UMI+UMDE implication is sound:

Theorem 1 (Soundness). *For any set $\Sigma \cup \{\sigma\}$ of PIA, UMI, and UMDE atoms,*

$$\text{If } \Sigma \vdash \sigma, \text{ then } \Sigma \models \sigma.$$

4   Completeness

In this section, we show that the axiomatization is complete, i.e., $\Sigma \models \sigma$ implies $\Sigma \vdash \sigma$ for every set $\Sigma \cup \{\sigma\}$ of PIA, UMI, and UMDE atoms. By combining this with the fact that all of the axioms are sound, we obtain the following theorem which states that the axiomatization characterizes PIA+UMI+UMDE implication:

Theorem 2. *For any set $\Sigma \cup \{\sigma\}$ of PIA, UMI, and UMDE atoms,*

$$\Sigma \models \sigma \text{ if and only if } \Sigma \vdash \sigma.$$

Since Theorem 1 covers the soundness of the axiomatization, we are left to prove the following theorem:

Theorem 3 (Completeness). *For any set $\Sigma \cup \{\sigma\}$ of PIA, UMI, and UMDE atoms,*

$$\text{If } \Sigma \models \sigma, \text{ then } \Sigma \vdash \sigma.$$

The idea of the proof is to show the contraposition: we assume that $\Sigma \nvdash \sigma$, and construct a probabilistic team that witnesses $\Sigma \nvDash \sigma$. We will handle the cases where σ is UMI, UMDE, or PIA separately in the following three lemmas. In the below, D is assumed to be the set of variables that appear in Σ.

Lemma 1. *For any UMI atom $x \approx y$, if $\Sigma \models x \approx y$, then $\Sigma \vdash x \approx y$.*

Proof. Suppose that $\Sigma \nvdash x \approx y$. We show that $\Sigma \not\models x \approx y$. Let $z_1, \ldots, z_n$ be a list of those variables $z_i \in D$ for which $\Sigma \vdash x \approx^* z_i$, and let $u_1, \ldots, u_m$ be a list of those variables $u_j \in D$ for which $\Sigma \nvdash x \approx^* u_j$. These lists are clearly disjoint, and $D = \{z_1, \ldots, z_n\} \cup \{u_1, \ldots, u_m\}$.

Let team $X = \{s\}$, where

$$s(v) = \begin{cases} 0, & \text{if } v \in \{z_1, \ldots, z_n\} \\ 1, & \text{if } v \in \{u_1, \ldots, u_m\}. \end{cases}$$

Define then $\mathbb{X} \colon X \to (0, 1]$ such that $\mathbb{X}(s) = 1$. Since $\Sigma \vdash x \approx x$ and $\Sigma \nvdash x \approx y$, we have $x \in \{z_1, \ldots, z_n\}$ and $y \in \{u_1, \ldots, u_m\}$. Hence, by the construction, $\mathbb{X} \not\models x \approx y$. Suppose that $\Sigma \vdash v \approx v'$. Now, because of the transitivity axiom UMI3, either $v, v' \in \{z_1, \ldots, z_n\}$ or $v, v' \in \{u_1, \ldots, u_m\}$. This means that $\mathbb{X} \models v \approx v'$. It is easy to see that all UMDEs and PIAs are satisfied by $\mathbb{X}$, so $\mathbb{X} \models \Sigma$.

Lemma 2. *For any UMDE atom $x \approx^* y$, if $\Sigma \models x \approx^* y$, then $\Sigma \vdash x \approx^* y$.*

Proof. Suppose that $\Sigma \nvdash x \approx^* y$. We show that $\Sigma \not\models x \approx^* y$.

First, note that $\Sigma \vdash x \perp\!\!\!\perp x$ and $\Sigma \vdash y \perp\!\!\!\perp y$ imply $\Sigma \vdash x \approx^* y$, so either $\Sigma \nvdash x \perp\!\!\!\perp x$ or $\Sigma \nvdash y \perp\!\!\!\perp y$. Without loss of generality, assume that $\Sigma \nvdash x \perp\!\!\!\perp x$.

Let $z_1, \ldots, z_n$ be a list of those variables $z_i \in D$ for which $\Sigma \vdash x \approx^* z_i$, and let $u_1, \ldots, u_m$ be a list of those variables $u_j \in D$ for which $\Sigma \nvdash x \approx^* u_j$. These lists are clearly disjoint, and $D = \{z_1, \ldots, z_n\} \cup \{u_1, \ldots, u_m\}$.

Let team X consist of all the tuples from the set

$$Z_1 \times \cdots \times Z_n \times U_1 \times \cdots \times U_m,$$

where $Z_i = \{0, 1\}$ and $U_j = \{0\}$ for $i = 1, \ldots, n$ and $j = 1, \ldots, m$. Define then $\mathbb{X}$ as the uniform distribution over X. It is easy to see that $\mathbb{X} \not\models x \approx^* y$. Suppose that $\Sigma \vdash v \approx v'$. Now, since $v \approx v'$ implies $v \approx^* v'$, because of the transitivity axiom UMDE3, either $v, v' \in \{z_1, \ldots, z_n\}$ or $v, v' \in \{u_1, \ldots, u_m\}$. This means that $\mathbb{X} \models v \approx v'$. The case $\Sigma \vdash v \approx^* v'$ is analogous.

Suppose that $\Sigma \vdash v \perp\!\!\!\perp v$. Suppose for a contradiction that $\mathbb{X} \not\models v \perp\!\!\!\perp v$. Then by the construction of $\mathbb{X}$, $v \in \{z_1, \ldots, z_n\}$. This means that $\Sigma \vdash x \approx^* v$, and thus by applying the axiom PIA & UMDE 1, we obtain $\Sigma \vdash x \perp\!\!\!\perp x$. This contradicts the assumption that $\Sigma \nvdash x \perp\!\!\!\perp x$.

Suppose then that $\Sigma \vdash \bar{w} \perp\!\!\!\perp \bar{w}'$. If $\mathsf{var}(\bar{w}) \cap \mathsf{var}(\bar{w}') \neq \emptyset$, then by the decomposition axiom PIA3, $\Sigma \vdash v \perp\!\!\!\perp v$ for all $v \in \mathsf{var}(\bar{w}) \cap \mathsf{var}(\bar{w}')$. By the previous case, we know that then $\mathbb{X} \models v \perp\!\!\!\perp v$. Thus, by the constancy axiom PIA5, we may assume that $\mathsf{var}(\bar{w}) \cap \mathsf{var}(\bar{w}') = \emptyset$. But then it is easy to see that by the construction, $\mathbb{X} \models \bar{w} \perp\!\!\!\perp \bar{w}'$.

The proof for the PIA case of the last lemma is a modified version of the one for the completeness of disjoint probabilistic independence implication from [8].

Lemma 3. *For any PIA atom $\bar{x} \perp\!\!\!\perp \bar{y}$, if $\Sigma \models \bar{x} \perp\!\!\!\perp \bar{y}$, then $\Sigma \vdash \bar{x} \perp\!\!\!\perp \bar{y}$.*

Proof. Suppose first that $\Sigma \not\vdash x\perp x$. Then the construction from the UMDE case shows that $\Sigma \not\models x\perp x$.

Suppose then that $\Sigma \not\vdash \bar{x}\perp\bar{y}$. We show that $\Sigma \not\models \bar{x}\perp\bar{y}$. First, assume that $\mathrm{var}(\bar{x}) \cap \mathrm{var}(\bar{y}) \neq \emptyset$. Let $v \in \mathrm{var}(\bar{x}) \cap \mathrm{var}(\bar{y})$. If $\Sigma \not\vdash v\perp v$, then $\Sigma \not\models v\perp v$ already follows from the previous case, and thus by the decomposition axiom PIA3, we also have $\Sigma \not\models \bar{x}\perp\bar{y}$. If $\Sigma \vdash v\perp v$, we can use the constancy axiom PIA5 to infer $\Sigma \not\vdash \bar{x}'\perp\bar{y}'$ where $\bar{x}'$ and $\bar{y}'$ are obtained from $\bar{x}$ and $\bar{y}$ by removing v. Hence, we may assume that $\mathrm{var}(\bar{x}) \cap \mathrm{var}(\bar{y}) = \emptyset$.

We may additionally assume that the atom $\bar{x}\perp\bar{y}$ is minimal in the sense that $\Sigma \vdash \bar{x}'\perp\bar{y}'$ for all $\bar{x}'$, $\bar{y}'$ such that $\mathrm{var}(\bar{x}') \subseteq \mathrm{var}(\bar{x})$, $\mathrm{var}(\bar{y}') \subseteq \mathrm{var}(\bar{y})$, and $\mathrm{var}(\bar{x}'\bar{y}') \neq \mathrm{var}(\bar{x}\bar{y})$. If not, we can remove elements from $\bar{x}$ and $\bar{y}$ until this holds. By the decomposition axiom PIA3, it suffices to show the claim for the minimal atom. Note that due to the trivial independence axiom PIA1 both $\bar{x}$ and $\bar{y}$ are at least of length one.

Let $\bar{x} = x_1 \ldots x_n$ and $\bar{y} = y_1 \ldots y_m$. Note that by the minimality of $\bar{x}\perp\bar{y}$, we have $\Sigma \not\vdash x_i\perp x_i$ and $\Sigma \not\vdash y_j\perp y_j$ for all $i = 1, \ldots, n$ and $j = 1, \ldots, m$. Let $\{u_1, \ldots, u_k\} \subseteq D$ be the set of those variables for which $\Sigma \vdash u_i\perp u_i$. Let

$$\{z_1, \ldots, z_l\} = D \setminus (\{x_1, \ldots, x_n\} \cup \{y_1, \ldots, y_m\} \cup \{u_1, \ldots, u_k\}).$$

Define a team X_0 over $D \setminus \{x_1\}$ such that it consists of all the tuples from the set

$$X_2 \times \cdots \times X_n \times Y_1 \times \ldots Y_m \times Z_1 \times \cdots \times Z_l \times U_1 \times \cdots \times U_k,$$

where $X_2 = \cdots = X_n = Y_1 = \ldots Y_m = Z_1 = \cdots = Z_l = \{0, 1\}$ and $U_1 = \cdots = U_k = \{0\}$. Let then $X = \{s \cup \{(x_1, a)\} \mid s \in X_0\}$, where

$$a = \sum_{i=2}^{n} s(x_i) + \sum_{i=1}^{m} s(y_j) \pmod{2}.$$

Define then $\mathbb{X}$ as the uniform distribution over X.

Now $\mathbb{X} \not\models \bar{x}\perp\bar{y}$. Let $s, s' \in X$ be such that $s(x_1) = 1$, $s(x_i) = 0$, and $s'(y_j) = 0$ for all $2 \leq i \leq n$ and $1 \leq j \leq m$. Then there is no $s'' \in X$ such that $s''(\bar{x}) = s(\bar{x})$ and $s''(\bar{y}) = s'(\bar{y})$.

Suppose that $\Sigma \vdash v \approx v'$. Suppose for a contradiction that $\Sigma \not\models v \approx v'$. Then one of v and v' must be in $\{u_1, \ldots, u_k\}$ and one in $D \setminus \{u_1, \ldots, u_k\}$[4]. Assume that $v' \in \{u_1, \ldots, u_k\}$. This means that $\Sigma \vdash v'\perp v'$. Since $\Sigma \vdash v \approx v'$, by applying UMI & UMDE and PIA & UMDE 1, we obtain $\Sigma \vdash v\perp v$. But then $v \in \{u_1, \ldots, u_k\}$, which is a contradiction. The case $\Sigma \vdash v \approx^* v'$. is analogous.

Suppose then that $\Sigma \vdash \bar{w}\perp\bar{w}'$. If $\mathrm{var}(\bar{w}) \cap \mathrm{var}(\bar{w}') \neq \emptyset$, then by the decomposition axiom PIA3, $\Sigma \vdash v\perp v$ for all $v \in \mathrm{var}(\bar{w}) \cap \mathrm{var}(\bar{w}')$. Then $v \in \{u_1, \ldots, u_k\}$, and thus $\mathbb{X} \models v\perp v$. Thus, by the constancy axiom PIA5, we may assume that $\mathrm{var}(\bar{w}) \cap \mathrm{var}(\bar{w}') = \emptyset$. Note that by a similar reasoning, we may more generally assume that $u_i \notin \mathrm{var}(\bar{w}\bar{w}')$ for all $1 \leq i \leq l$.

---

[4] Note that clearly $|\mathbb{X}_{w=0}| = 1$ for all $w \in \{u_1, \ldots, u_k\}$, and $|\mathbb{X}_{w=a}| = 1/2$ for all $a \in \{0, 1\}$ and $w \in D \setminus \{x_1, u_1, \ldots, u_k\}$. An easy induction proof shows that $|\mathbb{X}_{x_1=a}| = 1/2$ for all $a \in \{0, 1\}$.

Assume first that $\mathsf{var}(\bar{w}\bar{w}') \cap \mathsf{var}(\bar{x}\bar{y}) = \emptyset$. Then $\mathsf{var}(\bar{w}\bar{w}') \subseteq \mathsf{var}(\bar{z})$, where $\bar{z} = z_1 \ldots z_l$. It is clear by the definition of $\mathbb{X}$ that $\mathbb{X} \models \bar{w} \perp\!\!\!\perp \bar{w}'$.

Assume then that $\mathsf{var}(\bar{w}\bar{w}') \cap \mathsf{var}(\bar{x}\bar{y}) \neq \emptyset$, but $\mathsf{var}(\bar{x}\bar{y}) \not\subseteq \mathsf{var}(\bar{w}\bar{w}')$. Then $\mathbb{X} \models \bar{w} \perp\!\!\!\perp \bar{w}'$ because $|\mathbb{X}_{\bar{w}=\bar{a}}| = (1/2)^{|\bar{w}|}$ for all $a \in \{0,1\}^{|\bar{w}|}$ and $|\mathbb{X}_{\bar{w}'=\bar{a}}| = (1/2)^{|\bar{w}'|}$ for all $a \in \{0,1\}^{|\bar{w}'|}$.

Assume lastly that $\mathsf{var}(\bar{x}\bar{y}) \subseteq \mathsf{var}(\bar{w}\bar{w}')$. We show that this case is not possible. We may assume that $\bar{w} = \bar{x}'\bar{y}'\bar{z}'$ and $\bar{w}' = \bar{x}''\bar{y}''\bar{z}''$, where $\mathsf{var}(\bar{x}) = \mathsf{var}(\bar{x}'\bar{x}'')$, $\mathsf{var}(\bar{y}) = \mathsf{var}(\bar{y}'\bar{y}'')$, and $\mathsf{var}(\bar{z}'\bar{z}'') \subseteq \mathsf{var}(\bar{z})$. By the axiom PIA3, we have $\Sigma \vdash \bar{x}'\bar{y}' \perp\!\!\!\perp \bar{x}''\bar{y}''$. Note that by the minimality of $\bar{x} \perp\!\!\!\perp \bar{y}$, we have $\Sigma \vdash \bar{x}' \perp\!\!\!\perp \bar{y}'$. By using the exchange axiom PIA4 to $\bar{x}' \perp\!\!\!\perp \bar{y}'$ and $\bar{x}'\bar{y}' \perp\!\!\!\perp \bar{x}''\bar{y}''$, we obtain $\Sigma \vdash \bar{x}' \perp\!\!\!\perp \bar{y}'\bar{x}''\bar{y}''$. So now (by PIA3), $\Sigma \vdash \bar{x}' \perp\!\!\!\perp \bar{y}\bar{x}''$, and by the symmetry axiom PIA2, $\Sigma \vdash \bar{y}\bar{x}'' \perp\!\!\!\perp \bar{x}'$. Again, by the minimality of $\bar{x} \perp\!\!\!\perp \bar{y}$ and the symmetry axiom PIA2, we have $\Sigma \vdash \bar{y} \perp\!\!\!\perp \bar{x}''$. Then by using the exchange axiom PIA4 again, this time to $\bar{y} \perp\!\!\!\perp \bar{x}''$ and $\bar{y}\bar{x}'' \perp\!\!\!\perp \bar{x}'$, we obtain $\Sigma \vdash \bar{y} \perp\!\!\!\perp \bar{x}''\bar{x}'$. By (PIA3 and) the symmetry axiom PIA2, we have $\Sigma \vdash \bar{x} \perp\!\!\!\perp \bar{y}$, which is a contradiction.

This finishes the completeness proof. Hence, we have shown that the axiomatization is both sound and complete.

5 Complexity

In this section, we show that the implication problem for PIAs+UMIs+UMDEs has a polynomial-time algorithm. Recall that this implication problem is the decision problem of checking whether $\Sigma \models \sigma$ holds for a given set Σ and an atom σ such that $\Sigma \cup \{\sigma\}$ consists of PIAs, UMIs, and UMDEs. We first describe the idea of the algorithm and finally represent it in a more concise form in Algorithm 2.

Theorem 4. *PIA+UMI+UMDE implication is in polynomial-time.*

Let D be the set of the variables that appear in $\Sigma \cup \{\sigma\}$. We partition Σ into the sets of PIAs, UMIs, and UMDEs, and denote these sets by Σ_{PIA}, Σ_{UMI}, and Σ_{UMDE}, respectively.

For a UMI atom $\sigma := v \approx w$, it suffices to check whether $\Sigma_{\mathrm{UMI}} \models \sigma$ because no new UMIs can be obtained by using the inference rules for PIAs and UMDEs. As in [14], the set Σ_{UMI} can be viewed as an undirected graph $G(\Sigma_{\mathrm{UMI}}) = (D, \approx)$ such that each $x \approx y \in \Sigma_{\mathrm{UMI}}$ corresponds to an undirected edge between x and y. (We assume that each vertex has a self-loop and all of the edges are undirected.) Then $\Sigma_{\mathrm{UMI}} \models v \approx w$ iff w is reachable from v in $G(\Sigma_{\mathrm{UMI}})$. This can be checked in linear-time by using a breadth-first search.

Consider then the case for PIA or UMDE. We use ideas similar to [12] in order to isolate constancy atoms. Close the set Σ_{UMDE} under UMI & UMDE rule, i.e., define $\Sigma'_{\mathrm{UMDE}} := \Sigma_{\mathrm{UMDE}} \cup \{x \approx^* y \mid x \approx y \in \Sigma_{\mathrm{UMI}}\}$. Construct then the undirected graph $G(\Sigma_{\mathrm{UMDE}'}) = (D, \approx^*)$ for Σ'_{UMDE} analogously to the case Σ_{UMI} above. Let $\mathsf{Const}(\Sigma_{\mathrm{PIA}}) := \{v \in D \mid v \in \mathsf{var}(\bar{x}) \cap \mathsf{var}(\bar{y})$ for some $\bar{x} \perp\!\!\!\perp \bar{y} \in \Sigma_{\mathrm{PIA}}\}$.

Now, we can compute a set of variables Const and a graph G in polynomial-time by using Algorithm 1.

Algorithm 1 Comp(Σ)

Require: Σ_{PIA}, Σ_{UMI}, and Σ_{UMDE}
Ensure: Const and $G := (D, E)$

$\quad$ Const $\leftarrow$ Const(Σ_{PIA}) $\quad (= \{v \in D \mid v \in \text{var}(\bar{x}) \cap \text{var}(\bar{y})$ for some $\bar{x} \perp\!\!\!\perp \bar{y} \in \Sigma_{\text{PIA}}\})$

$\quad$ $G \leftarrow G(\Sigma'_{\text{UMDE}})$

$\quad$ **while** $E' := E \cap ((D \setminus \text{Const}) \times \text{Const}) \neq \emptyset$ **do**

$\quad\quad$ Const $\leftarrow$ Const $\cup \{x \mid \exists y : (x, y) \in E'\}$

$\quad$ **for all** $x, y \in$ Const, and $(x, y) \notin E$ **do** add (x, y) to E

Note that since constancy atoms can only be obtained from PIAs and UMDEs by applying the rules PIA3 or PIA & UMDE 1, for all $x \in D$, we have $\Sigma \models x \perp\!\!\!\perp x$ iff $x \in$ Const.

For $A \subseteq D$, denote by $\sigma(A)$, the restriction of a PIA σ to the variables in A. For example, if $\sigma := xyz \perp\!\!\!\perp uw$ and $A = \{x, y, u\}$, then $\sigma(A) = xy \perp\!\!\!\perp u$. Analogously, for set Σ of PIAs, we define $\Sigma(A) := \{\sigma(A) \mid \sigma \in \Sigma\}$. Consider then $\Sigma_{\text{PIA}}(D')$ and $\sigma(D')$ for $D' = D \setminus$ Const. We prove the following lemma:

Lemma 4. $\Sigma \models \sigma$ *if and only if* $\Sigma_{PIA}(D') \models \sigma(D')$.

Proof. By PIA3 and PIA5, it is clear that $\Sigma_{\text{PIA}}(D') \models \sigma(D')$ implies $\Sigma \models \sigma$.

Suppose that $\Sigma \models \sigma$. Note that for all $x \in D$ such that $\Sigma \models x \perp\!\!\!\perp x$, we have $x \in$ Const. Since PIAs interact with UMDEs only via constancy atoms, $\Sigma \models \sigma$ implies $\Sigma_{\text{PIA}} \cup \{x \perp\!\!\!\perp x \mid x \in \text{Const}\} \models \sigma$. Suppose then for a contradiction that $\Sigma_{\text{PIA}}(D') \not\models \sigma(D')$. Then there is a probabilistic team $\mathbb{X}$ over the variables D' such that $\mathbb{X} \models \Sigma_{\text{PIA}}(D')$, but $\mathbb{X} \not\models \sigma(D')$. Let Const $= \{y_1, \ldots, y_{|\text{Const}|}\}$. Consider then the probabilistic team $\mathbb{Y}: Y \to (0, 1]$ such that

$$Y := \{s \cup \{(y_1, 0), \ldots, (y_{|\text{Const}|}, 0)\} \mid s \in X\},$$

and $\mathbb{Y}(s \cup \{(y_1, 0), \ldots, (y_{|\text{Const}|}, 0)\}) = \mathbb{X}(s)$. Then clearly $\mathbb{Y}$ witnesses $\Sigma_{\text{PIA}} \cup \{x \perp\!\!\!\perp x \mid x \in \text{Const}\} \not\models \sigma$, and thus $\Sigma \models \sigma$ implies $\Sigma_{\text{PIA}}(D') \models \sigma(D')$, as wanted.

Now, we show how to use Const and G to decide whether $\Sigma \models \sigma$. Suppose that $\sigma := v \approx^* w$. Then it suffices to check whether w is reachable from v in G (by using a breadth-first search).

Suppose then that $\sigma := \bar{v} \perp\!\!\!\perp \bar{w}$. If $\text{var}(\bar{v}) \cap \text{var}(\bar{w}) \cap D' \neq \emptyset$, then $\Sigma \not\models \sigma$. Otherwise, by Lemma 4, it suffices to check whether $\Sigma_{\text{PIA}}(D') \models \sigma(D')$, which is now an instance of the implication problem for disjoint probabilistic independence that was shown to be in polynomial-time in [8]. This shows that the implication problem for PIAs+UMIs+UMDEs is in polynomial-time.

Let G be a graph and v and w two of its vertices. We write Reach(G, v, w) for the linear breadth-first search algorithm that outputs true if w is reachable from v in G and false otherwise. Algorithm 2 decides the implication problem for PIAs+UMIs+UMDEs.

Algorithm 2 PIA+UMI+UMDE-Implication(Σ, σ)

Require: Σ, σ
Ensure: true if and only if $\Sigma \models \sigma$
  if $\sigma = v \approx w$ **then return** Reach($G(\Sigma_{\text{UMI}}), v, w$)
  else
      construct Const and G using Comp(Σ)
      if $\sigma = v \approx^* w$ **then return** Reach(G, v, w)
      else if $\sigma = \bar{v} \perp \bar{w}$ **then**
         $D' \leftarrow D \setminus$ Const
         if var($\bar{v}$) $\cap$ var($\bar{w}$) $\cap D' \neq \emptyset$ **then return** false
         else
             return true if $\Sigma_{\text{PIA}}(D') \models \sigma(D')$ and false otherwise

---

6   Conclusion

We introduced a sound and complete finite axiomatization and a polynomial-time algorithm for the implication problem for probabilistic independence, unary marginal identity, and unary distribution equivalence. Since we saw that there is not much interaction between these three different kind of atoms, it would be interesting to extend the results to a larger set of atoms. The following questions are examples of some open questions related to this.

(i) Can we extend the axiomatization to nonunary marginal identity and marginal distribution equivalence?

(ii) Can we find an axiomatization for unary functional dependency, probabilistic independence, (unary) marginal identity and marginal distribution equivalence?

Implication problems for (disjoint) probabilistic independence and marginal identity have been axiomatized, respectively, in [8] and in [13]. In this paper, we have seen that when restricted to unary atoms, i.e. to the PIA+UMI+UMDE implication, the joint implication problem is quite simple, because the interaction between different atoms is characterized with three straightforward rules. The first question essentially asks what happens to the interaction if we drop the restriction to unary atoms.

Concerning the second question, note that the proof of undecidability of *conditional* independendence implication in [17] uses probabilistic independence and functional dependency in such a way that it follows that the implication problem for probabilistic independencies together with general functional dependencies is also undecidable. Therefore, we only want to consider unary functional dependencies. In the corresponding relational case, i.e., for unary functional dependency, independence (embedded multivalued dependence with an empty determining set) and unary inclusion, axiomatizations exists for both finite and unrestricted implication [12], so maybe we can also find an axiomatization in the probabilistic case.

Acknowledgments. The author was supported by grant 345634 of the Academy of Finland. I would like to thank the anonymous referees for valuable comments, and Miika Hannula, Matilda Häggblom, and Juha Kontinen for useful discussions and suggestions.

Disclosure of Interests. The author has no competing interests to declare that are relevant to the content of this article.

References

1. Armstrong, W.W.: Dependency structures of data base relationships. In: Proceedings of the IFIP World Computer Congress, pp. 580–583 (1974)
2. Beeri, C., Bernstein, P.A.: Computational problems related to the design of normal form relational schemas. ACM Trans. Database Syst. **4**(1), 30–59 (1979). https://doi.org/10.1145/320064.320066, http://doi.acm.org/10.1145/320064.320066
3. Casanova, M.A., Fagin, R., Papadimitriou, C.H.: Inclusion dependencies and their interaction with functional dependencies. J. Comput. Syst. Sci. **28**(1), 29–59 (1984)
4. Durand, A., Hannula, M., Kontinen, J., Meier, A., Virtema, J.: Approximation and dependence via multiteam semantics. Ann. Math. Artif. Intell. **83**(3–4), 297–320 (2018). https://doi.org/10.1007/s10472-017-9568-4
5. Durand, A., Hannula, M., Kontinen, J., Meier, A., Virtema, J.: Probabilistic team semantics. In: Foundations of Information and Knowledge Systems - 10th International Symposium, FoIKS 2018, Budapest, Hungary, 14–18 May 2018, Proceedings, pp. 186–206 (2018). https://doi.org/10.1007/978-3-319-90050-6_11
6. Galliani, P.: Game Values and Equilibria for Undetermined Sentences of Dependence Logic (2008). mSc Thesis. ILLC Publications, MoL-2008-08
7. Galliani, P.: Inclusion and exclusion dependencies in team semantics: on some logics of imperfect information. Ann. Pure Appl. Log. **163**(1), 68–84 (2012)
8. Geiger, D., Paz, A., Pearl, J.: Axioms and algorithms for inferences involving probabilistic independence. Inf. Comput. **91**(1), 128–141 (1991)
9. Grädel, E., Väänänen, J.: Dependence and independence. Stud. Log. **101**(2), 399–410 (2013). https://doi.org/10.1007/s11225-013-9479-2, http://dx.doi.org/10.1007/s11225-013-9479-2
10. Hannula, M.: Conditional independence on semiring relations (2023). arXiv:2310.01910 [cs.DB]
11. Hannula, M., Hirvonen, Å., Kontinen, J., Kulikov, V., Virtema, J.: Facets of distribution identities in probabilistic team semantics. In: Calimeri, F., Leone, N., Manna, M. (eds.) JELIA 2019. LNCS (LNAI), vol. 11468, pp. 304–320. Springer, Cham (2019). https://doi.org/10.1007/978-3-030-19570-0_20
12. Hannula, M., Link, S.: On the interaction of functional and inclusion dependencies with independence atoms. In: Pei, J., Manolopoulos, Y., Sadiq, S., Li, J. (eds.) DASFAA 2018. LNCS, vol. 10828, pp. 353–369. Springer, Cham (2018). https://doi.org/10.1007/978-3-319-91458-9_21
13. Hannula, M., Virtema, J.: Tractability frontiers in probabilistic team semantics and existential second-order logic over the reals. Ann. Pure Appl. Log. **173**(10), 103108 (2022). https://doi.org/10.1016/j.apal.2022.103108, https://www.sciencedirect.com/science/article/pii/S0168007222000239, logics of Dependence and Independence

14. Hirvonen, M.: The implication problem for functional dependencies and variants of marginal distribution equivalences. In: Varzinczak, I. (eds.) Foundations of Information and Knowledge Systems. FoIKS 2022. LNCS, pp. 130–146. Springer, Cham (2022). https://doi.org/10.1007/978-3-031-11321-5_8

15. Hodges, W.: Compositional semantics for a language of imperfect information. J. Interest Group Pure Appl. Log. 5(4), 539–563 (1997)

16. Hyttinen, T., Paolini, G., Väänänen, J.: A logic for arguing about probabilities in measure teams. Arch. Math. Log. 56(5–6), 475–489 (2017). https://doi.org/10.1007/s00153-017-0535-x

17. Li, C.T.: Undecidability of network coding, conditional information inequalities, and conditional independence implication. IEEE Trans. Inf. Theory 69(6), 3493–3510 (2023). https://doi.org/10.1109/TIT.2023.3247570

18. Väänänen, J.: Dependence Logic. Cambridge University Press, Cambridge (2007)

Logics and Semantics

A Complete Fragment of LTL(EB)

Flavio Ferrarotti[1](✉), Peter Rivière[2], Klaus-Dieter Schewe[2],
Neeraj Kumar Singh[2], and Yamine Aït Ameur[2]

[1] Software Competence Centre Hagenberg, Hagenberg, Austria
flavio.ferrarotti@scch.at
[2] Institut Nationale Polytechnique de Toulouse/ENSEEIHT, Toulouse, France
{peter.riviere,nsingh,yamine}@enseeiht.fr, kd.schewe@liwest.at

Abstract. The verification of liveness conditions is an important aspect of state-based rigorous methods. This article investigates this problem in a fragment □LTL of the logic LTL(EB), the integration of the UNTIL-fragment of Pnueli's linear time temporal logic (LTL) and the logic of Event-B, in which the most commonly used liveness conditions can be expressed. For this fragment a sound set of derivation rules is developed, which is also complete under mild restrictions for Event-B machines.

Keywords: Event-B · temporal logic · liveness · verification

1 Introduction

State-based consistency conditions such as state or transition invariants are included in rigorous state-based methods such as B [1], Abstract State Machines (ASMs) [6], TLA$^+$ [12] or Event-B [2], just to mention the most important ones. The verification of such conditions is well supported by appropriate logics such as the logics for Event-B [17], TLA$^+$ [14], deterministic ASMs [18] and arbitrary non-deterministic ASMs [9]. As the logics can be defined as definitional extensions of first-order logic with types, they are complete [19], which is a valuable asset for verification.

However, besides such consistency conditions other liveness conditions are likewise important. These conditions comprise (conditional) *progress*, i.e. any state satisfying a condition φ is always followed eventually (i.e. some time later) by a state satisfying ψ (for $\varphi = $ **true** we obtain unconditional progress also called *existence*), or *persistence*, i.e. eventually a condition φ will hold forever. Their verification requires the reasoning about complete runs of a specification, i.e. they are intrinsically connected to temporal logic [11]. Specific temporal logics

F. Ferrarotti—The research of Flavio Ferrarotti has been funded by the Federal Ministry for Climate Action, Environment, Energy, Mobility, Innovation and Technology (BMK), the Federal Ministry for Digital and Economic Affairs (BMDW), and the State of Upper Austria in the frame of the COMET Module Dependable Production Environments with Software Security (DEPS) within the COMET - Competence Centers for Excellent Technologies Programme managed by Austrian Research Promotion Agency FFG.

A. Meier and M. Ortiz (Eds.): FoIKS 2024, LNCS 14589, pp. 237–255, 2024.
https://doi.org/10.1007/978-3-031-56940-1_13

that have been used already for the verification of desirable liveness properties of sequential and concurrent (interleaved) systems are Linear-Time Temporal Logic (LTL) [15] and Computation Tree Logic (CTL) [7]. For many liveness conditions it suffices to consider only the UNTIL-fragment of LTL [13]. As these logics have been defined as temporal propositional logics, they require extensions when used in connection with any of the rigorous methods mentioned above.

Hoang and Abrial started to investigate the use of the UNTIL-fragment of LTL in connection with Event-B [10], and recently Rivière et al. provided a tool support using the EB4EB extension of RODIN [16]. Defining a logic that integrates LTL with the logic of Event-B is rather straightforward; instead of propositions consider formulae that can be defined for a given Event-B machine. In doing so, NEXT-formulae are already covered by the logic of Event-B, and hence the omission of the NEXT modal operator does no harm. Note that a similar argument is used for the logic of TLA$^+$ [14].

Naturally, with this integration we obtain a first-order modal logic, which cannot be complete. Nonetheless, Hoang and Abrial discovered a few derivation rules for invariance, existence, progress and persistence and proved their soundness, thus showing that if certain variant terms can be derived in an Event-B machine, such liveness properties can be verified. However, the question remains, if the derivation rules are also complete, at least for a well-defined fragment of LTL(EB).

Here we approach this problem defining a fragment □LTL of LTL(EB), for which we use the type of formulae in existence, progress and persistence conditions as defining constructors. Then we redo the soundness proofs from [10] with slight generalisations. We add a few standard derivation rules for modal formulae, and show that the set of all these derivation rules is also complete for the □LTL fragment. To be precise, all valid formulae are derivable, if appropriate variant terms can be defined in Event-B machines, a problem that was left open in [10], and the machines are tail-homogeneous, which means that the intrinsic non-determinism in Event-B is restricted. The tail-homogeneity restriction is necessary, as LTL is a linear time temporal logic and as such does not work well together with branching traces.

In order to show that such variant terms, which are needed for proofs of convergence or divergence properties, always exist, we use a streamlined version of Event-B, in which all sets used in an Event-B machine are defined as subsets of a single set HF(A) of hereditarily finite sets over a finite set A of atoms. In this case all values to which state variables can be bound, become hereditarily finite sets. This is similar to the special ASMs used in Choiceless Polynomial Time [4], and it is well known that this is no loss of generality, as sets can always be encoded in this way [3]. The advantage is that a few operators on HF(A) suffice to express all terms and consequently also all state formulae, which is exploited is the proof of the existence of variant terms in conservatively refined machines. That is, the logic □LTL is sound and complete for proofs on sufficiently refined, tail-homogeneous Event-B machines.

Organisation of the Paper. In Sect. 2 we first give a brief introduction to Event-B and to LTL, which give rise to the definition of the logic LTL(EB). As in [10] we highlight specific formulae for state transitions, deadlock-freeness, convergence and divergence. The former two of these are merely definitional extensions of first-order logic. For convergence and divergence, however, we need variant terms, so we will show that such terms always exist for sufficiently refined machines. For reason of space limitations full proofs have been outsourced to a report [8]. We continue in Sect. 3 with the definition of the □LTL fragment, the presentation of a set of derivation rules and the proofs of soundness and completeness for tail-homogeneous machines. The most common liveness properties can be expressed in the fragment. We conclude with a brief discussion of the value and limitations of the results in Sect. 4.

2   The Logic LTL(EB)

The logic LTL(EB) integrates the logic of Event-B into the UNTIL-fragment of LTL, which results in a first-order temporal logic. LTL(EB) formulae are interpreted over sequences of states, and thus can be used for stating and proving dynamic properties of computations of Event-B machines. We assume familiarity with the well-known Event-B method [2], and only recall some basic concepts fixing the notation needed in the remainder of this paper.

2.1   Event-B

Event-B is a state-based rigorous method. A *state* in Event-B is formed by a finite tuple of variables $\bar{v}$ taking values in certain sets with (explicitly or implicitly defined) auxiliary functions and predicates. The sets are usually specified in an Event-B *context*, but syntactical details are of no importance here.

Table 1 shows how an Event-B specification comprising a context and a machine looks like in general.

The basic schema views an Event-B *machine* (a.k.a. program or model) as offering a set of *events* E (operations), which are executed one at a time, i.e. only one event can be fired at any time point. Events are usually parameterised, where the parameters refer to externally provided input. This results in invariant-preserving state transitions. The firing of events is the only means for updating states.

For the sake of streamlining our proofs, however, we will adopt that all these sets are subsets of the set $\mathrm{HF}(A)$ of *hereditarily finite sets* over a finite set A of atoms. That is, if $\mathcal{P}$ denotes the powerset operator and we define inductively $\mathcal{P}^0(A) = A$ and $\mathcal{P}^{i+1}(A) = \mathcal{P}(\bigcup_{j \leq i} \mathcal{P}^j(A))$, then we have

$$\mathrm{HF}(A) = \bigcup_{i < \omega} \mathcal{P}^i(A) = A \cup \mathcal{P}(A) \cup \mathcal{P}(A \cup \mathcal{P}(A)) \cup \dots.$$

In particular, all values to which state variables in $\bar{v}$ can be bound are then hereditarily finte sets. It is well known that this is no loss of generality, as sets used in Event-B contexts can be encoded this way [3]. In particular, $\mathrm{HF}(A)$ contains a standard model of the set of natural numbers.

Then we use set operators $\in$, $\emptyset$, $Atoms$, $\bigcup$, $TheUnique$ and $Pair$. The predicate $\in$ and the constant symbol $\emptyset$ are interpreted in the obvious way, and $Atoms$ is interpreted by the set A of atoms. If $a_1, \ldots, a_k$ are atoms and $b_1, \ldots, b_\ell$ are sets, then $\bigcup\{a_1, \ldots, a_k, b_1, \ldots, b_\ell\} = b_1 \cup \cdots \cup b_\ell$. For $b = \{a\}$ we have $TheUnique(b) = a$, otherwise $TheUnique(b) = \emptyset$ denoting that it is undefined. Furthermore, we have $Pair(a, b) = \{a, b\}$. As shown in [4, Lemma 13] the usual set operations (union, intersection, difference) can be expressed by this term language.

Each $event$ $e_i \in E$ has the form **any** $\bar{x}$ **where** $G_i(\bar{x}, \bar{v})$ **then** $A_i(\bar{x}, \bar{v}, \bar{v}')$ **end**, where $\bar{x}$ are the $parameters$, the first-order formula $G_i(\bar{x}, \bar{v})$ is the $guard$ and $A_i(\bar{x}, \bar{v}, \bar{v}')$ is the $action$ of e_i.

An event e_i is $enabled$ in state S with state variables $\bar{v}$ as defined above, if there are values for its parameters $\bar{x}$ that make its guard $G_i(\bar{x}, \bar{v})$ hold in S. Otherwise, the event is $disabled$. If all events of a machine M are disabled in an state S, then M is said to be $deadlocked$ in S.

Table 1. Global structure of Event-B contexts and machines

Context	Machine
CONTEXT Ctx	**MACHINE** M
SETS s	**SEES** Ctx
CONSTANTS c	**VARIABLES** $\bar{v}$
AXIOMS A	**INVARIANTS** $I(\bar{v})$
THEOREMS T_{ctx}	**THEOREMS** $T_{mch}(\bar{v})$
END	**VARIANT** $V(\bar{v})$
	EVENTS
	EVENT e_i
	ANY $\bar{x}$
	WHERE $G_i(\bar{x}, \bar{v})$
	THEN
	$\bar{v} :\mid P_{A_i}(\bar{x}, \bar{v}, \bar{v}')$
	END
	...
	END
(a)	(b)

In general, an Event-B $action$ $A_i(\bar{x}, \bar{v}, \bar{v}')$ is a list of $assignments$ written in the form $v :\mid P(\bar{x}, \bar{v}, v')$, where v is a variable that occurs in the tuple $\bar{v}$ of state variables and P is a (so called) $before\text{-}after$ $predicate$ relating the value of v (before the action) and v' (after the action). The interpretation is that the value v' assigned to v is chosen non-deterministically[1] from the set of values v' that satisfy $P(\bar{x}, \bar{v}, v')$ for the given $\bar{v}$ and $\bar{x}$. Thus, each action $A_i(\bar{x}, \bar{v}, v')$ corresponds to a before-after predicate $P_{A_i}(\bar{x}, \bar{v}, \bar{v}')$ formed by the conjunction of all before-after predicates of the assignments in $A_i(x, \bar{v}, v')$. These predicates are defined using the language of set theory, i.e. first order logic with the binary relation-symbol $\in$. There are several dedicated notations for (typed) set operations such as set comprehension, cartesian product, etc. We do not discuss them here as

---

[1] It is commonly assumed that this choice is external, i.e. the values are provided by the environment and not by the machine itself.

they are definable in first-order logic and well known (for details see Abrial's monograph on Event-B [2]).

As shortcuts for this general form an action can also take assignments of the form $v := E(\bar{x}, \bar{v})$ and $v :\in E(\bar{x}, \bar{v})$, where $E(\bar{x}, \bar{v})$ is an expression. The assignment $v := E(\bar{x}, \bar{v})$ deterministically assigns the value of $E(\bar{x}, \bar{v})$ to v, i.e. it corresponds to the before-after predicate $v' = E(\bar{x}, \bar{v})$, while $v :\in E(\bar{x}, \bar{v})$ non-deterministically assigns an element of the set $E(\bar{x}, \bar{v})$ to v, i.e. it corresponds to the before-after predicate $v' \in E(\bar{x}, \bar{v})$.

The values of the variables in the initial state are set by means of an special event called *init* that has no parameters or guard. The values that variables $\bar{v}$ can take in a state are constrained by invariants $I(\bar{v})$. These invariants are to hold in every reachable state, which is achieved by proving that they are *established* by the initialisation event *init* and subsequently *preserved* by all other events.

In Event-B proof obligations are derived for all proofs. Table 2 shows the most important of these proof obligations.

Table 2. Relevant proof obligations for Event-B contexts and machines

(1)	Ctx Theorems (ThmCtx)	$A(s, c) \Rightarrow T_{ctx}$ (For contexts)
(2)	Mch Theorems (ThmMch)	$A(s, c) \wedge I(\bar{v}) \Rightarrow T_{mch}(\bar{v})$ (For machines)
(3)	Initialisation (Init)	$A(s, c) \wedge P_{A_i}(\bar{v}') \Rightarrow I(\bar{v}')$
(4)	Invariant preservation (Inv)	$A(s, c) \wedge I(\bar{v}) \wedge G(\bar{x}, \bar{v}) \wedge P_{A_i}(\bar{x}, \bar{v}, \bar{v}') \Rightarrow I(\bar{v}')$
(5)	Event feasibility (Fis)	$A(s, c) \wedge I(\bar{v}) \wedge G(\bar{x}, \bar{v}) \Rightarrow \exists \bar{v}' \cdot P_{A_i}(\bar{x}, \bar{v}, \bar{v}')$
(6)	Variant progress (Var)	$A(s, c) \wedge I(\bar{v}) \wedge G(\bar{x}, \bar{v}) \wedge P_{A_i}(\bar{x}, \bar{v}, \bar{v}') \Rightarrow V(\bar{v}') < V(\bar{v})$

Given an event e, we say that a state S' is an e-successor state of S, if S' is a possible after-state of the firing of e from the before-state S. Lifting the definition to a machine M, we say that S' is an M-successor state of S if there exists an event e of M such that S' is an e-successor of S.

Event-B defines a *computation* τ (or *trace* in Event-B terminology) of a machine M as a (possible infinite) sequence of states $S_0, S_1, S_2, \ldots$ such that S_0 is an initial state satisfying the after predicate defined by the event *init*, and for every pair of consecutive states S_i, S_{i+1} in τ, there is an event e such that S_{i+1} is an e-successor state of S_i. If the computation τ ends in an state S_n, i.e. the computation terminates, then M must be deadlocked in S_n.

Note that in general for a machine M and an initial state S_0 there exist multiple traces. This includes the possibility that infinite and finite traces occur together. As this is inconvenient for the proof of liveness properties, we introduce an additional event *ext*, by means of which all traces become infinite. The guard of *ext* is $\bigwedge_{e_i \in E} \forall \bar{x} \neg G_i(\bar{x}, \bar{v})$, so the event *ext* is enabled iff no other event $e_i \in E$ is enabled. The action of *ext* is given by a list of assignments $v : |v' = v$ for all variables v in $\bar{v}$, so a firing of *ext* does not change the state. That is, all infinite traces remain unchanged, and all finite traces are infinitely extended by repeating the final state. We call a machine $\tilde{M}$ that extends M by such an event *ext* the *trivial extension* of M.

Given a machine M we immediately obtain a language $\mathcal{L}$ of *state formulae* of M. If the state variables of M are $\bar{v}$, then the set of basic well formed formulae of $\mathcal{L}$ is formed by the set of first-order logic formulae over some signature τ with all free variables among those in $\bar{v}$. Such formulae are interpreted in any state S of M, where the value of the free (state) variables is interpreted by the value of these variables in S.

For any state formula φ we can also define the first-order formula

$$\mathcal{N}\varphi(\bar{v}) \equiv \bigwedge_{e_i \in E} \forall \bar{x} \Big(G_i(\bar{x}, \bar{v}) \rightarrow \forall \bar{v}'(P_{A_i}(\bar{x}, \bar{v}, \bar{v}') \rightarrow \varphi(\bar{v}')) \Big).$$

The formula $\mathcal{N}\varphi$ holds in a state S, if the formula φ holds in all M-successor states of S.

2.2 Linear Time Temporal Logic

Linear time temporal logic (LTL) is a well known propositional temporal logic with modal operators referring to time [15]. This logic has been used for the formal verification of computer programs for a long time [13]; only a fragment suffices to express the most important liveness conditions. Thus formulae are built from propositions, the usual Boolean operators $\neg, \wedge, \vee, \rightarrow$, and modal operators. There are different ways to define the basic modal operators of LTL; we will use only the three constructors $\square$ (always), $\Diamond$ (eventually, i.e. sometimes in the future), and $\mathcal{U}$ (until) [13].

Here we use state formulae of an Event-B machine instead of propositions, which defines the logic LTL(EB). Then the set of *well-formed formula* of LTL(EB) is defined as the closure of the set $\mathcal{L}$ of basic state formulae under the usual Boolean operators $\neg, \wedge, \vee, \rightarrow$ and modal operators $\square$ (always), $\Diamond$ (eventually) and $\mathcal{U}$ (until). Note that $\Diamond \varphi$ is merely a shortcut for $\mathbf{true}\,\mathcal{U}\,\varphi$, and $\square \varphi$ is a shortcut for $\neg\Diamond\neg\varphi$, as can be easily proven from the semantics we define below. As we saw above, the absence of the LTL modal operator $\mathcal{N}$ (next) does not matter, as conditions that are to hold in successor states are already covered by the first-order logic of Event-B.

LTL(EB) formulae are interpreted over traces of Event-B machines, which we now define formally. Let σ be a non-empty sequence of states $S_0, S_1, \ldots$. Let $\ell(\sigma) = n$ if the sequence σ is finite and has length n, and $\ell(\sigma) = \omega$ if it is infinite. Let $\sigma^{(k)}$ for $0 \leq k \leq \ell(\sigma)$ denote the sequence $S_k, S_{k+1}, \ldots$ obtained from σ by removing its first k elements. An LTL(EB) formula φ is satisfied by a sequence of states σ with state variables $\bar{v}$, denoted $\sigma \models \varphi$, iff the following holds:

- If $\varphi \in \mathcal{L}$, i.e. if φ is a first-order formula with all its free variables in $\bar{v}$, then $\sigma \models \varphi$ iff the values assigned by the first state S_0 of σ to the variables $\bar{v}$ satisfies φ.
- If φ is of the form $\neg\psi$, $\psi \wedge \chi$, $\psi \vee \chi$ or $\psi \rightarrow \chi$, where ψ and χ are well-formed LTL(EB) formulae, then $\sigma \models \varphi$ iff $\sigma \not\models \psi$, $\sigma \models \psi$ and $\sigma \models \chi$, $\sigma \models \psi$ or $\sigma \models \chi$, or $\sigma \models \chi$ whenever $\sigma \models \psi$, respectively.

- If φ is of the form $\Box\psi$, then $\sigma \models \varphi$ iff for all $0 \leq k \leq \ell(\sigma)$ it holds that $\sigma^{(k)} \models \psi$. That is, $\sigma \models \Box\psi$ iff all states of σ satisfy ψ.
- If φ is of the form $\Diamond\psi$, then $\sigma \models \varphi$ iff there is a $0 \leq k \leq \ell(\sigma)$ such that $\sigma^{(k)} \models \psi$. That is, $\sigma \models \Diamond\psi$ iff some state of σ satisfies ψ.
- If φ is of the form $\psi\,\mathcal{U}\,\chi$, then $\sigma \models \varphi$ iff there is a $0 \leq k \leq \ell(\sigma)$ such that $\sigma^{(k)} \models \chi$ and for all $0 \leq i < k$ it holds that $\sigma^{(i)} \models \psi$. That is, $\sigma \models \psi\,\mathcal{U}\,\chi$ iff some state S_k satisfies χ and all states in the sequence σ until S_k (where S_k is not included) satisfy ψ[2].

For an Event-B machine M with state variables $\bar{v}$ let φ be an LTL(EB) formulae such that a variable v_i is free in φ iff v_i appears in $\bar{v}$. We say that M *satisfies* property φ (denoted as $M \models \varphi$) iff all possible traces of M satisfy φ.

2.3 Variant Formulae

Our aim is to develop a proof system for LTL(EB) based on the derivation rules in [10] for reasoning about liveness properties in Event-B. The models in this proof system correspond to sequences of Event-B states. Thus, a sequence of Event-B states σ is a *model* of an LTL(EB) formula φ iff $\sigma \models \varphi$ holds. If Ψ is a set of formulae, then σ models Ψ (denoted as $\sigma \models \Psi$) iff $\sigma \models \varphi$ holds for every $\varphi \in \Psi$. A formula φ is a *logical consequence* of a set of formulae Ψ (denoted as $\Psi \models \varphi$) iff for all sequences of Event-B states σ whenever $\sigma \models \Psi$ holds, then also $\sigma \models \varphi$.

Let $\mathfrak{R}$ be a set of axioms and inference rules. A formula φ is *derivable* from a set Ψ of formulae using $\mathfrak{R}$ (denoted as $\Psi \vdash_{\mathfrak{R}} \varphi$, or simply $\Psi \vdash \varphi$ when $\mathfrak{R}$ is clear from the context) iff there is a deduction from formulae in Ψ to φ that only applies axioms and inference rules from $\mathfrak{R}$.

The notion of *validity* applies to a given Event-B machine M as explained in this section. That is, a formula φ is *valid for* M (denoted as $M \models \varphi$) iff $\sigma \models \varphi$ holds for all computations σ of M. If $M \models \varphi$ can be derived from a set of axioms and inference rules $\mathfrak{R}$, then we write $M \vdash_{\mathfrak{R}} \varphi$.

Before we recall and extend the LTL(EB) proof rules from [10], we define certain common LTL(EB) formulae used in those rules. For this let M be an Event-B machine with a set E of events and state variables $\bar{v}$. For each $e_i \in E$, let $G_i(\bar{x}, \bar{v})$ and $P_{A_i}(\bar{x}, \bar{v}, \bar{v}')$ denote the guard and the before-after predicate corresponding to the action $A_i(\bar{x}, \bar{v}, \bar{v}')$ of event e_i, respectively.

For state formulae φ_1 and φ_2 we say that M *leads from* φ_1 to φ_2 iff the following sentence holds:

$$\text{leadsto}(\varphi_1, \varphi_2) \equiv \bigwedge_{e_i \in E} \forall \bar{v}\bar{x}\bar{v}' \Big(\varphi_1(\bar{v}) \wedge G_i(\bar{x}, \bar{v}) \wedge P_{A_i}(\bar{x}, \bar{v}, \bar{v}') \rightarrow \varphi_2(\bar{v}')\Big).$$

---

[2] Note that this is a strong interpretation of until-formulae, as it includes that χ eventually holds. If this requirement is dropped, i.e. we allow ψ to hold forever, we obtain a weak notion of until-formulae, usually denoted as $\psi\,\mathcal{W}\,\chi$.

It implies that for every computation σ of M and every $0 \leq k \leq \ell(\sigma)$, it holds that whenever $\sigma^{(k)} \models \varphi_1$ then $\sigma^{(k+1)} \models \varphi_2$. We therefore call such formulae *state transition formulae*.

For a state formula φ we say that M *is deadlock-free in* φ iff following sentence is satisfied:

$$\mathrm{dlf}(\varphi) \equiv \forall \bar{v}\Big(\varphi(\bar{v}) \rightarrow \exists \bar{x}\big(\bigvee_{e_i \in E} G_i(\bar{x}, \bar{v})\big)\Big).$$

It expresses that whenever a state satisfies φ, there is at least one event e_i of M that is enabled. In particular, $\sigma^{\ell(\sigma)} \models \neg\varphi$ holds for every finite computation σ of M.

State transition formulae leadsto(φ_1, φ_2) and deadlock-freeness formulae dlf(φ) express properties of traces of an Event-B machine, but nonetheless they are defined in first-order logic. As first-order logic is complete, such formulae are derivable using a standard set of derivation rules for first-order logic. This also holds for the logic of Event-B, which is first-order with types.

This will no longer be the case for convergence and divergence formulae conv(φ) and div(φ), respectively, which we define next.

For a state formula φ we say that M *is convergent in* φ iff for every computation σ of M there is no k such that $\sigma^{(\ell)} \models \varphi$ holds for all $\ell \geq k$. Note that if a machine M satisfies conv(φ), then its trivial extension $\tilde{M}$ also satisfies conv(φ) and vice versa. Hoang and Abrial showed that conv(φ) can be derived by means of *variant* terms [10, p. 460]. As we adopted that all values are hereditarily finite sets in HF(A), we can exploit a canonical partial order $\leq$ on HF(A), defined by $x \leq y$ iff TC$(x) \subseteq$ TC(y), where TC(x) denotes the transitive closure of x. This order is well-founded with $\emptyset$ as the smallest element, and it subsumes set inclusion $\subseteq$ as well as the reflexive, transitive closure of the membership relation $\in$.

Suppose that $t(\bar{v})$ is a well-formed term called *variant* and var$_c(t, \varphi)$ denotes the formula

$$\bigwedge_{e_i \in E} \forall \bar{v}\bar{x}\bar{v}'\Big(\varphi(\bar{v}) \wedge G_i(\bar{x}, \bar{v}) \rightarrow \big(t(\bar{v}) \neq \emptyset \wedge (P_{A_i}(\bar{x}, \bar{v}, \bar{v}') \rightarrow t(\bar{v}') < t(\bar{v}))\big)\Big).$$

That is, a state S satisfies var$_c(t, \varphi)$ iff whenever φ holds and an event e_i is enabled, we have that $t(\bar{v})$ evaluates to a non-empty set, and an execution of e_i decreases $t(\bar{v})$. Hoang and Abrial showed the following:

Lemma 1. *If* var$_c(t, \varphi)$ *is a valid formula and no trace of M terminates in a state satisfying φ, then M is convergent in φ, in other words, the derivation rule*

$$\text{CONV:} \quad \frac{M \vdash var_c(t, \varphi) \quad M \vdash \mathrm{dlf}(\varphi)}{M \vdash \mathrm{conv}(\varphi)}$$

is sound.

Proof. If $M \models \mathrm{dlf}(\varphi)$ holds, then every finite trace of M terminates in a state satisfying $\neg\varphi$. If $M \models$ var$_c(t, \varphi)$, but $M \not\models$ conv(φ), then by the definitions of conv(φ) and var$_c(t, \varphi)$ there is an infinite subsequence $S_i, S_{i+1}, \ldots$ of states of some trace σ of M such that for the values b_j of $t(\bar{v})$ in S_j we have $b_i > b_{i+1} > \ldots$. As the order $\leq$ on HF(A) is well-founded, this is not possible. $\qquad\square$

Analogously, for a state formula φ we say that M *is divergent in* φ iff for every infinite computation σ of M there is a k such that $\sigma^{(k')} \models \varphi$ for every $k' \geq k$. Note that if $\tilde{M} \models \text{div}(\varphi)$ holds for the trivial extension, then also $M \models \text{div}(\varphi)$ holds, but the converse is false in general. However, if $M \models \text{div}(\varphi)$ holds and all finite traces terminate in a state satisfying φ, then also $\tilde{M} \models \text{div}(\varphi)$ follows.

Hoang and Abrial also showed that $\text{div}(\varphi)$ can be derived by means of *variant* terms [10, p. 460]. For this suppose that $t(\bar{v})$ is a well-formed term called *variant* and let $\text{var}_d(t, \varphi)$ denote the formula

$$\bigwedge_{e_i \in E} \forall \bar{v}\bar{x}\bar{v}' \Big(\neg\varphi(\bar{v}) \wedge G_i(\bar{x}, \bar{v}) \rightarrow \big(t(\bar{v}) \neq \emptyset \wedge (P_{A_i}(\bar{x}, \bar{v}, \bar{v}') \rightarrow t(\bar{v}') < t(\bar{v})) \big) \Big)$$

$$\wedge \Big(\varphi(\bar{v}) \wedge G_i(\bar{x}, \bar{v}) \wedge P_{A_i}(\bar{x}, \bar{v}, \bar{v}') \rightarrow t(\bar{v}') \leq t(\bar{v}) \big) \Big).$$

That is, a state S satisfies $\text{var}_d(t, \varphi)$ iff whenever $\neg\varphi$ holds and an event e_i is enabled, we have that $t(\bar{v})$ evaluates to a non-empty set, and an execution of e_i decreases $t(\bar{v})$, and whenever φ holds and an event e_i is enabled, we have that an execution of e_i does not increase $t(\bar{v})$.

Lemma 2. *If* $\text{var}_d(t, \varphi)$ *is a valid formula, then* M *is divergent in* φ, *in other words, the derivation rule*

$$\text{DIV:} \qquad \frac{M \vdash \text{var}_d(t, \varphi)}{M \vdash \text{div}(\varphi)}$$

is sound.

Proof. If $M \models \text{var}_d(t, \varphi)$, but $M \not\models \text{div}(\varphi)$, then by the definition of $\text{div}(\varphi)$ there is an infinite trace $\sigma = S_0, S_1, \ldots$ of M such that for all i there is some $k_i \geq i$ with $S_{k_i} \models \neg\varphi$. Let b_j be the value of $t(\bar{v})$ in S_j. Then by the definition of $\text{var}_d(t, \varphi)$ we have $b_i \geq b_{i+1}$ and $b_{k_i} > b_\ell$ for all i and all $\ell > k_i$. As the order $\leq$ on HF(A) is well-founded, this is not possible. $\qquad\square$

We call the first-order formulae $\text{var}_c(t, \varphi)$ and $\text{var}_d(t, \varphi)$ *variant formulae*. Then the derivation rules CONV and DIV allow us to reduce proofs of convergence and divergence properties to proofs of formulae in first-order logic, if we can find appropriate variant terms. We will show that this is always possible. Let $\text{var}_c(M, t, \varphi)$ and $\text{var}_d(M, t, \varphi)$ denote the formulae obtained from the sentences $\text{var}_c(t, \varphi)$ and $\text{var}_d(t, \varphi)$, respectively, by making $\bar{v}$ and $\bar{v}'$ quantifier-free. The M in this notation makes it explicit that the set of events E is taken from the event-B machine M.

Lemma 3. *Let* M *be an Event-B machine with state variables* $\bar{v} = (v_0, \ldots, v_m)$ *satisfying a convergence property* $\text{conv}(\varphi)$. *Then there exists an Event-B machine* M' *with state variables* $\bar{v}' = (\bar{v}, \bar{w}, l, s, u)$, *where* $\bar{v}$, $\bar{w} = (w_0, \ldots, w_m)$, l, s *and* u *are pairwise different variables, and a term* $t(\bar{v}, \bar{w}, l, s, u)$ *such that:*

(i) The formulae $var_c(M, t, \varphi)$ is valid for M'.

(ii) For each computation σ of M there exists a computation σ' of M' with $\sigma = \sigma'|_{s=1,\bar{v}}$ and vice versa, where $\sigma'|_{s=1,\bar{v}}$ is the sequence of states resulting from the selection of those with $s = 1$ and projection to the state variables $\bar{v}$.

A full proof is given in [8]. The key idea of the proof is sketched as follows. The machine M' uses a copy $\bar{w}$ of the state variables, and events are first executed on them. Furthermore, M' uses a status variable s. As long as the machine M' is in a state satisfying φ and $s = 0$ holds, the tuple $\bar{w}$ is added to a list l. In case of a state satisfying $\neg \varphi$ the machine will switch to status $s = 1$. As there can only be finite subsequences of states satisfying φ, such a status switch will occur, unless the machine runs into a deadlock. When the status $s = 1$ is reached, the collected tuples in the list ℓ will be one-by-one copied to the original state variables $\bar{v}$, until finally the machine switches back to status $s = 0$. In this way all firing of events are first executed on a copy $\bar{w}$, and the length of the list l defines the desired variant term, which is reset by each status switch from $s = 0$ to $s = 1$. In addition, a few subtle cases concerning deadlocks need to be considered separately, for which another status variable u is used.

Lemma 4. Let M be an Event-B machine with state variables $\bar{v} = (v_0, ..., v_m)$ satisfying a divergence property $div(\varphi)$. Then there exists an Event-B machine M' with state variables $\bar{v}' = (\bar{v}, \bar{c}, \bar{b})$, where $\bar{c} = (c_0, \ldots, c_m)$, $\bar{b} = (b_0, \ldots, b_m)$ and $\bar{v}$ are pairwise different variables, and a term $t(\bar{v}, \bar{c}, \bar{b})$ such that:

(i) The formulae $var_d(M', t, \varphi)$ is valid for M';

(ii) For each computation σ of M there exists a computation σ' of M' with $\sigma = \sigma'|_{\bar{v}}$ and vice versa, where $\sigma'|_{\bar{v}}$ is the sequence of states resulting from the projection to the state variables $\bar{v}$.

A full proof is given in [8]. The key idea of the proof is sketched as follows. In M' for each state variable v_i we add a state variable c_i, which we initialise as $\emptyset$, and into which a new value v' is inserted, whenever the machine makes a step in a state satisfying $\neg \varphi$. Then the tuple $(c_0, \ldots, c_m)$ is a monotone increasing sequence of tuples of sets, which are represented in $HF(A)$ using the common Kuratowsky encoding. As in every trace there are only finitely many states satisfying $\neg \varphi$, there exists a maximum tuple that will never be exceeded. In M' we initialise $(b_0, \ldots, b_m)$ by these maximum set values, and never update these state variables. As the order $\leq$ on $HF(A)$ subsumes set inclusion, we can see that $\#(b_0, \ldots, b_m) - \#(c_0, \ldots, c_m)$ defines the desired variant term.

Lemmata 3 and 4 imply that adding the derivation rules CONV and DIV to a sound and complete set of derivation rules for first-order logic yields a sound and complete set of derivation rules for the derivation of convergence and divergence formulae, provided that the Event-B machines are conservatively extended to guarantee the existence of the required variants. Of course, for a proof of a convergence or divergence property the appropriate variant must be defined; the lemmata above only guarantee that this is always possible.

Note that the extensions exploited in the lemmata above are indeed $(1, n)$-refinements. We therefore say that an Event-B machine M is *sufficiently refined* with respect to a finite set $\Phi \subseteq \mathcal{L}$ of state formulae iff for every $\varphi \in \Phi$ there exist terms t_c and t_d such that the variant formulae $\text{var}_c(t_c, \varphi)$ and $\text{var}_d(t_d, \varphi)$ are valid for M. We summarise this result in the following theorem.

Theorem 5. *Let $\mathfrak{R}$ be a sound and complete set of derivation rules for first-order logic with types. Then $\mathfrak{R} \cup \{\text{CONV}, \text{DIV}\}$ is a sound and complete set of derivation rules for the proof of transition, convergence, divergence and deadlock-freeness formulae* $\text{leadsto}(\varphi_1, \varphi_2)$, $\text{conv}(\varphi)$, $\text{div}(\varphi)$ *and* $\text{dlf}(\varphi)$ *for Event-B machines that are sufficiently refined with respect to* $\{\varphi\}$.

3   The □LTL Fragment

We now investigate a fragment of LTL(EB), in which selected liveness conditions can be expressed. Of particular interest are the following conditions:

Invariance. An *invariance condition* is given by an LTL(EB) formula of the form $\Box \varphi$ for some state formula φ. Such a condition is satisfied by a machine M iff all states S in all traces of M satisfy φ.

Existence. An *existence condition*—we also call it an *unconditional progress condition*—is given by an LTL(EB) formula of the form $\Box \Diamond \varphi$ for some state formula φ. Such a condition is satisfied by a machine M iff in every infinite trace of M there is an infinite subsequence of states satisfying φ, and every finite trace of M terminates in a state satisfying φ.

Progress. A *progress condition*—to emphasise the difference to existence conditions we also call it a *conditional progress condition*—is given by an LTL(EB) formula of the form $\Box(\varphi \to \Diamond \psi)$ for some state formula φ. Such a condition is satisfied by a machine M iff in every trace of M a state S_i satisfying φ is followed some time later by a state S_j $(j \geq i)$ satisfying ψ. A progress condition with $\varphi = \mathbf{true}$ degenerates to an existence condition.

Persistence. A *persistence condition* is given by an LTL(EB) formula of the form $\Diamond \Box \varphi$ for some state formula φ. Such a condition is satisfied by a machine M iff every infinite trace of M ends with an infinite sequence of states satisfying φ, i.e. for some k we have $S_i \models \varphi$ for all $i \geq k$, and every finite trace of M terminates in a state satisfying φ.

It therefore makes sense to define the sought fragment of LTL(EB) as the closure of the set $\mathcal{L}$ of state formulae under a more restrictive set of constructors, which basically have the form of the formulae above. We denote this fragment as □LTL. The set of well-formed formulae (wff) of □LTL is inductively defined by the following rules:

- If $\varphi \in \mathcal{L}$, then φ is a □LTL wff.
- If φ is a □LTL wff, then $\Box \varphi$, $\Box \Diamond \varphi$ and $\Diamond \Box \varphi$ are □LTL wff.
- If φ is a state formula and ψ is a □LTL wff, then $\Box(\varphi \to \Diamond \psi)$ is a □LTL wff.
- Nothing else is a □LTL wff.

In the remainder of this section we will present a sound set of derivation rules for □LTL, which modify and extend the derivation rules discovered by Hoang and Abrial [10]. We want to show that together with derivation rules for first-order logic with types and the rules CONV and DIV from the previous section we obtain a complete set of derivation rules.

However, LTL as a linear time logic is well suited for linear traces, whereas Event-B machines in general are non-deterministic and yield multiple traces with the same start state. This makes it rather unlikely that we could show completeness. Therefore, we restrict the Event-B machines under consideration.

We say that a machine M is *tail-homogeneous* for a state formula φ iff $\tilde{M} \models \mathrm{conv}(\neg\varphi)$ or $\tilde{M} \models \mathrm{div}(\neg\varphi)$ holds. M is called *tail-homogeneous* for set Φ of state formulae iff it is tail-homogeneous for all $\varphi \in \Phi$.

3.1 Sound Derivation Rules

For invariance conditions we can exploit a simple induction principle. In order to establish invariance of a state formula φ it suffices to show that φ holds in the initial state, and furthermore that for every $1 \leq k < \ell(\sigma)$ whenever $\sigma^{(k)} \models \varphi$ holds, then also $\sigma^{(k+1)} \models \varphi$ holds. In addition, invariance of a state formula φ implies invariance of a weaker state formula ψ. This gives rise to the following lemma.

Lemma 6. *For state formulae $\varphi, \psi \in \mathcal{L}$ the derivation rules*

$$\mathrm{INV}_1: \frac{\vdash \psi_{init} \to \varphi \quad M \vdash \mathrm{leadsto}(\varphi, \varphi)}{M \vdash \Box\varphi} \qquad \mathrm{INV}_2: \frac{\vdash \varphi \to \psi \quad M \vdash \Box\varphi}{M \vdash \Box\psi}$$

are sound for the derivation of invariance properties in □LTL.

For existence conditions we must have that finite traces terminate in a state satisfying φ, which is the case if $\mathrm{dlf}(\neg\varphi)$ holds. For infinite traces we must have infinite subsequences of states satisfying φ, which by definition is the case, if $\mathrm{conv}(\neg\varphi)$ holds. This establishes the following lemma, which was proven in [10, p. 462].

Lemma 7. *For a state formula $\varphi \in \mathcal{L}$ the derivation rule*

$$\mathrm{LIVE}: \frac{M \vdash \mathrm{conv}(\neg\varphi)}{M \vdash \Box\Diamond\varphi}$$

is sound for the derivation of existence properties in □LTL.

For (conditional) progress conditions Hoang and Abrial also showed the soundness of two derivation rules. However, these rules contain arbitrary UNTIL-formulae and thus refer to LTL(EB), but not to the fragment □LTL. Therefore, we need to combine the rules into a single derivation rule, which is further generalised.

Lemma 8. *For state formulae $\varphi_1, \varphi_2, \varphi_3 \in \mathcal{L}$ the derivation rule PROG defined as*

$$\frac{M \vdash \mathrm{div}(\neg\varphi_3) \quad M \vdash \mathrm{leadsto}(\varphi_3 \wedge \neg\varphi_2, \varphi_3 \vee \varphi_2) \quad M \vdash \Box(\varphi_1 \wedge \neg\varphi_2 \to \varphi_3)}{M \vdash \Box(\varphi_1 \to \Diamond\varphi_2)}$$

is sound for the derivation of progress properties in $\Box LTL$.

Proof. Let σ be an arbitrary trace of M, and consider k with $\sigma^{(k)} \models \varphi_1$. If also $\sigma^{(k)} \models \varphi_2$ holds, we get $\sigma^{(k)} \models \varphi_1 \to \Diamond\varphi_2$ by definition.

Otherwise, for $\sigma^{(k)} \models \neg\varphi_2$ the third antecedent of the PROG rule implies $\sigma^{(k)} \models \varphi_3$. The first antecedent of the rule implies that there exists some m such that $\sigma^{(m')} \models \neg\varphi_3$ holds for all $m' \geq m$.

Let m be minimal with this property, in particular $m > k$. Then the second antecedent of the rule implies that there exists some $\ell < m$ such that $\sigma^{(\ell')} \models \varphi_3 \wedge \neg\varphi_2$ holds for all $k \leq \ell' \leq \ell$. If we take ℓ maximal with this property, we must have that $\sigma^{(\ell)} \models \varphi_2$ holds by the definition of transition formulae. This shows again $\sigma^{(k)} \models \varphi_1 \to \Diamond\varphi_2$, hence $M \models \Box(\varphi_1 \to \Diamond\varphi_2)$ as claimed. □

For persistence conditions we must have that finite traces terminate in a state satisfying φ, which is the case if $\mathrm{dlf}(\neg\varphi)$ holds. Infinite traces must end with an infinite sequence of states satisfying φ, which by definition is the case, if $\mathrm{div}(\varphi)$ holds. This establishes the following lemma, which was proven in [10, p. 464]. Note that the antecedent $\mathrm{dlf}(\neg\varphi)$ can be dropped, if all traces of M are infinite, which is the case for trivial extensions.

Lemma 9. *For a state formula $\varphi \in \mathcal{L}$ the derivation rule*

$$\text{PERS:} \quad \frac{M \vdash \mathrm{div}(\varphi) \qquad M \vdash \mathrm{dlf}(\neg\varphi)}{M \vdash \Diamond\Box\varphi}$$

is sound for the derivation of persistence properties in $\Box LTL$.

The sound derivation rules INV_1, INV_2, LIVE, PROG and PERS in Lemmata 6–9 are restricted to state formulae. In order to be able to derive arbitrary $\Box LTL$ formulae further derivation rules are needed. The sound derivation rules in the following lemma are well known for LTL, and proofs follow easily from the definitions.

Lemma 10. *The following derivation rules are sound for the derivation of formulae in $\Box LTL$:*

$$\Box:\quad \frac{M \vdash \Box\varphi}{M \vdash \Box\Box\varphi} \qquad\qquad \Diamond\Box_1:\quad \frac{M \vdash \Diamond\Box\varphi}{M \vdash \Diamond\Box\Box\varphi}$$

$$\Box\mathrm{v}:\quad \frac{M \vdash \Box\neg\varphi}{M \vdash \Box(\varphi \to \Diamond\psi)}\ \textit{for } \varphi \in \mathcal{L} \qquad \Diamond\Box_2:\quad \frac{M \vdash \Box(\varphi_1 \to \Diamond\varphi_2)}{M \vdash \Diamond\Box\Box(\varphi_1 \to \Diamond\varphi_2)}$$

$$\Box\Diamond_1:\quad \frac{M \vdash \Box\Diamond\varphi_2}{M \vdash \Box(\varphi_1 \to \Diamond\varphi_2)}$$

$$\Diamond\Box_3:\quad \frac{M \vdash \Diamond\Box\varphi}{M \vdash \Diamond\Box\Diamond\Box\varphi}$$

$$\Box\Diamond_2:\quad \frac{M \vdash \Diamond\Box\varphi}{M \vdash \Box\Diamond\Box\varphi}$$

$$\mathrm{EXT}:\quad \frac{\tilde{M} \vdash \varphi}{M \vdash \varphi}$$

$$\Box\Diamond_3:\quad \frac{M \vdash \Box(\varphi_1 \to \Diamond\varphi_2)}{M \vdash \Box\Diamond\Box(\varphi_1 \to \Diamond\varphi_2)}$$

The last derivation rule EXT is based on the fact that invariance, existence, progress and persistence conditions hold for a machine M iff they hold for its trivial extension $\tilde{M}$.

3.2   Completeness

Taking all our lemmata together we obtain a sound system of derivation rules for $\Box$LTL formula, which comprises a sound and complete set of derivation rules $\mathfrak{R}$ for first-order logic with types, the derivation rules CONV, DIV for convergence and divergence, the derivation rules INV_1, INV_2, LIVE, PROG and PERS for invariance, existence, progress and persistence, and the auxiliary derivation rules for modal formulae in Lemma 10. In the following we denote this set of derivation rules as $\mathfrak{R}_{\Box\mathrm{LTL}}$. We will now show that $\mathfrak{R}_{\Box\mathrm{LTL}}$ is also complete in the sense that $M \models \varphi$ implies $M \vdash_{\mathfrak{R}_{\Box\mathrm{LTL}}}$ for machines that are tail-homogeneous with respect to all state formulae appearing in φ.

Theorem 11. *The system $\mathfrak{R}_{\Box LTL}$ of derivation rules is sound and complete for $\Box LTL$ on Event-B machines M that are sufficiently refined and tail-homogeneous with respect to the set Φ of state formulae appearing as subformulae of the formulae in $\Box LTL$ to be proven as well as their negations.*

In the proof we omit some easier cases. A full proof is given in [8].

Proof. We only need to show the completeness. For this assume that $M \models \varphi$ holds for $\varphi \in \Box$LTL, hance also $\tilde{M} \models \varphi$. We use induction over the nesting depth of modal operators in φ to show that $M \vdash_{\mathfrak{R}_{\Box\mathrm{LTL}}} \varphi$ holds. In the following let σ always be an arbitrary trace of $\tilde{M}$.

For $\varphi \in \mathcal{L}$, transition formulae $\varphi = \mathrm{leadsto}(\psi, \chi)$, convergence formulae $\varphi = \mathrm{conv}(\psi)$, divergence formulae $\varphi = \mathrm{div}(\psi)$ and deadlock-freeness formulae $\varphi = \mathrm{dlf}(\psi)$ we immediately get $M \vdash_{\mathfrak{R}_{\Box\mathrm{LTL}}} \varphi$ from Theorem 5. This leaves the remaining cases of invariance formulae $\varphi = \Box\psi$, existence formulae $\varphi = \Box\Diamond\psi$, progress formulae $\varphi = \Box(\psi \rightarrow \Diamond\chi)$, and persistence formulae $\varphi = \Diamond\Box\psi$.

Invariance. Consider first an invariance formula $\varphi = \Box\psi$ with $\psi \in \mathcal{L}$. Then $\sigma^{(k)} \models \psi$ holds for all k. In particular, for $k = 0$ we get $\models \psi_{init} \rightarrow \psi$ and hence $\vdash \psi_{init} \rightarrow \psi$, because $\mathfrak{R}$ is complete. Furthermore, by definition $M \models \text{leadsto}(\psi, \psi)$ holds, and the completeness of $\mathfrak{R}$ implies $M \vdash \text{leadsto}(\psi, \psi)$. Together with the derivation rule INV_1 we get $M \vdash \Box\psi$ as claimed.

For $\varphi = \Box\psi$ with $\psi \notin \mathcal{L}$ we exploit the derivation rules from Lemma 10 to get $M \vdash \Box\psi$. See the appendix for details.

Existence. Next consider an existence formula $\varphi = \Box\Diamond\psi$ with $\psi \in \mathcal{L}$. Then $\sigma^{(k)} \models \Diamond\psi$ holds for all k. If σ is infinite, this implies $M \models \text{conv}(\neg\psi)$. If σ is finite, it cannot terminate in a state satisfying $\neg\psi$, hence $M \models \text{dlf}(\neg\psi)$. Using Theorem 5 we get $M \vdash \text{dlf}(\neg\psi)$ and $M \vdash \text{conv}(\neg\psi)$. Then with the derivation rule LIVE we obtain $M \vdash \varphi$.

For general existence formulae $\varphi = \Box\Diamond\psi$ with $\psi \notin \mathcal{L}$ we exploit again the derivation rules from Lemma 10 to get $M \vdash \varphi$. See the appendix for details.

Progress. Next consider a progress formula $\varphi = \Box(\varphi_1 \rightarrow \Diamond\varphi_2)$ with $\varphi_1, \varphi_2 \in \mathcal{L}$. Then for every trace σ of M and every k with $\sigma^{(k)} \models \varphi_1$ there exists some $\ell \geq k$ with $\sigma^{(\ell)} \models \varphi_2$. As M is tail-homogeneous with respect to φ_2, we can distinguish two cases.

Case 1. Assume $\tilde{M} \models \text{conv}(\neg\varphi_2)$ holds. Then $\sigma \models \Box\Diamond\varphi_2$ holds for all traces of $\tilde{M}$. Hence $M \models \Box\Diamond\varphi_2$ and by induction $\tilde{M} \vdash \Box\Diamond\varphi_2$. Then we can apply rule $\Box\Diamond_1$ to obtain $M \vdash \Box(\varphi_1 \rightarrow \Diamond\varphi_2)$.

Case 2. Assume that $\tilde{M} \models \text{div}(\neg\varphi_2)$ holds. Then all traces of $\tilde{M}$ contain only a finite number of states satisfying φ_2, thus we consider all states in these traces that satisfy $\neg\varphi_2$ and for which there exists a later state satisfying φ_2. Let φ_3 be a common invariant for these states. More precisely, for a state S satisfying $\neg\varphi_2$ take its type, i.e. the set of all state formulae that hold in S, and let φ_S be an isolating formula for this type. Then define φ_3 as the disjunction of all these formulae φ_S. Then by construction $M \models \Box(\varphi_1 \wedge \neg\varphi_2 \rightarrow \varphi_3)$ holds.

As an infinite tail of any trace contains only states satisfying $\neg\varphi_2$, these states must also satisfy $\neg\varphi_1$. Then our construction yields $M \models \Box(\varphi_1 \wedge \neg\varphi_2 \rightarrow \varphi_3)$.

Furthermore, as M is sufficiently refined and $\tilde{M}$ is divergent in $\neg\varphi_2$, by Lemma 4 we get a variant term $t(\bar{v})$ such that $\text{var}_d(t, \neg\varphi_1 \wedge \neg\varphi_2)$ is valid, in particular, $t(\bar{v}) > v_{\min}$ is included in φ_3, and $t(\bar{v}) = v_{\min}$ holds in all tailing states satisfying $\neg\varphi_1 \wedge \neg\varphi_2$. This implies $M \models \text{div}(\neg\varphi_3)$.

By induction we get $M \vdash \Box(\varphi_1 \wedge \neg\varphi_2 \rightarrow \varphi_3)$, $M \vdash \text{leadsto}(\varphi_3 \wedge \neg\varphi_2, \varphi_3 \vee \varphi_2)$ and $M \vdash \text{div}(\neg\varphi_3)$. Thus, we can apply the rule PROG, which yields $M \vdash \Box(\varphi_1 \rightarrow \Diamond\varphi_2)$.

Next consider a progress formula $\varphi = \Box(\varphi_1 \rightarrow \Diamond\varphi_2)$ with $\varphi_2 \notin \mathcal{L}$. In case $\tilde{M} \models \text{conv}(\neg\varphi_1)$ holds, we immediately get $M \models \Box\Diamond\varphi_1$ and hence also $M \models \Diamond\varphi_1$. In this case we consider again four cases for φ_2. (1) For $\varphi_2 = \Box\chi$ it follows that $M \models \Diamond\Box\chi$ holds, hence by induction $M \vdash \Diamond\Box\chi$. With rule $\Box\Diamond_2$ we infer

$M \vdash \Box\Diamond\Box\chi$, and with rule $\Box\Diamond_1$ we get $M \vdash \Box(\varphi_1 \rightarrow \Diamond\Box\chi)$. (2) For $\varphi_2 = \Box\Diamond\chi$ we get $M \models \Diamond\Box\Diamond\chi$ and further $M \models \Box\Diamond\Box\Diamond\chi$ due to the soundness of $\Box\Diamond_2$, which holds not only for $\Box$LTL. By induction it follows that $M \vdash \Box\Diamond\Box\Diamond\chi$, and then the application of rule $\Box\Diamond_1$ yields $M \vdash \Box(\varphi_1 \rightarrow \Diamond\Box\Diamond\chi)$. (3) For $\varphi_2 = \Box(\chi_1 \rightarrow \Diamond\chi_2)$ we have $M \models \Diamond\Box(\chi_1 \rightarrow \Diamond\chi_2)$, hence also $M \models \Box\Diamond\Box(\chi_1 \rightarrow \Diamond\chi_2)$. By induction we get $M \vdash \Box\Diamond\Box(\chi_1 \rightarrow \Diamond\chi_2)$, hence the application of rule $\Box\Diamond_1$ yields again $M \vdash \Box(\varphi_1 \rightarrow \Diamond\Box(\chi_1 \rightarrow \Diamond\chi_2))$. (4) Finally, for $\varphi_2 = \Diamond\Box\chi$ we get $M \models \Diamond\Diamond\Box\chi$ and further $M \models \Diamond\Box\chi$. The soundness of rule $\Box\Diamond_2$ implies $M \models \Box\Diamond\Box\chi$, hence also $M \models \Box\Diamond\Diamond\Box\chi$. By induction we conclude $M \vdash \Box\Diamond\Diamond\Box\chi$, and finally the application of rule $\Box\Diamond_1$ yields $M \vdash \Box(\varphi_1 \rightarrow \Diamond\Diamond\Box\chi)$, i.e. $M \vdash \Box(\varphi_1 \rightarrow \Diamond\varphi_2)$.

To conclude the proof for progress formulae we look at the case that $\tilde{M} \models \text{div}(\neg\varphi_1)$ holds. Then for all traces σ there exists some k with $\sigma^{(\ell)} \models \neg\varphi_1$ for all $\ell \geq k$. If no trace σ exists with $\sigma^{(m)} \models \varphi_1$ for some m, we have $\tilde{M} \models \Box\neg\varphi_1$ and hence also $M \models \Box\neg\varphi_1$. By induction we obtain $M \vdash \Box\neg\varphi_1$, so the application of rule $\Box\lor$ implies again $M \vdash \Box(\varphi_1 \rightarrow \Diamond\varphi_2)$.

Therefore, we can assume that there exists a trace σ with $\sigma^{(m)} \models \varphi_1$. By exploiting equivalences among $\Box$LTL formulae φ_2 can be rewritten to take one of the forms $\Box\psi$, $\Box\Diamond\psi$, $\Diamond\Box\psi$ with either $\psi \in \mathcal{L}$ or $\psi = \Box(\chi_1 \rightarrow \Diamond\chi_2)$ with $\chi_1 \in \mathcal{L}$.

(1) In case $\varphi_2 = \Box\psi$ with $\psi \in \mathcal{L}$ there exists a trace σ and some $k \geq m$ with $\sigma^{(\ell)} \models \neg\varphi_1$ for all $\ell \geq k$. That is, $\tilde{M} \models \text{div}(\psi)$, which implies $\tilde{M} \models \Diamond\Box\psi$ and $\tilde{M} \models \Box\Diamond\Box\psi$. By induction we get $\tilde{M} \vdash \Box\Diamond\Box\psi$, so the application of rule $\Box\Diamond_1$ implies $\tilde{M} \vdash \Box(\varphi_1 \rightarrow \Diamond\Box\psi)$, i.e. $\tilde{M} \vdash \Box(\varphi_1 \rightarrow \Diamond\varphi_2)$. An application of rule EXT implies $M \vdash \Box(\varphi_1 \rightarrow \Diamond\varphi_2)$.

(2) In case $\varphi_2 = \Box\Diamond\psi$ with $\psi \in \mathcal{L}$ there exists a trace σ such that for all $k \geq m$ there exist some $\ell \geq k$ with $\sigma^{(\ell)} \models \psi$. That is, $\tilde{M} \models \text{conv}(\neg\psi)$ holds, which implies $\tilde{M} \models \Box\Diamond\psi$ and hence also $\tilde{M} \models \Box\Diamond\varphi_2$. By induction we get $\tilde{M} \vdash \Box\Diamond\varphi_2$, and further $\tilde{M} \vdash \Box(\varphi_1 \rightarrow \Diamond\varphi_2)$ by applying rule $\Box\Diamond_1$. A final application of rule EXT implies $M \vdash \Box(\varphi_1 \rightarrow \Diamond\varphi_2)$.

(3) In case $\varphi_2 = \Diamond\Box\psi$ with $\psi \in \mathcal{L}$ we get $\tilde{M} \models \text{div}(\psi)$ as in (1). Using the same arguments it follows that $\tilde{M} \models \Box\Diamond\varphi_2$ holds. By induction we get $\tilde{M} \vdash \Box\Diamond\varphi_2$, and then $M \vdash \Box(\varphi_1 \rightarrow \Diamond\varphi_2)$ follows from the application of the rules $\Box\Diamond_1$ and EXT.

(4) Next consider the case $\varphi_2 = \Box(\psi \rightarrow \Diamond\chi)$ with $\psi \in \mathcal{L}$. If $\tilde{M} \models \text{conv}(\neg\psi)$ holds, then every trace contains an infinite subsequence of states satisfying ψ and hence also an infinite subsequence of states satisfying χ. If $\tilde{M} \models \text{div}(\neg\psi)$ holds, then for every trace σ there exists some k with $\sigma^{(\ell)} \models \neg\psi$ for all $\ell \geq k$. For both cases we can imply $\tilde{M} \models \Box\Diamond\Box(\psi \rightarrow \Diamond\chi)$, i.e. $\tilde{M} \models \Box\Diamond\varphi_2$. By induction we get $\tilde{M} \vdash \Box\Diamond\varphi_2$, and $M \vdash \Box(\varphi_1 \rightarrow \Diamond\varphi_2)$ follows from the application of the rules $\Box\Diamond_1$ and EXT. The cases $\varphi_2 = \Box\Diamond(\psi \rightarrow \Diamond\chi)$ and $\varphi_2 = \Diamond\Box(\psi \rightarrow \Diamond\chi)$ with $\psi \in \mathcal{L}$ are handled in a completely analogous way.

Persistence. Finally, consider a persistence formula $\varphi = \Diamond\Box\psi$, and first assume $\psi \in \mathcal{L}$. For an arbitrary trace σ, as $M \models \Diamond\Box\psi$ holds, it follows that σ cannot end in a state satisfying $\neg\psi$ for finite σ, and for every infinite σ there must exist some k with $\sigma^{(\ell)} \models \varphi$ for all $\ell > k$. That is, both $M \models \text{div}(\psi)$ and $M \models \text{dlf}(\neg\psi)$ hold. By induction we obtain $M \vdash \text{div}(\psi)$ and $M \vdash \text{dlf}(\neg\psi)$, which allows the rule PERS to be applied to yield $M \vdash \Diamond\Box\psi$, i.e. $M \vdash \varphi$.

For a general persistence formula $\varphi = \Diamond\Box\psi$ with $\psi \notin \mathcal{L}$ we exploit again the derivation rules from Lemma 10 to get $M \vdash \varphi$. See the appendix for details. $\Box$

Note that the requirement that machines should be tail-homogeneous was only used in the proof for progress formulae. We therefore obtain the following.

Corollary 12. *The system $\mathfrak{R}_{\Box LTL}$ of derivation rules is sound and complete for proofs of invariance, existence and persistence conditions on Event-B machines that are sufficiently refined with respect to the set Φ of state formulae appearing as subformulae of the formulae in $\Box LTL$ to be proven.*

4   Conclusion

In this paper we defined a fragment of the logic LTL(EB) integrating the UNTIL-fragment of LTL and the logic of Event-B, and proved its completeness for Event-B machines that are sufficiently refined and tail-homogeneous. The former restriction guarantees that variant terms required in the proofs exist. It is no loss of generality, as the necessary refinements are an intrinsic part of the Event-B method. The latter restriction tames the non-determinism in Event-B, which enables a smoother integration with LTL. The $\Box LTL$ fragment supports the mechanical verification of selected liveness conditions such as conditional and unconditional progress or persistence for Event-B. Our development of the theory is generic enough to allow the conclusion that a transfer of the results to other rigorous state-based methods such as TLA$^+$ or ASMs is straightforward.

However, LTL is a linear-time temporal logic, and as such it is appropriate for deterministic systems, but less so for non-deterministic ones. In Event-B there are two sources of non-determinism. First, events may involve the selection of arbitrary values satisfying the before-after predicate. In most cases this form of non-determinism is considered to be linked to an external selection (see the discussion in [5]), i.e. the values are merely parameters in the computation. Consequently, in most cases the use of LTL(EB) will suffice. Second, in every state several events may be enabled, and only one is selected to fire. Though the Event-B refinement process emphasises the reduction of this form of non-determinism, it is not well supported by LTL. In particular, conditions for successor states can only be expressed for all successor states. So it seems a good idea to also consider CTL instead of LTL, though it is well known that persistence formulae cannot be expressed using CTL. Nonetheless, an open question for future research is the definition of a complete fragment of CTL(EB).

For ASMs the logic developed by Stärk and Nanchen is explicitly tailored to deterministic ASMs [18]. Thus, a combination with a fragment of LTL and a straightforward carry-over of the $\Box LTL$ fragment to ASMs is appropriate. For non-deterministic ASMs the problems of a generalisation have been intensively discussed in [6], which also shows that a combination with CTL would be too weak. The logic of non-deterministic ASMs is second-order, but complete with respect to Henkin semantics. This raises the open research question how to define a complete temporal extension, in which selected liveness properties can be expressed.

References

1. Abrial, J.R.: The B-book - Assigning Programs to Meanings. Cambridge University Press, Cambridge (2005)
2. Abrial, J.R.: Modeling in Event-B - System and Software Engineering. Cambridge University Press, Cambridge (2010). https://doi.org/10.1017/CBO9781139195881
3. Barwise, J.: Admissible Sets and Structures. Springer, Berlin, Heidelberg (1975). https://doi.org/10.1017/9781316717196
4. Blass, A., Gurevich, Y., Shelah, S.: Choiceless polynomial time. Ann. Pure Appl. Log. **100**, 141–187 (1999)
5. Börger, E., Gervasi, V.: Structures of Computing - A Guide into a Practice-Oriented Theory. Springer, Berlin, Heidelberg, New York (2024). forthcoming. https://doi.org/10.1007/978-3-031-54358-6
6. Börger, E., Stärk, R.: Abstract State Machines. Springer, Berlin, Heidelberg, New York (2003). https://doi.org/10.1007/978-3-642-18216-7
7. Clarke, E.M., Emerson, E.A.: Design and synthesis of synchronization skeletons using branching time temporal logic. In: Grumberg, O., Veith, H. (eds.) 25 Years of Model Checking. LNCS, vol. 5000, pp. 196–215. Springer, Heidelberg (2008). https://doi.org/10.1007/978-3-540-69850-0_12
8. Ferrarotti, F., Rivière, P., Schewe, K.D., Singh, N.K., Aït Ameur, Y.: A complete fragment of LTL(EB). CoRR abs/2401.16838 (2024). https://arxiv.org/abs/2401.16838
9. Ferrarotti, F., Schewe, K.D., Tec, L., Wang, Q.: A unifying logic for non-deterministic, parallel and concurrent Abstract State Machines. Ann. Math. Artif. Intell. **83**(3–4), 321–349 (2018). https://doi.org/10.1007/s10472-017-9569-3
10. Hoang, T.S., Abrial, J.-R.: Reasoning about liveness properties in Event-B. In: Qin, S., Qiu, Z. (eds.) ICFEM 2011. LNCS, vol. 6991, pp. 456–471. Springer, Heidelberg (2011). https://doi.org/10.1007/978-3-642-24559-6_31
11. Kröger, F., Merz, S.: Temporal Logic and State Systems. Texts in Theoretical Computer Science. An EATCS Series. Springer, Berlin, Heidelberg (2008). https://doi.org/10.1007/978-3-540-68635-4
12. Lamport, L.: Specifying Systems, The TLA$^+$ Language and Tools for Hardware and Software Engineers. Addison-Wesley, Boston (2002)
13. Manna, Z., Pnueli, A.: Adequate proof principles for invariance and liveness properties of concurrent programs. Sci. Comput. Program. **4**(3), 257–289 (1984). https://doi.org/10.1016/0167-6423(84)90003--0
14. Merz, S.: On the logic of TLA$^+$. Comput. Artif. Intell. **22**(3–4), 351–379 (2003)
15. Pnueli, A.: The temporal logic of programs. In: 18th Annual Symposium on Foundations of Computer Science (FoCS 1977), pp. 46–57. IEEE Computer Society (1977). https://doi.org/10.1109/SFCS.1977.32
16. Rivière, P., Singh, N.K., Aït Ameur, Y., Dupont, G.: Formalising liveness properties in Event-B with the reflexive EB4EB framework. In: Rozier, K.Y., Chaudhuri, S. (eds.) NASA Formal Methods. NFM 2023. LNCS, vol. 13903, pp. 312–331. Springer, Cham (2023). https://doi.org/10.1007/978-3-031-33170-1_19

17. Schmalz, M.: Formalizing the Logic of Event-B. Ph.D. thesis, ETH Zürich (2012)
18. Stärk, R.F., Nanchen, S.: A logic for abstract state machines. J. Univ. Comput. Sci. **7**(11), 980–1005 (2001)
19. Väänänen, J.: Second-order and higher-order logic. In: Stanford Encyclopedia of Philosophy (2019). https://plato.stanford.edu/entries/logic-higher-order/

Decomposing Analogy: A Logic Characterization

Mena Leemhuis(✉) [iD], Diedrich Wolter[iD], and Özgür L. Özçep[iD]

University of Lübeck, Lübeck, Germany
{m.leemhuis,diedrich.wolter,oezguer.oezcep}@uni-luebeck.de

Abstract. Analogical proportions, i.e., relational assertions of the form "a is to b as c is to d" are fundamental for analogical reasoning, a cognitively motivated form of reasoning that has several important applications in AI, including problem solving and learning. This paper contributes to the logic characterization of analogical reasoning by establishing a link between two perspectives. Analogical proportions can either be viewed atomically as a quaternary relation or as the implicit relation induced by applying analogical comparison $a : b$ to an element d in order to identify a suitable element c. For linking these views we tackle a general question: Given a quaternary relation between four elements a, b, c, d, how can it be decomposed into a representation $a : b :: c : d$ with "::" denoting a binary relation and ":" denoting a binary function— possibly under additional constraints on : and ::? In particular we show that for a whole class of analogical proportions such a decomposition is possible with ":" denoting the same function in all of the analogical proportions of the class.

Keywords: Analogical Proportions · Analogy · Axiomatization

1 Introduction

This paper considers analogical proportions, i.e., assertions of the form "a is to b as c is to d", which are usually abbreviated as "$a : b :: c : d$". Analogical proportions are at the heart of analogical reasoning, which is considered an important part of common sense reasoning and has also been discussed in philosophy and psychology [7]. In particular, analogical reasoning is an important topic in AI research—with applications in various subareas of AI [19]. For example, contemporary research on word embeddings [17] as well as knowledge graph embeddings as in TransE [1] are usually illustrated with analogical reasoning of the following kind, illustrated in Fig. 1: Assume that one of the entities of an analogical proportion $a : b :: c : d$, say d, has to be inferred given entities a, b, c and the fact that $a : b :: c : d$ holds. In other words: If $a : b :: c : d$ holds, then what is an appropriate, not necessarily unique d? By answering the question a new relation $c : d$ is established in order to complete a given knowledge graph [2]. In another kind of analogical reasoning one assumes that only two entities are given [14]. In

A. Meier and M. Ortiz (Eds.): FoIKS 2024, LNCS 14589, pp. 256–274, 2024.
https://doi.org/10.1007/978-3-031-56940-1_14

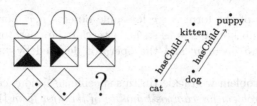

Fig. 1. Examples of analogical reasoning tasks. Raven's Progressive Matrices (left) require analogical progression pattern to be understood, knowledge graph completion using TransE [1] applies translation vectors in $\mathbb{R}^n$.

the wording of [18] (citing it with our adapted notation): for a given c, predict d such that the target pair (c, d) is in the same relation as another given source pair (a, b).

According to Hüllermeyer [13], analogical proportions may also act as the central building block in designing an explainable information system by exploiting analogical proportions, e.g., for explaining classification results of (black-box) machine learning (ML) classifiers.

But how can analogical proportions be characterized formally? Due to the diverse uses of analogical proportions it is not surprising that no concrete single relation has been singled out but manifold relations, sometimes informally defined, have been used. Following Prade and Richard [18], we are going to consider a minimal set of three axioms (reflexivity, symmetry, and central permutation) as those characterizing the family of operators that we will consider as analogical proportions. Even the most simple case where the compared objects a, b, c, d are Boolean values already results in a family of eight possible models of analogical proportions.

Why are Boolean values appropriate for building analogical proportions? The motivation of considering Boolean values is that they can represent whether a predicate holds or not, thus abstracting from an underlying language to represent domain knowledge. We, like previously [18], consider bit vectors to represent multiple predicates at once, allowing more complex analogies to be described. Our approach is further motivated by the assumption, which is shared with other computational approaches to analogy such as the structure mapping engine [4], that analogies are not build on a multi-valued validity of predicates, but on a crisp, Boolean one. Put differently, in context of a given task it has to be decided how a feature that is represented on a quantitative scale, e.g., size, is treated as a Boolean one, e.g., either small or large.

This paper investigates decomposition aspects for analogical proportions. The expression "$a : b :: c : d$" can be treated as denoting a quaternary relation, i.e., a relation of four arguments. The wording used in the English phrase "a is to b as is c to d" suggests such a reading. But another equally acceptable paraphrasing leads to another reading, as is suggested by the phrase "the relation of a to b is the same as the relation of c to d". Here, analogical proportion is decomposed into a binary relation $x :: y$ of two arguments x, y where in turn x and y are composed objects of the form $u : v$ for some objects u, v. For our purposes—and as we found no better names so far—we call the operator denoted by "$:$" the *analogical ratio operator* and the operator denoted by "$::$" the *analogical similarity relation*.

The general problem we tackle (in this specific situation) can be considered as an *extension problem for compositionality of the first form* [11, p.16]: given a language with a meaning specified for its sentences (in our case the analogical proportions $a : b :: c : d$ understood as a quaternary relation), find meanings for all other expressions of the language (in our case expressions built by : and :: (now understood as a binary relation)). As indicated above, we refer to this problem also as *decomposition problem (of the first form)* as it asks to decompose sentences in subsentential expressions.

Why is the compositionality problem mentioned above interesting for AI? The answer is that it allows us to bridge theoretical considerations on analogical proportions [18,19], treating them as quaternary relations, to practical approaches of analogical reasoning. For example, Lovett and Forbus [16] describe how to exploit analogical reasoning in visual problem solving in case of Raven's Progressive Matrices (RPM), see Fig. 1. In RPMs one is usually given a matrix of figures missing a single figure (marked '?' in Fig. 1). One has to identify the missing figure by understanding the progression of analogies in the matrix. As one of the steps in solving RPMs the authors consider identifying the differences $a : b$ (in our words: the ratio) between two given figures a, b and then applying them to the single figure d to yield a figure c as solution. So here the assumption is that there is a ratio $a : b$ and a mechanism of applying $a : b$ to a third object d to yield c such that $a : b :: c : d$ holds. "Applying" $a : b$ implicitly means that there is an analogical similarity :: between $a : b$ and $c : d$ which justifies applying a reconstruction of c out of $a : b$ and d. Quite often, but not necessarily always, this relation :: is the identity or an equivalence relation. So, analogical reasoning of this kind leads to an analogical proportion whose properties one may describe axiomatically, treating $a : b :: c : d$ as a quaternary relation. In the other direction, if one has described a class of analogical proportions one may tackle the problem of identifying those forms of analogical reasoning that are compatible with them by trying to give the : and the :: in $a : b :: c : d$ a meaning. This is an extension problem of the first form mentioned above which we tackle in this paper. The contributions of this paper are:

- We give results on how to extend the axioms of Prade and Richard [18] to represent each single model of the eight analogical proportions with additional axioms, treating :: as a 4-ary relation. The axioms belong to the core fragment of first order logic and hence allow for simple generalizations of analogical proportions.
- We solve the extension problem of the first form under the additional constraint that the analogical ratio has to be the same for all possible models of the three axioms of analogical proportion. For this purpose we identify a variant of the symmetric set difference operator as an appropriate candidate. We extend the results to hold also for domains of bit vectors of arbitrary

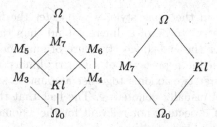

Fig. 2. Left: The Boolean algebra of analogical proportions. Right: The Boolean sub-algebra TGM of totally generic analogical proportions

length in order to apply analogical proportions to multiple predicates using the axioms identified.

- We consider the extension problem of the first form under a constraint imposed by the use of propositional language, namely that both : and :: have to be expressible in propositional logic. The outcome is that only one of the eight analogical proportions (namely Klein's analogical proportion) allows for this extension.

2 Preliminaries

We closely follow the presentation of Prade and Richard [18] to set up the main framework for pursuing our investigation of the decomposition of analogical proportions. The three properties any analogical proportional has to fulfill [18] are described formally by the following basic set of three axioms B_{ax}:

1. $\forall a \forall b \, (a : b :: a : b)$ (reflexivity);
2. $\forall a \forall b \forall c \forall d (a : b :: c : d \rightarrow c : d :: a : b)$ (symmetry);
3. $\forall a \forall b \forall c \forall d (a : b :: c : d \rightarrow a : c :: b : d)$ (central permutation).

These axioms together already entail further interesting properties such as outer permutation:

$$\forall a \forall b \forall c \forall d (a : b :: c : d \rightarrow d : b :: c : a) \qquad \text{(outer permutation)}$$

Another axiom discussed for a "natural analogy" [18, p. 237] is unicity: $\forall a \forall b \forall c$ $(a : a :: b : c \rightarrow c = b)$. Using the basic axioms B_{ax} (concretely using central permutation) unicity is equivalent to the following axiom which we will mainly use under the name "unicity":

$$\forall a \forall b \forall c (a : b :: a : c \rightarrow b = c) \qquad \text{(unicity)}$$

The property of reflexivity does not seem to be debatable: in any reading of the term "analogical proportion" the ratio of two objects should be similar to that ratio. The situation w.r.t. symmetry is different. At least for philosophical and psychological discussions regarding the similarity of perceptions (or mental states) symmetry is a highly debated if not rejected property [21].

Though presented in the same style, we consider the first two axioms (of reflexivity and symmetry) to be of a different kind than the third axiom: The former do not consider the embedded structure of analogical ratio denoted by ":" at all but rather define a property of a generic binary relation denoted by "::". Concretely, the first two axioms together amount to saying that $x::y$ is a similarity relation [10], usually denoted $\sim$. The fact that the domain of x and y are actually pairs of objects is not relevant for the axioms as these express a general property for any kind of object.

In contrast to the first two axioms, the third (central permutation) explicitly assumes some structure. The axiom of central permutation assumes that in $a : b$, as the notation suggests, at least a pair of objects a, b is involved and that the arguments of the pair can be arranged and substituted by other objects to get other objects of the kind of $a : b$. Note that we prefer to talk about "some" structure $a : b$ rather than "the structure" because, as we will discuss below, the type of object denoted by "$a : b$" is not determined beforehand and the whole idea is to find an appropriate one. Also note that analogical proportions are not necessarily equivalence relations, because $x :: y$ does not necessarily fulfill *transitivity*, i.e., $\forall a \forall b \forall c \forall d \forall e \forall f (a : b :: c : d \wedge c : d :: e : f \to a : b :: e : f)$—though most of the examples considered by [18] are in fact equivalence relations.

Prade and Richard [18] consider the domain of Boolean values $\{0, 1\}$ which may be motivated by understanding objects as the outcome of application-specific predicates (canFly, isRound, etc.). If the domain of the objects is assumed to be the set of Boolean values, then $a : b :: c : d$ can be understood to represent a Boolean function. As Prade and Richard [18] show, there are 8 different Boolean functions that fulfill the three axioms for analogical proportions. These functions form a lattice, actually even a Boolean algebra. Let us identify a Boolean function f on propositional variables a, b, c, d with the set of truth assignments $\mathcal{A}$ over $\{0, 1\}^4$ which are mapped to 1. Further we write those assignments as bit vectors of length four. With the notation of [18] the lattice elements are the following:

$$\Omega_0 = \{0000, 1111, 0101, 1010, 0011, 1100\}$$
$$Kl = \{0000, 1111, 0101, 1010, 0011, 1100\} \cup \{0110, 1001\}$$
$$M_3 = \{0000, 1111, 0101, 1010, 0011, 1100\} \cup \{1110, 1101, 1011, 0111\}$$
$$M_4 = \{0000, 1111, 0101, 1010, 0011, 1100\} \cup \{0001, 0010, 0100, 1000\}$$
$$M_5 = M_3 \cup \{0110, 1001\} = M_3 \cup Kl$$
$$M_6 = M_4 \cup \{0110, 1001\} = M_4 \cup Kl$$
$$M_7 = M_3 \cup \{0001, 0010, 0100, 1000\} = M_3 \cup M_4$$
$$\Omega = \{0, 1\}^4 = \{0000, 0001, 0010, \ldots, 1111\}$$

where Kl stands for Klein's model. The lattice structure of [18] is cited here on the left of Fig. 2.

3   Refined Axiomatization

The aim of this section is to characterize each individual structure in the lattice of analogical proportions axiomatically by adding additional axioms to the basic set of axioms B_{ax}. This will allow us to identify generalizations of analogical proportions from the domain $\{0,1\}$ to the domain of n-bit vectors (and beyond). The idea is to consider structures that satisfy the respective set of axioms.

All structures in the lattice are equal in the sense that they fulfill the three basic axioms of analogical proportions. Prade and Richard give—in particular—a (Kolmogorov) complexity theoretical argument for preferring the minimal structure Ω_0 over the others. From a logical point of view we consider all of the models in $TGM := \{\Omega_0, Kl, M_7, \Omega\}$, as illustrated on the right of Fig. 2, as equally natural analogical proportions. As already noted by Prade and Richard [18], these analogical proportions are invariant under the permutation of the Boolean variables $1 \mapsto 0, 0 \mapsto 1$ whereas the others are not (for example, $1110 \in M_3$ but $0001 \notin M_3$). In other words, for models outside of TGM we will not be able to define them in a so-called *totally generic language* (sometimes also called *domain-independent language*) [15, p. 255]. Prominent languages of the latter kind are Datalog or relational calculus.

Now let us consider first the question of axiomatizing each model m in the set TGM. We try to extend the three basic axioms B_{ax} with sets of formulae F_m such that the following conditions are fulfilled: 1.) $Mod(B_{ax} \cup F_m) = \{m\}$; 2.) F_m is "simple"; 3.) F_m is "general".

In the first condition $Mod(X)$ stands for the model operator in predicate logic, i.e., the set of FOL structures that make all sentences in X true.

As the signature of the formulae consists of the quaternary symbol "$a : b :: c : d$" these structures mainly describe the kind of relation used to interpret "$a : b :: c : d$" with the special constraint that $a, b, c, d \in \{0, 1\}$. So the first condition requires that F_m is made true exactly by m. But in general, these axiomatizations F_m can also be used to define analogical proportions for the case where a, b, c, d are not constraint to the Boolean values $0, 1$ (see end of Sect. 4). In that more general case the first condition cannot hold because, e.g., with any FOL structure being a model of a set of formulae F also all isomorphic structures are models of that formulae. So the first condition would be rather $m \in Mod(B_{ax} \cup F_m)$. Thus, the set of formulae F_m denotes a set of of models and m is in one of them. One might also add a separation condition:

$$Mod(B_{ax} \cup F_m) \cap Mod(B_{ax} \cup F_{m'}) = \emptyset \text{ for } m \neq m' \qquad (1)$$

The rationale behind the second condition is that F is formulated in a "simple" logic that minimally extends the logic in which B_{ax} is formulated. The logic in which B_{ax} is expressed is the so-called *core* fragment of FOL, i.e., the intersection of the Horn fragment and the Krom fragment.[1] The third item is intended to capture the idea that F should be applicable to arbitrary objects a, b, c, d,

---

[1] For a definition see [9]; roughly, the core fragment consists of rules with (possibly empty) antecedent and succedens being atoms.

not only Boolean values. In particular, it should handle the case where the variables range over bit vectors. If, as in the case of analogical proportions outside of TGM, we cannot guarantee total genericity, then fulfilling the third property is harder. Simplicity and genericity are not technically defined here but given on an intuitional level. We think that a technical definition of a general axiom is a foundational question. In particular, we think that the idea of generalizing axioms from a simple domain to a more complex domain has different facets and so there is no unique definition of generalization and of a general axiom.

The trivial analogical proportion Ω is captured by $\forall a \forall b \forall c \forall d (a : b :: c : d)$. Now we consider Kl. The basic intuition is that Kl (next to fulfilling unicity) forgets about the direction within the analogical ratio. This property is captured by an axiom we call *ratio symmetry*:

$$F_{Kl} = \{unicity\} \cup \{\forall a \forall b (a : b :: b : a)\}$$

We have $Mod(B_{ax} \cup F_{Kl}) = \{Kl\}$ and we stay in the core fragment. For the minimal structure Ω_0 we get the following set of formulae F_{Ω_0} fulfilling $Mod(B_{ax} \cup F_{\Omega_0}) = \{\Omega_0\}$.

$$F_{\Omega_0} = \{unicity\} \cup \{\forall a \forall b (a : b :: b : a \rightarrow a = b)\}$$

The axiom $\forall a \forall b (a : b :: b : a \rightarrow a = b)$ states that ratio symmetry is only possible if the inputs of the ratio are the same. Therefore, we call this axiom that of *ratio antisymmetry*. Instead of the unicity axioms the axiom of transitivity can be used in this case: $Mod(B_{ax} \cup \{trans\} \cup \{ratio\ antisym.\}) = \{\Omega_0\}$. (Proof: The only other models being transitive are Kl and Ω but in both models the axiom of antisymmetry is falsified.)

Last we give an axiomatization for M_7. M_7 is the only model in TGM that is not an equivalence relation. This model can be captured with the set of axioms F_{M_7}.

$$F_{M_7} = \{ratio\ antisym.\} \cup \{\forall a \forall b \forall c (a : a :: b : c)\}$$

It shares with F_{Ω_0} the axiom of ratio antisymmetry and contains the additional axiom $\forall a \forall b \forall c (a : a :: b : c)$. The latter axiom expresses some universal property of a neutral element in the sense that a ratio of an object with itself is similar w.r.t. :: to any other ratio. We call this axiom the *axiom of universal neutrality*.

Note that Ω_0 and Kl are the only analogical proportions fulfilling unicity and that Ω, Kl, Ω_0 are the only ones fulfilling transitivity. In particular this means that unicity entails transitivity in the domain $\{0, 1\}$. Over arbitrary domains this entailment does not necessarily hold. We summarize the observations in the following proposition.

Proposition 1. *The models $TGM = \{\Omega_0, Kl, M_7, \Omega\}$ are the only analogical proportions (over the domain $\{0, 1\}$ of Boolean values) that are domain independent. They can be expressed in the core fragment of FOL with identity with a single 4-ary relation $a : b :: c : d$.*

Proof. The models outside of TGM are not domain independent as they are not invariant under bit-complementation. We are left with showing that the given F_ms indeed lead to the axiomatizations of each of the analogical proportions.

Validating that each model $m \in TGM$ fulfills F_m only requires us to check each model:

Ω: As Ω contains all 4-bit vectors it fulfills $\forall a \forall b \forall c \forall d(a : b :: c : d)$. Kl: That Kl fulfills unicity is known (see, e.g., [18], but can be checked directly). Ratio symmetry holds in case of $a = b$ due to the fact all analogical proportions fulfill ratio reflexivity and ratio symmetry. For $a \neq b$ ratio symmetry holds due to the 4-bit vectors $0110, 1001$. Ω_0: Unicity follows directly or by considering the fact that $\Omega_0 \subseteq Kl$. Ratio antisymmetry says that bits $0110, 1001$ have to be excluded which is the case here. M_7: Ratio antisymmetry holds because the bits $0110, 1001$ are excluded. The axiom of universal neutrality holds because M_7 only excludes the 4-bit vectors $0110, 1001$.

The fact that no model m' makes F_m true (for $m \neq m'$) then follows from Proposition 3, proved below.

The refined axioms for the various models of analogical proportions do not explicitly state on how to use them for analogical reasoning, but only constrain the space of possible derivations. They thus contribute to showing how far models can be decomposed for analogical reasoning. Even in the constrained setting of a Boolean domain, the space of models of analogical proportions extends beyond the patterns found in mainstream applications [1,16]. For example, consider analogical reasoning with TransE [1] for knowledge graph completion: In this case, if three of a, b, c, d in an analogical proportion $a : b :: c : d$ are given, there is always a unique solution for the fourth element since TransE models all relations as vector translations in embeddings space $\mathbb{R}^n$, i.e., as functional relations. In particular, TransE fulfills unicity, which we saw is not fulfilled by some of the eight models of analogical proportions (and even stronger not by M_7 which is in TGM). A model of analogical proportion falsifying unicity allows for some form of uncertainty in analogical reasoning.

We end this section by describing models beyond those of TGM axiomatizations. Here we can only give non-totally-generic axiomatizations: they refer to constants $0, 1$. We can axiomatize M_3 by a weaker form of the axiom of universal neutrality that treats only $1 : 1$ as universally neutral element but not $0 : 0$.

$$F_{M_3} = \{\forall a \forall b(a : b :: b : a \to a = b)\} \cup \{\forall a \forall b(1 : 1 :: a : b)\} \cup$$
$$\{\forall a \forall b(0 : 0 :: a : b) \to a = b\}$$

Dually M_4 treats only $0 : 0$ as universally neutral element and hence leads to the following axiomatization:

$$F_{M_4} = \{\forall a \forall b(a : b :: b : a \to a = b)\} \cup \{\forall a \forall b(0 : 0 :: a : b)\} \cup$$
$$\{\forall a \forall b(1 : 1 :: a : b) \to a = b\}$$

For M_5 the following axiomatization is possible:

$$F_{M_5} = \{\forall a \forall b (a : b :: b : a\} \cup \{\forall a \forall b (1 : 1 :: a : b)\} \cup$$
$$\{\forall a \forall b (0 : 0 :: a : b) \rightarrow a = b\}$$

And dually for M_6 the following axiomatization works out:

$$F_{M_6} = \{\forall a \forall b (a : b :: b : a\} \cup \{\forall a \forall b (0 : 0 :: a : b)\} \cup$$
$$\{\forall a \forall b (1 : 1 :: a : b) \rightarrow a = b\}$$

We summarize this again in a proposition:

Proposition 2. *The models outside of TGM can be modeled in a core fragment of FOL with fixed constants 0, 1.*

Proof. Validating that each model $m \notin TGM$ fulfills F_m is again a matter of rechecking which we do in the following. Again, the fact that no model m' makes F_m true (for $m \neq m'$) then follows from Proposition 3, proved below. F_{M_3}: Ratio antisymmetry holds, as $1001, 0110$ are excluded. Universal neutrality w.r.t. 1 holds due to the fact that M_3 extends Ω_0 with the four 4-bit vectors $1110, 1101, 1011, 0111$. The axiom $\forall a \forall b (0 : 0 :: a : b) \rightarrow a = b$ holds due to the fact that no bit-vector of the form $00ab$ with $a \neq b$ is contained. F_{M_4}: Works dually to M_3 changing the roles of 0 and 1. F_{M_5}: Ratio symmetry holds since $0110, 1001$ are excluded. Universal neutrality w.r.t. 1 holds due to the fact that M_3 fulfills it and that $M_3 \subseteq M_5$. That $(0 : 0 :: a : b) \rightarrow a = b$ is fulfilled holds due to the fact that no bit-vector of the form $00ab$ with $a \neq b$ is contained. F_{M_6}: Works dually to M_5 changing the roles of 0 and 1.

Regarding the intended generalization of analogical proportions, we note that the class of the eight axiom sets F_m has the separation property expressed in (1), thus, that no model m' makes F_m true for $m \neq m'$.

Proposition 3. *For all pairs of axiom sets F_m and $F_{m'}$ with $m \neq m'$ the separation condition (1) is fulfilled over domains with at least two elements.*

Proof. The proof follows from the fact that each pair of axiom sets $F_m, F_{m'}$ contains a pair of clashing axioms, i.e., inconsistent axioms for the case where there are at least two elements. The matrix in Table 1 lists those clashing axioms for each pair of models. (We give only the upper triangle as the induced matrix is symmetric.) We abbreviate *ratio symmetry* by *sym*, *ratio antisymmetry* by *a-sym*, *unicity* by *unic*, *universal neutrality* by *neut*, *1 (0) universal neutrality* by *1(0)-neut*. Moreover, the axiom $\forall a, b, c, d (a : b :: c : d)$ is termed *super-totality* and abbreviated *s-tot*. And we call $\forall a \forall b (0 : 0 :: a : b) \rightarrow a = b$ the axiom of *anti-0-universal neutrality*, abbreviated as *a-0-neut* and we call $\forall a \forall b (1 : 1 :: a : b) \rightarrow a = b$ the axiom of *anti-1-universal neutrality*, abbreviated as *a-1-neut*.

This proposition can be verified by checking each pair of axiom sets $F_m, F_{m'}$ and noting that there is always a pair of complementary axioms (over domains

Table 1. Clashing axioms

	Ω_0	Kl	M_3	M_4	M_5	M_6	M_7	Ω
Ω_0		sym / a-sym	uni / 1-neut	uni / 0-neut	uni / 1-neut	uni / 0-neut	uni / neut	uni / s-tot
Kl			uni / 1-neut	uni / 0-neut	uni / 1-neut	uni / 0-neut	uni / neut	uni / s-tot
M_3				1-neut / a-neut	a-sym / sym	a-sym / sym	a-0-neut / neut	a-0-neut / s-tot
M_4					a-0-neut / 0-neut	a-sym / sym	a-1-neut / neut	a-1-neut / s-tot
M_5						1-neut / a-1-neut	a-0-neut / neut	a-0-neut / s-tot
M_6							a-1-neut / neut	a-1-neut / s − tot
M_7								a-sym / s-tot
Ω								

with at least two elements). For example, in case of F_{Kl} and F_{Ω_0} we have the axioms of ratio symmetry and ratio antisymmetry. Thus, for a domain with two elements $0, 1$ due to ratio symmetry, e.g., $1001 \in m$, a contradiction to ratio antisymmetry. The only non-contradictory options are $m = \{0000\}$ or $m = \{1111\}$, then, however, the domain consists of only one element.

4 A Basic Analogical Ratio Operator

We develop an operator to play the role of analogical ratios in all analogical proportions. The representation of an analogical proportion is by no means unique as can be shown already by the standard construction of rational numbers $\mathbb{Q}$ on the basis of pairs of integers.

Example 1. For this example, we leave the area of Boolean values and consider integers instead. Assume that "$a : b ::_{\mathbb{Q}} c : d$" says that the rational numbers $a : b$ and $c : d$ are the same. For "$:$" and "$::_{\mathbb{Q}}$" two readings are possible based on the standard construction of rational numbers on an equivalence relation $\equiv$. The equivalence is defined over pairs of integers and non-null integers $\mathbb{Z} \times \mathbb{Z} \setminus \{0\}$ and is given by $(a, b) \equiv (c, d)$ iff $a \cdot d = c \cdot b$. So, the first reading for $::_{\mathbb{Q}}$ is that of the equivalence relation $\equiv$ and for the analogical ratio $:$ is that of the pair (a, b). In this reading all relevant information of the analogical proportion is encoded in the analogical relation and no information in the analogical ratio. The second reading is that "$a : b$" stands for the equivalence class of the pair (a, b) w.r.t. $\equiv$, i.e., the set $\{(x, y) \in \mathbb{Z} \times \mathbb{Z} \setminus \{0\} \mid (x, y) \equiv (a, b)\}$, and $::_{\mathbb{Q}}$ stands for the identity relation over sets (namely equivalence classes). A similar duality holds for the more general case of similarity relations $\sim$ as shown by Hazen and Humberstone [10].

Now, we come back to the case of Boolean values: First, we develop an operator for analogical ratios in the simple case where the only objects occurring in an analogical proportion are Boolean truth values 0, 1—and then generalize it to the domain of n-bit vectors (over Boolean values). In order to define the following operator of symmetric difference also for the more general case of bit vectors we present Boolean values in a well-known way as sets: 0 is represented by the empty set $\emptyset$ and 1 is represented by the singleton set $\{\emptyset\}$ that contains the empty set as its single element. Let us denote the set of Boolean values in this representation $\mathbb{B}^s$ ("s" reminding us of set). The basic operator we consider maps pairs of objects to pairs of objects. The first argument of the resulting pair is calculated with a derivative of the symmetric difference named $\Delta^{\pm}$. It is essentially the symmetric difference but interpreting the union as disjoint union: $\Delta^{\pm}(a, b) = a \uplus b$. So, $\Delta^{\pm}$ is like the symmetric difference but preserves provenance information. Actually, we further represent the disjoint union as a pair.

$$\Delta^{\pm}(a, b) = (a \setminus b, b \setminus a)$$

For Boolean a, b the following mapping results:

$$00 \mapsto 00, 01 \mapsto 01, 10 \mapsto 10, 11 \mapsto 00$$

This is based on the intuition that for an analogy, the differences between a and b need to be resembled by the differences of c and d.

The second component of the pair outputted by the analogical ratio operator gives the summed-up cardinality of the input pair. If we would confine ourselves to binary domains this would amount to natural addition (over the reals). So we use here the symbol $+_s$ (disjoint addition) reminding us of addition

$$a +_s b = |a| + |b| = |a \uplus b|$$

With these components we can define our basic notion for the decomposition.

Definition 1. *The basic analogical ratio* operator *is defined as*

$$[\![a : b]\!] = a\!:\!b = (\Delta^{\pm}(a, b), a +_s b).$$

It is best to think of the analogical proportion as describing the ratio of a and b as the difference of a and b with provenance and cardinality information. The reason to work with a notion of cardinality is that we want to decompose any analogical proportion, in particular also those not in TGM (see Sect. 3). The mapping $(a, b) \mapsto a\!:\!b$ is a lossless mapping in that a and b can be reconstructed from $a\!:\!b$, thus it is injective. As an example, consider, e.g., $[\![1 : 1]\!] = (\Delta^{\pm}(1, 1), 1 +_s 1) = ((0,0), 2)$. $a +_s b = 2$ is only the case if $a = b = 1$. The other cases follow analogously.

As our notation suggests (no index at $:$), in this section, we will assume that all analogical proportions $a : b ::_i c : d$ rely on the same notion of analogical ratio. The main task is to define for all analogical proportions individual analogical similarity relations $::_i$.

We now give for the minimal model and Klein's model a representation based on the analogical ratio operator of Definition 1.

We describe first the denotation $[\![::_i]\!]$ of the analogical similarity and then the meaning of the analogical proportion that results by applying $[\![::_i]\!]$ onto the outputs of the basic analogical ratio. That all these representations are valid, i.e., really lead to the models on the left of Fig. 2 can be verified by applying them on all possible input assignments over $\{0, 1\}^4$. A proof is given in Proposition 4.

In case of the minimal model Ω_0 the semantics $[\![::_{\Omega_0}]\!]$ gives a similarity relation which is an equivalence relation, in fact, the identity on the first arguments x, u of its input pairs (x, y) and (u, v).

$$[\![::_{\Omega_0}]\!]((x, y), (u, v)) \quad \text{iff} \quad \pi_1(x, y) = \pi_1(u, v)$$
$$\text{iff} \quad (x = u) \tag{2}$$
$$a : b ::_{\Omega_0} c : d \quad \text{iff} \quad [\![::_{\Omega_0}]\!]([\![a : b]\!], [\![c : d]\!]) \tag{3}$$
$$\text{iff} \quad \Delta^{\pm}(a, b) = \Delta^{\pm}(c, d) \tag{4}$$

Here and below $\pi_i(x_1, x_2) = x_i$ for $i \in \{1, 2\}$ are the usual *projection functions*. Equation (4) exactly corresponds to Prade's equation (1) [18] that uses the propositional formula $(a \wedge \neg b \leftrightarrow c \wedge \neg d) \wedge (\neg a \wedge b \leftrightarrow \neg c \wedge d)$.

Consider Klein's model Kl. The idea is to extend the definition for the minimal model disjunctively, considering an additional condition to capture the additional 4-bit vectors added to Ω_0.

$$[\![::_{\Omega_{Kl}}]\!]((x, y), (u, v)) \quad \text{iff} \quad \pi_1(x, y) = \pi_1(u, v) \text{ or}$$
$$\pi_2(x, y) + \pi_2(u, v) = 2$$
$$a : b ::_{Kl} c : d \quad \text{iff} \quad [\![::_{Kl}]\!]([\![a : b]\!], [\![c : d]\!])$$
$$\text{iff} \quad \Delta^{\pm}(a, b) = \Delta^{\pm}(c, d) \text{ or}$$
$$(a +_s b) + (c +_s d) \in \{2\}$$

The template which we followed above in setting up the minimal models and Klein's model can be shown to work also for all the other six models of analogical proportions. Concretely, all of the definitions are of the following form:

$$a : b ::_i c : d \quad \text{iff} \quad \Delta^{\pm}(a, b) = \Delta^{\pm}(c, d) \text{ or}$$
$$(a +_s b) + (c +_s d) \in I_i \tag{5}$$

where I_i is a set of cardinalities $I_i \subseteq \{1, 2, 3\}$. In detail: $I_{\Omega_0} = \emptyset$, $I_{Kl} = \{2\}$, $I_{M_3} = \{3\}$, $I_{M_4} = \{1\}$, $I_{M_5} = \{2, 3\}$, $I_{M_6} = \{1, 2\}$, $I_{M_7} = \{1, 3\}$, $I_{\Omega} = \{1, 2, 3\}$. We summarize the result in the following proposition:

Proposition 4. *The extension problem for composition of the first form for analogical propositions can be solved under the restriction that in each of the models of analogical proportions according to [18], i.e., of the models of Fig. 2 (left), "$:$" is interpreted with the same operation of analogical ratio according to Definition 1.*

Proof. The restriction of the use of the same analogical ratio is fulfilled due to the fact that all analogical proportions have the form given in (5).

We are left with showing that indeed the presentations of (5) model each of the eight analogical proportions. We check this for each of the models one-by-one: Ω_0: Due to (4), $\Delta^{\pm}(a, b) = \Delta^{\pm}(c, d)$ holds iff $ab = cd$ or $ab = 00$ and $cd = 11$ or $ab = 11$ and $cd = 11$, which gives exactly the six 4-bit vectors of Ω_0. Kl: Klein's model extends Ω_0 with $0110, 1001$. These have cardinality 2. The only other 4-bit vectors with cardinality 2 are $1010, 0101, 0011, 1100$, which are already in Ω_0. M_3: extends Ω_0 with $1110, 1101, 1011, 0111$, the only 4-bit vectors of cardinality 3. M_4: extends Ω_0 with $0001, 0010, 0100, 1000$, the only vectors with cardinality 1. M_5: Due to the fact that M_5 is the union of M_3 and Kl. M_6: Due to the fact that M_4 is the union of M_4 and Kl. M_7: due to the fact that M_7 is the union of M_3 and M_4. Ω: Clear: any bit vector is captured as in addition to the vectors in Ω_0 all possible cardinalities of 4-bit vectors are captured.

Our definition of the basic analogical proportion in Definition 1 is applicable also for the case where a, b, c, d stand for bit vectors. The bit vector representation of an object can be understood as a representation of that object w.r.t. some specific fixed set of (Boolean) features.

Now, with bit vectors represented as sets we can apply the operator $\Delta^{\pm}(a, b)$. We represent the outcome of $\Delta^{\pm}(a, b)$ on n-bit-vectors $a = (a_1, \ldots, a_n)$ and $b = (b_1, \ldots, b_n)$ as a pair of vectors, applying $\Delta^{\pm}$ component-wise: $\Delta^{\pm}(a, b) = (\Delta^{\pm}(a_j, b_j))_{1 \leq j \leq n}$. We could also apply $+_s$ directly on the sets but this would not give generalized analogical proportions that are models of the axioms defined in Sect. 3, in particular, they may not verify the basic axioms B_{ax}. Instead, we redefine $+_s$ as bit-wise addition and similarly for $+$ (which in fact interprets $+_s$ and $+$ as vector additions), i.e., $a +_s b = (a_i +_s b_i)_{1 \leq i \leq n}$ and $a + b = (a_i + b_i)_{1 \leq i \leq n}$. And so the definition expressed in (5) works in this following adapted version (with a component-wise disjunction) also for n-bit vectors:

$$a : b :: {}_i c : d \text{ iff } (\Delta^{\pm}(a, b))_j = (\Delta^{\pm}(c, d))_j \text{ or } ((a +_s b) + (c +_s d))_j \in I_i$$
$$\text{for all } j \in \{1, \ldots, n\} \tag{6}$$

To capture also models outside of TGM we further generalize the 1 to the n-bit vector $(1, \ldots, 1)$ of ones only and similarly for 0. Note that the generalization of the minimal model Ω_0 corresponds exactly to the generalization of Ω_0 given by Prade and Richard [18]. We summarize this generalized result in the next proposition:

Proposition 5. *The extension problem for compositionality of the first form for the language of analogical propositions* over the domain of n-bit vectors *can be solved under the restrictions that each generalized analogical proportion* $::_i$ *fulfills the axiom set* F_i *and that* ":" *denotes always the same analogical ratio. One solution is to define* $::_i$ *as in (6).*

Proof. We first observe that $a : b ::_i c : d$ according to (6) is defined component-wise for each $j \in \{1, \ldots, n\}$ as $(\Delta^{\pm}(a,b))_j = (\Delta^{\pm}(c,d))_j$ or $((a +_s b) + (c +_s d))_j \in I_i$ which means nothing else than: for each $j \in \{1, \ldots, n\}$: $a_j : b_j ::_i c_j : d_j$ or equivalently that $\bigwedge_{1 \leq j \leq n} a_j : b_j ::_i c_j : d_j$. Now we can apply this to each of the eight analogical proportions $a_j : b_j ::_i c_j : d_j$ over bits a_j, b_j, c_j, d_j for each $j \in \{1, \ldots, n\}$. Proposition 1 shows that it fulfills F_i (for each j). As each F_i is defined in the core fragment (even the Horn fragment suffices) each rule can be represented in the form $X \to Y$ (where Y is an atom and X is either a tautology (for example in case of the axiom of ratio symmetry) or is an atom). So, to show that $a : b ::_i c : d$ fulfills $X \to Y$ we assume that $a : b ::_i c : d$ fulfills Y, which means that for all j $a_j : b_j ::_i c_j : d_j$ is fulfilled. Now with Proposition 1 it follows that for each j, $a_j : b_j ::_i c_j : d_j$ also fulfills Y and hence $a : b ::_i c : d$ fulfills Y.

The other part of the proposition (stating the decomposition with the same ratio operator) is directly given by (6).

The proposition above provides a solution to the extension problem for compositionality under a restriction stating that for a given class of analogical proportions the analogical ratio has to be the same. But the basic ratio operator used in the solution might seem to be unnecessarily complex. And so one might ask whether (for each individual analogical proportion) there is an analogical ratio operator that is definable directly by a propositional formula. In fact, as the following proposition shows, the complexity in our basic analogical proportion is necessary and a restriction to propositional functions for: and :: prohibits decomposability for six out of eight analogical proportions.

Proposition 6. *The only models of the lattice of analogical proportions that allow decomposition under the constraints that 1. "$a : b$" denotes a binary Boolean function and 2. "::" denotes another binary Boolean function are Ω and Klein's model. A decomposition for Klein's model is given by reading both : and :: as biimplication.*

Proof. Clearly for Klein's models Kl we get a simple representation:

$$a : b ::_{Kl} c : d = (a \leftrightarrow b) \leftrightarrow (c \leftrightarrow d)$$

So, both : and :: are biimplications. Of course this representation is not unique. Equally, we could have set up the following representation: $a : b ::_{Kl} c : d = (a \nleftrightarrow b) \leftrightarrow (c \nleftrightarrow d)$.

But already for the minimal model Ω_0 such a decomposition is not possible, though Ω_0 is the only other model for which :: is an equivalence relation. This can be shown as follows: Assume there is a propositional formula $A(a, b)$ for

$a : b$ and a propositional formula $B(x, y)$ for $x :: _{\Omega_0} y$. Let $A(0,0) = b_{00}$ for some bit $b_{00} \in \{0, 1\}$ and similarly $A(i, j) = b_{ij}$. W.l.o.g assume $b_{00} = 1$. We must have $B(1, 1) = 1$, as $0000 \in \Omega_0$. Now consider b_{10}. We have $0010 \notin \Omega_0$, so $B(b_{00}, b_{10}) = B(1, b_{10}) = 0$, hence $b_{10} \neq 1$ and hence $b_{10} = 0$. Now consider b_{01}. If $b_{01} = 1$, then $B(b_{01}, b_{00}) = B(1, 1) = 1$, contradicting the fact that $0001 \notin \Omega_0$. If $b_{01} = 0$ we get $B(b_{10}, b_{01}) = B(0, 0) = 1$, contradicting the fact that $1001 \notin \Omega_0$.

Now we consider M_7. We use the same abbreviations $A(a, b), B(x, y)$ and b_{ij}. The only bit vectors not contained in M_7 are 1001 and 0110. We must have $b_{01} \neq b_{10}$ (because of reflexivity of B, recalling that $::$ fulfills B_{ax}). Assume w.l.o.g. that $b_{01} = 1$. Then $b_{10} = 0$ and $B(1, 0) = B(0, 1) = 0$. Then $B(b_{10}, b_{11}) = 1 = B(0, b_{11})$, i.e. $b_{11} = 0$, but on the same hand $B(b_{01}, b_{11}) = 1 = B(1, b_{11})$, i.e. $b_{11} = 1$, a contradiction.

For M_5 we get with similar considerations as above that it cannot be represented as a propositional formula. As $1000 \notin M_5$ we have $b_{10} \neq b_{00}$. W.l.o.g. $b_{10} = 1$, so $b_{00} = 0$ and $B(1, 0) = 0$. Due to symmetry of B (remember that all analogical proportions fulfill B_{ax}) we have also $B(0, 1) = 0$. As $1111 \in M_5$ we have $B(b_{11}, b_{11}) = 1$, so $B(1, 1) = 1$ (for $b_{11} = 0$ follows $B(b_{11}, b_{10}) = B(0, 1) = 0$ and thus $1110 \notin M_5$, a contradiction). As $0000 \in M_5$ we have $B(b_{00}, b_{00}) = 1$, so $B(0, 0) = 1$. But this means that $B(x, y) = x \leftrightarrow y$. Now, as $1001 \in M_5$ we would have $b_{01} = 1$. This would fix $A(a, b)$ to $a \vee b$ and $(A(c, d)$ to $c \vee d)$. But the resulting formula $(a \vee b) \leftrightarrow (c \vee d)$ does not represent M_5 as, e.g., $0011 \in M_5$. Similar considerations lead to the non-decomposability of M_6.

For M_3 we note $1000 \notin M_3$. Assume w.l.o.g. $b_{10} = 1$, then $b_{00} = 0$. Also $1001 \notin M_3$. So $b_{01} = 0$ and $B(0, 1) = 0$ and $B(1, 0) = 0$. As $0111 \in M_3$ we get $b_{11} = 0$, but as $1011 \in M_3$, we get $b_{11} = 1$, a contradiction. Similarly one argues for M_4.

Finally, Ω is simply representable by choosing for example $A(a, b) = a \vee \neg a$ and $B(x, y) = x \leftrightarrow y$.

This result may be considered as a support for the intuition that propositional logic ontologically commits itself to propositions (and truth values) but not to objects (as in the case of first-order logic, say). Only in the special case of Klein's model this commitment is not reflected in limited expressivity.

5 Related Work

Analogical reasoning has been intensively studied in context of research in cognition, with both psychologically and neurally inspired approaches receiving attention. Some of these theories have been adapted into AI methods, most notably Genter's structure mapping theory [6] underlying the structure mapping engine (SME) [4], which has been used in several applications of analogical reasoning [5], including learning [8]. SME relies on knowledge represented in a graph structure (a semantic network) and characterizes analogical proportions by partial local graph isomorphisms.

Aside the development of algorithmic approaches and cognitive theories, researchers have also characterized logic properties of analogical reasoning. Schwering et al. [20] approach analogical reasoning as anti-unification in first-order theories. Their approach addresses limitations of approaches like SME that presuppose a similar structure between concepts when making analogical proportions. Anti-unification is applied to generalizes terms until isomorphy of terms is obtained. Following the work of Prade and Richard [18], this work takes a deep dive by focusing on how an operator for building analogical proportions can be characterized and decomposed.

Our solution for reaching decomposability for models of analogical proportions presented in Sect. 4 used, in particular, a difference operator $\Delta^\pm$ that combines two Boolean functions. A similar use of multiple Boolean functions can be found in the so-called *dependency quantified Boolean formula problem (DQBF)* [9]. An DQBF instance can be represented as a Boolean sentence of the form $\exists f_1 \ldots \exists f_m \forall p_1 \ldots \forall p_n \psi$ where each f_i is a Boolean function variable whose occurrences in ψ are of the form $f_i(p_{i_1}, \ldots p_{i_k})$, for some fixed sequence of proposition variables $p_{i_1}, \ldots p_{i_k}$. So, the question of decomposability of a given analogical proportion can be represented as a DQBF problem. And hence the extension problem of compositionality under the restriction of representabiltiy with Boolean functions can be automatized with a DQBF theorem prover. Quantification over functions also suggests a connection to the area of generalized quantifiers which, in particular, were introduced, to solve the problem of decomposition [22].

The use of analogical proportions for bit-vectors opens up the possibility to consider the analogies of each row not as equally important but as weighted. This also appears in the context of automata theory and weighted logics [3].

Hüllermeyer [13] envisions the use of analogical proportions for explainable AI. For example, assume that an ML algorithm has lead to categorizing an instance into some specific category. Using analogical proportions this categorization result may be explained to users. The example Hüllermeyer gives is the following: Assume a, b, c, d stand for journals that are categorized w.r.t. a ranking $A*, A, B, C, D$. The ranking can be described as a multi-class classification problem. An ML system can be trained based on some feature space to learn the classes by minimizing the errors on given training examples, i.e., journals represented in the feature space and their ranking. For end-users this system is a black-box whose results are going to be supported by analogical reasoning. Assume that a and c have the same ranking, say an A, and b and d have the same ranking B. Then the ranking of d can be justified if we know that $a : b :: c : d$ holds. Let us first assume that the ranking consists of two classes only, namely B and $\neg B$ (not B). The argument goes:

(AR) If there are a, b, c, d such that: $a : b :: c : d$ and $B(a)$ and $B(c)$ and $\neg B(b)$, then: $\neg B(d)$.

Things become interesting of course in the case the feature space for representing a, b, c, d has more dimensions, but for the sake of the argument assume it has exactly one feature. Then we can actually distinguish between two types of objects corresponding to the bits 1 and 0. If that feature indeed helps in distinguishing between objects of type B and $\neg B$, then say 1 corresponds to B and 0 corresponds to $\neg B$. Now, in order for an argument such as (AR) to work the principle of unicity would have to hold. So only the minimal analogical proportion Ω_0 or Klein's analogical proportion Kl would be an appropriate model for (AR). In fact, as Hüllermeyer argues, (AR) is a general principle that holds also for more complex domains. The idea is that the analogical proportion between objects "also applies to the properties caused by these objects (for example, the predictions produced by an ML model)" [13]. So, we can consider (AR) as a form of argumentation that relies on an extended unicity principle.

6   Conclusion and Future Work

We motivated our paper by observing that the AI community has two perspectives on analogical proportions—one axiomatic abstract, the other concrete with difference/ratio operators applied to analogical reasoning—and showed that we can bridge these perspectives by means of decompositions. Our example with RPMs shows how an analogical reasoning task can be tackled using analogical proportions. The proposed logic characterization complements the ML approaches of [12,23] that posed the task of mastering RPMs as a neuro-symbolic challenge. In future work it would be interesting to integrate the logic characterization with a ML model.

Coming back to the introductory example on RPMs and the approach by Lovett and Forbus [16], we also find motivation for the *extension problem of composition of the second form* [11, p.16]: Given the meanings of the sentences of a language (in our case the analogical proportions $a : b :: c : d$ understood as a quaternary relation) find also meanings for all other expressions of an extended language. Here we would consider expressions built by : and :: and some multiplication operator $*$ in order to "apply" a ratio $a : b$ to an element d. The task of finding c such that $a : b :: c : d$ becomes computing $(a : b) * d$. We see potential for a research agenda where the decomposition problem that we demonstrated for some class of models of analogical proportions and for some simple forms of analogical reasoning is conducted in a larger setting. As an outcome of such a long-term research we envision a full map of possible decompositions of analogical proportions.

Acknowledgment. The authors would like to thank the anonymous reviewers for their constructive and detailed feedback.

The research of Mena Leemhuis and Özgür L. Özçep is funded by the Federal Ministry of Education and Research of Germany (BMBF) within the project SmaDi under grant number 13XP5124A/B.

References

1. Bordes, A., Usunier, N., García-Durán, A., Weston, J., Yakhnenko, O.: Translating embeddings for modeling multi-relational data. In: Burges, C.J.C., Bottou, L., Ghahramani, Z., Weinberger, K.Q. (eds.) Advances in Neural Information Processing Systems 26: 27th Annual Conference on Neural Information Processing Systems 2013. Proceedings of a meeting held 5–8 December 2013, Lake Tahoe, Nevada, United States, pp. 2787–2795 (2013). https://papers.nips.cc/paper/5071-translating-embeddings-for-modeling-multi-relational-data

2. Chen, Z., Wang, Y., Zhao, B., Cheng, J., Zhao, X., Duan, Z.: Knowledge graph completion: a review. IEEE Access **8**, 192435–192456 (2020). https://doi.org/10.1109/ACCESS.2020.3030076

3. Droste, M., Gastin, P.: Weighted Automata and Weighted Logics, pp. 175–211. Springer, Berlin, Heidelberg (2009). https://doi.org/10.1007/978-3-642-01492-5_5

4. Falkenhainer, B., Forbus, K.D., Gentner, D.: The structure-mapping engine: algorithms and examples. Artif. Intell. **41**, 1–63 (1989)

5. Forbus, K.D.: Qualitative Representations: How People Reason and Learn about the Continuous World. MIT Press, Cambridge (2019)

6. Gentner, D.: Structure-mapping: a theoretical framework for analogy. Cogn. Sci. **7**(2) (1983)

7. Gentner, D., Smith, L.: Analogical Reasoning, 2 edn. In: Encyclopedia of Human Behavior, pp. 130–136. Elsevier, Amsterdam (2012)

8. Hancock, W., Forbus, K.D.: Qualitative spatiotemporal representations of episodic memory for strategic reasoning. In: Proceedings of the 34th International Workshop on Qualitative Reasoning (QR 2021) (2021)

9. Hannula, M., Kontinen, J., Lück, M., Virtema, J.: On the Complexity of Horn and Krom Fragments of Second-Order Boolean Logic, July 2020. https://doi.org/10.48550/arXiv.2007.03867. arXiv e-prints arXiv:2007.03867

10. Hazen, A., Humberstone, L.: Similarity relations and the preservation of solidity. J. Log. Lang. Inf. **13**(1), 25–46 (2004). https://www.jstor.org/stable/40180366

11. Hodges, W.: Formal features of compositionality. J. Log. Lang. Inform. **10**(1), 7–28 (2001). https://doi.org/10.1023/A:1026502210492

12. Hu, S., Ma, Y., Liu, X., Wei, Y., Bai, S.: Stratified rule-aware network for abstract visual reasoning. In: Proceedings of the AAAI Conference on Artificial Intelligence (AAAI-21), pp. 1567–1574 (2021)

13. Hüllermeier, E.: Towards analogy-based explanations in machine learning. In: Torra, V., Narukawa, Y., Nin, J., Agell, N. (eds.) MDAI 2020. LNCS (LNAI), vol. 12256, pp. 205–217. Springer, Cham (2020). https://doi.org/10.1007/978-3-030-57524-3_17

14. Klein, S.: Culture, mysticism & social structure and the calculation of behavior. In: Proceedings of the 5th European Conference on Artificial Intelligence, pp. 141–146. ECAI'82, North-Holland (1982)

15. Libkin, L.: Elements Of Finite Model Theory. Texts in Theoretical Computer Science, An EATCS Series (TTCS), Springer, Berlin, Heidelberg (2004). https://doi.org/10.1007/978-3-662-07003-1

16. Lovett, A., Kenneth, F.: Modeling visual problem solving as analogical reasoning. Psychol. Rev. **124**(1), 60–90 (2017)

17. Mikolov, T., Ilya Sutskever, I., Chen, K., Corrado, G., Dean, J.: Distributed Representations of Words and Phrases and their Compositionality, October 2013. ArXiv e-prints

18. Prade, H., Richard, G.: Analogical proportions: from equality to inequality. Int. J. Approx. Reason. **101**, 234–254 (2018). https://doi.org/10.1016/j.ijar.2018.07.005

19. Prade, H., Richard, G.: Analogical proportions: why they are useful in AI. In: Zhou, Z.H. (ed.) Proceedings of the Thirtieth International Joint Conference on Artificial Intelligence, IJCAI-21, pp. 4568–4576. International Joint Conferences on Artificial Intelligence Organization, August 2021. https://doi.org/10.24963/ijcai.2021/621, survey Track

20. Schwering, A., Krumnack, U., Kühnberger, K.U., Gust, H.: Syntactic principles of heuristic-driven theory projection. Cogn. Syst. Res. **10**(3), 251–269 (2009)

21. Tversky, A.: Features of similarity. Psychol. Rev. **84**(4), 327–352 (1977). https://doi.org/10.1037/0033-295X.84.4.327

22. Westerståhl, D.: Generalized Quantifiers. In: Zalta, E.N. (ed.) The Stanford Encyclopedia of Philosophy. Metaphysics Research Lab, Stanford University, Winter 2019 edn. (2019)

23. Zhang, C., Gao, F., Jia, B., Zhu, Y., Zhu, S.C.: RAVEN: a dataset for relational and analogical visual reasoning. In: Proceedings of the IEEE Conference on Computer Vision and Pattern Recognition (CVPR) (2019)

A Remark on the Expressivity
of Asynchronous TeamLTL and HyperLTL

Juha Kontinen[1], Max Sandström[1,2]([✉]), and Jonni Virtema[1,2]

[1] Department of Mathematics and Statistics, University of Helsinki, Helsinki, Finland
{juha.kontinen,max.sandstrom}@helsinki.fi
[2] Department of Computer Science, University of Sheffield, Sheffield, UK
j.t.virtema@sheffield.ac.uk

Abstract. Linear temporal logic (LTL) is used in system verification to write formal specifications for reactive systems. However, some relevant properties, e.g. non-inference in information flow security, cannot be expressed in LTL. A class of such properties that has recently received ample attention is known as hyperproperties. There are two major streams in the research regarding capturing hyperproperties, namely hyperlogics, which extend LTL with trace quantifiers (HyperLTL), and logics that employ team semantics, extending truth to sets of traces. In this article we explore the relation between asynchronous LTL under set-based team semantics (TeamLTL) and HyperLTL. In particular we consider the extensions of TeamLTL with the Boolean disjunction and a fragment of the extension of TeamLTL with the Boolean negation, where the negation cannot occur in the left-hand side of the Until-operator or within the Global-operator. We show that TeamLTL extended with the Boolean disjunction is equi-expressive with the positive Boolean closure of HyperLTL restricted to one universal quantifier, while the left-downward closed fragment of TeamLTL extended with the Boolean negation is expressively equivalent with the Boolean closure of HyperLTL restricted to one universal quantifier.

Keywords: Hyperproperties · Temporal Logic · Team Semantics · HyperLTL · Verification

1   Introduction

In 1977 Amir Pnueli [16] introduced a core concept in verification of reactive and concurrent systems: model checking of formulae of linear temporal logic (LTL). The idea is to view the accepting executions of the system as a set of infinite sequences, called traces, and check whether this set satisfies specifications expressed in LTL. The properties that can be checked by observing every execution of the system in isolation are called *trace properties*. An oft-cited example of a trace property is *termination*, which states that a system terminates if each of its computations terminates. Classical LTL is fit for the verification of such propositional trace properties, however some properties relevant in, for instance, information flow security are not trace properties. These properties profoundly speak of relations between traces. Clarkson and Schneider [3] coined the term *hyperproperties* to refer to such properties that lie beyond what LTL can express. *Bounded termination* is an easy to grasp example of a hyperproperty: whether every computation of a system terminates within some bound common for all traces, cannot be determined by looking at traces in isolation. In information flow security, dependencies between public observable outputs and secret inputs constitute possible security breaches; checking for hyperproperties becomes invaluable. Two well-known examples of hyperproperties from this field are noninterference [15,18], where a high-level user cannot affect what low-level users see, and observational determinism [21], meaning that if two computations are in the same state according to a low-level observer, then the executions will be indistinguishable. However, hyperproperties are not limited to information flow security; examples from different fields include distributivity and other system properties such as fault tolerance [6].

Given this background, several approaches to formally specifying hyperproperties have been proposed since 2010, with families of logics emerging from these approaches. The two major streams in the research regarding capturing hyperproperties are *hyperlogics* and logics that employ *team semantics*. In the hyperlogics approach, logics that capture trace properties are extended with trace quantification, extending logics such as LTL, computation tree logic (CTL) or quantified propositional temporal logic (QPTL), into HyperLTL [2], HyperCTL* [2], and HyperQPTL [4,17], respectively. An alternative approach is to lift the semantics of the temporal logics from being defined on traces to sets of traces, by using what is known as team semantics. This approach yields logics such as TeamLTL [9,14] and TeamCTL[9,13]. Since its conception, TeamLTL has been considered in two distinct variants: a synchronous semantics, where the team of traces agrees on the time step of occurrence when evaluating temporal operators; and an asynchronous semantics, where the temporal operators are evaluated independently on each trace. An example that illustrates the difference between these two semantics is the aforementioned termination and bound termination pair of properties. If we write F for the future-operator and terminate for a proposition symbol representing the trace terminating, we can write the formula F terminate, which under the synchronous semantics expresses the hyperproperty "bounded termination", while under the asynchronous semantics the same formula defines the trace property "termination". Not only is the above formulation of bounded termination clear and concise, it also illuminates a key difference between hyperlogics and team logics: while each formula of hyperlogic has a fixed number of quantifiers, which restricts the number of traces that can be referred to in a formula, which restricts the number of traces between which dependencies can be characterised by formulae, team logics have the ability to refer to an unbounded number of traces, even an infinite collection.

One of the original motivations behind team semantics [19] was to enable the definition of novel atomic formulae, and this is another important defining feature of team temporal logics as well. Among these atoms the *dependence atom* $\text{dep}(\bar{x}, \bar{y})$ and *inclusion atom* $\bar{x} \subseteq \bar{y}$ stand out as the most influential. They respectively state that the variables $\bar{y}$ are functionally dependent on the variables $\bar{x}$, and that the values of the variables $\bar{x}$ also occur among the values of variables $\bar{y}$. As an example of the use of the inclusion atom, let the proposition symbols $o_1, \ldots, o_n$ denote public observable bits and assume that the proposition symbol s is a secret bit. The atomic formula $(o_1, \ldots o_n, s) \subseteq (o_1, \ldots o_n, \neg s)$ expresses a form of non-inference by stating that an observer cannot infer the value of the confidential bit from the outputs.

While the expressivity of HyperLTL and other hyperlogics has been studied extensively, where the many extensions of TeamLTL lie in relation the hyperlogics is still not completely understood. The connections for the logics without extensions were already established in Krebs et al. [14], where they showed that synchronous TeamLTL and HyperLTL are expressively incomparable and that the asynchronous variant collapses to LTL. With regards to the expressivity of synchronous semantics, Virtema et al. [20] showed that the extensions of TeamLTL can be translated to HyperQPTL$^+$, which in turn extends HyperLTL with (non-uniform) quantification of propositions. Relating the logics to the first-order context, Kontinen and Sandström [11] defined Kamp-style translations from extensions of both semantics of TeamLTL to the three-variable fragment of first-order team logic. It is worth noting that recently asynchronous hyperlogics have been considered also in several other articles (see, e.g., [1,10]). An example of the significant rift between asynchronous and synchronous TeamLTL is that the asynchronous semantics is essentially a first-order logic, while the synchronous semantics has second-order aspects. Especially the set-based variant of asynchronous TeamLTL can be translated, using techniques in [11], into first-order logic under team semantics, which is known to be first-order logic [19]. Similarly, HyperLTL is equally expressive as the guarded fragment of first-order logic with the equal level predicate, as was shown by Finkbeiner and Zimmermann [7].

In this article we focus on exploring the connections between fragments of HyperLTL and extensions of TeamLTL. The set-based asynchronous semantics that we consider here was defined in Kontinen et al. [12] in order to further study the complexity of the model checking problem for these logics. Prior to that, the literature on temporal team semantics employed a semantics based on multisets of traces. In the wider team semantics literature, this often carries the name *strict semantics*, in contrast to *lax semantics* which is de facto a set-based semantics. This relaxation of the semantics enabled the definition of normal forms for the logics, which we use in this article to explore the connection with HyperLTL.

Our Contribution. We show correspondences in expressivity between the set-based variant of linear temporal logic under asynchronous team semantics and fragments of the Boolean closure of HyperLTL. In particular we show that LTL under team semantics with the Boolean disjunction, TeamLTL($\varovee$), is equiexpressive with the positive Boolean closure of HyperLTL restricted to only one universal quantifier, while the left downward closed fragment of TeamLTL($\sim$) is equi-expressive with the Boolean closure of HyperLTL restricted to one universal quantifier.

2   Preliminaries

We begin by defining the variant of TeamLTL and its extensions, as in [12].

Let AP be a set of *atomic propositions*. The formulae of LTL (over AP) is attained by the grammar:

$$\varphi ::= p \mid \neg p \mid \varphi \vee \varphi \mid \varphi \wedge \varphi \mid \varphi \mid G\varphi \mid \varphi U\varphi,$$

where $p \in$ AP. We follow the convention that all formulae of TeamLTL are given in negation normal form, where $\neg$ is only allowed before atomic propositions, as is customary when dealing with team semantics.

We will consider the extensions of TeamLTL with the Boolean disjunction $\varovee$, denoted TeamLTL($\varovee$), and Boolean negation $\sim$, denoted TeamLTL($\sim$).

A *trace* t over AP is an infinite sequence of sets of proposition symbols from $(2^{AP})^\omega$. Given a natural number $i \in \mathbb{N}$, we denote by $t[i]$ the $(i+1)$th element of t and by $t[i, \infty]$ the suffix $(t[j])_{j \geq i}$ of t. We call a set of traces a *team*.

We write $\mathcal{P}(\mathbb{N})^+$ to denote $\mathcal{P}(\mathbb{N}) \setminus \{\emptyset\}$. For a team $T \subseteq (2^{AP})^\omega$ a function $f: T \to \mathcal{P}(\mathbb{N})^+$, we set $T[f, \infty] := \{t[s, \infty] \mid t \in T, s \in f(t)\}$. For $T' \subseteq T$, $f: T \to \mathcal{P}(\mathbb{N})^+$, and $f': T' \to \mathcal{P}(\mathbb{N})^+$, we define that $f' < f$ if and only if

$$\forall t \in T' : \min(f'(t)) \leq \min(f(t)) \text{ and,}$$
$$\text{if } \max(f(t)) \text{ exists, } \max(f'(t)) < \max(f(t)).$$

Definition 1 (TeamLTL). *Let T be a team, and φ and ψ TeamLTL-formulae. The lax semantics is defined as follows.*

$$
\begin{aligned}
T \models l &\quad\Leftrightarrow\quad t \models l \text{ for all } t \in T, \text{ where } l \in \{p, \neg p \mid p \in \text{AP}\} \\
&\qquad\qquad \text{is a literal and "} t \models \text{" refers to LTL-satisfaction} \\
T \models \varphi \wedge \psi &\quad\Leftrightarrow\quad T \models \varphi \text{ and } T \models \psi \\
T \models \varphi \vee \psi &\quad\Leftrightarrow\quad \exists T_1, T_2 \text{ s.t. } T_1 \cup T_2 = T \text{ and } T_1 \models \varphi \text{ and } T_2 \models \psi \\
T \models \varphi &\quad\Leftrightarrow\quad T[1, \infty] \models \varphi \\
T \models G\varphi &\quad\Leftrightarrow\quad \forall f: T \to \mathcal{P}(\mathbb{N})^+ \text{ it holds that } T[f, \infty] \models \varphi \\
T \models \varphi U \psi &\quad\Leftrightarrow\quad \exists f: T \to \mathcal{P}(\mathbb{N})^+ \text{ such that } T[f, \infty] \models \psi \text{ and} \\
&\qquad\qquad \forall f': T' \to \mathcal{P}(\mathbb{N})^+ \text{s.t. } f' < f, \text{ it holds that } T'[f', \infty] \models \varphi \\
&\qquad\qquad \text{or } T' = \emptyset, \text{ where } T' := \{t \in T \mid \max(f(t)) \neq 0\}
\end{aligned}
$$

The semantics for the Boolean disjunction and Boolean negation, used in the extensions TeamLTL($\varovee$) *and* TeamLTL($\sim$), *are given by:*

$$
\begin{aligned}
T \models \varphi \varovee \psi &\quad\Leftrightarrow\quad T \models \varphi \text{ or } T \models \psi \\
T \models \sim \varphi &\quad\Leftrightarrow\quad T \not\models \varphi
\end{aligned}
$$

Note that the Boolean disjunction is definable in TeamLTL($\sim$), as the dual of conjunction, i.e. $T \models^l \varphi \varovee \psi$ if and only if $T \models^l \sim (\sim \varphi \wedge \sim \psi)$.

Two important properties of team logics are *flatness* and *downward closure*. A logic has the flatness property if $T \models^l \varphi$ if and only if $\{t\} \models^l \varphi$ for all $t \in T$, holds for all formulae φ of the logic. A logic is downward closed if for all formulae φ of the logic if $T \models^l \varphi$ and $S \subseteq T$ then $S \models^l \varphi$. The following Proposition was proven in [12].

Proposition 2. TeamLTL^l *has both the flatness and the downward closure properties, while* TeamLTL^l($\varovee$) *only has the downward closure property.*

We consider the *left-downward closed* fragment of TeamLTL^l($\sim$), denoted left-dc–TeamLTL^l($\sim$), where every subformula of the form $G \psi$ or $\psi \cup \theta$, the subformula ψ is a TeamLTL($\varovee$)-formula

It was established in [12] that any formula of TeamLTL^l($\varovee$) can be equivalently expressed in $\varovee$-*disjunctive normal form*, i.e. in the form

$$\bigvarovee_{i \in I} \alpha_i,$$

where α_i are LTL-formulae.

Similarly by [12], every formula of left-dc–TeamLTL^l($\sim$) can be equivalently stated in *quasi-flat normal form*, which means in the form

$$\bigvarovee_{i \in I} (\alpha_i \wedge \bigwedge_{j \in J_i} \exists \beta_{i,j}),$$

where α_i and $\beta_{i,j}$ are LTL-formulae, and $\exists \beta_{i,j}$ is an abbreviation for the formula $\sim \beta_{i,j}^d$, where $\beta_{i,j}^d$ is the formula obtained from $\neg \beta$, after $\neg$ has been pushed down to the atomic level.

Next we state the syntax and semantics of HyperLTL, as defined in [2], as well as the Boolean closure concepts we are concerned with.

Definition 3 (Syntax of HyperLTL). *Let* AP *be a set of propositional variables and* $\mathcal{V}$ *the set of all trace variables. Formulas of HyperLTL are generated by the following grammar:*

$$\psi ::= \exists \pi.\psi \mid \forall \pi.\psi \mid \varphi$$
$$\varphi ::= a_\pi \mid \neg \varphi \mid \varphi \vee \varphi \mid \varphi \mid \varphi \cup \varphi,$$

where $a \in$ AP *and* $\pi \in \mathcal{V}$.

We denote the set of all traces by TR and the set of all trace variables by $\mathcal{V}$. For a trace assignment function $\Pi: \mathcal{V} \to$ TR, we write $\Pi[i, \infty]$ for the trace assignment defined through $\Pi[i, \infty] = \Pi(\pi)[i, \infty]$, and $\Pi[\pi \mapsto t]$ for the assignment that assigns t to π, but otherwise is identical to Π.

Definition 4 (Semantics of HyperLTL**).** *Let* $a \in \mathrm{AP}$ *be a proposition symbol,* $\pi \in \mathcal{V}$ *be a trace variable,* T *be a set of traces, and let* $\Pi \colon \mathcal{V} \to \mathrm{TR}$ *be a trace assignment.*

$$
\begin{aligned}
\Pi \models_T \exists \pi.\psi \quad &\Leftrightarrow \quad \text{there exists } t \in T \colon \Pi[\pi \mapsto t] \models_T \psi \\
\Pi \models_T \forall \pi.\psi \quad &\Leftrightarrow \quad \text{for all } t \in T \colon \Pi[\pi \mapsto t] \models_T \psi \\
\Pi \models_T a_\pi \quad &\Leftrightarrow \quad a \in \Pi(\pi)[0] \\
\Pi \models_T \neg\varphi \quad &\Leftrightarrow \quad \Pi \not\models_T \varphi \\
\Pi \models_T \varphi_1 \vee \varphi_2 \quad &\Leftrightarrow \quad \Pi \models_T \varphi_1 \text{ or } \Pi \models_T \varphi_2 \\
\Pi \models_T \varphi \quad &\Leftrightarrow \quad \Pi[1,\infty] \models_T \varphi \\
\Pi \models_T \varphi_1 \,\mathsf{U}\, \varphi_2 \quad &\Leftrightarrow \quad \text{there exists } i \geq 0 \colon \Pi[i,\infty] \models_T \varphi_2 \\
&\qquad\qquad \text{and for all } 0 \leq j < i \text{ we have } \Pi[j,\infty] \models_T \varphi_1
\end{aligned}
$$

Definition 5 (Universal Fragments). *The universal fragment of* HyperLTL*, denoted by* $\forall^*$HyperLTL*, is the fragment of* HyperLTL *with no existential quantification. We write* $\forall$HyperLTL *for the one variable universal fragment of* HyperLTL*, and* QHyperLTL *for the one variable fragment of* HyperLTL*.*

Definition 6 ((Positive) Boolean Closure). *The Boolean closure of a logic* $\mathcal{L}$*, denoted by* $\mathrm{BC}(\mathcal{L})$*, is the extension of* $\mathcal{L}$ *that is closed under* $\wedge$*,* $\vee$ *and* $\neg$*. The positive Boolean closure of a logic* $\mathcal{L}$*, denoted by* $\mathrm{PBC}(\mathcal{L})$*, is the extension of* $\mathcal{L}$ *that is closed under* $\wedge$ *and* $\vee$*.*

The semantics for the Boolean closures are attained by relaxing the definition of conjunction $\wedge$, disjunction $\vee$, and $\neg$ to apply to any formula of the Boolean closure.

Using a suitable algorithm, all $\mathrm{BC}(\mathcal{L})$-formulae can be equivalently expressed in disjunctive normal form, i.e. as a disjunction of conjunctions with possibly a negation in front of each formula of $\mathcal{L}$. Similarly, all $\mathrm{PBC}(\mathcal{L})$-formulae can be equivalently expressed as

$$
\bigvee_{i \in I} \bigwedge_{j \in J} \varphi_{i,j}
$$

for some formulae $\varphi_{i,j} \in \mathcal{L}$ and index sets I and J. From here on we use I and J to denote arbitrary index sets.

3   Correspondence Between TeamLTL and HyperLTL

In this section we will explore the relationship between the logics by proving some correspondence theorems. First, however, we prove some pertinent propositions regarding the Boolean closure of HyperLTL, showing that conjunction, disjunction and negation distribute over the quantifiers in a manner analogous to first-order logic. We go through these propositions in some detail as, although they appear familiar from the first-order setting, HyperLTL is usually considered only in the prenex normal form and thus these basic results are not explicitly addressed in the literature. Moreover, the proofs feature arguments that will be useful in subsequent proofs.

As usual, for logics $\mathcal{L}$ and $\mathcal{L}'$, we write $\mathcal{L} \leq \mathcal{L}'$, if for every $\mathcal{L}$-formula there exists an equivalent $\mathcal{L}'$-formula. We write $\mathcal{L} \equiv \mathcal{L}'$, if both $\mathcal{L} \leq \mathcal{L}'$ and $\mathcal{L}' \leq \mathcal{L}$.

Proposition 7. $\mathrm{PBC}(\forall^*\mathrm{HyperLTL}) \equiv \forall^*\mathrm{HyperLTL}$

Proof. Let $\bigvee_{i \in I} \bigwedge_{j \in J} \psi_{i,j}$ be an arbitrary formula of $\mathrm{PBC}(\forall^*\mathrm{HyperLTL})$. If all $\psi_{i,j}$ are quantifier free, we are done, as then $\bigvee_{i \in I} \bigwedge_{j \in J} \psi_{i,j}$ is a $\forall^*\mathrm{HyperLTL}$-formula. Thus, we may assume that $\psi_{i,j} = \forall \pi_1 \cdots \forall \pi_n \varphi_{i,j}$ for some LTL-formula $\varphi_{i,j}$. Suppose

$$\Pi \models_T \bigvee_{i \in I} \bigwedge_{j \in J} \forall \pi_1 \cdots \forall \pi_n \varphi_{i,j}.$$

Without loss of generality, we may assume a uniform quantifier block in each conjunct, as one can rename variables and take the largest quantifier block as the common one, since redundant quantifiers do not effect evaluation. The previous is therefore equivalent with

$$\Pi \models_T \bigvee_{i \in I} \forall \pi_1 \cdots \forall \pi_n \bigwedge_{j \in J} \varphi_{i,j}.$$

At this point, we wish to push the disjunction past the quantifier block, but the variables would become entangled and different traces could satisfy different disjuncts. We need to distinguish the variables of the disjuncts from each other, so we rename the trace quantifiers. The previous evaluation is therefore equivalent with

$$\Pi \models_T \forall \pi_1^1 \cdots \forall \pi_1^i \cdots \forall \pi_n^1 \cdots \forall \pi_n^i \bigvee_{i \in I} \bigwedge_{j \in J} \varphi_{i,j}(\pi_1^1, \cdots, \pi_n^i).$$

This is a formula of $\forall^*\mathrm{HyperLTL}$.   □

The following remark, familiar from first-order logics, can be proven with a straight-forward induction over the length of the quantifier block.

Remark 8. For HyperLTL-formula $Q_1\pi_1 \cdots Q_n\pi_n\psi$ it holds that

$$\neg Q_1\pi_1 \cdots Q_n\pi_n\psi \equiv Q_1^-\pi_1 \cdots Q_n^-\pi_n\neg\psi,$$

where for every index i, Q_i are quantifiers $\forall$ or $\exists$, and Q_i^- is $\exists$ if Q_i is $\forall$ and vice versa.

Proposition 9. $\mathrm{BC}(\mathrm{HyperLTL}) \equiv \mathrm{HyperLTL}$.

Proof. Consider a $\mathrm{BC}(\mathrm{HyperLTL})$-formula $\bigvee_{i \in I} \bigwedge_{j \in J} \varphi_{i,j}$ in disjunctive normal form, with either $\varphi_{i,j} \in \mathrm{HyperLTL}$ or $\varphi_{i,j} = \neg\psi_{i,j}$ for some formula $\psi_{i,j} \in \mathrm{HyperLTL}$. By Remark 8 $\neg\psi_{i,j} \equiv Q_1^{i,j}\pi_1^{i,j} \cdots Q_n^{i,j}\pi_n^{i,j}\theta_{i,j}$, where $\theta_{i,j} \in \mathrm{LTL}$.

Thus we may assume that $\varphi_{i,j}$ only appears positively. By a similar argument to that of the proof of Proposition 7 we get the following:

$$\bigvee_{i \in I} \bigwedge_{j \in J} Q_1^{i,j} \pi_1^{i,j} \cdots Q_n^{i,j} \pi_n^{i,j} \psi_{i,j} \equiv Q_1^{1,1} \pi_1^{1,1} \cdots Q_1^{1,j} \pi_1^{1,j} \cdots Q_n^{i,j} \pi_n^{i,j} \bigvee_{i \in I} \bigwedge_{j \in J} \psi_{i,j}.$$

$\square$

One last remark before we get to the core results of this article, this time relating quantifier-free HyperLTL-formulae with LTL-formulae. The remark can again be proven by induction on the structure of the formula.

Remark 10. Let T be a team, Π be a trace assignment, π be a trace variable, φ be a LTL-formula, and let $\varphi(\pi)$ be the HyperLTL formula identical to φ, except every proposition symbol p is replaced by p_π. Suppose $\Pi(\pi) = t$ for some $t \in T$. Now the following equivalence holds

$$\Pi \models_T \varphi(\pi) \iff t \models \varphi.$$

Using the above propositions we may now proceed with proving our main results: correspondence theorems between team logics and the Boolean closures of hyperlogics.

Note that TeamLTL has no separation between closed and open formulae, and has no features to encode trace assignments. Thus, when φ is a formula of some team based logic $\mathcal{L}$ and ψ is a formula of a hyper logic $\mathcal{L}'$ without free variables, we say that φ and ψ are equivalent, if the equivalence $T \models \varphi \Leftrightarrow \emptyset \models_T \psi$, holds for all sets of traces T. The notations $\mathcal{L} \leq \mathcal{L}'$ and $\mathcal{L} \equiv \mathcal{L}'$ are then defined in the obvious way, by restricting $\mathcal{L}'$ to formulae without free variables.

Theorem 11. TeamLTL$^l(\oslash) \equiv$ PBC($\forall$HyperLTL)

Proof. Let T be an arbitrary team and φ an arbitrary TeamLTL$^l(\oslash)$-formula. By [12, Theorem 10], we may assume that φ is in the form $\bigotimes_{i \in I} \alpha_i$, where I in an index set and α_i are LTL-formulae. We let $\alpha_i(\pi)$ denote the HyperLTL-formulae obtained from α_i, by replacing every proposition symbol p by p_π. We obtain the following chain of equivalences:

$$T \models \bigotimes_{i \in I} \alpha_i \iff \text{there is } i \in I \text{ such that } T \models \alpha_i$$

$$\iff \text{there is } i \in I \text{ such that } t \models \alpha_i \text{ for all } t \in T$$

$$\iff \text{there is } i \in I \text{ such that } \emptyset \models_T \forall \pi \alpha_i(\pi)$$

$$\iff \emptyset \models_T \bigvee_{i \in I} \forall \pi \alpha_i(\pi),$$

where the first equivalence follows from the semantics of $\oslash$, the second equivalence holds by the flatness of α_i, the third equivalence is due to the semantics of $\forall$ and Remark 10, and the final equivalence follows from the semantics of $\lor$.

For the converse direction, consider an arbitrary PBC($\forall$HyperLTL)-sentence ψ. As noted above, ψ is equivalent to a sentence $\bigvee_{i \in I} \bigwedge_{j \in J} \forall \pi \varphi_{i,j}(\pi)$, where $\varphi_{i,j}(\pi)$, for every pair i and j, is a HyperLTL-formula with π as the only free variable. Now by an argument similar to the proof of Proposition 7, $\emptyset \models_T \bigvee_{i \in I} \bigwedge_{j \in J} \forall \pi \varphi_{i,j}(\pi)$ if and only if $\emptyset \models_T \bigvee_{i \in I} \forall \pi \bigwedge_{j \in J} \varphi_{i,j}(\pi)$. Equivalently then by the definition of the semantics of the disjunction, we may fix $i' \in I$ such that $\emptyset \models_T \forall \pi \bigwedge_{j \in J} \varphi_{i',j}(\pi)$. By the definition of the universal quantifier then we get that the previous is equivalent with $\emptyset[\pi \mapsto t] \models_T \bigwedge_{j \in J} \varphi_{i',j}(\pi)$ for all $t \in T$. Now by Remark 10, the previous holds if and only if $t \models \bigwedge_{j \in J} \varphi_{i',j}$ for all $t \in T$, which is equivalent to $T \models^l \bigwedge_{j \in J} \varphi_{i',j}$, due to the flatness property of TeamLTL. Finally, by the semantics of the Boolean disjunction, the previous is equivalent with $T \models \bigveedot_{i \in I} \bigwedge_{j \in J} \varphi_{i,j}$. $\square$

As a corollary we get that TeamLTL$^l(\veedot)$ is subsumed by the universal fragment of HyperLTL, which follows from Theorem 11 and the observations made in the proof of Proposition 7.

Corollary 12. TeamLTL$^l(\veedot) \leq \forall^*$HyperLTL

Note that another consequence of Theorem 11 is that $\forall$HyperLTL is strictly less expressive than PBC($\forall$HyperLTL), as the former is equivalent with LTL [5] and thus has the flatness property, while the latter is equivalent with TeamLTL($\veedot$), which does not satisfy flatness. This stands in contrast to the unrestricted universal fragment $\forall^*$HyperLTL, which by Proposition 7 is equivalent to its positive Boolean closure.

Theorem 13. *left-dc*–TeamLTL$^l(\sim) \equiv$ BC(QHyperLTL) $\equiv$ BC($\forall$HyperLTL)

Proof. Let φ be an arbitrary left-dc–TeamLTL$^l(\sim)$-formula. Now by the quasi-flat normal form $T \models^l \varphi$ if and only if $T \models^l \bigveedot_{i \in I} (\alpha_i \wedge \bigwedge_{j \in J} \exists \beta_{i,j})$. Equivalently, by the semantics of $\veedot$, we may fix an index $i' \in I$ such that $T \models^l \alpha_{i'} \wedge \bigwedge_{j \in J} \exists \beta_{i',j}$. By the semantics of the logic, flatness, and the interpretation of the shorthand $\exists$, the previous evaluation is equivalent with that $t \models \alpha_{i'}$ for all $t \in T$ and for all $j \in J$ there is a $t_j \in T$ such that $t_j \models \beta_{i',j}$. By Remark 10 the previous holds if and only if $\emptyset[\pi \mapsto t] \models_T \alpha_{i'}(\pi)$ for all $t \in T$ and for all $j \in J$ there is a $t_j \in T$ such that $\emptyset[\pi \mapsto t_j] \models_T \beta_{i',j}(\pi)$. Equivalently, by the semantics of $\forall$ and $\exists$, we have that $\emptyset \models_T \forall \pi \alpha_{i'}(\pi)$ and $\emptyset \models_T \bigwedge_{j \in J} \exists \pi \beta_{i',j}(\pi)$, which, finally by the semantics of $\vee$ and $\wedge$, holds if and only if $\emptyset \models_T \bigvee_{i \in I} (\forall \pi \alpha_i(\pi) \wedge \bigwedge_{j \in J} \exists \pi \beta_{i,j}(\pi))$.

On the other hand, let ψ be an arbitrary sentence of BC(HyperLTL). Now we get the following chain of equivalences, where $Q_{i,j} \in \{\exists, \forall\}$:

$$\emptyset \models_T \psi \iff \emptyset \models_T \bigvee_{i \in I} \left(\bigwedge_{j \in J} Q_{i,j} \pi \varphi_{i,j} \right)$$

$$\iff \emptyset \models_T \bigvee_{i \in I} \left(\forall \pi \alpha_i \wedge \bigwedge_{j \in J} \exists \pi \varphi_{i,j} \right)$$

$$\iff \text{there is } i \in I \text{ such that } \emptyset \models_T \forall \pi \alpha_i, \text{ and for all } j \in J$$

Table 1. Expressivity hierarchy of the logics considered in the paper. For the definition of left downward closure, we refer to the next section. Note that the equivalence in $*$ is over traces, whereas the other relations are over sets of traces. †: Follow by transitivity from the other results. ‡: Follow by slightly modifying the proof of [7, Lemma 2]. The one variable case does not require a equal time predicate, as only one trace can be specified at a time. **: Follows by a straightforward EF game argument.

$\mathrm{TeamLTL}^l$	$\overset{[12]}{\equiv}$	LTL	$\overset{[5]}{\equiv}$	$\forall\mathrm{HyperLTL}$	$\overset{[8]}{\equiv} *$	$\mathrm{FO}[\leq]$	
$\wedge$ [12]		$\wedge$†		$\wedge$ †		$\|\|\| *$	
$\mathrm{TeamLTL}^l(\varotimes)$	$\overset{\mathrm{Thm.\ 11}}{\equiv}$	$\mathrm{PBC}(\forall\mathrm{HyperLTL})$	$\overset{\mathrm{Cor.\ 12}}{\leq}$	$\forall^*\mathrm{HyperLTL}$	$\overset{\ddagger}{<}$	$\mathrm{FO}[\leq,\mathrm{E}]$	
$\wedge$ [12]		$\wedge$†				$\vee$**	
$\overset{\mathrm{left\text{-}dc\text{-}}}{\mathrm{TeamLTL}^l(\sim)}$	$\overset{\mathrm{Thm.\ 13}}{\equiv}$	$\mathrm{BC}(\forall\mathrm{HyperLTL})$	$\overset{\mathrm{Thm.\ 13}}{\equiv}$	$\mathrm{BC}(\mathrm{HyperLTL}^1)$	$\overset{\ddagger}{<}$	$\mathrm{FO}[\leq]$	

it holds that $\emptyset \models_T \exists\pi\varphi_{i,j}$

$\Longleftrightarrow$ there is $i \in I$ such that $\emptyset[\pi \mapsto t] \models_T \alpha_i$ for all $t \in T$, and for all $j \in J$ there exists $t_j \in T$ such that $\emptyset[\pi \mapsto t_j] \models_T \varphi_{i,j}$

$\Longleftrightarrow$ there is $i \in I$ such that $t \models \alpha_i$ for all $t \in T$, and for all $j \in J$ there exists $t_j \in T$ such that $t_j \models \varphi_{i,j}$

$\Longleftrightarrow$ there is $i \in I$ such that $T \models \alpha_i$, and for all $j \in J$ it holds that $T \models \exists\varphi_{i,j}$

$\Longleftrightarrow$ there is $i \in I$ such that $T \models \alpha_i \wedge \bigwedge_{j\in J} \exists\varphi_{i,j}$

$\Longleftrightarrow$ $T \models \bigvee_{i\in I}(\alpha_i \wedge \bigwedge_{j\in J} \exists\varphi_{i,j}),$

where the first equivalence is due to the normal form for a Boolean closure, the second equivalence is holds because the universally quantified conjuncts can equivalently be evaluated simultaneously, the third equivalence follows from the semantics of $\wedge$ and $\vee$, the fourth equivalence holds by the semantics of $\forall$ and $\exists$, the fifth equivalence holds by Remark 10, the sixth equivalences is due to flatness and the definition of the shorthand $\exists$, the seventh equivalence holds by the semantics of $\wedge$, and the final equivalence follows from the semantics of $\varotimes$.

The other equivalence in the theorem is a direct consequence of Remark 8.

□

4   Conclusion

In this article we explored the connections in expressivity between extensions of linear temporal logic under set-based team semantics ($\mathrm{TeamLTL}^l$) and fragments of linear temporal logic extended with trace quantifiers (HyperLTL). We showed that $\mathrm{TeamLTL}^l$, when extended with the Boolean disjunction, corresponds to the positive Boolean closure of the one variable universal fragment of HyperLTL. Furthermore we considered a fragment of TeamLTL^l extended with the Boolean negation, where the formulae are restricted to not to contain the Boolean negation on the left-hand side of the 'until' operator (U) or under the 'always going to' (G) operator. We showed a correspondence between that fragment and the Boolean closure of the one variable universal fragment of HyperLTL. From our results it follows that the logics considered are all true extensions of LTL. Decidability of the model checking and satisfaction problems for the team based logics was shown in [12], and by our correspondence results (and the translation implied by the proofs of the theorems), decidability of the problems extends to the hyperlogics in question as well. See Table 1 for a summary of the results.

It is fascinating to see that the restriction to left downward closed formulae in the latter correspondence on the team logic side disappears on the hyperlogic side. This hints at that the fragment considered is intuitive. It is an open question whether the downward closed fragment of TeamLTL$^l(\sim)$ is TeamLTL$^l(\varovee)$, or if some restricted use of the Boolean negation could be allowed and still maintain downward closure. Another open question is whether an analogous correspondence exists for the full logic TeamLTL$^l(\sim)$, or even for some lesser restriction of the logic than the left-downward closed fragment.

Acknowledgements. This work was supported by the Academy of Finland grant 345634 and the DFG grant VI 1045/1-1.

References

1. Baumeister, J., Coenen, N., Bonakdarpour, B., Finkbeiner, B., Sanchez, C.: A Temporal logic for asynchronous hyperproperties. In: Silva, A., Leino, K.R.M. (eds.) Computer Aided Verification. CAV 2021. LNCS, vol. 12759, pp. 694–717. Springer, Cham (2021). https://doi.org/10.1007/978-3-030-81685-8_33
2. Clarkson, M.R., Finkbeiner, B., Koleini, M., Micinski, K.K., Rabe, M.N., Sánchez, C.: Temporal logics for hyperproperties. In: Abadi, M., Kremer, S. (eds.) Principles of Security and Trust. POST 2014. LNCS, vol. 8414, pp. 265–284. Springer, Berlin, Heidelberg (2014). https://doi.org/10.1007/978-3-642-54792-8_15
3. Clarkson, M.R., Schneider, F.B.: Hyperproperties. J. Comput. Secur. **18**(6), 1157–1210 (2010)
4. Coenen, N., Finkbeiner, B., Hahn, C., Hofmann, J.: The hierarchy of hyperlogics. In: LICS 2019, pp. 1–13. IEEE (2019)
5. Finkbeiner, B.: Temporal hyperproperties. Bull. EATCS (123) (2017). http://eatcs.org/beatcs/index.php/beatcs/article/view/514
6. Finkbeiner, B., Hahn, C., Lukert, P., Stenger, M., Tentrup, L.: Synthesis from hyperproperties. Acta Informatica **57**(1–2), 137–163 (2020). https://doi.org/10.1007/s00236-019-00358-2
7. Finkbeiner, B., Zimmermann, M.: The first-order logic of hyperproperties. In: Vollmer, H., Vallée, B. (eds.), STACS 2017, volume 66 of LIPIcs, pp. 30:1–30:14. Schloss Dagstuhl - Leibniz-Zentrum für Informatik (2017)
8. Gabbay, D., Pnueli, A., Shelah, S., Stavi, J.: On the temporal analysis of fairness. In: Abrahams, P.W., Lipton, R.J., Bourne, S.R. (eds.), Conference Record of the Seventh Annual ACM Symposium on Principles of Programming Languages, Las

Vegas, Nevada, USA, January 1980, pp. 163–173. ACM Press (1980). https://doi.org/10.1145/567446.567462

9. Gutsfeld, J.O., Meier, A., Ohrem, C., Virtema, J.: Temporal team semantics revisited. In: Baier, C., Fisman, D. (eds.), LICS '22: 37th Annual ACM/IEEE Symposium on Logic in Computer Science, Haifa, Israel, 2–5 August 2022, pp. 44:1–44:13. ACM (2022). https://doi.org/10.1145/3531130.3533360

10. Gutsfeld, J.O., Muller-Olm, M., Ohrem, C.: Automata and fixpoints for asynchronous hyperproperties. Proc. ACM Program. Lang. 5(POPL), 1–29 (2021). https://doi.org/10.1145/3434319

11. Kontinen, J., Sandström, M.: On the expressive power of TeamLTL and first-order team logic over hyperproperties. In: Silva, A., Wassermann, R., de Queiroz, R. (eds.) WoLLIC 2021. LNCS, vol. 13038, pp. 302–318. Springer, Cham (2021). https://doi.org/10.1007/978-3-030-88853-4_19

12. Kontinen, J., Sandstrom, M., Virtema, J.: Set semantics for asynchronous teamltl: expressivity and complexity. In: Leroux, J., Lombardy, S., Peleg, D. (eds.), 48th International Symposium on Mathematical Foundations of Computer Science, MFCS 2023, August 28 to 1 September 2023, Bordeaux, France, volume 272 of LIPIcs, pp. 60:1–60:14. Schloss Dagstuhl - Leibniz-Zentrum für Informatik (2023). https://doi.org/10.4230/LIPIcs.MFCS.2023.60

13. Krebs, A., Meier, A., Virtema, J.: A team based variant of CTL. In: Grandi, F., Lange, M., Lomuscio, A. (eds.), 22nd International Symposium on Temporal Representation and Reasoning, TIME 2015, Kassel, Germany, 23–25 September 2015, pp. 140–149. IEEE Computer Society (2015). https://doi.org/10.1109/TIME.2015.11

14. Krebs, A., Meier, A., Virtema, J., Zimmermann, M.: Team semantics for the specification and verification of hyperproperties. In: Potapov, I., Spirakis, P., Worrell, J. (eds.), MFCS 2018, vol. 117, pp. 10:1–10:16, Dagstuhl, Germany. Schloss Dagstuhl-Leibniz-Zentrum fuer Informatik (2018)

15. McLean, J.: Proving noninterference and functional correctness using traces. J. Comput. Secur. 1(1), 37–58 (1992). https://doi.org/10.3233/JCS-1992-1103

16. Pnueli, A.: The temporal logic of programs. In: 18th Annual Symposium on Foundations of Computer Science, pp. 46–57. IEEE Computer Society (1977)

17. Rabe, M.N.: A Temporal Logic Approach to Information-Flow Control. PhD thesis, Saarland University (2016)

18. Roscoe, A.W.: CSP and determinism in security modelling. In: Proceedings of the 1995 IEEE Symposium on Security and Privacy, Oakland, California, USA, 8–10 May 1995, pp. 114–127. IEEE Computer Society (1995). https://doi.org/10.1109/SECPRI.1995.398927

19. Väänänen, J.: Dependence Logic. Cambridge University Press (2007)

20. Virtema, J., Hofmann, J., Finkbeiner, B., Kontinen, J., Yang, F.: Linear-time temporal logic with team semantics: expressivity and complexity. In: Bojanczyk, M., Chekuri, C. (eds.), 41st IARCS Annual Conference on Foundations of Software Technology and Theoretical Computer Science, FSTTCS 2021, 15–17 December 2021, Virtual Conference, volume 213 of LIPIcs, pp. 52:1–52:17. Schloss Dagstuhl - Leibniz-Zentrum für Informatik (2021). https://doi.org/10.4230/LIPIcs.FSTTCS.2021.52

21. Zdancewic, S., Myers, A.C.: Observational determinism for concurrent program security. In: 16th IEEE Computer Security Foundations Workshop (CSFW-16 2003), 30 June–2 July 2003, Pacific Grove, CA, USA, p. 29. IEEE Computer Society (2003). https://doi.org/10.1109/CSFW.2003.1212703

An Investigation of the Negationless Fragment of the Rescher-Härtig quantifier

Thomas L. Mayer[✉][iD]

Stanford University, Stanford, CA 94305, USA
mayert@cs.stanford.edu

Abstract. The Rescher quantifier and Härtig quantifier have been the subject of much theoretical inquiry, due to the ability of their respective languages to capture much of second-order logic. This paper deals with a hybrid of the two, which for clarity I have termed the Rescher-Härtig quantifier, the first-order language of which is expressively equivalent to that of the Rescher quantifier but contains language fragments with interesting properties. Specifically, the negationless fragment has the property of satisfiability of all sentences within a single model, yet the question of entailment in the language fragment has equal complexity to the question of entailment in the whole language. This can be demonstrated by embedding problems of entailment from the whole language into the language fragment. By additionally embedding the problem into propositional logic, in which entailment is known to be decidable, and reducing the first problem of entailment to the two embedded problems, we show that entailment in the whole language is no more complex than in the language fragment. The paper concludes with a discussion of the different notions of logical compactness and various open questions.

1 Introduction

The Rescher quantifier and the Härtig quantifier have both been studied extensively for their properties and the properties of the logical languages that utilize them. The Rescher quantifier is defined as in [4], inspired by [6], so that for any model $\mathcal{M}$,

$$\mathcal{M} \models Rx\phi(x)\psi(x) \iff |\{a : M \models \phi(a)\}| < |\{a : M \models \psi(a)\}|,$$

while the Härtig quantifier is defined by [5] so that for any model $\mathcal{M}$,

$$\mathcal{M} \models Ix\phi(x)\psi(x) \iff |\{a : M \models \phi(a)\}| = |\{a : M \models \psi(a)\}|.$$

It has been shown by [3,7] that the Rescher quantifier is strictly more expressive than the Härtig quantifier, with the latter able to be defined in terms of the former via the following equivalency (assuming the axiom of choice):

$$\mathcal{M} \models Ix\phi(x)\psi(x) \iff \mathcal{M} \models \neg Rx\phi(x)\psi(x) \land \neg Rx\psi(x)\phi(x).$$

A. Meier and M. Ortiz (Eds.): FoIKS 2024, LNCS 14589, pp. 287–297, 2024.
https://doi.org/10.1007/978-3-031-56940-1_16

The Härtig quantifier on its own is already quite expressive, and can capture many notions of second-order logic, such as the domain having infinite cardinality:

$$Iy(y = y)(Ix(x = x)(x \neq y)).$$

This means it is also not compact, as can be seen if one combines the negation of the above formula with the set of formulas that express "there are at least n distinct elements." Furthermore, its computational complexity is not Σ_2^1 or Π_2^1, as proved by [4]. Since the Rescher quantifier is strictly more expressive, it is a trivial corollary that all of these properties hold in its associated logic as well.

In addition to the quantifiers of Rescher and Härtig, one might consider a parallel third quantifier H that expresses that the quantity of domain elements satisfying one formula is at least as large as the quantity of domain elements satisfying the other formula. Formally, we say that for any model $\mathcal{M}$,

$$\mathcal{M} \models Hx\phi(x)\psi(x) \iff |\{a : M \models \phi(a)\}| \leq |\{a : M \models \psi(a)\}|.$$

However, in the context these quantifiers have usually been considered, such a quantifier would be redundant, since H is equally as expressive as R, which can be seen from their definitions in terms of each other (again, assuming the axiom of choice):

$$\mathcal{M} \models Hx\phi(x)\psi(x) \iff \mathcal{M} \models \neg Rx\psi(x)\phi(x);$$

$$\mathcal{M} \models Rx\phi(x)\psi(x) \iff \mathcal{M} \models \neg Hx\psi(x)\phi(x).$$

Thus, the language of the Härtig quantifier and the language of our third quantifier would be equivalently expressive, rendering further study of the third quantifier obsolete. For this reason, this third quantifier is often used interchangeably with the Härtig quantifier, as in [1].

On the other hand, these equivalencies depend not only on the axiom of choice, but also on the inclusion of FOL in our language, specifically negation. We could imagine fragments of these languages that do not take FOL for granted, which could differ significantly from each other. This paper will explore such a fragment of the language with our final quantifier, which for clarity and to differentiate it from the usual definition of the Rescher quantifier, I have termed the Rescher-Härtig quantifier. Specifically, it will look at the fragment without negation.

This paper will tackle two main questions that arise with any logical system: what sentences are satisfiable and what sentences are valid? As it turns out, the satisfiability problem ends up being trivial, and any sentence is satisfiable. In fact, there exists a model where every sentence in the language is satisfied simultaneously. From this, one might dismiss the fragment as uninteresting.

However, the more interesting question is what sentences are valid. It might seem as though this would be relatively simple as well, yet it turns out that this question is equally as complex as asking what sentences are valid in the whole language. This can be proven by embedding questions of entailment (and therefore questions of validity) from the whole language into the fragment. This shows that despite the simplicity of its satisfiability, the question of entailment in the fragment is not Σ_2^1 or Π_2^1.

Non-classical logics such as those discussed in this paper have played an important role in knowledge representation and reasoning. As discussed by [2], the greater expressive power of non-classical logics has better prepared agents for such contexts as belief revision. Much of the work in this area has been focused on extending the proof methods of these non-classical logics, a goal for which the results of this paper may provide assistance.

2   Definitions of Languages

For the remainder of the paper, our most important theoretical work and results will be restricted to three logical languages: $L_\#, L_\#^+$, and classical propositional logic (CPC) (although corollaries may involve other languages).

Just as in FOL, $L_\#$ takes for granted infinitely many variables and some number (possibly infinitely many or zero) of object constants, relational constants, and functional constants. It also takes for granted equality, as in FOL, and from these atoms, it uses the Rescher-Härtig quantifier to build up more complex formulas. To perhaps aid in readability, henceforth, the Rescher-Härtig quantifier, which in consistency with much of previous literature on these quantifiers was above denoted

$$H x \phi(x)\psi(x),$$

will be denoted

$$\#_x\phi(x) \preceq \#_x\psi(x).$$

To make the above explicitly clear, where P denotes an n-ary relational constant, t_i denotes a term and v denotes a variable, $L_\#$ will be built using two kinds of atomic formulas:

1. $P(t_1, t_2, ...t_n)$,
2. $t_1 = t_2$,

and one way to join and expand upon formulas:

3. $(\#_v\phi \preceq \#_v\psi)$.

As shown by [1], who proposed a similar formulation for the language of the Rescher-Härtig quantifier, if we replace $t_1 = t_2$ with $t_1 \neq t_2$, then the resulting language can express all of FOL.

In contrast to $L_\#$, $L_\#^+$ is the language that would most normally be associated with Rescher-Härtig quantifier (or equivalently with just the Rescher quantifier), which contains the above formulations as well as all of propositional logic. In particular it contains the additional atomic formula:

4. $\perp$,

and the additional way to join and expand upon formulas:

5. $\phi \rightarrow \psi$.

Note that since this fragment is capable of expressing all of propositional logic, it is also capable of expressing the quantifier $\forall$ (and therefore all of FOL) because of the following equivalence:

$$\mathcal{M} \models \forall x \phi(x) \iff \mathcal{M} \models \#_x \neg \phi(x) \preceq \#_x \neg x = x.$$

CPC will only include propositional constants, as well as the logical symbols $\perp$ and $\rightarrow$.

3   The Satisfiability Problem

In this section, we will consider the question of what sentences in $L_\#$ are satisfiable.

Theorem 1. *Every sentence in $L_\#$ is satisfiable. In fact, there is a single model in which every sentence in the language is satisfied.*

Proof. We will define our model $\mathcal{M}_0$ on a domain D such that D contains only one element d, i.e. so that $D = \{d\}$. This automatically means that any object constant c must be interpreted as d and that any n-ary function constant f must be interpreted as a function that maps the n-ary product of d onto d itself. The only other relevant property of our model is how we interpret each n-ary relational constant P, and we will interpret every such relational constant as all of D^n. We will now prove the stronger claim that given any variable assignment g and any formula ϕ, $\mathcal{M}_0 \models \phi[g]$

We shall prove the stronger claim by induction. It is clear that since this is a valid model, under any g, a term t must be interpreted as a definite object in the domain, which must be d. Thus, if our formula ϕ is of the form $t_1 = t_2$, both t_1 and t_2 must get interpreted as d, so $\mathcal{M}_0 \models \phi[g]$.

Similarly, if ϕ is of the form $P(t_1, t_2, ... t_n)$, then each t_i gets interpreted as d. Since we defined our model so that P gets interpreted as $\{d^n\}$, once again $\mathcal{M}_0 \models \phi[g]$.

Finally, we suppose that ϕ is of the form $(\#_v \psi \preceq \#_v \chi)$, and that for any choice of g, $\mathcal{M}_0 \models \psi[g]$ and $\mathcal{M}_0 \models \chi[g]$. That means under any assignment function h and any element b, $\mathcal{M}_0 \models \psi[h(v \mapsto b)]$ and $\mathcal{M}_0 \models \chi[h(v \mapsto b)]$. Therefore,

$$|\{b : M \models \psi[h(v \mapsto b)]\}| = |D| = |\{b : M \models \chi[h(v \mapsto b)]\}|,$$

which means that $\mathcal{M}_0 \models \phi[h]$.

Corollary 1. *$L_\#$ and $L_\#^+$ do not have equivalent expressive power.*

Proof. $L_\#$ cannot express $\perp$.

Corollary 2. *Let L_R be the language fragment defined identically to $L_\#$, except that the way of joining formulas, $(\#_v\phi \preceq \#_v\psi)$, is replaced by $(Rv\phi\psi)$. Then $L_\#$ and L_R do not have equivalent expressive power.*

Proof. The sentence $Rx(x = x)(x = x)$ is unsatisfiable, making it logically equivalent to $\perp$. There is no such formula in $L_\#$, so the two languages have different expressive power.

Corollary 3. *There is no formula $\phi \in L_\#$ such that $\neg\phi$ is expressible in $L_\#$.*

Proof. Suppose $\psi \in L_\#$ is logically equivalent to $\neg\phi$. Then since $\mathcal{M}_0 \models \phi$, $\mathcal{M}_0 \not\models \neg\phi$, so $\mathcal{M}_0 \not\models \psi$, which is impossible.

This means that our fragment lacks the ability to express both falsehood and negation.

4   The Validity Problem

The validity problem looks at what formulas are valid in the language. In this section, we will actually tackle a slightly broader problem, which is exactly when a finite set of sentences Γ entails another sentence ϕ.

Theorem 2. *The problem of entailment in $L_\#$ is of equal complexity to the problem of entailment in $L_\#^+$.*

Since $L_\# \subseteq L_\#^+$, it is clear that the problem of entailment in $L_\#$ is at most as complex as that in $L_\#^+$. To prove the reverse direction, we will reduce problems of entailment in $L_\#^+$ to problems of entailment in $L_\#$. To do this, we will need to prove a few preliminary results.

Lemma 1. *There is a sentence $\phi_{Unum} \in L_\#$ that expresses "the domain contains exactly one element."*

Proof. This is satisfied by the sentence

$$\#_x x = x \preceq \#_x(\#_y y = y \preceq \#_y y = x).$$

In order for this sentence to evaluate as true, we must have that

$$|\{a : \mathcal{M} \models \#_y y = y \preceq \#_y y = a\}| = |D|.$$

This is the case if and only if $|D| = 1$.

Lemma 2. *There is a computable function that maps any formula $\phi \in L_\#^+$ onto a formula $\phi' \in L_\#$ so that the two are equivalent in models with more than 1 element, under any assignment of free variables.*

Proof. We define ϕ' inductively on formulas in $L_\#^+$:

1. if ϕ is $P(t_1, t_2, \ldots t_n)$, then ϕ' is ϕ.
2. if ϕ is $t_1 = t_2$, then ϕ' is ϕ.
3. if ϕ is $\bot$, then ϕ' is ϕ_{Unum}.
4. if ϕ is $\#_v\psi \preceq \#_v\chi$, then ϕ' is $\#_v\psi' \preceq \#_v\chi'$,
5. if ϕ is $\psi \rightarrow \chi$ then ϕ' is $\#_v\psi' \preceq \#_v\chi'$, where v does not occur free in ψ' or χ'.

In cases 1 and 2, the equivalence is trivial, and in case 3, the equivalence is given by Lemma 1.

For case 4, consider some model $\mathcal{M}$ with domain D, $|D| > 1$. We assume inductively that for any assignment of variables on $\mathcal{M}$, ψ and ψ' are equivalent, as are χ and χ'. So

$$|\{d : \mathcal{M} \models \psi[g(v \mapsto d)]\}| = |\{d : \mathcal{M} \models \psi'[g(v \mapsto d)]\}|,$$

and likewise,

$$|\{d : \mathcal{M} \models \chi[g(v \mapsto d)]\}| = |\{d : \mathcal{M} \models \chi'[g(v \mapsto d)]\}|.$$

So under any variable assignment g, $\mathcal{M} \models \#_v\psi \preceq \#_v\chi$ if and only if $\mathcal{M} \models \#_v\psi' \preceq \#_v\chi'$.

For case 5, consider some model $\mathcal{M}$, with domain D, $|D| > 1$, and some assignment of free variables g. We assume inductively, that in $\mathcal{M}$ under g, ψ and ψ' are logically equivalent, as are χ and χ'. If v does not occur free in ψ', then the number of domain elements that satisfy ψ' is either $|D|$ or 0, depending on whether it is true or false, respectively. The same is true with respect to χ and χ'. We will first show that if ϕ is true then ϕ' is true, and then show that if ϕ is false, then ϕ' is false.

If ϕ is true, then ψ is false or χ is true. If ψ is false, then so is ψ', and so

$$|\{d : \mathcal{M} \models \psi'[g(v \mapsto d)]\}| = 0 \le |\{d : \mathcal{M} \models \chi'[g(v \mapsto d)]\}|,$$

so ϕ' is true. Additionally, if χ is true, then so is χ', and so,

$$|\{d : \mathcal{M} \models \chi'[g(v \mapsto d)]\}| = |D| \ge |\{d : \mathcal{M} \models \psi'[g(v \mapsto d)]\}|,$$

so ϕ' is true.

On the other hand, if ϕ is false, then ψ is true and χ is false. If ψ is true and χ is false, then the same will be true of ψ' and χ' respectively, so

$$|\{d : \mathcal{M} \models \psi'[g(v \mapsto d)]\}| = |D| > 0 = |\{d : \mathcal{M} \models \chi'[g(v \mapsto d)]\}|,$$

and so ϕ' is false.

Remark 1. We can think of ϕ_{Unum} as a kind of pseudo-falsum which only applies in multi-element models. The other four cases show that the absence of a proper way to express falsum is $L_\#$'s only barrier to total expressibility of FOL.

We now have a mapping between $L_\#^+$ and $L_\#$. For our proof of Theorem 2, we will also need a mapping between $L_\#^+$ and CPC.

Definition 1. *Given any formula $\phi \in L_\#^+$, we shall define the formula $\phi^\circ \in$ CPC inductively:*

1. *if ϕ is $P(t_1, t_2, ...t_n)$, then ϕ° is P*
2. *if ϕ is $t_1 = t_2$, then ϕ° is $\top$*
3. *if ϕ is $\bot$, then ϕ° is $\bot$*
4. *if ϕ is $\#_v\psi \preceq \#_v\chi$, then ϕ° is $\psi^\circ \to \chi^\circ$*
5. *if ϕ is $\psi \to \chi$ then ϕ° is $\psi^\circ \to \chi^\circ$*

Example 1. If ϕ is $\#_x p(x, c) \preceq \#_x c = x$, then ϕ° is $p \to \top$

Lemma 3. *For any formula $\phi \in L_\#^+$ and any set of formulas $\Gamma \subseteq L_\#$, $\Gamma \models \phi$ with respect to 1-element models if and only if $\Gamma^\circ = \{\gamma^\circ | \gamma \in \Gamma\} \models \phi^\circ$.*

Proof. First, we shall establish a bijection h between non-isomorphic 1-element models of $L_\#^+$ and non-isomorphic models of CPC. All domains of 1-element models are trivially isomorphic, and all object constants must be interpreted as that single element, making them isomorphic. Furthermore, all function constants must be interpreted to map any inputs onto that element as well, making them isomorphic. Thus, non-isomorphic models are differentiated only by their relation constants, which can be interpreted as either the empty set or D^n, for an n-ary relational constant. On the other hand, non-isomorphic models of CPC are differentiated by their interpretation of propositional constants, which can be interpreted as true or false.

Thus, if we fix the inventory of object constants, function constants, and relational constants in $L_\#^+$, we then allow our CPC language to include one propositional constant for every relational constant in $L_\#^+$, with each pair of constants denoted by a shared letter. We can then define h so that for any model $\mathcal{M}$ of $L_\#^+$, in $h(\mathcal{M})$, p is interpreted as false if and only if p is interpreted as the empty set in $\mathcal{M}$, and thus, we also have that p is interpreted as true if and only if p is interpreted as D^n in $\mathcal{M}$.

Now, we formulate a new claim that given a one-element model $\mathcal{M}$ of $L_\#^+$ and a formula $\phi \in L_\#^+$, under all variable assignments g, $\mathcal{M} \models \phi[g]$ if and only if in the corresponding model of propositional logic $h(\mathcal{M})$, $h(\mathcal{M}) \models \phi^\circ$.

We shall prove this by induction on ϕ, going through our cases in the definition of ϕ°. In the first case, if $\mathcal{M} \models P(t_1, t_2, ...t_n)[g]$ for all variable assignments g, then P must map to D^n. So in $h(\mathcal{M})$, P maps to true, meaning that $h(\mathcal{M}) \models \phi^\circ$. For the converse, if $h(\mathcal{M}) \models P$, then in $\mathcal{M}$, P must map to D^n, so $\mathcal{M} \models P(t_1, t_2, ...t_n)[g]$ for all variable assignments g.

In the second case, if $|D| = 1$, then t_1 and t_2 must map to the same element under any variable assignment. So for every one-element model $\mathcal{M}$ and every variable assignment g, $\mathcal{M} \models \phi[g]$. Similarly, for every corresponding model $h(\mathcal{M})$, $h(\mathcal{M}) \models \top$.

The third case is trivial, as there is no model of either system in which $\bot$ is satisfied.

In the fourth case, suppose that for a given model, under all variable assignments, $\mathcal{M} \models \psi$ if and only if $h(\mathcal{M}) \models \psi^\circ$, and $\mathcal{M} \models \chi$ if and only if $h(\mathcal{M}) \models \chi^\circ$.

Then $\mathcal{M} \models \psi^\circ \to \chi^\circ$ if and only if $h(\mathcal{M}) \not\models \psi^\circ$ or $h(\mathcal{M}) \models \chi^\circ$, which happens if and only if $\mathcal{M} \not\models \psi$ under all variable assignments or $\mathcal{M} \models \chi$ under all variable assignments.

If $\mathcal{M} \not\models \psi$ under all variable assignments, then under all variable assignments g,

$$|\{d : \mathcal{M} \models \psi[g(v \mapsto d)]\}| = 0 \leq |\{d : \mathcal{M} \models \chi[g(v \mapsto d)]\}|,$$

so $\mathcal{M} \models \phi$. If $\mathcal{M} \models \chi$ under all variable assignments, then under all variable assignments g,

$$|\{d : \mathcal{M} \models \chi[g(v \mapsto d)]\}| = |D| \geq |\{d : \mathcal{M} \models \psi[g(v \mapsto d)]\}|,$$

so $\mathcal{M} \models \phi[g]$.

On the other hand, if $\mathcal{M} \models \psi$ and $\mathcal{M} \not\models \chi$ under all variable assignments, then under all variable assignments g,

$$|\{d : \mathcal{M} \models \psi[g(v \mapsto d)]\}| = |D| > 0 = |\{d : \mathcal{M} \models \chi[g(v \mapsto d)]\}|,$$

so $\mathcal{M} \not\models \phi[g]$. Thus, ϕ evaluates the same under all variable assignments, and it evaluates to true if and only if ϕ° evaluates to true in the corresponding model.

Finally, in the fifth case, we suppose that for a given model $\mathcal{M}$, under all variable assignments, $\mathcal{M} \models \psi$ if and only if $h(\mathcal{M}) \models \psi^\circ$, and $\mathcal{M} \models \chi$ if and only if $h(\mathcal{M}) \models \chi^\circ$. Then $\mathcal{M} \models \phi$ if and only if $\mathcal{M} \not\models \psi$ or $\mathcal{M} \models \chi$, which occurs if and only if $h(\mathcal{M}) \not\models \psi^\circ$ or $h(\mathcal{M}) \models \chi^\circ$, which occurs if and only if $h(\mathcal{M}) \models \phi^\circ \to \chi^\circ$.

Now that we have proven our claim for all one-element models, all variable assignments, and all formulas, suppose $\Gamma \models \phi$, and suppose we have some model $\mathcal{M}$ of CPC such that $\mathcal{M}$ satisfies Γ°. Then $h^{-1}(\mathcal{M})$ satisfies Γ, and thus, also satisfies ϕ. So $\mathcal{M}$ satisfies ϕ°. So $\Gamma^\circ \models \phi^\circ$.

Conversely, suppose $\Gamma^\circ \models \phi^\circ$, and suppose some model $\mathcal{M}$ of $L_\#^+$ satisfies Γ. Then $h(\mathcal{M})$ satisfies Γ° and therefore ϕ°. So $\mathcal{M}$ satisfies ϕ. Thus, $\Gamma \models \phi$.

We are now ready to prove Theorem 2.

Proof. In order to prove that finite entailment in $L_\#$ is at least as complex as in $L_\#^+$, we will show that for any finite set of formulas $\Gamma \subseteq L_\#^+$ and any formula $\phi \in L_\#^+$, $\Gamma \models \phi$ if and only if $\Gamma' \models ((\phi \to \bot) \to \bot)'$ and $\Gamma^\circ \models \phi^\circ$, where $\Gamma' = \{\gamma' : \gamma \in \Gamma\}$ and $\Gamma^\circ = \{\gamma^\circ : \gamma \in \Gamma\}$. This means that any entailment problem in $L_\#^+$ can be reduced to an entailment problem in $L_\#$ and an entailment problem in CPC, the latter of which is known to be decidable, meaning that entailment in $L_\#^+$ can be no more complex than entailment in $L_\#$.

We will begin with an investigation of when $\Gamma' \models ((\phi \to \bot) \to \bot)'$. This is the case if and only if every one-element model of Γ' satisfies $((\phi \to \bot) \to \bot)'$ and every multi-element model of Γ' satisfies $((\phi \to \bot) \to \bot)'$. We will consider what both of these conditions mean.

Using our inductive definitions of ϕ', we get that

$$((\phi \to \bot) \to \bot)' = \#_v(\phi \to \bot)' \preceq \#_v\phi_{\text{Unum}}.$$

According to Lemma 1, ϕ_{Unum} holds in all one-element models $\mathcal{M}$, so

$$|\{d : \mathcal{M} \models \phi_{\text{Unum}}[(v \mapsto d)]\}| = |D| \geq |\{d : \mathcal{M} \models (\phi \rightarrow \perp)'[(v \mapsto d)]\}|,$$

and thus, $((\phi \rightarrow \perp) \rightarrow \perp)'$ is satisfied in all one-element models. In particular, every one-element model of Γ' satisfies $((\phi \rightarrow \perp) \rightarrow \perp)'$. This makes the first condition always true.

On the other hand, according to Lemma 2, a multi-element model satisfies Γ if and only if it satisfies Γ', and a multi-element model satisfies $((\phi \rightarrow \perp) \rightarrow \perp)$ if and only if it satisfies $((\phi \rightarrow \perp) \rightarrow \perp)'$. Thus every multi-element model of Γ' satisfies $((\phi \rightarrow \perp) \rightarrow \perp)'$ if and only if every multi-element model of Γ satisfies $(\phi \rightarrow \perp) \rightarrow \perp$. Since ϕ and $(\phi \rightarrow \perp) \rightarrow \perp$ are logically equivalent, this is the case if and only if every multi-element model of Γ satisfies ϕ.

Thus, putting the two conditions together, we see that $\Gamma' \models ((\phi \rightarrow \perp) \rightarrow \perp)'$ if and only if every multi-element model of Γ satisfies ϕ.

We now consider when $\Gamma^\circ \models \phi^\circ$. According to Lemma 3, this is the case if and only if every one-element model of Γ satisfies ϕ.

Putting everything together, this means that $\Gamma' \models ((\phi \rightarrow \perp) \rightarrow \perp)'$ and $\Gamma^\circ \models \phi^\circ$ if and only if every one-element model of Γ satisfies ϕ and every multi-element model of Γ satisfies ϕ, which is the case if and only if $\Gamma \models \phi$.

5   Compactness

It is worth considering the effect of these conclusions on various notions of compactness in $L_\#$. The traditional notion is that any set of formulas $\Gamma \subseteq L_\#$ is satisfiable if and only if every finite subset of Γ is satisfiable.

Theorem 3. $L_\#$ *is compact.*

Proof. As we showed in our proof of Theorem 1, every formula $\phi \in L_\#$ can be satisfied in the same model. Thus, every set of formulas is satisfiable, and compactness follows trivially.

There are, however, other ways to think about compactness that are equivalent under FOL. For instance, we could define a notion of compact entailment which says that for any set of formulas $\Gamma \subseteq L_\#$ and any formula $\phi \in L_\#$, $\Gamma \models \phi$ if and only if there is a finite subset $\Lambda \subseteq \Gamma$ such that $\Lambda \models \phi$.

Theorem 4. $L_\#$ *does not have compact entailment.*

Proof. For $n \geq 2$, let $\phi_n \in$ FOL be the sentence that expresses "there are at least n distinct elements," and let $\phi_\infty \in L_\#^+$ be the sentence that expresses "there are infinitely many distinct elements." Let

$$\Gamma = \{\phi_n' | n \geq 2\} \cup \{(\neg\phi_\infty)'\}.$$

If $\mathcal{M}$ is a multi-element model, $\mathcal{M} \models \phi_n'$ if and only if $\mathcal{M}$ has at least n distinct elements, and $\mathcal{M} \models (\neg\phi_\infty)'$ if and only if $\mathcal{M}$ does not have infinitely many elements. Since any model that has at least n distinct elements for all $n \geq 2$ must have infinitely many elements, this means that no multi-element model can satisfy Γ, so $\Gamma \models \phi_{\text{Unum}}$.

On the other hand, let $\Lambda \subseteq \Gamma$ be a finite subset. Then there is some $m \in \mathbf{N}$ so that

$$\Lambda \subseteq \Gamma_m = \{\phi'_n | 2 \leq n \leq m\} \cup \{(\neg\phi_\infty)'\}.$$

Since an model with exactly $m + 1$ distinct elements is a multi-element model, it will satisfy Γ_m and therefore Λ. However, it will not satisfy ϕ_{Unum}. So $\Lambda \not\models \phi_{\text{Unum}}$.

Thus, compact entailment fails.

6   Conclusion and Further Issues

We have successfully shown that problems of entailment in $L_\#^+$ can be transformed into problems of entailment in $L_\#$. This can potentially be used to reduce the complexity of future investigations, as $L_\#$ has fewer possible components than $L_\#^+$. This, in turn, can aid future investigations of second-order logic in general.

The language fragment also presents an interesting case study as a highly sophisticated and undecidable language fragment that cannot express falsehood or negation, forcing further investigations of precisely what we have come to expect from notions like compactness.

This can also be used as a jumping-off point for similar investigations into the Rescher quantifier and the Härtig quantifier. While the Rescher quantifier, together with equality, actually already contains the full expressive power of FOL, the Härtig quantifier does not, and the properties of the corresponding language fragment for the Härtig quantifier are not similarly trivial, warranting further investigation into their properties.

Acknowledgments. This work could not have been completed without the guidance and support of Professor Thomas Icard and access to his and Professor Johan van Benthem's paper on counting logics.

Disclosure of Interests. The author has no competing interests to declare that are relevant to the content of this article.

References

1. van Benthem, J., Icard, T.: Interleaving logic and counting. Bull. Symbol. Logic (2023)
2. Giordano, L., Gliozzi, V., Olivetti, N., Pozzato, G.L., Schwind, C.B.: Logiche non-classiche per la rappresentazione della conoscenza e il ragionamento. In: Il Milione: A Journey in the Computational Logic in Italy, pp. 76–81 (2008)
3. Hauschild, K.: Zum vergleich von härtigquantor und rescherquantor. Math. Log. Q. **27**(16–17), 255–264 (1981)

4. Herre, H., Krynicki, M., Pinus, A., Väänänen, J.: The härtig quantifier: a survey. J. Symbol. Logic **56**(4), 1153–1183 (1991)
5. Härtig, K.: Über einen quantifikator mit zwei wirkungsbereichen. In: Colloquium on the Foundations of Mathematics, Mathematical Machines and Their Applications, pp. 31–36 (1965)
6. Rescher, N.: Plurality quantification. J. Symb. Log. **27**, 373–74 (1962)
7. Weese, M.: Decidability with respect to härtig quantifier and rescher quantifier. Zeitschrift für Mathematische Logik und Grundlagen der Mathematik **27**, 569–576 (1981)

Composition of Stochastic Services
for LTL_f Goal Specifications

Giuseppe De Giacomo[1,2], Marco Favorito[3], and Luciana Silo[2,4(✉)]

¹ University of Oxford, Oxford, UK
² Sapienza University of Rome, Rome, Italy
{degiacomo,silo}@diag.uniroma1.it
³ Banca d'Italia, Rome, Italy
marco.favorito@bancaditalia.it
⁴ Camera dei Deputati, Rome, Italy

Abstract. Service composition *à la* Roman model consists of realizing a virtual service by orchestrating suitably a set of already available services. In this paper, we consider a variant where available services are stochastic systems, and the target specification is goal-oriented and specified in Linear Temporal Logic on finite traces (LTL_f). In this setting, we are interested in synthesizing a controller (policy) that maximizes the probability of satisfaction with the goal, while minimizing the expected cost of the utilization of the available services. To do so, we combine techniques from LTL_f synthesis, service composition *à la* Roman Model, reactive synthesis, and bi-objective lexicographic optimization on Markov Decision Processes (MDPs). This framework has several interesting applications, including Smart Manufacturing and Digital Twins.

Keywords: Service Composition · Linear Temporal Logic on finite traces · Markov Decision Process · Lexicographic Multi-Objective Optimization

1 Introduction

The service-oriented computing (SOC) paradigm uses services to support the development of rapid, low-cost, interoperable, evolvable, and massively distributed applications. Services are considered autonomous, platform-independent entities that can be described, published, discovered, and loosely coupled in novel ways [29]. Service composition, i.e., the ability to generate new, more useful services from existing ones, is an active field of research in the SOC area and has been actively investigated for over two decades.

Particularly interesting in this context is the so-called Roman Model [2,3,16] where services are *conversational*, i.e., have an internal state and are procedurally described as finite transition systems (TS), where at each state the service offers a certain set of actions, and each action changes the state of the service in some way. The designer is interested in generating a new service, called *target*, which

A. Meier and M. Ortiz (Eds.): FoIKS 2024, LNCS 14589, pp. 298–316, 2024.
https://doi.org/10.1007/978-3-031-56940-1_17

is described as the other service; however, it is virtual in the sense that no code is associated with its actions. So, for executing the target, one has to delegate each of its actions to some of the available services by suitably orchestrating the services, considering the current state of the target and the current states of the available services. Service composition amounts to synthesizing a controller that can suitably orchestrate the executions of the available services to guarantee that the target actions are always delegated to some service that can actually execute them in its current state. The original paper on the Roman Model [2] was awarded as the most influential paper of the decade at ICSOC 2013 and is, to date, the most cited paper in the ICSOC conference series.

Recently a renewed interest in service composition à la Roman Model is stemming out of applications in smart manufacturing, where, through digital twins technology, manufacturing devices can export their behaviour as transition systems and hence being orchestrated very much in the same way as service did back in the early 2000s, see e.g., [15,26,27].

Interestingly, these new applications are also pointing out several variations that are not typically considered in earlier literature on services. First, they advocate for considering a stochastic behaviour of services, such as those studied in [4,37]. Unlike the classical model, in which the target specification can either be satisfied or not with no middle ground, in the stochastic setting, it is possible to define a notion of "approximate solution" in case an exact one does not exist.

Second, the notion of goal-oriented target specification is increasingly championed [25–27]. That is, instead of having the target specified as a transition system, it is specified as a (possibly temporally extended) goal that the composition has to fulfill. Of particular interest are specifications in Linear Temporal Logic on finite traces (LTL$_f$) [18], which are at the base of declarative process specification in Business Process Management (BPM) through the so-called DECLARE paradigm [19,20,30].

Third, apart from satisfying the target, it is of interest to also minimize cost coming from the service utilization [12–14]. This concern, together with the satisfaction of the target, calls for resorting to Multi-Objective Optimization for computing a solution.

In this paper, we address the three above requirements and study goal-oriented stochastic service composition where as goals we adopt arbitrary LTL$_f$ specifications, under the DECLARE assumption of a single action executed at the time (see later). Specifically, we are given a goal specification, and we want to synthesize an orchestrator that, on the one hand, *proactively* chooses actions to form a sequence that satisfies the goal and, on the other hand, delegates each action to an available service in such a way that at the end of the sequence, all services are in their final states. The composition problem consists of maximizing the satisfaction probability of the LTL$_f$ objective, and conditioned on this, minimizing the expected cost of utilization of the services.

A first attempt to do so may resort to Multi-objective MDPs (MOMDPs) [8]. One common solution is to reduce the multi-objective reward/cost optimization to a single reward optimization via a linear weighting of different sources of rewards/costs. However, this means that the two objectives, namely the maximization of target rewards and the minimization of cost uses, are blurred into one scalar value, which hides precious information from the agent. Instead, the maximization of the target objective has the *highest priority*. Among those strategies that maximize the first objective, we aim to find those strategies that achieve the minimum utilization cost. In the literature of multi-objective optimization, the setting in which there is a strict preference order among objectives is called *lexicographic multi-objective optimization* [7,22,34,36]. It is known that, in general, single Markovian rewards cannot capture certain multi-objective tasks, such as ones with lexicographic preferences [33]; hence, such problem cannot be easily reduced to standard techniques on MDPs [31].

Among related works, one of the earliest attempts at combining stochastic planning models with service composition is [21]. There are works based on Markov-HTN Planning [9], multi-objective optimization [10,28], and lexicographic optimization [32], helpful to model the stochastic behaviour as well as complex QoS preferences. However, in all cases, either there are no stateful services, no high-level declarative specification of the desired solution, or no strict preference among objectives.

Our solution technique relies on solving a bi-objective lexicographic optimization [6] over a special MDP, allowing to minimize the services' utilization costs while guaranteeing maximum probability of goal satisfaction. We point out that although this paper has mainly a foundational nature, it also has a significant applicative interest since it gives the foundations and solution techniques of goal-oriented compositions, which are indeed envisioned in the current literature on smart manufacturing where the notion of goal-oriented target specification is increasingly championed [15,25–27].

The rest of the paper is structured as follows. Section 2 explains the theoretical concepts on which the paper is based. Section 3 introduces the service composition framework in stochastic settings that we model, showing the formalization of the problem in terms of bi-objective lexicographic optimization on MDPs and proposes a solution technique able to find an optimal orchestrator. Section 4 shows the application of the formal framework to an industrial case study of an electric motor assembly process, describing in detail the manufacturing goal and the manufacturing actors. Finally, Sect. 5 concludes the paper with final remarks and future works.

2 Preliminaries

LTL$_f$ is a variant of Linear Temporal Logic (LTL) interpreted over finite traces, instead of infinite ones [18]. Given a set $\mathcal{P}$ of atomic propositions, LTL$_f$ formulas φ are defined by $\varphi ::= a \mid \neg\varphi \mid \varphi \wedge \varphi \mid \bigcirc\varphi \mid \varphi\mathcal{U}\varphi$, where a denotes an atomic proposition in $\mathcal{P}$, $\bigcirc$ is the next operator, and $\mathcal{U}$ is the until operator. We use abbreviations for other Boolean connectives, as well as the following: eventually as $\Diamond\varphi \equiv true\,\mathcal{U}\,\varphi$; always as $\Box\varphi \equiv \neg\Diamond\neg\varphi$; weak next as $\bullet\varphi \equiv \neg\bigcirc\neg\varphi$ (note that, on finite traces, $\neg\bigcirc\varphi$ is not equivalent to $\bigcirc\neg\varphi$); and weak until as $\varphi_1\,\mathcal{W}\,\varphi_2 \equiv (\varphi_1\,\mathcal{U}\,\varphi_2 \vee \Box\varphi_1)$ (φ_1 holds until φ_2 or forever). LTL$_f$ formulas are interpreted on finite traces $a = a_0 \ldots a_{l-1}$ where a_i at instant i is a propositional interpretation over the alphabet $2^{\mathcal{P}}$, and l is the length of the trace. An LTL$_f$ formula can be transformed into equivalent *nondeteministic automata* (NFA) in at most EXPTIME and into an equivalent and *deterministic finite automata* (DFA) in at most 2EXPTIME [18]. A DFA is a tuple $\mathcal{A}_\varphi = \langle 2^{\mathcal{P}}, Q, q_0, F, \delta \rangle$ where: (*i*) $2^{\mathcal{P}}$ is the alphabet, (*ii*) Q is a finite set of states, (*iii*) q_0 is the initial state, (*iv*) $F \subseteq Q$ is the set of accepting states and (*v*) $\delta : Q \times 2^{\mathcal{P}} \to Q$ is a total transition function. Note that the DFA alphabet is the same as the set of traces that satisfies the formula φ. An NFA is defined similarly to DFA except that δ is defined as a relation, i.e. $\delta \subseteq Q \times 2^{\mathcal{P}} \times Q$. In particular, LTL$_f$ is used in declarative process specification in BPM, for example in the system DECLARE [30]. In this specific case, it is assumed that only one proposition (corresponding to an action) is true at every time point. We call this the DECLARE *assumption*, and we do adopt it in this paper.

Markov Decision Process. A *Markov Decision Process* (MDP) is a tuple $M = (S, A, P, s_0)$, where: (*i*) S is a finite set of states, (*ii*) s_0 is the initial state, (*iii*) A is a finite set of actions, and (*iv*) $P : (S \times A) \to \Delta(S)$ is the transition probability function, i.e. a mapping from state-action pairs to probability distributions over S. With $\mathsf{Supp}(d)$, we denote the support of a probability distribution d. An infinite path $\rho \in (S \times A)^\omega$ is a sequence $\rho = s_0 a_1 s_1 a_2 \ldots$, where $s_i \in S$, $a_{i+1} \in A$, and $s_{i+1} \in \mathsf{Supp}(P(s_i, a_{i+1}))$, for all $i \in \mathbb{N}$. Similarly, a finite path $\rho \in (S \times A)^* \times S$ is a finite sequence $\rho = s_0 a_1 s_1 a_2 \ldots a_m s_m$. For any path ρ of length at least j and any $i \leq j$, we let $\rho[i : j]$ denote the subsequence $s_i a_{i+1} s_{i+1} a_{i+2} \ldots a_j s_j$. We use $\mathsf{Paths}^\omega_\mathcal{M} = (S \times A)^\omega$ and $\mathsf{Paths}_\mathcal{M} = (S \times A)^* \times S$ to denote the set of infinite and finite paths, respectively. A policy $\pi : \mathsf{Paths}_\mathcal{M} \to A$ maps a finite path $\rho \in \mathsf{Paths}_\mathcal{M}$ to an action $a \in A$. We denote with $\mathsf{Paths}_{\mathcal{M}_\pi}$ the set of finite paths over $\mathcal{M}$ whose actions are compatible with π. Given a finite path $\rho = s_0 a_1 \ldots a_m s_m$, the *cylinder* of ρ, denoted by $\mathsf{Paths}^\omega_\mathcal{M}(\rho)$, is the set of all infinite paths starting with prefix ρ. The σ-algebra associated with MDP $\mathcal{M}$ and a fixed policy π is the smallest σ-algebra that contains the cylinder sets $\mathsf{Paths}^\omega_{\mathcal{M}_\pi}(\rho)$ for all $\rho \in \mathsf{Paths}_{\mathcal{M}_\pi}$. For a state s in S, a measure is defined for the cylinder sets as $\mathbb{P}_{\mathcal{M}_\pi,s}(\mathsf{Paths}^\omega_{\mathcal{M}_\pi}(s_0 a_1 s_1 \ldots a_m s_m)) = \prod_{k=0}^{m-1} P(s_{k+1}|s_k, a_{k+1})$ if $s_0 = s$ and for all k, $a_{k+1} = \pi(\rho[0 : k])$, otherwise 0. We also have $\mathbb{P}_{\mathcal{M}_\pi,s}(\mathsf{Paths}^\omega_{\mathcal{M}_\pi,s}(s)) = 1$ and $\mathbb{P}_{\mathcal{M}_\pi,s}(\mathsf{Paths}^\omega_{\mathcal{M}_\pi,s}(s')) = 0$ for $s' \neq s$. This can be extended to a unique probability measure $\mathbb{P}_{\mathcal{M}_\pi,s}$ on the aforementioned σ-algebra. In particular, if $\mathcal{R} \subseteq \mathsf{Paths}_{\mathcal{M}_\pi}$ is a set of finite paths forming pairwise disjoint cylinder sets, then $\mathbb{P}_{\mathcal{M}_\pi,s}(\bigcup_{\rho \in \mathcal{R}} \mathsf{Paths}^\omega_{\mathcal{M}_\pi}(\rho)) = \sum_{\rho \in \mathcal{R}} \mathbb{P}_{\mathcal{M}_\pi,s}(\mathsf{Paths}^\omega_{\mathcal{M}_\pi}(\rho))$. We denote with $\mathbb{E}_{\mathcal{M}_\pi,s}(X)$ the expected value of a random variable X with respect to the distribution $\mathbb{P}_{\mathcal{M}_\pi,s}$.

3   Composition of Stochastic Services for LTL$_f$ Tasks

In this section, we present our service composition framework in stochastic settings. We aim to realize an LTL$_f$ goal specification with the available services by modeling nondeterminism using probability distributions over the services' successor states. Moreover, we allow the specification to be approximately satisfied, by considering the objective of maximizing the satisfaction probability of the specification.

3.1   Stochastic Services Framework

A stochastic service is a tuple $\tilde{S} = \langle \Sigma, A, \sigma_0, F, P, C \rangle$, where: (i) Σ is the finite set of service states, (ii) A is the finite set of services' actions, (iii) $\sigma_0 \in \Sigma$ is the initial state, (iv) $F \subseteq \Sigma$ is the set of final states (i.e., states in which the computation may stop but does not necessarily have to), (v) $P : \Sigma \times A \rightarrow \Delta(\Sigma)$ is the *transition function* that returns for every state σ and action a a distribution over next states, and (vi) $C : \Sigma \times A \rightarrow \mathbb{R}^+$ is the *cost function* that assigns a (strictly positive) cost to each state-action pair. A *(stochastic) service community* is a collection of stochastic services $\tilde{C} = \{\tilde{S}_1, \ldots, \tilde{S}_n\}$. A *(stochastic) trace of* $\tilde{C}$ is a finite alternating sequence of the form $\tilde{t} = (\sigma_{10} \ldots \sigma_{n0}), (a_1, o_1), \ldots, (a_m, o_m), (\sigma_{1m} \ldots \sigma_{nm})$, where σ_{i0} is the initial state of every service S_i and, for every $1 \leq k \leq m$, we have (i) $\sigma_{ik} \in \Sigma_i$ for all $i \in \{1, \ldots, n\}$, (ii) $o_k \in \{1, \ldots, n\}$ is the service index chosen by the orchestrator at step k, (iii) $a_k \in A$, and (iv) for all i, $\sigma_{ik} \in \mathsf{Supp}(P_i(\sigma_{i,k-1}, a_{ik}))$ if $o_k = i$, and $\sigma_{ik} = \sigma_{i,k-1}$ otherwise. A *history of* C is a finite prefix of a trace of C. With $|h| = m$, we denote the length of such history, and with $\mathsf{last}(h)$ we denote the service state configuration at the last step: $(\sigma_{1m} \ldots \sigma_{nm})$. Given a trace t, we call $\mathsf{states}(t)$ *sequence of states* of t, i.e. $\mathsf{states}(t) = (\sigma_{10} \ldots \sigma_{n0}), (\sigma_{11} \ldots \sigma_{n1}), \cdots$. The *choices* of a trace t, denoted with $\mathsf{choices}(t)$, is the sequence of actions in t, i.e. $\mathsf{choices}(t) = (a_1, o_1), (a_m, o_m), \ldots$. Note that, due to nondeterminism, there might be many traces of C associated with the same run. Moreover, we define the *action run* of a trace t, denoted with $\mathsf{actions}(t)$, the projection of $\mathsf{choices}(t)$ only to the components in A. states, $\mathsf{choices}$ and $\mathsf{actions}$ are defined also on history h, in a similar way. Note that both $\mathsf{choices}(h)$ and $\mathsf{actions}(h)$ are empty if $h = (\sigma_{10} \ldots \sigma_{n0})$.

An *orchestrator* is a function $\gamma : (\Sigma_1 \times \cdots \times \Sigma_n)^* \rightarrow A \times \{1 \ldots n\}$ that, given a sequence of states $(\sigma_{10} \ldots \sigma_{n0}) \ldots (\sigma_{1m} \ldots \sigma_{nm})$, returns the action to perform $a \in A$, and the service (actually the service index) that will perform it. Next, we define when an orchestrator is a composition that satisfies φ. Given a trace t, with $\mathsf{histories}(t)$, we denote the set of prefixes of the trace t that ends with a services state configuration. A trace t is an *execution* of an orchestrator γ over C if for all $k \geq 0$, we have $(a_{k+1}, o_{k+1}) = \gamma((\sigma_{10} \ldots \sigma_{n0}) \ldots (\sigma_{1k} \ldots \sigma_{nk}))$. Let $\mathcal{T}_{\gamma, \tilde{C}}$ be the set of such executions. Note that due to the nondeterminism of the services, we can have many executions for the same orchestrator, despite the orchestrator being a deterministic function. If $h \in \mathsf{histories}(t)$ for some (infinite) execution $t \in \mathcal{T}_{\gamma, \tilde{C}}$, we call h a finite execution of γ over C.

Consider a goal specification φ expressed in LTL$_f$ over the set of actions A, and consider a community of n services $C = \{S_1, \ldots, S_n\}$, where each set of actions $A_i \subseteq A$. We say that some finite execution h is *successful*, denoted with $\mathsf{successful}(h)$, if the following two conditions hold: (1) $\mathsf{actions}(h) \models \varphi$, and (2)

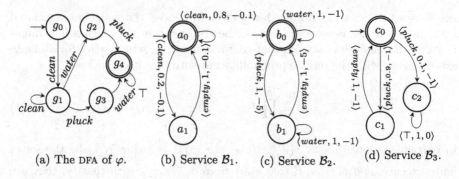

Fig. 1. The garden bot systems and the DFA of the LTL$_f$ goal.

all service states $\sigma_i \in \mathsf{last}(\mathsf{states}(h))$ are such that $\sigma_i \in F_i$. If for execution $t \in \mathcal{T}_{\gamma,\tilde{\mathcal{C}}}$ there exist a finite prefix history $h \in \mathsf{histories}(t)$ such that $\mathsf{successful}(h)$, we say that t is successful. Finally, we say that an orchestrator γ *realizes the* LTL$_f$ *specification* φ *with* $\mathcal{C}$ if, for all traces $t \in \mathcal{T}_{\gamma,\tilde{\mathcal{C}}}$, t is successful.

We are interested in orchestrators that maximize the probability of satisfaction of the goal specification, even when the specification cannot be surely satisfied (e.g. due to a stochastic misbehaviour of some service). Moreover, while guaranteeing the optimal probability of satisfaction, we aim to find those orchestrators that minimize the expected utilization cost of the services, conditioned on the achievement of the task.

Example 1. This example is inspired by the "garden bots system" scenario [37]. The goal is to *clean* the garden by picking fallen leaves and removing dirt, *water* the plants, and *pluck* the ripe fruits and flowers. The action *clean* must be performed at least once, followed by *water* and *pluck* in any order. In DECLARE LTL$_f$, the goal can be expressed as $\varphi = clean \wedge \bigcirc(clean\,\mathcal{U}((water \wedge \bigcirc pluck) \vee (pluck \wedge \bigcirc water)))$. We assume there are three available garden bots, $\mathcal{B}_1, \mathcal{B}_2, \mathcal{B}_3$, each with different capabilities and action rewards. In Fig. 1 the three services specifications and the DFA of the LTL$_f$ goal are shown. Transitions labels are of the form $\langle action, prob, reward \rangle$. We are interested in a composition of the bots to maximize the probability of the satisfaction of the goal φ, which also considers rewards/costs. The *clean* action can only be delegated to $\mathcal{B}_1$, and the optimal solution must take into account its stochastic behaviour in order to correctly compute the expected cost. Regarding the *pluck* action, both $\mathcal{B}_2$ and $\mathcal{B}_3$ can perform it; however, the optimal orchestrator will not dispatch it to $\mathcal{B}_3$ because, despite the cost being smaller than the one in $\mathcal{B}_2$, choosing $\mathcal{B}_3$ will lead to a probability of 0.1 of not reaching the final state configuration since the state c_2 is a failure state while choosing $\mathcal{B}_3$ does not compromise the optimal probability of goal satisfaction.

Before proceeding with a formalization of the optimization problem, we introduce additional auxiliary notions. Analogously to what has been done for MDPs, for a finite execution h of γ over $\tilde{\mathcal{C}}$, we use $\mathcal{T}_{\gamma,\tilde{\mathcal{C}}}(h)$ to denote the set of all (infinite) executions $t \in \mathcal{T}_{\gamma,\tilde{\mathcal{C}}}$ such that $h \in \mathsf{histories}(t)$. Moreover, the σ-algebra associated with the stochastic behaviour of the orchestrator γ over the stochastic community $\tilde{\mathcal{C}}$ is the smallest σ-algebra that contains the trace sets $\mathcal{T}_{\gamma,\tilde{\mathcal{C}}}(h)$, for all finite executions h, with the unique probability measure over it defined as:

$$\mathbb{P}_{\gamma,\tilde{\mathcal{C}}}(h) = \prod_{k=1}^{|h|} P_{o_k}(\sigma_{o_k,k} \mid \sigma_{o_k,k-1}, a_k) \tag{1}$$

In particular, note that $\mathbb{P}_{\gamma,\tilde{\mathcal{C}}}(\mathcal{T}_{\gamma,\tilde{\mathcal{C}}}(\langle\langle(\sigma_{10}\ldots\sigma_{n0})\rangle\rangle)) = 1$. Let $\mathcal{H}^{\varphi}_{\gamma,\tilde{\mathcal{C}}}$ be the set of finite executions h of γ on $\tilde{\mathcal{C}}$ that start from $\sigma_{10}\ldots\sigma_{n0}$ such that (i) they are successful, and (ii) there is no prefix history h that is successful. Intuitively, such a set only contains the executions that are successful for the first time. The *satisfaction probability* of φ under orchestrator γ and community $\tilde{\mathcal{C}}$ is given by:

$$\mathcal{P}^{\tilde{\mathcal{C}}}_{\varphi}(\gamma) = \mathbb{P}_{\gamma,\tilde{\mathcal{C}}}\left(\bigcup_{h \in \mathcal{H}^{\varphi}_{\gamma,\tilde{\mathcal{C}}}} \mathcal{T}_{\gamma,\tilde{\mathcal{C}}}(h) \right) \tag{2}$$

It is crucial to observe that since by definition there is no pair $h', h'' \in \mathcal{H}^{\varphi}_{\gamma,\tilde{\mathcal{C}}}(h)$ such that $h' \in \mathsf{prefixes}(h'')$, all trace sets $\mathcal{T}_{\gamma,\tilde{\mathcal{C}}}(h)$ for $h \in \mathcal{H}^{\varphi}_{\gamma,\tilde{\mathcal{C}}}$ are pairwise disjoint sets, which means that $\mathcal{P}^{\tilde{\mathcal{C}}}_{\gamma}$ is a well-defined probability.

Moreover, we define the *(conditioned) expected utilization cost* of services as the expected cost an orchestrator incurs in its successful executions, i.e.:

$$\mathcal{J}^{\tilde{\mathcal{C}}}_{\varphi}(\gamma) = \mathbb{E}_{h \sim \mathbb{P}_{\gamma,\tilde{\mathcal{C}}}}\left[\sum_{k=1}^{|h|} C_{o_k}(\sigma_{o_k,k-1}, a_k) \,\middle|\, \mathsf{successful}(h) \right] \tag{3}$$

Let $\Gamma(\tilde{\mathcal{C}})$ be the set of orchestrators for the community $\tilde{\mathcal{C}}$. Let $f : \Gamma(\tilde{\mathcal{C}}) \to \mathbb{R}$ be an objective function. We say an orchestrator $\gamma \in \Gamma(\tilde{\mathcal{C}})$ is f-optimal if $f(\gamma) = \sup_{\tau \in \Gamma(\tilde{\mathcal{C}})} f(\tau)$, and write Γ_f for the set of f-optimal orchestrators.

Finally, we define our optimization problem. We want to compute an orchestrator γ such that the following holds:

$$\gamma \in \Gamma_{\mathcal{P}^{\tilde{\mathcal{C}}}_{\varphi}} \text{ and } \mathcal{J}^{\tilde{\mathcal{C}}}_{\varphi}(\gamma) = \inf_{\gamma' \in \Gamma_{\mathcal{P}^{\tilde{\mathcal{C}}}_{\varphi}}} \mathcal{J}^{\tilde{\mathcal{C}}}_{\varphi}(\gamma') \tag{4}$$

Intuitively, we fix a lexicographic order on the objective functions $\mathcal{P}^{\tilde{\mathcal{C}}}_{\varphi}$ and $\mathcal{J}^{\tilde{\mathcal{C}}}_{\varphi}$, meaning that we aim to minimize the expected utilization cost to satisfy the specification, conditioned to the satisfaction of the specification, while guaranteeing the optimal probability of satisfying it. Interestingly, in case the specification is *exactly* realizable, the notion of optimal orchestrator according to Eq. (4) coincides with the notion of realizability, as shown in the following results.

Lemma 1. *If γ realizes the specification φ over $\tilde{\mathcal{C}}$, then* $\bigcup_{h \in \mathcal{H}^{\varphi}_{\gamma,\tilde{\mathcal{C}}}} \mathcal{T}_{\gamma,\tilde{\mathcal{C}}}(h) = \mathcal{T}_{\gamma,\tilde{\mathcal{C}}}(\langle\langle(\sigma_{10}\ldots\sigma_{n0})\rangle\rangle)$.

Proof. We prove (i) $\bigcup_{h \in \mathcal{H}^{\varphi}_{\gamma,\tilde{\mathcal{C}}}} \mathcal{T}_{\gamma,\tilde{\mathcal{C}}}(h) \subseteq \mathcal{T}_{\gamma,\tilde{\mathcal{C}}}(\langle\langle(\sigma_{10} \ldots \sigma_{n0})\rangle\rangle)$ and (ii) $\bigcup_{h \in \mathcal{H}^{\varphi}_{\gamma,\tilde{\mathcal{C}}}}$ $\mathcal{T}_{\gamma,\tilde{\mathcal{C}}}(h) \supseteq \mathcal{T}_{\gamma,\tilde{\mathcal{C}}}(\langle\langle(\sigma_{10} \ldots \sigma_{n0})\rangle\rangle)$ separately. Proposition (i) is immediate: every execution belongs to the set of executions starting from $\sigma_{10} \ldots \sigma_{n0}$. To prove proposition (ii), we start by observing that for all $t \in \mathcal{T}_{\gamma,\tilde{\mathcal{C}}}(\langle\langle(\sigma_{10} \ldots \sigma_{n0})\rangle\rangle)$, by definition of realizing orchestrator, they have a prefix $h' \in \mathsf{prefixes}(h)$ that is successful. In particular, if h'' is the shortest prefix of h that is successful, then $h'' \in \mathcal{H}^{\varphi}_{\gamma,\tilde{\mathcal{C}}}$ and $t \in \mathcal{T}_{\gamma,\tilde{\mathcal{C}}}(h'')$. This implies that $t \in \bigcup_{h'' \in \mathcal{H}^{\varphi}_{\gamma,\tilde{\mathcal{C}}}} \mathcal{T}_{\gamma,\tilde{\mathcal{C}}}(h'')$.

Theorem 1. *Let $\tilde{\mathcal{C}}$ be a community of stochastic services, and φ be a goal specification. The orchestrator γ realizes φ with community $\tilde{\mathcal{C}}$ iff $\mathcal{P}^{\tilde{\mathcal{C}}}_{\varphi}(\gamma) = 1$.*

Proof. ($\Rightarrow$) If an orchestrator γ realizes φ, then all infinite executions $t \in \mathcal{T}_{\gamma,\tilde{\mathcal{C}}}$ have a prefix $h' \in \mathsf{histories}(t)$ that is successful. Let h'' be the shortest of such prefixes. This implies that $t \in \bigcup_{h'' \in \mathcal{H}^{\varphi}_{\gamma,\tilde{\mathcal{C}}}} \mathcal{T}_{\gamma,\tilde{\mathcal{C}}}(h'')$. By Lemma 1, this set is equal to $\mathcal{T}_{\gamma,\tilde{\mathcal{C}}}(\langle\langle(\sigma_{10} \ldots \sigma_{n0})\rangle\rangle)$. Since by definition $\mathsf{Supp}(\mathbb{P}_{\gamma,\tilde{\mathcal{C}}}) \subseteq \mathcal{T}_{\gamma,\tilde{\mathcal{C}}}(\langle\langle(\sigma_{10} \ldots \sigma_{n0})\rangle\rangle)$, we have that $\mathcal{P}^{\tilde{\mathcal{C}}}_{\varphi}(\gamma) = \mathbb{P}_{\gamma,\tilde{\mathcal{C}}}(\bigcup_{h \in \mathcal{H}^{\varphi}_{\gamma,\tilde{\mathcal{C}}}} \mathcal{T}_{\gamma,\tilde{\mathcal{C}}}(h)) = \mathbb{P}_{\gamma,\tilde{\mathcal{C}}}(\mathcal{T}_{\gamma,\tilde{\mathcal{C}}}(\langle\langle(\sigma_{10} \ldots \sigma_{n0})\rangle\rangle)) = 1$.

($\Leftarrow$) Assume an orchestrator γ is such that $\mathcal{P}^{\tilde{\mathcal{C}}}_{\varphi}(\gamma) = 1$. This implies that for all orchestrator infinite executions $t \in \mathsf{Supp}(\mathbb{P}_{\gamma,\tilde{\mathcal{C}}}) \subseteq \mathcal{T}_{\gamma,\tilde{\mathcal{C}}}(\langle\langle(\sigma_{10} \ldots \sigma_{n0})\rangle\rangle)$, there is a prefix $h \in \mathsf{histories}(t)$ such that $h \in \mathcal{H}^{\varphi}_{\gamma,\tilde{\mathcal{C}}}$ and $t \in \mathcal{T}_{\gamma,\tilde{\mathcal{C}}}(h)$. This means t is successful, and therefore, all executions are successful, i.e. the definition of realizability.

Theorem 2. *Assume φ is realizable. If an orchestrator γ satisfies Eq. (4), then it realizes the specification φ.*

Proof. Since by assumption φ is realizable, then there exists an orchestrator γ' that realizes it. By Theorem 1, we can deduce that the optimal value of $\mathcal{P}^{\tilde{\mathcal{C}}}_{\varphi}(\gamma')$ is 1. Moreover, by assumption and by Eq. (4)), it follows that $\gamma \in \Gamma_{\mathcal{P}^{\tilde{\mathcal{C}}}_{\varphi}}$, i.e. $\mathcal{P}^{\tilde{\mathcal{C}}}_{\varphi}(\gamma) = 1$, by the arguments above. Finally, again by Theorem 1, we get that γ realizes φ.

Finally, we formally state the stochastic version of our problem:

Problem 1 (Stochastic Composition for LTL$_f$ *Specifications).* Given the pair $(\tilde{\mathcal{C}}, \varphi)$, where φ is an LTL$_f$ goal specification over the set of actions A, and $\tilde{\mathcal{C}}$ is a community of n stochastic services $\tilde{\mathcal{C}} = \{\tilde{\mathcal{S}}_1, \ldots, \tilde{\mathcal{S}}_n\}$, compute, if it exists, an orchestrator that is optimal according to Eq. (4).

Interestingly, Theorem 1 and Theorem 2 show that one can find an orchestrator even in a non-stochastic setting by considering arbitrary services' probability distributions for $P_i(\sigma_i, a)$, for any pair σ_i and a, whose support is compatible with δ_i, and then check whether $\max_{\gamma} \mathcal{P}^{\tilde{\mathcal{C}}}_{\varphi}(\gamma) = 1$.

3.2   Stochastic Services Solution Technique

Our solution technique is based on finding an optimal policy for a bi-objective lexicographic optimization on a specifically built MDP. In particular, we consider a variant of the framework introduced in [6]: while as the second objective, they considered the expected number of steps to a target, here we consider the expected cost. Our technique breaks down into the following steps: (1) first, we compute the equivalent NFA of an LTL$_f$ formula, $\mathcal{A}_\varphi$, and (2) we consider the DFA $\mathcal{A}_{\text{act}}$, as in the non-stochastic setting; then (3) we compute a *product of $\mathcal{A}_{\text{act}}$ with the stochastic services in $\tilde{C}$, obtaining a new MDP, $\mathcal{M}'$, that we call the* "composition MDP"; (4) we find a policy π for $\mathcal{M}'$ that is optimal w.r.t. the bi-objective lexicographic function, as in [6], and then (5) we derive an orchestrator γ from π that is optimal w.r.t. Eq. 4. We now detail each step.

Step 1. The NFA of an LTL$_f$ formula can be computed by exploiting a well-known correspondence between LTL$_f$ formulas and automata on finite words [17]. In particular, using the LTL$_f$2NFA algorithm [5], we can compute an NFA $\mathcal{A}_\varphi = (A, Q, q_0, F, \delta)$ that is equivalent to the specification φ which can be exponentially larger than the size of the formula. Note that the alphabet of the NFA is A since we assume the specification satisfies the DECLARE assumption: only one action is executed at each time instant.

Step 2. From the NFA of the formula φ, $\mathcal{A}_\varphi$, which is on the alphabet A, we define a *controllable* DFA on the alphabet $A \times Q$, $\mathcal{A}_{\text{act}} = (A \times Q, Q, a_0, F, \delta_{\text{act}})$, where everything is as in $\mathcal{A}_\varphi$ except δ_{act} that is defined as follows: $\delta_{\text{act}}(q, (a, q')) = q'$ iff $(q, a, q') \in \delta$. Notice that if a sequence of actions is accepted by the NFA $\mathcal{A}_\varphi$ as witnessed by the run $r = q_0, a_1, \ldots, q_n$, then the run itself is accepted by $\mathcal{A}_{\text{act}}$. Intuitively, with the DFA $\mathcal{A}_{\text{act}}$, we are giving to the controller not only the choice of actions but also the choice of transitions of the original NFA $\mathcal{A}_\varphi$, so that those chosen transitions lead to the satisfaction of the formula. In other words, for every sequence of actions $a_1, \ldots, a_n$ accepted by the NFA $\mathcal{A}_\varphi$, i.e. satisfying the formula φ, there exists a corresponding alternating sequence $q_0, a_1, \ldots, q_n$ accepted by the DFA $\mathcal{A}_{\text{act}}$, and viceversa. This means that when we project out the Q-component from the accepted sequences of $\mathcal{A}_{\text{act}}$, we get a sequence of actions satisfying φ. It can be shown that:

Proposition 1. $a_1 \ldots a_m \in \mathcal{L}(\mathcal{A}_\varphi)$ *iff* $(a_1, q_1) \ldots (a_m, q_m) \in \mathcal{L}(\mathcal{A}_{\text{act}})$, *for some* $q_1 \ldots q_m$.

Proof. By definition, $a_1 \ldots a_m \in \mathcal{L}(\mathcal{A}_\varphi)$ iff there exist a run $r = q_1 \ldots q_m$ s.t. for $1 \leq k \leq m$, $\delta(q_{k-1}, a_k) = q_k$ and $q_m \in F$. Consider the word $w' = (a_1, q_1) \ldots (a_m, q_m)$. By construction of $\mathcal{A}_{\text{act}}$, w' induces a run $r^d = r$. Since $q_m \in F$ by assumption, r^d is an accepting run for $\mathcal{A}_{\text{act}}$, and therefore $w' \in \mathcal{L}(\mathcal{A}_{\text{act}})$ is accepted. The other direction follows by construction because, if $(a_1, q_1) \ldots (a_m, q_m) \in \mathcal{L}(\mathcal{A}_{\text{act}})$, then by construction $q_1 \ldots q_m$ is a run of $\mathcal{A}_\varphi$ over word $a_1 \ldots a_m$, and since $q_m \in F$ by assumption $a_1 \ldots a_m \in \mathcal{L}(\mathcal{A}_\varphi)$.

Step 3. Consider a goal specification φ and a community of stochastic services $\tilde{C}$. Let $\mathcal{A}_{\text{act}} = (A \times Q, Q, q_0, F, \delta_{\text{act}})$ be the controllable DFA associated to the NFA $\mathcal{A}_\varphi$. We define the *Composition MDP* $\mathcal{M} = (S', A', P', s'_0)$ as follows: $S' = Q \times \Sigma_1 \times \cdots \times \Sigma_n$; $A' = A \times Q \times \{1 \ldots n\}$; $s'_0 = (q_0, \sigma_{10} \ldots \sigma_{n0})$; $P'(q', \sigma'_1 \ldots \sigma'_i \ldots \sigma'_n | q, \sigma_1 \ldots \sigma'_i \ldots \sigma_n, (a, q, i)) = P_i(\sigma'_i | \sigma_i, a)$ if $\delta_{\mathsf{act}}(q, (a, q')) = q'$. Moreover, let the composition cost function $C' : S' \times A' \to \mathbb{R}^+$ be defined as $C'((q, \sigma_1 \ldots \sigma_i \ldots \sigma_n), (a, q, i)) = C_i(\sigma_i, a)$.

We are interested in computing optimal policies for $\mathcal{M}$, where the optimality is defined as follows. Consider the target states $T = F \times F_1 \times \cdots \times F_n$. We consider the bi-objective lexicographic optimization over $\mathcal{M}'$, similarly to what has been done in [6]. In particular, we first consider the probability of reaching a set of target states T from $s \in S'$, following a policy π over the MDP $\mathcal{M}'$, denoted with $\mathbb{P}_{\mathcal{M}'_\pi, s}(\lozenge T)$; with $\Pi_{\mathcal{M}', s}(\lozenge T)$, we denote the set of policies with the maximum probability of reaching T, i.e. $\arg\max_\pi \mathbb{P}_{\mathcal{M}'_\pi, s}(\lozenge T)$. Then, we consider the cost of the shortest prefix of ρ that reaches one of the target states in T, i.e. $\mathsf{cost}_T(\rho) = \sum_{k=0}^i C'(s'_k, a'_k)$ if $\rho[i] \in T$ and for all $j < i$, $\rho[j] \notin T$. An optimal solution for $\mathcal{M}'$ is a policy π that minimizes the conditional expected cost of reaching a target state $\mathbb{E}_{\mathcal{M}'_\pi, s'_0}[\mathsf{cost}_T(\rho) | \lozenge T]$ among the policies in $\Pi_{\mathcal{M}, s'_0}(\lozenge T)$, that is, the policies which maximize $\mathbb{P}_{\mathcal{M}_\pi, s'_0}(\lozenge T)$, i.e.:

$$\pi \in \Pi_{\mathcal{M}', s_0}(\lozenge T) \text{ and } \pi \in \arg\min_{\pi'} \mathbb{E}_{\rho \sim \mathcal{M}'_\pi, s'_0}[\mathsf{cost}_T(\rho) | \lozenge T] \tag{5}$$

Step 4. The solution technique we will use is based on the work [6], where the authors propose a two-stage technique to find an optimal policy for a bi-objective lexicographic function in the form of Eq. (5). First, we compute the set of policies (in the form of a set of optimal actions for each state) that maximize the probability of reaching the target states; however, this set of policies also contains the "deferral" policies, i.e. policies that defer the actual reaching of the target states indefinitely, but in such a way that the target can still be reached with maximum probability at any moment. Then, we consider a "pruned MDP" in which (i) only optimal action can be taken, and (ii) only states from which the target can be reached are kept. The new MDP is used to find policies that minimize the expected cost of reaching the target. By construction, the optimal policy of the pruned MDP guarantees the target is always reached since any deferral policy will incur an infinite cost. The difference between our scenario and [6] is that they consider the length of the path, rather than its cost, as the second objective function. Nevertheless, it is easy to see that their approach works if, instead of considering the expected length of successful paths, we consider their expected total costs (i.e. minimizing path length can be seen as minimizing costs with each transition having unitary cost). Note that the techniques used to find the solutions are standard: the first stage requires solving the maximal reachability probability problem [1] on the composition MDP with the accepting end components as the set of states T. The second stage requires solving a stochastic shortest path problem [31] on the pruned MDP. The two subproblems can be solved efficiently using standard planning algorithms, e.g., Value Iteration or Linear Programming.

Step 5. Once an optimal policy is found, we can obtain its equivalent γ as follows: for any finite prefix of a run $\rho = (q_0, \sigma_{10} \ldots \sigma_{n0}), (a_1, q_1, o_1), \ldots (a_m, q_m, o_m), (q_m, \sigma_{1m} \ldots \sigma_{nm}), \ldots,$ we set $\gamma((\sigma_{10} \ldots \sigma_{n0}) \ldots (\sigma_{1m} \ldots \sigma_{nm})) = (a_{m+1}, o_{m+1})$, where $\pi(\rho) = (a_{m+1}, q_{m+1}, o_{m+1})$.

Now we aim to establish a relationship between optimal orchestrators according to Eq. (4), and optimal policies for $\mathcal{M}'$ according to Eq. (5). Given an infinite run $\rho = (q_0, \sigma_{10} \ldots \sigma_{n0}), (a_1, q_1, o_1) \ldots,$ we define the trace $t = \tilde{\tau}_{\varphi, \tilde{c}}(\rho) = (\sigma_{10} \ldots \sigma_{n0}), (a_1, o_1), \ldots$ The definition easily applies to finite prefixes of ρ but this time mapping into histories of t.

Now, we are going to prove a sequence of lemmata.

Lemma 2 shows that, once fixed a policy π over $\mathcal{M}'$, there is a one-to-one correspondence (modulo choices of $q_0 \ldots q_m$ in ρ) between paths ρ in $\mathcal{M}'$ following π and the executions $t \in \mathcal{T}_{\gamma, \mathcal{C}}$ of the equivalent orchestrator of π, γ; Lemma 3 shows that the probabilities of finite paths and histories are the same; Lemma 4 shows that paths that end with states in T correspond to successful histories; and Lemma 5 shows a correspondence between paths in $\mathsf{Paths}_{T, \mathcal{M}'_\pi}$ and $\mathcal{H}^\varphi_{\gamma, \tilde{c}}$.

Lemma 2. *Let π be a policy for $\mathcal{M}'$ and let γ be its equivalent orchestrator. Moreover, let $\rho \in \mathsf{Paths}^\omega_{\mathcal{M}'_\pi}$ and t be a trace such that $t = \tilde{\tau}_{\varphi, \tilde{c}}(\rho)$. Then, $\rho \in \mathsf{Paths}^\omega_{\mathcal{M}'_\pi}(\langle s'_0 \rangle)$ iff $t \in \mathcal{T}_{\gamma, \tilde{c}}(\langle (\sigma_{10} \ldots \sigma_{n0}) \rangle)$.*

Proof. Let the infinite path $\rho \in \mathsf{Paths}^\omega_{\mathcal{M}'_\pi}(\langle s'_0 \rangle)$, and the infinite trace $t = \tilde{\tau}_{\varphi, \tilde{c}}(\rho))$. We prove the claim by induction on the position of the run/trace.

Base case: we have the claim holds for position 0 because $\rho[0] = (q_0, \sigma_{10} \ldots \sigma_{n0})$, and $h[0] = \sigma_{10} \ldots \sigma_{n0}$. Therefore, $\langle h[0] \rangle$ satisfies the conditions of the definitions of history and execution of γ iff $s'_0 \in S'$.

Inductive case: assume the claim holds up to position $k \geq 0$. Consider the $(k+1)$-th action according to π, i.e. $\pi(\rho[0:k]) = (a_{k+1}, q_{k+1}, o_{k+1})$, and its successor state $\rho[k+1] = (q_{k+1}, \sigma_{1,k+1}, \ldots, \sigma_{n,k+1})$. By construction of $\mathcal{M}'$, we have that (i) $\sigma_{i,k+1} \in \Sigma_i$ for all services, (ii) $o_{k+1} \in \{1 \ldots n\}$, (iii) $a_{k+1} \in A$, and (iv) $\sigma_{k+1} \in \mathsf{Supp}(P_{o_{k+1}}(\sigma_{o_{k+1},k}, a_{k+1}))$. Moreover, by construction of γ, $(a_{k+1}, o_{k+1}) = \gamma(\mathsf{states}(t[0:k]))$, hence $h' = t[0:k], (a_{k+1}, o_{k+1}), (\sigma_{1,k+1} \ldots \sigma_{n,k+1})$ is a proper (finite) execution. The same arguments can be applied in the other direction by extending the actions of the trace with the next state $q_{k+1} \in Q$, where q_{k+1} is determined by the policy π (see above). By induction the claim also holds for any arbitrary position, and therefore $\rho \in \mathsf{Paths}^\omega_{\mathcal{M}'_\pi}(\langle s'_0 \rangle)$ iff $t \in \mathcal{T}_{\gamma, \tilde{c}}(\langle (\sigma_{10} \ldots \sigma_{n0}) \rangle)$.

Lemma 3. *Let π a policy on $\mathcal{M}'$, γ be its equivalent orchestrator, $\rho = s'_0 a_1 \ldots s'_m \in \mathsf{Paths}_{\mathcal{M}'_\pi}(s'_0)$ be a finite path on $\mathcal{M}'$, and $\tilde{h} = \tilde{\tau}_{\varphi, \tilde{c}}(\rho)$ be its associated history. Then, $\mathbb{P}_{\mathcal{M}_\pi, s'_0}(\mathsf{Paths}^\omega_{\mathcal{M}_\pi}(\rho)) = \mathbb{P}_{\gamma, \tilde{c}}(\mathcal{T}_{\gamma, \tilde{c}}(h))$.*

Proof.

$$\mathbb{P}_{\mathcal{M}'_\pi, s'_0}(\mathsf{Paths}^\omega_{\varphi, \tilde{\mathcal{C}}}(\rho)) = \prod_{k=1}^m P'(s'_k \mid s'_{k-1}, (a_k, q_k, o_k)) \tag{6}$$

$$= \prod_{k=1}^m P_{o_k}(\sigma_{o_k, k} \mid \sigma_{o_k, k-1}, (a_k, o_k)) \tag{7}$$

$$= \mathbb{P}_{\gamma, \tilde{\mathcal{C}}}(\mathcal{T}_{\gamma, \tilde{\mathcal{C}}}(h)) \tag{8}$$

where step 6 is by definition of the probability of a cylinder set, step 7 by definition of P' in $\mathcal{M}'$, and step 8 by Eq. (1).

Lemma 4. *Let* $\rho = s_0 a_1 \ldots s_m \in \mathsf{Paths}_{\mathcal{M}'_\pi}$ *be a finite path on* $\mathcal{M}'$, *and let* $h = \tilde{\tau}_{\varphi, \tilde{\mathcal{C}}}(\rho)$ *be its associated history. Then,* $s_m \in T$ *iff* $\mathsf{successful}(h)$.

Proof. By induction on the length of the run/history.
Base case: $\rho_0 = \langle s'_0 \rangle = \langle (q_0, \sigma_{10} \ldots \sigma_{n0}) \rangle$. Let $h_0 = \tilde{\tau}_{\varphi, \tilde{\mathcal{C}}}(\rho_0) = \langle (\sigma_{10} \ldots \sigma_{n0}) \rangle$. We have that $\rho_0[0] \in T$ iff (*i.a*) $q_0 \in F$ and (*i.b*) $\sigma_{i0} \in F_i$ for all $1 \le i \le n$. On the other hand, h is successful iff (*ii.a*) $\mathsf{actions}(h_0) = \epsilon \models \varphi$ and (*ii.b*) $\sigma_{i0} \in F_i$. The claim holds because (*i.b*) is precisely (*ii.b*), and (*i.a*) holds iff (*ii.a*) holds by the correctness of the construction of $\mathcal{A}_{\mathsf{act}}$.
Inductive case: assume the claim holds for $\rho_{k-1} = (q_0, \sigma_{10} \ldots \sigma_{n0}), (a_1, q_1, o_1),$ $\ldots, (a_{k-1}, q_{k-1}, o_{k-1}), (q_{k-1}, \sigma_{1, k-1} \ldots \sigma_{n, k-1})$ and $h_{k-1} = \tilde{\tau}_{\varphi, \tilde{\mathcal{C}}}(\rho)$. Let $a'_k = (a_k, q_k, o_k)$ be any valid next action taken from s_{k-1}, and let $s_k = (q_k, \sigma_{1k} \ldots \sigma_{nk}) \in \mathsf{Supp}(P_{o_k}(s_{k-1}, a_k))$ the next possible state. Consider the sequence $r = q_0 \ldots q_k$. By construction of $\mathcal{M}'$, and correctness of $\mathcal{A}^d$, we have that r is a run over $\mathcal{A}^d$, and that $q_k \in F$ iff $a_1 \ldots a_k \models \varphi$. By definition of $h_k = \tilde{\tau}_{\varphi, \tilde{\mathcal{C}}}(\rho_k)$, we also have that $\mathsf{actions}(h_k) = a_1 \ldots a_k$. Finally, we have that $s_k \in F$ iff (*i*) $q_k \in F$ and (*ii*) for all i $\sigma_{ik} \in F_i$ by construction of $\mathcal{M}'$; (*i*) holds iff (*iii*) $\mathsf{actions}(h_k) \models \varphi$ by the arguments above; finally, (*ii*) and (*iii*) hold iff $\mathsf{successful}(h)$.

Let $\mathsf{Paths}_{T, \mathcal{M}'_\pi}(s'_0)$ be the set of finite paths following π on $\mathcal{M}'$ such that they start with s'_0 and enter in a state in T only at the end of the path and for the first time, i.e. $\mathsf{Paths}_{T, \mathcal{M}'_\pi}(s'_0) = ((S' \setminus T) \times A)^* T \cap \mathsf{Paths}_{\mathcal{M}'_\pi}(s'_0)$.

Lemma 5. $\rho \in \mathsf{Paths}_{T, \mathcal{M}'_\pi}(s'_0)$ *iff* $\tilde{\tau}_{\gamma, \tilde{\mathcal{C}}}(\rho) \in \mathcal{H}^\varphi_{\gamma, \tilde{\mathcal{C}}}$

Proof. By Lemma 4, $\rho \in \mathsf{Paths}_{T, \mathcal{M}'_\pi}$ iff $h = \tilde{\tau}_{\gamma, \tilde{\mathcal{C}}}(\rho)$ is successful. Moreover, by Lemma 2, $\rho \in \mathsf{Paths}_{T, \mathcal{M}'_\pi} \subseteq \mathsf{Paths}_{\mathcal{M}'_\pi}$ iff h is an execution of γ. Furthermore, by assumption, any finite prefix ρ', say of length m, of ρ, is such that $\rho'[m] \notin T$. Then, again by Lemma 4, this holds iff $h' = \tilde{\tau}_{\varphi, \tilde{\mathcal{C}}}(\rho')$ is not successful, meaning that does not exist a prefix $h' \in \mathsf{prefixes}(h)$ with $h' \ne h$ such that h' is successful. But this is precisely the membership condition for $\mathcal{H}^\varphi_{\gamma, \tilde{\mathcal{C}}}$

This result shows the correctness of our technique:

Theorem 3. *Let $(\tilde{C}, \varphi)$ be an instance of Problem 2, and let $\mathcal{M}'$ be the composition MDP for $\tilde{C}$ and φ. We have that π is optimal (w.r.t. Eq. (5)) iff its equivalent orchestrator γ is optimal (w.r.t. Eq. (4)).*

Proof. First, we show that $\pi = \arg\max_{\pi'} \mathbb{P}_{\mathcal{M}'_\pi, s'_0}(\Diamond T)$ iff $\gamma = \arg\max_{\gamma'} \mathcal{P}^{\tilde{C}}_\varphi(\gamma')$. For any pair π and its equivalent γ, we have:

$$\mathbb{P}_{\pi, s'_0}(\Diamond T) = \sum_{\rho_T \in \mathsf{Paths}_{T, \pi}(s'_0)} \mathbb{P}_{\mathcal{M}'_\pi, s'_0}(\mathsf{Paths}^\omega_{\mathcal{M}'_\pi, s'_0}(\rho_T)) \tag{9}$$

$$= \sum_{\tilde{h} \in \mathcal{H}^\varphi_{\gamma, \tilde{C}}} \mathbb{P}_{\gamma, \tilde{C}}(\mathcal{T}_{\gamma, \tilde{C}}(\tilde{h})) \tag{10}$$

$$= \mathbb{P}_{\gamma, \tilde{C}}\left(\bigcup_{h \in \mathcal{H}^\varphi_{\gamma, \tilde{C}}} \mathcal{T}_{\gamma, \tilde{C}}(h) \right) \tag{11}$$

$$= \mathcal{P}^{\tilde{C}}_\varphi(\gamma) \tag{12}$$

where step 9 is by definition of probabilistic reachability, step 10 is by Lemma 3 and Lemma 5, step 11 is by disjointness of all $\mathcal{T}_{\gamma, \tilde{C}}(h)$ for $h \in \mathcal{H}^\varphi_{\gamma, \tilde{C}}$, and step 12 is by Eq. (2). From this, we obtain that $\pi^* = \arg\max_{\pi'} \mathbb{P}_{\mathcal{M}_{\pi'}, s'_0}(\Diamond T)$ iff $\gamma^* = \arg\max_{\gamma'} \mathcal{P}^{\tilde{C}}_\varphi(\gamma')$.

It remains to prove that π is cost-optimal iff γ is cost-optimal. We have:

$$\mathbb{E}_{\rho \sim \mathcal{M}'_\pi, s'_0}[\mathsf{cost}_T(\rho) \mid \Diamond T]$$

$$= \sum_{\rho_T \in \mathsf{Paths}_{T, \pi}(s'_0)} \mathbb{P}_{\mathcal{M}'_{\pi'}, s'_0}(\mathsf{Paths}^\omega_{\mathcal{M}'_\pi, s'_0}(\rho_T)) \cdot \sum_{k=0}^{|\rho_T|} C'(s'_k, a'_{k+1}) \tag{13}$$

$$= \sum_{\tilde{h} \in \mathcal{H}^\varphi_{\gamma, \tilde{C}}} \mathbb{P}_{\gamma, \tilde{C}}(\mathcal{T}_{\gamma, \tilde{C}}(\tilde{h})) \cdot \sum_{k=0}^{|h|} C_{o_{k+1}}(\sigma_{o_k, k}, a_{k+1}) \tag{14}$$

$$= \mathbb{E}_{h \sim \mathbb{P}_{\gamma, \tilde{C}}}\left[\sum_{k=1}^{|h|} C_{o_k}(\sigma_{o_k, k-1}, a_k) \,\middle|\, \mathsf{successful}(h) \right] \tag{15}$$

$$= \mathcal{J}^{\tilde{C}}_\varphi(\gamma) \tag{16}$$

where step 13 by definition of total expected cost conditioned on reaching of target states T, step 14 by construction of $\mathcal{M}'$ and by Lemma 3 and Lemma 5, step 15 by definition of total expected cost on successful executions of γ, and step 16 by Eq. (3). Therefore, if $\pi \in \arg\min_{\pi'} \mathbb{E}_{\rho \sim \mathcal{M}'_\pi, s'_0}[\mathsf{cost}_T(\rho) \mid \Diamond T]$ then $\gamma \in \arg\min_{\gamma'} \mathcal{J}^{\tilde{C}}_\varphi(\gamma')$. Combining both results, we get the thesis.

Computational Cost. Theorem 3 guarantees that we can reduce Problem 1 to the problem of finding an optimal policy for the lexicographic bi-objective optimization problem (Eq. (5)) over a composition MDP $\mathcal{M}'$. As explained above,

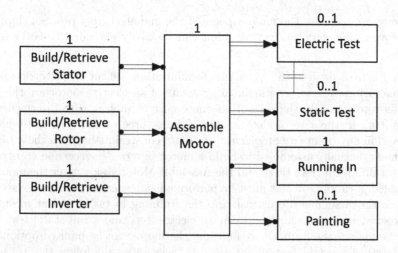

Fig. 2. The electric motor manufacturing process represented using DECLARE.

the two-stage technique requires solving a planning problem over MDPs. Since it is known that both steps require polynomial time complexity in the number of states and actions of the MDP [31] and that our Composition MDP has a state space that is a single-exponential in the size of the goal specification, we get this result:

Theorem 4. *Problem 1 can be solved in at most exponential time in the size of the formula, in at most exponential time in the number of services, and in polynomial time in the size of the services.*

Observe that, differently from the classical setting of LTL/LTL$_f$ synthesis on probabilistic systems [11,35], and analogously to our solution method for the non-stochastic case, we do not have unobservable "adversarial" nondeterminism in the composition MDP; hence, we do not need to determinize the NFA of the goal specification, thereby saving an exponential blow-up in time complexity.

4   Case Study

To introduce the proposed approach, its functionalities, and its capacity to address smart manufacturing, we consider the production process of an electric motor widely used in various applications such as industrial machinery, electric vehicles, household appliances, and many others [12]. To function properly, electric motors require certain materials that possess specific electrical and magnetic properties. Therefore, before the manufacturing processes start, the raw materials (i.e., copper, steel, aluminium, magnets, insulation materials, bearings) must be extracted and refined to obtain essential metals and polymers for electric motor parts manufacturing. When the materials are in the manufacturing facility, the effective manufacturing process can start. For the sake of brevity, in the following, we focus on the main aspects of the manufacturing process, skipping the provisioning, but the formalization can be easily extended to cover more details.

Goal. Figure 2 depicts the DECLARE formalization [30] of the electric motor manufacturing process. The main components of an electric motor are the stator, the rotor, and, in the case of alternate current motors with direct current power (e.g., in the case of electric cars). These three components are built or retrieved in any order (*no precedence* DECLARE constraints between these tasks) and then eventually assembled to build a motor (*alternate succession* constraint between Build/Retrieve tasks and the Assemble Motor task). After the motor is assembled, a running-in test must be performed (*alternate succession* constraint between the Assemble Motor task and the Running In task), and at most one (*not coexistence* constraint) between an electric test and a full static test (the latter comprises the former). In addition, the motor can be painted optionally. The Painting, Electric Test and Static Test tasks optionally follow the Assemble Motor task (*alternate precedence* constraints). The process depicts the manufacturing tasks involved in producing a *single motor* as indicated by the *existence constraints*. Machines and/or human operators can perform all these operations.

Services. The behaviour of each process actor can be described as a stochastic service, i.e., a state machine with a probabilistic behaviour used to model two types of actors involved in the manufacturing process, namely *machines* and *human operators*, shown in Fig. 3. Each transition edge has a label which indicates the operation, the probability of transition and the associated cost. Figure 3a depicts a simple stochastic service of human workers. Such services have an initial accepting state in which they are READY and accept operations, and a sink failure state from where no action can be taken. The transition triggered by the [OP] action has a probability of p^s of remaining in the same ready state (success), but a $1 - p^s$ probability of failing. The transition is associated with a certain cost $c_i^{[Op]}$ to perform the action (preceded by a $-$, i.e., the cost is thought of as a negative value, using the reward-based representation). Figure 3b depicts a generic stochastic service of machines. The machine is initially in the READY state, which is also the unique accepting state, where it can receive the CONFIG[DEV] command (the reader, in the following, can imagine the [DEV] trailer to be replaced with the name of the specific manufacturing actor). This action takes the service to the CONFIGURATION state where the actor is set up or warmed up. At the end of this phase, the CHECKED[DEV] action is performed. If the configuration is unsuccessful, with a probability p_i^u representing the possibility of finding the actor unemployable, the actor goes into the BROKEN state. If the configuration is successful, with a probability $1 - p_i^u$, the actor goes to the EXECUTING state, where a family of operations, denoted with [OP] in the picture, can be executed. For the sake of compactness, we only show a single operation, but the service can be easily generalized to the case where a single actor can perform multiple operations. The action [OP] represents one of those operations defined in Fig. 2. Executing an operation implies a certain cost

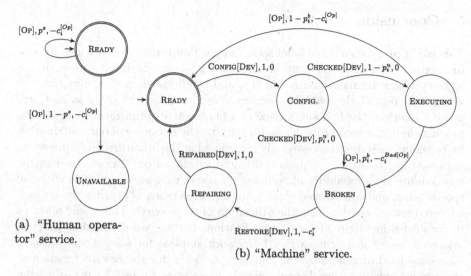

(a) "Human operator" service.

(b) "Machine" service.

Fig. 3. The two types of service we consider for the Electric Motor case study.

$c_i^{[Op]}$. In some cases, the execution of [OP] may take the actor i to the BROKEN state with probability p_i^b and also, in this case, the operation implies a high cost $c_i^{Bad[Op]}$. To take the actor back to the READY state, a RESTORE[DEV] task must be executed on the actor, which has a repair cost c_i^r depending on the actual conditions of the actor, and that takes the actor to the REPAIRING state. When the actor is repaired, a REPAIRED[DEV] event is received, making the actor available again for manufacturing. Noteworthy, the CONFIG[DEV], CHECKED[DEV], RESTORE[DEV], REPAIRED[DEV] operations do not leave any trace on the target process. Noticeably, we can imagine that some of these operations are triggered, in reality, as exogenous events, i.e., they should be reflected in the controller, but the actor will wait for these events instead of autonomously enacting them.

We are interested in the problem of maximising the probability that the smart factory succeeds in producing electric motors at a minimum utilization cost. A two-stage approach can achieve this: in the first stage, we aim to find the maximally permissive strategy that (i) determines the equally optimal sequences of actions to satisfy the goal specification and (ii) the equally optimal dispatching strategy that decides which services should perform the operation. The optimization must also consider configuration/checking/repairing action to bring the service back to a final configuration. This might require limiting the use of services with certain probability of leading to a failing configuration. In the second stage, we select, among the available strategies, those that also minimize the utilization cost. Crucially, the optimal solution might vary depending on the service available and their capabilities, as well as the probabilities p_i^s, p_i^u, p_i^b and costs $c_i^{[Op]}$, $c_i^{Bad[Op]}$ and c_i^r. Given the high degrees of freedom, it is paramount to use a technique, such as the one proposed in this work, that can automatically handle such a complex scenario.

5   Conclusion

This paper proposes a novel stochastic composition framework in which we aim to maximize the satisfaction probability of a goal specification, expressed as a high-level logic formalism such as LTL$_f$, and conditioned on this, minimize the utilization costs of the available services. We formalized the problem and proposed a solution based on a reduction to a bi-objective optimization over MDPs, proving the correctness. Finally, we highlighted the relevance of our contribution by providing an industrial case study considered in the literature. In future work, we would like to study the process-oriented variant of our framework, namely, to maximize the probability of realizing *all* traces that are compatible with the specification, and conditioned on this, maximize as much as possible the average expected reward coming from the utilization of the services. This would allow us to consider a hierarchy of target specifications (either goal-oriented or process-oriented), hence delivering a rich framework suitable for several applications. The same kind of generalization can be considered for the reward function of the services, where we can have more than one reward to consider regarding the service utilization. Moreover, we would like to implement our approach using state-of-the-art probabilistic model checkers such as PRISM [24] and Storm [23].

Acknowledgements. This work has been partially supported by the EU H2020 project AIPlan4EU (No. 101016442), the ERC-ADG WhiteMech (No. 834228), the EU ICT-48 2020 project TAILOR (No. 952215), the PRIN project RIPER (No. 20203FFYLK), and the PNRR MUR project FAIR (No. PE0000013). This work has been carried out while Luciana Silo was enrolled in the Italian National Doctorate on Artificial Intelligence run by Sapienza University of Rome.

References

1. de Alfaro, L.: Formal verification of probabilistic systems. Ph.D. thesis, Stanford University, USA (1997). https://searchworks.stanford.edu/view/3910936
2. Berardi, D., Calvanese, D., De Giacomo, G., Lenzerini, M., Mecella, M.: Automatic composition of E-services that export their behavior. In: Orlowska, M.E., Weerawarana, S., Papazoglou, M.P., Yang, J. (eds.) ICSOC 2003. LNCS, vol. 2910, pp. 43–58. Springer, Heidelberg (2003). https://doi.org/10.1007/978-3-540-24593-3_4
3. Berardi, D., Calvanese, D., De Giacomo, G., Mecella, M.: Composition of services with nondeterministic observable behavior. In: Benatallah, B., Casati, F., Traverso, P. (eds.) ICSOC 2005. LNCS, vol. 3826, pp. 520–526. Springer, Heidelberg (2005). https://doi.org/10.1007/11596141_43
4. Brafman, R.I., De Giacomo, G., Mecella, M., Sardiña, S.: Service composition in stochastic settings. In: Esposito, F., Basili, R., Ferilli, S., Lisi, F. (eds.) AI*IA 2017. LNCS, vol. 10640, pp. 159–171. Springer, Cham (2017). https://doi.org/10.1007/978-3-319-70169-1_12
5. Brafman, R.I., De Giacomo, G., Patrizi, F.: LTLf/LDLf non-Markovian rewards. In: AAAI, pp. 1771–1778. AAAI Press (2018)
6. Busatto-Gaston, D., Chakraborty, D., Majumdar, A., Mukherjee, S., Pérez, G.A., Raskin, J.: Bi-objective lexicographic optimization in Markov decision processes

with related objectives. In: André, É., Sun, J. (eds.) ATVA 2023. LNCS, vol. 14215, pp. 203–223. Springer, Cham (2023). https://doi.org/10.1007/978-3-031-45329-8_10

7. Chatterjee, K., Katoen, J.-P., Weininger, M., Winkler, T.: Stochastic games with lexicographic reachability-safety objectives. In: Lahiri, S.K., Wang, C. (eds.) CAV 2020. LNCS, vol. 12225, pp. 398–420. Springer, Cham (2020). https://doi.org/10.1007/978-3-030-53291-8_21

8. Chatterjee, K., Majumdar, R., Henzinger, T.A.: Markov decision processes with multiple objectives. In: Durand, B., Thomas, W. (eds.) STACS 2006. LNCS, vol. 3884, pp. 325–336. Springer, Heidelberg (2006). https://doi.org/10.1007/11672142_26

9. Chen, K., Xu, J., Reiff-Marganiec, S.: Markov-HTN planning approach to enhance flexibility of automatic web service composition. In: ICWS, pp. 9–16. IEEE Computer Society (2009)

10. Chen, Y., Huang, J., Lin, C., Shen, X.: Multi-objective service composition with QoS dependencies. IEEE Trans. Cloud Comput. (2019)

11. Courcoubetis, C., Yannakakis, M.: The complexity of probabilistic verification. J. ACM **42**(4), 857–907 (1995)

12. De Giacomo, G., Favorito, M., Leotta, F., Mecella, M., Monti, F., Silo, L.: AIDA: a tool for resiliency in smart manufacturing. In: Cabanillas, C., Pérez, F. (eds.) CAiSE 2023. LNBIP, vol. 477, pp. 112–120. Springer, Cham (2023). https://doi.org/10.1007/978-3-031-34674-3_14

13. De Giacomo, G., Favorito, M., Leotta, F., Mecella, M., Silo, L.: Digital twins composition via Markov decision processes. In: ITBPM@BPM. CEUR Workshop Proceedings, vol. 2952, pp. 44–49. CEUR-WS.org (2021)

14. De Giacomo, G., Favorito, M., Leotta, F., Mecella, M., Silo, L.: Modeling resilient cyber-physical processes and their composition from digital twins via Markov decision processes. In: PMAI@IJCAI. CEUR Workshop Proceedings, vol. 3310, pp. 101–104. CEUR-WS.org (2022)

15. De Giacomo, G., Favorito, M., Leotta, F., Mecella, M., Silo, L.: Digital twin composition in smart manufacturing via Markov decision processes. Comput. Ind. **149**, 103916 (2023)

16. De Giacomo, G., Mecella, M., Patrizi, F.: Automated service composition based on behaviors: the roman model. In: Bouguettaya, A., Sheng, Q., Daniel, F. (eds.) Web Services Foundations, pp. 189–214. Springer, New York (2014). https://doi.org/10.1007/978-1-4614-7518-7_8

17. De Giacomo, G., Patrizi, F., Sardina, S.: Automatic behavior composition synthesis. Artif. Intell. **196**, 106–142 (2013)

18. De Giacomo, G., Vardi, M.Y.: Linear temporal logic and linear dynamic logic on finite traces. In: IJCAI, pp. 854–860. IJCAI/AAAI (2013)

19. Di Ciccio, C., Montali, M.: Declarative process specifications: reasoning, discovery, monitoring. In: van der Aalst, W.M.P., Carmona, J. (eds.) Process Mining Handbook. Lecture Notes in Business Information Processing, vol. 448, pp. 108–152. Springer, Cham (2022). https://doi.org/10.1007/978-3-031-08848-3_4

20. Dumas, M., et al.: AI-augmented business process management systems: a research manifesto. ACM Trans. Manag. Inf. Syst. **14**(1), 11:1–11:19 (2023)

21. Gao, A., Yang, D., Tang, S., Zhang, M.: Web service composition using Markov decision processes. In: Fan, W., Wu, Z., Yang, J. (eds.) WAIM 2005. LNCS, vol. 3739, pp. 308–319. Springer, Heidelberg (2005). https://doi.org/10.1007/11563952_28

22. Hahn, E.M., Perez, M., Schewe, S., Somenzi, F., Trivedi, A., Wojtczak, D.: Model-free reinforcement learning for lexicographic omega-regular objectives. In: Huisman, M., Pǎsǎreanu, C., Zhan, N. (eds.) FM 2021. LNCS, vol. 13047, pp. 142–159. Springer, Cham (2021). https://doi.org/10.1007/978-3-030-90870-6_8

23. Hensel, C., Junges, S., Katoen, J., Quatmann, T., Volk, M.: The probabilistic model checker storm. Int. J. Softw. Tools Technol. Transf. **24**(4), 589–610 (2022)

24. Kwiatkowska, M., Norman, G., Parker, D.: PRISM 4.0: verification of probabilistic real-time systems. In: Gopalakrishnan, G., Qadeer, S. (eds.) CAV 2011. LNCS, vol. 6806, pp. 585–591. Springer, Heidelberg (2011). https://doi.org/10.1007/978-3-642-22110-1_47

25. Marrella, A., Mecella, M., Sardiña, S.: Supporting adaptiveness of cyber-physical processes through action-based formalisms. AI Commun. **31**(1), 47–74 (2018)

26. Monti, F., Silo, L., Leotta, F., Mecella, M.: On the suitability of AI for service-based adaptive supply chains in smart manufacturing. In: ICWS, pp. 704–706. IEEE (2023)

27. Monti, F., Silo, L., Leotta, F., Mecella, M.: Services in smart manufacturing: comparing automated reasoning techniques for composition and orchestration. In: Aiello, M., Barzen, J., Dustdar, S., Leymann, F. (eds.) SummerSOC 2023. CCIS, vol. 1847, pp. 69–83. Springer, Cham (2023). https://doi.org/10.1007/978-3-031-45728-9_5

28. Moustafa, Ahmed, Zhang, Minjie: Multi-objective service composition using reinforcement learning. In: Basu, Samik, Pautasso, Cesare, Zhang, Liang, Fu, Xiang (eds.) ICSOC 2013. LNCS, vol. 8274, pp. 298–312. Springer, Heidelberg (2013). https://doi.org/10.1007/978-3-642-45005-1_21

29. Papazoglou, M.P., Traverso, P., Dustdar, S., Leymann, F.: Service-oriented computing: state of the art and research challenges. Computer **40**(11), 38–45 (2007)

30. Pesic, M., Schonenberg, H., Van der Aalst, W.M.: Declare: full support for loosely-structured processes. In: EDOC (2007)

31. Puterman, M.L.: Markov decision processes (1994)

32. Sadeghiram, S., Ma, H., Chen, G.: A user-preference driven lexicographic approach for multi-objective distributed web service composition. In: 2020 IEEE Symposium Series on Computational Intelligence (SSCI) (2020)

33. Skalse, J., Abate, A.: On the limitations of Markovian rewards to express multi-objective, risk-sensitive, and modal tasks. In: UAI. Proceedings of Machine Learning Research, vol. 216, pp. 1974–1984. PMLR (2023)

34. Skalse, J., Hammond, L., Griffin, C., Abate, A.: Lexicographic multi-objective reinforcement learning. In: IJCAI, pp. 3430–3436. ijcai.org (2022)

35. Wells, A.M., Lahijanian, M., Kavraki, L.E., Vardi, M.Y.: LTLf synthesis on probabilistic systems. In: GandALF. EPTCS, vol. 326 (2020)

36. Wray, K., Zilberstein, S., Mouaddib, A.I.: Multi-objective MDPs with conditional lexicographic reward preferences. In: AAAI (2015)

37. Yadav, N., Sardiña, S.: Decision theoretic behavior composition. In: AAMAS, pp. 575–582. IFAAMAS (2011)

Argumentation

How to Manage Supports in Incomplete Argumentation

Marie-Christine Lagasquie-Schiex[1] , Jean-Guy Mailly[2] ,
and Antonio Yuste-Ginel[3(✉)]

[1] Université Paul Sabatier, IRIT, Toulouse, France
[2] Université Paris Cité, LIPADE, 75006 Paris, France
[3] Complutense University of Madrid, Madrid, Spain
antoyust@ucm.es

Abstract. The growing interest in generalizations of Dung's abstract argumentation frameworks has recently led to the simultaneous and independent discovery of a combination of two of these generalizations: Bipolar Argumentation Frameworks (BAFs), where a relation representing supports between arguments is added, and Incomplete Argumentation Frameworks (IAFs), where the existence of arguments and attacks may be uncertain, resulting in the so-called Incomplete Bipolar Abstract Argumentation Frameworks (IBAFs). This paper digs deeper into such a combination by: (i) providing a thoughtful analysis of the existing notions of completion (the hypothetical removal of uncertainty used in IBAFs to reason about argument acceptability); (ii) proposing, motivating and studying new notions of completion; (iii) throwing new complexity results on argument acceptability problems associated with IBAFs; (iv) encoding these reasoning problems into a lightweight version of dynamic logic.

Keywords: Argumentation Systems · Bipolarity · Support · Uncertainty · Incompleteness · Completions

1 Introduction

Formal argumentation has become a very popular approach to reasoning in Artificial Intelligence in recent decades. This popularity can be rooted in at least two reasons. First, argumentation is an essential component of human reasoning (if not the main one [35]), and therefore it is of crucial importance for human-machine interaction. Second, different ideas from this recently born subfield have found applications in other, well-established ones (e.g., in multi-agent systems [11]). Within this context, the studies of argument-based models of inference are almost ubiquitously influenced by the Abstract Frameworks (AFs) of Dung [21],

The second author benefited from the support of the project AGGREEY ANR-22-CE23-0005 of the French National Research Agency (ANR).
The third author gratefully acknowledges funding from the project PID2020-117871GB-I00 of the Spanish Ministry of Science and Innovation.

A. Meier and M. Ortiz (Eds.): FoIKS 2024, LNCS 14589, pp. 319–339, 2024.
https://doi.org/10.1007/978-3-031-56940-1_18

where nodes of a graph are used to represent arguments while the edges represent an attack relation among them. This way of approaching argumentation is *abstract*, as one ignores the nature and internal structure of arguments and their interactions in order to focus on more general, dialectical aspects. In this vein, different semantics are used for selecting *extensions* from a given AF, i.e. sets of arguments considered jointly acceptable because they satisfy some intuitive requirements.

Despite their popularity, Dung AFs come equipped with very limited expressivity, which makes them unsuitable to capture more fine-grained argumentative phenomena that do have an impact on argument acceptability. That partially explains the proliferation of very different generalizations of Dung's model. There are, at least, two important families of such generalisations. First, *the addition of new kinds of interactions among arguments*: among others, *support relations* [10,37,39], *higher-order frameworks* [6,12] (where attacks might target other attacks, not only arguments), or *collective interactions* (where the source of attacks might be a set of nodes, instead of a single one [36]). Second, *the addition of uncertainty to the model*, which can be done either by the introduction of *weights and preferences over arguments and interactions* [1,5,41], or by taking into account *uncertainty about the presence of the different elements* (both in a qualitative [34] and a probabilistic fashion [28]).

Before going any further, let us illustrate the kind of situations that motivate the development and study of combinations of frameworks from both families:

Example 1 ([31]*)*. The pension reform wanted by the government is the main topic of a heated discussion between people with the following arguments:

a_1: The pension reform is important and must be implemented.

a_2: Indeed. Because the pension financing system is in deficit (a_2 supports a_1).

a_3: This reform is the only way to avoid a reduction in the amount of pensions (a_3 supports a_1).

a_4: It would be surprising if this reform were the only way to avoid this reduction (a_4 attacks a_3).

a_5: Indeed, an increase in contributions would also prevent a reduction in the amount of pensions (a_5 supports a_4).

a_6: This reform is too premature; there are other reforms in progress and we do not yet know their impact (a_6 attacks a_1).

Clearly, uncertainty and incompleteness exist in this exchange. First, several politicians consider that the deficit of the pension system is not the real motivation of the government for reforming (so the support from a_2 to a_1 would be uncertain). Second, argument a_4 might not be even taken into consideration by part of the audience (hence its presence is uncertain). Finally, perhaps the impact of the previous reforms on the new one may have already been considered by the government so that the attack from a_6 to a_1 might be disregarded.   □

The intense interest that the mentioned generalizations of AFs illustrated by the previous example have awakened among formal argumentation practitioners is witnessed by the simultaneous, independent definition and computational study of a combination of two such generalizations. In the last few months, our technical report [31] and the ECAI paper [25] by Fazzinga and colleagues came up with the very same definition of *Incomplete Bipolar Argumentation Frameworks* (IBAFs).

This paper moves forward in the combination of argumentative bipolarity and argumentative uncertainty by providing several contributions to the study of IBAFs: (i) we compare in detail the existing notions of completions (the hypothetical removal of uncertainty used in IBAFs to reason about argument acceptability); (ii) we motivate and define a new notion of completion, which is somehow a compromise in between the proposals made by us [31] and Fazzinga et al. [25]; (iii) we throw new complexity results about argument acceptability problems in IBAFs; (iv) we encode these problems in the Dynamic Logic of Propositional Assignments (DL-PA) [2,3], a well-behaved variant of propositional dynamic logic that has been proven useful to reason about argumentation in recent years [18–20,27,43]. Apart from that, a significant part of the results that will be shown here were already presented in [31], so the current document can be seen as an improved and extended presentation, paper-style, of the mentioned technical report.

The rest of this paper is organized as follows: Sect. 2 gives the background on argumentation; the definition of IBAFs and the different notions of completion are given and discussed in Sect. 3; the complexity results are presented in Sect. 4; and a logical encoding of IBAFs in Sect. 5; Sect. 6 concludes the paper by giving some perspectives. Note that the proofs of our results can be found in the technical report [30].

2   Background

Basic Notions of Abstract Argumentation. We suppose the existence of a finite set of arguments $\mathbf{A}$. An abstract **argumentation framework** (AF) is a pair $\mathcal{F} = \langle \mathcal{A}, \mathcal{R} \rangle$ with $\mathcal{A} \subseteq \mathbf{A}$ the set of **arguments** and $\mathcal{R} \subseteq \mathcal{A} \times \mathcal{A}$ the set of **attacks**. For $a, b \in \mathcal{A}$, we say that a **attacks** b if $(a, b) \in \mathcal{R}$ (and we sometimes use the infix notation $a\mathcal{R}b$). If b attacks some $c \in \mathcal{A}$, then a **defends** c against b. Similarly, a set $S \subseteq \mathcal{A}$ attacks (resp. defends) an argument b if there is some $a \in S$ that attacks b (resp. if, for any $a\mathcal{R}b$, there is $c \in S$ that defends b against a). Let us consider Example 1 without taking into account the potential uncertainty, arguments a_4 and a_3 and their relationship can be represented by the graph (the simple plain arrow represents the attack from a_4 to a_3):

We classically use the concept of **extensions**, proposed by Dung [21], for evaluating the acceptability of arguments, i.e. sets of collectively acceptable arguments. The usual semantics are based on two main principles: conflict-freeness and admissibility. Given $\mathcal{F} = \langle \mathcal{A}, \mathcal{R} \rangle$ an AF, the set $E \subseteq \mathcal{A}$ is **conflict-free** iff $\forall a, b \in E, (a, b) \notin \mathcal{R}$; E is **admissible** iff it is conflict-free and $\forall a \in E, \forall b \in \mathcal{A}$ s.t. $b\mathcal{R}a, \exists c \in E$ s.t. $c\mathcal{R}b$. We use $\mathsf{cf}(\mathcal{F})$ (respectively $\mathsf{ad}(\mathcal{F})$) to denote the set of conflict-free (resp. admissible) sets of an AF $\mathcal{F}$. We focus on the four semantics proposed by Dung. Formally, the admissible set $E \subseteq \mathcal{A}$ is: a **complete** extension iff E contains all the arguments that it defends; a **preferred** extension iff E is a $\subseteq$-maximal admissible set; a **grounded** extension iff E is a $\subseteq$-minimal complete extension; and a **stable extension** iff $E \in \mathsf{cf}(\mathcal{F})$ and $\forall a \in \mathcal{A} \setminus E$, E attacks a. We use $\mathsf{co}(\mathcal{F})$, $\mathsf{pr}(\mathcal{F})$, $\mathsf{gr}(\mathcal{F})$ and $\mathsf{st}(\mathcal{F})$ for the sets of (resp.) complete, preferred, grounded and stable extensions of $\mathcal{F}$ (see more details in [4,21]).

Bipolar Argumentation Frameworks. This notion has been initially defined as a general approach taking into account two kinds of interactions between arguments: a negative one (attacks) and a positive one (supports), see [13].

A **Bipolar Argumentation Framework** (BAF) is a tuple $\mathcal{B} = \langle \mathcal{A}, \mathcal{R}, \mathcal{S} \rangle$ where $\mathcal{A} \subseteq \mathbf{A}$ are arguments, $\mathcal{R} \subseteq \mathcal{A} \times \mathcal{A}$ is an attack relation, and $\mathcal{S} \subseteq \mathcal{A} \times \mathcal{A}$ is a **support relation** (when $a \, \mathcal{S} \, b$ we say that a *supports* b). Given a (support) relation $\mathcal{S}$, we use $\mathcal{S}^+$ to denote its transitive closure (i.e. the smallest (w.r.t. $\subseteq$) transitive relation containing $\mathcal{S}$). Let us consider Example 1, arguments a_4, a_3 and a_1 and their relationship (ignoring uncertainty) can be represented by the graph (the double plain arrow represents the support from a_3 to a_1):

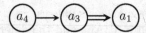

In the general approach to BAFs, semantics are defined using the addition of new attacks. Nevertheless, it turned out that such a general approach is not sufficient for encoding some real cases and sometimes the drawback is the lack of guidelines for choosing the appropriate definitions and semantics depending on the application. Consequently, various kinds of support relations have been defined in the literature as specializations of this general framework. Among others, one could mention the notion of necessary support [37], deductive support [10], evidential support [39], backing support [15], and monotonic support [26]. Here, we just focus on the two former notions, which have the following intuitive meaning: if a necessarily (resp. deductively) supports b then the acceptance of a is necessary for (resp. implies) the acceptance of b. Moreover, a duality exists between these two approaches: a necessarily supports b iff b deductively supports a (see [14]); so a deductive BAF is a necessary BAF in which the direction of the support arrows has been reversed (and vice-versa).

When the type of support is chosen, the reasoning is made once again with the notion of extension via the addition of new attacks. We focus on the deductive interpretation, as the necessary one follows from the mentioned duality by simply reversing support arrows. Let $\mathcal{B} = \langle \mathcal{A}, \mathcal{R}, \mathcal{S} \rangle$ be a BAF, let $a, b \in \mathcal{A}$, a **attacks** b **according to the deductive interpretation** iff either $a\mathcal{R}b$ *(Case 0: an existing direct attack)*, or there is $c \in \mathcal{A}$ s.t. $a\mathcal{R}c$ and $b\mathcal{S}^+c$ *(Case 1: a new attack)*, or there is $c \in \mathcal{A}$ s.t. $c\mathcal{R}b$ and $a\mathcal{S}^+c$ *(Case 2: a new attack)*. The following figure illustrates cases 1 and 2:[1]

$$a \longrightarrow c \Longleftarrow \cdots \Longleftarrow b \quad | \quad b \longleftarrow c \Longleftarrow \cdots \Longleftarrow a$$

---

[1] Case 1 (resp. 2) is also called "super-mediated" (resp. "supported") attack in the literature.

Obviously, the new attacks can therefore be used in turn to create new other attacks through a saturation process. Let ded and nec stand for 'deductive' and 'necessary', and let $t \in \{\text{ded}, \text{nec}\}$, we denote by $\mathcal{R}^t$ the set of attacks according to the interpretation t. Then the notions of conflict-freeness and acceptability in a BAF $\mathcal{B} = \langle \mathcal{A}, \mathcal{R}, \mathcal{S} \rangle$ under the interpretation t are defined using the classical argumentation framework $\langle \mathcal{A}, \mathcal{R}^t \rangle$ in which the support relation does not exist. So, given $\mathcal{B} = \langle \mathcal{A}, \mathcal{R}, \mathcal{S} \rangle$ a BAF, $\sigma^t(\mathcal{B}) = \sigma(\langle \mathcal{A}, \mathcal{R}^t \rangle)$ **is the set of extensions of the BAF under the interpretation t and for the semantics** σ ($\sigma \in \{\text{co}, \text{gr}, \text{pr}, \text{st}\}$). We say that $a \in \mathcal{A}$ is **credulously accepted** w.r.t. σ and t if it belongs to some extension in $\sigma^t(\mathcal{B})$, and **sceptically accepted** if it belongs to each extension.

In conclusion, the computation of the semantics for BAF is done in 3 steps: initially, the BAF is completed by the introduction of the new attacks due to the supports (depending on the meaning of these supports); secondly, the BAF produces an AF by removing the supports; and third, the extensions of the original BAF are exactly the Dung extensions of this AF.

Example 2. The following figure gives, on the left, a possible representation of the discussion described in Example 1 considering a deductive meaning for the support and ignoring uncertainty and, on the right, the corresponding classical AF in which the computation of extensions is made:

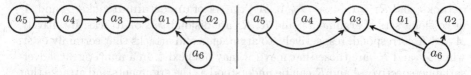

So in this example, if we ignore uncertainty, there is one preferred, grounded, complete and stable extension: $\{a_4, a_5, a_6\}$ (the reform is not the only way to avoid a reduction of the amount of pension; an increase in contributions is another way; the reform is too premature). Note that the existence of supports has a real impact on the acceptability of arguments. Consider for instance argument a_2 that is not directly attacked in the BAF. Since it deductively supports an argument that cannot be accepted, then a_2 cannot be accepted either. □

It is worth noticing that other semantics exist for deductive (resp. necessary) BAF, using some additional conditions for defining admissibility. One of them is the closure of the support defined as follows (see [13, 25]):[2] a set of arguments E is **closed for the deductive (resp. necessary) support relation** $\mathcal{S}$ iff $\nexists a \in \mathcal{A} \setminus E$ s.t. E "supports" (resp. "is supported by") a, with the following definitions: E supports (resp. is supported by) $a \Leftrightarrow \exists b \in E$ s. t. $(b, a) \in \mathcal{S}^+$ (resp. $(a, b) \in \mathcal{S}^+$). The σ-extensions for $\sigma \in \{\text{gr}, \text{co}, \text{pr}, \text{st}\}$ that are also closed for $\mathcal{S}$ are called the **c-σ-extensions** and the set of all these extensions is denoted by $\sigma_c^t(\mathcal{B})$, for $t \in \{\text{ded}, \text{nec}\}$. Nevertheless, it is easy to prove that c-σ-extensions

---

[2] These conditions have been first introduced in a very general approach by [13] then reused in the deductive case by [25]. Nevertheless, due to the duality between deductive and necessary supports, they can be trivially extended to the necessary case.

correspond exactly to σ-extensions (the next result is a rewriting of some of the principles described in [42]):

Proposition 1. *Let $\mathcal{B} = \langle \mathcal{A}, \mathcal{R}, \mathcal{S} \rangle$ be a BAF, $\mathsf{t} \in \{\mathsf{ded}, \mathsf{nec}\}$ be the interpretation of the support, and $\sigma \in \{\mathsf{co}, \mathsf{gr}, \mathsf{pr}, \mathsf{st}\}$ be a semantics. Then $\sigma_c^{\mathsf{t}}(\mathcal{B}) = \sigma^{\mathsf{t}}(\mathcal{B})$.*

Note that this result holds for the four studied semantics (complete, grounded, preferred and stable), but not for admissible sets. See for instance the very simple BAF: only 2 arguments a and b and the deductive support (a, b); in this case, the set $\{a\}$ is admissible (since the AF corresponding to the initial BAF contains only a and b without any attack) but not c-admissible (since b does not belong to $\{a\}$ whereas it is supported by a).

From a computational point of view, classical decision problems for BAFs under the necessary and deductive interpretations of support have the same complexity as their counterpart for standard AFs, since they can be solved by (polynomially) translating the BAF $\langle \mathcal{A}, \mathcal{R}, \mathcal{S} \rangle$ into the AF $\langle \mathcal{A}, \mathcal{R}^{\mathsf{t}} \rangle$ (see [17,22,29]).

Incomplete Argumentation Frameworks. They are AFs with qualitative uncertainty about the presence of some arguments or attacks [7,8,16,34]. Formally, an **Incomplete Argumentation Framework** (IAF) is a tuple $\mathcal{I} = \langle \mathcal{A}, \mathcal{A}^?, \mathcal{R}, \mathcal{R}^? \rangle$ where: $\mathcal{A} \subseteq \mathbf{A}$ is the set of **certain arguments**; $\mathcal{A}^? \subseteq \mathbf{A}$ is the set of **uncertain arguments**; $\mathcal{R} \subseteq (\mathcal{A} \cup \mathcal{A}^?) \times (\mathcal{A} \cup \mathcal{A}^?)$ the set of **certain attacks**; and $\mathcal{R}^? \subseteq (\mathcal{A} \cup \mathcal{A}^?) \times (\mathcal{A} \cup \mathcal{A}^?)$ the set of **uncertain attacks**. $\mathcal{A}$ and $\mathcal{A}^?$ are disjoint sets of arguments, and $\mathcal{R}$, $\mathcal{R}^?$ are disjoint sets of attacks. Intuitively, $\mathcal{A}$ and $\mathcal{R}$ correspond, respectively, to arguments and attacks that certainly exist, while $\mathcal{A}^?$ and $\mathcal{R}^?$ are those that may (or may not) exist. In a multi-agent, adversarial perspective, $\mathcal{A}$ and $\mathcal{R}$ can be understood as the arguments and attacks that an agent knows her opponent is aware of; while $\mathcal{A}^?$ and $\mathcal{R}^?$ are the arguments and attacks such that the agent does not know whether her opponent entertains. Note that a certain attack can exist between two uncertain arguments (these are usually called *conditionally certain* attacks); that means that, if the agent is *aware of these arguments*, then the attack is certain. Reasoning about IAFs is usually made through the notion of completion, i.e. a classical AF that represents a "possible world" w.r.t. the uncertain information encoded in the IAF. Formally, given $\mathcal{I} = \langle \mathcal{A}, \mathcal{A}^?, \mathcal{R}, \mathcal{R}^? \rangle$ an IAF, a **completion** of $\mathcal{I}$ is an AF $\langle \mathcal{A}_c, \mathcal{R}_c \rangle$ s.t. $\mathcal{A} \subseteq \mathcal{A}_c \subseteq \mathcal{A} \cup \mathcal{A}^?$ and $\mathcal{R} \cap (\mathcal{A}_c \times \mathcal{A}_c) \subseteq \mathcal{R}_c \subseteq (\mathcal{R} \cup \mathcal{R}^?) \cap (\mathcal{A}_c \times \mathcal{A}_c)$.

Reasoning tasks like credulous (or sceptical) acceptance or verification are defined over completions [7,8,34]. Hence, each classical task has two variants: the possible view (the property holds in some completion) and the necessary view[3] (the property holds in each completion). These reasoning tasks are, in most cases, computationally harder than their counterpart for standard AFs (under the usual assumption that the polynomial hierarchy does not collapse) [7,8]. This can be explained by the exponential number of completions. For instance,

---

[3] We are aware that we use the word "necessary" with two different meanings. We choose not to deviate from the standard terminology in the literature. However it will be clear from the context if we mean "necessary support" or "necessary in all the completions".

the acceptance problems for the grounded semantics are NP or coNP-complete in the case of IAFs whereas it is P-complete for AFs (see [7,34] for more details).

3 Incomplete Bipolar AFs

Incomplete Bipolar Argumentation Frameworks, which generalize both BAFs and IAFs were defined and studied independently by [25] and [31]. We recall their definition:

Definition 1 (Incomplete Bipolar AF - IBAF). *An* Incomplete Bipolar Argumentation Framework (IBAF) *is a tuple* $\mathcal{IB} = \langle \mathcal{A}, \mathcal{A}^?, \mathcal{R}, \mathcal{R}^?, \mathcal{S}, \mathcal{S}^? \rangle$, *where* $\mathcal{A}, \mathcal{A}^?$ *are disjoint sets of arguments and* $\mathcal{R}, \mathcal{R}^?, \mathcal{S}, \mathcal{S}^?$ *are disjoint relations between arguments. Elements of* $\mathcal{S}$ *(resp.* $\mathcal{S}^?$) *represent certain (resp. uncertain) supports.*[4]

Example 3. The following figure gives a possible representation of the debate described in Example 1, where supports are interpreted deductively, and where there is uncertainty of some elements (represented through dashed lines):

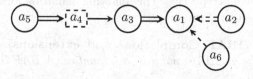

□

Before proposing different formal definitions for the notion of completions of an IBAF, let us informally present them together with their rationale. The key difference among these options is how they deal with certain supports that involve uncertain arguments, e.g., the deductive support from a_5 to a_4 in Example 3.

The simplest approach, concurrently proposed by [25] and [31], extends the notion of completion from IAFs by saying that each uncertain element can be present or not in each completion. We call this approach *plain* (or pla, for short) completions. In this case, the acceptance of a_5 implies the acceptance of a_4 *whenever* a_4 *is in the current completion*; this is what might be called a *conditionally certain support*. We believe that plain completions match well with a notion of completion that is independent of the interpretation of support.

A second possible approach, presented in [31] and that we call here *semantic completions*, is to consider that the meaning of support implies a semantic constraint that should be satisfied in any completion. In short, this constraint says that acceptance and support imply presence (in a completion). Following our running example, a completion in which a_5 would be accepted and not a_4 should be ruled out under this view. In more detail, and focusing on deductive supports, the principle we are after says: if a support is certain and its source is

---

[4] Note that this constraint could be relaxed by permitting $\mathcal{R}^?$ and $\mathcal{S}^?$ to have a (possibly) non-empty intersection. It will be the subject of future work.

accepted then its target must also be accepted, so it must be present in the completion even if it is uncertain.[5] Thus this second approach proposes to consider *unconditionally certain support (modulo argument acceptance)*, giving, therefore, some kind of "priority" to the notion of support over uncertainty whenever the source is accepted. We believe that this notion of completion captures the meaning of support together with its semantic impact.

A third approach, that has not been studied before, can be seen as a compromise between the previous two notions. The principle governing this approach simply states that if the source of a certain support belongs to a completion, then its target must also belong to this completion. The resulting notion is called *closed completions*. This approach also considers *unconditionally certain supports*, but it is simpler than the second one since the constraint is only syntactical. Moreover, it induces the same effect in terms of semantics: if the source of a certain support is accepted, then its target is also accepted whatever is the closed completion (since any extension is also closed for the support in a BAF). At the same time, it is also more specific and produces fewer completions (because the proposed principle is logically stronger). Thus this notion of completion is also dependent on the meaning of the support relation, but it follows a syntactical perspective. The following definition formally captures all the previous discussion:

Definition 2 (IBAF Completions and extensions). *Let $IB = \langle A, A^?, R, R^?, S, S^? \rangle$ be an IBAF and σ be a semantics. A BAF $B = \langle A_c, R_c, S_c \rangle$ is:*

1. *a pla-completion of IB (plain completion) iff $A \subseteq A_c \subseteq A \cup A^?$, $R \cap (A_c \times A_c) \subseteq R_c \subseteq (R \cup R^?) \cap (A_c \times A_c)$, $S \cap (A_c \times A_c) \subseteq S_c \subseteq (S \cup S^?) \cap (A_c \times A_c)$;*
2. *a t-completion of IB w.r.t. the semantics σ with $t \in \{nec, ded\}$ (semantic completion) iff B is a plain completion and $\forall (a, b) \in S, \forall E \in \sigma^t(B)$: (i) if $t = nec$ and $b \in E$, then $a \in E$ and (ii) if $t = ded$ and $a \in E$, then $b \in E$;*
3. *a t-completion of IB with $t \in \{cded, cnec\}$ (closed completion) iff B is a plain completion and $\forall (a, b) \in S$: (i) if $t = cnec$ and $b \in A_c$, then $a \in A_c$ and (ii) if $t = cded$ and $a \in A_c$, then $b \in A_c$.*

For $t \in \{pla, nec, ded, cded, cnec\}$, we denote as $\mathsf{completions}_\sigma^t(IB)$ the set of all t-completions of IB and the semantics σ; if σ is not used in the definition of this type of completion, the notation can be simplified as $\mathsf{completions}^t(IB)$ (see items 1 and 3 in Definition 2). The notation $\mathsf{completions}_\sigma^{ct}(IB)$ with $t \in \{ded, nec\}$ can also be used in place of $\mathsf{completions}_\sigma^t(IB)$ whenever $t \in \{cded, cnec\}$. We denote as $\sigma^{t_2}\text{-}t_1(IB)$ the set of all extensions of IB under the t_2 interpretation of the support ($t_2 \in \{nec, ded\}$), the semantics σ ($\sigma \in \{pr, gr, co, st\}$) and the t_1 type of the completions ($t_1 \in \{pla, nec, ded, cnec, cded\}$). So $\sigma^{t_2}\text{-}t_1(IB) = \{E \subseteq A \cup A^? | \exists B \in \mathsf{completions}_\sigma^{t_1}(IB)$ and $E \in \sigma^{t_2}(B)\}$. Some simplified notations can be used: $\sigma^t(IB)$ if $t = t_1 = t_2 \in \{ded, nec\}$; $\sigma^{ct}(IB)$ if $t = t_2$ and $t_1 = ct_2$. Each element of $\sigma^{t_2}\text{-}t_1(IB)$ is called a $\sigma^{t_2}\text{-}t_1$-extension.

---

[5] This principle can be straightforwardly adapted to necessary support by the mentioned duality.

In Definition 2, Item 1 represents the basic syntactical impact of uncertainty (an uncertain element is present or not in each completion), whereas the other items specify the impact of certain supports. Note that the last two items emphasize the closure of the *certain part* of the support relation assuming that *these certain supports must be kept* in the completions either through the semantics (Item 2), or by a syntactical constraint (Item 3).

It is worth remarking that pla-completions correspond exactly to the completions defined in [25]. Moreover, there exists a strong relationship between t-completions (and ct-completions) with $t \in \{nec, ded\}$ and the recently proposed *constrained IAFs* [27,32], and *IAFs with dependencies* [23,24]. In these works, a (set of) propositional formula(s) is added to an IAF in order to express constraints about the completions. These constraints could be used to filter among the completions of an IBAF for obtaining the set completions$^{ct}(\mathcal{IB})$. However, the constraints or dependencies in these related works only take into account syntactical information. So they are closer to ct-completions than to t-completions defined using semantics. Notice moreover that these related works only consider attack relations, so we would need to enrich their propositional language to take into account (uncertain) supports.

Example 4. Using Definition 2, the IBAF from Example 1 has 8 pla-completions (see Fig. 1). Moreover, with the pr semantics, only 4 ded-completions can be built: $\mathcal{B}_3$, $\mathcal{B}_4$, $\mathcal{B}_7$ and $\mathcal{B}_8$ that are also the only cded-completions whatever is the chosen semantics.

- for $\mathcal{B}_3$ (resp. $\mathcal{B}_7$), there is one preferred extension $\{a_1, a_2, a_4, a_5, a_6\}$; note that an additional attack from a_5 to a_3 is introduced for taking into account the deductive meaning of the support;
- for $\mathcal{B}_4$, there is one preferred extension $\{a_2, a_4, a_5, a_6\}$; note that two additional attacks are introduced: (a_5, a_3) and (a_6, a_3);
- for $\mathcal{B}_8$, there is one preferred extension $\{a_4, a_5, a_6\}$; note that 3 additional attacks exist: (a_5, a_3), (a_6, a_3) and (a_6, a_2).

For the other $\mathcal{B}_i$, a_5 belongs to the preferred extension whereas a_4 does not since a_4 is not in the completion, so they are not ded-completions.

So $pr^{ded}(\mathcal{IB}) = pr^{cded}(\mathcal{IB}) = \{\{a_1, a_2, a_4, a_5, a_6\}, \{a_2, a_4, a_5, a_6\}, \{a_4, a_5, a_6\}\}$, and pr^{ded}-pla$(\mathcal{IB}) = \{\{a_1, a_2, a_4, a_5, a_6\}, \{a_2, a_4, a_5, a_6\}, \{a_4, a_5, a_6\}, \{a_1, a_2, a_3, a_5, a_6\}, \{a_2, a_5, a_6\}, \{a_5, a_6\}\}$. □

Interestingly, the notion of "unconditional certainty" is useless when considering attacks. Indeed if an attack from a to b is certain whereas a or b are not, then only two kinds of completion exist: some completions contain a, b and the attack and so a and b cannot be accepted together; some others in which a or b are missing, so the attack too, and a and b cannot be accepted together; thus in each case, the meaning of the attack is captured by purely syntactical means.

Comparison of the Three Approaches. Two cases must be considered: a trivial case, where there is no uncertainty, and the general case:

Proposition 2. *Let $\mathcal{IB}$ be an IBAF, let t be an interpretation for supports (t $\in \{ded, nec\}$), and let $\sigma \in \{pr, gr, co, st\}$ be a semantics. We have that:*

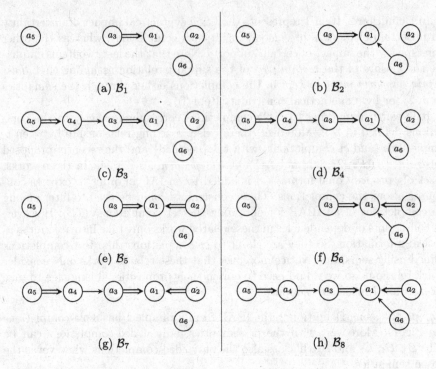

Fig. 1. The completions of $\mathcal{IB}$ from Example 1

- completions$^{\text{ct}}(\mathcal{IB}) \subseteq$ completions$^{\text{t}}_\sigma(\mathcal{IB}) \subseteq$ completions$^{\text{pla}}(\mathcal{IB})$. *The reverse does not hold in general.*
- $\sigma^{\text{ct}}(\mathcal{IB}) \subseteq \sigma^{\text{t}}(\mathcal{IB}) \subseteq \sigma^{\text{t}}$-pla$(\mathcal{IB})$. *The reverse does not hold in general.*
- *if* $\mathcal{A}^? = \mathcal{R}^? = \mathcal{S}^? = \varnothing$, *then* σ^{t}-pla$(\mathcal{IB}) = \sigma^{\text{t}}(\mathcal{IB}) = \sigma^{\text{ct}}(\mathcal{IB}) = \sigma(\langle \mathcal{A}, \mathcal{R}^{\text{t}} \rangle)$.

$\mathcal{B}_1$ in Example 4 is an example of a pla-completion that is not a ded-completion (whatever is the chosen semantics). An example of a ded-completion for a given semantics that is not a cded-completion can be obtained as follows: let consider a certain support (a, b) and a completion $\mathcal{B}$ such that (i) $a \in \mathcal{B}$, $b \notin \mathcal{B}$ and (ii) a is never accepted in $\mathcal{B}$ for this semantics.

Comparison with the Approach of [25]. First of all, let us recall that the interpretation of supports considered in [25] is only the deductive one. Moreover, Fazzinga et al. propose to transform the initial BAF into two types of AF: either a so-called **d-IBAF** obtained by the addition of three kinds of attacks (corresponding exactly to our cases 0 to 2, see Sect. 2), or a so-called **s-IBAF** obtained by the addition of only two kinds of attacks (corresponding to our cases 0 and 2). Then, they used three types of semantics, each kind being related to a specific notion of coherence: conflict-freeness (d-semantics), safety (s-semantics), and support-closedness (c-semantics). Thus they define 6 different sets of extensions, called i-extensions (one at each crossing point between the type of AF and the chosen semantics). So a comparison between our work and the work done in [25] makes sense only if we consider the same interpretation of the support relation: the deductive one with the same three additional attacks (our cases 0 to 2). It is interesting to note that, in this interpretation, conflict-freeness and safety are equivalent and thus d-semantics and s-semantics collapse. The following proposition gives the main points of this comparison, showing that both approaches collapse in the basic case (plain completions) but that our approach can also be more selective (semantic or closed completions):

Proposition 3. *Let $\mathcal{IB}$ be an IBAF with a deductive interpretation for the support. Let $\sigma \in \{\mathsf{pr},\mathsf{gr},\mathsf{co},\mathsf{st}\}$ be a semantics. Let $I_\sigma^c(\mathcal{IB})$ (resp. $I_\sigma^d(\mathcal{IB})$) be the set of i-extensions under the c-σ (resp. d-σ) semantics for $\mathcal{IB}$ as defined in [25].*

- σ^{t}-$\mathsf{pla}(\mathcal{IB}) = I_\sigma^d(\mathcal{IB}) = I_\sigma^c(\mathcal{IB})$.
- $\sigma^{\mathsf{cded}}(\mathcal{IB}) \subseteq \sigma^{\mathsf{ded}}(\mathcal{IB}) \subseteq I_\sigma^c(\mathcal{IB})$. *The reverse does not hold in general.*

Proposition 3 shows a link with the approach defined in [25] when the deductive interpretation is used for the support relation. Nevertheless, our approach is, at the same time, more general since it also proposes a direct definition for taking into account the "necessary" interpretation and more specific since it emphasizes the role of certain supports.

4   Complexity of Reasoning with IBAFs

Let us investigate the complexity of reasoning with IBAFs. We focus on acceptability problems, i.e. possible credulous acceptability (PCA), necessary credulous acceptability (NCA) and their counterparts for sceptical acceptability (PSA and NSA). Formally, given an IBAF $\mathcal{IB} = \langle \mathcal{A}, \mathcal{A}^?, \mathcal{R}, \mathcal{R}^?, \mathcal{S}, \mathcal{S}^? \rangle$ and $a \in \mathcal{A}$, and given $t_1 \in \{\mathsf{pla},\mathsf{nec},\mathsf{ded},\mathsf{cnec},\mathsf{cded}\}$ and $t_2 \in \{\mathsf{nec},\mathsf{ded}\}$ s.t. if $t_1 \in \{\mathsf{nec},\mathsf{ded}\}$, then $t_1 = t_2$ and if $t_1 \in \{\mathsf{cnec},\mathsf{cded}\}$, then $t_1 = ct_2$,

- σ^{t_2}-t_1-PCA: $\exists \mathcal{B} \in \mathsf{completions}_\sigma^{t_1}(\mathcal{IB})$, $\exists E \in \sigma^{t_2}(\mathcal{B})$ s.t. $a \in E$?
- σ^{t_2}-t_1-NCA: $\forall \mathcal{B} \in \mathsf{completions}_\sigma^{t_1}(\mathcal{IB})$, $\exists E \in \sigma^{t_2}(\mathcal{B})$ s.t. $a \in E$?
- σ^{t_2}-t_1-PSA: $\exists \mathcal{B} \in \mathsf{completions}_\sigma^{t_1}(\mathcal{IB})$, $\forall E \in \sigma^{t_2}(\mathcal{B})$ s.t. $a \in E$?
- σ^{t_2}-t_1-NSA: $\forall \mathcal{B} \in \mathsf{completions}_\sigma^{t_1}(\mathcal{IB})$, $\forall E \in \sigma^{t_2}(\mathcal{B})$ s.t. $a \in E$?

Reasoning with Plain Completions. For the case of $t_1 = \mathsf{pla}$, the results were recently given for $\sigma \in \{\mathsf{ad},\mathsf{st},\mathsf{gr},\mathsf{co},\mathsf{pr}\}$ by [25,31], which both independently show that (for any $t_2 \in \{\mathsf{ded},\mathsf{nec}\}$) PCA is NP-complete for all these semantics; NCA is coNP-complete for gr and Π_2^{P}-complete for the other semantics; PSA is NP-complete for $\sigma \in \{\mathsf{co},\mathsf{gr}\}$, Σ_2^{P}-complete for the stable semantics and Σ_3^{P}-complete for the preferred semantics; and finally NSA is coNP-complete for $\sigma \in \{\mathsf{st},\mathsf{gr},\mathsf{co}\}$ and Π_2^{P}-complete for pr.[6] Thus this case is not harder than the case of (non-bipolar) IAFs.

---

[6] As usual, sceptical reasoning is trivial with $\sigma = \mathsf{ad}$ since the empty set is always an admissible set.

Reasoning with Semantic Completions. Now we focus on semantic completions (conditions 1 and 2 in Definition 2), based on $t_1 \in \{\text{nec}, \text{ded}\}$. We start with showing that the problem "is a given BAF a t_1-completion of a given IBAF w.r.t. a given semantics?" is a hard problem (while it is polynomial for the pla case), except for the grounded semantics.

Proposition 4. Let $\mathcal{IB} = \langle \mathcal{A}, \mathcal{A}^?, \mathcal{R}, \mathcal{R}^?, \mathcal{S}, \mathcal{S}^? \rangle$ be an IBAF, and $\mathcal{B}^* = \langle \mathcal{A}^*, \mathcal{R}^*, \mathcal{S}^* \rangle$. Checking whether $\mathcal{B}^* \in \text{completions}_\sigma^t(\mathcal{IB})$ (for $t \in \{\text{nec}, \text{ded}\}$) is in P for $\sigma = \text{gr}$, coNP-complete for $\sigma \in \{\text{ad}, \text{co}, \text{st}\}$ and Π_2^P-complete for $\sigma = \text{pr}$.

Now, we study the complexity of acceptability problems, providing lower bounds and upper founds for all the problems and semantics considered.

Proposition 5. For $t \in \{\text{nec}, \text{ded}\}$ the following complexity results hold:

- For $\sigma \in \{\text{ad}, \text{st}, \text{co}, \text{pr}\}$, σ^t-t-PCA is NP-hard and in Σ_2^P, and NP-complete for $\sigma = \text{gr}$.
- For $\sigma \in \{\text{st}, \text{co}\}$, σ^t-t-NSA is coNP-hard and in Π_2^P, it is trivial for $\sigma = \text{ad}$, it is coNP-complete for $\sigma = \text{gr}$, and it is Π_2^P-hard and in Π_3^P for $\sigma = \text{pr}$.
- For $\sigma \in \{\text{ad}, \text{st}, \text{co}\}$, σ^t-t-NCA is Π_2^P-complete, it is coNP-complete for $\sigma = \text{gr}$, and it is Π_3^P-hard and in Π_3^P for $\sigma = \text{pr}$.
- For $\sigma = \text{gr}$, σ^t-t-PSA is NP-complete, it is trivial for $\sigma = \text{ad}$, NP-hard and in Σ_2^P for $\sigma = \text{co}$, it is Σ_2^P-complete for $\sigma = \text{st}$, and Σ_3^P-complete for $\sigma = \text{pr}$.

Reasoning with Closed Completions. Now we consider closed completions (i.e. $t_1 \in \{\text{cded}, \text{cnec}\}$, see conditions 1 and 3 in Definition 2), with the adequate support relation (i.e. $t_2 \in \{\text{nec}, \text{ded}\}$, and moreover $t_2 = \text{nec}$ if $t_1 = \text{cnec}$, and $t_2 = \text{ded}$ if $t_1 = \text{cded}$. As for pla-completions, we show that checking the (various kinds of) acceptability of arguments is in this case not harder than in the case of (non-bipolar) IAFs. This comes from the following observation:

Observation 1. Let $\mathcal{IB} = \langle \mathcal{A}, \mathcal{A}^?, \mathcal{R}, \mathcal{R}^?, \mathcal{S}, \mathcal{S}^? \rangle$ be an IBAF, and $\mathcal{B}^* = \langle \mathcal{A}^*, \mathcal{R}^*, \mathcal{S}^* \rangle$. Checking whether $\mathcal{B}^* \in \text{completions}^{ct}(\mathcal{IB})$ (for $t \in \{\text{ded}, \text{nec}\}$) can be done in polynomial time (w.r.t. the number of arguments $|\mathcal{A} \cup \mathcal{A}^?|$).

Proposition 6. For $t \in \{\text{nec}, \text{ded}\}$ the following complexity results hold:

- For $\sigma \in \{\text{ad}, \text{gr}, \text{st}, \text{co}, \text{pr}\}$, σ^t-ct-PCA is NP-complete.
- For $\sigma \in \{\text{gr}, \text{st}, \text{co}\}$, σ^t-ct-NSA is coNP-complete, it is trivial for $\sigma = \text{ad}$, and it is Π_2^P-complete for $\sigma = \text{pr}$.
- For $\sigma \in \{\text{ad}, \text{st}, \text{co}, \text{pr}\}$, σ^t-ct-NCA is Π_2^P-complete, and it is coNP-complete for $\sigma = \text{gr}$.
- For $\sigma \in \{\text{co}, \text{gr}\}$, σ^t-ct-PSA is NP-complete, it is trivial for $\sigma = \text{ad}$, it is Σ_2^P-complete for $\sigma = \text{st}$, and Σ_3^P-complete for $\sigma = \text{pr}$.

5   Logical Encoding of IBAFs

We will now encode acceptability problems for IBAFs in DL-PA. For space reasons, we only list here the main definitions and results. For more details, the reader is referred to previous papers on abstract models of argumentation and DL-PA [18–20, 27, 31, 43].

Syntax of DL-PA. We assume the existence of a denumerable set of propositional variables $\text{Prp} = \{p_1, p_2, \ldots\}$. We suppose that Prp contains several kinds of distinguished variables capturing the statuses of arguments and relations between them. First, given a set of arguments $\mathcal{A} \subseteq \mathbf{A}$ we define its set of **awareness variables**, $\text{AW}_{\mathcal{A}} = \{\text{aw}_x \mid x \in \mathcal{A}\}$ (these will be used to talk about the presence of arguments in completions), and its set of **acceptance variables** $\text{IN}_{\mathcal{A}} = \{\text{in}_x \mid x \in \mathcal{A}\}$. Second, given a relation $X \subseteq \mathbf{A} \times \mathbf{A}$ we define its set of **attack variables** $\text{ATT}_X = \{\text{r}_{x,y} \mid (x,y) \in X\}$ and its set of **support variables** $\text{SUP}_X = \{\text{s}_{x,y} \mid (x,y) \in X\}$. Summing up, we assume that $\text{Prp}_{\mathbf{A}} \subseteq \text{Prp}$ where $\text{Prp}_{\mathbf{A}} = \text{AW}_{\mathbf{A}} \cup \text{IN}_{\mathbf{A}} \cup \text{ATT}_{\mathbf{A} \times \mathbf{A}} \cup \text{SUP}_{\mathbf{A} \times \mathbf{A}}$. Note that the inclusion $\text{Prp} \subseteq \text{Prp}_{\mathbf{A}}$ is not assumed. The reason for this is that we will use fresh copies of variables in $\text{Prp}_{\mathbf{A}}$ at some points of the encoding process and hence we need Prp to be larger than $\text{Prp}_{\mathbf{A}}$. Formulas and programs of DL-PA are defined by mutual recursion:

> For formulas: $\varphi ::= p \mid \neg\varphi \mid (\varphi \wedge \varphi) \mid [\pi]\varphi \qquad (p \in \text{Prp})$
> For programs: $\pi ::= +p \mid -p \mid \varphi? \mid (\pi;\pi) \mid (\pi \cup \pi) \mid \pi^* \qquad (p \in \text{Prp})$

The intended meaning of formulas is as usual for atoms and the Boolean connectors. As for modal formulas, $[\pi]\varphi$ reads "φ is true after every possible execution of π", so that the dual $\langle\pi\rangle\varphi$, defined as $\neg[\pi]\neg\varphi$, reads "there is a possible execution of π that makes φ true". As for programs, their intended meaning is as follows: $+p$ (resp. $-p$) is the atomic program that makes p true (resp. false). $\varphi?$ is the program that tests whether φ is true. $(\pi;\pi')$ is the sequential composition of π and π' ("first execute π and then π'"). $(\pi \cup \pi')$ is the non-deterministic choice ("choose non-deterministically between π or π' and execute one of them"). Finally, π^* is the unbounded iteration of π ("execute π a finite number of times").

Semantics of DL-PA. Given a propositional valuation $v \subseteq \text{Prp}$ (so v is the set of the variables that are true), **truth for formulas** φ and the **meaning of programs** $||\pi||$ is given by mutual recursion:

> $v \models p$ if $p \in v$
> $v \models [\pi]\varphi$ if $(v, v') \in ||\pi||$ implies $v' \models \varphi$

and as usual for the Boolean connectives; moreover, considering that, given a binary relation R, R^* denotes the reflexive and transitive closure of R, the interpretation of programs is:

$$||+p|| = \{(v, v') \mid v' = v \cup \{p\}\} \qquad ||-p|| = \{(v, v') \mid v' = v \setminus \{p\}\}$$
$$||\varphi?|| = \{(v, v) \mid v \models \varphi\} \qquad ||\pi; \pi'|| = ||\pi|| \circ ||\pi'||$$
$$||\pi \cup \pi'|| = ||\pi|| \cup ||\pi'|| \qquad ||\pi^*|| = ||\pi||^*$$

Here are some useful abbreviations in our object language (where $\mathsf{P} = \{p_1, ..., p_n\}$ is a finite subset of Prp):

$$\mathsf{mkTrueSome(P)} = \overset{\bullet}{;}_{p\in\mathsf{P}}(+p \cup \mathsf{skip}) = (+p_1 \cup \mathsf{skip}); \ldots; (+p_n \cup \mathsf{skip})$$
$$\mathsf{mkFalseAll(P)} = \overset{\bullet}{;}_{p\in\mathsf{P}}(-p) = -p_1; \ldots; -p_n$$
$$\mathsf{vary(P)} = \overset{\bullet}{;}_{p\in\mathsf{P}}(+p \cup -p) = (+p_1 \cup -p_1); \ldots; (+p_n \cup -p_n)$$
$$\text{if } \varphi \text{ then } \pi \text{ else } \pi' = (\varphi?; \pi) \cup (\neg\varphi?; \pi')$$
$$\text{while } \varphi \text{ do } \pi = (\varphi?; \pi)^*; \neg\varphi?$$

From Valuations to (B)AFs and Backward. From our hypothesis that Prp contains $\mathsf{Prp_A}$, we can define for each valuation v the BAF $\mathcal{B}_v = \langle \mathcal{A}_v, \mathcal{R}_v, \mathcal{S}_v \rangle$ (called the **BAF represented by** v) where: $\mathcal{A}_v = \{x \in \mathbf{A} \mid \mathsf{aw}_x \in v\}$, $\mathcal{R}_v = \{(x, y) \in \mathcal{A}_v \times \mathcal{A}_v \mid \mathsf{r}_{x,y} \in v\}$, and $\mathcal{S}_v = \{(x, y) \in \mathcal{A}_v \times \mathcal{A}_v \mid \mathsf{s}_{x,y} \in v\}$. Note that the definition of $\mathcal{R}_v$ and $\mathcal{S}_v$ guarantees that $\mathcal{B}_v$ is always a well-defined BAF (even if $\mathsf{r}_{x,y} \in v$ but $\mathsf{aw}_x \notin v$ or $\mathsf{aw}_y \notin v$, or the analogous case for supports). The other way round, each BAF $\langle \mathcal{A}, \mathcal{R}, \mathcal{S} \rangle$ is represented by **its associated valuation** $v_{\langle \mathcal{A}, \mathcal{R}, \mathcal{S} \rangle} = \{\mathsf{aw}_x \mid x \in \mathcal{A}\} \cup \{\mathsf{r}_{x,y} \mid (x, y) \in \mathcal{R}\} \cup \{\mathsf{s}_{x,y} \mid (x, y) \in \mathcal{S}\}$. Note that both functions (from valuations to BAFs and backward) can be also defined for AFs, by just ignoring the supports. Finally, for each valuation v we define the **extension associated to** v as the set $\mathsf{E}_v = \{x \in \mathbf{A} \mid \mathsf{in}_x \in v\}$.

Argumentation Semantics in DL-PA. We rely on previous encoding of argumentation semantics in DL-PA (see [43, Theorem 1] for a comprehensive result). The main idea underlying these encodings is to write a generic DL-PA program mkExt^σ parametrised by each semantics σ, s.t. for every AF $\langle \mathcal{A}, \mathcal{R} \rangle$ we have that: $\sigma(\langle \mathcal{A}, \mathcal{R} \rangle) = \{\mathsf{E}_{v'} \mid (v_{\langle \mathcal{A}, \mathcal{R} \rangle}, v') \in ||\mathsf{mkExt}^\sigma||\}$. Due to space reasons, we only include here the instance of mkExt for capturing stable semantics as an illustration:

$$\mathsf{Well} = \bigwedge_{x \in \mathbf{A}}(\mathsf{in}_x \to \mathsf{aw}_x)$$
$$\mathsf{Stable} = \mathsf{Well} \wedge \bigwedge_{x \in \mathbf{A}}\left(\mathsf{aw}_x \to \left(\mathsf{in}_x \leftrightarrow \neg\bigvee_{y \in \mathbf{A}}(\mathsf{in}_y \wedge \mathsf{r}_{y,x})\right)\right)$$
$$\mathsf{mkExt}^{\mathsf{st}} = \mathsf{vary(IN_A)}; \mathsf{Stable}$$

Deductive and Necessary Supports in DL-PA. [31] was the first work capturing ded/nec supports in DL-PA. We sketch here the main ideas, taking deductive supports as the primitive notion and defining necessary ones by duality (the opposite strategy to the one followed in [31]). The first thing is to capture the transitive closure of the support relation associated with a valuation. This program computes one step of such closure:

$$\mathsf{step} = \overset{\bullet}{;}_{x,y,z\in\mathbf{A}}\left((\mathsf{aw}_x \wedge \mathsf{aw}_y \wedge \mathsf{aw}_z \wedge \mathsf{s}_{x,y} \wedge \mathsf{s}_{y,z})?; +\mathsf{s}_{x,z}\right)$$

Moreover, the following formula is true in those valuations where $\mathcal{S}_v$ is transitive:

$$\text{Transitive} = \bigwedge\nolimits_{x,y,z\in\mathbf{A}}\Big((\mathsf{aw}_x \wedge \mathsf{aw}_y \wedge \mathsf{aw}_z \wedge \mathsf{s}_{x,y} \wedge \mathsf{s}_{y,z}) \to \mathsf{s}_{x,z}\Big)$$

Hence, the following program computes the transitive closure of $\mathcal{S}_v$:

$$\text{transClosure} = \text{while } \neg\text{Transitive do step}$$

Now, we can capture complex attacks (see their description in Sect. 2):

$$\begin{aligned}
\mathsf{r}^{\mathsf{aw}}_{x,y} &= \mathsf{aw}_x \wedge \mathsf{aw}_y \wedge \mathsf{r}_{x,y} \quad \text{(direct attack)}\\
\mathsf{r}^{\mathsf{case1}}_{x,y} &= \mathsf{aw}_x \wedge \mathsf{aw}_y \wedge \bigvee\nolimits_{z\in\mathbf{A}}(\mathsf{aw}_z \wedge \mathsf{r}_{x,z} \wedge [\text{transClosure}]\mathsf{s}_{y,z})\\
\mathsf{r}^{\mathsf{case2}}_{x,y} &= \mathsf{aw}_x \wedge \mathsf{aw}_y \wedge \bigvee\nolimits_{z\in\mathbf{A}}\Big(\mathsf{aw}_z \wedge \mathsf{r}_{z,y} \wedge [\text{transClosure}]\mathsf{s}_{x,z}\Big)
\end{aligned}$$

And define a DL-PA program that adds these attacks to $\mathcal{B}_v$:

$$\begin{aligned}
\text{addAttacks}^{\mathsf{ded}} =\ & \mathbin{;}_{x,y\in\mathbf{A}}(\text{if } (\mathsf{r}^{\mathsf{aw}}_{x,y} \vee \mathsf{r}^{\mathsf{case1}}_{x,y} \vee \mathsf{r}^{\mathsf{case2}}_{x,y}) \text{ then } +\mathsf{r}'_{x,y}; \text{else skip});\\
& \text{mkFalseAll}(\text{ATT}_{\mathbf{A}\times\mathbf{A}});\\
& \mathbin{;}_{x,y\in\mathbf{A}}(\text{if } \mathsf{r}'_{x,y} \text{ then}+\mathsf{r}_{x,y} \text{ else skip}))
\end{aligned}$$

Note that this program makes use of a set of fresh copies of attack variables $\text{ATT}'_{\mathbf{A}\times\mathbf{A}} = \{\mathsf{r}'_{x,y} \mid (x,y)\in\mathbf{A}\times\mathbf{A}\}$. By duality (Sect. 2), we can easily go from one interpretation to the other using the following DL-PA program:

$$\begin{aligned}
\text{necessary2deductive} =\ & \mathbin{;}_{x,y\in\mathbf{A}}(\text{if } \mathsf{s}_{y,x} \text{ then } +\mathsf{s}'_{x,y}; \text{else skip});\\
& \text{mkFalseAll}(\text{SUP}_{\mathbf{A}\times\mathbf{A}});\\
& \mathbin{;}_{x,y\in\mathbf{A}}(\text{if } \mathsf{s}'_{x,y} \text{ then}+\mathsf{s}_{x,y}; \text{else skip})
\end{aligned}$$

Hence, we can abbreviate $\text{addAttacks}^{\mathsf{nec}} = \text{necessary2deductive}; \text{addAttacks}^{\mathsf{ded}}$.

Proposition 7. *Let $\mathcal{B} = \langle\mathcal{A},\mathcal{R},\mathcal{S}\rangle$ be a BAF, let $\mathsf{t}\in\{\mathsf{nec},\mathsf{ded}\}$, and let σ be an argumentation semantics, we have that*

$$\sigma^{\mathsf{t}}(\mathcal{B}) = \{\mathsf{E}_{v'} \mid (v_\mathcal{B},v')\in\|\text{addAttacks}^{\mathsf{t}}; \text{mkExt}^\sigma\|\}.$$

Computing Completions of IBAFs in DL-PA. All the notions of completion discussed in Sect. 3 can be computed by DL-PA programs. First, let us define the **valuation associated to** $\mathcal{IB} = \langle\mathcal{A},\mathcal{A}^?,\mathcal{R},\mathcal{R}^?,\mathcal{S},\mathcal{S}^?\rangle$ as $v_{\mathcal{IB}} = v_{\langle\mathcal{A},\mathcal{R},\mathcal{S}\rangle}$. Plain completions of $\mathcal{IB}$ are computed by:

$$\begin{aligned}
\text{mkComp}^{\mathsf{pla}}(\mathcal{IB}) =\ & \text{mkTrueSome}(\text{AW}_{\mathcal{A}?});\\
& \text{mkTrueSome}(\text{ATT}_{\mathcal{R}?}); \text{mkTrueSome}(\text{ATT}_{\mathcal{S}?})
\end{aligned}$$

For semantic and closed completions, it is necessary to check whether the corresponding additional constraint is satisfied after each execution of $\text{mkComp}^{\mathsf{pla}}(\mathcal{IB})$. We use yet another set of fresh copies $\text{SUP}''_{\mathbf{A}\times\mathbf{A}} = \{\mathsf{s}''_{x,y} \mid (x,y)\in\mathbf{A}\times\mathbf{A}\}$, and define the program:

$$\text{copy}''(\text{SUP}_{\mathbf{A}\times\mathbf{A}}) = \mathbin{;}_{x,y\in\mathbf{A}}(\text{if } \mathsf{s}_{x,y} \text{ then } +\mathsf{s}''_{x,y}; \text{else skip})$$

Now, the constraints corresponding to each kind of completion are:

$$\begin{aligned}
\mathsf{Constraint}^{\mathsf{nec}} &= \bigwedge_{x,y\in\mathbf{A}}((\mathsf{in}_x \wedge \mathsf{s}''_{y,x}) \to \mathsf{in}_y) \\
\mathsf{Constraint}^{\mathsf{ded}} &= \bigwedge_{x,y\in\mathbf{A}}((\mathsf{in}_x \wedge \mathsf{s}''_{x,y}) \to \mathsf{in}_y) \\
\mathsf{Constraint}^{\mathsf{cnec}} &= \bigwedge_{x,y\in\mathbf{A}}((\mathsf{aw}_x \wedge \mathsf{s}''_{y,x}) \to \mathsf{aw}_y) \\
\mathsf{Constraint}^{\mathsf{cded}} &= \bigwedge_{x,y\in\mathbf{A}}((\mathsf{aw}_x \wedge \mathsf{s}''_{x,y}) \to \mathsf{aw}_y)
\end{aligned}$$

For $t \in \{\mathsf{ded}, \mathsf{nec}\}$, we define:

$$\begin{aligned}
\mathsf{mkComp}^t_\sigma(\mathcal{IB}) = \ &\mathsf{copy}''(\mathsf{SUP}_{\mathbf{A}\times\mathbf{A}}); \mathsf{mkComp}^{\mathsf{pla}}(\mathcal{IB}); \\
&([\mathsf{addAttacks}^t; \mathsf{mkExt}^\sigma]\mathsf{Constraint}^t)?
\end{aligned}$$

and for $t \in \{\mathsf{cnec}, \mathsf{cded}\}$, we define:

$$\mathsf{mkComp}^t_\sigma(\mathcal{IB}) = \mathsf{copy}''(\mathsf{SUP}_{\mathbf{A}\times\mathbf{A}}); \mathsf{mkComp}^{\mathsf{pla}}(\mathcal{IB}); \mathsf{Constraint}^t?$$

Proposition 8. *Let* $\mathcal{IB} = \langle \mathcal{A}, \mathcal{A}^?, \mathcal{R}, \mathcal{R}^?, \mathcal{S}, \mathcal{S}^? \rangle$, $t \in \{\mathsf{pla}, \mathsf{nec}, \mathsf{ded}, \mathsf{cnec}, \mathsf{cded}\}$, *and let* σ *be a semantics. Then:*

- *If* $\langle v_{\mathcal{IB}}, v \rangle \in \|\mathsf{mkComp}^t_\sigma(\mathcal{IB})\|$, *then* $\langle \mathcal{A}_v, \mathcal{R}_v, \mathcal{S}_v \rangle \in \mathsf{completions}^t_\sigma(\mathcal{IB})$.
- *If* $\langle \mathcal{A}_c, \mathcal{R}_c, \mathcal{S}_c \rangle \in \mathsf{completions}^t_\sigma(\mathcal{IB})$, *then there is a* $v \subseteq \mathsf{Prp}$ *s.t.* $v \cap \mathsf{Prp}_{\mathbf{A}} = v_{\langle \mathcal{A}_c, \mathcal{R}_c, \mathcal{S}_c \rangle}$ *and* $\langle v_{\mathcal{IB}}, v \rangle \in \|\mathsf{mkComp}^t_\sigma(\mathcal{IB})\|$.

Argument Acceptance for IBAFs in DL-PA. Our final proposition is:

Proposition 9. *Let* $\mathcal{IB} = \langle \mathcal{A}, \mathcal{A}^?, \mathcal{R}, \mathcal{R}^?, \mathcal{S}, \mathcal{S}^? \rangle$, *let* $a \in \mathcal{A}$, *let* $\sigma \in \{\mathsf{co}, \mathsf{pr}, \mathsf{gr}, \mathsf{st}\}$, *let* $t_1 \in \{\mathsf{pla}, \mathsf{nec}, \mathsf{ded}, \mathsf{cnec}, \mathsf{cded}\}$ *and* $t_2 \in \{\mathsf{nec}, \mathsf{ded}\}$ *s.t. if* $t_1 \in \{\mathsf{nec}, \mathsf{ded}\}$, *then* $t_1 = t_2$; *and if* $t_1 \in \{\mathsf{cnec}, \mathsf{cded}\}$, *then* $t_1 = \mathsf{c}t_2$. *Then:*

- *The answer to* σ^{t_2}-t_1-*PCA with input* $\mathcal{IB}$ *and* a *is YES iff* $v_{\mathcal{IB}} \models \langle \mathsf{mkComp}^{t_1}_\sigma(\mathcal{IB}); \mathsf{addAttacks}^{t_2}; \mathsf{mkExt}^\sigma \rangle \mathsf{in}_a$.
- *The answer to* σ^{t_2}-t_1-*NCA with input* $\mathcal{IB}$ *and* a *is YES iff* $v_{\mathcal{IB}} \models [\mathsf{mkComp}^{t_1}_\sigma(\mathcal{IB})]\langle \mathsf{addAttacks}^{t_2}; \mathsf{mkExt}^\sigma \rangle \mathsf{in}_a$.
- *The answer to* σ^{t_2}-t_1-*PSA with input* $\mathcal{IB}$ *and* a *is YES iff* $v_{\mathcal{IB}} \models \langle \mathsf{mkComp}^{t_1}_\sigma(\mathcal{IB}) \rangle [\mathsf{addAttacks}^{t_2}; \mathsf{mkExt}^\sigma] \mathsf{in}_a$.
- *The answer to* σ^{t_2}-t_1-*NSA with input* $\mathcal{IB}$ *and* a *is YES iff* $v_{\mathcal{IB}} \models [\mathsf{mkComp}^{t_1}_\sigma(\mathcal{IB}); \mathsf{addAttacks}^{t_2}; \mathsf{mkExt}^\sigma] \mathsf{in}_a$.

Usefulness of the Encoding. Our translation of IBAFs to DL-PA follows a tradition of capturing abstract argumentation in this lightweight version of dynamic logic [18–20, 27, 43]. As such, the reasons given throughout this branch of the literature to justify the usefulness of this technique are naturally inherited by our approach. We here recall some of them and add a few more.

When compared to propositional encodings of argumentation formalisms (e.g., [9]), DL-PA permits representing notions that require maximality and minimality checkings (e.g., preferred and grounded semantics) more succinctly. While propositional formulas capturing these semantics are exponentially long (w.r.t. the size of the background set of arguments **A**), their DL-PA analogous are polynomially long (c.f. [19,43]).

When compared to encodings in equally succinct languages (e.g., Quantified Boolean Formulas QBFs), we are aware that not everything is advantageous. The main shortcoming of our encoding against those based on QBFs is the absence (up to date) of an efficient DL-PA solver, which prevents our approach from being empirically tested. However, this is by no means an essential limitation. Rather, it can be taken as an additional motivational reason to develop the missing tools because using DL-PA as a language for abstract argumentation formalisms has several strong advantages. First of all, it makes things simpler: it is enough to compare the rather complex encodings of IAFs in QBFs [7], to our simple DL-PA programs and formulas for IAFs. We think that this is in part due to the presence of imperative programming constructs in the DL-PA object language, which allows for assigning an intuitively clear meaning to programs that are later employed in the construction of more complex ones. That leads to the second advantage of our encoding approach: its modularity. Since we already had DL-PA programs for computing AFs extensions and IAFs completions, it was enough to plug them into programs capturing bipolarity (where "plugging-in" amounted most of the time to the use of the sequential composition operator ';'). As a third advantage, the dynamic nature of DL-PA makes it a more suitable logical tool for the study of dynamic extensions of IBAFs (e.g., IBAFs where new arguments, supports or attacks are added). Last but not least, although polynomial encodings of IBAFs in QBFs must exist (because QBFs and DL-PA are equally expressive and succinct [2]), they are still not known.

6   Conclusion

This paper was devoted to moving forward in the study of IBAFs: enriched frameworks for abstract argumentation taking into account two kinds of interaction between arguments (attacks and necessary or deductive supports) and considering at the same time that the elements (arguments or interactions) of this framework can be uncertain. Reasoning about IBAFs is done through the notion of completion: any uncertain element can be considered present or absent and so several "variants" of the IBAF may be built, each variant is called *completion* and corresponds to a classical BAF without uncertainty. Then, the semantics of IBAFs are defined by the application of the corresponding semantics on these completions. The focus of the paper has been the discussion and comparison of three different notions of completions. The first one, already studied in [25,31] and called *plain completions*, corresponds to the notion of *conditionally certain support* whereas the other ones introduce the notion of *unconditionally certain support* using either semantic constraint (an idea already presented in [31], that we call here *semantic completions*) or syntactical ones (*closed completions*, firstly studied here). Tight complexity results are given for plain and closed completions, while lower and upper bounds are provided for semantic ones. Finally, arguments acceptability problems with respect to IBAFs using any of the three variants of completions are shown to be reducible to DL-PA model checking.

In terms of future work, several directions can be explored. First, we could complete this study for IBAFs taking into account some other enriched abstract frameworks (for instance those with evidential support relations, or with higher-order interactions, or with collective ones). A second line of future work could be the study of instantiations of IBAFs into *structured* frameworks (see for instance [38,44] for recent instantiation of IAFs). A third interesting point could be to implement the computation of semantics of all these incomplete frameworks via the development of a DL-PA solver and to make some experiments for evaluating our encoding and comparing with other approaches (perhaps with a more direct computation of semantics without using logics). Finally, a fourth line of future research consists in focusing on the uncertainty aspect of IBAFs by, e.g., considering a recursive form of uncertainty [40], or proposing a direct approach (i.e. without using completions) to define extension-based semantics in the style of [33].

Acknowledgments. We want to acknowledge our colleague Sylvie Doutre for the very rich exchanges about the topic of this paper.

References

1. Amgoud, L., Cayrol, C.: A reasoning model based on the production of acceptable arguments. Ann. Math. Artif. Intell. **34**(1–3), 197–215 (2002). https://doi.org/10.1023/A:1014490210693
2. Balbiani, P., Herzig, A., Schwarzentruber, F., Troquard, N.: DL-PA and DCL-PC: model checking and satisfiability problem are indeed in PSPACE. arXiv preprint arXiv:1411.7825 (2014)
3. Balbiani, P., Herzig, A., Troquard, N.: Dynamic logic of propositional assignments: a well-behaved variant of PDL. In: Proceedings of LICS 2013, pp. 143–152 (2013). https://doi.org/10.1109/LICS.2013.20
4. Baroni, P., Caminada, M., Giacomin, M.: Abstract argumentation frameworks and their semantics. In: Baroni, P., Gabbay, D., Giacomin, M., van der Torre, L. (eds.) Handbook of Formal Argumentation, pp. 159–236. College Publications (2018)
5. Baroni, P., Giacomin, M., Guida, G.: Extending abstract argumentation systems theory. Artif. Intell. **120**(2), 251–270 (2000). https://doi.org/10.1016/S0004-3702(00)00030-8
6. Barringer, H., Gabbay, D., Woods, J.: Temporal dynamics of support and attack networks: from argumentation to zoology. In: Hutter, D., Stephan, W. (eds.) Mechanizing Mathematical Reasoning. LNCS, vol. 2605, pp. 59–98. Springer, Heidelberg (2005). https://doi.org/10.1007/978-3-540-32254-2_5
7. Baumeister, D., Järvisalo, M., Neugebauer, D., Niskanen, A., Rothe, J.: Acceptance in incomplete argumentation frameworks. Artif. Intell. **295**, 103470 (2021). https://doi.org/10.1016/J.ARTINT.2021.103470
8. Baumeister, D., Neugebauer, D., Rothe, J., Schadrack, H.: Verification in incomplete argumentation frameworks. Artif. Intell. **264**, 1–26 (2018). https://doi.org/10.1016/J.ARTINT.2018.08.001
9. Besnard, P., Doutre, S.: Checking the acceptability of a set of arguments. In: Delgrande, J.P., Schaub, T. (eds.) 10th International Workshop on Non-Monotonic Reasoning (NMR 2004), pp. 59–64 (2004)

10. Boella, G., Gabbay, D.M., van der Torre, L.W.N., Villata, S.: Support in abstract argumentation. In: Baroni, P., Cerutti, F., Giacomin, M., Simari, G.R. (eds.) Proceedings of COMMA 2010, pp. 111–122 (2010). https://doi.org/10.3233/978-1-60750-619-5-111
11. Carrera, Á., Iglesias, C.A.: A systematic review of argumentation techniques for multi-agent systems research. Artif. Intell. Rev. **44**(4), 509–535 (2015). https://doi.org/10.1007/S10462-015-9435-9
12. Cayrol, C., Cohen, A., Lagasquie-Schiex, M.: Higher-order interactions (bipolar or not) in abstract argumentation: a state of the art. In: Gabbay, D., Giacomin, M., Simari, G., Thimm, M. (eds.) Handbook of Formal Argumentation, vol. 2, pp. 3–118. College Publications (2021)
13. Cayrol, C., Lagasquie-Schiex, M.C.: On the acceptability of arguments in bipolar argumentation frameworks. In: Godo, L. (ed.) ECSQARU 2005. LNCS, vol. 3571, pp. 378–389. Springer, Heidelberg (2005). https://doi.org/10.1007/11518655_33
14. Cayrol, C., Lagasquie-Schiex, M.C.: Bipolarity in argumentation graphs: towards a better understanding. Int. J. Approx. Reason. **54**(7), 876–899 (2013). https://doi.org/10.1016/J.IJAR.2013.03.001
15. Cohen, A., García, A.J., Simari, G.R.: Backing and undercutting in abstract argumentation frameworks. In: Lukasiewicz, T., Sali, A. (eds.) FoIKS 2012. LNCS, vol. 7153, pp. 107–123. Springer, Heidelberg (2012). https://doi.org/10.1007/978-3-642-28472-4_7
16. Coste-Marquis, S., Devred, C., Konieczny, S., Lagasquie-Schiex, M., Marquis, P.: On the merging of Dung's argumentation systems. Artif. Intell. **171**(10–15), 730–753 (2007). https://doi.org/10.1016/J.ARTINT.2007.04.012
17. Čyras, K., Schulz, C., Toni, F.: Capturing bipolar argumentation in non-flat assumption-based argumentation. In: An, B., Bazzan, A., Leite, J., Villata, S., van der Torre, L. (eds.) PRIMA 2017. LNCS, vol. 10621, pp. 386–402. Springer, Cham (2017). https://doi.org/10.1007/978-3-319-69131-2_23
18. Doutre, S., Herzig, A., Perrussel, L.: A dynamic logic framework for abstract argumentation. In: Baral, C., Giacomo, G.D., Eiter, T. (eds.) Proceedings of KR 2014 (2014)
19. Doutre, S., Herzig, A., Perrussel, L.: Abstract argumentation in dynamic logic: representation, reasoning and change. In: Liao, B., Ågotnes, T., Wáng, Y.N. (eds.) CLAR 2018. LIAA, pp. 153–185. Springer, Singapore (2019). https://doi.org/10.1007/978-981-13-7791-4_8
20. Doutre, S., Maffre, F., McBurney, P.: A dynamic logic framework for abstract argumentation: adding and removing arguments. In: Benferhat, S., Tabia, K., Ali, M. (eds.) IEA/AIE 2017. LNCS, vol. 10351, pp. 295–305. Springer, Cham (2017). https://doi.org/10.1007/978-3-319-60045-1_32
21. Dung, P.M.: On the acceptability of arguments and its fundamental role in non-monotonic reasoning, logic programming and n-person games. Artif. Intell. **77**(2), 321–358 (1995). https://doi.org/10.1016/0004-3702(94)00041-X
22. Fazzinga, B., Flesca, S., Furfaro, F.: Probabilistic bipolar abstract argumentation frameworks: complexity results. In: Lang, J. (ed.) Proceedings of IJCAI 2018, pp. 1803–1809 (2018). https://doi.org/10.24963/IJCAI.2018/249
23. Fazzinga, B., Flesca, S., Furfaro, F.: Reasoning over argument-incomplete AAFs in the presence of correlations. In: Zhou, Z. (ed.) Proceedings of IJCAI 2021, pp. 189–195. ijcai.org (2021). https://doi.org/10.24963/IJCAI.2021/27
24. Fazzinga, B., Flesca, S., Furfaro, F.: Reasoning over attack-incomplete AAFs in the presence of correlations. In: Bienvenu, M., Lakemeyer, G., Erdem, E. (eds.) Proceedings of KR21, pp. 301–311 (2021). https://doi.org/10.24963/KR.2021/29

25. Fazzinga, B., Flesca, S., Furfaro, F.: Incomplete bipolar argumentation frameworks. In: Gal, K., et al. (ed.) Proceedings of ECAI 2023, pp. 684–691. IOS Press (2023). https://doi.org/10.3233/FAIA230332

26. Gargouri, A., Konieczny, S., Marquis, P., Vesic, S.: On a notion of monotonic support for bipolar argumentation frameworks. In: Dignum, F., Lomuscio, A., Endriss, U., Nowé, A. (eds.) Proceedings of AAMAS 2021, pp. 546–554 (2021). https://doi.org/10.5555/3463952.3464020

27. Herzig, A., Yuste-Ginel, A.: Abstract argumentation with qualitative uncertainty: an analysis in dynamic logic. In: Baroni, P., Benzmüller, C., Wáng, Y.N. (eds.) CLAR 2021. LNCS, vol. 13040, pp. 190–208. Springer, Cham (2021). https://doi.org/10.1007/978-3-030-89391-0_11

28. Hunter, A., Polberg, S., Potyka, N., Rienstra, T., Thimm, M.: Probabilistic argumentation: a survey. In: Gabbay, D., Giacomin, M., Simari, G., Thimm, M. (eds.) Handbook of Formal Argumentation, vol. 2, pp. 397–441. College Publications (2021)

29. Karamlou, A., Cyras, K., Toni, F.: Complexity results and algorithms for bipolar argumentation. In: Elkind, E., Veloso, M., Agmon, N., Taylor, M.E. (eds.) Proceedings of AAMAS 2019, pp. 1713–1721 (2019)

30. Lagasquie-Schiex, M.C., Mailly, J.G., Yuste-Ginel, A.: How to manage supports in incomplete argumentation frameworks. Technical report. IRIT/RR-2023-04-FR, IRIT - Institut de Recherche en Informatique de Toulouse (2023)

31. Lagasquie-Schiex, M.C., Mailly, J.G., Yuste-Ginel, A.: Incomplete bipolar argumentation frameworks. Technical report. IRIT/RR-2023-01-FR, IRIT - Institut de Recherche en Informatique de Toulouse (2023)

32. Mailly, J.G.: Constrained incomplete argumentation frameworks. In: Vejnarová, J., Wilson, N. (eds.) ECSQARU 2021. LNCS, vol. 12897, pp. 103–116. Springer, Cham (2021). https://doi.org/10.1007/978-3-030-86772-0_8

33. Mailly, J.G.: Extension-based semantics for incomplete argumentation frameworks. In: Baroni, P., Benzmüller, C., Wáng, Y.N. (eds.) CLAR 2021. LNCS, vol. 13040, pp. 322–341. Springer, Cham (2021). https://doi.org/10.1007/978-3-030-89391-0_18

34. Mailly, J.G.: Yes, no, maybe, I don't know: complexity and application of abstract argumentation with incomplete knowledge. Argument Comput. 13(3), 291–324 (2022). https://doi.org/10.3233/AAC-210010

35. Mercier, H., Sperber, D.: Why do humans reason? Arguments for an argumentative theory. Behav. Brain Sci. 34(2), 57–74 (2011). https://doi.org/10.1017/S0140525X10000968

36. Nielsen, S.H., Parsons, S.: A generalization of dung's abstract framework for argumentation: arguing with sets of attacking arguments. In: Maudet, N., Parsons, S., Rahwan, I. (eds.) ArgMAS 2006. LNCS, vol. 4766, pp. 54–73. Springer, Heidelberg (2007). https://doi.org/10.1007/978-3-540-75526-5_4

37. Nouioua, F., Risch, V.: Argumentation frameworks with necessities. In: Benferhat, S., Grant, J. (eds.) SUM 2011. LNCS, vol. 6929, pp. 163–176. Springer, Heidelberg (2011). https://doi.org/10.1007/978-3-642-23963-2_14

38. Odekerken, D., Lehtonen, T., Borg, A., Wallner, J.P., Järvisalo, M.: Argumentative reasoning in ASPIC+ under incomplete information. In: Marquis, P., Son, T.C., Kern-Isberner, G. (eds.) Proceedings of KR 2023, pp. 531–541 (2023). https://doi.org/10.24963/KR.2023/52

39. Oren, N., Norman, T.J.: Semantics for evidence-based argumentation. In: Besnard, P., Doutre, S., Hunter, A. (eds.) Proceedings of COMMA 2008, vol. 172, pp. 276–284. IOS Press (2008)

40. Rienstra, T., Thimm, M., Oren, N.: Opponent models with uncertainty for strategic argumentation. In: Rossi, F. (ed.) Proceedings of IJCAI 2013 (2013)
41. Rossit, J., Mailly, J.G., Dimopoulos, Y., Moraitis, P.: United we stand: accruals in strength-based argumentation. Argument Comput. **12**(1), 87–113 (2021). https://doi.org/10.3233/AAC-200904
42. Yu, L., Anaissy, C.A., Vesic, S., Li, X., van der Torre, L.: A principle-based analysis of bipolar argumentation semantics. In: Gaggl, S.A., Martinez, M.V., Ortiz, M. (eds.) JELIA 2023. LNCS, vol. 14281, pp. 209–224. Springer, Cham (2023). https://doi.org/10.1007/978-3-031-43619-2_15
43. Yuste-Ginel, A., Herzig, A.: Qualitative uncertainty and dynamics of argumentation through dynamic logic. J. Log. Comput. (2023). https://doi.org/10.1093/LOGCOM/EXAC098
44. Yuste-Ginel, A., Proietti, C.: On the instantiation of argument-incomplete argumentation frameworks. In: Alfano, G., Ferilli, S. (eds.) 7th Workshop on Advances in Argumentation in Artificial Intelligence. CEUR (2022)

Constrained Derivation
in Assumption-Based Argumentation

Giovanni Buraglio[1]([✉])[iD], Wolfgang Dvořák[1][iD], Anna Rapberger[2][iD],
and Stefan Woltran[1][iD]

[1] Institute of Logic and Computation, TU Wien, Vienna, Austria
{giovanni.buraglio,wolfgang.dvorak,stefan.woltran}@tuwien.ac.at
[2] Department of Computing, Imperial College London, London, UK
a.rapberger@imperial.ac.uk

Abstract. Structured argumentation formalisms provide a rich framework to formalise and reason over situations where contradicting information is present. However, in most formalisms the integral step of constructing all possible arguments is performed in an unconstrained way. For this, it may not be possible to represent situations where the reasoning process is subject to various kinds of restrictions; for example, where the possibility of communication is limited in a multi-agent setting. In this work, we introduce a general approach that allows constraining the derivation of arguments for assumption-based argumentation. We show that, under certain conditions, this reduces to eliminating rules from the given knowledge base while letting the derivation of arguments unconstrained. For this as well as for the general approach to derivation constraining, we provide an encoding into Answer Set Programming.

Keywords: Assumption-Based Argumentation · Normative Reasoning · Non-monotonic Reasoning

1 Introduction

Assumption-based argumentation (ABA) [5,6,11] is a well-studied formalism in the realm of structured argumentation with applications ranging from medical reasoning and decision-making to eXplainable AI [10,15,16]. Argumentative reasoning is hereby performed by instantiating ABA frameworks (ABAF) representing debates through (structured) arguments and an attack relation among them. Arguments are built as forward derivation supported by defeasible sentences called *assumptions*, using (strict) inference rules from the underlying knowledge base. Accordingly, attacks between arguments encode a consistency check among the assumptions that support them. As already noticed by Modgil and Prakken [30], assumption-based argumentation leaves the "set of inference rules unspecified" in the sense that rules are treated equally and no distinction can be made among them. However, in some domains of application, rules might be distinguished on the basis of their function. Such situations can be found, for

A. Meier and M. Ortiz (Eds.): FoIKS 2024, LNCS 14589, pp. 340–359, 2024.
https://doi.org/10.1007/978-3-031-56940-1_19

instance, in the area of normative reasoning. There it may become relevant to tell apart rules that produce obligations and permissions on the one hand from those that produce institutional facts on the other, based on Searle's famous distinction between regulative and constitutive norms [34]. To prevent instances of deontic paradoxes and fallacious conclusions, the combination of rules is subject to certain restrictions [27]. Another example that requires the separation of rules is the necessity to express a distinction between them based on their range of validity. In order to account for such situations, several argumentation formalisms separate strict and defeasible inference rules [8,28,29,32]. In the context of multi-agent systems [33,37], an agent's frame of reference may differ from that of others, giving rise to individual rule sets for each agent. Moreover, it can be the case that the communication among different agents is restricted and asymmentric in such a way that information is only partially distributed. Let us consider the following illustrative example.

Example 1. Our protagonist Alice wants to decide whether she will spend her weekend on a holiday at the seaside. In order for her to choose, she looks at her favourite weather forecast application, produced by company Y. She decides that she will go to the seaside only if the weather is sunny. Based on their available data and algorithms, company Y forecasts that there will be rain with probability of 95% in the weekend. Although she would be willing to take a risk, she considers bad weather for her holiday any forecast which assigns a probability greater than 80% to be rainy. There is a another company Z that produces the most precise and detailed weather forecast available. Indeed, company Z is able to soundly predict that while the probability that will rain is high, it is only going to be happening during night hours.

We model Alice's considerations via ABA as follows.[1] We consider the assumptions a ('Y is reliable') b ('sunny weather'), c ('not only rain in the night'), and d ('Z is reliable'), and atoms $\bar{b}$ ('bad weather'), $\bar{c}$ ('rain only during the night'), q ('P(rain) = 95%'), p ('P(rain) > 80%') and s ('seaside'). The relations between assumptions and atoms can be summarised as follows:

$$q \leftarrow a \qquad s \leftarrow b \qquad \bar{b} \leftarrow c, p \qquad p \leftarrow q \qquad \bar{c} \leftarrow d$$

From the reliability of company Y we can deduce bad weather; however, Alice also trusts company Z which predicts rain only in the night, and hence Alice decides to go to the seaside.   ◇

In the above setting, we assume that Alice has full information about all weather forecasting predictions. However, in the above example, we cannot capture the situation where the information is theoretically available but Alice has no knowledge about the predictions of company Z.

Example 2. Let us assume that Alice receives only updates from the weather forecasting company Y. Hence, although company Z predicts that rain only happens during the night, Alice cannot conclude that the weather is good enough for going to the seaside.   ◇

---

[1] For a formal definition of ABA, we refer to Sect. 2.

The knowledge of the three agents involved (Alice and the two companies) is not entirely distributed, and this prevents Alice to make a correct prediction. However, the situation cannot be modelled via ABA without deleting the predictions of company Z entirely. Since other agents might have access to the predictions of company Z it might not be desirable to simply delete the respective rule.

Let us consider a further modification of the example which shows that information flow and the possibility to share inference rules among each other can be asymmetric in a multi-agent setting.

Example 3. Let us assume that Alice witness an earthquake, modelled via a fact t ('Earthquake'). She knows that in this situation, Company Y always releases a safety alert on their application. We model this via an additional rule $u \leftarrow t$ where u stands for 'Safety alert is triggered'.

Unfortunately, Alice finds herself unable to communicate her information to Company Y, which cannot in turn spread this to their clients. Again, the formalisation of the ABA framework would let us wrongly conclude that the security alert is triggered.   ◊

We observe that standard ABA is not expressive enough to account for a distinction among inference rules that takes asymmetric and limited information flow into account. Consequently, it is not possible to constrain the rule combinations based on the specific relationship agents may display among each other in a multi-agent setting.

In this work, we propose first steps in order to close this gap. In particular, we (a) extend the ABA formalism with pairwise disjoint sets of rules in order to differentiate them; (b) equip this extension of ABA with formal constraints (called *derivation graphs*) that regulate its deductive machinery, by encoding applicability conditions for inference rules; (c) investigate the role of derivation constraints within the argument construction process. On the one hand, we examine the definition of constraints as pre-processing operations on the underlying knowledge base; on the other hand, we present a prototype encoding of our formalism in Answer Set Programming (ASP). Finally, we point out to the relation between the possibility of expressing conflicts in normative reasoning and the expressive power of non-flat ABA.

2   Background

In order to introduce our formalism, we first need to recall some preliminaries for assumption-based argumentation. In ABA, frameworks representing debates are built up from a rule-based knowledge base and defined in the following way:

Definition 1. *An ABA framework (ABAF) is a tuple $D = (\mathcal{L}, \mathcal{R}, \mathcal{A}, {}^{-})$ where: (i) $\mathcal{L}$ and $\mathcal{R}$ form together a deductive system and are respectively a set of atomic sentences in a language and a set of inference rules; (ii) $\mathcal{A} \subseteq \mathcal{L}$ is a non-empty set of atoms called assumptions; (iii) ${}^{-}$ is a total mapping from $\mathcal{A}$ into $\mathcal{L}$, where $\overline{a}$ is said to be the contrary of a, for each $a \in \mathcal{A}$.*

Following [9], we write rules as $r : \phi \leftarrow \phi_1, \ldots, \phi_m$ and we say that ϕ is the head of the rule and $\{\phi_1, \ldots, \phi_m\}$ is its body, formally $head(r) = \phi$ and $body(r) = \{\phi_1, \ldots, \phi_m\}$. For a set of rules R, we use $head(R)$ to indicate the set of atoms which are head of the rules contained in it. We consider here the finite flat version of ABAF, i.e. frameworks where $\mathcal{L}$ and $\mathcal{R}$ are finite and assumptions do not occur as conclusions of inference rules: there is no $r \in \mathcal{R}$ and $a \in \mathcal{A}$ for which $a = head(r)$. Arguments of an ABAF are based on proof-trees, constructed by forward-derivation from leaf-nodes to the root:

Definition 2 (deduction). *Let $D = (\mathcal{L}, \mathcal{R}, \mathcal{A}, \overline{})$ be an ABAF. A deduction for $p \in \mathcal{L}$ supported by $S \subseteq \mathcal{A}$ and $R \subseteq \mathcal{R}$, denoted $S \vdash^R p$ (or simply $S \vdash p$), is a finite rooted tree t with:*

i) a labelling function that assigns each vertex of t an element from $\mathcal{L} \cup \{\top\}$ s.t. the root is labelled by p and leaves are labelled by $\top$ or atoms in S;

ii) a surjective mapping m from the set of internal nodes of t onto rules R satisfying, for each vertex v, that the label of v is the head of the rule $m(v)$ and the children of v are (one-to-one) labelled with the elements of the body of $m(v)$.

In ABA, the attack relation is defined over sets of assumptions.

Definition 3 (attack). *Let $D = (\mathcal{L}, \mathcal{R}, \mathcal{A}, \overline{})$ be an ABAF, let $S, T \subseteq \mathcal{A}$ be two sets of assumptions. S attacks T $(S \rightarrow T)$ iff there is a set $S' \subseteq S$ such that $S' \vdash \overline{a}$ for some $a \in T$.*

Moreover, S defends a iff for every $B \subseteq \mathcal{A}$, if B attacks $\{a\}$, then S attacks B. Semantics can be defined then in the usual way.

Definition 4 (semantics). *Given ABAF $D = (\mathcal{L}, \mathcal{R}, \mathcal{A}, \overline{})$ and $S, T \in \mathcal{A}$. The set S is conflict-free iff it does not attack itself; admissible iff it is conflict-free and $T \rightarrow S$ implies $S \rightarrow T$; stable iff it is conflict-free and $a \in \mathcal{A} \setminus S$ implies $S \rightarrow \{a\}$; complete iff it is admissible and contains all arguments it defends. We write $S \in \sigma(D)$ with $\sigma \in \{cf, adm, stb, com\}$ to say that S is a conflict-free, admissible, stable or complete set of assumptions (or extension) of D.*

Likewise, we can define the corresponding AF for a given ABAF.

Definition 5. *For an ABAF $D = (\mathcal{L}, \mathcal{R}, \mathcal{A}, \overline{})$, we call $F = (\mathcal{A}, \mathcal{R})$ its corresponding AF with*

- $\mathcal{A} = \{S \vdash p \mid S \subseteq \mathcal{A}\}$;
- $\mathcal{R} = \{(S \vdash p, T \vdash q) \mid p = \overline{a}$ for some $a \in T\} \subseteq \mathcal{A} \times \mathcal{A}$.

3   ABA Frameworks with Multiple Rule-Sets

We can now define ABAFs with multiple rule-sets and derivation graphs. Jointly, these enable to trace rule kinds along with some constraint on their combination.

We consider only frameworks where rule-sets are pairwise disjoint. Further, it is sometimes desirable to evaluate scenarios where the same atom cannot be derived by rules of different kinds. Take for instance a legal debate built up using constitutive and regulative rules. The very difference between the two type of rules concerns their output (i.e. their heads): constitutive rules produce institutional facts whereas regulative rules produce deontic statements such as obligations or permissions. It is therefore an intuitive requirement to separate these two heterogeneous groups of statements. For this, we focus on the class of *separated n-ABAFs*, for which heads of rules in different rule-sets are pairwise disjoint.

Definition 6 (n-rule-sets ABA). *A n-rule-sets ABAF (n-ABAF) is a tuple $D = (\mathcal{L}, \{\mathcal{R}_i \mid 1 \le i \le n\}, \mathcal{A}, \overline{})$ such that $(\mathcal{L}, \bigcup_{i=1}^{n} \mathcal{R}_i, \mathcal{A}, \overline{})$ is an ABAF. Moreover, we call D separated whenever $head(\mathcal{R}_i) \cap head(\mathcal{R}_j) = \emptyset$ for all i, j with $i \ne j$.*

As mentioned earlier, one might want to represent some constraint on rules combinations on $\bigcup_{i \le n} \mathcal{R}_i$ depending on the particular application domain. Inspired by input/output combinations presented in [35], we introduce the more expressive concept of derivation graph to formalise combination constraints:

Definition 7 (derivation graph). *Let $D = (\mathcal{L}, \{\mathcal{R}_i \mid 1 \le i \le n\}, \mathcal{A}, \overline{})$ be an n-ABAF. A derivation graph $G = (V, E, \lambda)$ for D is a directed graph (V, E) with $|V| \ge n + 1$ and a labelling function $\lambda : V \to \{\mathcal{R}_i \mid 1 \le i \le n\}$ such that V contains:*

  i) a distinct vertex s (called "starting node") with no incoming edges;
  ii) at least one vertex r_i for each $\mathcal{R}_i$ (called "rule-node" for $\mathcal{R}_i$), i.e. $\lambda(\mathsf{r}_i) = \mathcal{R}_i$.

The outcome of the constraint encoded by some derivation graph is a limitation on the possibility of rules chaining. This affects the derivation process from the underlying deductive system. In particular, the idea consists in allowing only those sequential combinations of rules for which there is a path within the derivation graph. As a result, we extend the usual notion of deduction presented in ABA to accommodate this additional requirement.

Definition 8. *Let $D = (\mathcal{L}, \{\mathcal{R}_i \mid 1 \le i \le n\}, \mathcal{A}, \overline{})$ be an n-ABAF and let $G = (V, E, \lambda)$ be a derivation graph for D. A G-deduction for $p \in \mathcal{L}$ supported by $S \subseteq \mathcal{A}$ and $R = \bigcup_{i=1}^{n} R_i$ with $R_i \subseteq \mathcal{R}_i$, denoted $S \vdash_G^R p$ (or simply $S \vdash_G p$), is a deduction t with a function μ that maps every node v of t to a rule-node w in G such that:*

 - *i) each node v in t corresponds to a rule in the rule set of w, i.e. $m(v) \in \lambda(w)$ with $w = \mu(v)$.*
 - *ii) for each leaf-to-root-path $v_0 \ldots v_k$ in t, the corresponding series of nodes $w_0, \ldots, w_k$ form a path in G with $w_0 = \mathsf{s}$ and $w_i = \mu(v_i)$ for $1 \le i \le k$.*

Notions of G-attack, G-semantics and corresponding AF under G can be easily adapted from the standard ones by employing the notion of G-deduction instead of regular deduction.

To show our new adaption at work, let us revisit our introductory example.

Example 4. Consider again Example 1 from the introduction. We construct a 3-ABAF $D = (\mathcal{L}, \mathcal{R}_1, \mathcal{R}_2, \mathcal{R}_3, \mathcal{A}, {}^{-})$ where $\mathcal{R}_1$, $\mathcal{R}_2$ and $\mathcal{R}_3$ contain respectively inference rules of company Y, Alice and company Z. We recall the assumptions $\mathcal{A} = \{a, b, c, d\}$, given as follows:

$a = $ 'Y is reliable' $b = $ 'There is going to be sunny weather'

$d = $ 'Z is reliable' $c = $ 'It does not rain solely during the night'

We consider their contraries $\overline{x}$, $x \in \mathcal{A}$, and the claims

$p = $ 'The probability of rain is higher than 80%' $t = $ 'Earthquake!'

$q = $ 'There is 95% probability that will rain' $u = $ 'Safety alert'

$s = $ 'Alice will go to the seaside'

We consider three rule sets $\mathcal{R}_1$, $\mathcal{R}_2$, and $\mathcal{R}_3$ corresponding to Company Y, Alice, and Company Z, respectively. The rules are distributed as follows:

$$\mathcal{R}_1 : q \leftarrow a \quad u \leftarrow t \qquad\qquad \mathcal{R}_3 : \overline{c} \leftarrow d$$

Moreover, Alice's rule set $\mathcal{R}_2$ contains the following rules:

$$s \leftarrow b \qquad\qquad \overline{b} \leftarrow c, p \qquad\qquad p \leftarrow q \qquad\qquad t \leftarrow$$

It is possible to construct the relevant arguments: $\{b\} \vdash^{\{\}} b$ corresponding to the assumption b; $\{a, c\} \vdash^{\{\}} \overline{b}$ and $\{\} \vdash^{\{u \leftarrow t, t \leftarrow\}} u$ from the inference rules representing the knowledge of company Y and Alice; $\{d\} \vdash \overline{c}$ which is associated with the company Z. This would make $\{d, b, a\}$ an admissible set and $\{c\}$ not: both companies convey reliable information, and together these point out to the fact that in daylight hours the weather will be sunny, since it will rain only during the night. However, in our example we impose that Alice does not have access to the information disclosed by company Z and company Y does not have access to Alice's finding regarding the earthquake. This requirement can be captured with following derivation graph G:

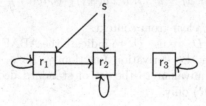

It can be easily seen that under G, we loose the argument $\{d\} \vdash \bar{c}$ that defends b from its attacker $\{a, c\}$. Indeed, it holds that $\{d\} \nvdash_G \bar{c}$, making $\{a, c\}$ an admissible set, to the detriment of $\{b\}$. Losing the information from company Z, Alice will believe that it will rain during the day. Moreover, we also get $\{\} \nvdash_G^{\{u \leftarrow t, t \leftarrow\}} u$, explaining the impossibility for company Y to receive information Alice holds in order to send a general safety alert to citizens.   ◇

4   Investigating Constraints in ABA

In the present section, we examine the role of derivation constraints in the n-ABA formalism. We show that under certain conditions it is possible to exploit the information given by derivation graphs to pre-process the knowledge base in order to obtain equivalent results in terms of ABAFs instantiation.

A core feature of ABA is that it comes with guidelines that specify how to instantiate a framework from a given knowledge base. This job is largely done by the notions of deduction and attack. In turn, derivation graphs work as a device for controlling and manipulating such instantiation process. An interesting research question would be that of asking under which conditions one can obtain an equivalent framework by pre-processing the knowledge base while leaving the derivation process untouched. Initial results show that if a derivation graph contains exactly one rule node for each rule set in the given n-ABAF, it is possible to define a *derivation function* that works in such a way. This is an operation on the knowledge base which automatically identifies and removes rules that would not be allowed under a derivation graph G, allowing unconstrained deductions. For each graph constraint G, there is a derivation function γ that extracts from the rules $\mathcal{R}$ of an n-ABAF the subset of rules whose application is allowed under G.

Definition 9. *Let D be an n-ABAF, $\mathcal{R}$ the rules appearing in D, $G = (V, E, \lambda)$ be some derivation graph with $V = \{s, r_1, \ldots, r_n\}$. The derivation function $\gamma_G : 2^{\mathcal{R}} \to 2^{\mathcal{R}}$ corresponding to G is defined as $\gamma(\mathcal{R}) = \mathcal{R} \setminus \{A \cup B\}$ with*

- $A = \{r \in \mathcal{R} \mid r \in \mathcal{R}_i, A \cap body(r) \neq \emptyset \text{ or } body(r) = \emptyset \text{ and } (s, r_i) \notin E\}$;
- $B = \{r \in \mathcal{R} \mid r \in \mathcal{R}_i, \exists j \leq n \text{ s.t. } head(\mathcal{R}_j) \cap body(r) \neq \emptyset \text{ and } (r_j, r_i) \notin E\}$.

We omit subscript G if clear from context.

Given some ABAF D, we use D_γ to indicate the ABAF obtained by restricting rule sets of D via the derivation function γ. As a result, the set of G-deductions for D is equivalent to the set of standard deductions that can be built using rules in $\gamma(\mathcal{R})$ only.

Lemma 1. *Let D be a separated n-ABA framework, $\mathcal{R}$ the rules appearing in D, $G = (V, E, \lambda)$ some derivation-graph with $V = \{s, r_1, \ldots, r_n\}$ and $\gamma : \mathcal{R} \to \mathcal{R}$ its corresponding derivation function. For any set of atomic sentences $S \subseteq \mathcal{L}$, $p \in \mathcal{L}$ and $R \subseteq \mathcal{R}$, $S \vdash_G^R p$ is a G-deduction for D if and only if $S \vdash^{\gamma(R)} p$ is a deduction for D_γ.*

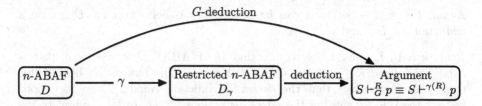

Fig. 1. Graphical representation of Lemma 1.

Proof (Sketch). ($\Rightarrow$) We prove the statement by first showing that our translation does not delete too many rules. Given a G-deduction $S \vdash_G^R p$ in D, we show that $S \vdash^{\gamma(R)} p$ is a deduction for D_γ. We show that $R = \gamma(R)$ which allows us to replace R with $\gamma(R)$ in $S \vdash_G^R p$, deriving that $S \vdash_G^{\gamma(R)} p$ is a G-deduction in D_γ. Hence, $S \vdash^{\gamma(R)} p$ is a deduction in D_γ.

($\Leftarrow$) For the other direction, suppose $S \vdash^{\gamma(R)} p$ is a deduction in D_γ. We show $S \vdash_G^R p$ is a G-deduction in D. Since $\gamma(\mathcal{R}) \subseteq \mathcal{R}$, we know that each rule in $\gamma(R)$ is contained in D, i.e. we can use each rule in $\gamma(R)$ under G. Hence, we can assume that $R = \gamma(R)$. We can thus replace $\gamma(R)$ with R in $S \vdash^{\gamma(R)} p$, thus showing that it is a deduction for D_γ (and *a fortiori* for D). It remains to prove that $S \vdash^R p$ is a G-deduction for D. For this, we start from a proof tree t for $S \vdash^R p$ in D' and show that the same proof tree can be constructed by adhering to the derivation graph G, i.e. each path in the proof tree t can be mapped to a path in the derivation graph G. $\square$

A graphical representation of the equivalence between G-deductions and deduction in D_γ is given in Fig. 1.

To see how the translation works from G-deduction of D to regular deductions in D_γ, consider the following example.

Example 5. Let $D = (\mathcal{L}, \mathcal{R}_1, \mathcal{R}_2, \mathcal{A}, {}^-)$ be a 2-ABAF with $\mathcal{L} = \{a, b, p, q, s\}$, $\mathcal{R}_1 = \{p \leftarrow a\}$, $\mathcal{R}_2 = \{q \leftarrow p, s \leftarrow b\}$ and $\mathcal{A} = \{a, b\}$. Let $G = (V, E)$ be a derivation graph with $V = \{s, r_1, r_2\}$ and $E = \{(s, r_1), (r_1, r_2)\}$ as follows:

$$s \longrightarrow \boxed{r_1} \longrightarrow \boxed{r_2}$$

Under G, the set of G-deduction that can be built are the following:

$$\{a\} \vdash_G a, \qquad \{b\} \vdash_G b \qquad \{a\} \vdash_G^{\{p \leftarrow a\}} p \qquad \{a\} \vdash_G^{\{p \leftarrow a, q \leftarrow p\}} q$$

However, $\{b\} \nvdash_G^{\{s \leftarrow b\}} s$ in D under G.

Let us now take the corresponding derivation function γ for G. By Definition 9, we have $\gamma(\mathcal{R}) = \mathcal{R} \setminus \{A \cup B\}$, where $A = \{s \leftarrow b\}$ and $B = \emptyset$ such that $D_\gamma = (\mathcal{L}, \gamma(\mathcal{R}), \mathcal{A}, {}^-)$. Eventually, for D_γ we obtain the following:

$$\{a\} \vdash a, \qquad \{b\} \vdash b \qquad \{a\} \vdash^{\{p \leftarrow a\}} p \qquad \{a\} \vdash^{\{p \leftarrow a, q \leftarrow p\}} q$$

Again, $\{b\} \nvdash^{\{s \leftarrow b\}} s$. As it can be seen, every G-deduction for D is also a deduction for D_γ, and vice versa.   ◇

Remark 1. In Lemma 1, we require that the n-ABAF D is *separated*, that is $head(\mathcal{R}_i) \cap head(\mathcal{R}_j) = \emptyset$ for all i, j with $i \neq j$. The motivation behind this choice lies in the fact that the derivation function could in some occasions restrict the rule-set causing the set of deductions for D_γ to be a subset of the set of G-deductions for D. To show this, let us consider the following example: take D such that $\mathcal{L} = \{a, b, p, q\}$, $\mathcal{R}_1 = \{p \leftarrow a, q \leftarrow p\}$, $\mathcal{R}_2 = \{p \leftarrow b\}$ and $\mathcal{A} = \{a, b\}$. D is not separated due to the fact that $p \in head(\mathcal{R}_1) \cap head(\mathcal{R}_2)$. Moreover, let $G = (V, E)$ be the following derivation graph:

As it can be seen easily, the rule $r : q \leftarrow p$ would be eliminated by the function γ since $r \in B$. Indeed, we have $p \in head(\mathcal{R}_2) \cap body(r)$, $r \in \mathcal{R}_1$ and $(r_2, r_1) \notin E$. Thus, $\{a\} \vdash^{\gamma(\mathcal{R})} q$ is not a deduction for D_γ. However, we would at the same time allow the rule r under G since $(s, r_1) \in E$ and $(r_1, r_1) \in E$, so that $\{a\} \vdash^{\mathcal{R}}_G q$ is a G-deduction for D. In order to avoid such undesired behaviour, we restrict our study to separated ABAFs.

From Lemma 1 it follows that the corresponding AF instantiated by means of G-deductions is equivalent to the one instantiated through standard deductions after its rule-set has been restricted by the derivation function. This assures that the same outcome is reached by limiting deductions via some derivation graph or by restricting the knowledge base accordingly.

Theorem 1 (Equivalence under instantiation). *Let D be a separated n-ABA framework, G some derivation graph with $V = \{s, r_1, \ldots, r_n\}$ and $\gamma : \mathcal{R} \rightarrow \mathcal{R}$ some derivation function. Let $F_G = (\mathcal{A}_G, \mathcal{R}_G)$ be the corresponding AF with respect to D under G and $F' = (\mathcal{A}', \mathcal{R}')$ the corresponding AF with respect to D_γ. For these, we derive that $F_G \equiv F'$, in the sense that:*

(1) $\mathcal{A}_G = \mathcal{A}'$;
(2) $\mathcal{R}_G = \mathcal{R}'$.

Proof. We start by considering (1). By Definition 5, we have $\mathcal{A}_G = \{S \vdash^{\mathcal{R}}_G p \mid S \subseteq \mathcal{A}\}$. Given Lemma 1, we know that for each argument in such set, there is an equivalent argument that can be obtained through some derivation function γ such that $\{S \vdash^{\gamma(\mathcal{R})} p \mid S \subseteq \mathcal{A}\} = \mathcal{A}'$. Hence, $\mathcal{A}_G = \mathcal{A}'$.

The proof of (2) is similar. By Definition 5, we have $\mathcal{R}_G = \{(S \vdash^{\mathcal{R}}_G p, T \vdash^{\mathcal{R}^*}_G q) \mid p = \bar{a}$ for some $a \in T\}$. Given Lemma 1, we know that for each pair of arguments in such set, there is an equivalent pair of arguments that can be obtained through some derivation function γ such that $S \vdash^{\mathcal{R}}_G p \iff S \vdash^{\gamma(\mathcal{R})} p$ and $T \vdash^{\mathcal{R}^*}_G q \iff T \vdash^{\gamma(\mathcal{R}^*)} q$. Since these arguments are pairwise equivalent, the attack relation among them will be equivalent as well. Thus, we obtain $\{(S \vdash^{\gamma(\mathcal{R})} p, T \vdash^{\gamma(\mathcal{R}^*)} q) \mid p = \bar{a}$ for some $a \in T\} = \mathcal{R}'$ as the set of attacks for F'. Finally, we can state $\mathcal{R}_G = \mathcal{R}'$, as desired.   □

A straightforward consequence of this is the semantics equivalence.

Corollary 1 (Equivalence). *Let D be a separated n-ABAF, D_γ its restriction under γ and G the corresponding derivation graph. Let $\sigma \in \{cf, adm, stb, com\}$ and let σ_G denote their constrained version. It holds that $\sigma_G(D) = \sigma(D_\gamma)$.*

We furthermore observe the following relationship between n-ABAFs.

Proposition 1. *Let D be an n-ABAF, $G_1 = (V_1, E_1)$ and $G_2 = (V_2, E_2)$ two derivation graphs such that $V_1 = V_2$ and $E_1 \subseteq E_2$. Further, let $F_1 = (\mathcal{A}_1, \mathcal{R}_1)$ and $F_2 = (\mathcal{A}_2, \mathcal{R}_2)$ be the corresponding argumentation frameworks for D under G_1 and G_2. Then, $F_1 \subseteq F_2$.*

Proof. In order to prove the statement, we only need to prove that $\mathcal{A}_1 \subseteq \mathcal{A}_2$. Hence, we show that for every argument $S \vdash_{G_1} p$ in $\mathcal{A}_1$ there is an identical argument $S \vdash_{G_2} p$ in $\mathcal{A}_2$. Assume that $S \vdash_{G_1} p \in \mathcal{A}_1$. By definition, $S \vdash_{G_1} p$ is a deduction t with a surjective mapping that maps every internal node v of t to a rule node w in G_1 such that i) v corresponds to a rule that is in some rule set $\mathcal{R}_i$ and $\mathcal{R}_i$ is mapped to some $w \in V_1$ and ii) for each leaf-to-root-path $v_0 \ldots v_k$ in t, the corresponding series of nodes $w_0 \ldots w_k$ in G_1 form a path in G_1 with $w_0 = \mathsf{s}$. Since $V_1 = V_2$ by hypothesis, i) is valid for $S \vdash_{G_2} p$ as well. Consider now ii). Each path $w_0 \ldots w_k$ in G_1 corresponds to the set of edges $(w_i, w_{i+1}) \in E_1$ with $0 \le i \le k - 1$. Given that $E_1 \subseteq E_2$ by hypothesis, for each edge in the path we have $(w_i, w_{i+1}) \in E_2$ with $0 \le i \le k - 1$. Therefore, $w_0 \ldots w_k$ is also a path in G_2. Hence, we can rewrite the former definition, substituting G_2 in place of G_1, obtaining $S \vdash_{G_2} p$ for F_2. □

5   Encoding Constrained n-ABA in ASP

In this section, we present an encoding[2] for our formalism in Answer Set Programming (ASP) that captures derivation constraints and their effect on the procedure of argument construction, inspired by the one provided in [22] for regular ABA frameworks and semantics.

Given an n-ABAF and derivation graph as input, our encoding provides an answer set M for each σ_G-extension of a given n-ABAF under the graph constraint G. Regarding the n-ABAF in input, we extend the encoding presented in [22] by introducing a new predicate specifying for each rule the (unique) ruleset $\mathcal{R}_i$ it belongs to. Let $D = (\mathcal{L}, \{\mathcal{R}_i \mid 1 \le i \le n\}, \mathcal{A}, \overline{})$ be an n-ABAF with $\mathcal{R}_i$ be the i-th set of rules. We use the following set of facts in ASP to represent D:

$$
\begin{aligned}
\mathtt{D} = &\{\mathbf{assumption}(a). \mid a \in \mathcal{A}\} \cup \\
&\{\mathbf{head}(m, b). \mid b \in head(r_m), r_m \in \mathcal{R}\} \cup \\
&\{\mathbf{body}(m, b). \mid b \in body(r_m), r_m \in \mathcal{R}\} \cup \\
&\{\mathbf{rule\_set}(r_m, rs_i). \mid r_m \in \mathcal{R}_i\} \cup \\
&\{\mathbf{contrary}(a, b). \mid b = \overline{a}, a \in \mathcal{A}\}.
\end{aligned}
$$

---

[2] Available at https://www.dbai.tuwien.ac.at/research/argumentation/abasp/.

Following [22], **assumption**(a) and **contrary**(a, b) labels a an assumption and b its contrary. Moreover, **head**(m, b) and **body**(m, b) mean that b is the head (resp. body) of the rule r_m within $\mathcal{R}$. In addition, we introduce the predicate **rule_set**(r_m, rs_i) to specify that r_m is in $\mathcal{R}_i$.

The derivation graph $G = (V, E, \lambda)$ is encoded as a labelled graph using predicates for nodes and edges, specifying which node corresponds to the starting node and each rule set.

$$G = \{\mathbf{node}(v). \mid v \in V\} \cup$$
$$\{\mathbf{edge}(v_1, v_2). \mid (v_1, v_2) \in E\} \cup$$
$$\{\mathbf{start}(v). \mid v \text{ is the starting node } \mathbf{s}\} \cup$$
$$\{\mathbf{rule\_node}(v, rs_i). \mid \lambda(v) = \mathcal{R}_i\}.$$

For an n-ABAF under G we use the ASP program π_G that mirrors the argument construction process (see Listing 1.1). To present this in a concise way, we say that "a rule R is in a node N" whenever such rule is contained in the rule-set corresponding to the node N in the derivation graph.

Listing 1.1. Module π_G

```
1   ← rule_set(R, I), rule_set(R, J), I! = J.
2   in(X) ← assumption(X), not out(X).
3   out(X) ← assumption(X), not in(X).
4   fact_rule(R) ← head(R, X), not non_fact_rule(R).
5   non_fact_rule(R) ← body(R, Y).
6   supp_by_node(X, N) ← in(X), start(N).
7   supp_by_node(X, N) ← head(R, X), rule_set(R, I), rule_node(N, I),
        non_fact_rule(R), supp_by_succ_of_node(Y, N) : body(R, Y)
8   supp_by_node(X, N) ← head(R, X), rule_set(R, I), rule_node(N, I),
        fact_rule(R), start(M), edge(M, N).
9   supp_by_succ_of_node(X, N) ← supp_by_node(X, M), edge(M, N).
```

A constraint in Line 1 checks that the same rule is not contained in two different rule sets, encoding the requirement that rule sets are pairwise disjoint. Lines 2 and 3 encode a guess of some possible extension in the set of assumptions, specifying which of them are taken to be **in** and **out** respectively. We label facts via the predicate **fact_rule**, telling them apart from rules with non-empty body (Lines 4 and 5). Lines 6–9 encode the construction process of G-deductions as forward derivations from subsets of $\mathcal{A}$ to supported claims. These establish the connection between nodes of a derivation graph, rules and supported atoms, represented by the predicate **supp_by_node**. As for Line 6, the set of assumptions $A \subseteq \mathcal{A}$ that is guessed to be **in** is set to be supported by the starting node of the derivation graph. Subsequently, as in [22], for some node $v \in V$ and any atom p that can be G-deduced from (a subset of) A, we obtain **supp_by_node**(p, v) in some answer set. Line 7 assures that each atom which is supported by some node M in the graph G remains supported by every node which is directly reachable from M. As for Line 8, an atom X is supported by the node N if (i) it occurs as the head of a non-fact rule R contained in the rule-set corresponding to N and (ii) the body of R is supported by a node M such that N is directly reachable from M. Finally, for fact-rules Line 9 makes sure that their head is supported by a node N whenever N can be reached directly from the starting node.

Eventually, each semantics-related module presented in [22] can be integrated into ours, after being carefully adapted to take into account rule-sets and derivation constraints. In the following, we refer as these encodings as π_G^σ, for each semantics σ. For G-constrained conflict-free sets, we simply extend π_G with the following two lines:

Listing 1.2. Module π_G

10 **defeated**$(X) \leftarrow$ **supp_by_node**$(Y, \_)$, **contrary**(X, Y).
11 $\leftarrow$ **in**(X), **defeated**(X).

This is obtained by simply substituting the **supported** predicate in Listing 1 of [22] with **supp_by_node**. Line 10 establishes that an atom is defeated when its contrary is supported by some node N in the derivation graph. Moreover, Line 11 enforces that those atoms which are defeated cannot be **in** at the same time. These rule out those assumption sets corresponding to the answer sets that include defeated atoms.

Similar considerations can be made regarding the module for admissible sets. This is obtained by making the predicate **derived_from_undef** compatible with the π_G module, taking rule-nodes and rule-sets into account. Thus, we get:

Listing 1.3. Module π_G^{adm}

```
12  derived_from_undef(X, N) ← assumption(X), not defeated(X), start(N)
13  derived_from_undef(X, N) ← head(R, X), rule_set(R, I), rule_node(N, I),
        non_fact_rule(R), derived_from_undef_by_succ_of_node(Y, N) : body(R, Y).
14  derived_from_undef(X, N) ← head(R, X), rule_set(R, I), rule_node(N, I),
        fact_rule(R), start(M), edge(M, N).
15  derived_from_undef_by_succ_of_node(X, N) ← edge(M, N),
        derived_from_undef(X, M).
16  attacked_by_undef(X) ← contrary(X, Y), derived_from_undef(Y, _).
17  ← in(X), attacked_by_undef(X).
```

The main idea underlying admissible semantics is that assumptions attacked by undefeated atoms cannot be **in** for any answer set, as stated in Line 17. Further, Line 16 enforces that atoms are attacked by undefeated assumptions if their contrary is derived from undefeated assumptions. Then, Lines 12–15 define which atoms are to be considered as derived in a node N from undefeated assumptions. In particular, these can be either (i) assumptions in the starting node which are not defeated (Line 12), (ii) heads of fact rules derived in a node which is directly reachable from the starting node (Line 15) or (iii) heads of non-fact rules whose body is constituted by atoms derived from undefeated assumptions (Lines 14). Moreover, every atom which is derived in a node M by an undefeated assumptions remains so in each node N directly reachable from M (Line 13).

The specifications of ASP programs for stable and complete semantics already presented in [22] extend the Modules π_G^{cf} and π_G^{adm} without the need for any adjustment in the syntax. In particular, the ASP program for stable semantics extends π_G^{cf} (see Listing 1.2) with

$$\leftarrow \mathbf{out}(X), not \ \mathbf{defeated}(X).$$

This encodes the requirement imposed by stable semantics that every assumption for which the predicate **out** holds must be attacked by the stb_G-extension. Similarly, complete semantics builds up on the notion of admissible set by requiring that every extension must not exclude any assumption that is defended by such extension. Hence, there is no assumption which is included in **out** but not in **attacked_by_undef**. As a consequence, π_G^{com} results from adding

$$\leftarrow \mathbf{out}(X), not \ \mathbf{attacked\_by\_undef}(X).$$

to the module for admissible sets (see Listing 1.3).

6 Non-flat ABA for Normative Reasoning

In the area of normative reasoning, it is often employed the famous distinction among constitutive and regulative norms, taken from Searle's theory of social reality [34]. Constitutive and regulative norms are statements of the form 'X count as Y in the context C' and 'if X is the case, the Y is obligatory', respectively. Following [24], we represent these as inference rules and set them apart based on the outcome they produce, namely institutional facts or obligations. In this context, conflicts may occur not only in presence of inconsistent information regarding brute facts, but also regarding institutional facts and norms [31]. Scenarios that concern the detachment of conflicting institutional facts are called *normative conflicts* and arise when more agents agree on the same brute fact, but assign conflicting institutional values to it. For example, an homosexual couple counts as married after having signed the marriage contract in some legal systems, but not in others. Similarly, conflicts among obligations can give rise to so-called *moral dilemmas*. Instances of these arise in presence of an obligation for p and for its opposite (formally, this translates to deriving p and $\overline{p}$ from assumptions by means of different regulative rules).

In assumption-based argumentation, conflicts between sentences are encoded by the contrary function over the assumption set. This represent a fundamental design property of ABA, since it allows in turn to define semantics directly on the assumption level. Because of this, in order to express normative conflicts and moral dilemmas, it is required that assumptions may not only consist of so-called brute facts, but also of institutional facts or obligations (produced by constitutive and regulative rules). Since these are always derived by rules in our knowledge base, flat ABA may not always be expressive enough to encompass such cases. Therefore, we anticipate here that the full expressiveness of non-flat ABA may be required for capturing instances of normative reasoning.

The higher expressive power of non-flat ABA requires some additional preconditions for the semantics based on admissible sets. In particular, given a non-flat ABAF D, for a set of assumptions of A to be admissible, it is necessary that both A and its attackers are *closed*.

Definition 10 (closed set). *A set of assumptions $A \subseteq \mathcal{A}$ is closed iff $A = Cl(A)$, where $Cl(A) = \{a \in \mathcal{A} | \exists A' \vdash a, \ A' \subseteq A\}$.*

In order to see why non-flat ABA is necessary, let us first consider an instance of Forrester's paradox [17]. In Standard Deontic Logic [36], Forrester's paradox, also known in the literature as "gentle murderer paradox", follows from the statements A: "One should not (under the law) commit murder" and B: "if someone commits murder, then they should do it gently". Moreover, B implies C: "if someone should commit murder gently, then they should commit murder". Under the assumption that D: "someone commits murder", this eventually creates a paradoxical situation whereby it is obligatory to commit and not to commit murder at the same time. Therefore, a moral dilemma is created where it is contradictory to assume that a law exists and someone violates it. In the following, we show that such an undesired outcome can be avoided by imposing some constraint by means of a derivation graph G.

Example 6. Take a non-flat 1-ABAF $D = (\mathcal{L}, \mathcal{R}_1, \mathcal{A}, \overline{})$ where $\mathcal{R}_1$ corresponds to the set of regulative rules. We recall the assumptions $\mathcal{A} = \{a, b\}$ as follows:

$$a = \text{'Bob commits a murder'} \qquad b = \text{'Bob ought not to commit murder'}$$

Moreover, we consider a language $\mathcal{L} = \{a, b, p, q\}$ with $q = \overline{b}$, containing the following claims:

$$p = \text{'Bob ought to murder gently'} \qquad q = \text{'Bob ought to commit murder'}$$

We have only one rule-set $\mathcal{R}_1$, which contains the following regulative rules:

$$p \leftarrow a \qquad\qquad q \leftarrow p \qquad\qquad b \leftarrow$$

Given that $q = \overline{b}$, we observe that $\{a\}$ attacks $\{b\}$. Moreover, $\{a, b\}$ is not a (closed) admissible set. Hence the contrary-to-duty paradox: the assumptions that murdering is forbidden and that someone murders are mutually exclusive and their union is not conflict-free. For this example, not every derivation graph will prevent the paradox to arise. Consider the following:

G_1 puts no restriction on deductions, G_2 restricts deductions to using only one rule, and G_3 restricts deductions to using only two rules per branch. In our example both G_1 and G_3 do not prohibit any of the possible deductions, while G_2 does and in fact is the only graph which prevents the paradox. In fact, by forbidding the iteration for rules, it blocks the derivation of $\bar{b}$ from the assumption a. Indeed, we get $\{a\} \nvdash_G^{\{p\leftarrow a,\bar{b}\leftarrow p\}} \bar{b}$. Therefore, $\{a\}$ does not G-attack $\{b\}$ and the assumption set $\{a,b\}$ is an admissible set.   ◇

In this example, an instance of a contrary-to-duty paradox is easily formalised in non-flat 1-ABA and solved through some constraints imposed by the chosen derivation graph.

As for paradoxes, the use of constraints could as well prevent fallacies of normative reasoning to occur. Consider the following situation comprising regulative and constitutive norms:

Example 7 (adapted from [31, *Example 3]).* Our protagonist Alice has been accepted to a study program with payment obligations. Every student whose application has been accepted counts as eligible student (constitutive norm). Moreover, every eligible student must pay their tuition fee (regulative norm) and every student who pays their tuition fee counts as a self-funding student (constitutive norm). We can derive that Alice must pay her tuition fee (since she is an eligible student), and hence she counts as a self-funding student.

However, Alice has furthermore received a study grant which means that she is not a self-funding student after all. Hence we derive a counter-intuitive conflict, deducing Alice to be both self-funding and have received a grant.   ◇

In the above example, we end up fallaciously deducing a contradiction from our assumptions. The underlying issue is that the application of constitutive rules after regulative ones may produce fallacious conclusions. This type of fallacy, called *institutional wishful thinking* was introduced in [24]. The undesired situation in Example 7 could be circumvented by preventing the application of the rule *"tuition fee → self-funding student"* after the rule *"eligible student → tuition fee"*. In the context of formal argumentation, similar issues have been addressed in recent works, based on an ASPIC-like formalism [24,25,31,35]. Formally, we can represent such a scenario as follows:

Example 8. We construct a 2-ABAF $D = (\mathcal{L}, \mathcal{R}_1, \mathcal{R}_2, \mathcal{A}, \overline{})$ where $\mathcal{R}_1$ and $\mathcal{R}_2$ contain our constitutive and regulative rules, respectively. Following Example 7, we have assumptions a ('Alice has been accepted'), b ('Alice received a grant') and c ('Alice is a self-funding student'), their contraries, and the claims p ('Alice is an eligible student') and q ('Alice ought to pay her tuition fee'). Moreover, $\mathcal{R}_1$ and $\mathcal{R}_2$ contain constitutive and regulative rules respectively:

$$\mathcal{R}_1 : p \leftarrow a \quad c \leftarrow q \quad \bar{c} \leftarrow b \qquad \mathcal{R}_2 : q \leftarrow p$$

Hence, the conflicting arguments $\{b\} \vdash^{\{\bar{c}\leftarrow b\}} \bar{c}$ and $\{a\} \vdash^{\{p\leftarrow a,q\leftarrow p,c\leftarrow q\}} c$ can be constructed. We conclude that $\{b\}$ attacks $\{a,c\}$. This represents a normative conflict arising from the assumption-set $\{a,b\}$: given the closeness requirement, assuming a forces us to take c as well and b to accept $\bar{c}$. However, there should not be any conflict between a student being accepted and receiving a grant. By prohibiting the application of constitutive rules in the scope of regulative ones, $\bar{c}$ is no longer derived from the assumption b. We consider the derivation graph G:

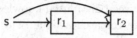

Since $(\mathsf{r}_2, \mathsf{r}_1) \notin E(G)$, we get $\{a\} \not\vdash_G^{\{p \leftarrow a, q \leftarrow p, c \leftarrow q\}} c$. Therefore, $\{b\}$ does no longer G-attack $\{a, c\}$, making $\{a, b\}$ a (closed) admissible set.   ◇

The examples above suggest that conflict resolution for normative reasoning requires the full expressiveness of non-flat n-ABA. Multiple kinds of inference rules can be distinguished and expressed, in particular conditional obligations and constitutive norms. This way, a graph-based constraint can be chosen in order to avoid paradoxes and fallacies in the deduction process.

7   Concluding Remarks

This work introduces a generalisation of assumption-based argumentation with multiple rule-sets together with some formal restrictions on its deductive machinery. These constraints, called *derivation graphs*, regulate the argument construction process from the underlying knowledge base, thereby limiting the procedure for its instantiation into an argumentation framework. Moreover, for the class of separated n-ABA frameworks we showed that this process reduces to eliminating rules from the knowledge base while letting the argument construction unconstrained. We presented an encoding of our formalism in ASP, building up on the work presented in [22]. Finally, we discussed the possibility to capture instances of normative reasoning in assumption-based argumentation, using the full expressive power of non-flat ABA to represent and reason about normative conflicts and moral dilemmas.

Within the broader field of knowledge representation and reasoning, related work can be found in the literature on multi-context systems [7], where reasoning in performed over a distributed knowledge base in which different modules (contexts) are linked together. In particular, in [13,20] possible conflicts arising from the interaction of contexts are taken into consideration. In the area of formal argumentation, another notion of modularity has been investigated at the abstract level, with a focus on splitting techniques for AFs [2,3] and ADFs [26] as well as on a principle-based analysis of argumentation semantics [1,23]. However, by exploiting the instantiation procedure of ABA, our approach combines the possibility of expressing (constrained) interactions among modules of a knowledge base with the possibility to perform reasoning at the abstract level on the corresponding argumentation framework.

Our work offers promising applications in relation to normative reasoning [24] and for distributed knowledge systems [14]. In the context of multi-agent settings, agents may be able to join forces to find solutions that elude each of them individually. This idea lies at the bottom of the study of *distributed knowledge* and *distributed belief* [14,21,38]. The proposed generalisation of ABA allows for constraints in the derivations which renders it a promising formalism to capture multi-agent scenarios with distributed knowledge among agents. We consider studies on the connection between distibuted knowledge systems and constraints in ABA as an exciting future research avenue. The derivation constraints presented in the paper successfully capture restrictions on the information flow among agents and avoid some paradoxes and fallacies in the domain of normative reasoning. While this allows to avoid undesired conclusions as shown in Examples 1, 6 and 8, such result is achieved at the expense of the deductive power of the ABA formalism. As a general direction for future research we want to investigate different kinds of reasoning constraints that minimise this loss. In doing so, we aim at positioning our formalism with respect to related frameworks: the work by Pigozzi and Van der Torre on constitutive and regulative norms in argumentation [31]; modular ABA [12] as it was proposed in connection with normative reasoning; Deontic ASP [19] encoding input/output logics. Although we restricted our studies on flat ABAFs so far, we anticipate that the full expressiveness of non-flat ABAFs may be needed to capture general instances of normative reasoning (cf. Example 6). Equipping non-flat ABAFs with derivation graphs might pose additional challenges since non-flat ABAFs require certain closure conditions on the set of acceptable assumptions. In addition, it would be interesting to investigate how our approach based on derivation constraints could be applied to other structured argumentation formalisms, like Defeasible Logic Programming (DeLP) [18], logic-based argumentation [4] and ASPIC+ [28].

Acknowledgments. The authors thank the reviewers for their helpful comments to improve the original version of this paper. This research has been supported by Vienna Science and Technology Fund (WWTF) through project ICT19-065 and by the European Research Council (ERC) under the European Union's Horizon 2020 research and innovation programme (grant agreement No. 101034440).

References

1. Baroni, P., Cerutti, F., Giacomin, M.: Decomposing semantics in abstract argumentation. FLAP **10**(3), 341–392 (2023). https://www.collegepublications.co.uk/downloads/ifcolog00059.pdf
2. Baumann, R.: Splitting an argumentation framework. In: Delgrande, J.P., Faber, W. (eds.) LPNMR 2011. LNCS (LNAI), vol. 6645, pp. 40–53. Springer, Heidelberg (2011). https://doi.org/10.1007/978-3-642-20895-9_6
3. Baumann, R., Brewka, G., Dvořák, W., Woltran, S.: Parameterized splitting: a simple modification-based approach. In: Erdem, E., Lee, J., Lierler, Y., Pearce, D. (eds.) Correct Reasoning. LNCS, vol. 7265, pp. 57–71. Springer, Heidelberg (2012). https://doi.org/10.1007/978-3-642-30743-0_5
4. Besnard, P., Hunter, A.: A logic-based theory of deductive arguments. Artif. Intell. **128**(1–2), 203–235 (2001). https://doi.org/10.1016/S0004-3702(01)00071-6
5. Bondarenko, A., Dung, P.M., Kowalski, R.A., Toni, F.: An abstract, argumentation-theoretic approach to default reasoning. Artif. Intell. **93**, 63–101 (1997). https://doi.org/10.1016/S0004-3702(97)00015-5

6. Bondarenko, A., Toni, F., Kowalski, R.A.: An assumption-based framework for non-monotonic reasoning. In: Pereira, L.M., Nerode, A. (eds.) Logic Programming and Non-monotonic Reasoning, Proceedings of the Second International Workshop, Lisbon, Portugal, June 1993, pp. 171–189. MIT Press (1993)

7. Brewka, G., Eiter, T.: Equilibria in heterogeneous nonmonotonic multi-context systems. In: Proceedings of the Twenty-Second AAAI Conference on Artificial Intelligence, 22–26 July 2007, Vancouver, British Columbia, Canada, pp. 385–390. AAAI Press (2007). http://www.aaai.org/Library/AAAI/2007/aaai07-060.php

8. Caminada, M., Modgil, S., Oren, N.: Preferences and unrestricted rebut. In: Parsons, S., Oren, N., Reed, C., Cerutti, F. (eds.) Computational Models of Argument - Proceedings of COMMA 2014, Atholl Palace Hotel, Scottish Highlands, UK, 9–12 September 2014. Frontiers in Artificial Intelligence and Applications, vol. 266, pp. 209–220. IOS Press (2014). https://doi.org/10.3233/978-1-61499-436-7-209

9. Cyras, K., Fan, X., Schulz, C., Toni, F.: Assumption-based argumentation: disputes, explanations, preferences. FLAP 4(8) (2017). http://www.collegepublications.co.uk/downloads/ifcolog00017.pdf

10. Cyras, K., Oliveira, T., Karamlou, A., Toni, F.: Assumption-based argumentation with preferences and goals for patient-centric reasoning with interacting clinical guidelines. Argument Comput. 12(2), 149–189 (2021). https://doi.org/10.3233/AAC-200523

11. Dung, P.M., Kowalski, R.A., Toni, F.: Assumption-based argumentation. In: Simari, G.R., Rahwan, I. (eds.) Argumentation in Artificial Intelligence, pp. 199–218. Springer, Boston (2009). https://doi.org/10.1007/978-0-387-98197-0_10

12. Dung, P.M., Thang, P.M.: Modular argumentation for modelling legal doctrines in common law of contract. Artif. Intell. Law 17(3), 167–182 (2009). https://doi.org/10.1007/s10506-009-9076-x

13. Eiter, T., Fink, M., Schüller, P., Weinzierl, A.: Finding explanations of inconsistency in multi-context systems. Artif. Intell. 216, 233–274 (2014). https://doi.org/10.1016/J.ARTINT.2014.07.008

14. Fagin, R., Halpern, J.Y., Moses, Y., Vardi, M.Y.: Reasoning About Knowledge. MIT Press (1995). https://doi.org/10.7551/MITPRESS/5803.001.0001

15. Fan, X.: On generating explainable plans with assumption-based argumentation. In: Miller, T., Oren, N., Sakurai, Y., Noda, I., Savarimuthu, B.T.R., Cao Son, T. (eds.) PRIMA 2018. LNCS (LNAI), vol. 11224, pp. 344–361. Springer, Cham (2018). https://doi.org/10.1007/978-3-030-03098-8_21

16. Fan, X., Toni, F., Mocanu, A., Williams, M.: Dialogical two-agent decision making with assumption-based argumentation. In: Bazzan, A.L.C., Huhns, M.N., Lomuscio, A., Scerri, P. (eds.) International conference on Autonomous Agents and Multi-Agent Systems, AAMAS 2014, Paris, France, 5–9 May 2014, pp. 533–540. IFAAMAS/ACM (2014). http://dl.acm.org/citation.cfm?id=2615818

17. Forrester, J.W.: Gentle murder, or the adverbial Samaritan. J. Philos. 81(4), 193–197 (1984)

18. García, A.J., Simari, G.R.: Defeasible logic programming: an argumentative approach. Theory Pract. Log. Program. 4(1–2), 95–138 (2004). https://doi.org/10.1017/S1471068403001674

19. Gonçalves, R., Alferes, J.J.: An embedding of input-output logic in deontic logic programs. In: Ågotnes, T., Broersen, J., Elgesem, D. (eds.) DEON 2012. LNCS (LNAI), vol. 7393, pp. 61–75. Springer, Heidelberg (2012). https://doi.org/10.1007/978-3-642-31570-1_5

20. Haque, H.M.U., Akhtar, S.M., Uddin, I.: Contextual defeasible reasoning framework for heterogeneous knowledge sources. Concurr. Comput. Pract. Exp. **35**(15) (2023). https://doi.org/10.1002/CPE.6446

21. Herzig, A., Lorini, E., Perrotin, E., Romero, F., Schwarzentruber, F.: A logic of explicit and implicit distributed belief. In: Giacomo, G.D., et al(eds.) ECAI 2020–24th European Conference on Artificial Intelligence, Santiago de Compostela, Spain, August 29 - September 8, 2020 - Including 10th Conference on Prestigious Applications of Artificial Intelligence (PAIS 2020). Frontiers in Artificial Intelligence and Applications, vol. 325, pp. 753–760. IOS Press (2020). https://doi.org/10.3233/FAIA200163

22. Lehtonen, T., Wallner, J.P., Järvisalo, M.: Declarative algorithms and complexity results for assumption-based argumentation. J. Artif. Intell. Res. **71**, 265–318 (2021). https://doi.org/10.1613/jair.1.12479

23. Liao, B.: Toward incremental computation of argumentation semantics: a decomposition-based approach. Ann. Math. Artif. Intell. **67**(3–4), 319–358 (2013). https://doi.org/10.1007/S10472-013-9364-8

24. Liao, B., Pardo, P., Slavkovik, M., van der Torre, L.: The jiminy advisor: moral agreements among stakeholders based on norms and argumentation. J. Artif. Intell. Res. **77**, 737–792 (2023). https://doi.org/10.1613/jair.1.14368

25. Liao, B., Slavkovik, M., van der Torre, L.W.N.: Building jiminy cricket: an architecture for moral agreements among stakeholders. CoRR abs/1812.04741 (2018). http://arxiv.org/abs/1812.04741

26. Linsbichler, T.: Splitting abstract dialectical frameworks. In: Parsons, S., Oren, N., Reed, C., Cerutti, F. (eds.) Computational Models of Argument - Proceedings of COMMA 2014, Atholl Palace Hotel, Scottish Highlands, UK, 9–12 September 2014. Frontiers in Artificial Intelligence and Applications, vol. 266, pp. 357–368. IOS Press (2014). https://doi.org/10.3233/978-1-61499-436-7-357

27. Makinson, D., van der Torre, L.W.N.: Input/output logics. J. Philos. Log. **29**(4), 383–408 (2000). https://doi.org/10.1023/A:1004748624537

28. Modgil, S., Prakken, H.: A general account of argumentation with preferences. Artif. Intell. **195**, 361–397 (2013). https://doi.org/10.1016/j.artint.2012.10.008

29. Modgil, S., Prakken, H.: The ASPIC$^+$ framework for structured argumentation: a tutorial. Argument Comput. **5**(1), 31–62 (2014). https://doi.org/10.1080/19462166.2013.869766

30. Modgil, S., Prakken, H.: Abstract rule-based argumentation. FLAP **4**(8) (2017). http://www.collegepublications.co.uk/downloads/ifcolog00017.pdf

31. Pigozzi, G., van der Torre, L.: Arguing about constitutive and regulative norms. J. Appl. Non Class. Logics **28**(2–3), 189–217 (2018). https://doi.org/10.1080/11663081.2018.1487242

32. Prakken, H.: An abstract framework for argumentation with structured arguments. Argument Comput. **1**(2), 93–124 (2010). https://doi.org/10.1080/19462160903564592

33. Rahwan, I.: Guest editorial: argumentation in multi-agent systems. Auton. Agents Multi Agent Syst. **11**(2), 115–125 (2005). https://doi.org/10.1007/s10458-005-3079-0

34. Searle, J.R.: Speech Acts: An Essay in the Philosophy of Language. Cambridge University Press, Cambridge (1969)

35. Sun, X., van der Torre, L.: Combining constitutive and regulative norms in input/output logic. In: Cariani, F., Grossi, D., Meheus, J., Parent, X. (eds.) DEON 2014. LNCS (LNAI), vol. 8554, pp. 241–257. Springer, Cham (2014). https://doi.org/10.1007/978-3-319-08615-6_18

36. von Wright, G.H.: Deontic logic. Mind **60**(237), 1–15 (1951). https://doi.org/10. 1093/mind/lx.237.1
37. Xie, J., Liu, C.C.: Multi-agent systems and their applications. J. Int. Council Electr. Eng. **7**(1), 188–197 (2017)
38. Ågotnes, T., Wáng, Y.N.: Resolving distributed knowledge. Artif. Intell. **252**, 1–21 (2017). https://doi.org/10.1016/j.artint.2017.07.002, https://www.sciencedirect. com/science/article/pii/S0004370217300759

Answer Set Programming

Model-Based Diagnosis with ASP for Non-groundable Domains

Moritz Bayerkuhnlein[1]([✉]) [ID] and Diedrich Wolter[2] [ID]

[1] University of Bamberg, Bamberg, Germany
moritz.bayerkuhnlein@uni-bamberg.de
[2] University of Lübeck, Lübeck, Germany
diedrich.wolter@uni-luebeck.de

Abstract. Model-based diagnosis is a technique for identifying malfunctioning components in systems. While it has successfully been applied to systems such as digital circuits, this paper aims to extend applicability to systems such as programs that process values from large domains, for example, term structures. In these cases, especially when multiple components may be faulty, it is challenging to identify a diagnosis that provides a consistent model with respect to the specified domain. This paper presents an Answer-Set Programming (ASP) based method for computing such diagnoses. We are particularly interested in functional circuits over domains of values, such as rational numbers and inductive data types, to diagnose faults in programming assignments in order to advance intelligent tutoring systems. This article shows how a consistent diagnosis, justified by intermediate values, can be achieved efficiently using ASP. Additionally, an adaption to Constraint Answer Set Programming with s(CASP) is presented that avoids grounding, allowing domain sizes to be handled that are too large to be grounded.

Keywords: Model-based Diagnosis · Abductive Reasoning

1 Introduction

Diagnosis is the process of identifying the cause of a fault in a system. Model-based reasoning can be used to identify a group of components that are not in line with the system's observed behaviour. Such components are said to be abnormal w.r.t. their specified behaviour [24]. Without an estimated likelihood for a component to fail, it becomes difficult to select one diagnosis from a set of plausible alternatives. In addition, the candidate set can be too large to handle when multiple faults may occur [18]. By restricting the set of possible causes through task-specific modelling, the set of possible diagnoses may be reduced [25].

In this paper, we propose a task-independent method to reduce the number of possible diagnoses in multi-valued domains by improving an Answer-Set Programming (ASP) encoding of Model-Based Diagnosis. We introduce a step that ensures a diagnosis to be consistent with the observations and to be justified by

© The Author(s), under exclusive license to Springer Nature Switzerland AG 2024
A. Meier and M. Ortiz (Eds.): FoIKS 2024, LNCS 14589, pp. 363–380, 2024.
https://doi.org/10.1007/978-3-031-56940-1_20

a possible internal state of the system. A possible internal state is reconstructed in the form of intermediate values within the given system, i.e., possible input and output values of system components that may either function correctly or abnormally.

Explicit reasoning about values introduced by abnormal components has the immediate benefit of providing a *fault model of impossibility* [10] for values outside the specified domain. Additionally, this allows for further reasoning about the possible causes of a fault. In this way, the encoding presented here reduces the candidate set of diagnoses and improves on previous approaches with respect to the quality of the diagnosis.

Finding sets of intermediate values that are consistent with the observed behaviour is computationally expensive and becomes more difficult with large domain sizes. We first develop an Answer Set Programming (ASP) [3] encoding that finds a consistent model already for small domain sizes but suffers from grounding larger domains. We then extend the model to a Constraint Answer Set Programming (CASP) approach that avoids grounding the domain values and becomes applicable to dense domains such as rational numbers and inductive data types [2]. This allows us to use model-based diagnosis with a high level of abstraction, for example, to diagnose program faults based on a representation of the program's abstract internal state.

In summary, the contributions of this paper are as follows:

- proposal of a diagnosis method that is consistent with a value-based view on the system;
- efficiency of ASP-based diagnosis is increased over the framework proposed in [28], especially for multi-valued domains;
- a CASP variant of the encoding is presented that avoids grounding for otherwise non-groundable dense domains, such as rational numbers or inductive data types.

2   Preliminaries

2.1   Model-Based Diagnosis

There are two dominant logical frameworks of model-based diagnosis, the *consistency-based* and *abductive* approaches [6]. Both approaches consider systems composed of individual *components* that either adhere to their specified behaviour (normal behaviour) or deviate from it (abnormal behaviour). Diagnosis is applied when the observed system behaviour deviates from the specified behaviour. The consistency-based approach is based on the idea of finding a set of components that, when assumed to be *abnormal*, re-establish a consistent system model. Abductive approaches use a *strong fault model* that explicitly models any faulty behaviour.

Following Reiter's foundational work on diagnosis [24] we define:

Definition 1 (Diagnosis Problem Instance). A diagnosis problem instance consists of a triple, $\langle SD, OBS, COMP \rangle$ where:

- system description (SD), specifying the behaviour of the systems components and their structure;
- a set of observations (OBS) on the system as facts;
- a set of constants c_i, representing the components (COMP).

Throughout this paper we specify SD as predicates of first-order logic, representing the relation of input and output for a functional component c of the form $b(c, i_1, \ldots, i_n, o_1, \ldots, o_m)$. Connections between components are relations between their ports, following a component connection model. Similarly, OBS are modeled as concrete values v of the domain of interest, related to a terminal x where the said value was observed, $value(x, v)$.

Diagnosis identifies *abnormal* components. In the *strong fault model*, abnormality is categorized by distinct fault models K using $ab(c_i, K)$. Thus observations are seen as logical consequences of the assumed abnormalities w.r.t. the explanatory fault models. In the *weak fault model*, abnormal behaviour is represented by $ab(c_i)$; if true, any behaviour of the flawed component c_i is feasible.

The system model SD describes the normal behaviour of component, constraints for components assumed to behave abnormally will be suspended [7].

Definition 2 (Consistency-Based Diagnosis Problem). *Given a diagnosis problem instance* $\langle SD, OBS, COMP \rangle$*, the consistency-based problem is to compute all minimal sets* $\Delta \subseteq COMP$ *of faulty components such that expression 1 is consistent.*

$$SD \cup OBS \cup \{ab(c) \mid c \in \Delta\} \cup \{\neg ab(c) \mid c \in COMP \setminus \Delta\} \qquad (1)$$

2.2 Answer Set Programming

Answer Set Programming (ASP) is a declarative programming paradigm based on the stable model semantics of logic programs. The effectiveness of this approach is demonstrated by its ability to solve difficult search problems quickly and accurately, its capacity for non-monotonic reasoning, and its conciseness in programming [3]. A program Π in ASP consists of *rules*

$$a_1 \vee \cdots \vee a_l \leftarrow a_{l+1}, \ldots, a_m, \neg a_{m+1}, \ldots, \neg a_n.$$

With $l, m, n \in \mathcal{N}$ such that $l \leq m \leq n$, each a_i is a *atom* or predicate $p(t_1, \ldots, t_n)$, with predicate name p and terms t_i.

In a process called *grounding*, a version of Π is computed in which all variables have been replaced by constant symbols, denoted $ground(\Pi)$. The domain of the constant symbols is implied by the symbols that appear in the program. A *rule* is a *fact* for some a if $a \leftarrow \top$. In ASP clauses of the form $\bot \leftarrow a_1, \ldots, a_m, \neg a_{m+1}, \ldots, \neg a_n$ are called *constraints* or *denials*, for clarity

```
c(×;△;∘). var(0..6).
edg(1,2). edg(4,5). edg(0,1). edg(0,2).
...

1 {lb(N,C) : c(C)} 1 ← var(N).
⊥ ← lb(N,C), lb(M,C), edg(N,M), c(C).
```

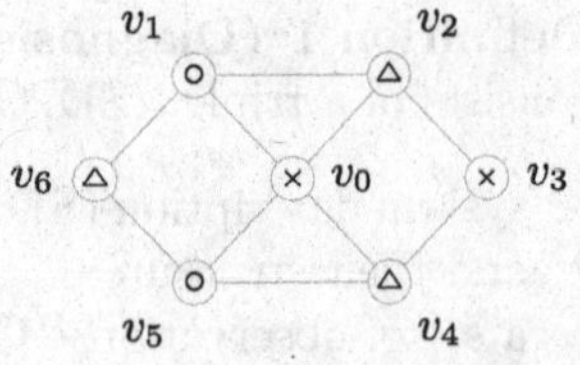

Fig. 1. Graph Coloring Problem and its ASP encoding

we will refer to this form as *global constraints*. A set of atoms is called an *interpretation* I. If $I \models \Pi$, I satisfying all the rules of Π, I is called a model. For more details we refer the reader to [3, 15].

The encodings presented in this paper rely on *choice* constructs, to select arbitrary values from a domain. We briefly illustrate the denials and choice constructs on a graph coloring problem.

For every node in the graph we have a variable v_i characterised by a predicate var/1 that can be assigned a color C from the set of colors c/1. The *choice* construct is used to select a label C for each node N, where the lower and upper bounds 1 guarantee exactly one color is selected for each variable. The *denial* is used to ensure that no two adjacent nodes have the same color. A stable model for the chosen labels is shown in Fig. 1.

Goal-Directed Constrained Answer Set Programming

Constraint Answer Set Programming is an extension to goal-directed ASP, which avoids the grounding phase by computing only *partial stable models* relevant to a *query* posed. Each *partial stable model* is a subset of a stable model that makes all non-negated atoms true, negated atoms non-provable, and satisfies all constraints, but only for atoms relevant to the *query*. Model generation is top-down, using *constructive negation* instead of Prolog's *negation as failure* [5], conversely the grounding phase is omitted [2, 22].

Constraint incorporation allows the search to gain efficiency by pruning parts of the search space that would cause a violation of the constraints. In particular, it allows continuous domains to be modeled and reasoning about *unsafe variables*, which are typically not allowed in conventional ASP systems due to grounding [1]. These restrictions on variables are also reflected in the answer sets.

To generate solutions from a program Π s(CASP) constructs an extension of Π that contains rules that assert the complementary propositions for *constructive negation*, this program is called the *dual program*. [2]. Unlike conventional ASP, where the order in which the propositions are written is not relevant, for s(CASP), the order is essential for the efficiency of its goal-directed evaluation procedure.

Listing 1. Goal-Directed ASP Version of (Figure 1) Graph Coloring Problem

```
lb(N,C)  ←  c(C), var(N), not adj_color(N,C), not other(N,C).
other(N,C)  ←  C\=C2, lb(N,C2).

adj_color(N,C)  ←  edg(N,N2), lb(N2,C).

?- lb(0,V0), lb(1,V1), lb(2,V2), lb(3,V3), lb(4,V4),
   lb(5,V5), lb(6,V6).
```

Again consider graph coloring, where we want to find a coloring for a graph with 7 nodes. Listing 1 shows an s(CASP) version of the encoding from Listing 1. Most notably the query ?- is used to specify the goal that has to be fulfilled by a partial stable model. Instead of a generate-and-test approach, we use local constraint not adj_color/2 to state that an adjacent node N must not be colored with C. While the ASP solver labels lb/2, this local constraint reduces the search space already during generation. The choice construct for lb/2 in Fig. 1 is implemented with a loop using the other/2 rule, which ensures that each node is assigned exactly one color. Note that the rule other/2 uses an unsafe variable C. Disequality \ = in other/2 forces the solver to proof that all the other colors are explicitly stated as not being assigned to that particular variable, building a set of colors which then constrains the choices for lb/2. The resulting partial stable model only assigns values to variables occurring in the query.

The concepts used in the example of the graph coloring problem are build upon in the encodings for diagnosis presented in this paper.

3 Reasoning About Intermediate Values

A problem with the consistency-based approach is that suspending constraints allows diagnoses that, on closer inspection, are not plausible. Usually when a weak fault model is used, the output of an abnormal component has no restriction on the value that is assumed. Adding a constraint to the system description, which forces the diagnosis to be explicit about these values, circumvents that problem.

For example, consider a circuit consisting of multiplier components {M1, M2, M3} and adder components {A1, A2} as shown in Fig. 2, where the components perform operations on 4-bit integer values in the range 0 to 15. Clearly we have a system-wide physical restriction w.r.t. the values that can be produced. Ports A–E are the inputs, and ports F and G are the observable system outputs. Therefore the system calculates $F = (A \cdot C) + (B \cdot D)$ and $G = (B \cdot D) + (C \cdot E)$. The inputs shown in Fig. 2 indicate a discrepancy, since $G = 10$ differs from the expected value $(3 \cdot 2) + (1 \cdot 2) = 8$.

The diagnosis generated by a consistency-based approach, without a constraint on physical plausability according to [28] gives the set of diagnoses Δ^* = {{M3}, {A2}, {M2, A1}, {M1, M2}}, i.e., four possible minimal sets of abnormal components. If we consider the diagnosis system as a system of equations

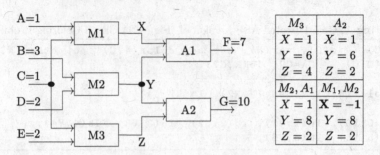

Fig. 2. Functional circuit on a domain of [0,15] (4-bit), diagnosed sets of components and their context as the corresponding values of the variables.

and the abnormal components output X, Y as free variables, we obtain the equations $X + Y = 7$ and $Y + 2 = 10$, so $X + 8 = 7$, which have no solution in the domain of non-negative 4-bit integers.

We can therefore conclude that diagnosis {M1, M2} is not a good explanation for the observed failure, as the values needed to justify that diagnosis are physically impossible.

Ruling out implausible diagnoses using physical impossibility as an alternative to fault models has been attempted for common sense reasoning about small domains and physical systems [10,25]. When modeling and reasoning about systems, we can identify quantities and quantity spaces as domains of values. Here, we use the presence of domains or quantities as a universal constraint to what is physically possible.

We propose to extend the system descriptions by requiring the diagnosis to be consistent with the domain values of the system. A diagnosis also states which values support the diagnosis based on the unobserved values that are passed between components. More formally, we are interested in a stable and exact numerical solution for ports in the system, essentially determining a satisfying model or context C such that:

$$C \models \forall p. (\text{port}(p) \Rightarrow \exists v.\text{value}(p, v) \land \text{domain}(v)) \tag{2}$$

Solving for this context can be phrased as a Constraint Satisfaction Problem (CSP) where an assignment of variables from a finite domain is searched, in our case the context C. The connections between components form variables of a CSP, searching for intermediate values thus enforces local consistencies. Where *node consistency* restricts the variables to only include the specified domain in their valuations [9]. The resulting model provides further qualitative information about the system, the process of obtaining these models is used by constraint programming is referred to as *constructive abduction* [21]. In addition to the use to eliminate inconsistent diagnoses, these models shall aid in characterization of a diagnosis.

Explicit reasoning about hidden values was already done in the later General Diagnostic Engine (GDE) [8]. However, the purpose of this representation is to retain information about which components must be functional to support a value on a variable in order to detect conflicts. In the literature, integration of diagnosis and CSP solving has been done on problems such as spreadsheet debugging [16,29], where parts of spreadsheets are compiled into constraints, where relaxation constraints act as identification of faulty components. In the context of program debugging, using a model for a programming language and a constraint representation of test cases, a CSP is formulated from small snippets of source code that identify lines of code as faulty [27,29].

However, improved quality comes at the cost of computational complexity, since suitable values must be found for all intermediate values. This is particularly challenging when functions implemented by components are not reversible, such as $x * 0 = 0$, where x can be any domain value and suitable hidden input values must be searched for. When dealing with large domains, such as integers or terms, the search does not scale.

4   Diagnosis with Answer Set Programming

The use of logic programming as a framework for diagnosis is favorable in cases where there is a need for different system models because the focus is on the system model, abstracting from general diagnosis techniques. Component behaviour can be declared, using a simple but general implementation of Prolog, without the need for application-specific techniques [11]. There is already an ASP-based approach to model-based reasoning.

In [28] the system is represented as components and their interconnections. Simulation rules and integrity constraints prevent conflicting port values. Diagnoses are generated by searching for minimum-cardinality sets of abnormal components.

In the context of consistency-based diagnosis, Kuhlmann et al. [19] explore inconsistency measures for knowledge bases. They provide an ASP coding to find the minimum facts to remove for restoring consistency. Their approach distinguishes between hard and soft constraints in propositional knowledge bases. By treating component behaviours as soft constraints and interconnections as hard constraints, the method of Kuhlmann et al. can be used directly for diagnosis.

We follow the notation for defining functional circuits as component connection models given in [11], where each component has a type that determines its behaviour. Components are connected to their ports, where they pass values. A circuit is composed of different components, the types of components, the connections between them and the observed values. Components and ports are derived from the connections and types specified by the circuit. Figure 2 is modelled as shown in Listing 2.

Listing 2. Component-Connection Model Representation of Figure 2

```
1   type(m1, mult).        type(m2, mult).      type(m3, mult).
2   type(a1, plus).        type(a2, plus).
3   conn(a, in1(m1)).      conn(c, in2(m1)).
4   conn(b, in1(m2)).      conn(d, in2(m2)).
5   conn(c, in1(m3)).      conn(e, in2(m3)).
6   conn(out(m1),in1(a1)).
7   conn(out(m2),in2(a1)). conn(out(m2),in1(a2)).
8   conn(out(m3),in2(a2)).
9   conn(out(a1), f).         conn(out(a2), g).
10  val(a,1). val(b,3). val(c,1). val(d,2). val(e,2).
        val(f,7). val(g,10).
```

4.1 Encoding Based on Satisfaction

We briefly explain the concepts used in the ASP encoding shown in the Listing 3, which we refer to as the *Satisfy*-encoding. Conceptually, the search for models is controlled by selecting values for the internal ports of a system.

To reason about the values that could exist in a circuit behaving abnormally, we say that a diagnosis is consistent only if it can explain the observations by justifying them with values that are accepted by the correctly behaving components. Ports are seen as existentially quantified variables in a formula, where the assignment to ports is the justifying model. Since a component can implement a non-reversible function, ASP encoding uses a *choice* operation and builds models by choosing a single satisfying value among options within the domain (line 6). The variable assignments must be the same for all connected ports, referred to as global constraints (lines 8 and 9). Each component can be abnormal or not, again realised using a choice operation, allowing for abductive inference (line 11).

Multi-shot ASP Diagnosis. Following Reiter's idea of parsimony [24], we search for minimal diagnoses. Sets generated by the diagnosis approach must be subset minimal, such that within the set there is no diagnosis which is a superset 'of another. To this end the number of components allowed to be abnormal is limited by the number $N = 0, 1, \ldots,$ (lines 11 and 12), which increases over multiple solving cicles, so that the smallest set of abnormal components that explains the observations, the cardinality minimal diagnosis, is found first. A model found by ASP is a conjunction of abnormality predicates ab, yielding a diagnosis Δ.

Multi-shot ASP solvers such as `clingo` can perform multiple searches on different cardinalities efficiently and without additional grounding overhead [12]. Solvers are instructed to search for a set cardinality N of abnormal components. Excluding the found diagnoses for cardinality N in the following iteration where $N + 1$ abnormal components are searched to exclude supersets [28].

Listing 3. ASP encoding for reasoning about intermediate Values

```
1   comp(C) ← type(C,T).
2   port(P) ← conn(P,P2).
3   port(P) ← conn(P1,P).
4
5   dom(0..200). %set domain here
6   1{val(P,V): dom(V)}1 ← port(P).
7
8   ⊥ ← conn(P1,P2),val(P1,V),val(P2,W),V!=W.
9
10  {ab(C)} ← comp(C).
11  no_ab(N) ← N = #count { C : ab(C) }.
12  ⊥ ← not no_ab(1). %set cardinality here
13
14  tuple(plus,X,Y,X+Y) ← dom(X+Y),dom(X),dom(Y).
15  tuple(mult,X,Y,X*Y) ← dom(X*Y),dom(X),dom(Y).
16
17  satisfied(C) ← val(in1(C),IN1), val(in2(C),IN2),
            val(out(C),OUT), tuple(T,IN1,IN2,OUT), type(C,T).
18  satisfied(C) ← comp(C), ab(C).
19  ⊥ ← not satisfied(C), type(C,T).
```

When only minimal cardinality diagnosis is required, Answer Set Optimization (ASO) provides an alternative by minimizing the number of abnormal components through objective functions or preferences.

The notion of consistency in terms of a diagnosis used in this encoding is identical to that of Definition 1. System behaviour is encoded as the specification of correct behaviour per component type. For example, (lines 14 and 15) the component of an adder component plus is specified as input/output tuple connecting inputs X, Y to output X+Y. Each component must behave as specified (line 17) or be abnormal (line 18) for the condition satisfied to evaluate to true.

The answers found by the ASP solver represent the diagnosis as a set of ab/1 predicates with the specified cardinality. Starting from a cardinality of zero (no error), the minimal diagnosis is found first. A more detailed description of the underlying algorithm using multi-shot ASP solving can be found in [28].

Since the port/1 predicates now act as variables within a CSP, the resulting model also provides information about the conditions that triggered the erroneous behaviour on the supporting scenario that further characterises the behaviour. The resulting diagnosis is a subset of the consistency-based solutions produced by previous ASP-based methods. The results of the diagnosis that are inconsistent w.r.t. specified domain, are suppressed, as illustrated by the example in the previous section. Because diagnoses are determined iteratively and depend on the exclusion of previously identified subsets, the suppressed diagnosis cannot exclude potentially relevant diagnoses in subsequent iterations.

Proposition 1. *The ASP encoding consisting of Listing 3 computes the cardi-nality minimal consistent diagnosis w.r.t. the specified domain.*

Proof (Proof Sketch). Assume that the minimal diagnosis set Δ^* comprises sets of components $\Delta_1,...,\Delta_k$, where $\Delta_j = \{c_1, ...c_l\}$ such that $0 \leq |\Delta_j| \leq n$ with n being the total number of components. The trivial (non-minimal) solution $|\Delta_j| = n$ for which a satisfying assignment C can always be constructed. The diagnoses with minimal cardinality $|\Delta_j|$ form a set Δ^{min} such that $\Delta^{min} \subseteq \Delta^*$. For each value $i = 0, \ldots, n$ for which ASP cannot find a satisfying assignment C, i.e., intermediate values, no consistent model for $SD \cup OBS \cup \{ab(c) \mid c \in \Delta_j\}$ exists with $|\Delta_j| = i$. Therefore, no consistent diagnosis for cardinality i exists and hence the minimal cardinal diagnosis must be found first.

4.2   Results and Analysis

ASP has already been shown to be capable of diagnosing Boolean circuits [28]. Here, we are particularly interested in diagnosing systems with value ranges over finite domains.

ASP solvers rely on a grounding phase. This adds a new dimension of complexity to the diagnostic process, in addition to the number of components within a system, as the domain size increases. As the domain required to represent the values of a system becomes large, the ground program becomes too large to be used in practice.

Table 1 shows how the specified domain sizes 100, 300 and 500 affect the time taken by an ASP solver to perform the diagnosis using the respective encoding. *Simulate* refers to the encoding proposed by [28], the encoding proposed in this paper is called *Satisfy*, referring to whether consistency checks are performed on simulated values, or consistency satisfying assignments to variables are found. We also compare this with the GDE [8], which does not require grounding.

The polycircuits with layers of alternating multiplier and adder components are identified by their naming scheme, where 4_2 stands for a circuit where the first layer has 4 components and the layer immediately before the output has 2 components. The intermediate layers are decreasing in the number of components. Errors are injected into random components by adding a random number in the range -5 to 5 to their outputs, staying within domain boundaries. The measurements in Table 1 are the median of the time taken to find a diagnosis. All measurements were performed using ASP Solver *clingo* version 5.5.2 with default settings on 32 x Intel(R) Xeon(R) Gold 6334 CPUs, each running at 3.60 GHz, distributed across 2 sockets. The server was equipped with 16 modules of 32 GB DDR-4 memory.

These circuits have the property of requiring domains that grow as the number of layers increases because non-negative numbers are added or multiplied. As a result, ASP techniques cannot find the desired solution if the required domain

Table 1. Comparing required domain size (0–100, 300, 500) for correct solving of single and double fault scenarios with total time to diagnosis for polycircuits. Simulation-encoding given by [28], Satisfy-encoding presented here and GDE from [8]. Total time (median) in seconds. Circuits ordered by total component count.

circ	Simulate-encoding						Satisfy-encoding [this paper]						GDE	
	single			double			single			double			single	double
	100	300	500	100	300	500	100	300	500	100	300	500	1500	1500
3_2	0.43	5.14	12.93	0.32	3.39	13.08	0.34	3.16	9.32	0.22	2.19	8.51	0.07	0.07
4_3	0.50	5.65	14.85	0.32	3.98	15.06	0.38	4.12	13.46	0.28	3.09	12.35	0.08	0.09
4_2	0.90	8.71	22.64	0.14	8.49	18.72	0.57	4.52	10.61	0.43	4.04	11.17	0.17	0.16
5_3	0.60	5.71	18.01	0.14	9.10	>30	0.69	6.14	17.23	0.54	4.98	15.40	2.12	2.08
5_2	1.78	15.23	>30	0.15	14.12	>30	0.89	8.93	25.86	0.69	13.08	>30	28.84	13.95
6_3	1.60	19.18	>30	0.14	13.30	>30	0.98	7.85	>30	0.91	9.11	18.57	>30	>30
7_4	2.04	21.96	>30	0.14	>30	>30	1.56	11.3	>30	1.11	11.27	>30	>30	>30

boundaries and specified domain boundaries do not match. Measurements that meet the required domain limits are highlighted in Table 1. The *Simulate* encoding indicates success because it does not detect violations when simulating values outside the domain. Conversely, the *Satisfy* encoding terminates without a consistent model and diagnosis due to an insufficiently specified range of values.

However, the time spent grounding and starting a futile solution attempt increases with domain size. A comparison with the classical GDE approach shows that it performs well on small circuits regardless of domain size, but does not scale to multi-layer polycircuits.

5   Diagnosis in Non-groundable Domains

Grounding large domains is not feasible for ASP grounders such as gringo [13]. The initial grounding phase and the combinatorial explosion when grounding, for example, the domain of arbitrary data structures such as lists, or values on a fine-grained, possibly continuous scale, would be intractable.

However, since the information relevant for diagnosis depends on the given circuit and the observations, the relevant part of the domain is bounded and can be grounded if necessary. The idea is to extend the subset of domain values to be considered by ASP whenever the subset considered so far does not allow a consistent model to be determined. For this purpose we use Constraint Answer Set Programming [2]. We adapt[1] the logical model presented in the previous section to constraint answer set programming using s(CASP) [14].

---

[1] s(CASP) does not yet fully implement the ASP Core 2 language standard, therefore, a direct translation is not always possible [4].

Listing 4. s(CASP) Diagnosis with intermediate Values

```
1   abnormals([],[]).
2   abnormals([C|T], T2) ← ok(C), abnormals(T,T2).
3   abnormals([C|T], [C|T2]) ← ab(C), abnormals(T,T2).
4
5   ab(C) ← not ok(C).
6   ok(C) ← not ab(C).
7
8   lstlength([], 0).
9   lstlength([_|List], Len) ← Len #= Len0+1, Len0 #>= 0,
10      lstlength(List, Len0).
11
12  not_sub([X|Xs],[]).
13  not_sub([E|Xs],[E|Ys]) ← not_sub(Xs,Ys).
14  not_sub([X|Xs],[Y|Ys]) ← X \= Y, not_subs([X|Xs],Ys).
15
16  satisfied(ID,plus,X,Y,OUT) ←OUT #= X+Y.
17  satisfied(ID,mult,X,Y,OUT) ←OUT #= X*Y.
18  satisfied(ID,_,X,Y,OUT) ← ab(ID).
```

5.1   Goal-Directed Constraint ASP

For example, assuming that most components function correctly and only a few are abnormal, we want to encode this information as a *default* when the solver constructs the diagnosis.

Therefore, in the s(CASP) model shown in Listing 4 the first case represents the correct functioning of a considered component as default, i.e., not abnormal, modelled by the predicate ok/1, which the solver should consider first (e.g. line 2,3).

s(CASP) does not have the syntactic sugar of the choice operator we used in the ASP encoding in Listing 3. One can rewrite the line as the loop in lines 5 and 6 to make the abnormal predicate abducible [14]. This simulates the ASP version, distinguishing between worlds where a component is either abnormal or not. The solver will however explicitly represent the negative atoms during solving and list them in the partial answer sets (e.g., { comp(a1), ab(a1), not ok(a1), ...}).

As a result of not grounding, the encoding can work with lists, which can be used as substitutes for the missing aggregate rules such as #count. In the case of checking whether one diagnosis is a subset of another, the implementation of the dual ab, ok bypasses the extensive equality checks otherwise required for constructive negation [14].

The *satisfied* property is encoded directly by the predicates that define the behaviour. Unlike conventional ASP encoding, there is no need to ground the variables within the clause by binding them to ports or connections. Instead, the variables representing ports and their constraints are managed directly within the solver.

Listing 5. s(CASP) Example Query

```
1  ?- Components = [m1,m2,m3,a1,a2], length(Diagnosis, 1),
2     %not_sub([a1],Diagnosis), not_sub([m1],Diagnosis),
3     listab(Components, Diagnosis),
4     A#= 1,B#= 3,C#=1, D#=2, E#=2,  G#=7, H#=10,
5     satisfied(m1, mult, A, C, X),
6     satisfied(m2, mult, B, D, Y),
7     satisfied(m3, mult, C, E, Z),
8     satisfied(a1, plus, X, Y, G),
9     satisfied(a2, plus, Y, Z, H).
```

In particular, this encoding avoids global constraints and reformulates them as goals in the query of Listing 5. For example, instead of searching for a model where there is no component such that its behaviour constraints are unsatisfied, we query for the goal that every component's behaviour constraints are satisfied.

s(CASP) does not yet support ASO, to the same degree as solvers like `clingo`. We can however rely on the same iterative approach (see Sect. 4.1) by posting constraints in the query. In this case, incremental diagnosis approach is implemented using lists of `lstlength(D, N)`, where N represents the expected number of abnormal components.

5.2 Results and Analysis

The query shown in Listing 5 yields models equivalent to those shown in Fig. 2. Notice how this also yields a model model where `Diagnosis = [m1,m2]` yet including the negative number X = -1 as an intermediate value. Natively s(CASP) interfaces with $CLP(\mathcal{R})$, which allows the efficient reasoning about numerical constraints, also over rational numbers. We analyze the performance over infinite domains using the same polycircuit examples as in the finite-domain scenario. There are some caveats that must be considered when applying diagnoses to dense domains, since only models using the finite domain can be acceptable answers in direct comparison with the ASP-based models. However, the intermediate values generated by s(CASP) can be negative or rational, since the domain no longer needs to be finite. But since these values are explicitly stated to justify the diagnosis, they can be filtered[2].

For evaluation, therefore, we only consider diagnoses of minimal cardinality. Figure 3 shows the time required until all single fault diagnoses were found for the polycircuits, exclusively searching for diagnoses of cardinality 1. Independent of the domain of the observed values, the time required for diagnosis is comparatively low rarely going beyond a couple of seconds.

---

[2] Since s(CASP) provides the option to interface with alternative constraint solvers where an integer constraint solver might be an alternative.

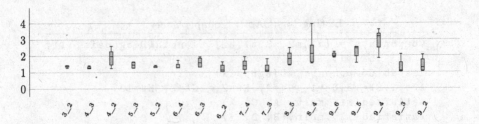

Fig. 3. Time (seconds) for minimal diagnosis with maximal cardinality of 1 for circuits with 1 faulty component.

6   Diagnosis with Domains of Structures

To further illustrate the benefit of representing large domains in consistency-based diagnosis, consider an application of model-based diagnosis in the context of automated feedback generation for programming assignments where it has been argued that providing feedback that singles out faults can be helpful to a learner [17].

An intuitive approach to modelling a computational system and diagnosing potential faults is to consider an abstract form of the data representation used, representing how data is constructed and modified, rather than how it is stored in memory. For example, we use a term such as `create_stack(3)` to represent an empty stack of capacity 3, rather than describing the memory layout. Model-based reasoning can then be used to explain which methods fail and under what conditions the failure occurs.

Abstract structures lack direct observability; their data is revealed by observer operations, such as testing the emptiness of a stack and reading the Boolean result. Inferences about the content of a structure rely on these observations. Observer functions are not injective; they map an output to an infinite domain of possible structures. For example, the input set for `is_empty`, which examines stack emptiness, includes all non-empty stacks if `is_empty` returns false. Next, the inherently large domain of structures leads to a combinatorial explosion when trying to list all instances of a given size - like stacks with N elements. Representing *faulty* structures further expands the domain. Consider binary search trees, for example. By specification, each element within the structure is unique, and the tree arranges elements in its subtrees from left to right. However, faulty components for manipulating a binary search tree can violate the order or introduce duplicates. To diagnose systems containing such components, it is necessary to consider arbitrary tree structures, not just binary search trees.

Listing 6. Stack type defined as a tuple and the list of elements, and its operations as predicates wth size constraint

```
create(MAX, stack(MAX, [])).
push(stack(MAX,SL),E,stack(MAX,[E|SL])) ←
   lstlength(SL,N), N #< MAX.
pop(stack(MAX,[E|R]),stack(MAX,R),E).

max_count(5).
virtual_size(stack(CAP,LST), SIZE) ←
   max_count(C), SIZE #=< C,
   lstlength(LST, SIZE).
```

6.1   Modelling Data Structures

We apply the model and logic framework from the non-groundable domain application to diagnose component systems handling data structures. Formally, structures are represented like abstract data types (ADTs), using algebraic structures with value sets and operations, alongside axioms defining their behaviour. These axioms set value constraints for diagnoses. Each ADT operation corresponds to a specific component type. The sequence of ADT operations forms a circuit akin to diagnosing electrical circuits.

With ASP, data structure operations can be encoded as domain predicates. We opt for CASP to accommodate non-ground variable clauses. An example is given for a limited-capacity stack datatype, including its operations and logic program (see Listing 6). $create : \langle nat, stack \rangle$,

$push : \langle stack \times e, stack \rangle$ and $pop : \langle stack, stack \times e \rangle$
defined by the axiom $pop(push(S, E)) = (S, E)$

For termination of diagnosis search, we must limit the structure size. This is achieved through a virtual size predicate, bounded by a parameterised maximum.

In this context, diagnosis parallels circuit diagnosis. Just as a circuit comprises individual operations, diagnosing ADT methods constructs a circuit from method call sequences. Inputs are transferred through method calls to generate outputs, which are then processed by subsequent operations. For instance, in a

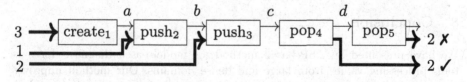

Fig. 4. Sequence of operations on the ADT stack in analogy to a functional circuit, variables $a, \dots, d$ represent the internal state of the ADT passed from a component to another. Inputs are shown on the left, outputs on the right. Thin arrows represent hidden values that are passed.

sequence of two consecutive push operations, each takes an element and a stack as input, producing a modified stack with the new value on top. As shown in Listing 6, we denote $push(i, v, o)$ to signify a push operation taking input i and yielding output o by pushing v onto the stack. Constructed circuits may have multiple components of the same type, differentiated by an index. For example, $\exists abcde.$ $\text{create}_1(2, a)$ $\text{push}_2(a, 1, b)$, $\text{push}_3(b, 2, c)$, $\text{pop}_4(c, d, 2)$, $\text{pop}_5(d, e, 2)$ is an abnormally behaving sequence (Fig. 4). We obtain a the cardinality minimal diagnosis diagnosis $\Delta = \{\text{push}_2, \text{push}_3, \text{pop}_4, \text{pop}_5\}$, with the supporting variable assignments constituting the alternate behaviours $\text{push}_2([], 1, [2])$, $\text{push}_3([1], 2, [2, 2])$, $\text{pop}_4([2, 1], [2 \mid \_], 2)$, $pop_5([1], \_, 2)$ using a list representation of the data on the stack.

For a single sequence, the diagnosis can only exclude create_1 as a single faulty component. When other call sequences are examined, they can be represented using shared components (assuming the components are deterministic), similar to the way polycircuits are built, thus narrowing down the diagnosis.

7   Related Work

The notion of explicitly considering system values is related to *constructive abduction* [20]. It improves coarse logical diagnosis through constraint programming, offering more insightful results. In analog value diagnosis, it is applied to validate logical diagnoses using numerical models [21].

The efforts for a semantically well-defined yet integrated language and reasoning engine for model-based diagnosis has been addressed with model generation as built into Prolog, resulting in a concise program called MOMO [11]. As a contemporary approach in the same direction, the use of ASP as a framework for efficient yet expressive model-based diagnosis has been explored for digital circuits [26] and with a refined model for analog circuits in [28]. In this paper we have extended the approach of [28] by altering the system description such that we identify intermediate values that lead to a consistent model, thereby providing an improved diagnosis. Previous solutions to this problem required intricate combinations of distinct solvers. For example, [23] employs a sophisticated strategy for the diagnosis of analog circuits, amalgamating qualitative and quantitative models. It leverages linear equation solvers for continuous domains and employs Prolog as a modeling language.

8   Conclusion

We have presented an ASP-based method for model-based diagnosis for systems processing values from large and dense domains. Our method improves on previous ASP encodings by incorporating intermediate values that improve the quality of the diagnosis by providing information that can help to further characterise a fault, as they are examples of conditions under which the fault occurs.

Using Goal-Directed Constrained Answer Set Programming, our method can bypass an initial grounding phase to cope with domains of larger size. We have also sketched how Constrained Answer Set Programming could be used to model diagnosis over inductive data types, demonstrating the capabilities of this new technology.

The ability of intermediate values to conditionalise faults opens up the possibility for future work to investigate means of more fine-grained diagnosis, which could help in the case of software fault diagnosis to locate bugs more easily.

Acknowledgments. This work has been carried out in the context of the VoLL-KI project (grant 16DHKBI091), funded by Bundesministeriums für Bildung und Forschung (BMBF).

Disclosure of Interests. The authors have no competing interests to declare that are relevant to the content of this article.

References

1. Arias, J., Carro, M., Chen, Z., Gupta, G.: Justifications for goal-directed constraint answer set programming. arXiv preprint arXiv:2009.10238 (2020)
2. Arias, J., Carro, M., Salazar, E., Marple, K., Gupta, G.: Constraint answer set programming without grounding. Theory Pract. Logic Program. **18**(3–4), 337–354 (2018)
3. Brewka, G., Eiter, T., Truszczyński, M.: Answer set programming at a glance. Commun. ACM **54**(12), 92–103 (2011)
4. Calimeri, F., et al.: ASP-Core-2 input language format. Theory Pract. Logic Program. **20**(2), 294–309 (2020). https://doi.org/10.1017/S1471068419000450
5. Clark, K.L.: Negation as failure. In: Gallaire, H., Minker, J. (eds.) Logic and Data Bases, pp. 293–322. Springer, Boston (1978). https://doi.org/10.1007/978-1-4684-3384-5_11
6. Console, L., Torasso, P.: A spectrum of logical definitions of model-based diagnosis. Comput. Intell. **7**(3), 133–141 (1991)
7. Davis, R.: Diagnostic reasoning based on structure and behavior. Artif. Intell. **24**(1–3), 347–410 (1984)
8. De Kleer, J., Williams, B.C.: Diagnosing multiple faults. Artif. Intell. **32**(1), 97–130 (1987)
9. Dechter, R., Cohen, D., et al.: Constraint Processing. Morgan Kaufmann, Burlington (2003)
10. Friedrich, G., Gottlob, G., Nejdl, W.: Physical impossibility instead of fault models. In: AAAI, vol. 90, pp. 331–336 (1990)
11. Friedrich, G., Nejdl, W.: MOMO-model-based diagnosis for everybody. In: Sixth Conference on Artificial Intelligence for Applications, pp. 206–213. IEEE (1990)
12. Gebser, M., Kaminski, R., Kaufmann, B., Schaub, T.: Multi-shot ASP solving with clingo. CoRR abs/1705.09811 (2017)
13. Gebser, M., Schaub, T., Thiele, S.: GrinGo: a new grounder for answer set programming. In: Baral, C., Brewka, G., Schlipf, J. (eds.) LPNMR 2007. LNCS, vol. 4483, pp. 266–271. Springer, Heidelberg (2007). https://doi.org/10.1007/978-3-540-72200-7_24

14. Gupta, G., et al.: Automating commonsense reasoning with ASP and s(CASP). In: Proceedings of 2nd Workshop on Goal-directed Execution of Answer Set Programs (GDE 2022) (2022)

15. Janhunen, T., Nimelä, I.: The answer set programming paradigm. AI Mag. **37**(3), 13–24 (2016)

16. Jannach, D., Schmitz, T.: Model-based diagnosis of spreadsheet programs: a constraint-based debugging approach. Autom. Softw. Eng. **23**, 105–144 (2016)

17. Keuning, H., Jeuring, J., Heeren, B.: Towards a systematic review of automated feedback generation for programming exercises. In: Proceedings of the 2016 ACM Conference on Innovation and Technology in Computer Science Education, pp. 41–46 (2016)

18. de Kleer, J.: Focusing on probable diagnoses. In: AAAI, vol. 91, pp. 842–848 (1991)

19. Kuhlmann, I., Gessler, A., Laszlo, V., Thimm, M.: A comparison of ASP-based and SAT-based algorithms for the contension inconsistency measure. In: Dupin de Saint-Cyr, F., Öztürk-Escoffier, M., Potyka, N. (eds.) SUM 2022. LNCS, vol. 13562, pp. 139–153. Springer, Cham (2022). https://doi.org/10.1007/978-3-031-18843-5_10

20. Ligeza, A.: Towards constructive abduction. In: KEOD, pp. 352–357 (2015)

21. Ligeza, A.: Constraint programming for constructive abduction. A case study in diagnostic model-based reasoning. In: Koscielny, J., Syfert, M., Sztyber, A. (eds.) DPS 2017. AISC, vol. 635, pp. 94–105. Springer, Cham (2018). https://doi.org/10.1007/978-3-319-64474-5_8

22. Marple, K., Salazar, E., Chen, Z., Gupta, G.: The s(ASP) predicate answer set programming system. The Association for Logic Programming Newsletter (2017)

23. Mozetič, I., Holzbaur, C., Novak, F., Santo-Zarnik, M.: Model-Based Analogue Circuit Diagnosis with CLP(R). In: Brauer, W., Hernández, D. (eds.) Verteilte Künstliche Intelligenz und kooperatives Arbeiten. Informatik-Fachberichte, vol. 291, pp. 343–353. Springer, Heidelberg (1991). https://doi.org/10.1007/978-3-642-76980-1_31

24. Reiter, R.: A theory of diagnosis from first principles. Artif. Intell. **32**(1), 57–95 (1987)

25. Struss, P., Dressler, O.: "Physical Negation" integrating fault models into the general diagnostic engine. In: IJCAI, vol. 89, pp. 1318–1323 (1989)

26. Wotawa, F.: On the use of answer set programming for model-based diagnosis. In: Fujita, H., Fournier-Viger, P., Ali, M., Sasaki, J. (eds.) IEA/AIE 2020. LNCS, vol. 12144, pp. 518–529. Springer, Cham (2020). https://doi.org/10.1007/978-3-030-55789-8_45

27. Wotawa, F., Dumitru, V.A.: The Java2CSP debugging tool utilizing constraint solving and model-based diagnosis principles. In: Fujita, H., Fournier-Viger, P., Ali, M., Wang, Y. (eds.) IEA/AIE 2022. LNCS, vol. 13343, pp. 543–554. Springer, Cham (2022). https://doi.org/10.1007/978-3-031-08530-7_46

28. Wotawa, F., Kaufmann, D.: Model-based reasoning using answer set programming. Appl. Intell. 1–19 (2022)

29. Wotawa, F., Nica, M., Moraru, I.: Automated debugging based on a constraint model of the program and a test case. J. Logic Algebraic Program. **81**(4), 390–407 (2012)

Integrating Competencies into Preventive Maintenance Scheduling with Answer Set Optimization

Anssi Yli-Jyrä[1]([⊠]) [iD], Heini Ikävalko[2] [iD], and Tomi Janhunen[1,2] [iD]

[1] Tampere University, Tampere, Finland
{anssi.yli-jyra,tomi.janhunen}@tuni.fi
[2] Aalto University, Espoo, Finland
heini.ikavalko@aalto.fi

Abstract. The maintenance optimization of multi-component machines has been recently formalized as an Answer Set Optimization (ASO) problem based on component selection and grouping of overlapping maintenance intervals. The motivation of the current work is to develop an extension that would integrate resources and availability constraints into this maintenance model. This article outlines an extended ASO model with the primary focus on modeling and optimizing costly maintenance resources, culminating in cost savings facilitated by the progressive development of workforce competence. The model presented in this work extends the cost function of the prior ASO formalization in a modular way with additional cost priorities concerning parallelism, workforce, and expertise. Due to the presented extensions, the complexity of the integrated maintenance model increases compared to the prior formalization.

1 Introduction

Maintenance optimization [16,25,27] contributes to the availability and reliability of industrial production lines by optimizing the cost-efficiency of the maintenance activities. For example, a lazy, evenly distributed care plan ensures a healthier machinery condition over the lifetime than a restlessly exhaustive plan that is completed early, leaving the aging machinery without spare parts. Therefore, the maintenance scheduling problem is dissimilar to the makespan minimization which is a common objective in job-shop scheduling problems.

It is natural to view optimized maintenance as a digitalized *product-service system* [20] that integrates into its industrial context. The focus of maintenance is then not limited to corrective maintenance operations but it extends to scheduled, opportunistic, condition-based, predictive, and prescriptive maintenance [25]. It also integrates tightly with the operation environment, taking into account the availability for production scheduling and the allocation of scarce maintenance resources [6,8,9,16,26], as illustrated in Fig. 1. Therefore, *integrated maintenance scheduling* differs vastly from classical planning and

A. Meier and M. Ortiz (Eds.): FoIKS 2024, LNCS 14589, pp. 381–400, 2024.
https://doi.org/10.1007/978-3-031-56940-1_21

Fig. 1. Integrated maintenance in the context of production and resource allocation

scheduling problems and presents a new set of layers and challenges to modeling and efficiency: Besides the stochastic nature of the failure occurrences that the models must reflect, there are challenges related to knowledge representation and scheduling algorithms. In this article, scheduling algorithms constitute the infrastructure on top of which more knowledge on the resource and production environment can be added.

The maintenance scheduling algorithms [16,37] can be viewed through the dichotomy of *online* and *offline* algorithms. Online algorithms such as *reinforcement learning* (RL) [32] can take significant advantage of the partial knowledge of the problem instance and the function computations before the rest of the problem is presented and the policy function is queried to determine the actions of a maintenance schedule. The system's state space is obtained from the machine specifications and state values and the policy function are then computed in advance, through a time-consuming iteration that estimates the value and the action policies at each state. Since the state space of the system grows exponentially to the number of components, a compact representation of the large state space is necessary (cf. the curse of dimensionality) [13]. The downside is that a compacted state space no longer guarantees to find the globally optimal schedule through its local policy. However, recent developments in *deep RL* approaches [7,33] help close the gap between the full and compact state-space representations. In line with this, reinforcement learning has been concluded as one of the most promising algorithms for maintenance optimization [25].

Logic-based frameworks such as *mixed-integer programming* (MIP) [34], *answer set programming/optimization* (ASP/ASO) [3,15,30], and *constraint programming* (CP) [28] are different from state-based methods such as RL. Solvers in logic-based frameworks are typically used as offline algorithms: the whole problem instance, including the machine specification, is provided as a input when the scheduling starts. After the start of the algorithm, some constraints on the feasible states are learned during the optimization. These algorithms can find global optima. However, since many formalizations of maintenance scheduling give rise to NP-hard decision problems (cf. [16] and [35]), the computation of optimal schedules is non-deterministic by nature. Although the search can be heavily constrained, the performance and scalability of these algorithms are rightful concerns in practice, giving a motivation for heuristic bounds, pruning constraints, and approximations in logic-based approaches. Nevertheless, logic-based optimization is widely used in practice. It is a promising alternative for interpretable model formulation, problem solving, and multi-target optimization as logical formalisms allow a high-level description of the problem knowledge.

The current work is methodologically framed within the logic-based ASO framework that is well-suited for scheduling and planning tasks [1,10,12,15,21]. The approach is based on an existing formulation [35] of the *preventive maintenance scheduling* (PMS) problem of multi-component machines. Due to the general intractability of the PMS problem [35], we assume parallel development of efficient solving techniques for the problem, potentially exploiting fixed parameters and machine specifications. For example, more scalable encodings based on decompositions, symmetry breaking and pruning constraints have contributed towards this direction [35,36]. More specifically, we extend existing ASP encodings and the related concepts of PMS [35] with some aspects of resource allocation. Maintenance requires sufficient resources to implement maintenance operations and to avoid delays and additional costs, such as hiring an outsourced workforce. For example, the number and duration of maintenance breaks must be adequate for the machine. Each break appears as an *opportunity* in maintenance scheduling, as a *bounded resource* in resource scheduling, and as a *lack of availability* in production scheduling. Seen this way, all three aspects of integrated maintenance (Fig. 1) will be visited although our extensions do not properly combine the planning or scheduling aspects of production to maintenance.

On a conceptual level, the current work advocates *competent maintenance professionals* as the most important type of resource in maintenance optimization. The claim is that the scheduling of the maintenance professionals can be easily integrated into maintenance scheduling. This integration is an important extension as employees form an infra-like long-term investment. The competencies of the employees should be developed and managed to reduce outsourced services and improve the company's efficiency. The recent study [22] recognizes that a manufacturer can develop its capability for service delivery, especially through infrastructure development and management. The hired employees represent a socially complex combination of human resources that are deployed to achieve a desired end goal in product-service systems [31]. At the operational level, developing maintenance capability deals with managing the competence and behavior of the workforce and the diversity in the individual *capabilities* of the maintenance personnel [18,23]. Overall, the current model divides personnel-related resources into three categories further characterized below:

1. **Quantitative Resources** – Realizing maintenance operations within a bounded time frame (i.e., the maximum duration of the maintenance break) by a bounded number of maintenance professionals.
2. **Competence Resources** – Delivering maintenance service with a bounded pool of experts for each component.

3. **Training Resources** – Developing professional competencies of the employees progressively via training.

These resource categories are dealt with by three extensions to the ASP encoding of the core PMS model [35]. Section 2 recaps the core model and outlines the formal interfaces between the three extensions. The three extensions will be called *resource models* (RM1, RM2, RM3) and described in the subsequent three sections. Their purpose is to formalize a minimal understanding of scheduling concerning the three categories of personnel resources as follows:

– Section 3 presents the time-bound service realization as RM1;
– Section 4 formalizes competence requirements as RM2; and
– Section 5 introduces apprenticeship and training as RM3.

The cost-based integration of the three resource models under the cost-based scheduling objective is outlined in Sect. 6. The ultimate goal of maintenance optimization is to improve the cost-effectiveness of maintenance operations from the product-service point of view. This goal assumes that everything can be uniformly measured as financial rewards or costs. It is easy to postulate some relative costs among different quantitative resources and individuals with the disclaimer that they are nearly arbitrary. Since maintenance scheduling, availability, and resources appear in the cost-based objective function side by side, it is perhaps fair to summarize that the current work *presents a uniformly weighted ASP-based model for integrated maintenance scheduling.*

Finally, Sect. 7 concludes this article with discussion. The article extends an existing logic-based approach to PMS optimization by formalizing a few aspects of resource allocation. The main contribution of the article resides in the incorporation of management insights into preventive maintenance scheduling.

2   Overview of Maintenance and Resourcing Problems

In the sequel, the preventive maintenance scheduling (PMS) problem is exclusively understood in the abstract sense of [35]. The problem plays a fundamental role as it lays out the scene for further constraints and objective functions, and it is parameterized by the number of maintenance breaks (b) and the time horizon (h). A *solution* to the PMS problem assigns for each break $i \in \{1, \ldots, b\}$,

– its discrete location b_i on the timeline, i.e., $1 \leq b_i \leq h$,
– a group of components $g_i = \{c \in C \mid s(i, c)\}$ to be maintained at i.

An optimal solution minimizes the objective function that measures the overall *miscoverage* of components in the schedule, reflecting the absolute deviation of component-wise renewals from their recommendations that are given in machine specifications. Miscoverage may take place in two different ways. *Under-coverage* means overdue component renewals, increasing the risk for aging-related component failures. *Over-coverage* arises if renewals occur too early in the component's lifetime, increasing the cost of maintenance. The optimal schedule on the left of

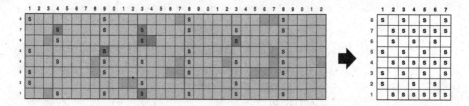

Fig. 2. A scheduling timeline with 32 time steps and 7 maintenance breaks [35].

Fig. 2 covers the maintenance of an 8-component machine over 32 time steps. Red and blue cells denote under- and over-service, respectively, for a particular component and time step. The maintenance breaks are indicated by blue vertical lines while the cells marked with letter "S" denote the renewal of the component in question. As a result, the component is valid for a component-specific time indicated by sequences of (blue or) green cells starting from cells where a component is renewed. For the components 1–8 in question, the respective recommended service intervals are 5, 10, 7, 4, 9, 11, 5, and 8.

The *integrated maintenance problem* of the present work focuses on combining the core maintenance scheduling model with maintenance-related resource models. Constraints related to production planning and scheduling are left for further work but the availability of the production machinery will be measured indirectly, through the total number of maintenance breaks that are excepted from the time available for production operation. In the following, we define an *interface* that extracts the core of an (optimal) solution, i.e., an optimal maintenance schedule in the space of feasible candidate schedules. The core is a projection of a full schedule. It views time as a sequence of breaks $1, \ldots, b$ rather than points of time, ignoring the corresponding time steps $b_1, \ldots, b_b$ in the scheduling timeline, see Fig. 2. The schedule on the right of Fig. 2 condenses service selection information $g_1, \ldots, g_b$ as the basis for resource allocation.

Several ASP encodings of the maintenance scheduling problem exist [35,36]. The shared core of the encodings is now assumed to define three predicates:

- i(I) – there is a maintenance break indexed by I;
- c(C) – there is a component whose identity is C; and
- s(I,C) – the component C is to be maintained (serviced) during a break I.

The maintenance scheduling problem is extended with maintenance-related resource scheduling that is divided into three scheduling needs, namely the quantitative resources (Sect. 3), competence resources (Sect. 4), and training resources (Sect. 5). Each of these extensions can be seen as a successive refinement to the maintenance scheduling problem, see Fig. 3. Each refinement narrows the search toward a smaller space of feasible maintenance schedules. The interface of core maintenance scheduling is shared by all refinements. The refinements, i.e. the resource models, constrain the space of feasible schedules through the interface. The operation scheduler extends the interface of maintenance scheduling with one predicate op(I,C,Q) denoting that during the break I, component C is being

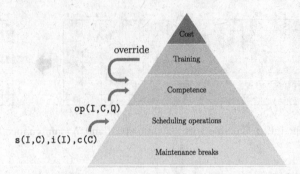

Fig. 3. Refining the maintenance scheduling problem

maintained by the required number of professionals at time slice Q. The result-ing interface builds on four predicates (i.e., i/1, c/1, s/2, and op/3) and it is employed by both the competence model and the training model. Since the training model is a proper extension of the competence model, it overrides and partially replaces the latter model if deployed.

The integration of the maintenance scheduler with the extensions is imple-mented first as hard resource models RM1–RM3. The *hard integration* restricts the space of feasible schedules since the resources are limited and non-negotiable. These restrictions may result in over-constrained problem instances and the fail-ure of integrated scheduling, as demonstrated in Sect. 6. In contrast, *soft inte-gration*, to be developed in the end of Sect. 6, assumes the availability of further resources, but with extra cost. There is a trade-off between additional resources and the miscoverage of a schedule. Some extra resources can be deployed, but the high costs of such resources force one to find a balance between an excellent but costly schedule and a moderate and affordable schedule.

3   Scheduling Service Operations During Breaks

Our first extension and refinement of maintenance scheduling (RM1) deals with quantitative personnel resources required by the implementation of maintenance operations during maintenance breaks. To characterize the organization of main-tenance operations serially and in parallel, and the workforce to carry out the operations, we assume three numeric parameters:

- q – the number *time slices* inside each maintenance break,
- t – the number of maintenance *tracks* running in parallel, and
- p – the number of *professionals* available for service operations.

In addition to these global parameters, there is a database of resource require-ments for each component. For simplicity, we assume that the resource require-ments of a particular component remain the same for every break when the component is maintained. Thus, it is possible to estimate the overall need for

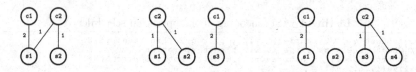

Fig. 4. Some ways to schedule the maintenance of components c1 and c2 during a maintenance break. Left: 2 tracks, 2 time slices, 3 professionals. Center: 1 track, 3 time slices, 2 professionals. Right: 1 track, 4 time slices, 2 professionals.

service personnel although for each break, the actual number of professionals depends on the set of components being serviced. The required resources are specified with predicates taking the component C as the first argument:

- durreq(C,D) – the maintenance of component C requires D time slices and
- proreq(C,P) – the maintenance of component C requires P professionals.

Example 1. Consider two components c1 and c2 whose requirements are given by durreq(c1,1) and proreq(c1,2), and durreq(c2,2) and proreq(c2,1), respectively. Then, suppose that these components are being maintained during the same break. If the number of professionals is two, the tasks during the break will take at least three time slices. However, if the number of professionals is increased by one, then the tasks can be completed within 2 time slices.

This situation is illustrated by the first diagram in Fig. 4. The upper row of vertices denotes components and the lower row denotes time slices. An edge between a component and a time slice indicates that the component is being maintained during the slice. The label of the edge indicates the resource taken, i.e., how may professionals are working on the component.   ∎

Following the idea in Example 1, the goal of the service operation scheduler is, for each maintenance break I, to

1. choose, for each scheduled service operation s(I,C), a time slice during which the service of C is started and, given the request durreq(C,D), reserve D consecutive time slices in total for completing the service of C;
2. check that at most t parallel operations are allocated to each time slice; and
3. ensure for each time slice Q that the number of professionals is not less than the number requested by components C being maintained during Q.

The allocation of a time slice Q to the component C during break I is encoded by a fact op(I,C,Q). If the component requires multiple time slices for service, there will be several such facts. It is also worth observing that there is no need to allocate tracks explicitly and, hence, it is possible to avoid certain symmetries arising from the identities of components. Since one component may require multiple professionals, the number t of parallel tracks can be exceeded by the total number P of professionals working simultaneously.

Listing 1. ASP encoding of the operation scheduler

```
1  % Assumes q, s/2, durreq/2, i/1, proreq/2. Provides: op/3.
2  % Choose one time slice to start each operation
3  resource_model1 :- not resource_model2, not resource_model3.
4  slice(1..q).
5  { opstarts(I,C,Q) : slice(Q), slice(Q+D-1) } = 1 :- s(I,C), durreq(C,D).
6
7  % Reserve the track from the starting slice to the slice of completion
8  op(I,C,J) :- opstarts(I,C,Q), durreq(C,D), J=Q..Q+D-1.
9
10 % Limit the tracks during any given slice
11 :- i(I), slice(Q), t < #count{ C : op(I,C,Q) }.
12
13 % Limit the professionals during any given slice
14 p(I,Q,M) :- i(I), slice(Q), M = #sum{ P,C: op(I,C,Q), proreq(C,P) }.
15 :- i(I), slice(Q), p(I,Q,P), p < P.
```

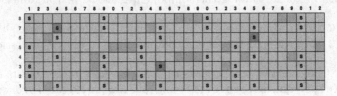

Fig. 5. The effect of enforcing resource constraints when the number of breaks is 9.

As regards encoding the service operation scheduler in ASP, it can be implemented in a few lines of code[1] (see Listing 1). The present encoding is not intended to be an efficient encoding of a knapsack-style packing problem. It merely demonstrates the purpose of the operation scheduler when checking the feasibility of service operations as well as the required personnel. Although some symmetries are already avoided, some remain as can be recalled from Fig. 4.

When it comes to more realistic industrial settings, one could introduce additional constraints that control the order in which service operations can be performed. To settle such further needs, an encoding that combines features from scheduling and planning problems might be in order.

Example 2. To illustrate the effect of resource constraints, we provide a maintenance schedule in Fig. 5. Due to resource requirements, fewer components can be serviced during maintenance breaks. To compensate, we increase the number of maintenance breaks to 9. The miscoverage of an optimal schedule is 27 which is one more than previously (cf. Fig. 2). This reveals that the number of service breaks is also an essential resource affecting the quality of schedules obtained. ∎

---

[1] The ASP encodings are publicly available under https://github.com/asptools and we have used CLINGO (v. 5.6.2, under MacBook Pro) as the solver in experiments.

4   Competence-Aware Maintenance

Our second resource-based extension of maintenance scheduling (RM2) addresses competencies required from the workforce. There are different kinds of skills and competencies that professionals can have. Some skills are specifically required by the machinery itself or necessary for maintenance professionals in general (cf. [19]). Key skills, such as language proficiency, professional certificates, safety and risk management cards and so on, are identified already in the job descriptions and interviews of the employees or sorted out during introductory courses. Further skills are identified through industrial benchmarks, external references, simulator hours, track records, and interviews.

Knowledge about crucial skills is commonly represented as a *competence matrix*, affecting permits, teams, and the financial rewards of individuals. In a simplified ASP encoding, a competence matrix can be represented by facts expert(P,C) stating that professional P has an expert-level proficiency of maintaining component C. In addition, predicate expreq(C,E) specifies how many experts are required by the component C. Then, based on such knowledge, the goal of *competence-aware* maintenance scheduling is to assign professionals to service operations so that component-specific requirements are met.

To find a schedule that implements the requirements in practice, there must be a sufficiently large pool of experts able to service the components of a machine as scheduled. Let us now assume that op(I,C,Q) holds, i.e., component C is being serviced during break I and at slice Q. The RM1 model ensures that there are sufficiently many professionals available for all maintenance operations occurring at each break I and slice Q. Among these, there are, according to expreq(C,E), E such experts of component C that are dedicated to C during the time slice.

The assignment of static experts in RM2 is formalized on lines 3–4 in Listing 2. Section 5 generalizes this assignment to dynamic experts that develop over time. To ensure the allocation of exactly E experts for each operation op(I,C,Q), the assignment of a professional P to a component C at break I and time slice Q is encoded (lines 3–4) with an atom e(I,(C,Q),P), where the pair (C,Q) links the component C to the slice Q. Similarly, the assignment of professionals that are not acting as experts is expressed using an atom o(I,(C,Q),P) (o=other professional) on lines 8–9. Experts (and other professionals) should work only on single component at a time (lines 5 and 10). Multi-tasking as an expert and a non-expert is also ruled out on lines 13–14.

The presented model of competence-awareness is simplistic and based on certification-based listings in the competence matrix. Such matrices tend to forget tacit, proactive knowledge and generic skills, such as the ability to deploy a growing range of digital services:

– **Proactive skills.** Maintenance work includes proactive tasks to foresee the breakdown of the system [29]. The daily tasks in maintenance involve monitoring the current situation and the overall quality status of the production line. As an example, a maintenance worker describes their role at work: "*Here, when production is underway, it is monitored for the condition of the line to*

Listing 2. ASP encoding of the competence scheduler

```
1   p(1..p).
2   resource_model2 :- not resource_model3.
3   { e(I,(C,Q),P) : p(P), expert(P,C) } = EN :-
4       op(I,C,Q), expreq(C,EN), resource_model2.
5   :- e(I,(C1,Q),P), e(I,(C2,Q),P), C1 < C2.
6
7   % For each C with PN>EN>0 assign PN-EN other pros to op(I,C,Q)
8   { o(I,(C,Q),P) : p(P), not e(I,(C,Q),P) } = PN-EN   :-
9       op(I,C,Q), expreq(C,EN), proreq(C,PN).
10  :- o(I,(C1,Q),P), o(I,(C2,Q),P), C1 <  C2.
11
12  % Check that nobody works in two roles at the same time
13  iso(I,Q,P) :- o(I,(C,Q),P).
14  :- iso(I,Q,P), e(I,(C,Q),P).
```

ensure everything is okay. I walk around, observe, and listen. Even the nose is in use, as it can reveal certain things. If I notice something, I record it in the fault log, noting down the symptoms and the location. It then moves on to job planning, and from there, we begin to determine the urgency of the matter."

– **Generic digital skills.** Individuals with strong digital skills and those who quickly adapt to new things can assist colleagues and support others at work. Their active engagement often makes them role models and educators in the workplace, beyond their designated roles. There is evidence of individual differences in using digital systems, based on workers' experiences. According to [18], the enactment of digital systems varies based on attitudes, competence, and individual activities. The study also notes instances where individuals, despite positive attitudes and strong skills, may not engage in helping others in their work due to being occupied with their own.

To model generic and proactive skills or a variety of skill types and their role in maintenance in general, the respective generalizations to the present model would be needed. Such generalizations go beyond our illustrative purposes.

5   Scheduling Training During Breaks

The resource model RM2 is naive in the sense that competencies are considered as static properties. A static competence model is quite limited as it ignores the dynamic development of skills and continuous learning:

– **Continuous learning.** The competencies of individuals develop over time. The longer one practices, the more competent the person becomes at a job. Similarly, the maintenance team's competence to execute maintenance actions changes dynamically over time.
– **Knowledge and experience sharing.** Sharing tacit and generic knowledge is crucial for the effectiveness of maintenance teams [18,29]. These skills are difficult to formalize as competence matrices, but they can be deployed and facilitated through adequate procedures and experiential learning [24].

Fig. 6. Five stages of proficiency according to Benner [2].

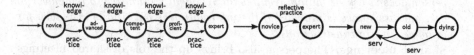

Fig. 7. States of the *From novice to expert* model (Left) and its simplification (Middle) vs. a simple model of component-wise deterioration and reset service (Right).

Our third resource model (RM3) addresses the limitations of the static competence model. The goal is to extend the notion of expertise to a more dynamic direction—partly capturing the effects of continuous learning and experience sharing. This process can be supported in many respects:

- **Instruction.** Some individuals may feel that following instructions is sufficient for their tasks. For instance, individuals with initially weak digital skills but a positive attitude may actively strive to enhance the efficient use of digital systems in their work. To cope with instructions, some individuals proactively record conversations with key users to learn from them [18].
- **E-Learning.** Competence of maintenance workers can also be enhanced through digitally facilitated knowledge processes [17]. Increasing knowledge through activities like reading instructions in ERP or watching videos represent such ways. According to one maintenance worker: *"Often, the video would be the best option [to develop competence] because, in my opinion, converting it into written form takes more time, and conveying every little nuance with pictures and words is much more challenging."*
- **Experience.** Competence can be developed through practical experience: *"Yes, I mainly believe that there's no other way than by doing, observing, walking around, and analyzing. One must understand the state of the process, whether this operating sound is now abnormal or if it is normal. In this, I have noticed that there are differences among people. It purely depends on long-term practice and experience."*
- **Proactive behavior.** The same person, working in the maintenance describes the role of proactivity in developing their competence: *"One who asks won't get lost; in that case, help and assistance are provided. I don't*

Listing 3. ASP encoding of the training scheduler

```
1   % Define expertise as a function of time, progressively:
2   expert(P,C,1)   :- p(P), expert(P,C),     i(1).
3   expert(P,C,I+1) :- p(P), expert(P,C,I),   i(I+1).
4   expert(P,C,I+1) :- p(P), practice(P,C,I), i(I+1).
5
6   % For each operation op(I,C,Q), with expreq(C,EN), assign EN dynamic experts
7   resource_model3.  % Turn off the earlier rule implementation
8   { e(I,(C,Q),P) : p(P), expert(P,C,I) } = EN :- op(I,C,Q), expreq(C,EN).
9
10  % Record apprenticeship as practice.
11  practice(P,C,I) :- o(I,(C,Q),P), expreq(C,EN), EN > 0.
```

know where one would suddenly go to tell someone what they should do if the person doesn't ask. It mainly requires the recipient's initiative to remember to ask, and assistance is provided if the information is not readily available, for example, in work instructions."

– **Shared meetings.** The person also brings up the role of shared meetings with their colleagues: "Often, in the morning, we have group discussions. If any issues arise or if there has been something showing symptoms, we monitor it through production displays. This leads to discussions, and we address it as a group."

These learning means are activated efficiently when an individual is in charge of carrying out maintenance activities with an expert. Novices can develop their competence with the support of experts sharing their tacit knowledge. The expert can explain the tasks in advance, request the novice to study on-line material, and provide support when the task is performed for the very first time.

Benner's *from novice to expert* model (Fig. 6) describes how an individual gains new knowledge and skills and develops from novice to expert [11]. The model identifies five stages of development: *novice, advanced beginner, competent, proficient,* and *expert* (Fig. 7a). The development takes place through knowledge acquisition and reflective practice. Since the immediate goal of this paper is to demonstrate the incorporation of proficiency development into integrated maintenance, two levels of proficiency are distinguished in a simplified version of Benner's model: *novice* and *expert* (Fig. 7b). The development is assumed progressive, i.e., the proficiency of an individual can only increase and no iteration or declining proficiency is considered. This differs from the stages of machine condition development that involves a reset mechanism (Fig. 7c).

An ASP encoding that takes into account progressive expertise and the effects of training is presented in Listing 3 that contains a streamlined *from novice to expert* model. In this model, the progression from novice to expert is easy: During operation op(I,C,Q), a novice professional P can gain practice on component C as an apprentice (line 11) if the component C requires some other professionals to be present besides the experts. If professional P was not an expert at break I, but gets practice under the supervision of an expert, P is considered an expert during the next break (line 4). The worker's existing expertise is propagated

Listing 4. Description of 8 components and the competence matrix of 8 professionals

```
1   comp(1,  5,2).   durreq(1,2).   proreq(1,2).   expreq(1,1).
2   comp(2,10,0).    durreq(2,1).   proreq(2,2).   expreq(2,1).
3   comp(3,  7,0).   durreq(3,1).   proreq(3,1).   expreq(3,1).
4   comp(4,  4,3).   durreq(4,1).   proreq(4,1).   expreq(4,1).
5   comp(5,  9,0).   durreq(5,3).   proreq(5,2).   expreq(5,2).
6   comp(6,11,2).    durreq(6,2).   proreq(6,3).   expreq(6,3).
7   comp(7,  5,4).   durreq(7,1).   proreq(7,1).   expreq(7,1).
8   comp(8,  8,0).   durreq(8,1).   proreq(8,2).   expreq(8,2).
9   cost(1,5).  expert(1,  1..8).   cost(2,2).  expert(2,  2..6).
10  cost(3,0).  expert(3,  7..8).   cost(4,2).  expert(4,  (1;4;7)).
11  cost(5,2).  expert(5,  (2;6)).  cost(6,0).  expert(6,  (1;5)).
12  cost(7,2).  expert(7,  6..8).   cost(8,0).  expert(8,  4..5).
```

further (lines 2–3). These kinds of dynamically computed experts replace static experts when the requirements are checked (lines 7–8).

6   Integration

Hard Integration. Integration with a hard, restrictive resource model increases the risk of an over-constrained problem instance that does not have any solution. A central question is whether there is a way to preserve at least one candidate solution even when all candidates violate at least one constraint. If the miscoverage function, i.e., the search space for core PMS problem [35], is itself total and not restricted by pruning constraints [36], the space contains even schedules that do not consume any resources and are, therefore, not affected by resource models. However, if the solution space is narrowed by both pruning constraints and resource restrictions, the search may be over-constrained, leading to no solution. This is likely in integrated maintenance because the two types of constraints are almost complementary: pruning constraints eliminate many suboptimal solutions while resource restrictions eliminate unrealizable optimal solutions.

Example 3. This example illustrates how resource restrictions degrade the miscoverage of schedules. The small database in Listing 4 specifies the recommended maintenance intervals R and the due times D of components ($comp(C,R,L)$) for the same eight components whose maintenance schedule appears in Fig. 2a. Resource requirements are also given for each component with $durreq/2$, $proreq/2$, and $expreq/2$. In addition, the expertise ($expert/2$) and hourly salary ($cost/2$) of the eight professionals ($p = 8$) is explicated by further facts in the listing.

Table 1 samples the output of the integrated maintenance scheduler when hard resource models RM1, RM2, and RM3 are activated. For the sake of easier comparison to prior work [35], assume $h = 32$ time steps and fix $b = 7$ breaks to the same locations of the timeline as in Fig. 2a. However, the maintained components at every break are reselected for optimization under integrated maintenance. This is executed by setting controlling parameters t, q, p as indicated in the table.

Table 1. The effect of hard constraints on miscoverage

PMS Core	b	t	q	p	Pruned?	RM1	RM2	RM3
26	7	3	4	5	yes	26	26	26
26	7	3	4	4	yes	27	UNSAT	UNSAT
26	7	3	4	4	no	27	54	54
26	7	2	4	5	no	31	31	31
26	7	2	4	4	no	31	55	55
26	7	2	3	4	no	54	77	**69**
26	7	2	3	3	no	74	83	83
26	7	2	2	2	no	124	140	140
26	7	1	1	1	no	206	206	206
26	7	0	0	0	no	245	245	245

The effect of over-constrained search is seen only when the search space is pruned with further constraints [36]. Pruning is harmless when the resource model is not restrictive ($\langle t, q, p \rangle = \langle 3, 4, 5 \rangle$). The search fails, however, when the solution space is narrowed both by pruning and resources where $p = 4$.

Consider now searching for globally optimal schedules without any pruning constraints [36]. The increasing resource sensitivity affects miscoverage clearly:

– In RM1, the bounded parallelism (t) and break duration (q) limit the size of groups g_i of maintained components, increasing miscoverage from the original 26 to the range 27–245.
– When RM2 is included, the limited competence of the small maintenance team restricts operational capacity even more. This degrades miscoverage even more, to the range 54–245, although sometimes the competence requirement has no effect on miscoverage.
– When RM2 is upgraded with RM3, the pool of experts grows dynamically towards the horizon. This reduces miscoverage when ($\langle t, q, p \rangle = \langle 2, 3, 4 \rangle$).

If no resources are given, i.e. ($\langle t, q, p \rangle = \langle 0, 0, 0 \rangle$), there still remains a trivial solution (no maintenance). In this empty schedule, 'green cells' occur at the beginning of the timeline only.   ■

Soft Integration. In soft integration, the quality of schedules is a function (e.g., a weighted sum or polynomial) of miscoverage and resource consumption. This function is intended to emulate the cost-efficiency of maintenance activities: (i) Miscoverage is an indirect measure for *component-related* cost-efficiency of a maintenance schedule [35]. Over-coverage oc(C,T) at a timestep T means loss in the remaining lifetime of component C while under-coverage uc(C,T) correlates to an increased risk of failure for component C during timestep T. An abrupt failure seldom goes without harm and loss in availability for production. (ii) The

Listing 5. ASP encoding of the integrated objective function

```
1   % Assumes s/2, op/3, i/1, uc/2, oc/2, cost/2, o/3, e/3.
2   maxb(M) :- M = #count{ I: s(I,C)    }.                    % used breaks
3   t(T)    :- T = #count{ C: op(I,C,Q) }, i(I), slice(Q).    % implicit tracks
4   maxt(M) :- M =   #max{ T: t(T); 0 }.                      % used tracks
5   maxq(M) :- M = #count{ Q: op(I,C,Q) }.                    % used slices
6   maxp(N) :- N =   #max{ P: p(I,Q,P); 0 }.                  % used pros
7   __usage(B,T,Q,P) :- maxb(B), maxt(T), maxq(Q), maxp(P). #show __usage/4.
8
9   % Minimize MC and resources at @2 (primary key) and MC at @1 (secondary key)
10  #minimize{ 20@2,C,T,mc   : uc(C,T)                  ;  % uc
11             20@2,C,T,mc   : oc(C,T)                  ;  % oc
12             50@2,I,breaks: I=1..M, maxb(M)           ;  % breaks
13             50@2,Q,slices: Q=1..M, maxq(M)           ;  % slices
14             50@2,T,tracks: T=1..M, maxt(M)           ;  % tracks
15             50@2,P,pros  : P=1..M, maxp(M)           ;  % pros
16             K@2,I,C,P    : o(I,(C,Q),P), cost(P,K) ;  % non-experts
17             K@2,I,C,P    : e(I,(C,Q),P), cost(P,K) }.  % experts
```

number of breaks has been previously fixed [35,36]. Now breaks can be seen as
a similar quantitative resource as tracks t, time slices q, and professionals p.
Every break $1, \ldots, b$ takes away some availability of the production machinery.
(iii) Additional time slices (q) prolong maintenance breaks, and additional parallel tracks (t) in maintenance operations increase the simultaneous duties of
professionals. Furthermore, simultaneous deployment of many professionals or
experts increases personnel costs. Reductions in these resource quantities contribute directly to the *resource-related* cost-efficiency of maintenance as the saved
time or salary costs can be used for production. (iv) Finally, the deployment of
in-house novices is typically cheap, while general experts and outsourced consultants cost more. This salary differentiation goes back to cost(P,M)-facts in the
database.

In ASO, we can encode the integrated objective function as a *pseudo-Boolean
expression* (Boolean variables with integer coefficients) that specifies costs being
minimized. For sake of flexibility, the hard bounds are first set sufficiently high to
make resource bounds compatible with acceptable (not necessarily optimal) solutions to the core PMS problem. Second, a sufficient number of experts (employees
or consultants) are ensured in the database to avoid infeasible schedules. This
would allow resource models to allocate resources whose balanced consumption
could be controlled by an objective function that compares schedules.

A possible ASP formalization of the objective function is given in Listing 5.
The unary predicates maxb/1, maxt/1, and maxq/1 indicate how many breaks,
tracks, and time slices are utilized in the schedule. The summands of the objective function are specified on lines 10–17 where notation @2 tells that this objective function forms the primary (i.e. higher) key to the optimizer. The core
PMS scheduler [35] contains another objective function (miscoverage) that will
now become a lower ranked key to the optimizer. The primary key is, in principle, enough for soft integration. The secondary key (miscoverage) has two roles:
It gives useful information about the solution and contributes to tie-breaking
between multiple optimal schedules in a way that is consistent with the core PMS
problem. The actual objective function (mc*20+resources*50+salaries) is merely

Table 2. Automatic parameter optimization in cost-based integration

Model	b	t	q	p	Used b	t	q	p	Cost (mc*20+resources*50+salaries)	Mc.
Core	7	7	7	5	7	0	0	0	870 $(26*20+(7+0+0+0)*50+0)$	26
RM1	7	7	7	5	7	2	5	4	1420 $(26*20+(7+2+5+4)*50+0)$	26
RM2	7	7	7	5	7	2	5	4	1535 $(26*20+(7+2+5+4)*50+115)$	26
RM3	7	7	7	5	7	2	5	4	1535 $(26*20+(7+2+5+4)*50+115)$	26
RM1	7	2	3	4	7	2	3	4	1880 $(54*20+(7+2+3+4)*50+0)$	54
RM2	7	2	3	4	7	2	3	4	2415 $(77*20+(7+2+3+4)*50+75)$	77
RM3	7	2	3	4	7	2	3	4	**2261** $(69*20+(7+2+3+4)*50+81)$	**69**

a suggestion based on our experience with the 8-component machine. Further details of the objective function are mainly ASP technicalities that implement the weighted sum. The behavior of the function can be tuned easily by changing the coefficients of the summands.

Example 4. Table 2 shows the results of applying cost-based optimization (Listing 5) in integrated maintenance. This example illustrates that cost-based integration balances between miscoverage and resources and adapts to the high resource costs by performing fewer operations. The pruning constraints [36] are *not* applied and the 7 breaks are still fixed to the same locations of the timeline as in Fig. 2a. In this experiment, resources are bounded from above by the input parameters b, t, q, and p as indicated in the table.

The scheduler returns two cost-function values: the integrated cost (primary key for optimization) and the miscoverage (secondary key for information and tie-breaking). No personnel-related resources are allocated with the core PMS scheduler. With enough resources, all resource models can find a schedule with the minimal miscoverage 26 and the table indicates that only a portion of the resources is actually used. But when the resources are bounded to 2 tracks, 3 slices, and 4 professionals, the miscoverage goes up in all resource models. First, RM1 introduces timing and personnel limits, and then RM2 enforces competence requirements. But, since RM3 can develop new competencies on the way, it pays off to hire some experts to teach. This increases the capacity of the professionals, and they can be more effective and perform more operations within the same time limits. The cost-efficiency of maintenance is improved as a result!   ■

7   Evaluation and Conclusion

In this article, prior work on *preventive maintenance scheduling* [35,36] (PMS) is extended towards *integrated maintenance* (Fig. 1) that incorporates aspects of production and resource allocation into maintenance. In the extended model, production aspects are implicitly present, as the numbers of maintenance breaks (and time slices within) affect indirectly the availability of the production machinery. The main focus is, however, on resources required by maintenance actions during maintenance breaks. Such resources relate to the availability of workforce, the recognition of the workers' competencies, and opportunities created by their enhancement via training.

These ingredients are embodied in the *resource models* RM1-3 whose formalization in Sect. 3–5 is our first contribution. These models reveal the desire for incorporating dynamic proficiency binding (i.e., *from novice to expert model* [2]), practice, and tacit knowledge into resource modeling. Continuous learning and experience sharing deserve much deeper and careful analysis than what was possible within this article. The RM3 model takes a step towards *from novice to expert model* in a quite simplified setting, nevertheless demonstrating the potential of logical approaches when modeling continuous learning in the context of PMS.

The encapsulation and interfacing of resource models is itself a technical challenge as this can be done in arbitrarily many ways. Our second contribution is to identify a *minimal interface* for coupling PMS with resource models. The given interface identifies the cores of maintenance schedules for resourcing purposes and enables the separation of concerns when it comes to implementing integrated maintenance. Such an abstraction is made possible by the ASO framework that supports modular knowledge representation and the incorporation of instance-specific information as simple collections of facts. The interface alleviates the development of more efficient encodings for both PMS and resource allocation in separation, although the overall performance depends on their combination.

On top of the three resource models, we further develop a *weight-based* approach to integrated maintenance that maps all resources to monetary values, making their uniform comparison and trade-off possible. Besides being immediately more conceivable by production economists and maintenance developers, it also addresses the consistency of integrated models when conflicting hard constraints cannot be strictly satisfied by any candidate solution. The benefits of this generic approach also include flexibility resulting from highly parameterized objective functions: the configuration of the scheduler can be delegated to the cost optimization process. This is enabled by the ASO framework that readily supports both integer-weighted constraints and objective functions.

In summary, the current article advances logic-based approaches to integrated maintenance scheduling by developing its underlying theory and knowledge presentation models. This research is interdisciplinary and promotes workforce and competence management in product-service applications such as maintenance optimization. It puts forth formal abstraction and knowledge representation related to these interests but does not compare formalisms, encodings, nor algorithms. Therefore, the formalism (ASO), existing encodings of PMS [35,36], and efficient solvers are merely prerequisites rather than contributions of this work.

In this work, we apply logic-based modeling and optimization in the context of scheduling and resource allocation. Due to logical representations, the scalability of our approach is expected to improve along the development of more efficient solver technology. Moreover, we anticipate the applicability of the presented resource models and ideas related to workforce allocation in other contexts such as multi-agent systems, Markov decision processes, and (deep) reinforcement learning—already combined with logical representations [4,5,14].

Acknowledgment. This research has been supported by the Research Council of Finland under projects AI-ROT (#335718,#335719) and XAILOG (#345633).

References

1. Banbara, M., et al.: *teaspoon*: solving the curriculum-based course timetabling problems with answer set programming. Ann. Oper. Res. **275**, 3–37 (2019). https://doi.org/10.1007/s10479-018-2757-7
2. Benner, P.: From novice to expert. Am. J. Nurs. **82**(3), 402–407 (1982). https://doi.org/10.1002/nur.4770080119
3. Brewka, G., Eiter, T., Truszczynski, M.: Answer set programming at a glance. Commun. ACM **54**(12), 92–103 (2011). https://doi.org/10.1145/2043174.2043195
4. Camacho, A., Icarte, R.T., Klassen, T.Q., Valenzano, R.A., McIlraith, S.A.: LTL and beyond: formal languages for reward function specification in reinforcement learning. In: IJCAI 2019, pp. 6065–6073. ijcai.org (2019). https://doi.org/10.24963/IJCAI.2019/840
5. Cao, Y., et al.: GALOIS: boosting deep reinforcement learning via generalizable logic synthesis. In: NeurIPS 2022, pp. 19930–19943 (2022)
6. Chansombat, S., Pongcharoen, P., Hicks, C.: A mixed-integer linear programming model for integrated production and preventive maintenance scheduling in the capital goods industry. Int. J. Prod. Res. **57**(1), 61–82 (2019). https://doi.org/10.1080/00207543.2018.1459923
7. Chen, J., Wang, Y.: A deep reinforcement learning approach for maintenance planning of multi-component systems with complex structure. Neural Comput. Appl. **35**(21), 15549–15562 (2023). https://doi.org/10.1007/s00521-023-08542-9
8. Chen, X., An, Y., Zhang, Z., Li, Y.: An approximate nondominated sorting genetic algorithm to integrate optimization of production scheduling and accurate maintenance based on reliability intervals. J. Manuf. Syst. **54**, 227–241 (2020). https://doi.org/10.1016/j.jmsy.2019.12.004
9. Do, P., Vu, H.C., Innovation, A., Berenguer, C.: Maintenance grouping for multi-component systems with availability constraints and limited maintenance teams. Reliab. Eng. Syst. Saf. **142**, 56–67 (2015). https://doi.org/10.1016/j.ress.2015.04.022
10. Dodaro, C., Maratea, M.: Nurse scheduling via answer set programming. In: Balduccini, M., Janhunen, T. (eds.) LPNMR 2017. LNCS, vol. 10377, pp. 301–307. Springer, Cham (2017). https://doi.org/10.1007/978-3-319-61660-5_27
11. Dreyfus, H.L., Dreyfus, S.E.: Mind over Machine: The Power of Human Intuition and Expertise in the Age of the Computer. Basil Blackwell, Oxford (1986)
12. Eiter, T., Geibinger, T., Musliu, N., Oetsch, J., Skocovský, P., Stepanova, D.: Answer-set programming for lexicographical makespan optimisation in parallel machine scheduling. In: KR 2021, pp. 280–290 (2021). https://doi.org/10.24963/kr.2021/27
13. El Akraoui, B., Daoui, C., Larach, A., Rahhali, K.: Decomposition methods for solving finite-horizon large MDPs. J. Math. 1–8 (2022). https://doi.org/10.1155/2022/8404716

14. Elsayed-Aly, I., Feng, L.: Logic-based reward shaping for multi-agent reinforcement learning. CoRR abs/2206.08881 (2022). https://doi.org/10.48550/ARXIV.2206.08881

15. Falkner, A.A., Friedrich, G., Schekotihin, K., Taupe, R., Teppan, E.C.: Industrial applications of answer set programming. Künstliche Intelligentz **32**(2–3), 165–176 (2018). https://doi.org/10.1007/S13218-018-0548-6

16. Geurtsen, M., Didden, J., Adan, J., Atan, Z., Adan, I.: Production, maintenance and resource scheduling: a review. Eur. J. Oper. Res. **305**(2), 501–529 (2023). https://doi.org/10.1016/j.ejor.2022.03.045

17. Hannola, L., Richter, A., Richter, S., Stocker, A.: Empowering production workers with digitally facilitated knowledge processes conceptual framework. Int. J. Prod. Res. **56**(14), 4729–4743 (2018). https://doi.org/10.1080/00207543.2018.1445877

18. Ikävalko, H., Saarelma, E., Martinsuo, M.: Innovation users profiles in implementing a digital innovation in maintenance. In: ISPIM Connects Salzburg The Sound of Innovation. LUT Scientific and Expertise Publications (2023)

19. Le Deist, F.D., Winterton, J.: What is competence? Hum. Resour. Dev. Int. **8**(1), 27–46 (2005). https://doi.org/10.1080/1367886042000338227

20. Lerch, C., Gotsch, M.: Digitalized product-service systems in manufacturing firms: a case study analysis. Res. Technol. Manag. **58**(5), 45–52 (2015). https://doi.org/10.5437/08956308X5805357

21. Luukkala, V., Niemelä, I.: Enhancing a smart space with answer set programming. In: Dean, M., Hall, J., Rotolo, A., Tabet, S. (eds.) RuleML 2010. LNCS, vol. 6403, pp. 89–103. Springer, Heidelberg (2010). https://doi.org/10.1007/978-3-642-16289-3_9

22. Marcon, É., et al.: Capabilities supporting digital servitization: a multi-actor perspective. Ind. Mark. Manag. **103**, 97–116 (2022). https://doi.org/10.1016/j.indmarman.2022.03.003

23. Martinsuo, M., Ikävalko, H.: Innovation users' view to implementing digital innovations in industrial operations. In: IPDMC 2023. European Institute for Advanced Studies in Management (2023)

24. Paukkunen, J.: Enhancing the transfer of tacit knowledge in maintenance: strategies and implications. Master's thesis, Aalto University School of Business, Information & Service Management (2023)

25. Pinciroli, L., Baraldi, P., Zio, E.: Maintenance optimization in industry 4.0. Reliab. Eng. Syst. Saf. **234**, 109204 (2023). https://doi.org/10.1016/j.ress.2023.109204

26. Rajaprasad, S.V.S.: Investigation of reliability, maintainability and availability of a paper machine in an integrated pulp and paper mill. Int. J. Eng. Sci. Technol. **10**(3), 43–56 (2018). https://doi.org/10.4314/ijest.v10i3.5

27. Raza, S., Hameed, A.: Models for maintenance planning and scheduling a citation-based literature review and content analysis. J. Qual. Maint. Eng. **28**(4), 873–914 (2022). https://doi.org/10.1108/JQME-10-2020-0109

28. Rossi, F., van Beek, P., Walsh, T. (eds.): Handbook of Constraint Programming, Foundations of Artificial Intelligence, vol. 2. Elsevier (2006)

29. Selcuk, S.: Predictive maintenance, its implementation and latest trends. J. Eng. Manuf. **231**(9), 1670–1679 (2017). https://doi.org/10.1177/0954405415601640

30. Simons, P., Niemelä, I., Soininen, T.: Extending and implementing the stable model semantics. Artif. Intell. **138**(1–2), 181–234 (2002). https://doi.org/10.1016/S0004-3702(02)00187-X

31. Story, V., Raddats, C., Burton, J., Zolkiewski, J., Baines, T.: Capabilities for advanced services: a multi-actor perspective. Ind. Mark. Manag. **60**, 54–68 (2017). https://doi.org/10.1016/j.indmarman.2016.04.015

32. Sutton, R.S., Barto, A.G.: Reinforcement Learning: An Introduction. A Bradford Book. MIT Press, Cambridge (2018)

33. Tassel, P., Gebser, M., Schekotihin, K.: An end-to-end reinforcement learning approach for job-shop scheduling problems based on constraint programming. In: ICAPS 2023, pp. 614–622. AAAI Press (2023). https://doi.org/10.1609/ICAPS.V33I1.27243

34. Wolsey, L.A.: Mixed Integer Programming. Wiley, Hoboken (2008). https://doi.org/10.1002/9780470050118.ecse244

35. Yli-Jyrä, A., Janhunen, T.: Applying answer set optimization to preventive maintenance scheduling for rotating machinery. In: Governatori, G., Turhan, A.Y. (eds.) RuleML+RR 2022. LNCS, vol. 13752, pp. 3–19. Springer, Cham (2022). https://doi.org/10.1007/978-3-031-21541-4_1

36. Yli-Jyrä, A., Rankooh, M.F., Janhunen, T.: Pruning redundancy in answer set optimization applied to preventive maintenance scheduling. In: Hanus, M., Inclezan, D. (eds.) PADL 2023. LNCS, vol. 13880, pp. 279–294. Springer, Cham (2023). https://doi.org/10.1007/978-3-031-24841-2_18

37. Zhang, X., Zeng, J.: Joint optimization of condition-based opportunistic maintenance and spare parts provisioning policy in multiunit systems. Eur. J. Oper. Res. **262**(2), 479–498 (2017). https://doi.org/10.1016/j.ejor.2017.03.019

Author Index

A. Meier and M. Ortiz (Eds.): FoIKS 2024, LNCS 14589, pp. 401–402, 2024.
https://doi.org/10.1007/978-3-031-56940-1

Printed in the United States
by Baker & Taylor Publisher Services